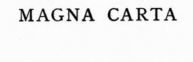

MAGNA CARTA

BURT FRANKLIN BIBLIOGRAPHICAL SERIES

1. Burt Franklin & G. Legman. David Ricardo and Ricardian theory. A bibliographical checklist. New York, 1949.

2. Francesco Cordasco. A Junius Bibliography. With a preliminary essay on the political background, text and identity. A contribution to 18th century constitutional and literary history. With eight appendices. New York, 1949.

3. Burt Franklin & Francesco Cordasco. Adam Smith: a bibliographical checklist. An international record of critical writings and scholarship relating to Smith and Smithian theory, 1876-1950. New York, 1950.

4. Edmund Silberner. Moses Hess: an annotated bibliography. New York, 1951.

5. Francesco Cordasco. The Bohn Libraries. A history and checklist. New York, 1951.

6. Jan M. Novotny. A Library of Public Finance and Economics.

7. Andrew George Little. Initia operum latinorum, quae saeculis XIII, XIV, XV, attribuuntur, secundum ordinem alphatbeti disposita. 13 + 275 pp. 8vo., cloth. (Manchester University Publications, n. 5 - 1905). New York: Burt Franklin, 1958.

8. John William Bradley. Dictionary of miniaturists, illuminators, calligraphers and copyists with references to their works, and notices of their patrons, compiled from sources, many hitherto inedited, from the establishment of Christianity to the 18th century. 3 volumes, lg. 8vo., cloth. (London, 1887-89) New York: Burt Franklin, 1958.

9. Frank Wadleigh Chandler. The literature of roguery. 2 vols., 8vo., cloth. (The Types of English Literature, ed. by W. A. Neilson). (Boston, 1907). New York: Burt Franklin, 1958.

10. Robert Huntington Fletcher. The Arthurian material in the chronicles, especially those of Great Britain and France, 9 + 313 pp., bibliography, 8vo., cloth ([Harvard] Notes and Studies in Philology 10, 1906) New York: Burt Franklin, 1958.

11. John Alexander Herbert. Illuminated manuscripts. 10 + 355 pp., 51 plates; index of manuscripts, scribes and illuminators; bibliography, lg. 8vo., cloth. (London, 1911). New York: Burt Franklin, 1958.

MAGNA CARTA

A COMMENTARY ON THE GREAT CHARTER OF KING JOHN

WITH AN
HISTORICAL INTRODUCTION

BY

WILLIAM SHARP McKECHNIE
M.A., LL.B., D.Phil.

LECTURER ON CONSTITUTIONAL LAW AND HISTORY IN THE UNIVERSITY OF GLASGOW
AUTHOR OF
'THE STATE AND THE INDIVIDUAL,' 'THE REFORM OF THE HOUSE OF LORDS'
'THE NEW DEMOCRACY AND THE CONSTITUTION,' ETC.

SECOND EDITION
REVISED AND IN PART RE-WRITTEN

BURT FRANKLIN
New York 25, N. Y.
1958

JN
147
·M21
Cp·2

Reprinted by

BURT FRANKLIN

514 West 113th Street

New York 25, N. Y.

This work was originally published

GLASGOW

1914

MANUFACTURED IN THE UNITED STATES OF AMERICA
NOBLE OFFSET PRINTERS, INC., 400 LAFAYETTE ST., NEW YORK, N. Y.

PREFACE TO SECOND EDITION.

THE numerous and weighty criticisms upon the first edition of this Commentary (published in 1905 and now out of print) were doubly welcome to the author as showing a widespread interest in the subjects discussed, and as enabling him to profit from the collaboration of eminent specialists in the elucidation of Magna Carta and of the age that gave it birth. The last eight years have been fertile in discussions on the form and contents, the historical setting, and the constitutional value of the Great Charter. Monographs and contributions to periodical literature, devoted exclusively to Magna Carta, have been published in France, Germany and the United States of America, as well as in Great Britain; while few books have appeared on English medieval history or on the development of English law without throwing light incidentally on one or more of the Charter's various aspects.

An endeavour has been made, by severe condensation, to find room in this new edition for whatever seemed relevant and of permanent value in this mass of new material, without sacrificing anything of importance contained in the first edition. Effect has been given, so far as space permitted, to the suggestions cordially offered by critics and fellow-workers, both privately and in published books and articles; while the author's own recent researches have supplied additional illustrations, and have led him to modify several of his earlier impressions. Although no reason has been found for altering fundamental propositions, the whole work has been recast; hardly a page, either of Commentary or of Historical Introduction, remains as originally written; and care has been taken to supply the reader with references to the most recent authorities on the various topics discussed or referred to.

The new material will be found mainly (1) in the portions of the Introduction treating respectively of scutages, the Coronation Charter of Henry I., the juridical nature of Magna Carta, its contemporary and permanent effects on constitutional development, its reissues by Henry III., and the nature of the so-called "unknown charter" of John; and (2) in chapters 12, 13, 14, 18, 20, 25, 27, 34, 38, 39 and 61 of the Commentary. In the Appendix, Professor Liebermann's amended text of Henry I.'s Charter of Liberties has been adopted, and the Great Charter of 1225 substituted for that of 1217; while an attempt has been made, by means of italics and foot-notes, to show at a glance the chief points in which the three reissues by Henry III. differ from one another and from the Charter as originally granted by John.

Latin Charters, of which the full text is given in the Appendix or elsewhere, have been printed *literatim* as in the authorities cited in each case; but for detached Latin words or phrases, whether occurring in the Historical Introduction or the Commentary, a uniform spelling has been adopted, in which the "ae" diphthong, where appropriate, has been substituted for the less familiar "e."

The author's grateful acknowledgments are due to the Trustees of the Carnegie Foundation, for a grant towards the expenses of this edition; to Professor Vinogradoff, for help courteously given in solving problems affecting the interpretation of chapter 34; and to Mr. David B. Mungo, LL.B., formerly the author's assistant in the University of Glasgow, for his services in reading the proof-sheets and for many useful suggestions.

THE UNIVERSITY,
GLASGOW,
December, 1913.

FROM PREFACE TO FIRST EDITION.

No Commentary upon Magna Carta has hitherto been written from the standpoint of modern research. No serious attempt has yet been made to supersede, or even adequately to supplement, the works of Coke and Richard Thomson, published respectively in 1642 and 1829, and now hopelessly out of date. That this conspicuous gap in our historical and legal literature should have remained so long unfilled is the more remarkable in view of the great advance, amounting almost to a revolution, which has been effected since Coke and Thomson wrote. Within the last twenty years, in especial, a wealth of new material has been explored with notable results. Discoveries have been made, profoundly affecting our views of every branch of law, every organ of government, and every aspect of social and individual life in medieval England. Nothing, however, has hitherto been done towards applying to the systematic elucidation of Magna Carta the new stores of knowledge thus accumulated.

With this object in view, I have endeavoured, throughout several years of hard, but congenial work, to collect, sift, and arrange the mass of evidence, drawn from many scattered sources, capable of throwing light upon John's Great Charter. The results have now been condensed into the Commentary which fills two-thirds of the present volume. This attempt to explain, point by point, the sixty-three chapters of Magna Carta, embracing, as these do, every topic—legal, political, economic and social—in which John and his barons felt a vital interest, has involved an analysis in some detail of the whole public and private life of England during the thirteenth century. The Commentary is preceded by a Historical Introduction, which describes the events leading to the crisis of 1215, analyzes the grievances which stirred the barons to revolt, discusses the contents and characteristics of the Charter, traces its connection with the subsequent course of English history, and gives some account of previous editions and commentaries.

February, 1905.

CONTENTS.

HISTORICAL INTRODUCTION.

PART I. EVENTS LEADING TO MAGNA CARTA :

PAGE

I. William I. to Henry II. : Main Problem, the Monarchy -   3

II. William I. to Henry II. : Problem of Local Government   13

III. William I. to Henry II. : Problem of Church and State -   16

IV. Richard I. and John - - - - - - -   19

V. The Years of Crisis (1213–15) - - - - -   27

VI. Runnymede, and after - - - - - - -   36

PART II. FEUDAL GRIEVANCES AND MAGNA CARTA :

I. The Immediate Causes of the Crisis - - - -   48

II. The Crown and Feudal Obligations - - - -   52

III. Royal Justice and Feudal Justice - - - - -   77

PART III. MAGNA CARTA : ITS FORM AND CONTENTS :

I. Its Prototypes : Earlier Charters - - - - -   93

II. Magna Carta : Its Form and Juridical Nature - -   104

III. Magna Carta : Its Contents and Characteristics - -   109

IV. Magna Carta : An Estimate of its Value - - -   120

V. Magna Carta : Its Defects - - - - - -   129

VI. Magna Carta : Value of Traditional Interpretations -   132

VII. Magna Carta : Its Traditional Relation to Trial by Jury   134

PART IV. HISTORICAL SEQUEL TO MAGNA CARTA:

PAGE

I. Reissues and Confirmations of the Great Charter - - 139

(i) Reissue of 1216 - - - - - - - 139

(ii) Reissue of 1217 - - - - - - - 145

(iii) Reissue of 1225 - - - - - - - 152

(iv) Confirmations (1237 to 1297) - - - - - 157

II. Magna Carta and the Reforms of Edward I. - - - 159

PART V. MAGNA CARTA; ORIGINAL VERSIONS, PRINTED
EDITIONS, AND COMMENTARIES:

I. Manuscripts of Magna Carta and Relative Documents - 165

II. Previous Editions and Commentaries - - - 176

MAGNA CARTA:
TEXT, TRANSLATION, COMMENTARY.

PREAMBLE.

I. The King's Title. II. The names of the consenting Nobles. III.
The Motives of the Grant - - - - - - - 186

CHAPTER ONE.

I. The Rights of the National Church : (1) *Quod Anglicana ecclesia
libera sit*; (2) Canonical Election. II. Civil and Political
Rights - - - - - - - - - - - 190

CHAPTER TWO.

I. Assessment of Reliefs. II. Units of Assessment : (1) *Feodum
militis integrum*; (2) *Baronia integra*; (3) *Baronia comitis
integra*. III. Liability of Church Property to " Relief " - - 196

CHAPTER THREE.

No Relief after Wardship - - - - - - - - 203

CHAPTER FOUR.

Wardship : (1) The Definition of Waste ; (2) Punishment of Wasteful Guardians ; (3) Provision against Recurrence - - - 205

CONTENTS

CHAPTER FIVE.

PAGE

I. The Obligations of the Warden of a Lay-fief. II. Wardship over
Vacant Sees - - - - - - - - - - 209

CHAPTER SIX.

The Marriage of Wards - - - - - - - - 212

CHAPTER SEVEN.

I. The Widow's Share of Real Estate : (1) Dower ; (2) *Maritagium* ;
(3) *Hereditas*. II. Her Share of Personal Estate. III. Provision for her Immediate Needs : (1) Quarantine ; (2) Estovers
of Common - - - - - - - - - - 215

CHAPTER EIGHT.

Marriage of Widows - - - - - - - - - 220

CHAPTER NINE.

Procedure for Enforcing Payment of Debts - - - - - 221

CHAPTER TEN.

Usury. I. The History of the Jews in England. II. Legal Position
of the Jews - - - - - - - - - - 223

CHAPTER ELEVEN.

Widows and Children of Debtors to be Protected against Creditors 230

CHAPTER TWELVE.

I. Protection of Crown Tenants from Arbitrary Exactions : (1)
Feudal Aids ; (2) Scutage. II. Protection of London from
Arbitrary Exactions : (1) Aid ; (2) Tallage ; (3) Comparison of
Aid and Tallage ; (4) London's attempts to escape Tallage ;
(5) Effects of Omission of Tallage from Magna Carta ; (6)
Nature of the Protection accorded to London ; (7) Later History
of the Crown's Right to Tallage the Towns. III. Magna Carta
and the Theory of Parliamentary Taxation - - - - 231

CHAPTER THIRTEEN.

Liberties and Free Customs of London - - - - - - 240

CHAPTER FOURTEEN.

Method of obtaining the Common Council of the Kingdom. I. Nature of the Summons. II. Composition of the Council. III. Position of "Minor Barons." IV. Representation. V. Powers of the Council. VI. Rights of Majorities and Minorities   248

CHAPTER FIFTEEN.

Restrictions on Mesne Lords taking Aids. I. Points of difference between tenants-in-chief and under-tenants. II. The influence of Magna Carta upon later practice   -   -   -   -   -   256

CHAPTER SIXTEEN.

No one to perform greater service for a tenement than is due -   -   260

CHAPTER SEVENTEEN.

Common Pleas. I. The Curia Regis as a Court of Law. II. Common Pleas and Royal Pleas. III. Influence of Magna Carta on Genesis of the three Courts of Common Law. IV. Evolution of the Court of Common Pleas. V. Common Pleas and the Exchequer   -   -   -   -   -   -   -   -   -   261

CHAPTER EIGHTEEN.

Petty Assizes. I. The Curia Regis and the Travelling Justices. II. Nature and Origin of the three Petty Assizes. III. Aims of Magna Carta. IV. Effects of Magna Carta. V. An Erroneous View. VI. Later History of the Justices of Assize   ·   -   -   269

CHAPTER NINETEEN.

Procedure at Petty Assizes   -   -   -   -   -   -   -   -   282

CHAPTER TWENTY.

Amercement. I. Three Stages of Criminal Law : (1) The blood-feud ; (2) Fixed money-payments ; (3) Amercements. II. Magna Carta and Amercements : (1) Of Freeholders ; (2) Of Merchants ; (3) Of Villeins ; (4) Fines and Amercements ; (5) Contenement -   -   -   -   -   -   -   -   -   284

CHAPTER TWENTY-ONE.

Amercement of Earls and Barons   -   -   ·   -   -   -   -   295

CONTENTS

CHAPTER TWENTY-TWO.

PAGE

Amercement of the Clergy - - - - - - - - 298

CHAPTER TWENTY-THREE.

I. Origin of Obligation to make Bridges. II. The King's Interest
in the Repair of Bridges. III. Erroneous Interpretations - - 299

CHAPTER TWENTY-FOUR.

I. Pleas of the Crown. II. Keeping and Trying Criminal Pleas.
III. The Intention of Magna Carta. IV. An Erroneous View.
V. Local Magistrates under John : (1) The Sheriff ; (2) The
Constable ; (3) The Coroner ; (4) The Bailiff - - - 304

CHAPTER TWENTY-FIVE.

Farms of Counties and Hundreds - - - - - - - 317

CHAPTER TWENTY-SIX.

Crown Debtors. I. Nature of the Grievance. II. The Right to
Bequeath - - - - - - - - - - 321

CHAPTER TWENTY-SEVEN.

Intestate Succession - - - - - - - - - 326

CHAPTER TWENTY-EIGHT.

I. Purveyance in General. II. Branches of it restricted by Magna
Carta. III. Its other Branches - - - - - - 329

CHAPTER TWENTY-NINE.

Castle-Guard - - - - - - - - - 333

CHAPTER THIRTY.

Purveyance of Horses and Carts - - - - - - - 334

CHAPTER THIRTY-ONE.

Purveyance of Timber - - - - - - - - - 336

CONTENTS

CHAPTER THIRTY-TWO.

PAGE

I. The Crown's Claim to Felons' Property : (1) Lands ; (2) Chattels. II. Indictment, Conviction, and Attainder   -   -   -   -   336

CHAPTER THIRTY-THREE.

Obstructions to be removed from Rivers   -   -   -   -   -   343

CHAPTER THIRTY-FOUR.

The Writ " *Praecipe*." I. Royal Writs and the Feudal Jurisdictions. II. The Intention of Magna Carta. III. Expedients for evading Magna Carta. IV. Influence upon Later Legal Development   -   346

CHAPTER THIRTY-FIVE.

Standards of Weights and Measures   -   -   -   -   -   -   356

CHAPTER THIRTY-SIX.

Writ *de Odio et Atia*. I. Trial by Combat prior to John's Reign. II. Writ of Life and Limb. III. Its Subsidiary Uses. IV. Later History of Appeal and Battle   -   -   -   -   -   359

CHAPTER THIRTY-SEVEN.

Prerogative Wardship   -   -   -   -   -   -   -   -   -   367

CHAPTER THIRTY-EIGHT.

No Bailiff to put anyone to his " law " without Witnesses. I. Medieval Interpretations. II. Modern Interpretations. III. Nature of the Grievance   -   -   -   -   -   -   -   369

CHAPTER THIRTY-NINE.

I. Its Main Object : (1) Judgment must precede execution ; (2) *Per judicium parium* ; (3) *Per legem terrae* ; (4) Meaning of " *vel*." II. The scope of the Protection afforded. III. What classes of men enjoyed it. IV. Reactionary Aspects. V. Genesis of this Chapter. VI. Later History of " Judgment of Peers." VII. Erroneous Interpretations   -   -   -   -   -   -   -   375

CHAPTER FORTY.

Justice not to be Sold, Refused, or Delayed   ·   -   -   -   -   395

CONTENTS

CHAPTER FORTY-ONE.

PAGE

Freedom of Trade. I. Magna Carta favours Alien Merchants. II. Customs and Tolls. III. The Motives prompting this Chapter. IV. English Boroughs and Merchant Strangers - - - 398

CHAPTER FORTY-TWO.

Liberty to leave the Kingdom—Writs *ne exeat regno* - - - 407

CHAPTER FORTY-THREE.

Tenants of Escheated Baronies - - - - - - - - 411

CHAPTER FORTY-FOUR.

I. The Royal Forests. II. Their Origin. III. Forest Officials. IV. Forest Courts. V. Chases, Parks, and Warrens. VI. Forest Rights and Forest Grievances. VII. Later History of Forests and Forest Laws - - - - - - - - - 414

CHAPTER FORTY-FIVE.

Justices, Castellans, Sheriffs, and Bailiffs to be law-abiding men - 431

CHAPTER FORTY-SIX.

Wardship over Vacant Abbeys - - - - - - - 433

CHAPTER FORTY-SEVEN.

Forests and River-banks encroached upon by John - - - 435

CHAPTER FORTY-EIGHT.

Procedure for abolishing Evil Customs of Forests and elsewhere - 438

CHAPTER FORTY-NINE.

Hostages and Charters to be restored - - - - - 441

CHAPTER FIFTY.

List of those excluded from offices of trust in future - - - 444

CHAPTER FIFTY-ONE.

Banishment of Foreign Mercenaries - - - - - - 447

CONTENTS

CHAPTER FIFTY-TWO.

PAGE

Procedure for redressing wrongful Disseisins - - . - - 448

CHAPTER FIFTY-THREE.

A Crusader's Respite allowed to John - - . . . - 450

CHAPTER FIFTY-FOUR.

Right of Appeal by Women - - . . . . . - 451

CHAPTER FIFTY-FIVE.

Remission of Unjust Fines and Amercements - - - 454

CHAPTER FIFTY-SIX.

Redress for Welshmen wrongfully disseised by John - - - 456

CHAPTER FIFTY-SEVEN.

Redress for Welshmen wrongfully disseised by Henry II. or Richard I. 457

CHAPTER FIFTY-EIGHT.

Welsh Hostages and Charters to be restored - - - - - 458

CHAPTER FIFTY-NINE.

Justice to be done to King of Scots ; Relations of England and
Scotland - - - - - - - - - - 459

CHAPTER SIXTY.

Extension of Provisions of Charter to Tenants of Mesne Lords - 463

CHAPTER SIXTY-ONE.

Forma Securitatis or Legal Sanction of the Charter. I. Nature of
the Security. II. Details of Scheme : (1) Twenty-five
Executors ; (2) A quorum may act ; (3) Sub-committee of
four ; (4) Local Agents ; (5) Co-operation of Public. III.
Relations to Contemporary Theory. IV. Modern Criticism.
V. Failure of Scheme - - - - - - - - 465

CHAPTER SIXTY-TWO.

Prelates to issue Letters Testimonial - - - - - - 478

CHAPTER SIXTY-THREE.

PAGE

Formal Clauses - - - - - - - - - 479

APPENDIX.

DOCUMENTS RELATIVE TO, OR ILLUSTRATIVE OF, JOHN'S
MAGNA CARTA :

I. The Charter of Liberties of Henry I. (1100) - - - 481

II. The Second or Oxford Charter of Stephen (1136) - - 483

III. Charter of Henry II. (*circa* 1154) · - - - - 485

IV. The so-called " Unknown Charter of Liberties " - - 485

V. The Articles of the Barons (1215) - - - - - 487

VI. Writs Supplementary of John's Great Charter - - 493

VII. The Great Charter of Henry III. (Third Re-issue, 1225) 497

VIII. Carta de Foresta (1217) - - - - - - - 508

SELECT BIBLIOGRAPHY AND LIST OF AUTHORITIES REFERRED
TO - - - - - - - - - - 513

INDEX OF STATUTES - - - - - - - 519

GENERAL INDEX - - - - - - - - 521

HISTORICAL INTRODUCTION

PART I.

EVENTS LEADING TO MAGNA CARTA.

THE Great Charter is too often treated as the outcome of accidental causes; its sources are traced no deeper than the personal tyrannies and blunders of King John. That monarch's misdeeds are held to have goaded into action a widespread opposition that never rested until it had achieved success; and the outcome of this success was the Great Charter of Liberties. The moving causes of events of tremendous moment are thus sought in the characteristics and vices of one man. If John had never lived and sinned, so it would appear, the foundations of English freedom would never have been laid.

Such shallow views of history fail to comprehend the magnitude and inevitable nature of the sequence of causes and effects upon which great issues depend. The compelling logic of events forces a way for its fulfilment, independent of the caprices, aims and ambitions of individual men. The incidents of John's career are the occasions, not the causes, of the movement that laid the foundations of English liberties. The origin of Magna Carta lies too deep to be determined by any purely contingent phenomena. It is as unwise as it is unnecessary to suppose that the course of constitutional development in England was violently wrested into a new channel, merely because of the incapacity or cruelties of the temporary occupant of the throne. The source of the discontent fanned to flame by John's oppressions must be sought in earlier reigns. The genesis of the Charter cannot be understood apart from its historical antecedents.

It is thus necessary briefly to narrate how the scattered Anglo-Saxon and Danish tribes and territories, originally unconnected, were slowly welded together and grew into England; how this fusion was made permanent by the growth of a strong centralized government which crushed out local independence, and threatened to become the most absolute despotism in Europe; how, finally, the Crown, because of the very plenitude of its power, called into play opposing forces, which set limits to royal prerogatives and laid the foundations of the reign of law.   Such a survey of the early history of England reveals two leading movements; the establishment of a strong Monarchy able to bring order out of anarchy, and the establishment of safeguards to prevent this source of order from degenerating into an unrestrained tyranny, and so crushing out not merely anarchy but legitimate freedom as well.   The later movement, in favour of liberty and the Great Charter, was the natural complement, and, in part, the consequence of the earlier movement in the direction of a strong government able to enforce peace.   In historical sequence, order precedes freedom.

These two problems, mutually complementary, arise in the history of every nation, and in every age : the problem of *order,* or how to found a central government strong enough to suppress anarchy, and the problem of *freedom,* or how to set limits to an autocracy threatening to overshadow individual liberty.   Deep political insight may still be acknowledged in Æsop's fable of Jupiter and the frogs. King Log proves as ineffective against foreign invasion as he is void of offence to domestic freedom; King Stork secures the triumph of his subjects in time of war, but devours them in time of peace.   All nations in their early efforts to obtain an efficient government have to choose between these two types of ruler—between an executive, harmless but weak; and one powerful to direct the business of government at home and abroad, but ready to use powers entrusted to him for the good of all, for his own selfish aims and the trampling out of his subjects' liberties.

On the whole, the miseries of the long centuries of Anglo-

Saxon rule were the outcome of the Crown's weakness;
while, at the Norman Conquest, England escaped from the
mild sceptre of inefficiency, only to fall under the cruel
sceptre of selfish strength.   Yet the able kings of the new
dynasty, powerful as they were, had to struggle to maintain
their mastery; for the unruly barons fought vigorously to
shake off the royal yoke.

During a century of Norman rule, constant warfare was
waged between two great principles—the monarchic, standing on the whole for order, seeking to crush anarchy, and
the oligarchic or baronial, standing on the whole for local
autonomy, protesting against the tyranny of autocratic
power.   Sometimes one of these gained the ascendant;
sometimes the other.   The history of medieval England is
the swing of the pendulum between.

The main plot, then, of early English history, centres
in the attempt to found a strong monarchy, and yet to
set limits to its strength.   With this main plot subordinate
plots are interwoven.   Chief among these must be reckoned
the necessity of defining the relations of the central to the
local government, and the need of an acknowledged frontier
between the domains of Church and State.   On the other
hand, all that interesting group of problems connected with
the *ideal form* of government, much discussed in the days of
Aristotle as in our own, is notably absent, never having
been forced by the logic of events upon the mind of medieval
Europe.   Monarchy was accepted as the only possible
scheme of government; the merits of aristocracy and democracy, or of the much-vaunted constitution known as
"mixed" were not discussed, since these forms of constitution did not lie within the sphere of practical politics.
The student of history will do well to begin by concentrat-
ing his attention on the main problem, to which the others
are subsidiary.

I. William I. to Henry II.—Main Problem: the Monarchy.

The difficulties that surrounded the English nation in its
early struggles for existence were formidable.   The great
problem was, first, how to get itself into being, and there-

after how to guard against the forces of disintegration, which strove without rest to tear it to pieces again. The dawn of English history shows the beginning of that long slow process of consolidation in which unconscious reason played a deeper part than human will, whereby many discordant tribes and races, many independent provinces, were crushed together into something bearing a rude likeness to a united nation. Many forces converged to the achievement of this result. The coercion of strong tribes over weaker neighbours, the pressure of outside foes, the growth of a body of law, and of public opinion, the influence of religion as the friend of peace, all helped to weld together a chaos of incongruous and warring elements.

It is notable that each of the three influences, destined ultimately to aid in this process of unification, threatened at one time a contrary effect. Thus the rivalries of the smaller kingdoms tended towards disruption before Wessex gained undisputed supremacy; the Christianizing of England, partly by Celtic missionaries from the north and partly by emissaries from Rome, threatened to split the country into two, until mutual rivalries were stilled after the Synod of Whitby in 664; and one effect of the settlements of the Danes was to create a barrier between the lands that lay on either side of Watling Street, before the whole country succumbed to the unifying pressure of Canute and his sons.

The stern discipline of foreign conquest was required to make national unity possible; and, with the restoration of the old Wessex dynasty in the person of Edward Confessor, the forces of disintegration again made headway. England threatened once more to fall to pieces, but the iron rule of the Normans came to complete what the Danes had begun half a century before. As the weakness of the Anglo-Saxon kings and the disruption of the country had gone hand in hand; so the complete unification of England was the result of the Norman despotism.

Thereafter, it was the strength of its monarchy that rendered England unique in medieval Europe. Three kings in particular contributed to this result—William the Conqueror, Henry Beauclerk, and Henry Plantagenet.

In a sense, the work of all three was the same; to build up the central authority against the disintegrating effects of feudal anarchy. But the policy of each was modified by changing times and needs. The foundations of the edifice were laid by the Conqueror, whose character and circumstances combined to afford him an opportunity unparalleled in history. The difficulties of his task, and the methods by which he secured a successful issue, are best understood in relation to the nature of the obstacles to be overcome. Feudalism was the great current of the age—a tide formed by many converging streams, all flowing in the same direction, unreasoning like the blind powers of Nature, carrying away or submerging every obstacle in its path. In other parts of Europe—in Germany, France, and Italy, as in Scotland—the ablest monarchs found their thrones endangered by this feudal current. In England alone the monarchy stood firm. William I. refrained from any attempt to stay the torrent; but, while accepting it, he made it serve his own purposes. He watched and modified the tendencies making for feudalism, which he found in England, and he profoundly altered the feudal usages and rights transplanted from Norman soil. The special expedients used by him for this purpose are well known, and are all closely connected with his crafty policy of balancing Anglo-Saxon against Norman elements, and of selecting what suited him in either. He encouraged the adoption in England of feudalism, considered as a system of land tenure and of social distinctions based on the possession of land; but he successfully checked the evils of its unrestrained growth as a system of local government and jurisdiction.

William's policy was one of balancing. Not content to depend entirely on the right of conquest, he insisted on having his title confirmed by a body claiming to represent the Witenagemot, and alleged that he had been named successor by his kinsman, Edward Confessor, a nomination strengthened by the renunciation of Harold in his favour. Thus, to Norman followers claiming to have set him by force of arms on his throne, William might point to the election by the Witan, while for his English subjects, claiming to have elected him, the presence of foreign troops was an effective argument. Throughout his reign, he played off the old English laws and institutions against the new Norman ones, with himself as umpire over all. He retained, too, the popular moots or meetings of the shire and hundred as a counterpoise to the feudal jurisdictions; the fyrd or militia of all free men as a set-off to the feudal levy; and whatever incidents of the Anglo-Saxon land tenures he thought fit.

Thus the Norman feudal superstructure was built on a basis of Anglo-Saxon usage and tradition. William, however, did not shrink from innovations where these suited his purpose. The great earldoms into which England had been divided, even down to the Norman Conquest, were abolished. New earldoms were indeed created, but on a different basis. Even the great officers subsequently known as Earls Palatine, always few in number, never attained to the independence of the Anglo-Saxon Ealdormen. William was chary of creating even ordinary Earls, and such as he did create soon became mere holders of empty titles of honour, ousted from all real power by the Norman *vicecomites* or sheriffs. No English earl was a "Count" in the continental sense of a real ruler of a "County." No earl was allowed to hold too large an estate within his titular shire.

Ingenious devices were used for checking the feudal excesses so prevalent on the Continent. Rights of private war, coinage, and castle-building, were jealously circumscribed; while private jurisdictions, although tolerated as a necessary evil, were kept within bounds. The manor was in England the normal unit of seignorial jurisdiction; the higher courts of Honours were exceptional. No appeal lay from the manorial court of one magnate to that of his over-lord, while, in later reigns at least, appeals were encouraged to the *Curia Regis*. The results of this policy have been aptly summarized as "a strong monarchy, a relatively weak baronage, and a homogeneous people."

During the reign of William II. (1087-1100) the Constitution made no conspicuous advance. The foundations had been laid; but Rufus was more intent on his hunting and enjoyments, than on the deeper matters of statecraft. Minor details of feudal organization were doubtless settled by the King's Treasurer, Ralph Flambard; but the extent to which he innovated on the practice of the elder William is matter of dispute. On the whole, the reign must be reckoned a time of comparative rest between two periods of advance.

Henry I. (1100-35) took up, with far-seeing statesmanship and much vigour, the work of consolidation. His policy shows an advance upon that of his father. William had been content to curb the main vices of feudalism. Henry introduced within the *Curia Regis* itself a new class of men, representing a new principle of government. The great offices of state, previously filled by holders of baronies, were now given to creatures of Henry's own, men of humble birth, whose merit had raised them to his favour, and whose only title to power lay in his goodwill. Henry's other great achievement was the organization of the Exchequer, as a source of royal revenue, and as an instrument for making his will felt in every corner of England. For this great work he was fortunate to secure in Roger, Bishop of Salisbury, the help of a minister who combined genius with painstaking ability. At the Exchequer, as organized by the King and his minister, the sheriff of each county twice a year, at Easter and at Michaelmas, rendered account of every payment that had passed through his hands. His balance was adjusted before all the great officers of the King's household, who subjected his accounts to close scrutiny. Official records were drawn up, one of which—the famous Pipe Roll of 1130—is extant at the present day. As the sums received by the sheriff affected every class of society in town and country, these half-yearly audits enabled the King's advisers to scrutinize the lives and conduct of high and low. These half-yearly investigations were rendered more effective by the existence at the Exchequer of a great record of every landed estate in England. With this the sheriffs' returns could be compared and checked. Henry's Exchequer thus found one of its most powerful weapons in the great Domesday Survey, the most enduring proof of the statesmanship of the Conqueror, by whose orders and under whose direction it had been compiled.

The central scrutiny conducted within the Exchequer was supplemented by occasional inspections conducted in each county. The King's representatives, including among them the officers who presided over the half-yearly audit, visited, at intervals still irregular, the various shires. These Eyres, as they were called, were at first undertaken chiefly for financial purposes. The sheriffs' accounts rendered at Westminster were checked locally on the scene of their labours. These investigations necessarily involved the trial of pleas. Complaints of oppression at the hands of the local tyrant were made and determined on the spot; gradually, but not until a later reign, the judicial business became equally important with the financial, and ultimately even more important.

Henry, before his death in 1135, seemed to have carried to completion the congenial task of building a strong monarchy on the foundations laid by William. Much of his work was, however, for a time undone, while all of it seemed in imminent danger of perishing for ever, because he left no male heir of his body to succeed him. His daughter's claims were set aside by Stephen, son of the Conqueror's daughter, and a cadet of the House of Blois, to whom Henry had played the indulgent uncle, and who repaid his benefactor's generosity by constituting himself his heir. Stephen proved unequal to the task of preserving the monarchy intact from the forces that beat around the throne. His failure is attributed by some to personal characteristics; by others, to the defective nature of his title, combined with the presence of a rival in the field in the person of his cousin, Henry's daughter, the ex-Empress Matilda. The nineteen years of anarchy which nominally formed his reign did nothing—and worse than nothing—to continue the work of his great ancestors. The power of the Crown was humbled: England was almost torn in fragments by the claims of rival magnates to local independence.

With the accession of Henry II. (1154) the tide quickly turned, and turned for good. Of the numerous steps taken by him to complete the work of the earlier master-builders of the English Monarchy, only a few need here be mentioned. Ascending the throne in early manhood, he brought with him a statesman's instinct peculiar to himself, together with the unconquerable energy common to his race. He rapidly overhauled every institution and every branch of administration. The permanent *Curia Regis* was not only restored to working order, but improved in each of its many aspects—as the King's household, as a financial bureau, as the administrative centre of the kingdom, and as the vehicle of royal justice. The Exchequer, which was originally merely the *Curia* in its financial aspect, received the re-organization so urgently needed after the terrible strains to which it had been subjected. The Pipe Rolls were revived and financial reforms effected. The old popular courts of hundred and county, and the feudal jurisdictions were brought under more effective control of the central government by the restoration of the system of Eyres with their travelling justices, whose visits were now placed on a more systematic basis. Equally important were the King's care in the selection of fit men for the duties of Sheriff, the frequent punishment and removal from office of offenders, and the restored control over all in authority. Henry was strong enough to employ more substantial men than the *novi homines* of his grandfather without suffering them to get out of hand. Another expedient for controlling local courts was the calling up of cases to his own central feudal *Curia,* or before those benches of professional judges, the future King's Bench and Common Pleas, that formed as yet merely committees of the *Curia* as a whole.

Closely connected with these innovations was the new system of procedure instituted by Henry. The chief feature was that each litigation must commence with an appropriate royal writ issued from the Chancery. Soon for each class of action was devised a special writ, and the system came to be known as " the writ system."   A striking feature of Henry's policy was the bold manner in which he threw open the doors of his royal Courts of Law to all-comers (excepting villeins), and provided there—always in return for hard cash, be it said—a better article in name of justice than could be procured elsewhere in England, or, for that matter, elsewhere in Europe.   Thus, not only was the Exchequer filled with fines and fees, but, insidi-ously and without the danger involved in a frontal attack, Henry sapped the strength of the great feudal magnates, and diverted the stream of litigants from manorial courts to his own.   The same policy had a further result in facili-tating the growth of a body of common law, uniform throughout the length and breadth of England, opposed to the varying usages of localities and individual baronial courts.

The reorganization of the army was another reform that helped to strengthen the throne of Henry and his sons. This was effected in various ways : partly by the revival and more strict enforcement of obligations connected with the Anglo-Saxon fyrd, under the Assize of Arms (1181), which compelled every freeman to maintain at his own expense weapons and warlike equipment suited to his station in life; partly by the ingenious method of increasing the amount of feudal service due from Crown tenants, based upon an investigation instituted by the Crown and upon the written replies returned by the barons, known to historians as " the *Cartae* of 1166 "; and partly by the development of the principle of scutage, a means whereby unwilling military service, limited as it was by annoying restrictions as to time and place, might be exchanged at the option of the Crown for money, with which a more flexible army of mercenaries might be hired.

By these expedients and many others, Henry raised the English monarchy, always in the ascendant since the Con-quest, to the very zenith of its power, and left to his sons the entire machinery of government in perfect working order, combining high administrative efficiency with great strength. Full of bitter strifes and troubles as his reign of thirty-five years had been, nothing had interfered with the vigour and success of the policy whereby he tightened his hold on England. Neither the long struggle with Becket, ending as it did in Henry's personal humiliation, nor the unnatural warfare with his sons, which hastened his death in 1189, was allowed to interfere with his projects of reform in England.

The last twenty years of life had been darkened for him, and proved troubled and anarchic in the extreme to his continental dominions; but in England profound peace reigned. The last serious revolt of the powers of feudal anarchy had been suppressed in 1174 with characteristic thoroughness and moderation. After that date, the English monarchy retained its supremacy almost without an effort.

II. William I. to Henry II.—Problem of Local Government.

It is necessary to retrace our steps in order to consider the subsidiary problem of local government. The failure of the Princes of the House of Wessex to devise adequate machinery for keeping the Danish and Anglian provinces in subjection to their will was one main source of the weakness of their monarchy. When Duke William solved this problem, he took an enormous stride towards establishing his throne on a securer basis.

Every age has to face, in its own way, a group of difficulties essentially the same, although assuming different names as Home Rule, Local Government, or Federation. Problems as to the proper nature of the local authority, the extent of its powers, and its relation to the central government, require constantly to be re-stated and solved anew. The difficulties involved, always great, were unspeakably greater in an age when no proper administrative machinery existed, and when rapid communication and serviceable roads were unknown. Lively sympathy is excited by consideration of the difficulties that beset the path of King Edgar or King Ethelred, endeavouring to rule from Winchester the distant and alien races of North-

umbria, Mercia, and East Anglia. If a weakling governed
a distant province, anarchy would result and the King's
authority might suffer with that of his inefficient representative; while a powerful viceroy might consolidate his
own authority and then defy his King. The two horns of
this dilemma are amply illustrated by the course of early
English history. The West-Saxon Princes vacillated
between two lines of policy: spasmodic attempts at
centralization alternated with periods of local autonomy.
The scheme of Edgar and Dunstan has sometimes been
described as a federal or home-rule policy—as a frank
surrender of the attempt to control exclusively from one
centre the mixed populations of Northern and Midland
England. Their solution was to relax rather than tighten
the bond; to entrust with wide powers the local viceroy in
each district, and to aim at a loose federal empire—a union
of hearts, rather than a centralized despotism founded on
coercion. The dangers of such a system are obvious,
where each ealdorman commanded the troops of his
province.

Canute's consolidating policy has been the subject of
much discussion, and has sometimes been misunderstood.
The better opinion is that, with his Danish troops behind
him, he felt strong enough to reverse Dunstan's tactics by
decisive action in the direction of centralization. His
provincial viceroys (jarls or earls, as they were now called)
were appointed on a new basis: England was mapped out
into new administrative districts under viceroys having no
hereditary connection with the provinces they governed.
In this way Canute sought to arrest the process by which
England was breaking up into a number of petty kingdoms.
If these viceroys were a source of strength to the powerful
Canute, they proved a source of weakness to the saintly
Confessor, who was forced to submit to the control of his
provincial rulers, such as Godwin and Leofric, as each in
turn gained the upper-hand in the field or among the Witan.
The process of disintegration continued until the coming of
the Conqueror changed the relations between the monarchy
and the other factors in the national life.

Among the expedients adopted by the Norman Duke for curbing his feudatories in England, one of the most important was the reorganization of the system of provincial rulers. The real representative of the King in each group of counties was now the sheriff, not the earl. His Latin name of *vicecomes* is misleading, since that officer in no sense represented the earl or *comes*, but acted as the direct agent of the Crown. The name "viceroy" more accurately describes his actual position and functions.

The problem of local government, however, was not eradicated: it only took a different form. The sheriffs themselves, relieved from the earl's rivalry, tended to become too powerful. If they never dreamed of openly defying the royal authority, they thwarted its exercise, appropriated to their private uses items of revenue, pushed their own interests, and punished their own enemies, while acting in the King's name. The office threatened to become territorial and hereditary,[1] and its holders aimed at independence. Safeguards were found against the sheriffs' growing powers, partly in the organization of the Exchequer and partly in the itinerant justices, who took precedence of the sheriff and heard complaints against his misdeeds in his own county. By such measures, Henry I. seemed almost to have solved these problems before his death; but his success was apparent rather than real.

The incompleteness of Henry's solution became evident under Stephen, when the leading noble of each locality tried, generally with success, to capture *both* offices for himself: great earls like Ralph of Chester and Geoffrey of Essex compelled the King not only to confirm them as sheriffs in their own titular counties, but also to confer on them exclusive right to act as justices.

With the accession of Henry II. some advance was made towards a permanent solution. That great ruler was strong enough to prevent the growth of the hereditary principle as applied to offices either of the Household or of local magistrates. The sheriffs were frequently changed, not only by the drastic and unique measure known as the

---

[1] In one county, Westmoreland, the office did become hereditary.

Inquest of Sheriffs, but systematically, and as a matter of routine. Their power tended in the thirteenth century to decrease, chiefly because they found important rivals not only in the itinerant judges, but also in two new officers first heard of in the reign of Richard I., the forerunners of the modern Coroner and Justice of the Peace respectively. All fear that the sheriffs as administrative heads of districts might defy the Crown was thus ended. Yet each of them remained a petty tyrant over the inhabitants of his own bailiwick. While the Crown was able and willing to avenge neglect of its own interests, it was not always sufficiently alert to punish wrongs inflicted upon its humble subjects. The problem of local government, then, was fast taking a new form, namely, how best to protect the weak from unjust fines and oppressions inflicted on them by local magistrates. The sheriff's local power was no longer a source of danger to the monarch, but had become an effective part of the machinery which enabled the Crown to levy with impunity its always increasing taxation.

III. William I. to Henry II.—Problem of Church and State.

The Church had been, from an early date, in tacit alliance with the Crown. The friendly aid of a line of statesman-prelates from Dunstan downwards had given to the Anglo-Saxon monarchy much of the little strength it possessed. Before the Conquest the connection between Church and State had been exceedingly close, so much so that no one thought of drawing a sharp dividing line between. What afterwards became two separate entities were at first merely two aspects of one society, which comprehended all classes of the people. Change came with the Norman Conquest; for the English Church was brought into closer contact with Rome, and with the ecclesiastical ideals prevailing on the Continent. Yet no fundamental alteration resulted; the friendly relations that bound the prelates to the English throne remained intact, while English Churchmen continued to look to Canterbury, rather than to Rome, for guidance.

Gratitude to the Pope for moral support in effecting the Conquest never modified William's determination to allow no unwarranted papal interference in his new domains. His letter, both outspoken and courteous, in reply to papal demands is still extant :—" I refuse to do fealty nor will I, because neither have I promised it, nor do I find that my predecessors did it to your predecessors." Peter's pence he was willing to pay at the rate recognized by his Saxon predecessors; but all encroachments would be politely repelled.

In settling the country newly reduced to his domination, the Duke of Normandy found his most valuable adviser in a former prior of the Norman Abbey of Bec, whom he raised to be Primate of all England. No record has come down to us of any serious dispute between William and Lanfranc. Friendly relations between King and Archbishop continued, notwithstanding Anselm's condemnation of the evil deeds of Rufus. Anselm supported that King's authority over the Norman magnates, even while he resented his evil practices towards the Church. He contented himself with a dignified protest (made emphatic by a withdrawal of his presence from England) against unfair exactions from English prelates, and against the long intervals during which vacancies remained unfilled.

Returning at Rufus's death from a sort of honourable banishment at Rome, Anselm found himself compelled, by his conscience and the recent decrees of a Lateran Council, to enter on the great struggle of the investitures.

In many respects, the spiritual and temporal powers were still indissolubly locked together. Each bishop was a vassal of the king, holder of a Crown barony, as well as a prelate of Holy Church. By whom, then, should a bishop be appointed, by the spiritual or by the temporal power? Could he without sin perform homage for the estates of his See? Who ought to invest him with ring and crozier? Anselm adopted one view; Henry the other. A happy compromise, suggested by the King's statesmanship, or possibly by Bishop Ivo of Chartres,[1] healed the breach for

[1] Adams, *Pol. Hist. of Engl.*, II. 141. See, however, Davis, *England under Normans*, 132.

B

the time being. The symbols of spiritual authority were to be conferred by the Church, but each prelate must perform fealty to the King before receiving them, and do homage thereafter, but before he was actually anointed as bishop. This compromise of 1106 did not embrace, it would appear, any final understanding as to the method of appointing bishops : "Canonical election" formed no part of Henry's express concessions. [1]

Henry, however, does not seem to have rejected openly the claims of the capitular clergy, but only to have taken steps to render them nugatory in practice. Some of the leading prelates, administrative officials on whom the Monarch could depend, took part in the election of bishops and were usually able to secure the appointment of a candidate acceptable to the King.

The Church gained in power during Stephen's reign, and deserved the power it gained, since it remained the only stable centre of good government, while other institutions crumbled around it. It was not unnatural that Churchmen should advance new claims, and we find them adopting the watchword, afterwards so famous, "that the Church should be free," a vague phrase, destined to be embodied in Magna Carta. The extent of immunity thus claimed was never defined : an elastic phrase might be expanded with the ever-growing pretensions of the Church. Churchmen made it clear, however, that they meant it to include at least two principles—"benefit of clergy," and "canonical election."

Henry II. attempted to define the position in the Constitutions of Clarendon (1164), clause 12 of which provided that in filling vacant Sees the King should summon *potiores personas ecclesiae* and that the "election" should take place in the King's chapel with consent of the King and *consilio personarum regni*, vague words which seem to reserve to Henry the decision as to who constituted "the more influential persons of the church," whom he ought to summon, thus enabling him to control elections (as his

[1] Adams, *Pol. Hist. of Engl.*, II. 148. Contrast the older view in Stubbs, *Const. Hist.*. I. 342-3.

grandfather had done) by means of ecclesiastics whose loyalty to the Crown was undoubted. Henry, in consequence of his humiliation following on Becket's murder, had to release the bishops from their oath to observe the Constitutions. In 1173 he gave a definite promise to allow greater liberty in elections, and it was part of a new agreement with Rome in 1176, that in normal circumstances vacant sees should not be kept in the King's hands for more than a year.[1] Yet, in practice, he continued to exercise a control not inferior to that enjoyed by his grandfather. On the whole, the rights of the Church at the close of the reign of Henry Plantagenet were not far different from what had been set down in the Constitutions of Clarendon. A new definition of the frontier between the spiritual and temporal powers was the outcome of John's need of allies on the eve of Magna Carta.

IV. Richard I. and John.

Henry II., before his death, had fulfilled the task of restoring order : to effect this, he had brought to perfection machinery of rare excellence, equally adapted for purposes of taxation, of dispensing justice, and of general administration. Great as was the power for good of this new instrument in the hands of a wise and justice-loving king, it was equally powerful for evil in the hands of an arrogant, or even of a careless monarch. All the old enemies of the Crown had been crushed. Local government, now systematized, formed a source of strength, not of weakness ; while the Church, whose highest offices were filled with officials trained in Henry's own Exchequer (differing widely from the type of saintly monks like Anselm), still remained the fast friend of the Crown. The monarchy was strong enough to defy any one section of the nation.

The very thoroughness with which the monarchy had surmounted its early difficulties, induced in Henry's successors an exaggerated feeling of security. The very abjectness of the various factors of the nation, now prostrate beneath the heel of the Crown, prepared them to sink their

[1] Makower, *Const. Hist. of Church*, 24-26.

mutual suspicions and to form a tacit alliance in order to join issue with their common oppressor. Powers used moderately and on the whole for national ends by Henry, were abused for selfish ends by both his sons. Richard's heavy taxation and contemptuous indifference to English interests reconciled men's minds to thoughts of change, and prepared the basis of a combined opposition to a power that threatened to grind all other powers to powder.

In no direction were these abuses felt so severely as in taxation. Financial machinery had been elaborated to perfection, and large additional sums could be squeezed from every class by an extra turn of the screw. Richard did not even require to incur the odium, since ministers, his instruments, shielded him from the unpopularity of his measures, while he pursued his own good pleasure abroad in war and tournament without visiting the subjects he oppressed. Twice only, for a few months in either case, did Richard visit England during a reign of ten years.

In his absence new methods of taxation were devised, affecting new classes of property; in particular, personal effects—merchandise and other chattels—only once before (in 1187, for the Saladin tithe) placed under contribution—now became a regular source of royal revenue. The isolated precedent of Henry's reign was followed when an extraordinarily heavy levy was required for Richard's ransom. The very heartiness with which England made sacrifices to succour the Monarch in his hour of need was turned against the tax-payers. Richard showed no gratitude; and, being devoid of kindly interest in his subjects, he argued that what had been paid once might equally well be paid again. With exaggerated notions of the revenue to be extracted from England, he sent from abroad demand after demand to his overworked justiciars for ever-increasing sums of money. The chief lessons of the reign are connected with this excessive taxation; the consequent discontent prepared the way for a new grouping of political forces under John.

Some minor lessons may be noted :

(1) In Richard's absence the odium for his exactions fell

upon his ministers at home, who bore the burden meet for his own callous shoulders, while he enjoyed an undeserved popularity by reason of his bravery and achievements, exaggerated as these were by the halo of romance which surrounds a distant hero. Thus may be traced some dim foreshadowing of the doctrine of ministerial responsibility, although analogies with modern politics must not be pushed too far.

(2) Throughout the reign, parts of Henry's system, technical details of taxation and reforms in the administration of justice, were elaborated by Archbishop Hubert Walter, connected with trial by jury on the one hand and with election on the other.

(3) Richard is sometimes said to have inaugurated the golden age of municipalities. Many Charters, still extant, bear witness to the lavish hand with which he granted, on paper at least, privileges to the nascent towns. John Richard Green finds the true interest of the reign not in the King's Crusade and French wars, so much as in his supposed fostering care over the growth of municipal enterprise.

The death of Richard on 6th April, 1199, brought with it at least one important change; England was no longer to be governed by an absentee. John endeavoured to shake himself free from the restraints of powerful ministers, and conduct the work of government in his own way. The result was an abrupt end to the progress made in the previous reign towards ministerial responsibility. The odium formerly exhausting itself on the justiciars of Richard was now expended on John. While, previously, men had sought redress in a change of minister, such expectations could no longer deceive. A new element of bitterness was added to injuries long resented, and the nobles who felt the pinch of heavy taxation were compelled to seek redress in a new direction. All the forces of discontent played openly around the throne.

As is usual at the opening of a reign, the discontented hoped that a change of sovereign would bring relief. Heavy taxation had been the result of exceptional circum-

stances : the new king would revert to the less burdensome
scale of his father's exactions. Such hopes were quickly
disappointed. John's needs proved as great as Richard's :
the excessive demands, both for money and for service,
coupled with the unpopular uses to which these were put,
form the keynote of the reign : they form also the background of Magna Carta.

The reign falls naturally into three periods; the years
in which John waged a losing war with the King of France
(1199-1206), the quarrel with the Pope (1206-13), the great
struggle with the barons (1213-16).

The first seven years were for England comparatively
uneventful, except in the gradual deepening of disgust with
the King and all his ways. The continental dominions
were ripe for losing, and John precipitated the catastrophe
by injustice and dilatoriness. The ease with which Normandy was lost showed something more than the incapacity
of the King as a ruler and leader—John Softsword as
contemporary writers call him. It showed that the feudal
army of Normandy had come to regard the English Sovereign as an alien. The unwillingness of the English
nobles to succour John has also its significance. The
descendants of the men who helped William I. to conquer
England had now a less vital interest in the land from
which they came. The estates of many of the original
Norman baronage, not unequally divided on both sides of
the Channel, had been split up by inheritance or escheat.
Some of John's barons were purely English landowners
with no interest at stake in France.

By his arbitrary and selfish home policy, the King had
alienated their sympathies. Some of his father's innovations had been unpopular from the first, and became the
objects of bitter opposition in John's tactless hands. The
whole administration of justice, along with the entire feudal
system of land-tenure, with its military obligations, aids
and incidents, were degraded into instruments of extortion,
of which details will be given under appropriate chapters
of the subjoined commentary. English discontent contributed to the loss of Normandy, and that in turn left

English barons more free to attend to' insular matters, and so prepared the way for Magna Carta.

The death of Archbishop Hubert Walter on 13th July, 1205, deprived John of the services of the most experienced statesman in England. It did more, for it marked the termination of the long friendship between the English Crown and the English Church : its immediate effect was to create a vacancy, the filling of which led to a quarrel with Rome.

John failed, as usual, to recognize the merits of abler men, and saw in the death of his great Minister merely the removal of an unwelcome restraint, and the opening to the Crown of a desirable piece of patronage. He prepared to strain to the utmost his rights in the election of a successor to the See of Canterbury, in favour of one of his own creatures, John de Grey, already by royal influence Bishop of Norwich. Unexpected opposition to his will was offered by the canons of the Cathedral Church, who determined to appoint their own nominee, without waiting either for the King's approval or the co-operation of the suffragan bishops of the Province, who, in the three last vacancies, had participated in the election, and had invariably used their influence on behalf of the King's nominee. Reginald, the sub-prior, was secretly elected by the monks, and hurried abroad to obtain confirmation at Rome before the appointment was made public. Reginald's vanity prevented his keeping his pledge of secrecy, and a rumour reached the ear of John, who brought pressure to bear on a section of the monks, now frightened at their own temerity, and secured de Grey's appointment in a second election. The Bishop of Norwich was enthroned at Canterbury, and invested by the King with the temporalities of the See. All parties now sent representatives to Rome. This somewhat petty squabble benefited none of the original disputants; for Innocent III. was quick to seize his opportunity. Both elections were set aside by decree of the Papal Curia, in favour of the Pope's own nominee, a certain Cardinal, English-born, but hitherto little known in England, Stephen Langton by name, destined to play an important part in the history of the land of his birth.

John refused to view this triumph of papal arrogance in the light of a compromise—the view diplomatically suggested by Innocent. The King, with the hot blood common to his race, and the bad judgment peculiar to himself, rushed headlong into a quarrel with Rome which he was incapable of carrying to a successful issue. Full details of the struggle, the interdicts and excommunications hurled by the Pope, and John's measures of retaliation against the unfortunate English clergy, need not be here discussed; but it should. be noted that Innocent, in 1211, released the English people from allegiance to their King.[1]

John was one day to reap the fruits of this quarrel in bitter humiliation and in the defeat of his most cherished aims; but, for the moment, the breach with Rome seemed to lead to a triumph for the King. The papal encroachments furnished him with a pretext for confiscating the property of the clergy. Thus his Exchequer was amply replenished, while he was able for a time to conciliate his most inveterate opponents, the northern barons, by remitting during several years the hated burden of a scutage. John had no intention, however, to forego his right to resume the practice of annual scutages: on the contrary, he executed a measure intended to make them more remunerative. This was the Inquest of Service, ordered on 1st June, 1212.[2]

During these years, however, John temporarily relaxed the pressure on his feudal tenants. His doing so failed to gain back their goodwill, while he broadened the basis of future resistance by shifting his oppressions to the clergy and through them to the poor. Meanwhile, his power was great. Speaking of 1210, a contemporary chronicler declares : " All men bore witness that never since the time of Arthur was there a King who was so greatly feared in England, in Wales, in Scotland, or in Ireland." [3]

Some incidents of the autumn of 1212 require brief

---

[1] Petit-Dutaillis, *Louis VIII.*, 30.   [2] See Round, *Commune of London*, 273.
[3] *Histoire des ducs*, p. 109.

notice, as well from their inherent interest as because they find an echo in Magna Carta. Serious trouble had arisen with Wales. Llywelyn (who had married John's natural daughter Joan, and had consolidated his power under protection of the English King) now seized the occasion to cross the border, while John was preparing for a new continental expedition. The King changed his plans, and prepared to lead his troops to Wales instead of France. A muster was summoned for September at Nottingham, and John went thither to meet his troops. Before tasting meat, in Roger of Wendover's graphic narrative, he hanged twenty-eight Welsh hostages, boys of noble family, whom he held as sureties that Llywelyn would keep the peace.[1]

Almost immediately thereafter, two messengers arrived simultaneously from Scotland and from Wales with unexpected tidings. John's daughter, Joan, and the King of Scots, each independently warned him that his English barons were prepared to revolt, under shelter of the Pope's absolution from their allegiance, and either to slay him or betray him to the Welsh. In a panic he disbanded the feudal levies; and, accompanied only by his mercenaries, moved slowly back to London.[2]

Two of the barons, Robert Fitz-Walter, afterwards the Marshal of the army which opposed John at Runnymede, and Eustace de Vesci, showed their knowledge of John's suspicions by withdrawing secretly from his Court and taking to flight. The King caused them to be outlawed in their absence, and thereafter seized their estates and demolished their castles.[3]

These events of September, 1212, rudely shook John out of the false sense of security in which he had wrapped

---

[1] R. Wendover, III. 239.

[2] W. Coventry, II. 207 ; R. Wendover, III. 239.

[3] From their possible connection with chapter 39 of Magna Carta, it may be worth while to quote the words of Ralph de Coggeshall, *Chronicon Anglicanum*, p. 165 : "Rex Eustachium de Vesci et Robertum filium Walteri, in comitatibus tertio requisitos, cum eorum fautoribus utlaghiari fecit, castra eorum subvertit, praedia occupavit."

himself. In the spring of the same year, he had still seemed to enjoy the full tide of prosperity; and he must have been a bold prophet who dared, like Peter of Wakefield, to foretell the speedy downfall of the King.[1]

John's apparent security was deceptive; he had underestimated the powers arrayed against him. In January, 1213, by Innocent's command, formal sentence of excommunication was passed on John, and Philip of France was appointed as its executor. The chance had come for which the barons, particularly the eager spirits of the North, had long been waiting. The King, on his part, realised that the time had arrived to make his peace with Rome.

On 13th May, 1213, John met Pandulf, the papal legate, and accepted unconditionally the same demands which he had refused contemptuously some months before. Full reparation was to be made to the Church. Stephen Langton was to be received as archbishop in all honour with his banished bishops, friends and kinsmen. All church property was to be restored, with compensation for damage done. One of the minor conditions of John's absolution was the restoration to Eustace de Vesci and Robert Fitz-Walter of the estates which, they persuaded Innocent, had been forfeited because of their loyalty to Rome.[2]

Two days later, apparently on his own initiative, he resigned the Crowns of England and Ireland, and received them again as the Pope's feudatory, promising to perform personal homage should occasion allow. John hoped thus to be free to avenge himself on his baronial enemies. The surrender was embodied in a formal document which bears to be made by John, "with the common council of our barons." Were these merely words of form? They may have been so when first used; yet two years later the envoys of the barons claimed at Rome that the credit (so they now represented it) for the whole transaction lay with them. In any case, no protest seems to have been raised at the time of the surrender. This step, so repugnant to later

[1] See Miss Norgate, *John Lackland*, 170, and authorities there cited.
[2] *Ibid.*, 292-3.

writers, seems not to have been regarded by contemporaries as a disgrace. Matthew Paris, indeed, writing in the next generation, describes it as " a thing to be detested for all time "; but events had ripened in Matthew's day, and he was a keen politician rather than an impartial onlooker.[1]

Stephen Langton, now assured of a welcome to the high office into which he had been thrust against John's will, landed at Dover and was received by the King at Winchester on 20th July, 1213. John swore on the Gospels to cherish and defend Holy Church, to restore the good laws of Edward, and to render to all men their rights, repeating practically the words of the coronation oath. He agreed further to make reparation of all property taken from the Church or churchmen.

V. The Years of Crisis, 1213-15.

Once more the short-sighted character of John's abilities was illustrated : a brief triumph led to a deeper fall. For a season, however, after he had made his peace with Rome, he seemed to enjoy substantial fruits of his diplomacy. Philip's threatened invasion had to be abandoned; the people renewed their allegiance on the removal of the papal sentence; the barons had to make their peace as best they could, awaiting a better opportunity to rebel. If John had confined himself to home affairs, he might have postponed the final explosion : he could not, however, reconcile himself to the loss of the continental heritage of his ancestors. His attempts to recover Normandy and Anjou led to new exactions and new murmurings, while their complete failure left him, discredited and penniless, at the mercy of the malcontents at home.

His projected campaign in Poitou required all the levies he could raise. More than once John demanded, and his barons refused, their feudal service. Many excuses were put forward. At first they declined to follow a King who had not yet been fully absolved. After 20th July, 1213,

---

[1] For the complacency with which contemporary opinion viewed John's surrender, see Petit Dutaillis, *Louis VIII.* p. 39. *Cf. ibid.* p. 181. See also Cardinal Manning, *Contemp. Rev.*, December, 1875 ; Adams, *Origin Engl. Const.*, 152 n.

their new plea was that the tenure on which they held their lands did not compel them to serve abroad : they added that they were already exhausted by expeditions within England.[1] John took this as defiance, and determined, with troops at his back (*per vim et arma*), to compel obedience. Before his preparations were completed, an important assembly met at St. Albans on 4th August, to make sworn inquest as to the extent of damage inflicted on church property during John's quarrel with Rome.[2] From this Council directions were issued in the King's name commanding sheriffs, foresters, and others to observe the laws of Henry I. and to abstain from unjust exactions, as they valued their lives and limbs.[3]

On 25th August, after John had set out with his mercenaries to punish his northern magnates, Stephen Langton held a meeting with the great men of the south. Many bishops, abbots, priors and deans, together with some lay magnates of the southern counties, met him at St. Paul's, London, ostensibly to determine what use the Archbishop should make of his power to grant partial relaxation of the interdict, still casting its blight over England. In the King's absence, Stephen reminded the magnates that John's absolution had been conditional on a promise of good government. He showed them Henry I.'s coronation charter : " by which, if you desire, you can recall your long lost liberties to their pristine state." [4] All present swore to " fight for those liberties, if it were needful, even unto death." The Archbishop promised his help, " and a confederacy being thus made between them, the conference was dissolved." [5]

[1] R. Coggeshall, p. 167.

[2] For the latest views on this council and the writs of summons, see Prof. A. B. White, *Am. Hist. Rev.*, XVII. 12-16.

[3] R. Wendover, III. 261-2.

[4] R. Wendover, III. 263-6. Blackstone (*Great Charter*, Introduction, p. vi.), makes the apposite comment that it seems unlikely that the discovery of a charter probably already well known " should be a matter of such novelty and triumph."

[5] R. Wendover, III. 263-6. Ramsay, *Angevin Empire*, 444, doubts the authenticity of this meeting, the incidents of which have a suspicious resemblance to what took place some fourteen months later at Bury St. Edmunds : see *infra*, p. 32.

Stephen Langton desired a peaceable solution. We find him, accordingly, at Northampton, on the 28th of August, striving to avert civil war. His line of argument is worthy of note : the King must not levy war on his subjects before he had obtained a legal judgment against them (*absque judicio curiae suae*). These words should be compared with the " unknown charter " [1] and with chapter 39 of Magna Carta.

John continued his march to Nottingham, bidding the archbishop not to meddle in affairs of state; but threats of excommunication caused him to consent to substitute legal process for violence, and to appoint a day for the trial of defaulters before the *Curia Regis*—a trial which never took place.[2] John apparently continued his journey as far north as Durham, but returned to meet the new papal legate Nicholas, to whom he performed the promised homage and repeated the act of surrender in St. Paul's on 3rd October.[3] Having completed his alliance with Rome, he was confident of worsting his enemies in France and England.

Yet most, if not all, of the magnates were against him, and this fact may possibly explain John's issue of writs, on 9th November, 1213, inviting four discreet men of each county to discuss with him affairs of the Kingdom.[4] This has sometimes been interpreted as a deliberate design to broaden the basis of the *commune concilium* by adding to it representatives of classes other than Crown-tenants.[5] Miss Norgate, indeed, lays stress on the fact that these writs were issued after the death of the great Justiciar, Geoffrey Fitz-Peter, and before any successor had been appointed. John, she argues, acted on his own initiative, and is thus entitled to the credit of being the first statesman to introduce representatives of the counties into the national assembly. Knights who were tenants of mesne lords (Miss Norgate says " yeomen ") were invited to act as a counter-

---

[1] See Appendix.   [2] R. Wendover, III. 262-3.

[3] The charter recording this act may be read in *New Rymer*, I. 115. It was sealed not in perishable wax, but in gold.

[4] *Sel. Chart.* 287.   [5] *John Lackland*, 195.

poise to the barons. This innovation is held to have
anticipated the line of progress afterwards followed by
de Montfort and Edward I. : compared with it, the often-
praised provisions of chapter 14 of Magna Carta are
regarded as antiquated and even reactionary.

Recent research and criticism, however, have tended to
throw doubts on the authenticity and purport of these writs,
and to postpone the introduction of the representative
principle into the central council to a considerably later
date. It would be unwise to build far-reaching inferences
on the supposed participation of county representatives in
the debates of November, 1213.[1]

In the early spring of 1214, John considered his home
troubles ended, and that he was now free to use against
France the coalition formed by his diplomacy. He went
abroad early in February, leaving Peter de Roches, the
unpopular Bishop of Winchester, as Justiciar, to guard his
interests, in concert with the papal legate.[2] Deserted by
the northern barons, John relied partly on his mercenaries,
but chiefly on the Emperor Otto and his other powerful
allies. Fortune favoured him at first, only to ruin him
more completely in the end. On 2nd July, 1214, John had
hastily to abandon the siege of Roches au Moine, leaving
his baggage to the enemy. The final crash came on
Sunday, 27th July, when the King of France triumphed
over John's allies at the decisive battle of Bouvines. On
18th September, John was compelled to sign a five years'
truce with Philip, abandoning all pretensions to his
continental dominions.

He had left even more dangerous enemies at home, to
watch with trembling eagerness the vicissitudes of his
fortunes abroad. His earlier successes struck dismay into
the malcontents in England, apprehensive of the probable
sequel to his triumphant return home. They waited with
anxiety, but not in idleness, the culmination of his campaign, wisely refraining from open rebellion until news
reached them of his failure or success. Meanwhile, they
quietly organized their programme of reform and their

---

[1] See *e.g.* Adams, *Origin*, 340-1.   [2] See *Rol. Pat.* I. 110, 110, *b*.

measures of resistance. John's strenuous endeavours to exact money and service, while failing to fill his Exchequer, had ripened dormant hostility into an active confederacy organized for resistance. The English barons felt that the moment for action had arrived when news came of the disaster at Bouvines.

Even while abroad, John had not relaxed his efforts to wring exactions from England. Without consent or warning, he had imposed a scutage at the unprecedented rate of three marks on the knight's fee. Writs for its collection had been issued on 26th May, 1214, an exception being indeed allowed for tenants personally present in the King's army in Poitou. The northern barons, who had already refused to serve in person, now refused likewise to pay the scutage. This repudiation was couched in words peculiarly bold and sweeping; they denied liability to follow the King not merely to Poitou, but to any part of the Continent.[1]

When John returned, vanquished and humiliated, on 15th October, 1214, he found himself confronted with a crisis unique in English history. During his absence, the opponents of his misrule had drawn together, formulated their grievances, and matured their plans. The embarrassments on the Continent which weakened the King, heartened the opposition. The northern barons took the lead. Their cup of wrath, which had long been filling, overflowed when the scutage of three marks was imposed. Within three weeks of his landing, John held parley with the malcontents at Bury St. Edmunds (on 4th November).[2] No compromise was possible: John pressed for payment, and the barons refused.

It seems probable that, after John's retiral, a conference of a more private nature was held at which, under cloak of attending the Abbey for worship, a conspiracy against John was sworn. Roger of Wendover gives a graphic account: the magnates came together "as if for prayers; but there was something else in the matter, for after they had held much secret discourse, there was brought forth

[1] See W. Coventry, II. 217.   [2] See Norgate, *John Lackland*, p. 221.

in their midst the charter of King Henry I., which the same barons had received in London . . . from Archbishop Stephen of Canterbury."[1] A solemn oath was taken to withdraw their fealty (a threat carried into effect on 5th May of the following year), and to wage war on the King, unless he granted their liberties. A date—soon after Christmas—was fixed for making their formal demands. Meanwhile they separated to prepare for war. The King also realized that a resort to arms was imminent. While collecting mercenaries, he tried to sow dissension among his opponents : he hoped to buy off the hostility of the Church by a charter, issued on 21st November, professing to be granted " of the common consent of our barons." Its object was to gain the Church's support by granting freedom of election to vacant sees. The appointment of prelates should henceforth really lie with the canons of the various cathedral or conventual churches and monasteries, saving, however, to the Crown the right of wardship during vacancies. John promised never to deny or delay his consent to an election, and conferred powers on the electors, if he should do so, to proceed without him. The King was bitterly disappointed in his hope that by this bribe he would bring over the Church from the barons' side to his own.

John held what must have been an anxious Christmas at Worcester, but tarried only for a day, hastening to the Temple, London, where the proximity of the Tower gave him a feeling of security. There, on 6th January, 1215, a deputation from the insurgents met him without disguising that their demands were backed by force. These demands, they told him, included the confirmation of the laws of Edward, with the liberties set forth in Henry's Charter. On the advice of the Archbishop and the Marshal, who acted as mediators, John asked a truce till Easter, which was granted on his promise that he would then give reasonable satisfaction. The Archbishop, the Marshal, and the Bishop of Ely were named as the King's sureties.

John was in desperate straits for money : " the pleas of

---

[1] R. Wendover, III. 293. *Cf. supra* 28.

the exchequer and the counties ceased throughout England, for nobody was found who would pay tax to the King, or obey him in anything."[1] On 15th January, he reissued the Charter to the Church, and demanded a renewal of homage. The sheriffs in each county were instructed to administer the oath in a stringent form; all Englishmen must now swear to "stand by him against all men." Meanwhile, emissaries were dispatched by both sides to Rome. Eustace de Vesci, as spokesman of the malcontents, asked Innocent, as overlord of England, to compel John to restore the ancient liberties, and claimed consideration on the ground that John's surrender to the Pope had been made under pressure put on the King by them—all to no effect. John thought to propitiate the Pope by swearing to go upon Crusade, a politic oath which would serve to protect him from personal violence, and which afforded him, as is well illustrated by several chapters of Magna Carta, a fertile excuse for delay in remedying abuses. In April, the northern barons met in arms at Stamford, and after Easter (when the truce had expired) marched southward to Brackley, in Northampton. There they were met, on 27th April, by the Archbishop and the Marshal, as emissaries from the King, to enquire as to their demands. They received in reply, and took back with them to John, a certain schedule, which, so Roger of Wendover informs us, consisted for the most part of ancient laws and customs of the realm, with an added threat that, if the King did not immediately adhibit his seal, the rebels would constrain him by seizing his castles, lands, and goods.[2]

John's answer when he read these demands, was emphatic. "Why do not the barons, with these unjust exactions, ask my kingdom?" Then furious, he declared with an oath that he would never grant them liberties which would make him a slave.[3]

A metrical chronicle[4] records the threat to depose the King, unless he fully amended the law and furnished

---

[1] R. Wendover, III. 301.

[2] R. Wendover, III. 298.   For the schedule see *infra*, pp. 37-9.

[3] R. Wendover, III. 298.   [4] *Chronica de Mailros, sub anno* 1215.

undoubted guarantees for a lasting peace. On 5th May, the barons went through the ceremony of *diffidatio,* or formal renunciation of allegiance,[1] a recognised feudal right, and not involving treason if justified by events and properly intimated to the overlord.[2] They chose as their commander, Robert Fitz-Walter, who, as though conducting a Crusade, styled himself piously and grandiloquently, " Marshal of the army of God and Holy Church."

The insurgents, still shivering on the brink of civil war, delayed to march southwards. Much would depend on the attitude of London, with its wealth and central position; and John bade high for the support of its citizens. On 9th May a new charter[3] was granted to the Londoners, who now received a long-coveted privilege, the right to elect their mayor annually and to remove him at the year's end. This marked the culmination of a long series of progressive grants in their favour. Previously the mayor had held office for life, and Henry Fitz-Aylwin, the earliest holder of the office (appointed perhaps in 1191), had died in 1212.

Apparently no price was paid for this charter; but John doubtless expected in return the grateful support of the Londoners, exactly as he had expected the support of churchmen when he twice granted a charter in their favour. In both instances he was disappointed. Next day he made, probably as a measure of delay, an offer of arbitration to the barons. In the full tide of military preparations, he issued a writ in these words : [" Know that we have conceded to our barons who are against us that we shall not take or disseise them or their men, nor go against them *per vim vel per arma,* unless by the law of our land, or by the judgment of their peers in *curia nostra,* until consideration shall have been had by four whom we shall choose on our part and four whom they shall choose on their part, and the lord Pope who shall be oversman over them "—

---

[1] Blackstone, *Great Charter,* p. xiii, citing *Annals of Dunstable* (p. 43), says they were absolved at Wallingford by a Canon of Durham.

[2] *Cf.* Adams, *Origin,* 181 n. ; 306, 312 ; *cf.* also *infra* under c. 61.

[3] The Charter appears *Rot. Chart.,* p. 207. *Cf.* under chapter 13 *infra,* where the rights of the Londoners are discussed.

words worthy of careful comparison with chapter 39 of Magna Carta. The offer could not be taken seriously, since it left the decision of every vital issue virtually to the Pope, whom the barons distrusted.[1]

Another royal writ, of two days later, shows a rapid change of policy, doubtless due to the contemptuous rejection of arbitration. On 12th May, John ordered the sheriffs to do precisely what he had offered not to do. They were told to take violent measures against the rebels without waiting for a " judgment of peers." Lands, goods, and chattels of the King's enemies were to be seized and applied to his benefit.[2] The barons, rejecting all offers, marched by Northampton, Bedford, and Ware, towards the capital. London opened its gates on 17th May.[3] The example was quickly followed by other towns and by many hesitating magnates. The confederates felt strong enough to issue letters to all who still adhered to John, bidding them forsake him on pain of forfeiture.

John found himself, for the moment, without power of effective resistance; and, probably with a view of gaining time rather than of committing himself irretrievably to any abatement of his prerogatives, agreed to a conference. As a preliminary, he issued, on 8th June, a safe-conduct for the barons' representatives to meet him at Staines within the three days following. This was too short notice : on 10th June, John, now at Windsor, granted an extension of the safe-conduct till Monday, 15th June. William Marshal and other envoys were dispatched from Windsor to the barons in London with a message of surrender : John " would freely accede to the laws and liberties which they asked," if they would appoint a place and day of meeting. The intermediaries, in the words of Roger of Wendover,[4] " without guile carried back to the barons the

[1] The writ is given in *Rot. Pat.*, I. 141, and also in *New Rymer*, I. 128.

[2] For writ, see *Rot. Claus.*, 204.

[3] Some authorities give 24th May, but *New Rymer*, p. 121, under 17th May, prints a writ of John, informing Rowland Blaot of the surrender of London. This was followed on 20th May (*N. R.*, p. 121) by another writ, ordering bailiffs and other to molest the Londoners in every possible way.

[4] III. 301.

message which had been guilefully imposed on them."
The barons, *immenso fluctuantes gaudio,* fixed as the time
of meeting, the last day of the extended truce, Monday,
15th June, at a certain meadow between Staines and
Windsor, known as Runnymede.

VI. Runnymede, and after.

On 15th June, 1215, a five days' conference between
King and Barons began.   On the side of the insurgents
appeared a great host; on the monarch's, a small band of
magnates, loyal to the person of the King, but only half-
hearted, at the best, in his support.   Their names may be
read in the preamble to the Charter : the chief among them,
Stephen Langton, still nominally neutral, was known to be
in full sympathy with the rebels.

Dr. Stubbs,[1] maintaining that the whole baronage of
England was implicated in these stirring events, analyses
its more conspicuous members into four groups : (1) the
Northumbrani or *Norenses* of the chroniclers, the first to
raise the standard of revolt; (2) other barons from various
parts of England, who had shown themselves ready to
co-operate with the Northerners—" the great baronial
families that had been wise enough to cast away the feudal
aspirations of their forefathers, and the rising houses which
had sprung from the ministerial nobility "; (3) the moderate
party, who followed the lead of London, including even the
King's half-brother (the Earl of Salisbury), the loyal
Marshal, Hubert de Burgh, and other Ministers of the
Crown, whose names may be read in the preamble to the
Charter; and (4) the tools of John's misgovernment, mostly
men of foreign birth, tied to John by interest as well as
loyalty, since their differences with the baronial leaders lay
too deep for reconciliation, a few of whom are branded by
name in Magna Carta as for ever incapable of holding
office.   These men of desperate fortunes alone remained
whole-hearted on John's side when the crisis came.[2]

---

[1] *Const. Hist.,* I. 581-3.

[2] The names may be read in Stubbs, *Ibid.* ; and readers in search of biographical
knowledge are referred to Bémont, *Chartes,* 39-40, and for fuller, less reliable
information, to Thomson, *Magna Charta,* 270-322.

When the conference began, the fourth group was in command of castle garrisons or of troops actually in the field; the third group, a small one, was with John; the first and second groups were, in their imposing strength, arrayed against him.

Unfortunately, the vagueness of contemporary accounts prevents us from reproducing with certainty the progress of negotiations on that eventful 15th of June and the few following days. Some inferences, however, may be drawn from the words of the completed Charter and of several closely related documents. One of these, the Articles of the Barons,[1] is sometimes supposed to be identical in its terms with the schedule which had been already presented to the King's emissaries at Brackley, on 27th April. It is more probable that during seven eventful weeks the original demands had been somewhat modified. The schedule of April was probably only a rough outline of the Articles as we now know them, and these formed in turn the draft on which the Charter was based. Articles and Charter are alike authenticated by the impress of the King's seal. There is thus a strong presumption that an interval elapsed between the King's acceptance of the first and the completion of the second; since it would have been absurd to seal a superseded draft at the same time as the principal instrument. The probability of such an interval must not be lost sight of in any attempt to reconstruct the stages of negotiations at Runnymede.

A few undoubted facts form a starting-point on which inferences may be based. John's headquarters were at Windsor from Monday, 15th June, to the afternoon of Tuesday the 23rd. On each of these nine days (with the possible exception of the 16th and 17th) he visited Runnymede to confer with the barons.[2] Two crucial stages were reached on Monday the 15th (the date borne by Magna Carta itself) and on Friday the 19th (the day on which John

[1] See Appendix.

[2] So far there can be no doubt. Either on *Close* or *Patent Rolls* (q.v.) copies of writs are preserved dated from Windsor on each of these days, and also one or more dated from Runnymede on 15th, 18th, 19th, 20th, 21st, 22nd, and 23rd June.

in more than one writ stated that peace had been concluded).
What happened exactly on each of these two days is matter
of conjecture. It is here maintained, with some confidence,
that on Monday the substance of the barons' demands was
provisionally accepted and that the Articles were then
sealed; while on Friday this arrangement was confirmed
and Magna Carta itself, in several duplicates, was sealed.

To justify these inferences, a more detailed examination
of the evidence available is required. The earliest meeting
between John and the baronial leaders, all authorities are
agreed, took place on Monday, 15th June, probably in the
early morning. The barons undoubtedly brought to the
conference a list of grievances they were determined to
redress. On the previous 27th of April the rebels had sent
a written schedule to the King;[1] they are not likely to
have been less fully prepared on 15th June.

John, on his part, would naturally try a policy of evasions
and delays; and, when these were clearly useless, would
then endeavour to secure modifications of the terms offered.
These tactics met with no success. His opponents asked
a plain acceptance of their plainly expressed demands.
Before nightfall, John, overawed by their firmness and by
the numbers of the armed force behind them, was constrained to surrender, and signified his acceptance of the
barons' demands, as contained in a list of 49 Articles
(apparently drawn out on the spot), by imprinting his great
seal on the wax of its label, where it may still be seen.[2]
Ralph of Coggeshall's brief account gives the contemporary opinion : "By intervention of the archbishop of
Canterbury, with several of his fellow-bishops and some
barons, a sort of peace was made."[3] The document bears
traces of the discussions that preceded it. The first article
postpones a definition of the customary "relief," leaving
this to be expressed "in carta."[4] Articles 45 and 46 (less
vital to the barons as affecting their allies, not themselves)
are joined by a rude bracket; and their suggested modifica-

---

[1] R. Wendover, III. 298.
[2] In the British Museum. See *infra* under Part V.
[3] R. Coggeshall, 172.   [4] See *infra*, c. 2

tion in favour of John is referred to Stephen Langton's decision.[1] The last article, or *forma securitatis,* the dregs of John's cup of humiliation, is separated by a blank space from the rest.[2]

The document is in a running hand and appears to have been rapidly though carefully written : a diligent copyist would be able to complete his task within a few hours. There are thus ample reasons for holding that it was not the identical schedule of the preceding April, but that it was written out between two conferences on Monday, 15th June, by one of the clerks of the royal Chancery. This is in keeping with the contemporary heading : " *Ista sunt capitula quae barones petunt et dominus rex concedit.*"

Comparison with the final Charter suggests that further conferences led to alterations in regard to various details : [3] thus, chapter 14 contains provisions not contained in the *Articuli,* though forming a necessary supplement to the substance of article 32. New influences would seem to have been at work, favourable to the claims of the English Church; effecting some slight modifications in favour of the Crown ; [4] and apparently not too careful of the interests of the towns or of native traders.[5]

It is not difficult to infer the nature of the forces at work. John was fighting for his own hand; the barons merely demanded a fair statement of their just rights, and had no desire to take undue advantage of the King; the towns found the barons more ready to meet the King by sacrificing their allies' rights than their own ; Stephen Langton, while acting as mediator, looked well after the interests of the Church.

Tuesday, Wednesday and Thursday were probably consumed in adjusting these matters of detail ; in reducing the

[1] See *infra,* cc. 58 and 59. *Cf.* Blackstone, *Great Charter,* xvii. : " subjoined in a more hasty hand, . . . as if added at the instance of the King's commissioners upon more mature deliberation."

[2] See *infra,* c. 61.

[3] Blackstone, *Great Charter,* xviii., has given a careful analysis of the points of difference.

[4] *E.g.* chapters 48 and 52 *infra.*   [5] *E.g.* chapters 12, 13, 35, and 41 *infra.*

heads of agreement to the more binding form of a feudal Charter; and in engrossing several copies for greater security. Everything was ready for settlement on Friday, the 19th. On that day, the final concord probably included several steps; the nomination by the opposition, with the King's acquiescence, of twenty-five barons to act as "Executors" under chapter 61,[1] the solemn sealing and delivery of several originals of the Charter in its final form, the taking of an oath by all parties to abide by its provisions, and the issue of the first batch of writs of instructions to the sheriffs.

The barons on that day renewed their oaths of fealty and homage : this was the stipulated price of "the liberties." They promised a guarantee in any form John wished, except the delivery of hostages or the surrender of strongholds—a promise they failed to keep.[2]

The statement that Friday, 19th June, was the day on which peace was finally concluded rests on unmistakable evidence. On 21st June, John wrote from Windsor to William of Cantilupe, one of his captains, instructing him not to enforce payment of any unpaid balances of "tenseries "[3] demanded since the preceding Friday, "on which day peace was made between the King and his barons."[4]

It has been usually assumed that peace was concluded, and the Charter sealed on the 15th. The fact that all four copies of Magna Carta still extant bear this date seems to have been regarded as conclusive. Elaborate charters, however, which occupied time in preparation, usually bore the date, not of their actual execution, but of the day on which occurred the transactions they record. Thus it is

---

[1] The powers and constitutional position of these " executors " are fully discussed *infra* under c. 61.

[2] See Protest in Appendix.

[3] Round explains this (*Geoffrey de Mandeville*, 414) as "blackmail," *i.e.* " money extorted under pretence of protection or defence."

[4] See *Rot. Claus.*, p. 225. This writ does not stand alone. In another writ, dated 19th June, John informs his half-brother that he has just concluded peace. See also *Annals of Dunstable*, III. 43, reporting peace made "*die Gervassi et Protasii*," *i.e.* on 19th June.

far from safe to infer from Magna Carta's mention of its own date that the seal was actually adhibited on 15th June.

Such presumption as exists is all the other way. The Great Charter is a lengthy document, and it is barely possible that any one of the four originals known to us could have been engrossed (to say nothing of the adjustment of substance and form) within one day. Not only is it much longer than the Articles on which it is founded; but even the most casual comparison will convince any unbiassed mind of the slower rate of engrossment of the Charter. All four copies show marks of deliberation, while those at Lincoln and Salisbury are models of leisurely and exquisite penmanship. The highly finished initial letters of the first line and other ornamental features may be instructively compared with the plain, business-like, rapid hand of the Articles. How many additional copies, now lost, were once in existence bearing the same date, it is impossible to say; but each of those still extant may well have occupied more than one day in the writing.[1]

In addition to the various originals of the Charter issued under the great seal, chapter 62 provides that authenticated copies should be made and certified as correct by " Letters Testimonial," under the seals of the two archbishops with the legate and the bishops.[2] These were intended for the

---

[1] Miss Norgate, *John Lackland*, p. 234, in fixing on Monday as the day of final concord, relies for evidence on a more than doubtful interpretation of an error in the copy of a writ, which in the *Patent Rolls* bears to be dated 18th June (erroneously as will be shown), addressed to Stephen Harengod, announcing that terms of peace had been agreed upon "last Friday." Miss Norgate contends that on the Friday preceding the 18th negotiations had not even begun, and is confident that the " die Veneris" which occurs three times in the writ is an unaccountable error for "die Lunae." Yet, it is unlikely that a scribe writing three days after so momentous an event could have mistaken the day of the week. It is infinitely more probable that is writing xxiij. he formed the second " x " so carelessly that it was mistaken by the enrolling clerk for a " v." The correct date is thus the 23rd, and the reference is to Friday the 19th. This presumption becomes a certainty by comparison with the words of the writ to William of Cantilupe, dated the 21st, and other evidences cited *supra*, p. 40.

[2] No specimen of these Letters is known, but a copy is preserved on folio 234, *Red Book of Exchequer*. See *infra* under c. 62 and also R. L. Poole, *Eng. Hist. Rev.*, XXVIII. 448.

sheriffs, whose writs of instructions dated 19th to 27th June, to publish the terms of the charters, are preserved in the Patent Rolls. Each sheriff was instructed to cause all in his bailiwick to make oath, according to the form of the Charter, to the twenty-five barons or their attorneys, and further, to see to the appointment of twelve knights of the county in full County Court, to declare upon oath all evil practices as well of sheriffs as of their servants, foresters, and others.[1] This was held to apply chiefly to the redress of forest grievances.

A week elapsed before these writs, with copies of the Charter, could be sent to every sheriff. During the same few days, orders were sent to military commanders to stop hostilities. A few writs, dated mostly 25th June, show that some obnoxious sheriffs had made way for better men; while Hubert de Burgh became Justiciar in room of Peter des Roches. On 27th June, new writs directed the sheriffs and the elected knights to punish, by forfeiture of lands and chattels, all who refused to swear to the twenty-five Executors within a fortnight.

The barons were still unsatisfied as to the King's sincerity, and demanded further securities. The interesting question thus arises, how far they were justified in doubting John's intentions. Prof. Petit-Dutaillis, founding mainly on the writs dispatched to sheriffs and constables, credits John with perfect though perhaps short-lived good faith.[2] He rightly refuses to believe Wendover's unlikely story of John's immediate retiral to the Isle of Wight, and of the war preparations he made there in a delirium of fury.[3] Proof of John's sincerity is sought in the reputed quarrel with his Flemish mercenaries, for whom the King's " villain

---

[1] See Appendix.

[2] He might here have strengthened his argument by referring to the evidences of extreme care shown in revising the original Articles of the Barons when translating them into charter form. This would have been thrown away, if John intended to break faith. On the other hand, this care, equally with the issue of writs, might have been a blind.

[3] See *Louis VIII.*, p. 57, and also Hardy's *Introd.* to *Litt. Pat.*, XXIX., where the story was disproved by dates of writs issued elsewhere.

peace" meant that his purse would be closed to them and led them to desert his cause.[1]

In brief, according to M. Petit-Dutaillis, John's conduct was above reproach during June and July, and until the bad faith of his opponents forced him to protect himself.[2]

Yet John's punctilious observance, for a short space, of the letter of his bargain may be equally consistent with studied duplicity, dictated by urgent need of gaining time, as with any loyal intention to submit permanently to restraints which, in his own words, "made him a slave," and were to be enforced by "five-and-twenty over kings";[3] while his negotiations with Rome are difficult to reconcile with any intention of permanently keeping faith.

Justified or not, the barons demanded that the City and Tower of London should be placed in their hands as pledges of good-faith until 15th August, or until the reforms were completely carried out. John had to surrender the city to the rebels, but the Tower was placed in the neutral custody of Stephen Langton. These terms may be read in a supplementary treaty headed: "*Conventio facta inter Regem Angliae et barones ejusdem regni.*"[4] John, equally distrustful on his side, demanded the security promised at the renewal of allegiance; but the barons refused to embody the terms of their homage in a formal Charter. The Archbishops of Canterbury and Dublin, with several suffragans, appealed to as umpires by the King, recorded a protest narrating the barons' breach of faith.[5]

The same prelates, alarmed apparently lest drastic measures of reform should lead to the total abolition of the forests, entered a second protest. As mediators, bound to see fair-play, they declared in writing that the words of the Charter must be read in a restricted sense: customs needful for preserving the forests should remain in force.[6] The provisions referred to were, as is now well known, chapters

---

[1] See *Hist. des ducs de Norm.*, pp. 149-151.   [2] *Louis VIII.*, p. 57.

[3] See Norgate, *Lackland*, 235, citing M. Paris, II. 611.

[4] *New Rymer*, I. 133. See Appendix. It is undated, but must be later than the letters of 27th June to which it alludes.

[5] *Rot. Pat.*, 181. See Appendix.   [6] See *Rot. Pat.* and *New Rymer*, I. 134.

47, 48, and 53 of Magna Carta itself, and not, as Roger of Wendover states, a separate Forest Charter.[1] That writer was led into error by confusing John's Charter with its reissue by his son. Sir William Blackstone was the first commentator to correct this mistake.[2]

These are not the only pieces of evidence that point to lack of moderation on the barons' part, revealed even before the four days' conference was ended. Matthew Paris narrates how it was found necessary to curb the excesses of the twenty-five Executors of the Charter by the nomination of a second body of thirty-eight barons, drawn from both parties.[3]

From a contemporary chronicler there comes a strange tale of the arrogance of the twenty-five : one day when they went to the King's court " to make a judgment," John, ill in bed, asked them to come to his chamber as he was unable to go to them; but they curtly refused, demanding that the King, unable to walk, should be carried into their presence.[4]

John looked for aid to Rome. Three weeks before granting the Charter, he had begun his preparations for its repudiation. In a letter of 29th May, addressed to the Pope, there may still be read his own explanation of the causes of quarrel, and how he urged, with low cunning, that the rebels prevented fulfilment of his vow of crusade. In conclusion, he expressed his willingness to abide by the Pope's decision on all matters at issue. He followed up this letter, shortly after 19th June, by dispatching Richard de Marais to plead his cause at Rome.[5] Delay was doubly in his favour; since the combination formed against him was certain, in a short time, to break up. It was, in the happy phrase of Dr. Stubbs,[6] a mere " coalition," not an " organic union "—a coalition, too, in momentary danger of dissolving into its original factors. The barons were without sufficient sinews of war to carry a protracted struggle to a successful issue.

Soon, both sides to the treaty of peace were preparing

---

[1] See R. Wendover, III. 302-318. [2] *Great Charter*, p. xxi.
[3] M. Paris, II. 605-6. [4] *Hist. des ducs de Normandie*, 151.
[5] *New Rymer*, I. 129. [6] Stubbs, *Const. Hist.*, II. 3.

for war. The northern barons, anticipating the King in direct breach of the compact, began to fortify their castles, and maltreated the royal officials.[1] John, in equally bad faith, wrote for foreign allies, whilst he anxiously awaited the Pope's answer to his appeal. Langton and the bishops still struggled to restore harmony. The 16th July was fixed for a new conference. John did not attend; but it was probably at this Council that in his absence a papal bull was read conferring upon a commission of three—the Bishop of Winchester, the Abbot of Reading, and the legate Pandulf—full powers to excommunicate all "disturbers of the King and Kingdom." No names were mentioned, but these powers might clearly be used against Langton and his friends. The execution of this sentence was delayed, in the groundless hope of a compromise, till the middle of September, when two of the commissioners, Pandulf and Peter of Winchester, demanded that the archbishop should publish it; and, on his refusal, they forthwith suspended him from office (a sentence confirmed by the Pope on 4th November).[2]

Stephen left for Rome, and his absence at a critical juncture proved a national misfortune. The insurgents lost in him, not only their bond of union, but also a wholesome restraint. After his departure, a papal bull arrived (in the end of September) dated 24th August. This is an important document in which Innocent, in the plainest terms, annuls and abrogates the Charter, after adopting all the facts and reproducing all the arguments furnished by the King. Beginning with a full description of John's wickedness and repentance, his surrender of England and Ireland, his Crusader's oath, his quarrel with the barons; it goes on to describe Magna Carta as the result of a conspiracy, and concludes, " We utterly reprobate and condemn any agreement of this kind, forbidding, under ban of our anathema, the foresaid king to presume to observe it, and the barons and their accomplices to exact its performance, declaring void and entirely abolishing both the Charter itself and the obligations and safeguards made, either for its enforcement

---

[1] Walter of Coventry, 222.   [2] See Petit-Dutaillis, *Louis VIII.*, 61.

or in accordance with it, so that they shall have no validity at any time whatsoever." [1]

A supplementary bull, of one day's later date, reminded the barons that the suzerainty of England belonged to Rome, and that therefore nothing could be done in the kingdom without papal consent.[2] Thereafter, at a Lateran Council, Innocent excommunicated the English barons who had persecuted "John, King of England, crusader and vassal of the Church of Rome, by endeavouring to take from him his kingdom, a fief of the Holy See." [3]

Meanwhile, the points in dispute had been submitted to the rude arbitrament of civil war, in which the first notable success fell to John, who took Rochester Castle by assault on 30th November. The barons had already made overtures to Louis, the French King's son, offering him the crown of England. Towards the end of November, seven thousand French troops arrived in London, where they spent the winter, while John marched from place to place, meeting, on the whole, with success, especially in the east of England. John's best ally was once more the Pope, who did not intend to allow a French Prince to usurp his vassal's throne. Gualo was dispatched from Rome to Philip, King of France, forbidding his son's invasion, and asking protection and assistance for John. Philip, anxious to break the force of the Pope's arguments by proving some right to intervene, endeavoured to find defects in John's title as King of England, and to argue that therefore John was not *in titulo* to grant to the Pope the rights of an over-lord: John had been convicted of treason while Richard was King, and this involved forfeiture of all rights of succession. Thus the Pope's claim of intervention was invalid, while Prince Louis justified his own interference by some imagined right which, he ingeniously argued, had passed to him through the mother of his wife.

John had not relied solely on papal protection; but the

---

[1] The bull with the seal attached is in the British Museum (Cotton, Cleopatra E 1), and is carefully printed by Bémont, *Chartes*, 41. It may also be read in Rymer and Blackstone.

[2] The text is given by Rymer.   [3] See Rymer, and Bémont, *Chartes*, XXV.

fleet, collected at Dover to block Louis with his smaller
vessels in Calais harbour, was wrecked on 18th May, 1216.
The French Prince, setting sail on the night of the 20th
May, landed next morning unopposed. John, reduced to
dependence on mercenaries, dared not risk an engagement.
Gualo, now in England, on 28th May excommunicated
Louis by name, and laid London under interdict. On 2nd
June, the French Prince entered London, received homage
from the Mayor and others, and took oath to uphold good
laws and restore invaded rights.[1] It was probably on this
occasion that Louis confirmed the Charter.[2] Into the
vicissitudes of the war and the royalist reaction, to which
the arrogance of the French troops contributed, it is unnecessary here to enter. At a critical juncture, when
fortune still trembled in the balance, John's death at Newark
Castle, on the morning of 19th October, 1216, altered the
situation, rendering possible, and indeed inevitable, a new
arrangement of parties and forces in England. The heir to
the throne was an infant, whose advisers found it prudent to
reissue voluntarily, and to accept as their rule of government, the essential principles of the Charter that had been
extorted from the unwilling John.

[1] *Cronique de Merton*, cited Petit-Dutaillis, *Louis VIII.*, 514.
[2] *Ibid.*, 115

PART II.

FEUDAL GRIEVANCES AND MAGNA CARTA.

I. The Immediate Causes of the Crisis.

Many attempts have been made to show why the storm, long brewing, broke at last in 1214, and culminated precisely in June of the following year. Sir William Blackstone [1] shows how carefully historians have sought for some one specific feature or event, occurring in these years, of such moment as by itself to account for the rebellion crowned with success at Runnymede. Matthew Paris, he tells us, attributes the whole movement to the sudden discovery of Henry I.'s Charter, and most of the chroniclers assign John's inordinate debauchery as the cause of the dissensions, dwelling on his personal misdeeds, real and imaginary.[2] "Sordida foedatur foedante Johanne, gehenna." [3] Blackstone himself suggests a third cause, the appointment as Regent in John's absence of the hated alien and upstart, Peter des Roches, and his misconduct in that office.

Of John's arrogance and cruelty there is abundant testimony; [4] but the causes from which Magna Carta took its rise were more deeply rooted in the past. The very success of Henry Plantagenet in restoring order in Eng-

---

[1] *The Great Charter*, p. vii. [2] R. Wendover, II. 535.

[3] M. Paris, II. 669. Several of the most often-repeated charges of personal wrongs inflicted by King John upon the wives and daughters of his barons have been in recent years refuted. See Miss Norgate, *John Lackland*, p. 289.

[4] See, *e.g.*, the harrowing account of how he starved to death Matilda de Braose and her son (Davis, *Engl. under Normans*, 363). For his conduct in Ireland, see Orpen, *Ireland*, II. 96-105; and in Normandy, Powicke, *Loss of Normandy*, 190-2.

land, for effecting which special powers had been allowed
to him, made the continuance of these powers unnecessary.
From the day of Henry's death, if not earlier, forces were
at work which only required to be combined in order to
control the licence of the Crown. When the battle of order
had been won—the complete overthrow of the rebellion of
1173-4 may here be taken as the crucial date—the battle of
liberty had, almost necessarily, to be begun.

The wonder is that the crisis was so long delayed.
Events, however, were not ripe for rebellion before John's
accession, and a favourable occasion did not occur previous
to 1215. The doctrine of momentum accounts in politics
for the long continuance of old institutions in a condition
even of unstable equilibrium; an entirely rotten system of
government may remain for ages until at the destined
moment comes the final shock. John conferred a boon on
future generations, when by his arrogance and his misfortunes he combined against him all classes and interests
in the community.

The chief factor in the coalition that ultimately triumphed
over John was the baronial party, led by those strenuous
nobles of the north, who were goaded into opposition by
their own personal and class wrongs, not by any altruistic
promptings to sacrifice themselves for the common good.
Their complaints, as they appear in the imperishable record
of Magna Carta, are grounded on technical rules of feudal
usage, not upon any broad basis of constitutional principle.

The grievances most bitterly resented may be ranged
under one or other of two heads—increase in the weight of
feudal obligations and infringement of feudal jurisdictions :
the Crown, while it exacted the fullest measure of services
legally exigible, curtailed those rights and privileges which
had originally balanced the obligations. The barons were
compelled to give more, while they received less. Each of
these heads calls for separate and detailed treatment.[1]

The grievances of the barons, however, were not the only
wrongs calling for redress. It is probable that the baronial
party, if they had acted in isolation, would have failed in

[1] See *infra* the two sections (II. and III.) immediately following.

D

1215 as they had already failed in 1173. If the Crown had retained the active sympathy of Church and common people, the King might have successfully defied the baronage as his father had done before him. John had, on the contrary, broadened the basis of opposition by oppressing the mercantile classes and the peasantry. The order-loving townsmen had been willing to purchase protection from Henry at the price of heavy taxation : John continued to exact the price, but failed to furnish good government in return. Far from protecting the humble from oppression, he was himself the chief oppressor; and he let loose his foreign favourites as deputy oppressors in all the numerous offices of sheriff, castellan, and bailiff. Far from using the perfected machinery of Exchequer, Curia, and local administration in the interests of good government, John valued them merely as instruments of extortion and outrage —as ministers to his lust and greed.

The lower orders were by no means exempt from the increased taxation which proved so galling to the feudal tenants. When John, during his quarrel with Rome, repaid each new anathema of the Pope by fresh acts of spoliation against the English Church, the sufferings of the clergy were shared by the poor. In confiscating the goods of monasteries, he destroyed the chief provision for poor-relief known to the thirteenth century. The alienation of the affections of the great masses of lower-class Englishmen thus effected was never wholly undone, even after the reconciliation of John with the Holy See. Notwithstanding the completeness and even abjectness of John's surrender, he took no special pains to reinstate himself in the good graces of the Church at home. Innocent, secure at the Lateran, had issued his thunderbolts; and John's counterstrokes had fallen, not on him, but on the English clergy. The measures taken, in 1213 and afterwards, to make good to these victims some part of the heavy losses sustained, were inadequate.

After 1213, John's alliance with Rome brought new dangers in its train. The united action of two autocrats, each claiming supreme powers, lay and spiritual respectively, threatened to annihilate the freedom of the English nation and the English Church. "The country saw that the submission of John to Innocent placed its liberty, temporally and spiritually, at his mercy; and immediately demanded safeguards."[1]

This union of tyrants led to another union which checkmated it, for the baronial opposition allied itself with the ecclesiastical opposition. The urgency of their common need brought prelates and barons into line—for the moment. A leader was found in Stephen Langton, who succeeded in preventing the somewhat divergent interests of the two estates from splitting them asunder.

All things were thus ripe for rebellion, and even for *united* rebellion; an opportunity only was required. Such an opportunity came in a tempting form in 1214; for the King had then lost prestige and power by his failure in the wars with France. He had lost the friendship of the English Church. His unpopularity and vacillating nature had been thoroughly demonstrated. Further, he had himself, in 1191, when plotting against his absent brother Richard, successfully ousted the Regent Longchamp from office, thus furnishing an example of successfully concerted action against the central government.

The result was that, when the barons began active operations, not only had they no opposition to dread from churchman or merchant, from yeoman or peasant, but they might count on the sympathy of all and the active co-operation of many. Further, John's policy of misrule had combined against him two interests usually opposed to each other, the party of progress and the party of reaction. The influence of each of these may be clearly read in various chapters of Magna Carta.

The progressive party consisted mainly of the heads of the more recently created baronial houses, men trained in the administrative methods of Henry II., who desired that his system of government should be properly enforced. They demanded that the King should conduct the business of Exchequer and Curia according to the rules laid down by

[1] Stubbs, *Select Charters*, 270.

Henry.   Routine and order under the new system were
what this party desired, and not a return to the unruly days
of Stephen.   Many of the innovations of the great Angevin
had now been loyally accepted by all classes of the nation;
and these accordingly found a permanent resting-place in
the provisions of the Charter.   In temporary co-operation
with this party, the usually rival party of reaction was
willing to combine for the moment against the common
enemy.   There still existed, in John's reign, magnates of
the old feudal school, who hoped to wrest from the King's
weakened hand some measure of feudal independence.
They had accepted such reforms as suited them, but still
bitterly opposed many others.   In particular, they resisted
the encroachments of the royal courts of law which were
gradually superseding their private jurisdictions.   For the
moment, John's crafty policy, so well devised to gain
immediate ends, and so unwise in the light of subsequent
history, combined these two streams, usually ready to
thwart each other, into a united opposition to his throne.
Attacked at the same moment by the votaries of traditional
usage and by the votaries of reform, by the barons, the
trading classes, and the clergy, he had no course left him
but to surrender at discretion.   The movement which culminated at Runnymede may thus best be understood as
the resultant of a number of different but converging
forces, some of which were progressive and some reactionary.

II. The Crown and Feudal Obligations.

Among the evils calling loudly for redress in England at
the commencement of the thirteenth century, none spoke
with more insistent voice than those connected with feudal
abuses.   The refusal of the northern barons to pay the
scutage demanded on 26th May, 1214, was the spark that
fired the mine.   The most prominent feature of the Charter
is its solicitude to define the exact extent of feudal services
and dues, and so to prevent these from being arbitrarily
increased.   A detailed knowledge of feudal obligations
forms a necessary preliminary to the study of Magna Carta.

The precise relations of the Norman Conquest to the growth of feudalism in England are complicated, and have formed the subject of much controversy. The view now generally accepted, and with reason, is that the policy of the Conqueror accelerated the process in one direction, but retarded it in another. Feudalism, regarded as a system of government, had its worst tendencies checked by the great upheaval that followed the coming of Duke William; feudalism, considered as a system of land tenure, and as a social system, was, on the contrary, formulated and developed. It is mainly as a system of land tenure that it falls here to be considered. Originally, the relationship between lord and tenant, dependent upon the double owner-ship of land (of which each was, in a different sense, proprietor), implied obligations on both sides: the lord gave protection, while the tenant owed services of various sorts. It so happened, however, that, with the changes wrought by time, the legal obligations of the lord ceased to be of much importance, while those of the vassal became more and more burdensome. The tenant's services varied in kind and in extent with the nature of the tenure. It is difficult to frame an exact list of the various tenures formerly recognized as distinct in English law: partly because the classical authors of different epochs, from Bracton to Black-stone, contradict each other; and partly because of the obscurity of the process by which these tenures were gradually differentiated. Sir William Blackstone,[1] after explaining the dependent nature of all real property in England, thus proceeds: " The thing holden is therefore styled a *tenement*, the possessors thereof *tenants*, and the manner of their possession a *tenure*." Tenure thus comes to mean the conditions on which a tenant holds real estate under his lord.

The ancient classification differs materially from that in use at the present day. The modern English lawyer (unless of an antiquarian turn of mind) concerns himself only with three tenures: freehold (now practically identical with socage), copyhold and leasehold. The two last-mentioned

[1] *Commentaries*, II. 59.

may be rapidly dismissed, as they were of little importance in the eyes of Littleton, or of Coke : leasehold embraces only temporary interests, such as those of a tenant-at-will or for a limited term of years; while copyhold is the modern form of tenure into which the old unfree villeinage has slowly ripened. The ancient writers were, on the contrary, chiefly concerned with holdings both permanent and free. Of these, seven at least may be distinguished in the thirteenth century, all of which have now come to be represented by the modern freehold or socage. These seven are knight's service, free socage, fee-farm, frankalmoin, grand serjeanty, petty serjeanty, and burgage.

(1) *Knight's Service.* Medieval feudalism had many aspects; it was almost as essentially an engine of war as it was a system of land-holding. The normal return for which an estate was granted consisted of the service in the field of a specific number of knights. Thus the normal feudal tenure was known as knight's service, or tenure in chivalry—the conditions of which must be constantly kept in view, since by them the relations between John and his recalcitrant vassals fell to be determined. When finally abolished at the Restoration, there fell with knight's service, it is not too much to say, the feudal system of land tenure in England. " Tenure by barony " is sometimes spoken of as a separate species, but may be more correctly viewed as a variety of tenure in chivalry.[1]

(2) *Free Socage.* The early history of socage, with its division into ordinary and privileged, is involved in obscurities which do not require to be here unravelled. The services returned for both varieties were not military but agricultural, and their exact nature and amount varied considerably. Although not so honourable as chivalry, free socage was less burdensome, in respect that two of the most irksome of the feudal incidents, wardship and marriage, did not apply. When knight's service was abolished those who had previously held their lands by it, whether of the Crown or of a mesne lord, were henceforward to hold

[1] See Pollock and Maitland, *Hist. Engl. Law*, 1st ed., I. 218.

in free socage, which thus came to be the normal holding throughout England after the Restoration.[1]

(3) *Fee-farm* was the name applied to lands held in return for services which were neither military nor agricultural, but consisted only of an annual payment in money. The " farm " thus indicates the rent paid, which apparently might vary without limit, although it was long maintained that a fee-farm rent must amount at least to one quarter of the annual value. This error seems to have been founded on a misconstruction of the Statute of Gloucester.[2] Some authorities [3] reject the claims of fee-farm to rank as a tenure separate from socage; although chapter 37 of Magna Carta seems to recognize the distinction.

(4) *Frankalmoin* was a favourite tenure with founders of religious houses. It was also the tenure on which much of the glebe lands of England was held by the village priests. The grant was made *in liberam eleemosinam* or " free alms" (that is, no *temporal* services were to be rendered).[4] In Scots charters the return formally stipulated was *preces et lacrymae.*

(5) *Grand serjeanty* was a highly honourable tenure, sharing the distinctions and the burdensome incidents of knight's service, but distinct in this, that the tenant, in place of ordinary military duties, performed some specific service, such as carrying the King's banner or lance, or filled some important office at the coronation.[5] An often-quoted example of a serjeanty is that of Sir John Dymoke and his family, who have acted as the Sovereign's champions at successive coronations from Richard II. to William IV., ready to defend the Monarch's title to the throne by battle in the ancient form.

Grand serjeanties were liable to wardship and marriage, as well as to relief, but not to payment of scutage.[6]   William

---

[1] See Statute 12 Charles II., c. 24.   [2] See Pollock and Maitland, I. 274 n.

[3] Pollock and Maitland, I. 218.

[4] Littleton, II. viii. s. 133. See, on whole subject, Maitland, *Coll. Papers*, II. 205-222.

[5] Littleton, II. viii. s. 153.

[6] Littleton, II. viii. s. 158. *Cf.* Round, *Kings Serjeanties*, 21.

Aguilon, we are told by Madox,[1] "was charged at the Exchequer with several escuages. But when it was found by Inquest of twelve Knights of Surrey that he did not hold his lands in that county by military tenure, but by serjeanty of finding a Cook at the King's coronation to dress victuals in the King's kitchen, he was acquitted of the escuages."

(6) *Petty serjeanty* may be described in the words of Littleton as " where a man holds his lands of our lord the king to yield to him yearly a bow or sword, or a dagger or a knife...or to yield such other small things belonging to war." [2] The grant of lands on such privileged tenures was frequently made in early days on account of some great service rendered at a critical juncture to the King's person or interests. Serjeanties, Miss Bateson tells us, " were neither always military nor always agricultural, but might approach very closely the service of knights or the service of farmers. ... The serjeanty of holding the King's head when he made a rough passage across the Channel, of pulling a rope when his vessel landed, of counting his chessmen on Christmas Day, of bringing fuel to his castle, of doing his carpentry, of finding his potherbs, of forging his irons for his ploughs, of tending his garden, of nursing the hounds gored and injured in the hunt, of serving as veterinary to his sick falcons, such and many other might be the ceremonial or menial services due from a given serjeanty." [3]

The line between grand and petty serjeanties, like that between the greater and smaller baronies of chapter 14 of Magna Carta, was at first vaguely drawn. The distinction, which Dr. Horace Round considers an illustration of " non-technical classification," [4] may possibly have originated in

[1] *History of Exchequer*, I. 650, citing *Pipe Roll* of 18 Henry III.

[2] See Littleton, II. ix. s. 159. With this may be compared the definition given in chapter 37 of Magna Carta, where John speaks of land thus held by a vassal as "quam tenet de nobis per servitium reddendi nobis cultellos, vel sagittas vel hujusmodi."

[3] *Mediaeval England*, 249-250. A similar tenure exists in Scotland under the name of " blench"—wherein the reddendo is elusory, viz., the annual rendering of such things as an arrow or a penny or a peppercorn, "if asked only" (*si petatur tantum*).

[4] Round, *Peerage, and Pedigree*, 359.

the Great Charter. At a later date, however, petty serjeanties, while liable for "relief," escaped the onerous incidents of wardship and marriage which grand serjeanties shared with lands held in chivalry.[1] The way was thus prepared for the ultimate amalgamation of petty serjeanty with ordinary socage.

(7) *Burgage*, confined to lands within free boroughs, is mentioned as a separate tenure by Littleton,[2] and his authority receives support from chapter 37 of Magna Carta. Our highest modern authorities,[3] however, treat it rather as a variety of socage. In Scotland, where several of the English tenures have failed to obtain recognition, burgage has established itself beyond a doubt. Even the levelling process consummated by the Act of 1874 has not abolished its separate existence.[4]

Of these tenures, originally six or seven, frankalmoin and grand serjeanty still exist, but rather as ghosts than realities; the others have been swallowed up in socage, which has thus become identical with "freehold."[5] This triumph of socage is the result of a long process : fee-farm, burgage, and petty serjeanty, always with features in common, were gradually assimilated in almost all respects, while a statute (12 Charles II. c. 24) transformed tenure in chivalry also into socage. The once humble socage has thus risen high, and now embraces most of the land of England.[6]

The interest of historians centres in tenure by knight's service, which is the very kernel of the feudal system.

---

[1] Littleton, II. viii. s. 158.　　　[2] *Ibid.*, II. x. s. 162.

[3] Pollock and Maitland, I. 218.

[4] Littleton and Coke seem almost to countenance two additional tenures, viz., scutage or escuage, and castle-guard. Pollock and Maitland consider both as alternative names for knight's service. (See I. 251 and I. 257.) The latter is discussed *infra* under c. 29 of Magna Carta.

[5] Jenks, *Modern Land Law*, 14.

[6] It has been well described by Pollock and Maitland (I. 294) as "the great residuary tenure." In Scotland the "residuary tenure" is not socage but "feu" (resembling the English fee-farm). Holdings in feu are still originated by charter, followed by registration (the modern equivalent of infeftment or feudal investiture), thus preserving an unbroken connection with the feudal conveyancing of the Middle Ages.

Lack of definition in the middle ages was a fruitful source of quarrel : for a century and more after the Norman Conquest, the exact amount and nature of military services due by a tenant to his lord were vague and undetermined. Each Crown tenant (except favoured foundations like Battle Abbey) held his lands on condition of furnishing a certain number of fully armed and mounted soldiers in the event of war.   High authorities differ as to when and by whom the amount of each vassal's service was fixed.   The common view (promulgated by Professor Freeman [1]) attributes the allocation of specific service to Ranulf Flambard, the unscrupulous tool of Rufus.   Mr. J. H. Round [2] urges convincing reasons in support of the older view which attributes the innovation to William I.   Two facts, apparently, are certain : that within half a century from the Conquest each military tenant was burdened with a definite amount of service; and that no written record of the amount was made at the time of granting : there were, as yet, no written charters, and thus disputes arose.   Probably, such grants were made in full *Curia,* and the only record of the conditions would lie in the memory of the Court.

Long before Magna Carta, the various obligations had been grouped into three classes, which may be arranged in order of importance, as *services, incidents,* and *aids.* Under each of these three heads, disputes continually arose.[3]   The essence of the feudal tie consisted in the liability to render " suit and service," that is, to follow the

[1] *Norman Conquest,* V. 377 ; *Hist. of William Rufus,* 335-7.

[2] *Feudal England,* p. 228 *et seq.*

[3] All three forms of feudal obligation—service, incidents, and aids—have long been obsolete in England.   The statute 12 Charles II. c. 24 swept away the feudal *incidents* along with the feudal system ; centuries before, *scutages* in lieu of military *service* had become obsolete in the transition from the system of feudal finance to that of national finance, effected by the Crown in the thirteenth and fourteenth centuries.   Feudal *aids* were also long obsolete, although James I., in desperate straits for money, had attempted to revive two of them.   In France the feudal system, with all its burdensome obligations, remained in full vigour until it was abolished in one night by the famous decree of the National Assembly of 4th August, 1790.   In Scotland, the feudal system of land tenure still exists, and certain of its incidents (*e.g.* reliefs and compositions or fines for alienation) are exacted at the present day.

lord's banner in time of war, and attend his court in time of peace. It will be more convenient, however, to reserve full consideration of these services until the comparatively uncomplicated obligations, known as incidents and aids, have been first discussed.

I. *Feudal Incidents.* In addition to " suit and service," the lord reaped, at the expense of his tenants, a number of casual profits, which thus formed irregular supplements to his revenue. These profits, accruing, not annually, but on the occurrence of exceptional events, came to be known as " feudal incidents." They were gradually defined with more or less accuracy, and their number may be given as six : reliefs, escheats, wardships, marriages, primer seisins, and fines for alienation.[1]

(*a*) *Relief* is easily explained. The fee, or *feudum,* or hereditary feudal estate, seems to have been the result of a gradual evolution from the old *beneficium* (or estate held for one lifetime), and that again from the older *precarium* (or estate held during the lord's will). Grants originally subject to revocation, gradually attained fixity of tenure for the life of the original grantee, and, later on, became transmissible to descendants : the Capitulary of Kiersey (A.D. 877) is said to be the first authoritative recognition of the heir's absolute right to succeed. It would seem that even after the Norman Conquest, this rule of hereditary descent was not established beyond possibility of dispute.[2] The heir's right to succeed remained subject to one condition, namely, the payment of a sum known as a " relief." This was an acknowledgment that the new tenant's right to ownership was incomplete, until recognized by his superior —a reminiscence of the earlier *precarium* from which the *feudum* had developed. The amount remained long undefined, and the lord frequently asked exorbitant sums.[3]

(*b*) *Escheat,* it has been said, " signifies the return of

---

[1] Blackstone, *Commentaries,* II. 63, arranges these in a different order, and mentions as a seventh incident "aids," which are here reserved for separate treatment.

[2] See Pollock and Maitland, I. 296.

[3] See *infra,* under c. 2, for the process whereby this evil was redressed.

an estate to a lord, either on failure of issue from the tenant
or upon account of such tenant's felony." [1] This lucid
description conveys a good general conception of escheat;
but it is inaccurate in at least two respects. It does not
exhaust the occasions on which escheat occurs, and it errs
in speaking of "the return" of an estate to a lord, when
more accurately, that estate had always remained his property, subject only to a burden, which was now removed.
In theory, the feudal grant of lands was always conditional:
when the condition was broken, the grant fell, and the lord
found himself, automatically as it were, once more the
absolute proprietor, as he had been before the grant was
made. Thereafter, he held the land in demesne, unless
he chose to make a new grant to another tenant. The word
"escheat" was applied indifferently to the lord's right to
such reversions, and to the actual lands which had reverted.
In warlike times the right was valuable, for whole families
might become rapidly extinct. Further, when a landholder
was convicted of felony, his blood became, in the phrase of
a later day, attainted, and no one could succeed to any
estate through him. If a man failed in the ordeal of water
provided by the Assize of Clarendon in 1166 for those
accused of heinous crimes, his estates escheated to his lord.
A complication arose when treason was the crime of which
the tenant had been convicted; for the king, as the
injured party, had prior rights which excluded those of
the lord: the lands of traitors were forfeited to the Crown.
Even over the lands of ordinary felons the king had rights
during a period which was defined by Magna Carta. [2]

Felony and failure of issue were two main grounds of
escheat, but not the only ones; the goods of fugitives from
justice and of those who had been formally outlawed also
escheated, and Glanvill adds another case, [3] namely, female
wards guilty of unchastity (an offence which spoiled the
king's market). Failure to obey the royal summons in
time of war or to pay scutage in lieu thereof might also be
a ground of forfeiture. [4]

[1] R. Thomson, *Magna Charta*, p. 236.   [2] *Infra*, c. 32.   [3] VII. c. 17.
[4] Pollock and Maitland, I. 247 and 250, citing *Hist. Abingdon*, II. 128.

Escheat was thus a valuable right both to the Crown and to mesne lords. Its effect was simply this : one link in the chain was struck out, and the links on either side were fitted together. If the defaulter was a Crown tenant, all his former sub-tenants, whether freeholders or villeins, moved up one rung in the feudal ladder and held henceforward directly of the king, who took over the entire complexus of legal rights previously enjoyed by the defaulter : rents, crops, timber, casual profits, and advowsons of churches falling vacant; jurisdictions and their profits; services of villeins; reliefs, wardships, and marriages of freeholders, as these became exigible.

The Crown, however, while taking everything the defaulter might have taken before default, must take nothing more—so Magna Carta[1] provides. The rights and status of innocent sub-tenants must not be prejudiced by the misdeeds of defaulting lords.

(c) *Wardships* are described in the *Dialogus de Scaccario* as "escheats along with the heir" (*escaeta cum herede*).[2] This expression does not occur elsewhere, but it would be impossible to find any description of wardship which throws more light on its nature and consequences. When the heir of a deceased tenant was unfitted to bear arms by reason of his tender years, the lands were, during his minority, without an effective owner : the lord treated them as temporarily escheated, entered into possession, drew the revenues, and applied them to his own purposes, subject only to the obligation of maintaining the heir in a manner suited to his station in life. Considerable sums might thus be spent : the *Pipe Roll* of the seventeenth year of Henry II. shows how out of a total revenue of £50 6s. 8d. from the Honour of "Belveeir," £18 5s. had been expended on the children of the late tenant.[3] Wardship came to an end with the full age of the ward, that is, in the case of a military tenant, on the completion of his twenty-first year, " in that of a holder in socage on the completion of the fifteenth, and in the case of a burgess

[1] See *Infra*, c. 43.   [2] See Hughes' edition, p. 133.
[3] See *Dialogus*, p. 222 (citing *Pipe Roll*, p. 27).

when the boy can count money, measure cloth, and so forth."[1] Wardship of females normally ended at the age of fourteen, "because that a woman of such age may have a husband able to do knight's service." An heiress who did not succeed to the estate until she was fourteen thus escaped wardship altogether, but if she became a ward at a younger age, the wardship continued till she attained sixteen years unless she married earlier.[2]

All the remunerative consequences flowing from escheat flowed also from wardship—rents, casual profits, advowsons, services of villeins, and reliefs. Unlike escheats, however, the right of the Crown here was only temporary, and Magna Carta sought[3] to provide that the implied conditions should be respected by the Crown's bailiffs or nominees: the lands must not be wasted or exhausted, but restored to the son when he came of age, in as good condition as when his father died.

One important aspect ought to be emphasized: Wardship affected bishoprics as well as lay baronies, extending over the temporalities of a See between the death of one prelate and the instalment of his successor. It was to the king's interest to keep sees vacant, while his Exchequer drew the revenues and casual profits.[4] This right was carefully reserved, even in the comprehensive charter in which John granted freedom of election.[5]

(d) *Marriage* as a feudal incident is difficult to define; for its meaning changed. Originally it seems to have implied little more than the right of a lord to forbid an

---

[1] Glanvill, VII. c. 9. In socage and burgage tenures no wardship was recognized; the guardianship went to the relations of the ward, and not to his feudal lord. Complicated, but equitable, rules applied to socage. The maternal kindred had the custody, if the lands came from the father's side; the paternal kindred, if from the mother's side (Glanvill, VII. c. 11). In plain language, the boy was not entrusted to those who had an interest in his death. *Cf. infra*, cc. 3, 4 and 37.

[2] Littleton, II. iv. s. 103.   [3] See under c. 5.

[4] What these were may be read in the *Pipe Rolls*, *e.g.*, in that of 14 Henry II. when the Bishopric of Lincoln was vacant.

[5] See *Sel. Chart.*, 288. Contrast Stephen's Oxford Charter; *Sel. Chart.*, 120-1. *Cf. supra*, p. 32, and *infra*, under c. 1.

heiress to marry his personal enemy. Such veto was reasonable, since the husband of the heiress would become the tenant of the lord. The claim to concur in the choice of a husband gradually expanded into an absolute right to dispose of the lands and person of the female ward : the prize might be a bribe to any unscrupulous gentleman of fortune who placed his sword at the King's disposal, or it might go to the highest bidder. The lady passed as a mere adjunct to her own estates. At fourteen she might be sent to market, and the only way in which she could protect herself against an obnoxious husband was by out-bidding her various suitors.

This right seems, at some uncertain date, to have been extended from females to males, and instances of sums thus paid occur in the *Pipe Rolls*. It is difficult at first sight to imagine how the Crown found a market for such wares as male wards; but probably wealthy fathers were ready to purchase desirable husbands for their daughters. Thus in 1206 a certain Henry of Redeman paid forty marks for the hand and lands of the heir of Roger of Hedon, " *ad opus filiae suae*,"[1] while Thomas Basset secured a prize in the person of the young heir of Walerand, Earl of Warwick, to the use of any one of his daughters.[2] This extension to male heirs is usually explained as founded on a strained construction of chapter 6 of Magna Carta; but the beginnings of the practice can be traced before 1215.[3] The lords' right to sell their wards was recognized and defined by the Statute of Merton, chapter 6. The attempts made to remedy some of the most serious abuses may be read in Magna Carta.[4] Hallam [5] considers that " the rights, or feudal incidents, of wardship and marriage were nearly peculiar to England and Normandy," and that the French kings never " turned this attribute of sovereignty into a means of revenue." [6]

(e) *Primer Seisin*, which is usually regarded as a separate

[1] *Rotuli de oblatis et finibus*, p. 354.   [2] *Rot. Claus.*, 37, 55.

[3] Pollock and Maitland, I. 305.   [4] See *infra*, under chapters 6, 7, and 8.

[5] *Middle Ages*, II. 429.   [6] p. 437.

incident, and figures as such in Blackstone's list, is perhaps
better understood, not as an incident at all, but as a special
procedure—effective and summary—whereby the Crown
could enforce the four incidents already described.   It was
an exclusive prerogative of the Crown, denied to mesne
lords.[1]   When a Crown tenant died, the King's officers
had the right to enter into immediate possession, and to
exclude the heir, who could not touch his father's lands
without permission from the Crown : he had first to prove
his title by inquest, give security for any balance of relief
or other debts, and perform homage.[2]   It will be readily
seen what a strong strategic position all this assured to the
King in any disputes with the heir of a dead vassal.   If
the Exchequer had doubtful claims against the deceased,
its officials could satisfy themselves before admitting the
heir to possession.   If the heir showed any tendency to
evade payment of feudal incidents, the Crown could check-
mate his moves.   If the succession was disputed, the King
might favour the claimant who pleased or paid him most ;
or, under colour of the dispute, refuse to disgorge the estate
—holding it in custody analogous to wardship, and meanwhile drawing the profits.   If the son happened to be
abroad when his father died, he would experience difficulty
in forcing the Crown to restore the estates.   Such was the
experience of William Fitz-Odo on returning from Scotland
in 1201 to claim his father's carucate of land in Bam-
borough.[3]   Primer seisin was thus not so much a separate
incident, as a right peculiar to the Crown to take summary
measures for the satisfaction of all claims against a deceased
tenant or his heir.   Magna Carta contains no direct reference to it, but chapters 37 and 53, providing against the

[1] The Bishop of Durham enjoyed it, so it seems to be stated in a charter of 1303
(Lapsley, *Pal. of Durham*, 133).   But this forms no real exception ; since the
Bishop, as an Earl Palatine, enjoyed the *regalia* of a king.

[2] See Pollock and Maitland, I. 292.   From Statute of Marlborough, c. 16,
primer seisin extended over serjeanty as well as knight's service.   Statute of
Merton, c. 7, provided that a ward might refuse a marriage on undertaking to
pay the offered price when he came of age.   Under c. 8, double the value might
be exacted for a secret marriage or one in fraud of the lord's right.

[3] *Rotuli de oblatis*, p. 114.

abuse of prerogative wardship, have a bearing on the subject.[1]

(f) *Fines for alienation* occupy a place by themselves. Unlike the incidents already discussed, they became exigible not on the tenant's death, but on his parting with his estate during his lifetime, either as a gift or in return for a price. How far could he effect this without consent of his lord? This was, for many centuries, a subject of heated disputes, often settled by compromises, under which the new tenant paid a fine to the lord for recognition of his title. Such fines are payable at the present day in Scotland (under the name of "compositions") from feus granted prior to 1874; and, where no sum has been mentioned in the Feu Charter, the law of Scotland defines the amount exigible as one year's rent. Magna Carta contains no provisions on this subject. Disputes, long and bitter, took place in the thirteenth century; but their history is irrelevant to the present inquiry.[2]

II. *Feudal Aids.* The feudal tenant was expected to come to the aid of his lord in any special crisis or emergency. At first, the occasions on which these "aids" might be demanded were varied and undefined. Gradually they were limited to three. Glanvill,[3] indeed, mentions only two: the knighting of the overlord's eldest son, and the marriage of his eldest daughter; but he intends these, perhaps, as illustrations rather than as an exhaustive list. Before the beginning of the thirteenth century the recognized aids were the ransoming of the King and the two already mentioned.[4] This understanding was embodied in Magna Carta.[5]

[1] Sir Edward Coke (*Coke upon Littleton*, 77 A) is the original source of much confusion as to the nature of primer seisin, which he seems to have considered as a second and additional relief exacted by the Crown, amounting to the whole rent of the first year. The Popes, he further held (erroneously), were imitating this practice when they exacted a year's rent from every newly granted benefice under name of "first fruits." These errors have been widely followed (*e.g.* Thomson, *Magna Charta*, p. 416; Taswell Langmead, *Const. Hist.*, 50).

[2] See Taswell Langmead, *Const. Hist.*, pp. 51-2; also Pollock and Maitland, II. 326.

[3] IX. c. 8.

[4] An aid to marry the king's eldest sister might be taken, if not previously exacted by her father.

[5] See *infra*, under chapter 12.

E

A tradition has been handed down from an early date, that these aids were voluntary offerings made as a mark of affection.[1]   Long before John's reign, however, the obligation had become fixed by law; the tenant dared not refuse to pay the recognized three.   But, when the Crown exacted contributions for any other reason, it required consent of the *commune concilium*.

The Great Charter, while confirming this tacit compromise, left the *amount* of aids undefined, merely stipulating that they should be "reasonable."   Examples of such payments, both before and after the Charter, are readily found in the Exchequer Rolls.   Thus, in his fourteenth year Henry II. took one mark per knight's fee for his daughter's marriage; Henry III. took 20s., and Edward I. 40s. for a similar purpose.   For Richard's ransom, 20s. had been exacted from each knight's fee (save those owned by men actually serving in the field); and Henry III. took 40s. in his thirty-eighth year at the knighting of his son.   The Statute of Westminster I.[2] fixed the "reasonable" aid payable to mesne lords at 20s. per knight's fee, and 20s. for every estate in socage of £20 annual value.   This rate, it will be observed, is one-fifth of the knight's relief.[3]   The Crown, in thus enforcing "reason" on mesne lords, seems never to have intended that the same limit should hamper its own dealings with Crown tenants, but continued to exact larger sums whenever it thought fit.[4]   Thus £2 per fee was taken in 1346 at the knighting of the Black Prince.

A statute of Edward III.[5] at last extended to the Crown the same measure of "reasonableness" as had been applied

---

[1] Thus, the Abingdon *Chronicle* (II. 113) speaks of "auxilia quod barones michi dederunt"; while Bracton says (Book II. c. 16, s. 8): "Auxilia fiunt de gratia et non de jure; cum dependeant ex gratia tenentium, et non ad voluntatem dominorum."

[2] 3 Edward I. c. 36.   [3] Fixed at 100s. by c. 2 of Magna Carta.

[4] *Cf.* Pollock and Maitland, I. 381-2.   One entry in the *Memoranda Roll* of 42 Henry III. (cited Madox, I. 615) seems to admit that the Crown could not exact more than 20s.; but in 1258 the baronial opposition would be strong in the Exchequer as elsewhere.

[5] 25 Ed. III. stat. 5, c. 11.

three-quarters of a century earlier to mesne lords. The
last instances of the exaction of aids in England occur as
late as the reign of James I., who, in 1609, demanded one
for the knighting of the ill-fated Prince Henry, and in 1613
another for the marriage of his daughter Elizabeth.

III. *Suit and Service.* This phrase expresses the
essential obligations inherent in the very nature of the
feudal tie. It may be expanded (as regards tenure in
chivalry) into the duty of attendance at the lord's court,
whether met for administrative or judicial purposes, or for
reasons of mere display, and the further duty of military
service under that lord's banner in the field. Suit had
ceased to be an urgent question before the reign of John.
Indeed, the barons were gradually approaching the modern
conception, which regards it as a privilege rather than a
burden to attend the *commune concilium*—the embryo
Parliament—of the King.

It was otherwise with the duties of military service,
which were rendered every year more unwillingly, partly
because of the increased frequency of warlike expeditions,
partly because of the greater cost of campaigning in distant
lands like Poitou, partly because the English barons were
completely out of sympathy with John's foreign policy and
with him. We have seen that the want of definition in
the Conqueror's reign left to future ages a legacy of strife.
William and his barons lived in the present; and the
present did not urgently call for definition. Therefore, the
duration of the military service, and the conditions on
which exemption could be claimed, were originally vague;
but the return due (*servitium debitum*) for each knight's fee
was gradually fixed by custom at the service of one fully
armed horseman during forty days. There were still, however, innumerable minor points on which disputes might
arise, and these remained even in 1215. Indeed, although
several chapters of the Charter attempted to settle certain
of these disputed points, others were left as bones of contention to subsequent reigns : for example, the exact equipment of a knight; the liability to serve for more than forty
days on receiving pay for the extra time; what exemption

might be claimed by churchmen; how far a tenant might compromise for actual service by tendering money; whether attendance and money might not both be withheld, if the King did not lead his forces in person; and whether service was due for foreign wars equally as for home ones.[1]

Difficulties increased as time went on. The Conqueror's followers had estates on both sides of the Channel: his wars were theirs. Before John's reign, these simple relations had become complicated by two considerations. By forfeitures and the division of inheritances, holders of English and of Norman fiefs had become distinct. On the other hand, the expansion of the dominions of the English kings increased the number of their wars, and the expense of each expedition. The small wars with Wales and Scotland formed sufficient drain on the resources of English magnates without their being summoned to fight in Maine or Gascony.

Were the barons bound to follow John in a forlorn attempt, of which they disapproved, to recover his lost fiefs from the French Crown? Or were they bound to support him only in his legitimate schemes as King of England? Or were they, by way of compromise, liable for services in the identical possessions held by William the Conqueror at the date when their ancestors first got their fiefs—that is, for wars in England and Normandy alone? So early as 1198 the Knights of St. Edmunds refused to serve in Normandy, while offering to pay scutage.[2] The northern barons in 1213 declared that they owed no service whatsoever out of England.[3] This extreme claim put them clearly in the wrong, since John could produce precedents to the contrary. When, on his return from the unfortunate expedition of 1214, he demanded a scutage from all who

---

[1] Some of these questions might be answered by the terms of special charters: the *Hundred Rolls* (1279) relate how Hugh de Plesens must go with the King for forty days at his own, and thereafter at the King's expense. *Rot. Hund.*, II. p. 710; *cf.* for France, *Établissements de St. Louis*, I. c. 65.

[2] Jocelin of Brakelond, 63, cited by Pollock and Maitland, I. 250 n.

[3] See R. Coggeshall, p. 167; the barons argued *non in hoc ei obnoxios esse secundum munia terrarum suarum.*

had not followed him to Poitou, the malcontents declared
that they had no obligation either to follow him out of the
kingdom, or to pay a scutage in lieu thereof.[1] Pope
Innocent was probably correct in condemning this contention
as founded neither on English law nor on feudal custom.[2]
There is some ground for believing that a compromise was
mooted on the basis that the barons should agree to serve
in Normandy and Brittany, as well as in England, on being
exempted from fighting elsewhere abroad.[3]

A definite understanding was never arrived at : chapter
16 of Magna Carta provided that existing services were not
to be increased, without defining what these were.   This
was to shelve the difficulty : the dispute went on under
varying forms and led to an unseemly wrangle between
Edward I. and his Constable and Marshal, dramatized in
a classic passage by Walter of Hemingburgh.[4] Strangely
enough, the *Confirmatio Cartarum* of 1297, which was,
in part, the outcome of this later quarrel, omits (like Magna
Carta itself)[5] all reference to foreign service.   The omission
from both charters of all mention of the chief cause of
dispute is noteworthy.   It must be remembered, however,
that the question of liability to serve abroad had practically
resolved itself into that of liability to scutage, and that
chapters 12 and 14 of the Charter of 1215 provided an
adequate check on the levy of all scutages; but this is a
subject that requires separate and detailed treatment.

IV. *Scutage*. The Crown did not always insist on
personal service, but was frequently willing to accept a
commutation in the form of a money payment.   The subject of scutage is one of the most vexed of questions, all
received opinions of yesterday having to-day been thrown
into the melting pot.   The theories of Stubbs and Freeman,
once universally accepted, require substantial modifications.
Four propositions may be stated with some confidence : (1)

---

[1] W. Coventry, II. 217.

[2] See his letter dated 1st April, 1215, in *New Rymer*, I. 128.

[3] See "unknown charter" in Appendix.   [4] *Chronicon*, II. 121.

[5] See, however, *infra* under c. 16.

that scutage is an ambiguous term with a vague general meaning as well as a narrow technical meaning; (2) that the importance of the changes introduced by Henry II. in 1156 and 1159 has been much exaggerated; (3) that scutage was always in the option of the King, never of the barons, his tenants; and (4) that at a later time, probably during John's reign, scutage changed its character, and became, partly through altered circumstances and partly by the King's deliberate policy, a much more burdensome exaction.   Each of these propositions requires explanations :

(1) The proper technical meaning of *scutagium* or " shield-money " is a money payment of so much per " shield " (that is, per knight's fee) by a tenant in lieu of actual attendance in the army of his feudal lord : it is, as Dr. Stubbs explains,[1] " an honourable commutation for personal service."   The word, however, is also more loosely used for any exaction assessed on a feudal basis, irrespective of the occasion of its levy ; and, in this wider sense, includes feudal aids and other payments as well.[2]

(2) Professor Freeman, Dr. Stubbs, and their adherents held that one of Henry's most important reforms was the invention of scutage; that he allowed his Crown tenants at their discretion to substitute payments in money for the old obligation of personal service in the field—this option being granted to ecclesiastics in 1156, and to lay barons in 1159.   Such a theory had *a priori* much to recommend it. A measure of this nature, while giving volume and elasticity to the resources of the Crown, was calculated subtly to undermine the basis of the feudal tie; but Henry, far-seeing statesman as he was, could not discard the ideals of his own generation : no evidence that he made any sweeping change is forthcoming.   On the contrary, his grandfather, Henry I., is shown by the evidence of extant charters to have accepted money in place of the services of knights *when it suited him* (notably from church fiefs in 1109),[3] and there is no evidence (direct or indirect) to show that the

---

[1] *Const. Hist.*, I. 632.   [2] Madox, I. 619.
[3] See Round, *Feudal England*, 262 ff., 532.

grandson accepted such commutation *when it did not suit him*.   Scutage was thus known in England half a century before 1156—the traditional date of its introduction.

(3) Further, neither before nor after the reign of Henry II. had the individual baron any option of tendering at his discretion money in place of personal service.   The conclusions on this subject formulated by Dr. Horace Round lie implicitly in the examples from the *Pipe Rolls* stored in the famous work of Madox.   From these it would appear that the procedure of the Exchequer of the great Angevin and his two sons might be explained in some such propositions as these :

(*a*) The option to convert service into scutage lay with the Crown; not with the tenants, either individually or as a body.   When the King summoned his army, no baron could (as Professor Freeman would have us believe) simply stay away under obligation of paying a small fixed sum to the Exchequer.   On the contrary, Henry and his sons jealously preserved the right to insist on *personal* service whenever it suited them; efficient substitutes were not always accepted, much less money payments.

(*b*) If the individual wished to stay at home he required to make a special bargain with the King, paying such sum as the King thought fit to demand and sometimes having to find a substitute in addition.   Exorbitant sums (not properly " scutages " at all) might thus be extorted from stay-at-homes *ne transfretent* or *pro remanendo ab exercitu* —phrases which appear in the *Pipe Rolls* of Richard.   A Crown vassal in John's twelfth year made fine " that he might send two knights to serve for him in the army of Ireland." [1]   In such cases, each baron made his own bargain with the Crown : a scutage, on the contrary, " when it ran in the land " was at a uniform rate.

(*c*) The tenant-in-chivalry who stayed at home without first making his bargain was in much worse plight.   He had broken faith, and in strict feudal theory had forfeited his fief by failing to perform the service for which he held it.   He was " in mercy," and might be glad to accept such

[1] Madox, I. 658.

terms of pardon as a gracious king might offer him.[1]
Sometimes, quite small amercements were inflicted : the
Abbot of Pershore in 1196 escaped with 40s :[2]   But the
Crown sometimes insisted on total forfeiture.[3]

It was the duty of the Barons of Exchequer to determine
whether lands had thus escheated by default, and also to
determine the amount of " forfeit " to be taken where con-
fiscation was not justified or insisted on.   The barons
wished to refer such questions to the *judicium parium*.[4]

(4) Scutage tended continually to become more burdensome :

(*a*) With new inventions and more complicated fashions
in arms and armour for man and horse, and increased rates
payable for the hire of mercenaries, the expenses of a
campaign steadily increased.   It was not unnatural that
the normal rate of scutage should increase in sympathy.
Under Henry the recognized maximum had been two
marks, the exact equivalent of 40 days' wages at the normal
rate of 8d. *per diem*.[5]   Usually he was content with a
smaller sum per knight's fee : 20s., 13s. 4d. or even 10s.
being sometimes taken.

(*b*) A second method of increasing the yield of scutage
was to readjust the assessment on which it was based,
by increasing the number of contributory knights' fees.
Henry II. in 1166 had invited his unsuspecting barons to
furnish him with details of the number of knights actually
enfeoffed on their lands both before and after the death of
his grandfather; and then treated the latter as a sort of
unearned increment, the benefit of which should be shared
by the Crown.   The amount of *servitium debitum* as previously reckoned was increased by the addition of the
number of knights of the *novum feoffamentum*, that is, of

---

[1] Pollock and Maitland, I. 247, noted this distinction under Edward ; it
existed, as the above-cited instance proves, under John.

[2] *Pipe Roll* of Richard I., cited Madox, I. 663.

[3] *Pipe Roll* of 12 John, cited *ibid*.   [4] *Cf. infra*, under cc. 39 and 21.

[5] Interesting details are given by Vinogradoff, *English Society*, 15 ff.   *Cf.*
Round, *Feudal England*, 277 ff.

those created subsequent to the death of Henry I.[1] The
basis of assessment thus fixed in 1166 remained unaltered
at John's accession.

(c) The third respect in which scutages tended to become
more burdensome was in their increased frequency. This
was, in part, a consequence of the growth of the Empire
of the Kings of England, bringing with it a widening of
interests and ambitions, and an increase in the number and
expense of wars. Much depended, however, on the spirit
in which this feudal prerogative was used, on the amount
of consideration given to the needs and interests of the
barons. Neither Henry nor Richard seems to have
regarded it as other than an expedient to be reserved for
special emergencies, not as a permanent source of revenue
in normal times.

Henry II. seems to have levied money in name of scutage
only when actually at war—on seven occasions in all
during a reign of thirty-five years; and only once at a rate
exceeding 20s., if we may trust Mr. Round,[2] and that when
he was putting forth a special effort against Toulouse.
Richard I., rapacious as he was, levied, apparently, only
four scutages during ten years, and the rate of 20s. was
never exceeded even in the King's hour of urgent need,
—in 1194, when the arrears of his ransom had to be paid
and preparations simultaneously made for war in Normandy.

If it can be shown that John altered established usages
under every one of these heads, breaking away from all
restraints, and that too in the teeth of the keen opposition
of a high-spirited baronage whose members felt that their
pride and prestige as well as their money-bags were
attacked, a distinct step is taken towards understanding
the crisis of 1215. Such knowledge would explain why a
storm, long brewing, burst in John's reign, neither sooner
nor later; and even why some of the disreputable stories
told by the chroniclers and accepted by Blackstone and
others, found inventors and believers.

It is here maintained that John did make changes in all

---

[1] Round, *Feudal England*, 237-9.   [2] *Feudal England*, 277 *seq.*

of these directions; and, further, that the incidence of this increase in feudal burdens was rendered even more unendurable by two considerations :—because at his accession there remained unpaid (particularly from the fiefs of the northern knights) large arrears of the scutages imposed in his brother's reign,[1] and because in June, 1212, he drew the feudal chain tight by a drastic and galling measure.

That John elevated scutage from a weapon reserved for emergencies into a regular source of revenue, and that he raised the rate demanded beyond the recognized maximum of two marks, becomes apparent from a glance at the table[2] of scutages extorted during his reign :

First scutage of reign—1198-9 — 2 marks per knight's fee.

Second	„	„	1200-1	2 „ „
Third	„	„	1201-2	2 „ „
Fourth	„	„	1202-3	2 „ „
Fifth	„	„	1203-4	2 „ „
Sixth	„	„	1204-5	2 „ „
Seventh	„	„	1205-6	20s. „
Eighth	„	„	1209-10	2 marks „
Ninth	„	„	1210-11	2 „ „
Tenth	„	„	1210-11	20s. „
Eleventh	„	„	1213-14	3 marks „

It will be seen that, in his very first year, John took a scutage at two marks per *scutum*. Next year he wisely allowed a breathing space; then without a break in each of the third, fourth, fifth, sixth and seventh years of his reign, scutages were extorted in quick succession at the same high rate. *Fines*, in addition to this scutage of two marks, were exacted from those who had not made the necessary compromise for personal service in due time.[3]

These scutages were collected with increasing difficulty, and arrears accumulated; but the spirit of opposition

---

[1] Norgate, *John Lackland*, p. 122.

[2] Norgate, *John Lackland*, p. 123 note, correcting Swereford's lists in the *Red Book of Exchequer*. Further corrections are perhaps necessary: R. Wendover III. 173, mentions a scutage of 2½ marks in January, 1204.

[3] See Ramsay, *Angevin Empire*, 390, and authorities there cited.

increased even more rapidly. In 1206, apparently, the breaking point was almost reached.[1] Accordingly, in that year, some slight relaxation was allowed—the annual scutage was reduced from two marks to 20s. John's needs, however, were as great as ever, and would prevent further concessions, unless something untoward happened. Something untoward *did* happen in the summer of 1207, when John quarrelled with the Pope. This postponed his quarrel with the baronage. John had, for the time being, the whole of the confiscated property of the clergy in his clutches. The day of reckoning for this luxury was still far distant, and the King could meanwhile enjoy a full exchequer without goading his Crown tenants to rebellion. For three years no scutage was imposed. In 1209, however, financial needs again closed in on John, and a new scutage of two marks was levied; followed in the next year actually by two scutages, the first of two marks against Wales, and the second of 20s. against Scotland. John had no sense of moderation. These three levies, amounting to a total of five-and-a-half marks per fee within two years, strained the tension almost to breaking point.

During the two years following (Michaelmas, 1211, to Michaelmas, 1213) no scutage was imposed. John, however, although he thus a second time relaxed the tension, had no intention to do so for long. On the contrary, he determined to ascertain if scutages could not be made to yield more in the future. By writs, dated 1st June, 1212, he instituted a strict Inquest into the amount of service exigible from every estate in England. Commissioners were appointed to take the sworn verdicts of local juries as to the amount of liability due by each Crown vassal. Mr. Round [2] considers that previous writers have unaccountably ignored the importance of this measure, " an Inquest worthy to be named in future by historians in conjunction with those of 1086 and 1166,"[3] and describes it as an effort " to revive rights of the Crown alleged to have lapsed." John

[1] Cf. Norgate, *John Lackland*, 125.   [2] *Commune of London*, 273-4.

[3] Yet, of recent historians, Ramsay (*Angevin Empire*, 432) treats it briefly, and Miss Norgate (*John Lackland*, 163) barely notices it.

intended by this Inquest, the returns to which were due on the 25th June, to prepare the necessary machinery for wringing the uttermost penny out of the next scutage when occasion for one again arose.   That occasion came in 1214.

Up to this date, even John had not dared to exact a rate of more than two marks per knight's fee; but the weight of his constant scutages had been increased by the fact that he sometimes exacted personal services in addition, and that he inflicted crushing fines upon those who neither went nor arranged beforehand terms of composition with the King.[1]

Thus insidiously throughout the entire reign, the stream of feudal obligations steadily rose until the barons feared that nothing of their property would be saved from the torrent.   The normal rate of scutage had been raised, the frequency of its imposition had been increased, the conditions of foreign service had become more burdensome, and the objects of foreign expeditions more unpopular; while attempts were sometimes made to exact both service and scutage in the same year.   The limit of the barons' endurance was reached when, under circumstances peculiarly inauspicious, John, in May, 1214, demanded a new scutage at the unprecedented rate of three marks on every fee, grounded doubtless on the searching inquest of 1212.[2]

This outline of the history of scutage makes plain that grievances connected with its abuse formed one of the chief incentives to the insurrection that resulted in the winning of the Great Charter.

[1] Miss Norgate (123) describes the exactions supplementing the scutages: "These scutages were independent of the fines paid by the barons who did not accompany the King on his first return to Normandy in 1199, of the money taken from the host as a substitute for its service in 1201, of the equipment and payment of the 'decimated' knights in 1205, and the fines claimed for all the tenants-in-chivalry after the dismissal of the host in the same year, as well as of actual services which many of those who had paid the scutage rendered in the campaigns of 1202-4 and 1206."

[2] See Miss Norgate, *John Lackland*, 210, and *cf. supra*, 31.   For a minor grievance connected with scutage and the writ *de habendo scutagio*, see *infra*, under c. 15.   The later history of scutage is outlined in Pollock and Maitland, I. 254.   *Cf. infra*, under c. 12.

III. Royal Justice and Feudal Justice.

A well-known aphorism describes the King as " the sole fountain of justice." It would be an anachronism to transport this metaphor into the thirteenth century. In John's reign there still were, not one, but many competing jurisdictions. It was by no means certain that the King's Courts were the proper tribunals to which a wronged individual must repair. On the contrary, the great bulk of the rural population, the villeins, had no *locus standi* except in the court of the manor to which they belonged; while the doors of the royal Courts had been opened to the ordinary freeman no earlier than the reign of Henry II. Royal justice was still the exception, not the rule. Each man must seek redress, in the ordinary case, in his own locality. To dispense justice to the nation at large was no part of the normal business of a medieval King.

I. *Rival systems of Law Courts.* In the thirteenth century, there existed not one source of justice, but many. Rival courts, eagerly competing to extend their own sphere of usefulness and to increase their own fees, existed in a bewildering multitude. Putting aside for the moment the Courts Christian, the Borough Courts, the Forest Courts, and all exceptional or peculiar tribunals, there existed three great rival systems of jurisdiction which may be named in the order in which they became in turn prominent in England.[1]

(1) *Local or District Courts.* Justice was originally a local product, administered in rude tribunals which partook more or less of a popular character. Each shire had its assembly for hearing pleas, known as a " shire-moot " in Anglo-Saxon days, and as a " *comitatus* " after the Norman Conquest; while each of the smaller districts subdividing the shire, and forming units of administration for purposes

---

[1] Too absolute a line must not be drawn between the three types of court. In one sense all tribunals were, or tended to become, royal courts. The king's representatives presided in the "popular courts," and the king received a share of the fines levied there; while, in Prof. Vinogradoff's words (*English Society*, 108), "all the well-known franchises or liberties of the feudal age were chips from the block of royal authority."

of taxation, defence, justice, and police, had a moot or council of its own, serving as a court of law, to which the inhabitants of the villages brought their pleas in the first instance.   These smaller districts were known as hundreds in the south, and as wapentakes (a name of Danish derivation) in the north.

The theory generally received is that all freemen were originally suitors in the courts of shire and hundred, and that the whole body of those present, the ordinary peasant ("ceorl") equally with the man of noble blood ("eorl"), took an active part in the proceedings, pronouncing (or, at least, concurring in) the judgments or dooms there declared; but that, as time progressed, the majority of the Anglo-Saxon ceorls sank to the half-servile position of villeins—men tied for life to the soil of the manor, and passing, like property, from father to son.   These villeins, although still subjected to the burden of attendance, and to some of the other duties of their former free estate, were deprived of those rights which had once formed the counterpart of the obligations.   Another school of historians, it is true, denies that the mass of the population, even in very early times, ever enjoyed an active share in the dispensation of justice.   It is unnecessary here to attempt a solution of the intricate problems of the courts of shire and hundred; or to discuss the still more vexed question how far the small assembly of each township is worthy to be reckoned a formal Court of Law.[1]

(2) *Feudal Courts.*   Centuries before the Norman Conquest, the system of popular or district justice found itself confronted with a rival scheme of jurisdictions—the innumerable private courts belonging to the feudal lords. These private tribunals, known as feudal, manorial, or seignorial courts, slowly gained ground on the older public courts of shire, hundred, and wapentake.[2]

[1] John's Charter makes no mention of these courts, although c. 25, forbidding increase of the farms of shires, may have a bearing on the subject.   Henry's Charters of 1217 and 1225 regulate their times of meeting.   *Cf. infra*, Part IV.

[2] This account of the relations of the two sets of courts would receive the support of recent writers, such as Maitland and Round, as well as of the older generation,

Practically every holder of land in England came to be also the holder of a court for the inhabitants of that land. The double meaning of the word " *dominus* " illustrates the double position of the man who was thus both owner and lord.[1]   In the struggle between two schemes of justice, the tribunals of the feudal magnates triumphed over, but never abolished their rivals.   The earlier popular courts lived on ; but the system of district justice, which had once embraced the whole of England, was honeycombed by the growth of feudal courts.   As each village passed under the domination of a lord, the village-moot became a manorial court endowed with wider powers and more effective sanctions for enforcing them.   Further, as complete hundreds fell under control of powerful magnates, the courts of these hundreds were also transformed into feudal courts : franchises thus took the place of many of the old popular moots. Still, the older system retained part of the disputed ground, thanks to the protection of the Crown.   Many hundreds never bowed to the exclusive domination of any one lord, and the courts of the shires were guarded by the Norman Kings against the encroachment of even the most powerful barons.

Although it was the policy of the Norman Kings to prevent their barons from gaining excessive powers of jurisdiction, it was by no means their policy to suppress these jurisdictions altogether.   The Conqueror and his sons were glad that justice should be administered, even in a rough-and-ready manner, in those districts whither the Crown's arm was not long enough to reach, and where the popular courts were likely to prove inefficient.   The old system and the new existed side by side; it was to the interest of the central government to play off the one against the other.

In later days (but not till long after Magna Carta), each manorial court had three distinct aspects, according to the

such as Stubbs and Freeman.   Mr. Frederic Seebohm may be mentioned as perhaps the most weighty upholder of the opposite view, which regards the manorial courts as of earlier origin than those of hundred and shire.

[1] *Cf.* "landlord."

class of pleas it was called upon to try. Later writers distinguish absolutely from each other, the Court Baron, settling civil disputes between freeholders of the manor; the Court Customary, deciding non-criminal cases among the villeins; and the Court Leet, a petty criminal court enforcing order and punishing small offences. The powers of these courts might vary, and in many districts the jurisdiction over misdemeanours belonged not to the steward of the manor, but to the sheriff in his half-yearly Circuits or "Tourns" through the county. In imperfectly feudalized districts the Tourn of the sheriff performed the same functions as the Court Leet did within a franchise.

(3) *Royal Courts*. Originally, the King's Court had been merely one among many feudal courts—differing in degree rather than in kind from those of the great earls or barons. The King, as feudal lord, dispensed justice among his tenants, just as any baron or freeman dispensed justice among *his* tenants, bond or free. No one dreamed, in the time of the Norman Kings, that the *Curia Regis* could undertake the labour of dispensing justice for the whole nation. The monarchy had no machinery at command for a task which no Anglo-Saxon King, nor even William I., could have undertaken. No attempt in this direction was made until the reign of Henry II., who was placed in a position of unprecedented power, partly by circumstances, but chiefly by his great abilities. Even he, born reformer as he was, would never have increased so greatly the labours of government, if he had not seen that the change would enhance the security of his throne and the revenue of his exchequer.

From an early date, however, the business of the Monarch was wider than the business of any other lord. In a dim way, too, it must have been apparent from the first, that offences against the established order were offences also against the King, and that to redress these was the King's business competent in the King's Courts. The Crown, further, asserted a right to investigate pleas of special importance, whether civil or criminal. Still, under William and his sons, royal justice had made no deliberate attempt to become national justice, or to supersede feudal justice: the struggle came with the reforms of Henry II.[1]

Thus the three great systems of jurisdiction, popular justice, feudal justice, and royal justice succeeded each other, on the whole, in the order in which they are here named. Yet the sequence is in some ways logical rather than chronological. No absolute line can be drawn, showing where one system ended and the next began. The germs of manorial jurisdiction may have been present from an early date. Shire-courts and hundred courts alike were continually in danger of falling under the domination of powerful local magnates. Yet, the shire-courts were successful in maintaining till the last (thanks to royal favour) their independence of the manorial jurisdictions; while only a proportion of the hundred courts fell into bondage. The royal courts, again, from an early date, withdrew causes from the Shire Courts and interfered with manorial franchises. The Courts Baron were silently undermined, until they sank into decrepitude without ceasing to exist. With these caveats, the three systems may be regarded, in some measure, as following one another in the order named:—popular justice, feudal justice, royal justice.

II. *Legal Procedure.* The procedure adopted in litigation in Anglo-Saxon and Norman times was similar in essentials in all three classes of tribunals, and differed materially from the practice of courts of law at the present day. Some knowledge of the more glaring contrasts between ancient and modern procedure will conduce to an understanding of several obscure provisions of Magna Carta.

Avoiding technical language, and eliminating special procedure peculiar to any one court or country, the principal stages in a litigation in a modern court of law may be given briefly as follows: (1) On the complaint of the party aggrieved a summons, or writ, is issued by an officer of

---

[1] The stages in the process, extending from the reign of Henry I. to that of Edward I., by which royal justice encroached on feudal justice, may be studied in Maitland's preface to *Sel. Pleas in Manorial Courts*, pp. liii. ff. See also Pollock and Maitland, I. 181-2.

the Court. Proceedings are opened by the command addressed to the defendant to appear in Court and answer what is alleged against him.

(2) In the usual case each party lodges written statements of his facts and pleas—that is, of the circumstances as they appear to him (or such of them as he hopes to bring evidence to prove)—on which he founds his claim or his defence, and of the legal principles he intends to deduce from these circumstances. When these statements of facts and pleas have been revised and adjusted, the complete data are before the Court; each party has stated what he considers essential to his case.

(3) Proof is, in due course, led; that is, each party is afforded an opportunity of proving such facts as he has alleged (and as require proof through the denial of his opponent). This he may do by documents, witnesses, or oath. Each party has the further privilege of shaking his opponent's evidence by cross-examination.

(4) The next important stage is the debate, the main object of which is to establish by legal arguments the pleas founded on; to deduce the legal consequences inherent in the facts which have been proved.

(5) Finally, the Judge gives his decision. He has to determine, after weighing the evidence led by either party, what facts have really been established, and how far the various pleas of plaintiff and defendant respectively are implied in these facts. Reasoning of such a kind as can be successfully performed only by a trained legal mind is thus necessary before the final decree or sentence can be pronounced by a Judge in a modern court of law.

A trial in Anglo-Saxon and early Norman times stands in notable contrast to all this in its stages and procedure, and even more in the spirit which pervades the whole. Thus, the proceedings, from first to last, were purely oral, there being no original writ or summons, no written pleadings, no record kept of the decision except in the memories of those present. The functions of " the Judges " were entirely different, and called for no previous training, since they were not required either to weigh a mass of evidence or to determine the bearing of subtle legal arguments, but merely to see fairplay, and to decide, according to simple rules, well established by centuries of custom, by what test the allegations of plaintiff and defendant were respectively to stand or fall. Finally, the arrangement of the stages of the litigation was entirely different: it is with something of a shock that the modern lawyer learns that in civil and criminal causes alike " judgment" invariably preceded " trial." Reflection will convince him that each of these words had in the Middle Ages a meaning different from what it bears to-day. That this is so can be best understood by following the stages of the old procedure.

(1) The initial difficulty was to obtain the presence of the defendant in Court, since there existed a strange reluctance either to compel his attendance or to allow judgment to pass against him by default. No initial writ was issued commanding him to appear; almost endless delays were allowed.

(2) When both parties had been, after many adjournments, actually brought face to face before the Court, the statements alike of the claim and of the defence were made verbally and in set *formulae,* the slightest slip or stumble in the words of which involved complete failure. This is merely one illustration of the tremendously formal and technical nature of early legal procedure, a trait common to all primitive systems of jurisprudence.

(3) Before the plaintiff could put the defendant on his defence, he required to show some presumption of the probability or *bona fides* of his case. This he usually did by producing two friends ready to substantiate his claim, known sometimes as his " suit " (Latin *secta*), or his " fore-witnesses." Their testimony had no reference to the particular facts of the case; it was not weighed against the " proof " afterwards led by the defendant; its object was merely to warrant the Court in demanding " proof " from the latter at all.[1]

---

[1] Sometimes no fore-witnesses were required; for example, where the claim was for restoration of stolen cattle, traced by "hue and cry" to defendant's house or byre. The presumption was here so strong as to render corroborative evidence unnecessary.

(4) Then came the judgment or " doom," which partook in no respect of the nature of the judgment of a modern tribunal. It came *before* the proof or trial, not after it, and was therefore called a " medial " judgment. It consisted in decreeing whether or no, on the strength of the previous procedure, the defendant should be put to his proof at all; and if so, *what* " proof " should be demanded.

Now, the exact test to be appointed by the court varied somewhat, according to circumstances, but long-established custom had laid down with some exactitude a rule applicable to every case likely to occur; and, further, the possible modes of proof were limited to some four or five at the outside. In Anglo-Saxon times, these were mainly compurgation, ordeal, witnesses (whose functions were, however, widely different from those of witnesses in modern law), and charters. The Norman Conquest introduced for the new-comers, a form of proof previously unknown in England—" trial by combat "—which tended, for the upper classes at least, to supersede all earlier procedures. The " proof," of whatever kind it might be, thus appointed by the " judges " for the defendant's performance was technically known as a " law " (Latin *lex*) in the sense of a " test " or " trial " or " task," according to success or failure in which his case should stand or fall.[1] To pronounce a " judgment " in this sense was a simple affair, a mere formality in the ordinary case, where room for dubiety could hardly be admitted: thus it was possible for " judgment " to be delivered by all the members of a feudal court, or all the suitors present at the hundred or shire-moot.

(5) The crucial stage, this " trial " which thus came after " judgment," consisted in one party (usually the defendant) essaying, on the day appointed, to satisfy the court as to the truth of his allegations by performing the task or " law " which had been set or " doomed " to him. When this consisted in the production of a charter, or of " transaction witnesses " (that is, the testimony of those officials appointed in each market-town to certify the conclusion of such bargains as the sale of cattle), it commends itself readily to

---

[1] See *infra* under cc. 38 and 39, where *lex terrae* is discussed.

modern approval. More frequently it took the form of
"an oath with oath-helpers," the plaintiff bringing with
him eleven or twelve of his trusty friends or dependents
to swear after him the words of a long and cumbrous oath,
under risk of being punished as perjurers for any slip in
the formula. Sometimes the decision was referred to the
intervention of Providence by appealing to the ordeal of
the red-hot iron or the more dreaded ordeal of water.
After the Norman Conquest, the trial in all litigations
between men of high rank, took the form of *duellum* or
legally regulated combat between the parties. The defendant gained his case if he caused the plaintiff to own himself a "craven," or if he held out till nightfall against the
plaintiff's attempts to force him to utter that fateful
word.[1]

This earlier form of "*lex*" or trial (which is referred to
in several clauses of Magna Carta)[2] was thus entirely
different from the modern "trial." It may be said without
exaggeration that there was no "trial" at all in the current
meaning of the word—no balancing of the testimony of
one set of witnesses against another, no open proof and
cross-examination, no debate on the legal principles
involved. The ancient "trial" was merely a formal test,
which was, except in the case of battle, entirely one-sided.
The phrase "burden of proof" was inapplicable. The
litigant to whom "a law" was appointed had rather the
"privilege of proof," and usually won his case—especially
in compurgation, and even in ordeal if he had arranged
matters properly with the priest who presided. In one
sense, the final "trial" was determined by the parties
themselves, or by one of them; in another and higher
sense the facts at issue were left to Providence; a miracle,
if necessary, would attest the just claim of the innocent.[3]

[1] Details may be studied in Neilson's *Trial by Combat*.

[2] See *infra*, cc. 38 and 39, where ordeal and compurgation and other forms of
lex are further discussed.

[3] Cf. Thayer, *Evidence*, p. 8. "The conception of the trial was that of a
proceeding between the parties, carried on publicly, under forms which the
community oversaw."

The essentials of this procedure[1] were the same in Norman as in Anglo-Saxon England, and that in all three classes of tribunals—popular, manorial, and royal courts. Two innovations the Normans did make; they introduced trial by combat and "*inquisitio*." Among the prerogatives of the Norman Dukes was this right to compel the sworn evidence of reliable men of any district—men specially picked for the purpose, and put on oath before answering the questions asked of them. This procedure was known as *inquisitio* (or the seeking of information) from the point of view of the government making the inquiry, and as *recognitio* (or the giving of information) from the point of view of those supplying it. This device was capable of endless extension to new uses in the deft hands of the Norman Kings. William employed it in compiling Domesday Book; while his successors made it the instrument of experiments in the science of taxation. It has a double claim to the interest of the constitutional historian, because it was one of the influences that helped to mould our Parliamentary institutions; and because several of the new uses to which it came to be put had a close connection with the origin of trial by jury. The recognitors, indeed, were simply local jurors in a rude or elementary form.[2]

III. *Reforms of Henry II. in Law Courts and Legal Procedure.* It was reserved for Henry of Anjou to inaugu-

[1] These stages of procedure are fully illustrated by recorded cases. Two of these, both from the reign of John, may here be cited. (1) "Hereward, the son of William, appeals Walter, the son of Hugh, of assaulting him, in the King's peace, and wounding him in the arm with an iron fork, and giving him another wound on the head; and this he offers to prove on his body as the Court shall appoint. And Walter defends all of it by his body. And it is testified by the coroners and by the whole county that the same Hereward showed his wounds at the proper time, and has made sufficient suit. Therefore it is decreed that there should be 'battle.' . . . Let them come armed, a fortnight from St. Swithin's day, at Leicester." *Sel. Pleas of Crown* (Selden Society), p. 18. (2) "Walter Trenchebof was said to have handed to Inger of Faldingthorpe the knife with which he killed Guy Foliot, and is suspected of it. Let him purge himself by water that he did not consent to it. He has failed and is hanged." *Ibid.*, p. 75.

[2] The relation of "recognition" to trial by jury is discussed *infra*, Part III., section 7.

rate a new era in the relations of the three classes of courts. He was the first king deliberately to plan the overthrow of the feudal jurisdictions by insidiously undermining them, if not yet by open attack. He was the first king to reduce the old district courts so thoroughly under the control of royal officials as to turn them practically into royal courts. He was the first king also to throw open the doors of his own courts of law to all-comers, to all freemen, that is to say, for the villein had for centuries still to seek redress in the Court of that very lord of the manor who was too often his oppressor.[1]

In brief, then, Henry's policy was twofold: to convert the County Courts completely into Royal Courts, since in them royal officials now dispensed royal justice according to the same rules as prevailed at the King's *Curia*; and to reduce all manorial or private Courts to insignificance by diverting pleas to his own *Curia*, and leaving the rival tribunals to die gradually from inanition. Both branches of this policy met ultimately with success, although the event hung in the balance until long after his death. The barons, though partially deceived by the insidious nature of Henry's reforms, did what they could to thwart him; but the current was with the Crown. Royal justice steadily encroached upon feudal justice. One of the last stands made by the barons has left its traces in several chapters of Magna Carta.[2] These contain what

---

[1] The trend of learned opinion for the moment is towards transferring the chief share of credit for remedial changes from Henry II. to his grandfather. Prof. Haskins, too, has shown reason for holding that the younger Henry found precedents in the procedure of his Angevin father as well as of his Norman grandfather (*Amer. Hist. Rev.*, VIII. 618). There is some evidence also that Henry II. avoided any violent breaking with the past. Mr. Davis (*Engl. under the Normans*, p. 283) shows Henry and his Justice Glanvill acting in a spirit friendly to the private courts. It is possible, however, to found erroneous estimates upon such items of evidence. The true inventor is the man who adapts for common use what was before exceptional: Henry II. can afford to be judged by this test. To him, rather than to Henry I., belongs the credit for revolutionizing the whole system of dispensing justice. *Cf.* G. B. Adams (*Origin of Engl. Const.*, 106-7): "It is in his time that these changes are finally made and the new methods become permanently a part of the constitution."

[2] *E.g.* 34 and 39.

seem, at first sight, to be merely trivial alterations of technical points of court procedure; but inextricably bound up with them are principles of wide constitutional importance.   It was Henry's good fortune or policy to disguise radical reforms until they looked like small changes of procedure; it follows that the framers of Magna Carta, while appearing merely to seek the reversal of these trivial points, were really seeking to return to the totally different conditions which had prevailed prior to the reforms of Henry.

The short account of that monarch's system of procedure, necessary to a comprehension of Magna Carta, falls naturally into two divisions.

(1) *Criminal Justice.*   (a) By his Assizes of Clarendon and Northampton, Henry reserved important crimes for the exclusive consideration of his own judges either on circuit or at his court; and he demanded entry for these judges into all franchises for that purpose.   In this part of his policy, the King was completely successful; heinous crimes were, in the beginning of the thirteenth century, admitted on all hands to be " pleas of the Crown " (that is, cases reserved exclusively for royal jurisdiction); and Magna Carta made no attempt to reverse this part of the Crown's policy: all that was attempted in 1215 was to obtain a promise that these functions, now surrendered to the Crown forever, should be discharged by the Crown's officials in a proper manner.

(b) Henry's usual good sense, in this matter stimulated by some notable miscarriages of justice, led him to question the equity of the procedure usually adopted in criminal pleas : for private " appeal " (or accusation by the injured party or his nearest surviving relative), he substituted, whenever possible, communal accusation; that is, the duty of indicting suspected criminals before the King's Justices was no longer left to private initiative, but was laid on a body of neighbours—the predecessors of the Grand Jury of later days.   Appeals were discouraged and rules laid down restricting the right of accusation.[2]

[1] See *infra*, under cc. 24 and 45.   [2] See *infra*, under chapter 54.

(c) A necessary complement was the discouragement of
" trial by combat." An ingenious device was invented and
extended to an increasing number of cases; an accused
individual might apply for a writ known as *de odio et atia*,
and evade the *duellum* by a reference to what was practically
a jury of neighbours.[1]

(2) *Civil Justice.* Henry's innovations under this head
were equally important. In his reign justice, it is sometimes said, was pigeon-holed. Much attention was
bestowed on the formalities of litigation; while pleas
began to be classified into stereotyped groups, each form
of grievance having its appropriate remedy, to be obtained
only by means of the appropriate writ.

(a) *The Writ System.* An unflinching rule was established that no case could be brought before the royal court
until a writ had been obtained from chancery. This had
to be paid for, sometimes at a fixed rate, and sometimes at
whatever sum the Crown demanded. The whole procedure
in the royal courts, which followed the issuing of such a
writ, came to be known as " the writ system." From an
early date, much attention was directed to the devising of
forms of writ applicable to various cases. The system,
somewhat inflexible from the first, had become absolutely
rigid long before the close of the thirteenth century. If
a proper writ was not selected, or if no such writ had been
invented, the wronged individual had no remedy in the
King's courts of common law. Registers of writs were
drawn up, copied and enlarged, and transmitted from one
generation to another.[2]

(b) *Control of Feudal Courts.* Whether devised for that
purpose or not, this writ system proved a useful instrument
for diverting the stream of litigation from the barons' courts
to the *curia regis*. Henry, if we may credit Glanvill,
succeeded in establishing the somewhat astounding rule
that no plea concerning land could be commenced in *any*
court without the authority of a royal writ.[3] Even if such

[1] See *infra*, under chapter 36.   [2] See Maitland, *Collected Papers*, II., 110-173.
[3] Glanvill xii, 25. For a discussion of the difficulties involved in accepting
Glanvill see Adams, *Origin*, 96.

writs were issued as matter of course, the mere need of asking for them would supply Henry with information doubly valuable in relation to certain other expedients still to be explained.   That King, applying to his own needs procedure known to the Carolingian Kings, secured an effective means of evoking suits regarding freehold from the seignorial courts to his own.   This was done by procedure initiated by two types of writs : " writs of right " addressed to the holder of a court, bidding him do justice under penalty of interference by the royal court; and " writs *praecipe* " addressed to the sheriff, bidding him require the holder of a piece of land to hand it over to a claimant or explain to the King why he has not done so.[1]

It is probable that even in 1215 the Crown had not fully developed the consequences afterwards seen to be involved in the writ of right, properly so called; but Henry II. and his sons seem freely to have used the writ *praecipe* in such a manner as to cause their barons to lose their jurisdiction—an abuse struck at by chapter 34 of Magna Carta.

(c) *Royal Pleas and Common Pleas.*   The mass of new business made it necessary to increase the staff of judges and apportion the work.   A natural division was that between ordinary (or common) pleas and pleas of the Crown.   This distinction is recognized in many separate chapters.[2]   Thus two groups of judges were formed which, in later years, developed into separate courts—the Court of Common Pleas (known as " the Bench," that is, the ordinary Bench), and the King's Bench (known earlier as the court *Coram Rege,* supposed to be held in the King's presence).

(d) *The Petty Assizes.*   Special procedure for determining titles to land or rights of possession was also invented by Henry to supersede trial by battle.   These Assizes, as they were called, are fully discussed elsewhere.[3]   While the Grand Assize is not mentioned in Magna Carta, its abuse was indirectly struck at by the clause concerning

---

[1] See Brunner, *Schwurgerichte*, 78-80.   Details are discussed *infra*, under c. 34.

[2] See *infra*, under chapters 17 and 24.   [3] See *infra*, under chapter 18.

writs *praecipe* in chapter 34 : the Petty Assizes, however, would seem to have won favour with the barons, who in chapter 18 demanded that regular sessions for hearing them should be held four times a year.

These were the chief innovations that enabled Henry II. to effect a revolution in the relations of royal to feudal justice. As time went on, new writs were continually devised to meet new types of cases; and litigants flocked readily to the King's Courts, leaving the seignorial courts empty of business and of fees. Nor was this the only grievance of the barons. When one of their own number was amerced or accused of any offence involving loss of liberty or lands, he might be compelled by the Crown, under Henry and his sons, to submit to have the amercement assessed, or the criminal proceedings conducted, by one of the new Benches (by a tribunal composed of some four or five of the King's officials), in place of the time-honoured judgment of his peers assembled in the *Commune Concilium* (the predecessor of the modern Parliament).

Can we wonder that the barons objected to be amerced and judged by their inferiors?[1] Can we wonder that they resented the complete though gradual supersession of their own profitable jurisdictions by the royal courts?[2] or that they looked with suspicion on every new development of the royal justice? Can we wonder that, when they seemed to have King John for the moment in their power, they demanded redress of these grievances, as well as of those connected with increase of feudal burdens? The cause for wonder rather is that their demands were not more sweeping: the barons, in their hour of triumph, accepted cordially one half of the royal innovations.

The chapters bearing on jurisdiction may be arranged in two groups, some reactionary, and some favourable to Henry's reforms. On the one hand, no lord of a manor shall be robbed of his Court by the King evoking before the royal courts pleas between two freeholders of the lord's manor;[3] no freeman shall be judged or condemned by the

---

[1] See *infra*, under chapters 21 and 39.   [2] See *infra*, under chapter 34.
[3] c. 34.

King's officials, but only before the full body of his peers;[1] earls and barons must be amerced only by their equals.[2] On the other hand, in prescribing remedies for abuses connected with numerous branches of legal procedure, the barons accepted by implication this new procedure itself and the royal encroachments implied therein. For example, the Crown's right to hold "Common Pleas" was impliedly admitted, when the barons asked and obtained that these should be tried in some certain place (that is, at Westminster).[3] Yet these very pleas must have included many cases which, prior to Henry II.'s reforms, would have been tried in a seignorial court. Again, in regulating the petty assizes, chapters 18 and 19 admit the Crown's right to hold them. Here, as in chapter 40, the ground of complaint is not that there is too much royal justice, but rather that there is too little of it: henceforth it must be neither delayed nor denied. Further, the encroachments made by Henry II. in 1166 on the private franchises in the matter of criminal jurisdiction are tacitly accepted by the acquiescence in the King's definition of "Pleas of the Crown" implied in chapter 24.

These, then, are the two groups into which the innovations made by Henry and his sons naturally fell, as viewed by John's opponents in 1215: some of them had come to be warmly welcomed; while others, it was insisted, must be swept away.

[1] c. See *infra*, under chapter 39.   [2] c. 21.   [3] c. 17.

PART III.

MAGNA CARTA: ITS FORM AND CONTENTS.

I. Its Prototypes: Earlier Charters.

The traditional view makes Magna Carta the direct descendant of Henry Beauclerk's Coronation Charter, which is, in turn, regarded as merely an amplification of the old coronation oath sworn by the Conqueror and his sons, in terms borrowed from a long line of Anglo-Saxon kings, stretching back from Edward Confessor to Edgar, Alfred and Egbert, until its origin is lost in the mists of antiquity. According to this time-honoured view, which insists on an exclusively Anglo-Saxon pedigree for the charters of Norman and Angevin kings, the charters of Henry I. and John were regarded as confirmations to the nation at large of the essential principles of the old laws of Alfred and of Edward, thus bridging over, alike in form and substance, the gulf of the Norman Conquest.

The accuracy of these preconceptions has of late years been rudely questioned. The simple formula for solving all problems of English constitutional origins by assuming an unmixed Anglo-Saxon ancestry, has been challenged from more sides than one. Magna Carta, like the Constitution itself, is of mixed parentage, tracing its descent not entirely from Teutonic, but partly from Norman, and even Danish and Celtic sources. In the first place, John's Charter derives some of its vital clauses from documents not couched in charter form. The Constitutions of Clarendon of 1164 and the *Forma Procedendi* of 1194 are as undoubtedly antecedents of Magna Carta as is the Coronation Charter of Henry itself. The same is true of many grants made by successive kings of England to the Church, to London and other cities, and to individual prelates and barons. In a sense, the whole previous history of England went to the making of Magna Carta.

Then, again, the exclusively Anglo-Saxon origin of the antecedents of Henry's Charter is by no means left unchallenged. A recent American writer, attacking the older theories as advanced by Bishop Stubbs, has formulated these three propositions: that Henry's charter was feudal in character rather than constitutional or national, promising " a regulated feudal government " purged of Rufus' misdeeds rather than a return to a "national" type of government; that its substance was derived from Norman innovations rather than from the Confessor's or Canute's laws; and that its form was founded on continental models, possibly on some Norman borough charter, and by no means on the old coronation oath.[1]

These iconoclastic theories require to be modified: the claims of Magna Carta, on its formal side, at least, to an Anglo-Saxon ancestry have found a powerful advocate in Mr. W. H. Stevenson,[2] who holds that the Anglo-Norman charters of liberties "are developments of the Anglo-Norman writ charter, and that in its turn is . . . merely the Anglo-Saxon writ translated into Latin."[3]

Looking both to the contents and the formalities of execution of John's Great Charter, the safer opinion would

[1] See Dr. H. L. Cannon's article, *Amer. Hist. Rev.*, XX. 37. Some of his theories, however, had been anticipated (see, *e.g.* Prothero, *S. de Montfort*, 16), and others have not been substantiated.

[2] *Engl. Hist. Rev.*, XXVII. 1-8. Dr. R. L. Poole is also an advocate of the traditional view: see *ibid.*, XXVIII. 444.

[3] *Ibid.*, XXVII. 4. Mr. Stevenson explains further that "the Anglo-Saxon writ was in its origin a letter from the King to a shire-moot, and this characteristic clung closely to the Anglo-Norman writ-charter of the twelfth century" (p. 5). He also shows how the double-faced pendant seal, in the use of which William and his sons followed the Confessor, was not derived by Edward from the Normans, who in his day used (like the Kings of France) a seal *plaqué*. The whole article throws much light on the diplomatics of the genesis of Magna Carta.

seem to be, that, like the English Constitution, it is of mixed origin, deriving elements from ancestors of more races than one; but that the traditional line of descent from the oaths and writs of Anglo-Saxon kings, through the Charter of Henry I., is one that cannot be neglected.

The promises of good government that connect King John with the old kings of Wessex are thus the outcome of an essential feature of the ancient monarchy, and of the rules that regulated succession to the Crown. Two rival principles, the elective and the hereditary, from an early date, had struggled for the mastery. In an unsettled state of society, nations cannot allow the sceptre to pass to an infant or a weakling. When a king died, leaving a son of tender age and a brother of mature ability, the magnates of the kingdom, the so-called Witan, claimed the right to choose a fitting successor. The exact relations between the elective and the hereditary principles were never laid down with absolute precision : the practice usually followed by the Witenagemot was to select some near kinsman of the late king competent for the post. The king-elect had still to be solemnly anointed, and this gave to the Church an important share in deciding who should be king. Not later than the days of Edgar, it became the practice for the officiating archbishop to exact an oath of good government from the new sovereign before his final coronation. The terms of this oath became stereotyped; and, as administered by Dunstan to King Ethelred, they are still extant.[1]

This may be analyzed into three promises—peace to God's Church and people; repression of violence in men of every rank; justice and mercy in all judgments. When William I., anxious in all things to fortify the legality of his title, took the oath in solemn form, he created a precedent of tremendous importance, although he may have regarded it at the moment as an empty formality.[2] The

[1] See *Memorials of St. Dunstan* (Rolls Series), p. 355.

[2] Florence of Worcester and the Worcester version of the *Chronicle* agree that the Conqueror took the oath. " William of Poitiers and Guy are silent about the oath" (Freeman, *Norman Conquest*, III. 561, note).

quasi-elective character of the kingship, the need for coronation by the Church, and this tripartite oath were all preserved.

This was of vital moment, because limits were thereby placed, in theory at least, to prerogatives that threatened to become absolute. The power of the Norman kings might almost be described as irresponsible despotism, tempered by fear of rebellion. Three forces, indeed, acted as curbs: the necessity for consulting the Curia Regis; the restraining influence of the Church; the growth of a body of public opinion, confined as yet to the upper classes.

These elements counted for something, but failed to restrain sufficiently even an average king; while they were powerless against a strong ruler, like William I. The moment at which the Crown might be taken at disadvantage was during the interregnum that followed a king's death. Thus, William Rufus, anxious to prevent his elder brother Robert from making good his claim to the English throne, succeeded chiefly through the friendship of Lanfranc. To gain this, he was compelled to make promises of good government, taking oath in the ancient form. In the same reign, began the practice of supplementing verbal promises by sealed charters. No such charter was indeed issued either by Rufus or his father when they were crowned; but the younger William, at a critical period in his reign, granted a short Charter of Liberties, the text of which has not come down to us. By a treaty made at Caen in 1091, Duke Robert and Rufus agreed that each should constitute the other his heir. Thus, at Rufus' death, Henry was, in a sense, a usurper, and this made it necessary for him to bid high for influential support.[1] It is to this doubtful title that Englishmen owe the first Charter of Liberties that has come down to us.[2]

Roger of Wendover relates how " as many charters were made as there are counties in England, and by the King's command they were deposited in the abbeys of every county

---

[1] Stubbs, *Const. Hist.*, I. 328-9, and authorities there cited.

[2] See text in Appendix. For textual criticism see Liebermann, *Trans. R. H. S.*, VIII. 21 ff.

as a memorial," and this is confirmed by an analysis of the copies still preserved.[1]

Henry's coronation charter was the price paid for support in his candidature for the Crown. Its terms contain, however unconsciously, an indictment of his brother Rufus' government and, perhaps, in part also of his father's. The new king was merely " playing to the gallery " : when his purpose was served, his promises were broken.[2] On the bearing of these promises there is room for diversity of opinion. Dr. Stubbs' contention that Henry " definitely commits himself to the duties of a national king " [3] has been rejected, as already explained, by recent critics. The more modern view is strengthened by an analysis of the Charter, revealing important concessions to the barons and the Church, while those to the people at large were few and vague. Of the fourteen chapters into which it is usually divided, chapter one proceeds on the narrative that the kingdom had been oppressed by unjust exactions. Henry, in the first place, makes free the holy Church of God, " so that I shall neither sell nor farm out nor, on the death of archbishop, or bishop or abbot, accept anything from the demesne of the church or from its feudal-tenants until a successor has been inducted to it."

It seems doubtful whether the regrettably vague phraseology of the qualifying clause is intended merely to apply the generalities of the church's " freedom " to specific instances, or whether it must be taken as a deliberate restriction. The prohibition of selling has been read as referring to the simoniacal practice of taking money from aspirants to episcopal preferments; but more probably it was meant to prohibit the alienation of the property of a vacant see, a practice that must have been often resorted to, if we judge from the efforts at recovery made by successive archbishops, notably by Becket. This reading is the more probable from the fact that " selling " is here coupled with

---

[1] See Liebermann, *op. cit.* On the whole subject of publication of charters by Henry I., Stephen and John, see Poole, *Engl. Hist. Rev.*, XXVIII. 444-453.

[2] Round, *Feudal England*, 227.   [3] *Const. Hist.*, I. 331.

G

"farming out," an expedient clearly inapplicable to pre-
latical appointments and referring to the Crown's practice
of granting leases of the lands of vacant sees for nominal
annual returns in consideration of a heavy *grassum* paid
to the Treasury at the commencement of the lease.   The
rest of the clause is best interpreted as a renunciation of the
claim to exact either a " relief " from a prelate on his
appointment or payments in lieu of relief from tenants of
a vacant see or royal abbey.[1]

The last clause of the chapter abrogates evil customs
whereby the kingdom was unjustly oppressed, and then
proceeds to define them—a process that occupies the
remaining thirteen chapters of the document.   Chapter 2
promises that reliefs of feudal tenants should be " just and
legitimate." [2]   Chapters 3 and 4 guard against abuse of
the feudal incidents of marriage and wardship.[3]   Chapter 5
abolishes as an innovation "the common mintage " (an
exaction levied by the mints when the coinage was altered),[4]
and enjoined the punishment of any one taken with false
money—provisions finding no echo in John's Charter.

Chapter 6 remits a number of arrears, reliefs, and
penalties due to Rufus at his death.   Chapter 7 confirms
crown-tenants in the right to dispose of their personal
estate by will, and provides for the division of the property
of intestates among their wives, children, relations, and
vassals, and for the good of their own souls.[5]   Chapter 8
seems to promise the total abolition of the Norman system
of forfeitures and amercements (in respect of petty offences,
as opposed to treasons and crimes) and a return to the
Anglo-Saxon system of a fixed tariff of *bots* and *wites*.[6]

[1] The use of the word "*donec*" is ambiguous, and might grammatically be
strained to make the clause a prohibition of wardship, coupled with an endorse-
ment of relief : the King must take nothing *until* the new bishop gets possession.
Another interpretation would stretch the prohibition to include both wardship and
relief, and indeed to include the taking of profits of any sort whatever.   It has
also been read as mainly a prohibition against the Crown's permanent appropriation
of "escheats " falling to a see during a vacancy.   See Makower, *Const. Hist. of
Church*, 17.

[2] *Cf. infra*, under cc. 2 and 3 of 1215.   [3] *Cf. infra*, cc. 3 to 6.
[4] See Stubbs, *Early Engl. Hist.*, 113.   [5] See *infra*, cc. 26 and 27.
[6] See Pollock and Maitland, II. 512-3.   See also *infra*, c. 20.

Chapter 9 is concerned with the " *murdrum* " fine—a payment exacted by the Norman kings from all the inhabitants of a hundred in which a corpse had been found, where the slayer remained undiscovered and the dead man's identity as a person of English birth could not be proved. " Murder" was thus primarily secret slaying, in the sense that the perpetrator was not known, and, secondarily, the fine exacted on that account. This heavy fine, whose original amount is variously given as 40 or 46 marks, was intended as a protection to Normans against the native Englishry they oppressed.

Henry remitted all " murder-fines " incurred before his coronation, and promised that those incurred after that date should be " justly " paid for " in accordance with the law of King Edward "—a clause difficult to reconcile with the recognized opinion that the *murdrum* was unknown in England prior to 1066, unless on the supposition that the draftsman of the Charter of 1100 was strangely ignorant of the usages of thirty-four years earlier. Perhaps the " murder-fine " was not an invention of the Conqueror and his sons, but an old English institution put by the Normans to new uses. An alternative suggestion may be hazarded that here (as perhaps elsewhere in the charter) the reference to the good laws of Edward was a mere tag or " common form," meant to please his subjects without committing the King to anything in particular.

Chapter 10 contains no concession (unless it be an implied renunciation of Rufus' encroachments), but, on the contrary, a blunt intimation that Henry, with his barons' consent, would retain the forests as his father had had them. The barons' consent may be partly explained by their expectation to enjoy, as more or less habitually in attendance upon Henry, a share in the pleasures of the hunt of which the King was " master." By chapter II., Henry concedes " *proprio dono meo* to knights holding their lands *per loricas* [that is, by knight's service] to have the lands of their demesne ploughs quit of all gelds and of every [non-military] service, in order that, as being relieved by so great a relief, so they might effectually provide themselves with horses and arms for my service and the defence of my kingdom." In thus exempting Crown-tenants holding by the "hauberk" (that is to say his "barons," in the wider sense of the word) from Danegeld, on the distinct understanding that they should keep in readiness an efficient military equipment, Henry aimed at making hard-and-fast an old and fluctuating rule that prohibited Crown-tenants from being subjected to a double set of burdens. The lands of knights and churchmen, who already served the King in other ways, were not expected to contribute Danegeld in respect of their home-farms. Holders of knight's fees, however, must keep proper weapons and armour for themselves and their horses—an obligation involving an expenditure constantly increasing with every advance in the art of war. The chapter thus recognizes a contrast between land subject to military service and land subject to geld; "the *inland* and *warland* of old English fiscal arrangements, the *dominium* and *terra geldabilis* respectively of the Geld Roll of 1084."[1] The fact that Henry's Charter draws so sharp a line between the two, suggests that the barons may have made this a condition of their support of his claims against those of Robert. Henry's promise, however, was never strictly carried out: the practice continued to fluctuate. Under Henry II., only the barons of the Exchequer and a few privileged religious persons enjoyed exemption.[2] Gradually the distinction between *inland* and *warland* became extinct.

The remaining clauses of the Charter of Henry I. are mainly of a formal character. Chapter 12 declares a firm peace for the future throughout his kingdom—thus marking the end of the *interregnum* consequent on his brother's death. Chapter 13, on the strength of which wide-reaching theories have sometimes been built, seems to be merely an amplification of the purely formal chapter that precedes it: it restores the law of Edward, with the reforms his father

---

[1] See Prof. Vinogradoff, in a review of the first edition of this book, *Law Quarterly Review*, XXI., 250-7. See also his *Growth of the Manor*, 226-7, and his *Engl. Society*, 191.

[2] *Dialogus de Scaccario*, I. c. 11.

had effected with the barons' consent. The old law was vague; the innovations definite and well known. Chapter 14 proclaims terms and conditions of indemnity, extended to those guilty of acts of spoliation during the *interregnum* now brought to an end.

These provisions, taken as a whole, contain little to justify Henry's claim to rank as a constitutional or national sovereign. The bulk of the concessions are made to the barons. The Church, it is true, obtains a definite promise in chapter one: but the individuals who would chiefly benefit were newly-appointed prelates, who became feudal vassals on entering upon the lands of their sees. Chapters 2 and 4 confine their benefits to Crown-tenants and sub-tenants, and are therefore purely feudal and not " national " in their range. They may be compared with the clauses of John's Charter that extend some of its provisions to sub-tenants. Chapters 12 and 13, with their vague affirmation of a firm peace, and of the old English law, now half-forgotten (undefined and declared valid only so far as unaltered by William I.), are the only grants " to the people at large." The baronial element clearly triumphs over the " national," in the tenor and outlook of the famous coronation charter.[1]

There are three intermediate links in the chain of charters connecting those of Henry I. and John, namely, the two charters of Stephen and that of Henry II.[2] The circumstances of the accession of the earlier King were peculiar. Henry I. had nominated his only child Matilda as his heir: his nephew, Stephen, and all the English barons had done homage to her as their future liege lady. Stephen, however, taking advantage of Matilda's absence and unpopularity, and of the barons' reluctance to be ruled by a woman, made a bold dash for the Crown. From the moment of the old King's death, " the Norman barons treated the suc-

[1] See Charter in Appendix. For text and textual criticism, see Liebermnan, *Trans. R.H.S.*, VIII. 21-48. On whole subject, see Vinogradoff, *Law Quart.*, *Rev.*, as above cited.

[2] The discussions on the " unknown charter " (*infra*, p. 175) would seem however, in another sense, to leave these three links out of the chain.

cession as an open question ": in these words of Stubbs,[1]
Dr. Round finds [2] the keynote of the reign. Stephen
was prepared to bid higher for support than Henry had
felt compelled to do : like William of Orange, five centuries
later, he agreed to become "king upon conditions." A
Charter of Liberties and a solemn oath securing "the
liberty of the Church" together formed the price of
Stephen's consecration; and this price was not perhaps
too high when we remember that "election was a matter
of opinion, coronation a matter of fact." [3] The process by
which he built up a title to the Crown culminated in the
Easter of 1136, when he secured the support of Matilda's
half-brother Robert, Earl of Gloucester, whose lead was
quickly followed by influential nobles who, however, performed homage under an important reservation; their
future loyalty would be strictly conditional on the treatment extended to them by Stephen.

These transactions took place at Oxford;[4] at the same
time the King issued his second or Oxford Charter, which
combined the provisions of the oath to the Church and of
the vague earlier charter, with the conditions extorted by
Earl Robert and his followers. The opening words contain a laboured attempt to set forth a valid title to the
throne. All reference to predecessors is avoided, and
Stephen declares himself king "by appointment of the
clergy and people, by consecration of the Archbishop and
papal legate, and by the Pope's confirmation.[5]

Perhaps its chief provisions are those in favour of the
Church, supplementing a vague declaration that the Church
should be "free" by specific promises that the bishops
should have exclusive jurisdiction and power over ecclesiastics and their goods, with the sole right to superintend
their distribution after death. Here was a clear confirma-

---

[1] Stubbs, *Const. Hist.*, I. 345.   [2] Round, *Geoffrey de Mandeville*, p. 1.

[3] Round, *Geoffrey de Mandeville*, p. 6.   Dr. Round, *ibid.*, p. 438, explains that
this earlier charter of Stephen was supplemented by the verbal promise recorded
by William of Malmesbury, *de libertate reddenda ecclesiae et conservanda*.

[4] Round, *Geoffrey*, 22.

[5] Stephen was not justified in this last assertion.   See Round, *Geoffrey*, 9.

tion of the right of the Courts Christian to a monopoly of all pleas affecting the clergy or their property. Stephen also renounced wardship over church lands during vacancies—a surrender never dreamt of by Henry I. or Henry II. Grants to the people at large followed. A general clause promising peace and justice was supplemented by specific concessions of more practical value, namely, a promise to extirpate all exactions, unjust practices, and "miskennings" by sheriffs and others, and to observe good, ancient, and just customs in respect of murder-fines, pleas, and other causes.

Strangely enough, there is only one provision specially benefiting feudal magnates, the King's renunciation of all tracts of land afforested since the time of the two Williams. The omission of further feudal concessions must not be attributed either to Stephen's strength, or to any spirit of moderation or self-sacrifice in the magnates. Each baron of sufficient importance had already extorted a private charter, more valued than a general provision in favour of all and sundry. Such grants often included the right to maintain a feudal stronghold, whose owner would enjoy a position of practical independence.

It is instructive to compare these wide promises of Stephen with the meagre words of the charter granted by Henry of Anjou at or soon after his coronation.[1] Henry II. omits all mention of Stephen and his charters, not because he did not wish to acknowledge a usurper, but because of that usurper's lavish grants to the Church. Henry had no intention to confirm "benefit of clergy" in so sweeping a form, or to renounce wardship over vacant sees.

To the Church, as to the barons, Henry confirms only what his grandfather had already conceded. Even compared with the charter of Henry I., that of the younger Henry is shorter and less explicit—features that justified Stephen Langton in his preference for the older document. If Henry II. granted a short and grudging charter, neither of his sons, at their coronations, granted any charter at all.

[1] See Bémont, *Chartes*, 13, and *Select Charters*, 135.

Reasons for the omission readily suggest themselves; the Crown had grown strong enough to dispense with this unwelcome formality, partly because of the absence of rival competitors for the throne, and partly because of the perfection to which the machinery of government had been brought. The utmost the Church could extract from Richard and John, as the price of their consecration, was the renewal of the three vague promises contained in the oath, now taken as a pure formality. John, however, was not to be allowed to shake himself free from the obligations of his oath. Stephen Langton, before absolving him in 1213, compelled him to swear it anew.[1]

Not only were the terms of the ancient oath riveted anew on John's conscience, but, as has been shown, the coronation Charter of Henry I., exhibited by the Primate in times of crisis to the nobles, and used in preparing the schedules that formed the rough drafts of the *Articuli Baronum,* was made a curb for royal caprice. It is thus impossible to neglect the importance of the sequence of coronation oaths and charters as contributors both to the form and substance of Magna Carta, although that is only one of the many lines of descent through which the Great Charter can trace its ancestry.

II. Magna Carta: its Form and Juridical Nature.

The juridical nature of the document to which John set his seal at Runnymede will be differently estimated according as it is judged by present-day or by medieval standards.

(1) *The Modern Point of View.* Much ingenuity has been expended in the effort to discover which particular category of modern jurisprudence most accurately describes the Great Charter. Is it an enacted law, or a treaty; the royal answer to a petition; or a declaration of rights? Is it a simple pact, bargain, or agreement between contracting parties? Or is it a combination of two or more of these? Something has been said in favour of almost every possible

---

[1] See *supra*, p. 27, and Round, *Eng. Hist. Rev.*, VIII. 292.

view, perhaps more to the bewilderment than to the en-
lightenment of students of history uninterested in legal
subtleties.

The claim of Magna Carta to rank as a formal act of
legislation has been supported on the ground that it was
promulgated in what was practically a *commune concilium*.
King John, it is maintained, met in a national assembly
all the estates of his realm who had any political rights,
and these concurred with him in the grant.   The consent
of all who claimed a share in the making of laws—archbishops, bishops, abbots, earls, and crown-tenants, great
and small—entitles the Charter to rank as a statute.

Against this view, however, technical informalities may
be urged.   Both the composition of the Council and the
procedure adopted there, were irregular.   No formal writs
of summons had been issued, and, therefore, the meeting
was never properly constituted.   Further, the whole proceedings were tumultuary; the barons, assembled in military array, compelled the consent of John by show of force.
On these grounds, modern jurisprudence, if appealed to,
would reject the claim of the Charter to be enrolled as an
ordinary statute.   It may be argued also that Magna Carta,
while something less than a law, is also something more.
A law made by the king in one national assembly might
be repealed by the king in another; whereas the Great
Charter was intended by the barons to be unchangeable.
It was granted to them and their heirs for ever; and, in
return, a price had been paid, namely, the renewal of their
allegiance.[1]

Magna Carta has also been described as a treaty.   Such
is the verdict of Dr. Stubbs.[2]   "The Great Charter,
although drawn up in the form of a royal grant, was really
a treaty between the King and his subjects. . . . It is the
collective people who really form the other high contracting
party in the great capitulation." [3]   This view receives some

---

[1] The *quid pro quo* was *conditional* homage, dependent (as we learn from
chapter 63) on observance of the Charter.

[2] *Const. Hist.*, I. 569.

[3] *Cf.* Prothero *Simon de Montfort*, 15; Pike, *House of Lords*, 312.

support from words contained in chapter 63 of the Charter:
"*Juratum est autem tam ex parte nostra quam ex parte baronum, quod haec omnia supradicta bona fide et sine malo ingenio observabuntur.*" There is, however, a radical objection. A treaty is a public act between two contracting powers, who must, to meet the requirements of modern jurisprudence, be independent States or their accredited agents; while John and his opponents were fragments of one State, torn asunder by mutual jealousies.

For other authorities, Magna Carta is a contract, pact, or private agreement. M. Emile Boutmy is of this opinion :—" Le caractère de cet acte est aisé à définir. Ce n'est pas précisément un traité, puisqu'il n'y a pas ici deux souverainetés légitimes ni deux nations en présence; ce n'est pas non plus une loi; elle serait entachée d'irrégularité et de violence; c'est un compromis ou un pacte." [1] Thus considered, the proudest act of the national drama would take its place in the legal category which includes the hire of a waggon or the sale of a load of corn. There are, however, objections to this theory also. It is difficult to see how the plea of " force," if sufficient (as M. Boutmy urges) to render null the enactment of a public law, would not be even more effective in reducing a private agreement. If Magna Carta has no other basis than the consent of the contracting parties, it seems safer to describe it as a public treaty than a private pact.

Other theories also are possible; as, for example, that the Great Charter is of the nature of a Declaration of Rights, such as have played so prominent a part in France and the United States; while a recent American writer on English constitutional development regards it as a code, creating a formal constitution for England—in a rude and embryonic form, it is true :—" If a constitution has for its chief object the prevention of encroachments and the harmonizing of governmental institutions, Magna Carta answers to that description, at least in part." [2] It would be easy to cite compromises between these competing

---

[1] *Études de droit constitutionnel*, 41.

[2] Prof. Jesse Macy, *English Constitution*, 162.

theories. Thus, a high authority declares that "the Great Charter is partly a declaration of rights, partly a treaty between Crown and people." [1]

The essential nature of what took place at Runnymede, in June, 1215, is plain, when stripped of legal subtleties. A bargain was struck, between the King and his rebel magnates, that, in return for a renewal of fealty and homage, John would grant "to the freemen of England and their heirs for ever" the liberties enumerated in sixty-three chapters. No one thought of asking whether the transaction thus concluded was a "treaty" or a private "contract." The terms had to be drawn up in legal form, so as to bear record to the exact nature of the provisions, and also to the authenticity of John's consent. It was, therefore, reduced to writing, and the resulting document was naturally couched in the form invariably used for all irrevocable grants intended to descend from father to son, namely, a feudal charter, authenticated by the impression of the granter's seal—just as in the case of a grant of land, and with many of the clauses appropriate to such a grant. [2]

John grants to the freemen of England and their heirs certain specified rights and liberties, as though these were so many hides of land. [3] The legal effect of such a grant is hard to determine; and insuperable difficulties beset any attempt to expound its legal consequences in terms of modern law. [4] In truth, the form and substance of Magna

---

[1] Anson, *Law of the Constitution*, I. 14. *Cf. Report on Dignity of a Peer*, I. 63, which makes it both a contract and a treaty.

[2] In strict legal theory the complete investiture of the grantee required that "charter" should be followed by "infeftment" or delivery (real or constructive) of the subject of the grant. In the case of such intangible things as political liberties, the parchment on which the Charter was written would be the natural symbol to deliver to the grantees.

[3] See chapter I. The grant which purports to be perpetually binding on John's heirs, was in practice treated as requiring confirmation by his son.

[4] Prof. Maitland, *Township and Borough*, p. 76, explains some of the absurdities involved: "Have you ever pondered the form, the scheme, the main idea of Magna Charta? If so, your reverence for that sacred text will hardly have prevented you from using in the privacy of your own minds some such words as 'inept' or 'childish,' etc."

Carta are badly mated. Its substance consists of a number of legal enactments and political and civil rights; its form is borrowed from the feudal lawyer's book of styles for conferring a title to landed estate.[1]

The results of this part of the inquiry seem, then, to be mainly negative. It is misleading to describe phenomena of the thirteenth century in modern phraseology which would have been unintelligible to contemporaries. Yet, if it is necessary to make the attempt, Magna Carta may perhaps be regarded as an agreement partaking of the natures alike of a statute and a royal grant, of a public treaty and a private contract, yet identical with no one of these, but (in any view) enacting or proclaiming a number of rules and customs as binding in England, and reducing them to writing in the unsuitable form of a feudal charter granted by King John to the freemen of England and their heirs.[2]

(2) *The Contemporary Standpoint.* It is perhaps more profitable to enquire under what category of medieval jurisprudence Magna Carta would have fallen, if its contemporaries had consciously attempted its classification. In Dr. Vinogradoff's phrase: "The best way to solve these problems is perhaps to locate our document in the pigeon-holes of medieval and not of modern rubrication."[3]

Answering his own question, he proceeds to range it, partly as a unilateral grant by John to his subjects and partly as of the nature of the medieval expedient known to the continent of Europe as an "establishment" (*stabilimentum* or *établissement*). No exact definition of a *stabilimentum* need be expected from an age accustomed to a vague use of words; but its essence seems to have been

---

[1] Pollock and Maitland, I. 150, emphasize this disparity. "In form a donation, a grant of franchises freely made by the king, in reality a treaty extorted from him by the confederate estates of the realm, . . . it is also a long and miscellaneous code of laws." Cf. also *Ibid.*, I. 658.

[2] See Prof. Adams (*Origin*, 212), who has a suggestive note on "the diplomatic form of the Great Charter."

[3] *Law Quarterly Review*, XXI. 250-7.

a legislative act, more or less of an institutional and exceptional nature, affecting the general welfare of the country, and thus requiring collective action by all classes or estates. The elements of authority dispersed among the various participants in legislative or sovereign power had to be concentrated round the King, somewhat as the consent of all first-class States has to be obtained at the present day for effecting a change in the rules of International Law observed by civilized nations.[1]

Legislative acts similar to the *établissements* of Capetian Kings were not unknown in England. The main purport of the Statute of York (1322), for instance, according to its latest interpreter,[2] would seem to be that consent of " the community " (or " commonalty," as it is usually rendered), as well as of the prelates, earls and barons, should be needed for any change of the nature of an " establishment," which thus means an alteration in the framework of government. Magna Carta contemplated in chapter 61 an institutional innovation, parallels to which may be found in the more or less oligarchical schemes of 1244, 1258, 1264 and 1311. The historical importance of such restrictions upon the method of legislation required for changing the framework of government, lies in their bearing on the development of a system of Estates and of the future Parliament of the three Estates.[3]

III. Magna Carta: its Contents and Characteristics.

The rights enumerated in the sixty-three chapters of the Charter, representing the price paid by John for renewed allegiance, are fully discussed in the main part of the present volume : a brief description of their more prominent characteristics, when viewed as a collective whole, is, therefore, all that is here required.

As to externals, the want of orderly, logical arrangement has often been noted. As John Reeves[4] says : " The

---

[1] *Cf.* Vinogradoff, *op. cit.*, who cites an example from a French ordinance of 1223.

[2] G. Lapsley, *Eng. Hist Rev.* XXVII., p. 118.

[3] *Cf.* Vinogradoff, *op. cit.*   [4] *History of Law*, I. 266.

whole is strung together in a disorderly manner, with very little regard to the subject matter"; while a recent writer maintains that "no portion of this famous document can possibly be described as a good piece of drafting."[1] Thirteenth-century standards, however, were different from our own; and the lengthy document, with its specific remedies for many abuses, contains evidence of a carefully weighed scheme and of a deep-rooted conviction of the need of reform. The barons and royal officials who helped in framing it were ignorant of the abstract principles of political science. Their ideas, it has been truly said,[2] "seem to have been concrete and practical, and in their remedies they went no further than the correction of the specific abuses from which they suffered." The framers of the document observed (with few exceptions) great legal accuracy in defining the traditional rights of the Crown, proceeding with praiseworthy moderation and scrupulous fairness towards John.[3]

Three closely connected characteristics of the document, as a whole, will be brought out in the succeeding analysis: Magna Carta is feudal, contractual, and (in parts, at least) reactionary in tone. Professor Adams of Yale, giving voice to opinions now widely admitted by historians, emphasizes the crucial place occupied by "the feudal contract" as the basis alike of Magna Carta and of the medieval English constitution;[4] and maintains that, from the narrower point of view of 1215, the essence of John's Charter "in spirit, in method, and in principle," was reaction.[5]

In the attempt to analyze the leading provisions, various principles of classification have been adopted: the chapters may be arranged according to the functions of the central government they were intended to limit; according to their own nature as progressive, reactionary, or declaratory; and, finally, according to the classes of the community which reaped the greatest benefit.

[1] Harcourt, *Steward*, 215.   [2] Adams, *Origin*, 250.
[3] Adams, *ibid.*, 256.   [4] *Ibid.*, 150, 169, 203, 232.
[5] *Ibid.*, 249.

I. *Provisions classified according to the prerogatives affected.*

Dr. Gneist[1] arranges the chapters in five groups according as they place restraints (1) on the military power of the Crown, (2) on its judicial power, (3) on its police power, (4) on its financial power, or (5) furnish a legal sanction for the enforcement of the whole. In spite of Dr. Gneist's high authority, it is doubtful whether an analysis of Magna Carta upon these somewhat arbitrary lines throws much light on its main objects or results. Such a division is founded on distinctions not clearly formulated in the thirteenth century, when the various functions of government were still undifferentiated.[2]

II. *Provisions classified according as they are of a progressive, reactionary, or declaratory nature.*

Blackstone,[3] writing in 1759, expresses the generally accepted views: " It is agreed by all our historians that the Great Charter of King John was for the most part compiled from the ancient customs of the realm, or the laws of King Edward the Confessor, by which they usually mean ne common law, which was established under our Saxon princes, before the rigours of feudal tenures and other hardships were imported from the continent." Substantially the same doctrine has been enunciated only the other day, by our highest authority. " On the whole, the charter contains little that is absolutely new. It is restorative. John in these last years has been breaking the law; therefore the law must be defined and set in writing." [4] This view seems, on the whole, a correct one : the insurgents in 1215 professed to be demanding nothing new. Yet the Great Charter contained much that was unknown to the days of the Confessor and had no place in the promises of Henry I.

Thus it is not sufficient to describe Magna Carta merely

---

[1] *Hist. Engl. Const.*, Chapter XVIII.

[2] Dr. Gneist indeed confesses this, when, in discussing the limitations of the financial power, he admits that many of these are "already comprised in the provisions touching the feudal power."

[3] *Great Charter*, vii.   [4] Pollock and Maitland, I. 151.

as a declaratory enactment : it is necessary to distinguish between the different sources of what it declared. A fourfold division may be suggested. (1) Magna Carta handed on some of the usages of the old English law unchanged by the Conqueror or his successors, now confirmed and purified from abuses. (2) In defining feudal incidents and services, it confirmed many rules of the feudal law brought into England by the Normans after 1066. (3) It also embodied many provisions of which William I. and even Henry I. knew no more than did the Anglo-Saxon kings— innovations introduced for his own purposes by Henry of Anjou, but, after half a century of experience, now accepted loyally even by the most bitter opponents of the Crown. In the words of Mr. Prothero, " We find . . . the judicial and administrative system established by Henry II. preserved almost intact in Magna Carta, though its abuse was carefully guarded against." [1] Finally, (4) in some few points, the Charter aimed at going farther than Henry II. had intended to go : to mention only two particulars, the petty assizes are to be taken four times a year, while sheriffs are prohibited from holding pleas of the Crown.

History, indeed, has proved that a purely declaratory enactment is impossible : the mere lapse of time, by producing an altered context, changes the purport of any statute re-enacted in a later age. It is no unusual device for innovators to render their reforms more palatable by presenting them disguised as returns to the past. Further, it is important to bear in mind the nature of the provisions confirmed. A re-statement of some of the reforms of Henry II. leads logically to progress rather than to mere stability ; while the confirmation of Anglo-Saxon usages or of ancient feudal customs, fast disappearing under the new *régime*, may imply retrogression rather than standing still. Chapters 34 and 39 of Magna Carta, for example, really demand a return to the system in vogue prior to the innovations of Henry of Anjou, when they favour feudal jurisdictions. Thus, some of the provisions of the Great Charter which, at a casual glance, appear declaratory,

[1] *Simon de Montfort,* 17.

are, in reality, innovations; while others tend towards reaction.

III. *Provisions classified according to the estates of the community in whose favour they were conceived.*

Here we are face to face with a fundamental question of immense importance : Does the Great Charter really, as the orthodox view so vehemently asserts, protect the rights of the whole mass of humble Englishmen equally with those of the proudest noble? Or is it rather a series of concessions to feudal selfishness wrung from the King by a handful of powerful aristocrats? On such questions, learned opinion is sharply divided, although an overwhelming majority of authorities range themselves on the popular side, from Coke down to writers of the present day. Lord Chatham, in one of his great orations,[1] insisted that the barons who wrested the Charter from John established claims to the gratitude of posterity because they " did not confine it to themselves alone, but delivered it as a common blessing to the whole people"; and Sir Edward Creasy[2] caps these words with more ecstatic words of his own, declaring that one effect of the Charter was " to give and to guarantee full protection for property and person to every human being that breathes English air." Staid lawyers and historians like Blackstone and Hallam use similar expressions. " An equal distribution of civil rights to all classes of freemen forms the peculiar beauty of the charter "; so we are told by Hallam.[3] Bishop Stubbs unequivocally enunciated the same doctrine. " Clause by clause the rights of the commons are provided for as well as the rights of the nobles. . . . This proves, if any proof were wanted, that the demands of the barons were no selfish exactions of privilege for themselves."[4] " The rights which the barons claimed for themselves," says John Richard Green,[5] " they claimed for the nation at large."

[1] House of Lords, 9th January, 1770.   [2] *History of English Constitution*, 151.
[3] *Middle Ages*, II. 447.   [4] *Const. Hist.*, I. 570-1.
[5] *Short History*, 124. *Cf.* Gneist, *Const. Hist.* (trans. by P. A. Ashworth), 253; " A separate right for nobles, citizens, and peasants, was no longer possible." See also Gneist, *Hist. of Engl. Parl.* (trans. by A. H. Keane), 103, and Hannis Taylor, *Engl. Const.*, I. 380.

It would be easy to add to this "cloud of witnesses," but enough has been said to prove that it has been a common boast of Englishmen, for many centuries, that the provisions of the Great Charter were intended to secure, and did secure, the liberties of every class and individual, not merely those of the feudal magnates.

It is a usual corollary to this theory, to attribute credit to Stephen Langton for broad-minded statesmanship: the so-called "Articles of the Barons" are really, it would seem, articles of the archbishop. In Miss Norgate's words, the original articles "are obviously not the composition of the barons mustered under Robert Fitz-Walter," who could never have risen to "the lofty conception embodied in the Charter—the conception of a contract between King and people which should secure equal rights to every class and every individual in the nation."[1]

It is not safe, however, to accept, without a careful consideration of the evidence, opinions cited even from such high authorities. "Equality" is essentially a modern ideal: for many centuries after the thirteenth, class legislation maintained its prominent place on the Statute Rolls, and the interests of the various classes were by no means always identical. A vigorous minority has always protested against the popular view of Magna Carta. "It has been lately the fashion," Hallam confesses, "to depreciate the value of Magna Charta, as if it had sprung from the private ambition of a few selfish barons, and redressed only some feudal abuses."[2]

Two different parts of the Charter have a bearing on this question: chapter 1, which explains to whom the rights were granted; and chapter 61, which declares by whom they were to be enforced. The liberties were confirmed "to all freemen of my kingdom and their heirs for ever." This opens the question—who were *freemen* in 1215? An enthusiasm that seeks to enhance the merits of Magna Carta by extending its provisions as widely as possible,

---

[1] Norgate, *John Lackland*, 233.

[2] *Middle Ages*, II. 447. See, *e.g.* Robert Brady, *A Full and Clear Answer* (1683).

has led commentators to stretch the meaning of " freeman "
to embrace the entire population of England, including
not only churchmen, merchants, and yeomen, but even
villeins.

Now, *homo* in medieval law-Latin, was originally
synonymous with *baro*—all feudal vassals being described
as " men " or " barons." Magna Carta is a feudal grant,
and the presumption is in favour of the technical feudal
meaning. The word, indeed, occasionally bore a looser,
wider sense; but any room for ambiguity seems to be
precluded by the use of the qualifying word " free." No
villein was fully a " *liber homo*." In chapter 34, for
example, the " *liber homo*" is assumed to be a landowner
with a manorial court. Even a burgess might not be
reckoned for all purposes as " free "; for the *Dialogus de
Scaccario* discusses how far a *miles* or other *liber homo*
might lose his status by engaging in commerce in order
to make money.[1] The word " freeman," it would appear,
as used in the Charter is synonymous with " freeholder ";
and therefore only a limited class could, as grantees or the
heirs of such, make good a *legal* claim to share in the
liberties secured by it.[2] To the question, who had
authority to enforce its provisions, the Great Charter has
likewise a definite answer, namely, a quasi-committee of
twenty-five barons. It is clear that no support for democratic interpretations of Magna Carta can be founded on

[1] *Dialogus*, II. xiii. c.

[2] In addition to its appearance in the two places mentioned in the text, the
word "freeman" appears in five other chapters, 15, 20, 27, 30, and 39. The
last three instances throw no light on the meaning of the word. It is different,
however, with chapter 15, where freemen are necessarily feudal tenants of a
mesne lord—that is, freeholders; and with chapter 20, where, in the matter of
amercement, freeman is contrasted with *villanus*. Further, where men of servile
birth are clearly meant, they are described generally as *probi homines* (*e.g.* in
cc. 20, 29, and 48), and in one place, perhaps, c. 26, as *legales homines*.
Chapter 44 mentions *homines* without any qualification. It seems safe to infer
that the Great Charter never spoke of "freemen" when it meant to include the
ordinary peasantry or villagers. In chapter 39 of the reissue of 1217, *liber homo*
is clearly used as synonymous with "freeholder." In later centuries, it is true,
the "freeman" of the Charter came to be read in an ever less restricted sense,
until it embraced all Englishmen.

the choice of executors; since these formed a distinctly aristocratic body.

Magna Carta, indeed, contains positive evidences which point to the existence of class legislation. At the beginning and end of the Charter, clauses are inserted to secure to the Church its " freedom " and privileges. Many chapters, again, have no value except to landowners; a few affect tradesmen and townsmen exclusively; while chapters 20 to 22 adopt distinct sets of rules for the amercement of the ordinary freeman, the churchman, and the earl or baron respectively. A distinction is made (for example, in chapter 20) between the freeman and the villein, and the latter was carefully excluded from many of the benefits conferred on others by Magna Carta.[1]

(1) *The Feudal Aristocracy.* A casual glance at the clauses of the Great Charter shows how prominently feudal rights and obligations bulked in the eyes of its promoters. Provisions of this type must be considered chiefly as concessions to the feudal aristocracy—although the relief, primarily intended for them, indirectly benefited other classes as well.

(2) *Ecclesiastics.* The position of the Church is easily understood when we neglect the privileges enjoyed by its great men *quâ* barons rather than *quâ* prelates. The special Church clauses found no place whatsoever in the Articles of the Barons, but bear every appearace of having been added as an after-thought, due probably to the influence of Stephen Langton.[2] Further, they are mainly confirmatory of the separate Charter already twice granted within the few preceding months.

(3) *Tenants and Mesne Lords.* When compelling John to grant Magna Carta by parade of armed might, the barons were obliged to rely on the support of their own freeholders. It was necessary that these under-tenants should receive some recognition of their claims, and concessions in their favour are contained in two clauses (couched apparently in no generous spirit), chapters 15 and 60. The former limits the number of occasions on

---

[1] See *infra*, under c. 39.   [2] Cf. *supra*, p. 39.

which aids might be extorted from sub-tenants to the same three as were recognized in the Crown's case. Chapter 60 provides generally that all customs and liberties which John agrees to observe towards his vassals shall be observed by mesne lords, whether prelates or laymen, towards their sub-vassals. This provision has met with a chorus of applause from modern writers. Dr. Hannis Taylor [1] declares that, "animated by a broad spirit of generous patriotism, the barons stipulated in the treaty that every limitation imposed for their protection upon the feudal rights of the king should also be imposed upon their rights as mesne lords in favour of the under-tenants who held of them." [2] A vague general clause, however, affords little protection in a rude age and might readily be infringed when occasion arose. The barons were compelled to do something, or to pretend to do something, for their under-tenants. Apparently they did as little as they, with safety or decency, could.

(4) Something was also done for the *merchant and trading classes*. The existing privileges of London were confirmed in the Articles of the Barons; and some slight additions were made. An attentive examination suggests, however, that these privileges were refined away in the final form of Magna Carta. The right to tallage London and other towns was reserved to the Crown, while the rights of trading granted to foreigners were inconsistent with the policy of monopoly dear to the hearts of the Londoners. A mere confirmation of existing customs, already bought and paid for at a great price, seems a poor return for support given to the movement of insurrection at a critical moment, when their adherence was sufficient to turn the scale. The marvel is that so little was done for them. [3]

---

[1] *English Constitution*, I. 383.

[2] Bishop Stubbs, Preface to *W. Coventry*, II. lxxi., represents the barons, in their fervour for abstract law, as actually supporting their own vassals against themselves: "the Barons of Runnymede guard the people against themselves as well as against the common tyrant."

[3] For details, see *infra* under cc. 12, 13, 33, 35, and 41. Compare with the corresponding Articles of the Barons (viz. 32, 23, 12, and 31). The alterations,

(5) The relation of the *villein* to the benefits of the Charter has been hotly discussed. Coke claims for him, in regard to chapter 39 at least, that he must be regarded as a *liber homo*, and therefore as a participant in the advantages of the clause.[1] This contention, it has been already shown, is not well founded. Yet the villein, it may be argued, though excluded from participating in the rights of freemen, has certain rights secured to him in his own name. For example, in chapter 20, John promises that he will not so cruelly amerce villeins—other people's villeins at least—as to leave them utterly destitute.

The villein was protected, however, not as the acknowledged subject of legal rights, but because he formed a valuable asset of his lord.[2] This attitude is illustrated by a somewhat peculiar expression used in chapter 4, which prohibited injury to the estate of a ward by " waste of men or things." For a guardian to raise a villein to the status of a freeman was to benefit the enfranchised peasant at the expense of his young master.[3]

Other clauses of John's Charter and of the various reissues show scrupulous care to avoid infringing the rights of property enjoyed by manorial lords over their villeins. The King could not amerce other people's villeins harshly, although those on his own farms might be amerced at his discretion. Chapter 16, while carefully prohibiting any arbitrary increase of service from freehold property, leaves by inference all villein holdings unprotected. The " farms " or rents of ancient demesne might be raised by the Crown,[4] and tallages might be arbitrarily taken (measures likely to press hardly on the villein class). The villein was deliberately left exposed to the worst forms of purveyance, from which chapters 28 and 30 rescued his betters. The horses and implements of the *villanus* were still at the mercy of

---

slightly inimical to the towns, seem to show that the barons were more willing to sacrifice their allies' interests than their own to John's insistence, when the final terms were being haggled over.

[1] See Coke, *Second Institute*, p. 45, "for they are free against all men, saving against their lord." Contrast *ibid.*, p. 27.

[2] Cf. under c. 20 *infra*.   [3] Cf. under c. 4 *infra*.   [4] See under c. 25 *infra*.

the Crown's purveyors.   The reissue of 1217 confirms this
view: while demesne waggons were protected, those of
villeins were left exposed.[1]   Again, the chapter that takes
the place of the famous chapter 39 of 1215[2] makes it clear
that lands held in villeinage are not to be protected from
arbitrary disseisin or dispossession.   The villein was left
by the common law merely a tenant-at-will—subject to
arbitrary ejectment by his lord—whatever meagre measure
of protection he might obtain under the " custom of the
manor" as interpreted by the court of the lord who
oppressed him.

When taken together, the significance of these somewhat
trivial points is clear.   The bulk of the English peasantry
were protected by Magna Carta merely because they formed
valuable assets of their lords.   The Charter viewed them as
" villeins regardant "—as chattels attached to a manor, not
as members of an English commonwealth.[3]

The conclusion derived from this survey is that the
baronial leaders are scarcely entitled to the excessive lauda-
tion they have sometimes received.   The rude beginnings
of features prominent later on (such as the conceptions of
patriotism, nationality, equality before the law, and tender
regard for the rights of the humble) may possibly be found
in germ in parts of the completed Charter; but the Articles
of the Barons were what their name implies, a baronial
manifesto, seeking chiefly to redress the private grievances
of the promoters, and mainly selfish in motive.

Yet, when all deductions have been made, the Great
Charter stands out as a prominent landmark in the sequence
of events that have led, in an unbroken chain, to the consolidation of the English nation, and to the establishment
of a free and constitutional form of polity upon a basis so

---

[1] See chapter 26 of 1217.   [2] See chapter 35 of 1217.

[3] Dr. Stubbs takes a different view.   Admitting that there is " so little notice
of the villeins in the charter," he explains the omission on two grounds: (1) they
had fewer grievances to redress than members of other classes; (2) they participated in all grants from which they were not specially excluded.   " It was not
that they had no spokesman, but that they were free from the more pressing
grievances, and benefited from every general provision."   Preface to *W. Coventry*,
II. lxxiii.

enduring that, after many centuries of growth, it still retains —or, until a few years ago, did retain—the vigour and buoyancy of youth.

IV. Magna Carta: an Estimate of its Value.

The importance of the Charter for the men of 1215 did not lie in what forms its main value for the constitutional theorists of to-day. To the barons at Runnymede its merit was that it was something definite and utilitarian—a legal document with specific remedies for current evils. To English lawyers and historians of a later age it became something intangible and ideal, a symbol for the essential principles of the English Constitution, a palladium of English liberties.

To trace the growth of these modern estimates lies outside the scope of the present treatise; but it should be noted that admiration for John's Charter and its numerous reissues and confirmations was more measured among contemporaries than among its votaries of the seventeenth or nineteenth centuries; and that, for a long intervening period, it suffered almost complete neglect.

There is some reason to suppose that the *Carta Libertatum* or *Carta Baronum* (as it is usually cited by contemporary authorities) was first described as "great" in the reign of Henry III., and that it was then "great" mainly in a material sense, a "large" charter as contrasted with a certain *parva carta* granted by Henry in 1237.[1]

When, after many confirmations, the Charter had established itself as a permanent part of the law of the land, it seems to have fallen into the background of men's thoughts. It played no conscious or conspicuous part in the "constitutional experiments" of the Yorkist kings; and friends of popular liberties under the Tudors seem to have made few appeals to its authority; Shakespeare's *King John* has nothing to say of Runnymede or what happened there.[2] It was during the struggles of Parliament with the first two Stewart Kings and in part through the influence of Coke,

---

[1] See *infra*, p. 157.   [2] See A. F. Pollard, *Henry VIII.*, 33 ff.

with his strange combination of black-letter lore and enthusiasm for the old Constitution as interpreted by him, that the Charter, now " great " in a sense higher than material, took hold of the popular imagination. Thereafter estimates of its worth steadily expanded. In many a time of national crisis, Magna Carta has been appealed to as a fundamental law too sacred to be altered—as a talisman containing some magic spell, capable of averting national calamity.

Are these modern estimates of its value justified by facts, or are they gross exaggerations? Did it really create an epoch in English history? If so, wherein did its importance exactly lie?

The numerous factors which contributed towards the worth of Magna Carta may be distinguished as of two kinds, inherent and accidental. (a) Its intrinsic value depends on the nature of its own provisions. The reforms demanded by the barons were just and moderate : avoidance of extremes tended towards a permanent settlement. Its aims were practical as well as moderate; the language in which they were framed, clear and straightforward. A high authority has described the Charter as " an intensely practical document." [1] This *practicability* is an English characteristic, and strikes the key-note of almost every great movement for reform which has succeeded in English history. Closely connected with this is another feature, the markedly *legal* nature of the Charter. As Magna Carta, after Coke's day, was rarely absent from the thoughts of statesmen, a practical and legal direction was thus given to the efforts of Englishmen in many ages.[2] Therein lies another English characteristic. While democratic enthusiasts in France and America have often sought to found their liberties on a lofty but unstable basis of philosophical theory embodied in Declarations of Rights; Englishmen have occupied lower but surer ground, aiming at practical

[1] Maitland, *Social England*, I. 409.

[2] Cf Gneist *Const. Hist.*, Chapter XVIII. : " By Magna Carta English history irrevocably took the direction of securing constitutional liberty by administrative law."

remedies for actual wrongs, rather than enunciating theoretical platitudes with no realities to correspond.

Further, the nature of the provisions bears witness to the broad basis on which the edifice was intended to be built. The Charter, notwithstanding the prominence given to feudal grievances, redressed other grievances as well. Another intrinsic merit was that it made definite what had been vague before. Definition is a valuable protection for the weak against the strong : vagueness favours the tyrant who can interpret while he enforces the law. Misty rights were now reduced to a tangible form, and could no longer be broken with impunity. Where previously the vagueness of the law lent itself to evasion, its clear re-statement in 1215 pinned down the King to a definite issue. He could no longer plead that he sinned in ignorance; he must either keep the law, or openly defy it—no middle course was possible.

(b) Part of the value of Magna Carta may be traced to extrinsic causes; to its vivid historical setting. The importance of its provisions is emphasized by the object-lessons that accompanied its inauguration. Christendom was amazed by the spectacle of a King obliged to surrender at discretion to his subjects. The fact that John was compelled to accept the Charter meant a loss of royal prestige, and great encouragement to future rebels. What once had happened, might happen again : the King's humiliation was stamped as a powerful image on the minds of future generations.

A separate treatise would be required for any serious attempt to discuss the various estimates formed of Magna Carta as viewed in successive centuries and in different aspects. Some commentators have concerned themselves mainly with individual clauses; others have treated it as one whole. Historians look mainly to its immediate effects; lawyers and publicists to its ultimate consequences, as it affected the development of the English law and Constitution.

(1) *Value of Individual Provisions.* To judge from the reforms that attracted the notice of the only contemporary

chronicler [1] whose opinion has come down to us, the clauses considered of most importance in his day were those treating of the "disparagement" of women, loss of life or member for killing beasts of the forest, reliefs, the restoration of seignorial jurisdiction ("*hautes justices*") and the appointment and powers of the twenty-five barons over the King's government and over the appointment of bailiffs.

Some at least of these clauses are among those usually considered reactionary, and there seems little doubt that the barons in 1215 were deeply interested in the restoration of their feudal franchises, which Henry and his sons were taking away from them. In the words of the French historian, who was perhaps the first to sound the reaction from the "traditional" view of Magna Carta: "The barons had no suspicion that they would one day be called the founders of English liberty. . . . They were guided by a crowd of small and very practical motives in extorting this form of security from John Lackland." [2]

Of modern writers' estimates of the relative importance of particular clauses it seems unnecessary to speak, as their number and variety are great. [3]

(2) *Its Legal Value.* The value of the Charter as a whole, however, is more than a mere sum of the values of its separate parts. Its great importance lay, not in the exact terms of any or all of its provisions, but in the fact that it enunciated a definite body of law, claiming to be above the King's will and admitted as such by John. As our supreme authorities say of Magna Carta: "For in brief it means this, that the King is, and shall be below the law." [4] The

---

[1] *Histoire des ducs* (A.D. 1220), 149-150.

[2] Petit-Dutaillis, *Louis* VIII., 58. *Cf.* Adams, *Origin*, 249.

[3] Prof. Adams (*Origin*, 176 n.) condenses its essence into three general rules. Prof. Maitland (*Collected Papers*, II. 38), from a temporary angle of observation, declares that "Magna Carta is an act for the amendment of the law of real property and for the advancement of justice." John Lilburne (*Just Man's Justification*, p. 11) was also thinking of particular clauses when he wrote, "Magna Carta itself being but a beggarly thing containing many marks of intolerable bondage."

[4] Pollock and Maitland, I. 152. See, however, Petit-Dutaillis, *Studies Supplementary*, 143 (criticising Pollock and Maitland): "That again, it seems to

King, by granting the Charter, admitted that he was not
an absolute ruler—that he had a master in the laws he had
often violated, but which he now swore to obey. Magna
Carta has thus been truly said to enunciate "the reign of
law" or "rule of law" in the phrase made famous by Professor Dicey.[1]

This conception of the existence of a definite body of
clearly formulated rights (now set down in the Charter in
black and white under John's seal), which the King was
bound to observe, was supplemented by the King's acceptance of the barons' claim to a right of compulsion. This
was a principle of abiding value, apart from any or all of
the clauses redressing specific grievances. "In the slowly
developing crisis of Henry III.'s reign, what men saw in
the charter in its bearing on their differences with the King
was not a body of specific law, but that the King's action
was bound and limited, and that the community possessed
the right to coerce him."[2]

(3) *Its Value for the future Development of the Constitution.* Magna Carta marks the commencement of a
new grouping of political forces in England; indeed, without such a rearrangement, the winning of the Charter would
have been impossible. Throughout the reign of Richard I.
the unity of interests between King and lower classes had
been endangered by the heavy drain of taxation; but the
actual break-up of the old tacit alliance only came in the
crisis of John's reign. Henceforward can be traced a
change in the balance of parties in the commonwealth. No
longer are Crown and people united, in the name of law and
order, against the baronage, standing for feudal disintegration. The mass of humble freemen and the Church form a
league with the barons, in the name of law and order,
against the Crown, now the chief law-breaker.

Such an alliance involved the adoption of a new baronial

us, is to assign too glorious a rôle to the baronage of John Lackland and to
its political conceptions, which are childish and anarchical. The English
nobility of that day had not the idea of law at all."

[1] A. V. Dicey, *Law of the Constitution*, Part II.

[2] Adams, *Origin*, 251.

policy. Hitherto each great baron had aimed at his own independence, striving to gain new franchises for himself, and to keep the King outside. This policy, which succeeded both in France and Scotland, had before John's reign already failed in England; and the English barons, now admitting the hopelessness of the struggle for feudal independence, substituted a more progressive policy. The King, whose interference they could no longer hope completely to shake off, must at least be taught to interfere justly and according to rule; he must walk by law and custom, not by the caprices of his evil heart. The barons sought to control henceforward the royal power they could not exclude: they desired some share in the national councils, if they could no longer hope to create little nations of their own within the four corners of their fiefs. Magna Carta was the fruit of this new policy.

It has been often repeated, and with truth, that the Great Charter marks also a stage in the growth of national unity or nationality. Here, however, it is necessary to guard against exaggeration. It marks merely a stage in a process, rather than a final achievement. It is necessary somewhat to discount the Charter's claims to be " the first documentary proof of the existence of a united English nation " and the often-quoted words of Dr. Stubbs, that " the Great Charter is the first great public act of the nation, after it has realised its own identity." [1]

A united English nation, whether conscious or unconscious of its identity, cannot be said to have existed in 1215, except under several qualifications. The conception of " nationality," in the modern sense, is of recent origin, and requires that the lower as well as the higher classes should be comprehended within its bounds. Further, the coalition which wrested the Charter from the royal tyrant was essentially of a temporary nature, and quickly fell to

---

[1] *Const. Hist.*, I. 571. Cf. *Ibid.*, I. 583, "The act of the united nation, the church, the barons, and the commons, for the first time thoroughly at one." Who were " the commons " in 1215? Cf. also Prothero, *Simon de Montfort*, 18, "The spirit of nationality of which the chief portion of Magna Carta was at once the product and the seal."

pieces. Even while the alliance continued, the interests of the various classes, as has been already shown, were far from identical. Political rights were treated as the monopoly of the few; [1] and civil rights were far from universally distributed. The leaders of the "national" movement gave no *political* rights to the despised villeins, who comprised more than three quarters of the population of England; while their *civil* rights were almost completely ignored in the provisions of the Charter. Magna Carta marked an important step, in the process by which England became a nation; but that step was neither the first nor yet the final one. [2]

In treating of the juridical nature of Magna Carta as partly of the type of legislation known on the Continent as an *établissement,* requiring all participants in political power to be assembled round the King in order that they might give consent, it has already been suggested that what took place at Runnymede may have had an influence on the development of the conception of a series of estates and therefore on the genesis of the modern Parliament. [3] The Charter's greatest contribution, however, to constitutional advance lay undoubtedly in its admission (tacitly implied in its every clause) that the royal prerogative was limited by the customary feudal rights of the barons (if not of other classes as well).

In a sense there was nothing new in this: the feudal relation, with its inherent conceptions of mutual, contractual obligations and the rights of *diffidatio* and rebellion, needed no official proclamation: it was known to all. But the formal embodiment of a great mass of feudal custom in a document, destined to be consulted and reinterpreted in future ages, created, as it were, a bridge between the older monarchy, limited by medieval, feudal restraints, and the modern, constitutional monarchy, limited by a national

---

[1] See *infra*, under c. 14.

[2] The possibility that the movement leading to the Great Charter may have also helped forward the growth of the idea of a separate national Church is discussed *infra*, under c. one.

[3] *Supra*, p. 109.

law enforced by Parliament.   This is the main thesis upon which Professor Adams so emphatically insists, " the unintended result " of Magna Carta.[1]   In light of it, he claims to have located the origin of the English Constitution in Magna Carta, and in these two principles of it which assert the limitations of the King's prerogative and the barons' right to compel him to respect the rights of others.

These estimates of the rôle played by Magna Carta would seem to be somewhat excessive and to attempt to find too simple an origin for a system of which complexity and compromise between conflicting elements are the very essence.   On the one hand, there is more in the English Constitution than the mere principle of limited monarchy : on the other, the main line by which that monarchy has progressed from medieval to modern ideals has not been by the method, unsuccessfully attempted in 1215, 1244, 1258, 1265 and 1311 (to name only the best-known instances), of subjecting the King to the dictation of a Committee of his adversaries; but rather the method of using the counsellors of his own appointment to curb his own caprice, while making it progressively difficult for him to appoint any minister of whom the national council did not approve. The revolutionary expedient of the Committee of twenty-five was not destined to be on the direct line of development that led, through the doctrine of ministerial responsibility, to the Cabinet system of government that reached and perhaps passed its highest point of achievement in the nineteenth century.

(4) *Its Moral or Sentimental Value.*   After every allowance has been made for the great and beneficent influence of Magna Carta, it may still be doubted whether the belief of enthusiasts in its excessive importance has been fully justified.   Many other triumphs, almost equally important, have been won in the cause of liberty; and statutes have been passed embodying them.   Why then should Magna Carta be extolled as the palladium of English liberties? Is not, when all is said, the extreme merit attributed to it mainly of a sentimental or imaginative nature?   Such

[1] Adams, *Origin*, 250.

questions must be answered partly in the affirmative. Much of its value *does* depend on sentiment. Yet all government is, in a sense, founded upon sentiment—sometimes affection, sometimes fear : psychological considerations are all-powerful in the practical affairs of life. Intangible and even unreal phenomena have played an important part in the history of nations. The tie that binds the British colonies at the present day to the Mother Country is largely one of sentiment; yet the troopers from Canada and New Zealand who responded to the call of Britain in her hour of need produced practical results of an obvious nature. The element of sentiment in politics can never be ignored.

It is no disparagement of Magna Carta, then, to confess that part of its power has been read into it by later generations, and lies in the halo, almost of romance, that has gathered round it in the course of centuries. It became a battle cry for future ages, a banner, a rallying point, a stimulus to the imagination. For a King, thereafter, openly to infringe the promises contained in the Great Charter, was to challenge public opinion—to put himself palpably in the wrong. For an aggrieved man, however humble, to base his rights upon its terms was to enlist the sympathy of all. Time and again, from the Barons' War against Henry III. to the days of John Hampden and Oliver Cromwell, the possibility of appealing to the words of Magna Carta has afforded a practical ground for opposition; an easily intelligible principle to fight for; a fortified position to hold against the enemies of national freedom. To explain the exact way in which this particular document —dry as its details at first sight may seem—has fired the popular imagination, is a task that lies rather within the sphere of psychology than of history, as usually conceived. However difficult it may be to explain this phenomenon, there is no doubt of its existence. The importance of the Great Charter has increased, as traditions, associations, and aspirations have clustered more thickly round it.

Thus Magna Carta, in addition to its legal and political value, has a moral value of an equally emphatic kind.

Apart from and beyond the salutary effect of the useful laws it contains, its moral influence has contributed to an advance in the national spirit, and therefore in the national liberties. Such considerations justify enthusiasts, who hold that the granting of Magna Carta was the turning-point in English history.

V. Magna Carta. Its defects.

The great weakness of the Charter was the absence of an adequate sanction. The only expedient for compelling the King to keep his promises was clumsy and revolutionary; quite worthless as a working scheme of government. Indeed, it was devised not so much to prevent the King from breaking faith as to punish him when he had done so. In other words, instead of constitutional machinery to turn the theories of Magna Carta into realities, "a right of legalized rebellion" was conferred on an executive committee of twenty-five of the King's enemies.[1]

This is the chief defect, but not the only one. Many minor faults and omissions may be traced to a similar root. Constitutional principles are conspicuously absent. The importance of a council or embryo parliament, framed on national lines; the right of such a body to influence the King's policy in normal times as well as in times of crisis; the doctrine of ministerial responsibility; the need of distinguishing the various functions of government, legislative, judicial, and administrative—all these cardinal principles are completely ignored. Only five of the sixty-three chapters can be said to bear directly on the subject of constitutional (as opposed to purely legal) machinery, and these do so only incidentally, namely, chapters 14, 21, 39, 52, and 61.

The *Commune Concilium* is indeed mentioned; and its composition and mode of summons are defined in chapter 14. But this chapter appears as an afterthought—an appendix to chapter 12 : it has no counterpart in the Articles of the Barons. The rebel magnates were interested

---

[1] See *infra*, c. 61, for details.

I

in the narrow question of scutage, not in the wide possibilities involved in the existence of a national council. The *Commune Concilium* was dragged into the Charter, not on its own merits, but merely as a convenient method of preventing arbitrary increase of feudal exactions. This is further proved by the omission of the Council from the reissue of 1217, when an alternative way of checking the increase of scutage had been devised.

If the framers of John's Magna Carta had possessed the grasp of constitutional principles, with which they have been sometimes credited, they would have seized the opportunity afforded them by the mention of the Common Council, in chapters 12 and 14, to define carefully the powers they claimed for it. On the contrary, no list of its functions is drawn up; nor do the words of the Charter contain anything to suggest that it exercised powers other than that of consenting to scutages and aids. Not a word is said of any right to a share in legislation, to control or even to advise the Executive, or to concur in choosing the great ministers of the Crown. Neither deliberative, administrative, nor legislative powers are secured to it, while its control over taxation is strictly limited to scutages and aids—that is to say, it only extends over the exactions that affected the military tenants of the Crown. It is true that chapters 21 and 39 may possibly be read as confirming the *judicial* power of the Council in a certain limited group of cases. Earls and barons are not to be amerced except by their peers (*per pares suos*), and the natural place for these " equals " of a Crown vassal to assemble for this purpose would be the *Commune Concilium*. This, however, is matter of inference; chapter 21 makes no mention of the Council; and it is equally possible that its requirements would be met by the presence among the officials of the Exchequer of a few Crown tenants.[1] Similar reasoning applies to the provisions of chapter 39 (protecting persons and property of freemen, by insisting on the necessity of a " trial by peers ") so far as they affect earls and barons.

[1] This is the view of Pike, *House of Lords*, 204. See *infra*, c. 21.

It is clear that the leaders of the opposition in 1215 did not consider the constitutional powers of a national Parliament to be the best safeguard of the rights and liberties theoretically guaranteed by the Charter. They relied rather on the revolutionary powers of the twenty-five barons to be appointed under chapter 61.

The same inability to devise practical remedies may be traced in minor clauses of the Charter.[1] When John promised in chapter 16 that no one should be compelled to do greater service than was due, no attempt was made to provide machinery to define such service; while chapter 45, providing that only men who knew the law and meant to keep it, should be made justiciars, sheriffs and bailiffs, laid down no criterion of fitness, and contained no suggestion of the way in which so laudable an ambition might be realized.

Thoughtful and statesmanlike as were many of the provisions of Magna Carta, and wide as was the ground they covered, important omissions can be pointed out. Some crucial questions seem not to have been foreseen; others, for example the liability to foreign service, were deliberately shelved[2]—thus leaving room for future misunderstandings. The praise, justly earned, by its framers for the care and precision with which they defined a long list of the more crying abuses, must be qualified in view of the failure to provide procedure to prevent their recurrence. Men had not yet learned the force of the maxim, so closely identified with all later reform movements in England, that a right is valueless without an appropriate remedy to enforce it.[3]

---

[1] Magna Carta has been described, in words already quoted with approval, as "an intensely practical document," Maitland, *Social England*, I. 409 ; but this requires qualification. If it was practical in preferring condemnation of definite grievances to enunciation of philosophical principles, it was unpractical in omitting machinery for giving effect to its provisions.

[2] Except in so far as affected by cc. 12 and 16.

[3] Mr. Prothero estimates more highly the constitutional value of Magna Carta : "The constitutional struggles of the following half-century would to a great extent have been anticipated had it retained its original form." *Simon de Montfort*, 14.

V. Magna Carta : Value of Traditional Interpretations.

The Great Charter has formed a favourite theme for orators and politicians, partly from its intrinsic merit, partly from its dramatic background, but chiefly because it has been, from the time of its inception to the present day, a rallying cry and a bulwark in every crisis that threatened to endanger the national liberties.

The uses to which it has been put, and the interpretations read into it, are so numerous and varied, that they would require a separate treatise to describe them all. Not only was Magna Carta frequently reissued and confirmed, but its provisions have been asserted and reasserted times without number in Parliament, in the courts of justice, and in institutional works on jurisprudence. Its influence has thus been threefold; and any attempt to explain its bearing on the subsequent history of English liberties would require to distinguish between these three separate and equally important aspects :—(1) It proved a powerful weapon in the hands of politicians, especially of the parliamentary leaders in the seventeenth century, when waging the battle of constitutional freedom against the Stewart dynasty. (2) Its legal aspect has been equally important as its political one : in the course of legal debate and in judicial opinions, it has been the subject of many and conflicting interpretations, some of them accurate and some erroneous.[1] (3) Finally, it has been discussed in many commentaries either exclusively devoted to its elucidation or treating of it incidentally in the course of general expositions of the law of England.

In light of the part played by Magna Carta throughout centuries of English history, it is not surprising that an increasing veneration has tended at times to overstep all bounds. It is unfortunate, however, that it has been more frequently described in terms of inflated rhetoric than of sober methodical analysis.[2] Nor has this tendency to un-

---

[1] As early as 1231 the " carta de Runemede " was cited in a plea. See Bracton's *Notebook*, No. 513. See also No. 1478, dating from 1221 ; others in Index.

[2] Extravagant estimates of its value will readily suggest themselves. Sir James Mackintosh (*History of England*, I. 218, edn. of 1853) declares that we are

thinking adulation been confined to popular writers; judges
and institutional authors, even Sir Edward Coke, have too
often lost the faculty of critical and exact scholarship when
confronted with the virtues of the Great Charter. There
is scarcely one great principle of the modern English
constitution calculated to win the esteem of mankind,
which has not been read by commentators into Magna
Carta. The political leaders of the seventeenth century
discovered among its chapters every reform they desired
to introduce into England, disguising revolutionary projects by dressing them in the garb of the past.

Instances of constitutional principles and institutions
erroneously credited to the Great Charter will be expounded
under appropriate chapters of the sequel. It will be sufficient, in the meantime, to enumerate trial by jury; Habeas
Corpus; abolition of arbitrary imprisonment; prohibition
of monopolies; the close tie between taxation and representation; equality before the law; a matured conception
of nationality: all these, and more, have been discovered
in various clauses of the Great Charter.[1]

If these tendencies to excessive and sometimes ignorant
praise have been unfortunate from one point of view, they
have been most fortunate from another. The legal and
political aspects must be sharply contrasted. If the vague
and inaccurate words of Coke have obscured the bearing
of many chapters, and diffused false notions of the development of English law, the service these very errors have
done to the cause of constitutional progress is measureless.
If political bias has coloured interpretation, the ensuing
benefit has accrued to the cause of national progress in its
widest and best developments.

"bound to speak with reverential gratitude of the authors of the Great Charter.
To have produced it, to have preserved it, to have matured it, constitute the im-
mortal claim of England upon the esteem of mankind. Her Bacons and Shake-
speares, her Miltons and Newtons, etc., etc."

[1] Edmund Burke (*Works*, II. 53) credits Magna Carta with creating the House
of Commons! "Magna Charta, if it did not give us originally the House of
Commons, gave us at least a House of Commons of weight and consequence." As
will be shown in the sequel, chapter 14 of the Great Charter (the only one bearing
on the subject) is in reality of a reactionary nature, confining the right of attendance
at the *commune concilium* to the freeholders of the Crown.

Thus the historian of Magna Carta, while bound to correct errors, cannot afford to despise traditional interpretations. The meanings read into it by learned men have had a potent effect whether they were historically well or ill founded. The stigma of being banned by the Great Charter was something to excite dread. If the belief prevailed that an abuse was really prohibited by Magna Carta, the most arbitrary king had difficulty in finding judges to declare it legal, or ministers to enforce it. The prevalence of such a belief was the main point; whether it was well or ill founded was, for political purposes, immaterial. The greatness of Magna Carta lies not so much in what it was to its framers in 1215, as in what it afterwards became to the political leaders, to the judges and lawyers, and to the entire mass of the men of England in later ages.

VII. Magna Carta. Its traditional relation to Trial by Jury.

One persistent error, adopted for many centuries, and even now hard to dispel, is that the Great Charter guaranteed trial by jury.[1] This belief is now held by all competent authorities to be unfounded. Not one of the three forms of a modern jury trial had taken definite shape in 1215, although the root principle from which all three subsequently grew had been in use since the Norman Conquest.[2]

Jury trial in each of the three forms in which it is known to modern English law (the grand jury, the petty criminal jury, and the jury of civil pleas) is able to trace an unbroken pedigree (though by three distinct lines of descent) from the same ancestor, that principle known as *recognitio* or *inquisitio*, which was introduced into England by the Normans, and was simply the practice whereby the Crown

[1] The source of this error was the identification of jury trial with the *judicium parium* of c. 39. *q.v.*

[2] For the origin of the jury see Brunner, *Schurgerichte* (1871): Haskins, *Am. His. Rev.*, VIII. 613 ff., traces the steps made towards the civil jury in Normandy, particularly under Henry's father, Geoffrey.

obtained information on local affairs from the sworn testimony of local men. While thus postulating a foreign origin, we are afforded some consolation by remembrance of a fact which modern authorities are inclined to neglect, namely, that the soil was prepared by Anglo-Saxon labour for its planting.[1]

The old English institution of frithborh—the practice of binding together little groups of neighbours for preservation of the peace—and the custom of sending representatives of the villages to the Hundred Courts, had accustomed the natives to corporate action, and formed precedents for asking them to give evidence on local matters jointly and on oath. Further, one form of the jury—the jury of accusation—is clearly foreshadowed by the directions given to the twelve senior thegns of each Wapentake by a well-known law of Ethelred. Yet the credit of establishing the jury system as a fundamental institution in England is undoubtedly due to the Norman and Angevin kings, although they had no clear vision of the consequences of what they did. The uses to which *Inquisitio* was put by William and his sons in framing *Domesday Book,* collecting information, and dispensing justice, have already been discussed.[2] It was reserved for Henry II. to start the institution on a further career of development : he thus laid the foundations of the modern jury system not merely in one of its forms, but in all three of them.

(1) In reorganizing machinery for the suppression and punishment of crime by the Assizes of Clarendon and Northampton, he established the principle that criminal trials should (in the normal case) begin with indictment of the accused by a representative body of neighbours sworn

---

[1] The theory now generally accepted that the origin of trial by jury must be sought in procedure introduced by Norman dukes, not in any form of popular Anglo-Saxon institutions, is ably maintained by Pollock and Maitland, I. 119, and by the late Professor J. B. Thayer, *Evidence,* p. 7. Undoubtedly their conclusions are in the main correct ; but trial by jury may have had more than one root, and appreciation of the Norman contribution need not lead to neglect of the Anglo-Saxon. See, *e.g.* Hannis Taylor, *English Constitution,* I. 308 and I. 323 ; Vinogradoff, *Growth of the Manor,* 193 : 'something more than a Norman device."

[2] See *supra,* p. 86.

to speak the truth.[1] This was merely a systematic enforcement of one of the many forms of *inquisitio* already in use :
criminal prosecution was not to be begun on mere suspicion
or irresponsible complaints. The jury of accusation (or
presentment), instituted in 1166, has continued in use ever
since, passing by an unbroken development into the grand
jury of the present day.[2]

(2) By insisting that ordeal should supersede compurgation as the test of guilt or innocence, Henry unconsciously
prepared the way for a second form of jury. When the
fourth Lateran Council in the very year of Magna Carta
forbade priests to countenance ordeal by their presence or
blessing, a death-blow was dealt to that form of procedure
or " test," since it depended for its authority on supersti-
tion. A canon of the Church had struck away the pivot
on which Henry had made his criminal system to revolve.
Some substitute was urgently required and so the petty
jury (or its rude antecedent) came into existence. The man
publicly accused as *presumably* guilty was asked if he
would stand or fall by reference to the verdict of a second
jury of neighbours. This second verdict, then, was the
new " test " or " law " substituted, if the accused man
agreed, for his old right of proving himself innocent by
ordeal. By obscure steps, on which those best entitled to
speak with authority are not yet agreed, this jury, giving
a second and final verdict, gradually developed into the
criminal jury of twelve, the petty jury of to-day, which has
had so important an influence on the development of constitutional liberties in England, and even on the national
character. Another expedient of Henry's invention aided
the movement towards the criminal jury, namely, the writ
de odio et atia by applying for which a man " appealed "

[1] See Pollock and Maitland, I. 131. It was part of Henry's policy to substitute
indictment by a representative jury for the older appeal by the wronged individual
or his surviving relatives. The older procedure, however, was not completely
abolished : its continuance and its unpopularity may be traced in chapter 54 of
Magna Carta, *q.v.*

[2] Chapter 38 of Magna Carta, according to a plausible interpretation of an
admittedly obscure passage, seems to insist on the necessity of such an accusation
by the jury :—" *non . . . sine testibus fidelibus ad hoc inductis.*"

of a crime might substitute what was practically a jury's verdict for the " battle " which had previously followed " appeal " as matter of course.[1]

(3) The Civil Jury owes its origin to quite a different set of reforms, though inaugurated by the same reformer. Among the evil legacies from Stephen's reign, not the least troublesome were the claims advanced by rival magnates to estates and franchises which had been bestowed with lavish prodigality by Matilda and Stephen. Henry realized the urgent need of protecting vested interests by a more rational expedient than trial by combat. Here again he had recourse to a new development of " inquisition." In such cases an option was given to the tenant (the man in possession) to refer the question at issue to the verdict of local recognitors.

This new expedient was applied at first only to a few special cases. It was used to settle claims of ultimate title —the out-and-out ownership of land—and then it was known as the Grand Assize; it was also used to settle a few well-defined groups of pleas of disputed possession, and then it was known as a Petty Assize (of which there were three distinct varieties).[2] The King by a high-handed act of power deprived the demandant of that remedy which was his right by feudal law, the resort to the legal duel. It was because the new procedure was founded on a royal Ordinance, that the name " Assize " was applied to it.

By consent of *both* parties, however, disputes of almost every description might be similarly determined; being referred (under supervision of the King's judges) to the verdict of local recognitors, usually twelve in number, who were then known as a *jurata* (not an *assisa*). While the *assisa* was narrowly confined to a few types of cases, the *jurata* was a flexible remedy capable of indefinite expansion, and thus soon became the more popular and the more important of the two. Sometimes the twelve recognitors, summoned as an *assisa* by the King's command, were by

[1] For details see *infra* under chapter 36, and *supra*, p. 89.

[2] The three Petty Assizes are mentioned by name in c. 18, *q.v.*

consent of both litigants turned into a *jurata* to try a broader issue that had unexpectedly arisen. This explains the phrase, *assisa vertitur ad juratam*. The *assisa* and *jurata,* always closely connected and resembling each other in essential features, can both claim to be ancestors of the modern civil "jury,"—the name of the more popular institution having survived. Magna Carta, in providing for the frequent holding of the three petty assizes, marked a stage in the development of the Civil Jury; while, by enforcing the criminal procedure of Henry Plantagenet, and guarding it from abuse, the Charter had also a vital bearing on the genesis of the Grand Jury and the Petty Jury alike.

These tentative measures, however, still vague and unconsolidated, must not be identified with the definite procedure into which at a later date they coalesced : Magna Carta did not promise " trial by jury " to anyone.

PART IV.

HISTORICAL SEQUEL TO MAGNA CARTA.

I. Reissues and Confirmations of the Great Charter.

King John had accepted the reforms contained in Magna Carta unwillingly and insincerely; but the advisers of his son accepted them in good faith. Three reissues of the Charter were granted in 1216, in 1217, and in 1225, and these were followed by many confirmations. The scheme of this Historical Introduction is restricted to such facts as have direct bearing on the genesis and contents of John's Charter. Yet no account of Magna Carta would be complete without some notice of the more important alterations effected in its text during the reigns of later kings.

(I.) *Reissue of* 1216. On 28th October, 1216, Henry of Winchester was crowned at Gloucester before a small assemblage.[1] The young King took the usual oath as directed by the Bishop of Bath, and he also performed homage to the Pope's representative Gualo; for the King of England was now a vassal of Rome.[2] At a Council held at Bristol, on 11th November, William Marshal, Earl of Pembroke, was appointed *Rector regis et regni;* and, next day, the Charter was reissued in the King's name. This was a step of extreme importance, marking the acceptance by those in power for the time being of the programme of the baronial opposition.

[1] See *Annals of Waverley*, p. 286.

[2] For the question of the Regency and the position of England as a fief of Rome, see Norgate, *Minority*, 10-62 ; Turner, *Trans. R.H.S.* (1904), 268 ff. In a plea roll of 1237 (Bracton's *Notebook*, No. 1219) Gualo is described as "*quasi tutor domini regis et custos regni.*"

The Charter in its new provisional form was really a manifesto issued by the moderate men who rallied round the throne of the young King; it may be viewed in two aspects, as a declaration by the Regent and his co-adjutors of the policy on which they accepted office, and as a bid for the support of the barons who still adhered to the faction of the French prince. Its issue was, indeed, dictated by the crucial situation created by the presence in England of Prince Louis of France, supported by a foreign army and by a large faction of the English barons who had sworn homage to him as King. It was, therefore, framed in terms meant to conciliate such of the opposition as were still open to conciliation.

Yet the new Charter could not be a verbatim repetition of the old one. Vital alterations were required by altered circumstances.[1] It was no longer an expression of reluctant consent by the government of the day to the demands of its enemies, but a set of rules deliberately accepted by that government for its own guidance. The chief tyrant against whom the original provisions had been directed was dead, and certain forms of tyranny, it was confidently hoped, had died with him. Restraints now placed on the Crown's prerogatives would only hamper the free action of the men who framed them, not of their political opponents. The Regent, while willing to do much for the cause of conciliation, could not afford to paralyze his own efficiency at a time when foreign invaders were in possession of one-half of England, from which it would require a supreme effort to dislodge them. It was imperative that the government should retain a free hand in exacting feudal services and levying scutages.

Miss Norgate argues,[2] somewhat unconvincingly, that the omission of chapters 12 and 14 was a concession to Gualo and the Holy See. Rome had regarded these pro-

---

[1] The cause for wonder is rather how few changes required to be made. "It is, however, by no means the least curious feature of the history, that so few changes were needed to transform a treaty won at the point of the sword into a manifesto of peace and sound government." Stubbs, *Const. Hist.*, II. 21.

[2] *Minority*, 15.

visions as dangerous innovations of so marked a kind as
to justify the annulling of the Charter of 1215, and papal
sanction could be obtained in 1216 only by their jettison.
William Marshal, however, is not likely to have required
external pressure : he naturally preferred to leave his own
hands untied.

Yet the issue of the Charter under papal sanction, however obtained, was of material value to Henry's cause.
It had the immediate effect of bringing over eleven bishops
to the young King's side. M. Petit-Dutaillis[1] sums up
the situation in two propositions : the French invasion
saved the Great Charter, and then papal support saved
England from Louis.[2]

The Charter of 1216[3] is notable for its omissions, which
may be arranged under five groups.[4] (1) Restraints placed
in 1215 on the taxing power of the Crown now disappeared.
The chapters which forbade the King to increase the
" farms " or fixed rents of the counties and hundreds, those
which defined the King's relations with the Jews, and those
which restricted the lucrative rights derived from the
rigorous enforcement of the forest laws, were discarded.
An even more important omission was that of chapter 12,
which abolished the Crown's rights to increase feudal contributions arbitrarily, without consent of the Common
Council.[5]

(2) No reference is made to John's charter of May, 1215
to the Church, granting liberty of elections, although the
vague declaration that " the English Church should be
free " was retained. Chapter 42, allowing liberty to leave
the kingdom, and to return without the King's consent (a
privilege chiefly valuable to the clergy in their intercourse
with Rome) was entirely omitted : and the same is true of

---

[1] See Petit-Dutaillis, *Louis*, 130-1.   [2] *Ibid.*, 181.

[3] In the Appendix, an attempt is made to show at a glance the main differences
between the various Great Charters.

[4] This classification takes no account of alterations merely verbal or inserted to
remove ambiguities, *e.g.* cc. 22, 28, and 30 of the original Charter.

[5] See, however, Adams (*Origin*, 261 ; 220), who maintains that the omission
was not intended to leave the Crown a freer hand (whatever might be the practical
result).

chapter 27, which had placed in the church's hands the supervision of all distributions of chattels of men who had died intestate.[1]

(3) A great number of provisions of purely temporary interest disappeared, among them those providing for disbandment of mercenary troops and dismissal from office of obnoxious individuals.

(4) A number of omissions of a miscellaneous nature may be grouped together; for example, chapter 45, by which the Crown restricted itself in the choice of justiciars and other officers; the latter half of chapter 47, relating to the banks of rivers and their guardians; and some of the provisions affecting the forest laws.

(5) These alterations implied, incidentally rather than deliberately, the omission of such constitutional machinery as had found a place in John's Great Charter. The twenty-five Executors fell with the other temporary provisions; while chapter 14, which defined the composition and mode of summons of the *Commune Concilium*, was omitted with chapter 12, to which it had formed a supplement.[2]

Magna Carta as granted by Henry is thus concerned with matters which lie within the sphere of private law, and contains no attempt to devise machinery of govern-

[1] Are these omissions mainly accidental? Are they the result of some influence at work hostile to English ecclesiastics? Or, are they due to the personal wishes and ambitions of Gualo? The Legate may have preferred to keep the patronage of vacant sees in his own hands rather than confirm the rival rights of chapters. It is notable that when John made his peace with Rome, no suggestion of "free elections" was hinted at, whereas that concession was the essence of his charters to the English Church. Again, freedom of intercourse with Rome would facilitate appeals from the Legate to the Pope, and so diminish Gualo's authority. In the months to follow, Gualo exercised almost despotic power over the Church, excommunicating all who supported Louis. On 27th October, 1217, he entered London, "went to the church of St. Paul, . . . and he put in new canons; and the old ones who had chanted the service in defiance of him he deprived of all their benefices." *Hist. des ducs*, 206. See also Adams, *Origin*, 258. Honorius had conferred on Gualo authority to appoint to vacant sees and benefices; see Bouquet, XIX. 623.

[2] Minute points of difference, which are numerous, will be discussed under appropriate chapters of the Commentary. Cf. Norgate, *Minority*, 10-14; Adams, *Origin*, 256-7, who holds these changes to strengthen the theory "that in the original charter the barons intended to state the law accurately and were not trying to take unjust advantage of the King."

ment or to construct safeguards for national liberties. The King's minority implied a constitutional check, in the necessary existence of guardians, but when Henry III. attained majority, Magna Carta, deprived of its original sanctions, would, with the disappearance of the Regency, tend to become an empty record of royal promises. The machinery of government remained exclusively monarchic; the King, once out of leading-strings, would be restrained only by his own sense of honour and by the fear of armed resistance—by moral forces rather than legal or constitutional. The logical outcome was the Barons' War.

The importance of the omissions is minimized by two considerations. (*a*) Many of the original provisions were declaratory, and their omission in 1216 by no means implied that they were then abolished. The common law remained what it had been previously, although it was not deemed advisable to emphasize those particular parts of it in black and white. In particular, throughout the reign of Henry, the *Commune Concilium* was always consulted before a levy was made of any scutage or aid. (*b*) It is stated in the new charter that the omitted clauses were reserved for further consideration. In the so-called " respiting clause " (chapter 42) six topics were thus reserved because of their " grave and doubtful " import : levying of scutages and aids; rights of Jews and other creditors; the liberty of going from and returning to England; the forest laws; the " farms " of counties; and the customs relating to banks of rivers and their guardians. This respiting clause amounts to a definite engagement by the King to consider at some future time (probably as soon as peace had been restored) how far it would be possible to re-enact the omitted provisions.[1]

A practical difficulty confronted the advisers of the young

---

[1] Dr. Stubbs propounds the theory that this reissue of 1216 represents a compromise whereby the central government, in return for increased taxing powers, allowed to the feudal magnates increased rights of jurisdiction. He gives, however, no reasons for this belief, either in *Select Charters*, p. 339, or in his *Constitutional History*, II. 27. The Crown reserved a freer hand in taxation, but there seems no evidence that feudal justice gained ground against royal justice in 1216, not already gained in 1215.

King.   Neither law nor custom afforded precedents for the execution of documents during a king's minority.   The seal of a king was not available for his heir : the custom was to destroy the matrix when a death occurred, to prevent its being put to improper uses.[1]   Henry was made to explain that, in the absence of a seal of his own, the Charter had been sealed with the seals of Cardinal Gualo and of William Marshal, Earl of Pembroke, "*rectoris nostri et regni nostri.*"

In the Red Book of the Dublin Court of Exchequer there is a copy of an Irish version of this Charter,[2] bearing to be executed at the same place and date as the English one (Bristol, 12th November, 1216).   It is possible that it was not issued till some months later.   After the coronation, the Marshal wrote to Geoffrey de Marsh, Justiciar of Ireland, promising to send a confirmation to the Irish of the liberties just granted to Henry's English subjects.[3]   It was not till 6th February, 1217, that this promise was fulfilled by the sending of an Irish version of the Charter, in the King's name, as a reward to his Irish subjects for their fidelity.[4] If this is the original transcribed into the Red Book, it would seem to have been antedated by nearly three months; while its terms suggest that little trouble was taken to adapt the purport of the English Charter to Irish needs : four perfunctory alterations substitute the freedom of the Irish Church for that of the English Church; the liberties of Dublin for those of London; prohibit weirs in the Liffey, instead of the Thames and Medway; and make the " quarter of Dublin," not of London, the measure of corn.   The value

[1] It is unnecessary to invent a catastrophe to account for the loss of John's seal. Blackstone (*Great Charter*, xxix.) says, " King John's great seal having been lost in passing the washes of Lincolnshire."

[2] On pp. 69-73.   Text is given in *Early Statutes of Ireland* (Rolls Series, H. F. Berry), 5-19, and in Gilbert's *Hist. and Mun. Docs. of Ireland*, 65-72.

[3] *New Rymer*, I. 145.

[4] *Rot. Pat.*, I. 31.   *Cf.* Norgate, *Minority*, p. 93 : " On 6th February, 1217, a copy of the Charter was sent to Ireland with a letter in the King's name addressed to all the King's faithful servants in Ireland, expressing his desire that . . . they and their heirs should, *of his grace and gift*, enjoy the same liberties which his father and he had granted to the realm of England."   This was the Marshal's policy.

of the grant must have lain rather in the principle involved than in the phraseology of particular clauses.

(II.) *Reissue of* 1217. The effect of the new Charter in England was disappointing : apart from the bishops, only four submissions were made to Henry in three months.[1] The vicissitudes of the war need not be traced : on 19th May, 1217, the royalists gained a decisive victory at the battle known as the " Fair of Lincoln "; and, on 24th August following, Hubert de Burgh destroyed the fleet on which Louis depended. The French prince was glad to accept honourable terms. Negotiations, beginning on the 8th, resulted, on 12th September, 1217, in the Treaty of Lambeth or Kingston. " The treaty of Lambeth is, in practical importance, scarcely inferior to the charter itself." [2]   It marked the final acceptance by the advisers of the Crown of the substance of Magna Carta as the permanent basis of government for England in time of peace, not merely as a provisional expedient in time of war. Its terms were equally honourable to both parties : to the Regent and his supporters, because of the moderation they displayed; and to Louis who, while renouncing all claim to the English Crown, did so only on condition of a full pardon to his lay allies, and a guarantee of the principles they fought for. He strove in vain to make better terms for the clergy, who were left exposed to Gualo's vindictive greed.[3]

It must have been an impressive scene when, on 12th September, at an eyot in the Thames near Kingston, between rival armies lining opposite banks, Louis (who had already granted a confirmation of the substance of John's Charter) and Henry, laying their hands on the Gospels, swore with the Legate and the Marshal to restore to the barons of England and all other men of the realm their rights and heritages, with the liberties formerly demanded.[4] Henry promised to pay to Louis 10,000 marks nominally as an indemnity for his expenses, an

---

[1] Davis, *Engl. under Normans*, 392.   [2] Stubbs, *Const. Hist.*, II. 25.

[3] Petit-Dutaillis, *Louis VIII.*, 171.

[4] Wendover, IV. 31-32 ; cited Norgate, *Minority*, 59, where full details are given.

amount partly raised by a scutage of two marks "*ad Angliam deliberandam de Francis.*"[1]   Louis, on his side, restored all cities, lands and property taken by him in England.   One version of the treaty mentions particularly the Rolls of Exchequer, charters of the Jews, charters of liberties made in the time of King John, and all other exchequer writings.[2]   The restoration of rights and liberties by Henry was the main provision of the treaty, and this was fulfilled on 6th November, 1217, by the issue of a revised Charter of Liberties and a separate Forest Charter.[3]

The issue of these two Charters put the coping stone to the general pacification.   After the havoc wrought by two years of civil war, the moment had come for a declaration by the Regent of his policy for ruling an England once more at peace.   Not only was he bound in honour to this course by the Treaty of Lambeth, but the opportunity was a good one for fulfilling the promise made in chapter 42 of the Charter of 1216.   Accordingly the respiting clause of that document disappeared, and some new clauses took its place.   The matters then reserved for further discussion

[1] *Pipe Rolls*, 2 and 3 Henry III., cited Petit-Dutaillis, 177.   Miss Norgate (*Minority*, 85) gives the rate *per incuriam* as "two shillings."

[2] Martene and Durand, *Thesaurus Novus Anecdotorum* (1717), I. 858, cited Norgate, *Minority*, 59.   Blackstone thinks that under this clause the original of the Articles of the Barons, captured by Louis with other national archives, was restored and deposited at Lambeth Palace until the seventeenth century. See *Great Charter*, xxxix.

[3] The Charter of Liberties of 1217, found among the archives of Gloucester Abbey and now in the Bodleian Library at Oxford, still bears the impression of two seals—that of Gualo in yellow wax, and that of the Regent in green.   See Blackstone, *Great Charter*, p. xxxv.   The existence of the separate Forest Charter was only surmised by Blackstone, *Ibid.*, p. xlii; but, shortly after he wrote, an original of it was found among the archives of Durham Cathedral.   For an account of this and of its discovery, see Thomson, *Magna Charta*, pp. 443-5.   This Forest Charter bears the date 6th November, 1217, and that, in itself, affords presumption that the Charter of Liberties (undated) to which it forms a supplement was executed at the same time.   M. Bémont accepts this date; see his *Chartes*, xxviii., and authorities there cited.   Blackstone, *Great Charter*, xxxix., gives the probable date as 23rd September.   Dr. Stubbs gives 6th November in *Const. Hist.*, II. 26; and both dates alternatively in *Sel. Chart.*, 344.   Prof. Lawlor, *Engl. Hist. Rev.*, XXII. 514-6, contended for two independent issues, one of each date; but Prof. Powicke's researches, *Eng. Hist. Rev.*, XXIV. 232, prove that there is only one genuine charter of that year, dated as in the text.

as " *gravia et dubitabilia* " had now been reconsidered and were either finally abandoned, or accepted with or without amendment. Of the six topics " respited " in 1216, one (concerning forests and warrens) was dealt with in the Forest Charter which took the place of chapters 36 and 38 of 1216 and of the omitted provisions of 1215; two others (concerning scutage and enclosure of rivers) formed the subjects of special chapters (44 and 20 respectively); while the remaining three (the rights of Jews, free egress from and ingress to England, and the " farms " of shires) were not mentioned, although some of the grievances involved may have been indirectly affected by certain newly added chapters (*e.g.* that which regulated the times of meeting of shire and hundred courts) or by the " saving clause " in chapter 42.

To take the chief alterations in the order in which they occur,[1] chapter 7 of 1217 defines further a widow's rights of dower; chapters 13, 14 and 15 alter the procedure for taking the three petty assizes; chapter 16 makes it clear that the King's villeins do not share in the protection from harsh amercement; chapter 20, as already mentioned, treats of river enclosures; chapters 23 and 26 treat of purveyance, the former extending the term of payment allowed to Crown officials, the latter exempting entirely the carts of people of the better classes—" parsons," knights and ladies. The two provisions, taken together, speak eloquently against the " democratic " interpretation of the Charter. Chapter 34 further limits or defines Crown bailiffs' rights in regard to legal tests or " trials " where there is no evidence except their own unsupported testimony; chapter 38 makes clear a previously doubtful point concerning the King's rights over escheats. Chapters 39, 42, 43, 44 and 46 will immediately receive separate discussion; while chapter 47 ordains " of common counsel " the demolition of all " unlicensed " strongholds built or rebuilt since the outbreak of the war between John and his barons.

[1] Details are discussed *infra*, under appropriate chapters of John's charter. The points in which this reissue differs from earlier and later charters are shown in the Appendix, in the footnotes to the text of 1225.

Chapter 44, generally regarded as replacing chapter 12 of 1215, declares that scutages should be taken in future as they had been wont to be taken under Henry II. If, as has already been suggested, the scutage question was the immediate cause of the revolt of 1215, the importance and difficulty of this subject are obvious. Professor Adams[1] thinks that the leaders in 1217, at their wits' end for a solution, fell back on a vague, non-committal formula as " an effort of despair." Yet the old rates of scutage could still be read in the Exchequer Rolls, and the practice of a reign that had closed only twenty-six years before must have been familiar to many others besides the aged Marshal who set seal to the Charter. In reality John's innovations were now swept away; these included the habit of making an annual tax of what was meant for special emergencies, the assessment under the Inquest of 1212, the demand for scutage and service cumulatively, and, above all, the high rate of three marks *per* knight's fee.[2]

The essence of the barons' demands in 1217 must undoubtedly have been the return to the normal maximum rate of 2 marks. The substitution of this reference to the usage of Henry for the discarded chapters 12 and 14 of John's Charter (which made " common consent " necessary for *all* scutages, whatever the rate) was a natural compromise; and the barons in agreeing to it were justified in thinking, from their own medieval point of view, that they were neither submitting to unfair abridgments of their rights, nor yet countenancing reactionary measures hurtful to the growth of liberty.[3] Yet when this alteration is viewed by modern eyes, in the light cast by the intervening centuries of constitutional progress, the conclusion suggests itself that, unconsciously, retrograde tendencies were at

[1] *Origin*, 260.

[2] Pollock and Maitland, I. 250 n., suggest that this chapter absolved under-tenants from the obligation of personal attendance in the army.

[3] Mr. Hubert Hall (*Eng. Hist. Rev.*, IX. 344) takes a different view, considering that a reduction of scutages to the old rate of Henry II. was impossible; he speaks of " the astounding and futile concession in c. 44 of the charter of 1217." The clause is neither astounding nor futile if we regard it as a promise by Henry III. that he would not exact more than two marks per fee *without consent*, and if we

work. All mention of the *Commune Concilium*—that predecessor of the modern Parliament, that germ of all that has made England famous in the realm of constitutional laws and liberties—disappears. If (as it was once the fashion to maintain) the control of taxation by a national assembly, the conception of representation, and the indissoluble connection of these two principles with each other, really found place in Magna Carta in 1215, they were ejected in 1216, and failed to find a champion in 1217 to demand their restoration.

A modern statesman, with a grasp of constitutional principles, would have seized the occasion of the revision of the Charter, to define the functions of the Great Council with precision and emphasis. He would not lightly have thrown away the written acknowledgment implied in chapters 12 and 14 of 1215—in the germ, at least—of the right of a national council to control the levying of taxes. The magnates in 1217 were content, however, to abandon abstract principles; they were selling, not indeed their birthright, but their best means of gaining new rights from the Crown, for "a mess of pottage."

Such considerations, however, must not be pressed too far: no one seriously thought in 1217, any more than in 1216, of dispensing with future meetings of the feudal tenants in *Commune Concilium*. Great Councils continued to meet with increasing frequency throughout the reign of Henry III., and the consent of the magnates was habitually asked to scutages even at a lower rate than that which had been normal in Henry II.'s reign. Sometimes such consent was given unconditionally: sometimes in return for a new confirmation of the Charters; sometimes a demand was met by absolute refusal—the first distinct instance of which seems to have occurred in January, 1242.[1]

Chapters 39, 42 and 43, treating of topics not mentioned

further note that it was the practice of his reign to ask such consent from the *Commune Concilium* for scutages even of a *lower* rate. A levy of 10s., for example, was granted by a Council in 1221. See Stubbs, *Const. Hist.*, II. 33.

[1] M. Paris, 581-2 ; *Sel. Chart.*, 369.

in John's Charter, fall (strictly considered) outside the scope of this treatise, but a short account of their main provisions may prove useful here. Chapter 42, from its possible connection with the omitted chapter 25 of 1215, may be taken first. The shire court is not to meet oftener than once a month; less often, where local custom so ruled it. No sheriff or bailiff is to make his tourn through the hundreds oftener than twice a year—after Easter and after Michaelmas respectively—and only in the accustomed places. Careful provision is made for holding view of frankpledge at Michaelmas, with due regard to "liberties" upon the one hand, and to the King's peace and keeping the tithings full upon the other. Finally, the sheriff is not to make "occasions," but shall content himself with what he used to have for holding view of frankpledge in Henry of Anjou's time—a reference, it would seem, to that "Sheriff's aid" which was the cause of a famous quarrel in 1163 between Henry and his recently appointed Archbishop, Thomas à Becket.[1]

Chapters 39 and 43 link themselves rather with the future than the past, showing that new problems were thrusting themselves to the front since the days of John—topics round which much controversy was to rage. These chapters anticipate the principles underlying two famous measures of Edward's reign : the statutes of *Quia Emptores*[2] and of Mortmain.[3] Chapter 39 forbade for the future that any freeman should give away or sell so much of his land as would not leave sufficient to furnish the service due from the fief to the feudal lord.

Chapter 43 marks the growing hostility against the accumulation by the monasteries of wealth in the form of landed estates. The times were not ripe for a final solution of this problem, and the charter only attempted to remedy one of the subsidiary abuses of the system, not to abolish the main evil. An ingenious expedient had been devised by lawyers to enable tenants to cheat their lords out of some of the lawful feudal incidents. Religious houses

---

[1] *Sel. Chart.*, 129.   [2] 18 Edward I., also known as Westminster III.
[3] 7 Edward I., also known as the Statute *de religiosis*.

made bad tenants, since, as they never died, the lord of the fief was deprived of wardship, relief, and escheat. This was not unfair, provided the transaction was *bona fide*. Sometimes, however, collusive agreements were made, whereby a freeholder bestowed his lands on a particular house, which then subinfeudated the same subjects to the original tenant, who thus got his lands back, but now became tenant of the church, not of his former lord. The lord was left with a corporation for his tenant; and all the profitable incidents would, under the new arrangement, accrue to the church. Such expedients were prohibited, under pain of forfeiture, by chapter 43 of the reissue of 1217; and this prohibition was interpreted liberally by the lords in their own favour.[1]

The only remaining provision that calls for comment is the " saving clause " in chapter 46, intended, perhaps, to cover the gaps left in the Charter as conceived in 1215, by the decision not to restore some of the *dubitabilia* of 1216: this chapter reserves to archbishops, bishops, abbots, priors, templars, hospitallers, earls, barons, and all other persons, cleric and lay, the liberties and free customs they previously had. The vagueness of this provision deprived it of value.

These were the main alterations made in 1217 in the tenor of the Great Charter. This reissue is of great importance, since it represents practically the final form taken by the Charter. On 22nd February, 1218, copies of the Great Charter, in this new form, were sent to the sheriffs to be published and enforced. In the writs accompanying them, the special attention directed to the clause against unlicensed castles shows the importance attached to their demolition.[2] These remained in 1217, as in 1154, a result of past civil war, and a menace to good government in the future. It was the aim of every efficient ruler to abolish all fortified castles—practically impregnable in the thirteenth century when artillery was unknown—except those of the King, and to see that royal castles were under command of castellans of approved loyalty. John

[1] See Pollock and Maitland, I. 314.   [2] See *Rot. Claus.*, I. 377.

had placed his own strongholds under creatures of his own, who, after his death, refused to give them up to his son's Regent. The attempt to dislodge these soldiers of fortune, two years later, led to new disturbances in which the famous Falkes de Breauté played a leading part.[1] The destruction of "adulterine" castles and the resumption of royal ones were both necessary accompaniments of any real pacification.

Attempts have been made to estimate the motives and forces at work in these considerable changes in the text of the revised Charter. Attention to minute points of detail in practice and phraseology are rightly held to indicate a return towards more normal conditions under which "problems of everyday government" and the more accurate statement of the law receive attention.[2] The new Charter, in its desire to profit by the actual experience of the past two years, has some analogy to a modern amending statute. Other alterations, however, of a more fundamental nature would seem to have been deliberately made; and, as changing the old customs of the realm, they are of a legislative character in the strictest sense. Evidence of pressure from the baronage, in pursuance of their own selfish interests, can be traced in some at least of these innovations; but, on the other hand, the destruction of their "adulterine" castles shows that there were limits to their power.

The sincerity with which Magna Carta, thus amended, had been accepted by those in power is shown by the issue, seven months later, of letters to the sheriffs ordering them to publish the Charter in their shires and see that it was put in force; while orders were also given to respect the franchises of the city of London.[3]

(III.) *Reissue of* 1225.[4] Henry's second Charter, like his first, had been authenticated by the seals of the Legate and the "Rector." The objection to providing a seal of Henry's own was that it might be used to prejudice the royal prerogatives by alienating Crown lands and fran-

---

[1] Stubbs, *Const. Hist.*, II. 32.   [2] Cf. Adams, *Origin*, 258-260.

[3] *New Rymer*, I. 147, 150.   [4] See text in Appendix.

chises during the King's minority. But, shortly before
Gualo left England, his task as Legate well done, instructions were given to a goldsmith to prepare a royal seal of
silver, 5 marks in weight. Apparently the first use to
which it was put was to attest letters patent, issued after
Michaelmas, 1218, warning all men that no grant in perpetuity was to be sealed with it till the King came of age.[1]

The full twenty-one years would not be completed until
1st October, 1228; but by letters dated 13th April, 1223,
Pope Honorius declared his ward to be of full age under
certain reservations. A few months earlier (30th January,
1223) consternation had been created by writs issued in
the King's name to the sheriffs for a sworn inquest as to
the customs and liberties enjoyed by John in the various
shires, before the war; and Henry's advisers thought it
prudent to issue second writs on 9th April ordering that
the results of the inquest should be held back till 25th June,
and disclaiming all intention of raising up " evil customs."[2]

It was not, apparently, until December, 1223, that the
Pope's declaration of the partial ending of Henry's nonage was given effect to, with consent of the Council; and
on 13th January, 1224, Henry was asked by Stephen
Langton for a new confirmation of the Charters.[3] In
the ensuing debate, William Brewer answered for the
King : " The liberties you ask ought not to be observed
of right, because they were extorted by force," words which,
coming from a royal favourite, were sufficient to justify
suspicion. When the Archbishop had rebuked this rash

---

[1] See Norgate, *Minority*, 102 ; Stubbs, *Const. Hist.*, II. 30. *Annals of
Waverley*, 290, speak of a reissue of the charters about this date ; but this
probably results from confusion with what happened a year earlier.

[2] *New Rymer*, I. 168 ; *Rot. Claus.*, I. 569.

[3] R. Wendover, IV. 84, who dates the demand a year earlier. Miss Norgate's
chronology is here followed (*Minority*, 215 n.). The request would be a natural
corollary to the King's coming of age. There may have been special reasons for
uneasiness, *e.g.* the suspicions aroused by the recent inquest, the resumption of
royal castles from their former wardens, and the Crown's need of increased sources
of taxation. See Adams, *Origin*, 281 n. ; Turner, *Trans. R.H.S.*, I. 205 ff.
Miss Norgate (*Ibid.* 215) suggests that Langton desired some modification of the
terms of the charter of 1217.

adviser : " William, if you loved the King, you would not endanger thus the peace of his realm," the young King said : " We have all sworn these liberties, and what we have sworn we are bound to keep." [1]

No formal charter seems at this time to have been granted; but the barons' opportunity came in December of the same year, when Henry's necessities forced him to demand a contribution of one-fifteenth of moveables. A bargain on these terms was struck, and on 11th February, 1225, the Charter of Liberties and the Forest Charter were both reissued.[2] The new Forest Charter was practically identical with that issued in 1217; while the alterations in the new Charter of Liberties were the result of a determination to place on record the circumstances in which it had been granted. In the preamble Henry stated that he acted " *spontanea et bona voluntate nostra* " and all reference to consent was omitted, although many magnates appear as witnesses. These alterations were intended to emphasize the fact that no pressure had been brought to bear, and thus to meet the objection urged by Brewer in 1224, that the Charter had been extorted by force.[3]

The "consideration" also appears in the concluding portion of the Charter, where it is stated that in return for the foregoing gift of liberties along with those granted in the Forest Charter, the archbishops, bishops, abbots, priors, earls, barons, knights, free tenants, and all others of the realm had given a fifteenth part of their moveables to the King.

[1] R. Wendover, *Ibid.*

[2] Miss Norgate (*Minority*, 262), for reasons not fully explained, speaks of this purchasing of admitted rights by payments of hard cash as an "irretrievable blunder." Does she not neglect, however, the effect of the legal doctrine of "valuable consideration" and the force underlying Brewer's argument that earlier charters were voidable because granted under duress?

[3] Dr. Stubbs thinks that in avoiding one danger, a greater was incurred. "It must be acknowledged that Hubert, in trying to bind the royal conscience, forsook the normal and primitive form of legislative enactment, and opened a claim on the king's part to legislate by sovereign authority without counsel or consent." (*Const. Hist.*, II. 37.) This seems to exaggerate the importance of an isolated precedent, the circumstances of which were unique. The confirmation was something far apart from an ordinary "legislative enactment." It had been asked and paid for.

The prominence given to this feature brings the transaction embodied in the reissue of 1225 (as compared with the original grant of 1215) one step nearer the legal category of "private bargain." In another important new clause—founded probably on a precedent taken from chapter 61 of John's Charter—Henry is made to declare: "And we have granted to them for us and our heirs, that neither we nor our heirs shall procure any thing whereby the liberties in this charter shall be infringed or broken; and if any thing shall be procured by any person contrary to these premises, it shall be held of no validity or effect." This provision was clearly directed against future papal dispensations; the clause, however, was diplomatically made general in its terms.

One original copy of this third reissue of the Great Charter is preserved at Durham with a still perfect impression of Henry's recently made seal in green wax, though the parchment has been "defaced and obliterated by the unfortunate accident of overturning a bottle of ink."[2] A second original is to be found at Lacock Abbey, in Wiltshire. The accompanying Forest Charter is also preserved at Durham.[3]

This third reissue brings the story of the genesis of the Great Charter to an end. It marked the final form assumed by Magna Carta; the identical words were then used which afterwards became stereotyped and were confirmed, time after time, without further modification. It is this Charter of 1225 which (in virtue of the confirmation of Edward I.) still remains on the statute book.[4]

Henry, however, was not yet, in 1225, fully of age; and suspicions seem still to have been entertained as to what would be his attitude when he became of full age for all purposes. It was apparently in January, 1227, that the

[1] A few minor alterations, such as the omission of the clause against unlicensed castles (now unnecessary) and some verbal changes need not be mentioned. A list of these is given by Blackstone, *Great Charter*, l.

[2] See Blackstone, *Ibid.*, xlvii. to l.   [3] *Ibid.*

[4] One slight exception should be noted. In one point of detail a change had occurred between 1225 and 1297; the rate of relief payable from a barony had been reduced from £100 to 100 marks. See *infra*, under chapter 2.

Council authorized the King to issue writs to his sheriffs that all grants of lands, tenements, or liberties, to be held valid, must be confirmed under Henry's seal. Writs in these terms went forth on 21st January. This was tantamount to an official declaration that the minority was ended.[1]

Under feudal theory, the close personal relations between lord and vassal had to be renewed when a death occurred : every new King exacted payments for confirmation of earlier grants, and Henry's previous recognitions had been provisional. The King was enunciating no general doctrine of contempt for vested interests : his abuse of power lay in the exorbitant sums charged for charters confirming earlier, informal " precepts." [2] There is no substantial ground for the opinion, once widely held,[3] that the King intended to annul the Great Charter, and that, accordingly, it was not in force from 1227 to 1237. Nor, in the instructions to the sheriffs, is there a word said about the Forest Charter. Henry, indeed, dared not openly repudiate either of the Charters, which had received full papal authority.

Yet he was far from scrupulous in observing the letter of their provisions : there was good warrant for the complaint contained in article 7 of the Petition of 1258,[4] that Henry broke his bargain, by extending the forests beyond the boundaries to obtain which the fifteenth had been paid. The process was begun by the issue of letters close, on 9th February, 1227.[5] Henceforward, Henry's attitude towards the charters was a settled one : he confirmed them with a

---

[1] A bull of Gregory IX., dated 13th April, 1227, confirmed this. See Blackstone, *Great Charter*, li., and Stubbs, *Const. Hist.*, II. 39.

[2] See Powicke, *Eng. Hist. Rev.*, XXIII. 221.

[3] R. Wendover, IV. 140, is apparently the source of the error. See Norgate, *Minority*, 266 n.

[4] *Sel. Chart.*, 383.

[5] See *Rot. Claus.*, II. 169. The best account is in Turner's *Select Pleas of the Forest*, pp. xcix. to cii., who gives a full and convincing account of Henry's procedure and motives. " The king neither repudiated the Charter of the Forest nor annulled the perambulations which had been made in his infancy. He merely corrected them after due inquiry." See also Adams, *Origin*, 283 n.

light heart when he could obtain money in return, and then acted as though they did not exist.

(IV.) *Confirmations* (1237 to 1297). After the close of Henry's minority history is concerned not with reissues of the Charter but with confirmations. Matthew Paris refers to the circumstances under which the first of these was executed on 28th January, 1237 : as the express condition of a grant of "a thirtieth part of the kingdom, to wit of all moveables," Henry promised that thenceforward the "*libertates Magnae Cartae*" should be inviolably observed.[1] This Charter differs fundamentally from those of 1215, 1216, 1217 and 1225. It does not rehearse the substance of any one of the "liberties" it confirms, but contents itself with a brief reference : "We have granted and by this our charter confirmed . . . all liberties and free customs contained in our charters which we caused to be made to our subjects during our minority, to wit as well in *magna carta nostra* as in *carta nostra de foresta*." [2] Even with the long list of witnesses, occupying half of its extent, this document is a small one when compared with the voluminous parchments of earlier grants. It has been suggested [3] that the marked contrast in size may have given rise to the practice of alluding to the earlier charter (whether of John or Henry) as *Magna Carta*, in distinction from the new *parva carta*.[4]

In support of the suggestion, it may be argued that the phrase "Magna Carta" is never used by Roger of Wendover, and that its first appearance in the narrative of Matthew Paris is in the passage just quoted, *sub anno* 1237, "*carta libertatum*" being the usual description. The words "Magna Carta" appear a second time in his account of a famous debate in 1242,[5] where pointed reference is

---

[1] M. Paris, 435 ; *Sel. Chart.*, 326-7.

[2] Its facsimile is given in *Statutes of the Realm* ; its text in *Sel. Chart.*, 365-6.

[3] By Dr. George Neilson, *Juridical Review*, XVII. 137.

[4] Henry I.'s charter was also described as "Magna Carta" but not till the thirteenth century. Leibermann, *Trans. R.H.S.*, VIII. 21.

[5] M. Paris, 581-2 ; *Sel. Chart.*, 369-370. Bracton's *Notebook* (see its Index) mentions the Charter eight times under various descriptions, but never as the Great Charter.

made to the bargain struck in 1237, when Henry conceded
the liberties contained in " *Magna Carta* " in return for the
thirtieth of moveables " *et inde fecit eis quandam parvam
cartam suam.*" The antithesis is here emphatic.

The adoption of this *parva carta* means that the Charter
had become stereotyped as it stood in 1225, and no longer
moved with the times. For ten years previous it had, like
a living thing, adapted itself to changing needs and
grievances. The new style possibly corresponds with a
new attitude on the part of both King and barons. Henry
had abandoned any intention of repudiating the Charter
or even of infringing its specific promises as to wardships,
reliefs or the like : his practice was to evade its spirit,
while observing its letter. The opposition, on their part,
may unconsciously have come to consider the Charter's
value to lie, not in its specific clauses, but in its assertion
of the existence of a fixed body of law to which successful
appeal could be made against the King's caprice. Changes
in the texture of that law are no longer reflected in reaffirmations of the Charter; but must be sought for in a
series of supplementary documents such as those of 1258,
1297, 1300, 1311, 1406 and 1628.

After 1237 little is heard of the charters until 1253, when
complaint was raised of infractions, particularly in regard
to the privileges of the Church. Both charters were
republished, and on 13th May, the sentence of excommunication, which had accompanied the reaffirmations of
1225 and 1237, was repeated in a peculiarly impressive
manner.[1]

In 1265 Simon de Montfort, during his brief period of
power, exacted from Henry and his son a new confirmation, dated 14th March, notable for its clause empowering
" all of the realm to rebel against us and use their utmost
resources and efforts to our hurt " in imitation of chapter 61
of John's grant. After Simon's overthrow and death, the
King and the young Edward, of their own initiative,
affirmed the charters by chapter five of the Statute of
Marlborough (1267). Of the confirmations of Edward's

[1] Blackstone, *Great Charter*, 70-72 ; Stubbs, *Sel. Chart.*, 373.

reign, it is only necessary to mention the emphatic *Confirmatio Cartarum* of 1297, accompanied by an *Inspeximus* of the issue of 1225, granted under conditions that are well known. It contains new clauses which impose restrictions on the taxing power of the Crown; and these, to some extent, take the places of those chapters (12 and 14) of the original grant of John, which had been omitted in all intervening grants.

Of later confirmations, Coke[1] has counted 15 under Edward III., 8 under Richard II., 6 under Henry IV. and one under Henry V. Of these, only the statute of 1369 (42 Edward III. c. 1) requires special notice : it commands that "the Great Charter and the Charter of the Forest be holden and kept in all points, and if any statute be made to the contrary that shall be holden for none." Parliament in 1369 thus sought to deprive future Parliaments of the power to effect any alterations upon the terms of Magna Carta. Yet, if Parliament in that year had the power to add anything, by a new legislative enactment, to the ancient binding force of the Great Charter, it follows that succeeding Parliaments, in possession of equal powers, might readily undo by a second statute what the earlier statute had sought to effect. If Parliament had power to alter the sacred terms of Magna Carta, it had power to alter the less sacred statute of 1369 which declared it unalterable. The terms of that statute, however, are interesting as perhaps the earliest example on record of the illogical theory that the English Parliament might so use its present legislative supremacy as to limit the legislative supremacy of other Parliaments in the future.[2]

II. Magna Carta and the Reforms of Edward I.

The Great Charter, alike from its excellences and its defects, exercised a potent influence throughout the two succeeding reigns. It is hardly too much to say that the failure of Magna Carta to provide adequate machinery for

[1] *Second Institute*, p. 1.

[2] Many further details will be found in Bémont, *Chartes, xxx.-lxx.*, and authorities there cited.

its own enforcement is responsible for the protracted struggles and civil war that made up the troubled reign of Henry III.; while the difference of attitude assumed by Henry and his son respectively towards the scheme of reform it embodied, explains why one reign was full of conflicts and distress, while the other was prosperous and progressive. The fundamental difference between the policies of Henry and Edward lies in this, that while Henry, in spite of numerous nominal confirmations of Magna Carta, never loyally accepted the settlement it contained, Edward acquiesced in its main provisions honestly on the whole, with a sincere intention to carry them into practice.

At the same time, the attitude of Henry III. indicates an advance upon that of John. Henry, on attaining majority, had confirmed the charters freely and on his own initiative, and found himself thereafter unable openly to repudiate the bargain he had made. Yet the settlement between Crown and baronage was nominal rather than real: the King was bound by bonds of parchment which he could break at pleasure. In the absence of sanctions for its enforcement, the Charter became an empty expression of good intentions: no constitutional expedient existed to obviate a final recourse to the arbitrament of civil war. Thus, part of the blame for the recurring and devastating struggles of the reign of Henry must be attributed to the defects of the Great Charter.

The whole interest of the reign, indeed, lies in the attempts made to evolve adequate machinery for enforcing " the liberties." Experiments of many kinds were tried in the hope of turning theory into practice. The system of government outlined in the Provisions of Oxford of 1258, for example, reproduced the defects of the scheme contained in chapter 61 of the Great Charter, and added new defects of its own. The baronial committee was not designed to enter into friendly co-operation with Henry in the normal work of government, but rather to supersede entirely certain of the royal prerogatives. No glimmering was yet apparent of the true solution afterwards adopted with success: it was not yet realized that the best way to control the Crown was through the agency of its own Ministers.

If Simon de Montfort had any vague conception of the real remedy for the evils of the reign, his ideals were overruled in 1258 by the more extreme section of the baronial party. Earl Simon, indeed, had one opportunity of putting his theories into practice : during the brief interval between the battle of Lewes, which made him supreme for the moment, and the battle of Evesham, which ended his career, he enjoyed an unfettered control ; and some authorities find in the provisional scheme of the closing months of 1264, traces of the constitutional expedient afterwards successfully adopted as a solution of the problem. In one respect, the Earl of Leicester did influence the development of the English constitution ; he furnished the first precedent for a true Parliament, reflecting interests wider than those of Crown tenants and free-holders, when he invited representatives of the boroughs to take their places by the side of representatives of the counties in a national council summoned to meet in January, 1265. His schemes of government, however, were not fated to be realized by him in a permanent form : the utter overthrow of his faction followed his decisive defeat and death on 4th August, 1265.

The personal humiliation of Simon, however, assured the ultimate triumph of the cause he had made his own. Prince Edward, from the moment of his brilliant victory at Evesham, was not only supreme over his father's enemies, but also within his father's councils. He found himself in a position to realize some of his political ideals ; and he adopted as his own, the main constitutional conceptions of his uncle Earl Simon, who had been his friend and teacher before he became his deadliest enemy.

Edward Plantagenet, alike when acting as chief adviser of his aged father and after he had succeeded to his throne, not only accepted the main provisions of the Great Charter,[1]

[1] The best proof of this will be found in a comparison of Magna Carta with the statute of Marlborough, and the chief statutes of Edward's reign, notably that of Westminster I.

L

but adopted also a new scheme of government which formed their necessary counterpart. The very fact of the adoption of Earl Simon's ideals by the heir to the throne altered their chances of success. All such schemes had been foredoomed to failure so long as they emanated from an opposition leader, however powerful; but their triumph was assured when accepted by the monarch himself. Under the protection of Edward I.—the last of the four great master-builders of the constitution—the *Commune Concilium* of the Angevin kings grew into the English Parliament. This implied no sudden dramatic change, but a long process of adjustment, under the guiding hand of Edward.

The main features of his scheme may be briefly summarized : Edward's conception of his position as a national king achieving national ends, the funds necessary for which ought to be contributed by the nation, led him to devise a system of taxation which would fill the Exchequer while avoiding unnecessary friction with the tax-payer. In broadening the basis of finance, he was led to broaden the basis of Parliament; and thus he advanced from the feudal conception of a *Commune Concilium,* attended only by Crown tenants, towards the nobler ideal of a national Parliament containing representatives of every community and every class in England. The principle of representation (foreshadowed in a vague way for centuries before the Conquest in English local government), now found a home, and, as it proved, a permanent home, in the English Parliament.

The powers of this assembly widened almost automatically, with the widening of its composition. To its original function of taxation, legislation was soon added. The functions of hearing grievances and of proffering advice had, even in the days of the Conqueror, belonged to such of the great magnates as were able to make their voices heard in the Curia Regis; and similar rights were gradually extended to the humbler members of the augmented assembly. The representatives of counties and towns retained rights of free discussion even after Parlia-

ment had split into two Houses.   These rights, fortified
by command of the purse strings, tended to increase, until
they secured for the Commons some measure of control
over the executive functions of the King, varying in extent
and effectiveness with the weakness of the King, with his
need of money, and with the political situation of the hour.

The new position and powers of Parliament logically
involved a corresponding alteration in the position and
powers of the smaller but more permanent council or *Concilium Ordinarium* (the future Privy Council).   This had
long been increasing in power, in prestige, and in independence, a process quickened by the minority of Henry
III.   The Council was now strengthened by the support
of a powerful Parliament, usually acting in alliance with
the leaders of the baronial opposition.   The Council was
recruited from Parliament, and the appointment of King's
ministers was influenced by the proceedings in the larger
assembly.[1]

The Council thus became neutral ground on which the
conflicting interests of King and baronage might be discussed and compromised.   Wild schemes like that of
chapter 61 of Magna Carta or that typified in the Committee
appointed by the Mad Parliament of 1258, were now
unnecessary.   The King's own ministers, backed by Parliament, became an adequate means of enforcing the constitutional restraints embodied in royal Charters.   The problem
was thus, for the time being, solved.   The bargain made
at Runnymede between the English monarch and the
English nation found its counterpart and sanction, before
the close of the thirteenth century, in the conception of a
King ruling through responsible ministers and in harmony
with a national Parliament.   Edward Plantagenet, though
merely the unconscious instrument by whose agency the
new conception was for a time partially realized, yet merits
the gratitude of posterity for his share in the elabora-
tion of a working scheme of government which took the

[1] The doctrine that the *Commune Concilium* should have some voice in the
appointment of Ministers had been acted upon on several occasions even in the
reign of Henry III.   See Stubbs, *Const. Hist.*, II. 41.

place of the clumsy expedients designed as constitutional sanctions in 1215. The ultimate triumph of the principles underlying Magna Carta was assured not through any executive committee of rebellious barons, but through the constitutional machinery devised by Edward Plantagenet.

PART V.

MAGNA CARTA: ORIGINAL VERSIONS, PRINTED EDITIONS AND COMMENTARIES.

I. Manuscripts of Magna Carta and Relative Documents.

The barons who had forced the Great Charter on King John were determined that its contents should be widely known and permanently preserved. It was not sufficient that the great seal should be formally impressed upon one parchment. Those who compelled John to submit were not content even with the execution of its terms in duplicate or in triplicate : copies were to be distributed throughout the land, to be preserved in important strongholds and among the archives of the chapters of cathedral churches.[1]

I. *The extant original versions.* Of the many sealed copies, four have escaped the destroying hand of time : (1) *The British Museum Magna Carta, number one*—formally cited as " Cotton, Charters XIII. 31A." The recent history of this document, which is possibly the original copy delivered to the barons of the Cinque Portes, is well known. It was discovered in the seventeenth century, among the archives of Dover Castle, by the Warden, Sir Edward Dering, and by him presented to Sir Robert Cotton.[2] In the fire of 23rd October, 1731, this Charter was rendered in parts illegible, while the yellow wax of the seal was melted. It is possible that the accident has added to the prestige of this particular copy of Magna Carta.

---

[1] For methods of publishing Great Charters see R. L. Poole, *Eng. Hist. Rev.* XXVIII. 444 (July, 1913); and *infra* under c. 62.

[2] The accompanying letter, dated 10th May, 1630, is also preserved in the British Museum, as " Cotton, Julius, C. III. Fol. 191."

Like the three others still extant, it is written continu-
ously, though with many contractions, in a neat, running,
Norman hand. Some omissions seem to have been made
in the body of this version and to have been supplied at
the foot. These are five in number.[1] It is possible to
regard them as corrections of clerical omissions due to
carelessness or hurry in engrossing the deed; but the fact
that one of the additions is distinctly in the King's favour
raises a presumption that they embodied additions made
as afterthoughts to what had been originally dictated to
the engrossing clerk, and that they were inserted at
the King's suggestion before he would adhibit the great
seal.

The importance of this document was recognized, and a
facsimile was prepared by John Pine, a well-known en-
graver, some eighteen months after the great fire. The
engraving bears a certificate, dated 9th May, 1733, that the
copy is founded on the original, which had been shrivelled
up by the heat; but that, where two holes had been burned,
the words obliterated had been replaced from the other
version (to be immediately described) preserved in the
Cottonian collection.

(2) *The British Museum Magna Carta, number two—*
cited as " Cotton, Augustus, II. 106." [2]   The early history
of this document is unknown, but it came into the possession of Mr. Humphrey Wyems, and by him was presented
to Sir Robert Cotton on 1st January, 1628-9. Unlike the
other Cottonian copy, this one is happily in an excellent

[1] These are carefully noted among the variations described by the editors of the
Charters of Liberties forming Part I. of the first volume of the *Statutes of the Realm.*
These addenda are (1) at the end of c. 48, "*per eosdem, ita quod nos hoc sciamus
prius, vel justiciarius noster, si in Anglia non fuerimus,*" providing that the King
should receive intimation of all forest practices branded as " evil " before they are
abrogated ; (2) ; two small additions, near the beginning of c. 53, (a), " *et eodem
modo de justicia exhibenda,*" and (b) "*vel remansuris forestis*" ; (3) in c. 56, these
four words, "*in Anglia vel in Wallia*"; and (4) in c. 61 the words "*in perpetuum*" after "*gaudere.*" In the 2nd British Museum MS. three of these
addenda appear at the foot, viz. (1), (2a) and (2b) ; but the words of (3) and (4)
are incorporated in the body of that MS.

[2] Reproductions of this are sold at the British Museum for 2s. 6d.

state of preservation; but there is no trace left of any seal.[1] Three of the five addenda inserted at the foot of the copy previously described are found in a similar position here; but the substance of the two others is included in the body of the deed. On the left-hand margin, titles intended to be descriptive of several chapters occur in a later hand. Thus for the preservation of two original copies of the national charter of liberties the nation is indebted to Sir Robert Cotton. Several authors[2] gravely record how Sir Robert discovered "the palladium of English liberties" in the hands of his tailor at the critical moment when scissors were about to transform it into shapes for a suit of clothes. This detail is a fable, since both manuscripts of Magna Carta in the Cottonian collection are otherwise accounted for.

(3) *The Lincoln Magna Carta.* This copy is under the custody of the Dean and Chapter of Lincoln Cathedral, where it has lain for many centuries. The word "Lincolnia" is endorsed in a later hand in two places on folds of the parchment. It has no corrections or additions inserted at the foot, but embodies in their proper places all those which occurred in the versions already discussed. Further, it is executed with flourishes and in a more finished manner: the inference is that it took longer to engross. The Record Commissioners, in preparing the *Statutes of the Realm,* considered this version of superior authority to the others and have chosen it for their engraving published in 1810 in that valuable work, and also in the first volume of their edition of Rymer's *Foedera* in 1816.[3]

(4) *The Salisbury Magna Carta*—preserved in the archives

---

[1] " The fold and label are now cut off, though it is said once to have had slits in it for two seals, for which it is almost impossible to account; but Dr. Thomas Smith, in his Preface to the *Cottonian Catalogue,* Oxford, 1695, folio, states that they were those of the barons" (Thomson, *Magna Carta,* 425). The facsimile published by the Trustees of the British Museum shows slits for *three* seals.

[2] See Isaac D'Israeli, *Curiosities of Literature,* I. 18, and Thomson, *Magna Carta,* 424.

[3] The engraving was executed to their order by James Basire.

of the Cathedral there. The early history of this manuscript has not been traced, but its existence was known
at the close of the seventeenth century.[1] Sir William
Blackstone, in April, 1759,[2] instituted a search for it, but
without success—his inquiries being met with the statement that it had been lost some thirty years before, during
the execution of repairs in the Cathedral library. As its
disappearance had taken place during the tenure of the see
by Gilbert Burnet, his political adversaries accused him of
appropriating it—an undoubted calumny, as will be hereafter explained. The document had not been re-discovered
in 1800 when the royal commission published a report of
its inquiries for national records.[3] Two sub-commissioners
visited Salisbury in 1806 in search of it, but obtained no
satisfaction. It seems, however, to have been re-discovered
within the next few years, since it is mentioned in a book
published in 1814,[4] and it is now exhibited to the public
by order of the Dean and Chapter of Salisbury Cathedral.
It resembles the Lincoln copy both in its fine, leisurely
penmanship and also in the absence of additions at the
bottom of the parchment.[5]

II. *Comparison of the Originals.* Prior to Sir William
Blackstone's work, extraordinary confusion seems to have
prevailed concerning the various Charters of Liberties.
Not only was John's Magna Carta confused with reissues
by Henry; but these latter were known only from an official
copy of the Charter of 1225 contained in the *Inspeximus*

[1] See James Tyrrell, *History of England*, Vol. II. 821 (1697-1704).

[2] Blackstone, *Great Charter*, p. xvii.

[3] See *Report* (1800), p. 341.

[4] Dodsworth, *Historical Account of the Cathedral*, 202.

[5] It is unnecessary to treat in detail of the copies of the charter not authenticated
by John's Great Seal, though some of these are of value as secondary authorities.
The four most important are (*a*) a copy appearing in the Register of Gloucester
Abbey, (*b*) the Harleian MS., British Museum No. 746 (which also contains the
names of the twenty-five Executors in a hand probably of the reign of Edward I.).
(*c*) in the Red Book of the Exchequer. There is also (*d*) an early French version,
printed in D'Achery, *Spicilegium*, Vol. XII. p. 573, together with the writ of 27th
September addressed to the Sheriff of Hampshire. See Blackstone, *Great Charter*,
p. xviii., and Thomson, *Magna Carta*, pp. 428-430.

of the twenty-eighth year of Edward I. Neither Madox[1] nor Brady[2] was aware of the existence of any one of the four originals; and no mention is made of them in the first edition of Rymer's *Foedera*, which appeared in 1704. Mr. Tyrrell, indeed, seems to have known of the second original in the British Museum and also of the Salisbury version.[3] Mr. Care[4] showed no clear knowledge of the various manuscripts, though he mentioned the existence of several. Even Blackstone in 1759 collated only the two Cottonian copies, since he failed to find that of Salisbury, and was unaware of the existence of the Lincoln manuscript.[5]

As these four versions are practically identical in their substance, no important question seems to be involved in the discussion as to whether any one of them has greater authority than the others. The Record Commissioners considered that the Lincoln copy was the first to be completed (and therefore that it possessed special authority), because it contained no insertions at the foot of the instrument. Yet it seems more plausible to argue that this very immunity from clerical errors, or from additions made after engrossment, proves that it was of later and less hurried execution than the others, and therefore of less

---

[1] Thomas Madox, *Firma Burgi* (1726). On p. 45, Madox refers only to the *Inspeximus* of Edward I.

[2] Robert Brady, *Complete History of England*, p. 126 of Appendix to Vol. I. (1685), takes his text of the Charter from Matthew Paris "compared with the manuscript found in Bennet College Library," *i.e.* Corpus Christi, Cambridge.

[3] James Tyrrell, *History of England* (1697-1704). In p. 9 of Appendix to Vol. II. p. 821, Tyrrell prints a text of John's Charter founded on that of M. Paris, collated with those two originals.

[4] Henry Care, *English Liberties in the Freeborn subjects' inheritance ; containing Magna Charta*, etc. (1719), p. 5. The first edition, with a somewhat different title, is dated 1691.

[5] Strangely enough, Sir Thomas Duffus Hardy, so recently as 1837, in publishing his *Rotuli Chartarum* (Introduction, p. ii. note 5) declared that no original of John's Charter existed ; "notwithstanding all the care taken by multiplication of copies, it is singular that no contemporary copy of King John's Magna Carta has yet been found." The Lincoln MS. he dismissed as "certainly not of so early a date." He further reasserts the fallacy, exposed by Blackstone eighty years earlier, that John had issued a separate *Carta de Foresta*.

authority, if any distinction is permissible. Mr. Thomson
has much ground for his contention, in speaking of the
fire-marked version, that "the same circumstances may
probably be a proof of its superior antiquity, as having
been the first which was actually drawn into form and
sealed on Runnymede, the original whence all the most
perfect copies were taken." [1]

In all printed texts of Magna Carta, the contents are
divided into a preamble and sixty-three chapters. There
is no warrant for this in any one of the four originals : the
" chapters " are a modern invention, made for convenience
of reference.

III. *Articles of the Barons.* Of hardly inferior interest
is the parchment which contains the heads of agreement
made between John and the rebels on 15th June, 1215.
This is now in the British Museum, cited officially as
"Additional MSS. 4838." The seven centuries that have
passed over it have left surprisingly few traces; it is legible
throughout, and still bears the impression of John's seal
in brown wax. It was apparently deposited in Lambeth
Palace, where it remained until the middle of the seventeenth century. Archbishop Laud, when threatened with
impeachment, thought it prudent to set his papers in order;
and on 18th December, 1640, he dispatched for that purpose
to his episcopal palace, his friend Dr. John Warner,
Bishop of Rochester. A few hours later, Laud was committed to custody of Black-Rod, and an official messenger
was sent by the House of Lords to seal up his papers.
Bishop Warner had, meanwhile, escaped with the Articles
of the Barons. He kept this till he died, and at his death
it passed to one of his executors named Lee, and from him
to his son Colonel Lee, who presented it to Gilbert Burnet.
When the Salisbury Magna Carta disappeared, Burnet
was suspected of appropriating it. What gave apparent
weight to these misrepresentations of his political opponents
was that special facilities had been granted him to search
public records in the prosecution of his historical labours,
and that he actually had in his possession—quite lawfully,

---

[1] Thomson, *Magna Carta*, 422.

as we know—the Articles of the Barons, which was confused by the carelessness of early historians with Magna Carta itself. The calumny was so widely spread that Burnet thought it necessary formally to refute it, explaining that he had received the Articles as a gift from Colonel Lee:—" So it is now in my hands, and it came very fairly to me." [1]

Bishop Burnet left it as a legacy to his son Sir Thomas Burnet; and on his death it passed to his executor David Mitchell, whose permission to print it Blackstone obtained in 1759. It was purchased from Mr. Mitchell's daughter by another historian, Philip, second Earl of Stanhope, who presented it to the British Museum in 1769. It is now exhibited along with the two Cottonian copies of Magna Carta. The Record Commissioners have reproduced it in *Statutes of the Realm* in 1810, and also in the *New Rymer* in 1816. [2]

The document begins with this headline: "*Ista sunt Capitula quae Barones petunt et dominus Rex concedit.*" Then the articles follow in 49 paragraphs of varying length, separate, but unnumbered, each new chapter (unlike the chapters of Magna Carta, which run straight on) beginning a new line. The numbers, which appear in all printed editions, have no warrant in the original. [3]

IV. *The so-called " unknown Charter of Liberties."* At Paris is preserved a copy of what looks like a charter granted by John, but irregular in its form. This document is preserved among the *Archives du Royaume* in the *Section Historique* and numbered J. 655. [4] A copy of this copy was discovered at the Record Office in London by Dr. Horace Round in 1893. Before that date it seems to have been practically unknown to English historians, although it had been printed by a French writer thirty years earlier. [5] As the interpretation of this document has proved a

---

[1] See Burnet's *Own Time*, I. 32 (edition of 1724).

[2] Reproductions are sold by the British Museum at 2s. 6d.

[3] Cf. *supra*, p. 39, and Blackstone, *Great Charter*, xvii.

[4] See the account by Mr. Hubert Hall, *Eng. Hist. Rev.*, IX. 326.

[5] Teulet, *Layettes du Trésor des Chartes*, I. p. 423 (1863).

puzzle attracting many to attempt its solution, it may be well to give a brief analysis of its tenor.[1] The text of the supposed Charter is preceded, in the manuscript (which is in a French hand of the early quarter of the thirteenth century), by a copy of the Charter of Liberties of Henry I., from which it is separated by this sentence, in Latin: " This is the Charter of King Henry, by which the barons seek their liberties, and these following are granted by King John," words which invite comparison with the heading of the *Articuli Baronum,* and suggest that the document under description may have formed a link between Henry I.'s charter and these *Articuli.*

The first clause runs in the third person (*concedit rex Johannes*) and grants that he will arrest no man without judgment, nor accept anything for justice, nor commit injustice. The remaining eleven clauses are all in the first person singular (whereas regular charters run in the plural). The second clause restricts relief; the third regulates wardship; the fourth, marriage; the fifth, testate and intestate succession; the sixth, the rights of widows. The seventh, opening with the word " *adhuc* " (as though later additions were now made to provisions previously written), concedes that Crown vassals need not go on military service outside of England except in Normandy and Brittany; and seems further to suggest, in certain circumstances, a diminution of the *servitium debitum.* Clause 8 limits scutage to one mark unless by counsel of the barons.

Clause 9, again beginning with *adhuc,* agrees to give up the forests made by Henry II. and Richard. Clause 10 (also with its *adhuc*) grants remission, in several particulars, of the strictness of the forest laws. Clause 11 prohibits Jews from taking interest during a debtor's minority; and clause 12 concedes that no one shall lose life or limbs for the killing of a deer.

At least seven solutions have been attempted of the problems raised by this manuscript. (1) Dr. Round, in communicating his discovery to the *English Historical Review,* maintained that the document was a copy, in a mangled

[1] See text in Appendix.

form perhaps, of a charter actually granted in the year 1213 by King John to the northern barons, containing concessions which they had agreed to accept in satisfaction of their claims.[1] (2) Mr. Prothero preferred to view it as an abortive proposal made by the King early in 1215 and rejected by the barons.[2] (3) Mr. Hubert Hall dismissed the document as a forgery, describing it as " a coronation charter attributed to John by a French scribe in the second decade of the thirteenth century "—probably between November, 1216, and March, 1217, when King Philip desired to prove that John had committed perjury by breaking his promises, and had thereby forfeited his right to the Crown of England.[3]

(4) In the first edition of this work, published in 1905, the tentative suggestion was made that the document might be a copy of the actual " schedule " which we know from Roger of Wendover [4] to have been drawn up by the barons prior to 27th April, 1215, and at that date forwarded to John with the demand, under threat of civil war, that he should forthwith set his seal to it. In this view the schedule would be merely a precursor of the Articles of the Barons, with which it had been previously identified. The fact that this " schedule " was hurriedly drawn up by unskilful hands was suggested as an explanation of the peculiar features of the " unknown charter " emphasized by Mr. Hall; its archaisms, its erroneous royal style running in the singular, and its transition from the third to the first person. (5) Mr. Davis,[5] in rejecting this theory, maintained that the document contained the jottings made by some one present while negotiations were actually in progress between the barons and John's representatives at some date between the drawing up of the *Articuli Baronum* and the sealing of the Great Charter, presumably, therefore, between 15th and 19th June, 1215.

(6) Mr. Petit-Dutaillis [6] modifies Mr. Davis's theory

---

[1] *Eng. Hist. Rev.*, VIII. 288-294.   [2] *Ibid.*, IX. 117-121.

[3] *Ibid.*, IX. 326-335.   [4] Wendover, III. 298, and cf. *supra*, 33.

[5] *Eng. Hist. Rev.*, XX. 719 ff.   [6] *Studies Supplementary*, 120 ff.

materially. The conference, at which the unofficial note-
taker was present, must have taken place shortly before
the framing of the *Articuli Baronum,* and the note-taker
himself may have been an emissary of Philip Augustus,
possibly a spy of humble origin, collecting information in
furtherance of Philip's designs on England. (7) The
most recent, detailed, and ingenious theory is that of Dr.
Ludwig Riess of Berlin,[1] who thinks that a copy of the
first Henry's Charter was sent to John for convenience of
reference when the latter, amid the misfortunes of the ill-
starred campaign of 1214, was trying to make terms with
the rebellious northern barons, and that jottings subsequently made on the blank space at the foot of the parchment, as to concessions granted by John, constitute the
so-called " unknown charter."

Successive clauses of the document tell the story of its
genesis—and a romantic story it is. When the northern
barons met the demand of 26th May, 1214, for a scutage,
by the counter demand for a confirmation of Henry Beauclerk's Charter, John's Regent, Peter des Roches, wrote
to the King, then in Poitou, for instructions, enclosing a
transcript of Henry's Charter, to which he had appended
a jotting to remind John of the promise already made on
28th August, 1213, through Stephen Langton. This note
forms, in Dr. Riess's theory, clause one of the much discussed document. Thereafter a period of haggling ensued
between John and the distant rebels, with Peter and
perhaps also the archbishop as intermediaries, the King
making a careful memorandum from time to time of each
concession wrung from him by the obduracy of the barons.
The King is thus the author of clauses 2 to 12 inclusive,
couched in the informal first person singular, each new
group opening with the word " *adhuc.*"

The original document, which thus represented the stages
of unsuccessful negotiations extending over several months,
was captured, so it is inferred, by the French. After a
copy had been made for preservation at Paris, the original
was sent by Philip to the barons that they might embarrass

[1] *Historische Vierteljahrschrift,* 1910, 449-458.

John by confronting him with concessions in his own handwriting which he now desired to repudiate. When Henry's Charter was produced by Stephen Langton at Bury St. Edmunds on 4th November, 1214, it was the royal jottings appended to it, not the familiar, century-old charter itself, that produced the sensation which modern writers have found so hard to explain.

Such is Dr. Riess's brilliant effort at historical reconstruction : the main difficulties to its acceptance are that it involves too many unproved assumptions; that John, before the failure of his schemes, was unlikely to authorize substantial concessions, or to make careful memoranda of them as though he meant to keep his promises; and that five months, between May and October, would not suffice for the conduct of protracted negotiations between John in Poitou and the malcontents scattered through the north of England.

It is beyond doubt, however, that offers and counter-offers, of which the schedule of Easter was only one, passed to and fro, between March and June of the year 1215. The negotiations of which our document contains a record may have taken place between the respective dates of the " schedule " and the *Articuli*. It would be easy to explain the presence of a copy in the French archives on the assumption that the original was among " the charters of liberties " surrendered by Louis in 1217. This trifling amendment would meet some of the objections to Dr. Riess's theory, which in all essentials seems to be the most convincing yet suggested. In any view, the " unknown charter " would appear to be a link between the Charter of 1100 and the *Articuli*.

It would clearly be inadvisable to found conclusions upon a document, the nature and authenticity of which form the subject of so many rival theories; but even if further investigation proves it to be a forgery, a forgery of contemporary date may still throw light on otherwise obscure passages in genuine charters. Instances of this will be found in the sequel.

II. Previous Editions and Commentaries.

I. *Printed Editions of the Text.* Prior to 1759, even the best informed writers on English history laboured under much confusion in regard to the various charters of liberties. Few seem to have been aware that fundamental differences existed between the charter granted by John and the reissues of Henry. Much of the blame must be borne by Roger of Wendover, who, in his account of the transactions at Runnymede, incorporated, in place of John's Charter, the text of the two charters granted by Henry.[1]

Early editions of " Magna Carta," then, are not of John's Charter at all, but give the text of Edward's *Inspeximus* of Henry's reissue of 1225. The very earliest of these to be printed was apparently that published on 9th October, 1499, by Richard Pynson, the King's printer.[2] The same document was followed in numerous editions by Pynson, Redman, Berthelet, Tottel, Marshe and Wight, from 1499 to 1618. It was not until Blackstone's day, however, that John's Charter appeared in print. Of the numerous editions that have since appeared, only four call for separate notice.

(1) In 1759 appeared Sir William Blackstone's scholarly work entitled *The Great Charter and the Charter of the Forest,* containing accurate texts of all the important issues of the Charters of Liberties carefully prepared from the original manuscripts so far as these were known to him.[3]

(2) In some respects the Record Commissioners have improved even on Blackstone's work, in their edition of the *Statutes of the Realm,* published in 1810. A special section of the volume is devoted to Charters of Liberties, where not only the grants of John and Henry III., but also the charters which led up to them, and their subsequent confirmations, have received exhaustive treatment.

---

[1] R. Wendover, III. 302-318.

[2] This date is given by Bémont, *Chartes,* lxxi., but Robert Watt in his *Bibliotheca Britannica,* Thomson, *Magna Carta,* 450, and Lowndes, *Bibliographer's Manual,* 1449, all give the date of the earliest edition as 1514.

[3] The substance of this admirable edition, now unhappily scarce, has been reproduced in the same author's *Tracts* (1762).

(3) A carefully revised text, *Magna Carta regis Johannis,* was published by Dr. Stubbs in 1868; and the various charters are also to be found, arranged in chronological order, in his well-known *Select Charters,* first published in 1870.

(4) In 1892, M. Charles Bémont published carefully edited texts of the charters of 1215 and 1225, printing as footnotes to the latter the variants of 1216 and 1217.

II. *Commentaries and Treatises.* Within five years of the peace made at Runnymede, a minstrel attached to Robert of Béthune, one of John's familiars, included an incomplete but not inaccurate summary of the Charter in his *Histoire des ducs de Normandie et des rois d'Angleterre,* supposed to have been composed in 1220.[1] This first rude commentary has already been alluded to.[2] Posterity would gladly have bartered it, such as it is, for a few words of explanation from one who was well able to speak but preferred to keep silence. The discreet biographer of William the Marshal excuses himself from drawing upon his intimate sources of information : he must pass over, he says, the war which was in England between the King and his barons, for there were too many incidents which it would not be honourable to recount.[3]

Later in the century, comes the mysterious medieval lawbook known as the *Mirror of Justices,* complaining of " the damnable disregard " of Magna Carta and containing a chapter on that document with some claims to rank as a commentary, although it represents the opinions of a political pamphleteer rather than those of an unbiassed judge. The date of this treatise is still the subject of dispute. It has been usual to place it not earlier than the years 1307-27, mainly because it makes mention of " Edward II." Prof. Maitland, however, dates it earlier, maintaining on general grounds that it was " written very soon after 1285, and probably before 1290." [4] He explains

---

[1] Published in 1840 (edited by F. Michel).   [2] *Supra,* p. 123.

[3] *G. le Maréchal,* 15031 ff.

[4] See *The Mirror of Justices* (edited for the Selden Society by W. J. Whittaker), Introduction (by Maitland), xxiii. to xxiv.

the reference to " Edward II." as applying to the monarch now generally known in England as Edward I., but sometimes in his own reign known as Edward II., to distinguish him from an earlier Edward still enshrined in the popular imagination, namely, Edward Confessor. Mr. Maitland is not disposed to treat this work of an unknown author too seriously, and warns students against " his ignorance, political bias, and deliberate lies." [1]

Reference has already been made to the comparative neglect of Magna Carta in the fifteenth and sixteenth centuries, and to the influence of Coke in reviving interest in its provisions. Of the commentaries that have subsequently appeared, it is not, perhaps, necessary to mention more than the following thirteen. (1) The elaborate treatise of Sir Edward Coke, King James's deposed Chief Justice, comprising the second of his four *Institutes,* was published in 1642 under direction of the Long Parliament, the House of Commons having given the order on 12th May, 1641.[2]

Although this commentary, like everything written by Coke, was long accepted as a work of great value, its method is in reality uncritical and unhistorical. The great lawyer reads into Magna Carta the entire body of the common law of the seventeenth century, of which he was admittedly a master. He seems almost unconscious of the changes wrought by the experience and vicissitudes of four eventful centuries. The clauses of Magna Carta are merely occasions for expounding the law as it stood, not at the beginning of the thirteenth century, but in Coke's own day. In the skilful hands of Sir Edward, the Great Charter is made to attack abuses of James or Charles, rather than those of John or Henry. In expounding the *judicium parium,* for example, he explains minute details of procedure before the Court of the Lord High Steward, and the nature of the warrants to be issued prior to arrest of any one by the Crown; while in the clause of Henry's Charter which secures an open door to foreign merchants in England " unless publicly prohibited," he discovers a declara-

---

[1] See *The Mirror of Justices,* xxxvii. Cf. xlviii.
[2] See *Dictionary of National Biography,* XI. 243.

tion that Parliament shall have the sole power to issue such prohibitions, forgetful that "Parliament" did not exist in 1215, and that the regulation of trade was then an exclusive prerogative of the Crown.

(2) In 1680 Edward Cooke, barrister, published a small volume entitled *Magna Charta made in the ninth year of King Henry III. and confirmed by King Edward I. in the twenty-eighth year of his reign.* This contained a translation of Henry's Magna Carta with short explanatory notes founded mainly on the commentary of Sir Edward Coke. Mr. Cooke declared that his object was to make the Great Charter more accessible to the public at large, since, as he said, " I am confident, scarce one of a hundred of the common people, know what it is."

(3) Sir William Blackstone's *Introduction* to his edition of the charters, published in 1759, as already mentioned, contains valuable information as to the documents he edits; but he explicitly disclaims all intention of writing a Commentary. He is careful to state "that it is not in his present intention, nor (he fears) within the reach of his abilities, to give a full and explanatory comment on the matters contained in these charters." [1]

(4) Daines Barrington published in 1766 his *Observations upon the Statutes from Magna Charta to 21 James I.* This book contains some notes on the Charter also founded chiefly upon Coke's *Second Institute*; his original contributions are not of outstanding value.

(6) In 1772 Prof. F. S. Sullivan issued a course of lectures under the title *An Historical Treatise on the Feudal Law, with a Commentary on Magna Charta*: " I shall therefore proceed briefly to speak to *Magna Charta,* and in so doing shall omit almost all that relates to the feudal tenures, which makes the greatest part of it, and confine myself to that which is now law." [2]

(7) John Reeves' invaluable *History of English Law,* which appeared in 1783-84, marked the commencement of a new epoch in the scientific study of the genesis of English law. Treating incidentally of Magna Carta, he shows

---

[1] Introduction, p. ii.   [2] P. 375 of work cited.

wonderful insight into the real purport of many of its provisions, but the state of historical knowledge when he wrote
rendered serious errors inevitable.

(8) In 1829 Richard Thomson published an elaborate
edition of the charters, combined with a commentary which
makes no serious attempt to supplement the unhistorical
explanations of Coke by the results of more recent investigations. His work is a storehouse of information which
must, however, be used with caution.

(9) In many respects, the most valuable contribution yet
made to the elucidation of the Great Charter is that contained in M. Charles Bémont's preface to his *Chartes des
Libertés Anglaises*, published in 1892. Although he has
subjected himself to the severe restraints imposed by the
slender size of his volume and by a rigid desire to state
only facts of an undisputed nature, leaving theories strictly
alone; he has done much to help forward the study of
the charters, insisting upon the close mutual connection
between the various Charters of Liberties. It is doubtful,
however, whether by this very insistence upon the continuity
of this one series of documents, he does not lay himself
open to the misconception that he takes too narrow a view
of the scope and relations of the Charter. Magna Carta's
antecedents must not be looked for exclusively among
documents couched in the form of charters, nor its results
merely in their subsequent confirmations. It is impossible
to understand it aright, except in close relation to all the
varied aspects of the national life and development. Every
Act appearing on the Statute Rolls is, in a sense, an Act
amending Magna Carta; while such enactments as the
Statutes of Marlborough and Westminster I. have as
intimate a connection with John's Great Charter as the
Confirmatio Cartarum or the *Articuli super Cartas* have.
This is a truth which M. Bémont recognizes, though the
scheme of his book led him to emphasize another aspect
of his subject. His object was not to explain the numerous
ways in which the Charters of Liberties are entwined with
the whole of English history, but merely to furnish a basis
for the accurate study of one of their most important

features. His book is indispensable, but is not intended to form, in any sense, a commentary on Magna Carta.

(10) A brilliant article by Mr. Edward Jenks appeared in *The Independent Review* for November, 1904, whose title, *The Myth of Magna Carta,* indicates the iconoclastic lines on which it proceeds. He argues that the Charter was the product of the selfish action of the barons pressing their own interests, and not of any disinterested or national movement; that it was not, by any means, " a great landmark in history "; and that, instead of proving a material help in England's advance towards constitutional freedom, it was rather " a stumbling block in the path of progress," being feudal and reactionary in its intention and effects. Finally, for most of the popular misapprehensions concerning it, he holds Coke responsible.

(11) In *The Magna Carta of the English and of the Hungarian Constitution* (1904), Mr. Elemér Hantos ably analyzes the numerous and interesting parallels between John's Charter and the *Bulla Aurea* of Andreas II., dating from 1222, and furnishes a brief commentary on both.

(12) M. Charles Petit-Dutaillis, in his *Étude sur la vie et le règne de Louis VIII.* (1894), was one of the first of modern historians to deprecate exaggerated estimates of the value of Magna Carta, insisting that " the barons had no suspicion that they would one day be called the founders of English liberty." [1] More recently, in his *Studies and Notes supplementary to Stubbs' Constitutional History* [2] he has included a brief but valuable discussion of the Great Charter.

(13) The whole of Prof. G. B. Adams' *The Origin of the English Constitution* (1912) is virtually a discussion of the Great Charter, and abounds in valuable suggestions for estimating its tenor and value, and for elucidating its various clauses. It does not aim at being an exhaustive

---

[1] P. 57 of work cited.

[2] This is the title of the English translation by Mr. W. E. Rhodes (1908) of the Appendices to the first volume of a French version of Stubbs' *Const. Hist.,* published in 1907.

treatise, but is intended to supplement rather than supersede existing commentaries.[1]

[1] Of the books and articles containing incidental references to Magna Carta, it is unnecessary to speak; those containing comments on isolated chapters or particular aspects are mentioned *infra* in their appropriate places. The late Mr. Harcourt's *His Grace the Steward and Trial of Peers* contains a vigorous commentary on chapter 39, and his article " The Amercement of Barons by their Peers " (*Eng. Hist. Rev.*, XXII. 732), on chapter 21. The first edition of the present work (published, 1905) evoked a number of valuable contributions to various aspects of the subject; among these may be mentioned Vinogradoff, *Law Quart. Rev.*, XXI. 250-7; Liebermann, *Historische Vierteljahrschrift*, 1907, 231-5; Bémont, *Revue Historique*, 1907, 122-4; Petit-Dutaillis, *Le Moyen Age*, 1906, 277-282; H. W. C. Davis, *Eng. Hist. Rev.* (1905), XX. 719-726 ; Neilson, *Juridical Review*, June, 1905, 128-144. See also *Jurid. Rev.*, March, 1905, 61 ; and *Law Notes* (New York), August, 1905, 94-6 for some legal decisions, Scotch and American respectively.

TEXT, TRANSLATION, AND
COMMENTARY

MAGNA CARTA.

PREAMBLE.[1]

JOHANNES Dei gratia rex Anglie, dominus Hibernie, dux Normannie et Aquitannie, et comes Andegavie, archiepiscopis, episcopis, abbatibus, comitibus, baronibus, justiciariis, forestariis, vicecomitibus, prepositis, ministris et omnibus ballivis et fidelibus suis salutem. Sciatis nos intuitu Dei et pro salute anime nostre et omnium antecessorum et heredum nostrorum, ad honorem Dei et exaltationem sancte Ecclesie, et emendacionem regni nostri, per consilium venerabilium patrum nostrorum, Stephani Cantuariensis archiepiscopi tocius Anglie primatis et sancte Romane ecclesie cardinalis, Henrici Dublinensis archiepiscopi, Willelmi Londoniensis, Petri Wintoniensis, Joscelini Bathoniensis et Glastoniensis, Hugonis Lincolniensis, Walteri Wygorniensis, Willelmi Coventriensis, et Benedicti Roffensis episcoporum; magistri Pandulfi domini pape subdiaconi et familiaris, fratris Aymerici magistri milicie Templi in Anglia; et nobilium virorum Willelmi Mariscalli comitis Penbrocie, Willelmi comitis Sarresburie, Willelmi comitis Warennie, Willelmi comitis Arundellie, Alani de Galeweya constabularii Scocie, Warini filii Geroldi, Petri filii Hereberti, Huberti de Burgo

---

[1] The division of Magna Carta into a preamble and sixty-three chapters is a modern device for which there is no warrant in the Charter. Cf. *supra*, 170. No title or heading precedes the substance of the deed in any one of the four known originals, but on the back of the Lincoln MS. (cf. *supra*, 167) these words are endorsed ; " *Concordia inter Regem Johannem et Barones pro concessione libertatum ecclesie et regni Anglie.*" The form of the document is discussed *supra*, 104-9. The text is taken from that issued by the Trustees of the British Museum founded on Cottonian version No. 2. Cf. *supra*, 166.

senescalli Pictavie, Hugonis de Nevilla, Mathei filii Here-
berti, Thome Basset, Alani Basset, Philippi de Albiniaco,
Roberti de Roppeleia, Johannis Mariscalli, Johannis filii
Hugonis et aliorum fidelium nostrorum.

> John, by the grace of God, king of England, lord of Ireland,
> duke of Normandy and Aquitaine, and count of Anjou, to the
> archbishops, bishops, abbots, earls, barons, justiciars, foresters,
> sheriffs, stewards, servants, and to all his bailiffs and liege
> subjects, greeting. Know that, having regard to God and for
> the salvation of our souls, and those of all our ancestors and
> heirs, and unto the honour of God and the advancement of
> holy Church, and for the reform of our realm, [we have
> granted as underwritten] [1] by advice of our venerable fathers,
> Stephen, archbishop of Canterbury, primate of all England and
> cardinal of the holy Roman Church, Henry archbishop of
> Dublin, William of London, Peter of Winchester, Jocelyn of
> Bath and Glastonbury, Hugh of Lincoln, Walter of Worcester,
> William of Coventry, Benedict of Rochester, bishops ; of master
> Pandulf, subdeacon and member of the household of our lord
> the Pope, of brother Aymeric (master of the Knights of the
> Temple in England), and of the illustrious men [2] William
> Marshal, earl of Pembroke, William, earl of Salisbury, William,
> earl Warenne, William, earl of Arundel, Alan of Galloway
> (constable of Scotland), Waren Fitz Gerald, Peter Fitz Herbert,
> Hubert de Burgh (seneschal of Poitou), Hugh de Neville,
> Matthew Fitz Herbert, Thomas Basset, Alan Basset, Philip
> d'Aubigny, Robert of Roppesley, John Marshal, John Fitz
> Hugh, and others, our liegemen.

The Great Charter of John opens, in the form common
to royal charters of the period, with a greeting from the
sovereign to his magnates, officials, and faithful subjects,
and announces, in the pious legal formula used by impious
and pious kings alike, that he had made certain grants by
the advice of counsellors whom he names. Three features
call for comment.

I. *The King's Title.* Points of interest are suggested by
the form of royal style here adopted. John's assumption
of the royal plural " *Sciatis Nos* " reads, in the light of

---

[1] The sentence is concluded in chapter one (see *infra*)—the usual division, here
followed, being a purely arbitrary one.

[2] The phrase "*nobiles viri*" was not used here in any technical sense ; the
modern conception of a distinct class of "noblemen" did not take shape until
long after 1215. Cf. what is said of "peerage" under cc. 14 and 39.

subsequent history, as a tribute to his arrogance rather than his greatness, when compared with the humbler first person singular used by his father. In this particular, however, Richard, not John, had been the innovator.[1] For a further alteration, John was alone responsible : to the titles borne by his father and brother, he added that of " lord of Ireland." When the wide territories of Henry II., had been distributed among his elder sons, the young John (hence known as " John Lackland ") was left without a heritage, until his father bestowed on him the island of Ireland, recently appropriated; and this brought with it the right to style himself " *dominus Hiberniae,*" a title retained after he had outlived his brothers and inherited their wide lands and honours.

John began his reign in 1199 as ruler over the undivided possessions of the House of Anjou from the Cheviots to the Pyrenees. These lands were held, by him as by his father, under a variety of titles and conditions. Anjou, the original fief of the Plantagenet race, still carried with it only the title of count. Henry II. had, at an early age, become duke of Normandy in his mother's right, and thereafter duke of Aquitaine by marriage with Eleanor, its heiress.[2] These fiefs were held by Henry and his sons under the King of France as Lord Paramount. Long before 1215, John had lost these wide dominions, except the most distant of them all, his mother's dowry of Aquitaine. Anjou and Normandy were irretrievably lost, but he still retained their empty titles; and in this Henry III. followed him at first, until, by the Treaty of 1259, he surrendered to Louis IX. all claim to Normandy and Anjou with their dependencies, in return for a confirmation of his claims on Aquitaine.[3]

Of Ireland, John was still, as formerly, " lord " not " king." [4] The exact denotation of " *dominus* " has formed

---

[1] Coke (*Second Institute*, pp. 1-2) errs in attributing the change to John.

[2] Aquitaine included Poitou and Gascony with the four dependent counties of Angoulême, La Marche, Limoges and Perigord. See Norgate, *Minority*, 132.

[3] See Giry, *Manuel de diplomatique*, 798.

[4] Henry VIII. was the first to call himself " King of Ireland "—a singular proof "of the success of Henry's policy." Gairdner, *Lollardy*, ii. 473.

the subject of learned controversy. It is not, as has sometimes been suggested, an inferior title to that of *rex*,
appropriate only to a preliminary stage of the process
culminating in kingship. The two words imply distinct
relationships differing in kind. The one is national and
the other personal and feudal. Kingship is conferred by
" election " (or at least proclamation) followed by coronation; lordship depends on the feudal contract made with
the individual vassal, by homage and fealty.[1] England,
alone of John's possessions, was held by the style of
" Rex," implying sovereign rule, although John in 1213
had accepted Innocent as feudal overlord. In calling himself " *Rex Angliae*," in place of " *Rex Anglorum* " (as
Henry I. had done), he followed precedents of Stephen and
of Henry II.[2]

No vindication of John's title is given. The simple
words, " *Dei gratia rex Angliae*," may be contrasted with
the laboured attempt of Stephen's second and more formal
charter of liberties (of April, 1136) to set forth a valid title
to the throne; where he describes himself as appointed
(" *electus* ") by consent of clergy and people; consecrated
by William, Archbishop of Canterbury and Legate of Holy
Roman Church; and thereafter confirmed by Innocent,
Pontiff of the Holy See of Rome.[3]

Conscious of the claims of his cousin Matilda, Stephen
here ignores the element of hereditary succession in determining the title to the Crown, and emphasizes the element
of appointment or "election," both of which were blended
in the twelfth, as in earlier centuries, in proportions not
easy to define with accuracy. Professor Freeman pushed
to excess the supposed right of the Witenagemot to elect
the King, and transferred it to the Norman *Curia*. A
recent German writer, Dr. Oskar Rössler,[4] denies that the

---

[1] Cf. *supra*, p. 95. See Orpen, *Ireland*, I. 300 and II. 31, where it is pointed
out that William Marshal refused to support his King against his "lord." For
other theories, see Round's *Mandeville*, 70; Rössler's *Matilde*, 291-4 and 424;
Ramsay's *Foundations*, II. 403; Davis, *England under Normans*, 170.

[2] Stubbs, *Early English History*, p. 122, seems to be in error here.

[3] See Charter in Appendix.   [4] *Matilde, passim.*

Normans admitted the elective element at all. The theory now usually held is a mean between these extremes, namely, that the Norman *Curia* had a limited right of selecting among the sons, brothers, or near relations of the last King, the individual best suited to succeed him.[1] Such a right, never authoritatively enunciated, gradually sank to an empty formality. Its place was taken, to some extent, by the successful assertion by the spiritual power of a claim to give or withhold the consecrating oil, without which no one could be recognized as *rex*. John, secure in possession, contents himself with the terse assertion of the fact of kingship: "John, by God's grace, King of England."

II. *The Names of the consenting Nobles.* It was natural that the Charter should place on record the assent of those magnates who remained in at least nominal allegiance, and were therefore capable of acting as mediators.[2] The leading men in England during this crisis may be arranged in three groups: (1) the leaders of the host opposed to John at Runnymede; (2) the agents of John's oppressions, extreme men, mostly aliens, many of whom were in command of royal castles or of mercenary levies; and (3) moderate men, churchmen or John's ministers or relations, who, whatever their sympathies might be, remained in allegiance to the King and helped to arrange terms of peace—a comparatively small band, as the paucity of names recited in Magna Carta testifies.[3] The men, here made consenters to John's grant, are again referred to,

---

[1] See, however, Chadwick, *Anglo-Saxon Institutions*, p. 355 ff.

[2] Dr. Stubbs, *Const. Hist.*, I. 582, gives the motive of thus naming them as "the hope of binding the persons whom it includes to the continued support of the hard-won liberties." Those named were all moderate men. M. Paris (*Chron. Maj.*, II. 589) describes them as "*quasi ex parte regis.*" Cf. *Annals of Dunstable*, III. 43. The neutrality of the prelates is proved by other evidence. (1) C. 62 gave them authority to certify by letters testimonial the correctness of copies of the Charter. (2) The 25th of the Articles of the Barons left to their decision whether John should enjoy a crusader's privileges; while c. 55 gave Langton a special place in determining what fines were unjust. (3) The Tower of London was placed in the custody of the archbishop. (4) Copies are preserved of two protests by the prelates in favour of the King. See Appendix.

[3] Cf. *supra*, 36; for biographical information see authorities there cited.

though not by name, in chapter 63, in the character of witnesses.

III. *The Motives of the Grant.* The preamble contains a statement of John's reasons for conceding the Charter. These are quaintly paraphrased by Coke :[1] " Here be four notable causes of the making of this great charter rehearsed. 1. The honour of God. 2. For the health of the King's soul. 3. For the exaltation of holy church, and fourthly, for the amendment of the Kingdom." The real reason must be sought in another direction, namely, in the army of the rebels; and John in after days did not scruple to plead consent given under threat of violence, as a reason for voiding his grant. The technical legal " consideration," the *quid pro quo* which John received as the price of this confirmation of their liberties was the renewal by his opponents of the homage and fealty that they had solemnly renounced. This " consideration " was not stated in the charter, but the fact was known to all.[2]

CHAPTER ONE.

IN primis concessisse Deo et hac presenti carta nostra confirmasse, pro nobis et heredibus nostris in perpetuum, quod Anglicana ecclesia libera sit, et habeat jura sua integra, et libertates suas illesas; et ita volumus observari; quod apparet ex eo quod libertatem electionum, que maxima et magis necessaria reputatur ecclesie Anglicane, mera et spontanea voluntate, ante discordiam inter nos et barones nostros motam, concessimus et carta nostra confirmavimus, et eam obtinuimus a domino papa Innocencio tercio confirmari; quam et nos observabimus et ab heredibus nostris in perpetuum bona fide volumus observari.[3] Concessimus eciam omnibus liberis hominibus regni nostri, pro nobis et heredibus nostris in perpetuum, omnes libertates sub-

---

[1] *Second Institute,* 1 n.   [2] Cf. *supra,* 40.

[3] Some editions place here the division between c. 1 and c.

scriptas, habendas et tenendas eis et heredibus suis, de nobis et heredibus nostris.

> In the first place we have granted to God, and by this our present charter confirmed for us and our heirs for ever that the English church shall be free, and shall have her rights entire, and her liberties inviolate ; and we will that it be thus observed ; which is apparent from this that the freedom of elections, which is reckoned most important and very essential to the English church, we, of our pure and unconstrained will, did grant, and did by our charter confirm and did obtain the ratification of the same from our lord, Pope Innocent III., before the quarrel arose between us and our barons : and this we will observe, and our will is that it be observed in good faith by our heirs for ever. We have also granted to all freemen of our kingdom, for us and our heirs forever, all the underwritten liberties, to be had and held by them and their heirs, of us and our heirs forever.

This first of the sixty-three chapters of Magna Carta places side by side, bracketed equal as it were, (*a*) a general confirmation of the privileges of the English church, and (*b*) a declaration that the rights to be afterwards specified were granted " to all freemen " of the kingdom and to their heirs for ever. The manner of this juxtaposition of the church's rights with the lay rights of freemen, suggests an intention to make it clear that neither group was to be treated as of more importance than the other. If the civil and political rights of the nation at large occupy the bulk of the Charter, and are defined in their minutest details, the church's rights receive a prior place.[1] A twofold division thus suggests itself.

I. *The Rights of the Church.* A general promise that the English church should be free was accompanied by specific confirmation of the separate charter, guaranteeing freedom of canonical election, granted on 21st November, 1214. (1) *Quod Anglicana ecclesia libera sit.* This emphatic declaration, which has no counterpart in the Articles of the Barons, is repeated twice in Magna Carta, at the beginning and the end respectively. If the original scheme of the barons showed no special tenderness for churchmen's privileges, Stephen Langton and his bishops were careful to have that defect remedied. It is interesting

[1] Cf. *supra*, p. 39.

to note that, where the charters of Henry II. and earlier Kings spoke of "holy church," Magna Carta speaks of "*ecclesia Anglicana.*" When English churchmen found that the tyrant, against whom they made common cause with English barons and townsmen, received sympathy and support from Rome, the conception of an English church that was something more than a mere branch of the church universal, began to take clearer shape. The use of the words *ecclesia Anglicana* may indicate, perhaps, that under the influence of Stephen Langton, English churchmen were beginning to regard themselves as members of a separate community, that looked for guidance to Canterbury rather than to Rome. John was now the feudal dependent of the Holy See, and the "liberty of the English church" had to be vindicated against the King and his lord paramount : the phrase had thus an anti-papal as well as an anti-monarchical bearing.

In promising that the English church should be free, John used a phrase that was deplorably vague; it scarcely needed stretching, to cover the widest encroachments of clerical arrogance. Yet the formula was by no means a new one : both Henry I. and Stephen had confirmed the claim of holy church to its freedom.[1]

Henry II. had agreed in 1173 to give greater freedom of elections, and in 1176 that he would not keep sees vacant for longer than one year,[2] but avoided sweeping promises of unlimited freedom. His whole reign, indeed, was an effort, not unsuccessful, in spite of the disastrous consequences of Becket's murder, to deprive the English church of what she considered her freedom. John in 1215 receded from the ground occupied by his father, confirming by the Great Charter the promise given by the weakest of his Norman predecessors, in a phrase repeated in all subsequent confirmations.

It by no means follows that "freedom of the church," as promised by Stephen, meant exactly the same thing as "freedom of the church" promised by John and his succes-

[1] See their Charters in Appendix.
[2] See Makower, *Const. Hist. of the Church,* 26, 315.

sors. The value to be attached to such assurances varied in inverse ratio to the strength of the Kings who made them, and this is well illustrated by a comparison of the charters of Henry I., Stephen, and John. Henry used words, which may possibly be interpreted as defining and restricting the grant of freedom,[1] until it meant little more than freedom from the graver abuses of Rufus' reign. Stephen's charter, on the contrary, supplements the same phrase by definite declarations that the bishops should have sole jurisdiction over churchmen and their goods, and that all rights of wardship over church lands were renounced, thus making it a " large and dangerous promise." [2]

" Freedom of the church " had come in 1136 to include " benefit of clergy " in a specially sweeping form, and much besides.[3] It is easy to understand why churchmen cherished an elastic phrase which, wide as were the privileges it already covered, might readily be stretched wider. Laymen, on the contrary, contended for a more restrictive meaning; and the Constitutions of Clarendon must be viewed as an attempt to settle disputed points of interpretation. Henry II. substantially held his ground, in spite of his nominal surrender after Becket's murder. Thanks to his firmness, " the church's freedom " shrank to more reasonable proportions, so that the well-known formula, when repeated by John, was emptied of much of the content found in it by Stephen's bishops. Chapter 18 of Magna Carta embodied, apparently with the approval of all classes, the principle that questions of church patronage (assizes of darrein presentment) [4] should be settled before the King's Justices, a concession to the civil power inconsistent with the more extreme interpretations formerly put by churchmen on the phrase.

In later reigns, the pretensions of the church to privileged treatment were reduced to narrow bounds, and the process of compression was facilitated by that very elasticity on which the clergy had relied as being favourable to the expansion of their claims. It was the civil government

---

[1] Cf. *supra*, p. 97.　　　　　[2] Cf. Pollock and Maitland, I. 74.
[3] Cf. *supra*, pp. 102-3.　　　　[4] For explanation see *infra*, c. 18.

N

which benefited in the end from the vagueness of the words in which Magna Carta declared *quod Anglicana ecclesia libera sit.*[1]

(2) *Canonical Election.* The charter, granted to the church on 21st November, 1214, had been reissued on 15th January.[2] Its tenor may be given in three words, " freedom of election." In all cathedral and conventual churches and monasteries, the appointment of prelates was to be free from royal intervention for the future, provided always that licence to fill the vacancy had first been asked of the King. The bishops present at Runnymede succeeded in having this concession inserted in the very forefront of Magna Carta.

Henry III. in his reissues was made to repeat the phrase *quod Anglicana ecclesia libera sit,* but omitted all reference alike to canonical election and to John's charters to the church. With the Pope's connivance or support, he reduced the rights of cathedral chapters to the sinecure they had been before 1215. It is true that Henry was prone to lean on the papal arm, and that the *Curia* at Rome rather than the *Curia Regis* often dominated appointments to vacant sees : the canons elected the nominee of king or pope, as each was, for the moment, in the ascendant.[3] In spite of Magna Carta, the independence of the English church retrograded during the long alliance between Henry III. and successive occupants of the papal throne.[4]

---

[1] Mr. J. H. Round (*Geoffrey de Mandeville,* 3), speaking of Stephen's " oath " to restore the church her " liberty," describes this as " a phrase the meaning of which is well known." If " well " known, it was known chiefly as something which baffled definition, because churchmen and laymen could never agree as to its contents, while it tended also to vary from reign to reign. Mr. Round attempts no definition. Sir James Ramsay (*Angevin Empire,* p. 475), writing of the phrase as used in John's Charter, is less prudent. " It would relieve the clergy of all lay control, and of all liability to contribute to the needs of the State beyond the occasional scutages due from the higher clergy for their knights' fees." This definition would not have satisfied John.

[2] Cf. *supra,* p. 33. The text will be found in *Statutes of the Realm,* I. 5, and in *New Rymer,* I. 126-7. It was confirmed by Innocent on 30th March, 1215. See Potthast, *Regesta pontificum romanorum,* No. 4963.

[3] Cf. *supra,* p. 141.

[4] Cf. Prothero, *Simon de Montfort,* p. 152. " The English church was indeed

II. *Civil and Political Rights.* After providing thus briefly for the church, chapter one proceeds to give equal prominence, but at greater length, to the grant or confirmation of secular customs and liberties. A general enacting clause leaves details to the remaining sixty-two chapters of the Charter. Some of the more important points involved have already been discussed in the Historical Introduction —for example, the feudal form of the grant, better suited, according to modern ideas, to the conveyance of a specific piece of land, than to the securing of the liberties of a mighty nation; and the vexed question as to what classes were intended, under the description of "freemen," to participate in these rights.[1]

Another interesting point, though of minor importance, calls for separate treatment. John does not state that his grants of civil and political rights had been made spontaneously. Whether deliberately or not, there is here a marked distinction between the phraseology applied to secular and to ecclesiastical rights respectively. While the concessions to churchmen are said to have been granted *"mera et spontanea voluntate,"* no such statement is made about the concessions to freemen. John may have favoured this omission with an eye to the future repudiation of the Great Charter on the ground that it had been sealed by him under compulsion. Perhaps it was to anticipate the repetition of such arguments that the words *spontanea et bona voluntate nostra* were inserted in the preamble of the reissue of 1225, which had been purchased by a liberal grant.[2]

less independent of the king in 1258 than in 1215, and far less independent of the Pope than in the days of Becket."

[1] See *supra*, pp. 104 and 114. For the meaning of "freeman" and Coke's inclusion of villeins under that term for some purposes but not for others, see *infra*, cc. 20 and 39.

[2] Cf. *supra*, 154, where the bearing of these words is discussed.

CHAPTER TWO.

Sɪ quis comitum vel baronum nostrorum, sive aliorum
tenencium de nobis in capite per servicium militare, mortuus
fuerit, et cum decesserit heres suus plene etatis fuerit et
relevium debeat, habeat hereditatem suam per antiquum
relevium; scilicet heres vel heredes comitis de baronia
comitis integra per centum libras; heres vel heredes baronis
de baronia integra per centum libras; heres vel heredes
militis de feodo militis integro per centum solidos ad plus;
et qui minus debuerit minus det secundum antiquam consuetudinem feodorum.

> If any of our earls or barons, or others holding of us in chief
> by military service shall have died, and at the time of his death
> his heir shall be full of age and owe "relief" he shall have his
> inheritance on payment of the ancient relief, namely the heir or
> heirs of an earl, £100 for a whole earl's barony; the heir or
> heirs of a baron, £100 for a whole barony; the heir or heirs of
> a knight, 100s. at most for a whole knight's fee; and whoever
> owes less let him give less, according to the ancient custom
> of fiefs.

Preliminaries concluded, the Charter attacked what was,
in the barons' eyes, the chief of John's abuses, his arbitrary
increase of feudal obligations.   The Articles of the Barons,
indeed, had plunged at once into this most crucial question
without a word by way of pious phrases or legal formulas.

I. *Assessment of Reliefs*.   Each " incident " had its own
possibilities of abuse, and the Great Charter deals with these
in turn.   The present chapter defines the reliefs to be henceforth paid to John.[1]   Vagueness as to the amount due was
a natural corollary of doubts as to whether the hereditary
principle was binding : the lord took as much as he could
grind from the inexperience or timidity of the youthful
vassal.

A process of definition, however, was early at work : some
conception of a " reasonable relief " was evolved.   Yet the
criterion varied.[2]   Henry I., when bidding against duke

---

[1] Cf. *supra*, p. 59.

[2] At an early date, in the midland counties, the thegn with more than six

Robert for the throne, was willing, in words if not in practice, to accept the limits set by contemporary opinion. His
Charter of Liberties promised that reliefs should be " just
and lawful "—an elastic phrase, liberally interpreted by
exchequer officials in their royal master's favour. When
Glanvill wrote the sums to be taken by mesne lords had
been fixed; but the Crown remained free to exact higher
rates. *Baroniae capitales* were charged relief at sums which
varied *juxta voluntatem et misericordiam domini regis*.[1]

Every year, however, made for definition; custom pointed
towards 100s. for a knight's fee, and £100 for a barony.
Two entries on the Pipe Roll of 10 Richard I. amusingly
illustrate the unsettled practice : £100 is described as a
" reasonable relief " for a barony, and yet a second entry
records an additional payment by way of " fine " to induce
the King to accept the sum his own roll had just declared

"manors" paid £8 of relief to the King ; the thegn with six or fewer paid three
marks to the sheriff. See *Domesday Book*, I. 280, b (Derby and Notts). Contrast
Ibid., I. 56, where, however, relief seems to be confused with heriot.

[1] Glanvill's words (IX. c. 4) are ambiguous. He distinguishes three cases :
(*a*) the normal knight's fee, from which 100s. was due as relief (whether this
extends to fees of Crown-tenants does not appear) ; (*b*) socage lands, from which
one year's rent might be taken ; and (*c*) "*capitales baroniae*" were left subject to
the King's discretion. Now "barony" was a loose word : baronies, like barons,
might be small or great (cf. *infra*, c. 14) ; all Crown fiefs being "baronies" in one
sense, but only certain larger "honours" being so reckoned in another. Glanvill
leaves this vital point undetermined, but *Dialogus de Scaccario* (II. x. E. p. 135
and II. xxiv. p. 155) supports the distinction between Crown-tenants and tenants
of mesne lords : only the latter had their reliefs fixed. Madox (I. 315-6) cites
from *Pipe Rolls* large sums exacted by the Crown : in one case £300 was paid for
six fees—or ten times what a mesne lord could have exacted. (*Pipe Roll*, 24
Henry II.) There is further evidence to the same effect : where a barony had
escheated to the Crown, reliefs of the former under-tenants would in future be
payable directly to the Crown ; but it was the practice of Henry II. (confirmed by
c. 43 of Magna Carta, *q.v.*) to charge, in such cases, only the lower rates exi ble
prior to the escheat. A similar rule applied to under-tenants of baronies in
wardship ; see the case of the knights of the see of Lincoln in the hands of a royal
warden in *Pipe Roll*, 14 Henry II. cited by Madox, *ibid.*). It would thus appear
that all holders of Crown fiefs (not merely *barones majores*) were in Glanvill's day
still liable to arbitrary extortions in name of reliefs. The editors of the *Dialogus*
(p. 223) are of this opinion. Pollock and Maitland (I. 289) maintain the opposite
—that the limitation to 100s. was binding on the Crown as well as on mesne
lords.

"reasonable."[1] John was more openly regardless of reason. The Pipe Roll of 1202 shows how an unfortunate heir failed to get his heritage until he paid 300 marks, with the promise of an annual "acceptable present" to the King.[2]

If John could ask so much, what prevented him asking more? He might name a prohibitive price, and so defeat the hereditability of fiefs altogether. Such arbitrary exactions must end, so the barons were determined in 1215: custom must be defined, so as to prevail henceforth against royal discretion. The first demand of the Articles of the Barons is, "that heirs of full age shall have their heritage by the ancient relief to be set forth in the Charter," as though the final bargain had not yet been made. Here it is, then, duly set forth and defined as £100 for an "earl's barony," £100 for "a baron's barony," 100s. for a knight's fee, and a proportional part of 100s. for every fraction of a knight's fee. This clause produced the desired effect. These rates were strictly observed by the exchequer of Henry III., as we know from the Pipe Rolls of his reign. Thus, when a certain William Pantoll was charged with £100 for his relief on the mistaken supposition that he had a "barony," he protested that he held only five knights' fees, and got off with the payment of £25.[3] The relief of a barony was subsequently reduced from £100 to 100 marks. The date of this change, if we may rely on Madox,[4] lies between the twenty-first and thirty-fifth years of Edward I.[5]

Apparently all who paid reliefs to the King were mulcted in a further payment (calculated at 9 per cent. of the relief) in name of "Queen's Gold," to the private purse of the Queen Consort, collected by an official representing her at the exchequer.[6]

The charter here says nothing of socage or serjeanty.[7]

[1] Madox, I. 316.   [2] Ibid., I. 317.   [3] Ibid., I. 318.   [4] Ibid., I. 321.

[5] Apparently its first appearance is in the Inspeximus of 10th October, 1297. See Madox, 318; Pollock and Maitland, I. 289; Bémont, Chartes, p. 47.

[6] See note by editors of Dialogus, p. 238; Poole, Exchequer, 16, 170. The barons in 1258 (Sel. Charters, 382) protested against this, and the practice was discontinued.

[7] Cf. supra, pp. 54-6.

(a) *Socage*. The barons were not vitally interested in socage, that being, in the normal case, the tenure of humbler men.[1] In later reigns the King, like an ordinary mesne lord, contented himself with one year's rent of socage lands in name of relief. (b) *Serjeanty*. The barons cannot have been indifferent to the fate of serjeanties, since many of them held great estates by such tenures. Possibly they assumed that the rules applied to knights' fees and baronies would apply to serjeanties as well. The Crown acted on quite a different view; large sums were frequently extorted by Henry III. By the reign of Edward I., however, the exchequer limited itself to one year's rent[2] for petty serjeanties, which thus fell into line with socage.[3]

II. *Units of Assessment*. Some explanation is required of the three groups into which Crown estates were thus divided—knights' fees, barons' baronies, and earls' baronies.

(1) *Feodum militis integrum*. There is little doubt, in light of evidence accumulated by Mr. Round in his *Feudal England*, that William I. stipulated verbally for the service of a definite number of knights from every fief bestowed by him on his Norman followers. A knight's fee (or *scutum*) became the measure of feudal assessment : *servitium unius militis* was a well-known legal unit. But difficult problems emerge when it is asked what equation, if any, existed between land and service. Unsuccessful attempts have been made to identify the knights' fee with a fixed area of five hides on the one hand, or with a fixed annual value of £20 upon the other. Prof. Vinogradoff[4] has shown conclusively that no fixed ratio exists. Fees have been found as small as one hide and as large as 48; and they vary in

---

[1] It is possible to argue that the custom as to socage was already too well settled to require confirmation : Glanvill (IX. c. 4) stated the relief for socage at one year's value. It is not clear, however, whether this restriction applied to the Crown. Further, no custom, however well established, was safe against John's greed.

[2] See Littleton, *Tenures*, II. viii. s. 154, and Madox, I. 321, who cites the case of a certain Henry, son of William le Moigne, who was fined in £18 for the relief of lands worth £18 a year held " by the serjeanty of the King's Lardinary."

[3] Cf. *supra*, p. 57. See Round, *King's Serjeanties*, p. 33.

[4] *Engl. Soc. in Eleventh Century*, pp. 42-48.

value from place to place, as well as from reign to reign. William I. allowed himself a wide discretion in saddling estates with service : favoured foundations like Gloucester and Battle Abbey enjoyed complete exemption. Yet he did not distribute burdens in pure wantonness; and the majority of holdings approximated to a normal standard of extent and value. Under Henry II. two types appear, the larger of 16 marks and the smaller of 10. Under Edward I. a general appreciation of values seems to have raised the former standard to £20.[1]

The Crown tenant's holding consisted of a fixed number of knights' fees—usually a multiple of five (a troop of ten mounted soldiers forming the military unit of the Norman Kings); and each fee, whatever might be its acreage or rental, owed the service of one knight. Each fee, under the Great Charter, paid relief at 100s., unless the estate, of which it formed part, was reckoned as a barony.

(2) *Baronia integra.* The word "barony" has undergone many changes.[2] A "barony" at the Norman Conquest differed in almost every respect from a "barony" at the present day. The word *baro* was originally synonymous with *homo,* meaning, in feudal usage, a vassal of any lord. It soon became usual, however, to confine the word to king's men; "*barones*" were identical with "crown tenants"—a considerable body at first; but a new distinction arose (possibly as a consequence of the procedure for summoning them to a Great Council as stipulated for in chapter 14 of Magna Carta) between the great men and the smaller men (*barones majores* and *minores*). The latter were called knights (*milites*), while "baron" was reserved for the greater tenants.[3] For determining what constituted a "barony," however, it was impossible to lay down any

---

[1] *Engl. Soc. in Eleventh Century,* pp. 49-50.

[2] See Pollock and Maitland, I. 262, and authorities there cited. "An honour or barony is thus regarded as a mass of lands which from of old have been held by a single title." See also Pike, *House of Lords,* pp. 88-9.

[3] This change was not complete in 1215, but Magna Carta, when it uses "*barones*" alone, seems to refer to "*barones majores*" (see cc. 2, 21, 61). *Cf. infra* under c. 14.

absolute criterion. Mere size was not sufficient. Under Henry II. baronies still paid relief at the King's good pleasure.[1] Richard and John were more rapacious than their father. John, indeed, forced William de Braose, who was heir to the barony of Limerick, to promise a relief of 5000 marks—a sum he was quite unable to pay.[2] Magna Carta, here not merely declaratory, but making an addition to existing custom, fixed £100 as the relief for a full barony (a sum afterwards reduced to 100 marks) irrespective of size or value.[3]

(3) *Baronia comitis integra.* Where a modern eye expects to find "earldom," the text reads "earl's barony."[4] But "earldom" originally meant an office, the chief magistracy of a county, not a title of dignity nor the ownership of land : whereas "relief" was due for the land, not the office. Therein lies also the explanation why the earl originally paid no more for his barony than the baron paid for his.

The position of an earl under the Norman Kings had been something far different from a modern "earldom" : it did not pass, as matter of course, from father to son without the King's confirmation; it did not carry with it any right to demand entry to the King's Council; it was not one of several "steps in the peerage," a conception that did not then exist.[5]

The policy of the Conqueror had been to bring each county as far as possible under his own direct authority; many districts had no earls, while in others the connection

---

[1] *Dialogus*, II. xxiv.   [2] *New Rymer*, I. 107.

[3] Madox, I. 216 ff. As the Exchequer, from the time of Edward I., exacted 100 marks from a barony and 100s. from a knight's fee, the false equation of extent " 1 barony=13⅓ knights' fees" was deduced. Coke (*On Littleton*, IV. s. 112, and *Second Inst.*, 7) is sometimes credited with originating this error, but it appears in *Modus tenendi Parliamentum* (*Sel. Chart.*, 503). To suit the proportion given in John's Charter the equation would need to be " 1 barony=20 fees." There is, of course, no fixed equation ; baronies might be of any size ; we read of land held "*in baronagio per servitium feodi unius militis*" (Northumberland Eyre Roll, 7 Ed. I. ; *Surtees Soc.*, 88, p. 327).

[4] In the *Inspeximus* of Edward I., however, *comitatus* (earldom) displaces the *baronia comitis* of the text. See *Statutes of Realm*, I. 114.

[5] See Pike, *House of Lords*, 57.

of an earl with his titular shire was reduced to a shadow, the only points of connection being the right to enjoy "the third penny" (that is, the third part *pro indiviso* of the profits of the county court) and the right to bear its name. It is true that, in addition, the earl usually held valuable estates in the shire, but he did this only as any other land-owner might. For purposes of taxation the whole of his lands were reckoned as one unit, here described as *baronia comitis integra,* the relief on which was taxed at £100.

Very gradually, in after ages, the conception of an earldom suffered change. The official character made way for the idea of tenure, and later on for the modern conception of a hereditary dignity conferring rank and privileges. The period of transition, when the tenurial idea prevailed, is illustrated by the successful attempt of Ranulf, earl of Chester and Lincoln, in the reign of Henry III. to dispose of one of his two earldoms—described by him as the *comitatus* of Lincoln.[1] Earls are now, like barons, created by letters patent, and need not be land-owners. Thus the words "barony" and "earldom," so diverse in their origin and early development, became closely united in their later history.

III. *Liability of Church Property to "Relief."* The Charter of John, unlike that of Henry I., makes no mention of the lands of vacant sees in this connection, probably because the main question had long been settled in favour of the church. The position of a bishopric was, however, a peculiar one : each prelate was a Crown tenant, and his fief was reckoned a "barony," entitling its owner to all the privileges, and saddling him with all the feudal obligations of a baron.[2]

It was not unnatural that, when a prelate died, the Crown should demand "relief" from his successor. Thus, in

---

[1] See Pike, *House of Lords,* 63. This term *comitatus* was a word of many meanings. Originally designating the "county" or "the county court," it came to mean also the office of the earl who ruled the county, and later on it might indicate either his titular connection with the shire, his estates, his share of the profits of justice, or his rank in the peerage.

[2] This was affirmed in 1164 by Article 11 of the Constitutions of Clarendon, which stipulated that each prelate should hold his lands *sicut baroniam.*

1092, Herbert Losinga paid £1000 of relief for the see of Thetford, an act of simony for which his conscience pricked him. Such demands met with bitter opposition. The Crown, unwilling to forego its feudal dues, endeavoured to shift their incidence from the revenues of the see to the shoulders of the feudal under-tenants. After bishop Wulfstan's death on 18th January, 1095, a writ was issued in William's name to the freeholders of the see of Worcester, calling on each of them to pay, as a relief due on their bishop's death, a specified sum, assessed by the barons of exchequer.[1]

In revenge for such extortions, the historians of the day, recruited from the clerical class, have heartily commended Rufus and Flambard to the opprobrium of posterity. Henry I., in his coronation Charter, promised to exact nothing during vacancies from the demesne of the church or from its tenants.[2] No corresponding promise was demanded from John, a proof that such exactions had ceased. The Crown no longer extorted relief from church lands, although wardship was, without protest, enforced during vacancies.

CHAPTER THREE.

Si autem heres alicujus talium fuerit infra etatem et fuerit in custodia, cum ad etatem pervenerit, habeat hereditatem suam sine relevio et sine fine.

> If, however, the heir of any one of the aforesaid has been under age and in wardship, let him have his inheritance without relief and without fine when he comes of age.

The Crown is here forbidden to exact relief where it had already enjoyed wardship. It was hard on the youth, escaping from leading-strings, to be met, when he " sued

---

[1] *Sicut per barones meos disposui.* The writ is given in Heming's *Cartulary*, I. 79-80, and reprinted by Round, *Feudal England*, 309.

[2] See *supra*, p. 98.

out his livery," with the demand for a large relief by the exchequer which had appropriated all his revenues.[1]

Such double extortion had long been forbidden to mesne lords; Magna Carta was extending similar limitations to the King. The grievance complained of had been intensified by an unfair expedient which John sometimes adopted. In cases of disputed succession he favoured the claims of a minor, enjoyed the wardship, and thereafter repudiated his title altogether, or confirmed it only in return for an exorbitant fine. The only safeguard was to provide that the King should not enjoy wardship until he had allowed the heir to perform homage, which pledged the King to "warrant" the title against all rival claimants. This expedient was actually adopted in the revised Charter of 1216.[2]

The alterations in that reissue were not altogether in the vassal's favour. Another addition made a reasonable stipulation in favour of the lord, which illustrates the theory underlying wardship. Only a knight was capable of bearing arms; hence, the lord held the lands in ward until the minor should reach man's estate. Ingenious attempts had apparently been made to defeat these legitimate rights of feudal lords by making the infant heir a "knight," thus cutting away the basis on which wardship rested. The reissue of 1216 provided that the lands of a minor should remain in wardship, although he was made a knight.[3] Incidentally, the same Charter declared twenty-one years to

[1] Where there had already been a wardship, the relief was thus the price paid by the heir in order to escape from the heavy hand of the King, and was therefore known as "*ousterlemain.*" Taswell-Langmead (*Engl. Const. Hist.*, 51 n.) states the amount at half a year's profits. He cites no authorities, and is probably in error. *Dialogus*, II. x. E. p. 135, forbids relief to be taken, when wardship had been exercised *per aliquot annos*.

[2] See chapter 3 of 1216, which stipulates that no lord shall have wardship "*antequam homagium ejus ceperit.*" See Coke, *Second Institute*, 10. Cf. Adams, *Origin*, 204, on "homage as a recognition of title."

[3] Coke, *Ibid.*, p. 12, makes a subtle and unwarranted distinction depend on whether the minor was made a knight before or after his ancestor's death. The proviso, he argues, does not apply to the former case, because lands cannot "remain" in wardship if they were not in it before.

be the period at which a military tenant came of age, a point on which John's Charter is silent.

In one case, exceptionally, wardship and relief might both be exacted on account of the same death, though not by the same lord.   Where the dead man had formerly held two estates, one of the Crown and one of a mesne lord, the Crown might claim the wardship of both, and then the disappointed mesne lord was allowed to exact relief as a solatium for his loss.[1]

CHAPTER FOUR.

CUSTOS terre hujusmodi heredis qui infra etatem fuerit, non capiat de terra heredis nisi racionabiles exitus, et racionabiles consuetudines, et racionabilia servicia, et hoc sine destructione et vasto hominum vel rerum; et si nos commiserimus custodiam alicujus talis terre vicecomiti vel alicui alii qui de exitibus illius nobis respondere debeat, et ille destructionem de custodia fecerit vel vastum, nos ab illo capiemus emendam, et terra committatur duobus legalibus et discretis hominibus de feodo illo, qui de exitibus respondeant nobis vel ei cui eos assignaverimus; et si dederimus vel vendiderimus alicui custodiam alicujus talis terre, et ille destructionem inde fecerit vel vastum, amittat ipsam custodiam, et tradatur duobus legalibus et discretis hominibus de feodo illo qui similiter nobis respondeant sicut predictum est.

> The guardian of the land of an heir who is thus under age, shall take from the land of the heir nothing but reasonable produce, reasonable customs, and reasonable services, and that without destruction or waste of men or goods; and if we have committed the wardship of the lands of any such minor to the sheriff, or to any other who is responsible to us for its issues, and he has made destruction or waste of what he holds in wardship, we will take of him amends, and the land shall be committed to two lawful and discreet men of that fee, who shall be responsible for the issues to us or to him to whom we shall

[1] See *Coke on Littleton*, Book II. c. iv. s. 112 ; and cf. *infra*, cc. 37 and 43 for the "prerogative wardship" of the Crown.

assign them ; and if we have given or sold the wardship of any such land to anyone and he has therein made destruction or waste, he shall lose that wardship, and it shall be transferred to two lawful and discreet men of that fief, who shall be responsible to us in like manner as aforesaid.

This chapter and the next treat of wardship,[1] a much-hated feudal incident, which afforded opening for grave abuses. It is a mistake, however, to regard its mere existence as an abuse : it seems to have been perfectly legal in England from the date of the Norman Conquest, although some writers[2] consider it an innovation devised by William Rufus and Flambard. Their chief argument is that Henry I., in promising redress of several inventions of Rufus, promised also to reform wardship. This shows that wardship was abused, but does not prove it an innovation.

The Charter of Henry committed him to drastic remedies, which would have altered the character of wardship altogether. Clause 4 of that document removed from the lord's custody both the land and the person of the heir, and gave them to the widow of the deceased tenant (or to one of the kinsmen, if such kinsman had, by ancient custom, rights prior to those of the widow).[3] This was one of the many promises which the " lion of justice " never kept. Wardship continued to be exercised as before, over lay fiefs, throughout the reigns of Henry I. and Stephen. Article 4 of the Assize of Northampton (1176) merely confirmed the existing practice when it allowed wardship to the lord of the fee.[4] The barons in 1215 made no attempt to revert to the drastic remedies of the Charter of Henry I., although the evils complained of had become worse under John's misgovernment.

It must be remembered that " wardship " placed the property and person of the heir at the mercy of the Crown. Even if the popular belief as to the fate met by prince

---

[1] The nature of wardship is more fully explained *supra*, pp. 61-2.

[2] *E.g.* Taswell-Langmead, *Eng. Const. Hist.*, p. 51 n.

[3] " This, it would seem, was the old English rule ; " see Ramsay, *Foundations of England*, II. 230.

[4] It is a common error to suppose that this Assize restores wardship to the lord.

Arthur at his uncle's hands was unfounded, John was not the guardian to inspire confidence in the widowed mother of a Crown tenant whose estates the King might covet. Further, the King might confer the office, with the delicate issues involved, upon whomsoever he would. When such a trust was abused, it was difficult to obtain redress. In 1133, a guardian, accused *de puella quam dicitur violasse in custodia sua,* paid a fine to the Crown, if not as hush money, at least in order to obtain protection from being sued elsewhere than in the *Curia Regis.*[1]

Guardians were of two kinds. The King might entrust the lands to the sheriff of the county where they lay (or to one of his bailiffs), such sheriff drawing the revenues on the Crown's behalf, and accounting in due season at the exchequer. Alternatively, the King might make an out-and-out grant of the office, with all its profits, to a royal favourite or the highest bidder. Commentators of a later date [2] apply the word "committee" to the former type of guardian, reserving "grantee" for the latter. This distinction, mentioned by Glanvill,[3] obtains recognition in this passage of the Charter. Neither type was likely to have the interests of the minor at heart. They had always strong inducements to exhaust the soil, stock, and timber, uprooting and cutting down whatever would fetch a price, and replacing nothing. The heir too often found impoverished lands and empty barns.

William Marshal's experience affords apt illustration. Early in Richard's reign, he married Isabel of Clare, but John, *Dominus Hiberniae,* refused seisin of the bride's Irish lands. When Richard was appealed to, John tried to make conditions : "provided the grants of lands I have made to my men hold good and be confirmed," to which the King aptly replied : "That cannot be : for what would then remain to him, seeing that you have given all to your people ? " [4]

The remedies proposed by Magna Carta were too timid

---

[1] See *Pipe Roll,* 29 Henry II., cited Madox, I. 483.

[2] *E.g.* Coke, *Second Institute,* p. 13.

[3] VII. c. 10. [4] Orpen, *Ireland,* II. 203.

and half-hearted; yet something was effected. It was unnecessary to repeat the recognized rule that the minor must receive, out of the revenues, maintenance and education suited to his station; but the Crown was restrained by chapter 3 from exacting relief where wardship had already been enjoyed; chapter 37 forbade John to exact wardship in certain cases where it was not legally due; while here in chapter 4 an attempt was made to protect the estate from waste.

The promised reforms included a definition of " waste "; punishment of the wasteful guardian; and protection against repetition of the abuse. Each of these calls for comment. (1) *The definition of waste.* The Charter uses the words *" vastum hominum vel rerum "* (a phrase which occurs also in Bracton).[1] It is easy to understand waste of goods; but what is " waste of men " ? An answer may be found in the " unknown Charter of Liberties," [2] which binds guardians to hand over the land to the heir *" sine venditione nemorum et sine redemptione hominum."* To enfranchise villeins was one method of " wasting men." The young heir, when he came to his estates, must not find his praedial serfs emancipated.[3] In 1259, the Provisions of Westminster (c. 20) forbade " farmers " to make waste, or sale, or exile, of woods, or houses, or men. The statute of Marlborough placed such defaulters at the King's mercy.

(2) *Punishment of wasteful guardians.* The Charter provides appropriate punishment for each of the two types of guardian. John promises to take " amends," doubtless of the nature of a fine, from the " committee " who had no personal interest in the property; while the " grantee " is to

---

[1] II. folio 87.   [2] See Appendix.

[3] Another way of " wasting " villeins was by tallaging them excessively. (For meaning of tallage cf. *infra,* c. 12.) Thus Bracton's *Note Book* reveals how one guardian *destruxit villanos per tallagia* (v. case 485); how another exiled or destroyed villeins to the value of 300 marks (case 574); how a third destroyed two rich villeins so that they became poor and beggars and exiles (case 632). Cf. also case 691. Daines Barrington, writing towards the middle of the eighteenth century, went too far when he inferred from this passage " that the villeins who held by servile tenure were considered as so many negroes on a sugar plantation " (*Observations,* p. 7).

forfeit the guardianship, thus losing a valuable asset for which he had probably paid a high price. While the Statute of Westminster [1] merely repeated the words of Magna Carta, the Statute of Gloucester [2] enacted that the grantee who had committed waste should not only lose the custody, but should, in addition, pay to the heir any balance between the value of the wardship thus forfeited and the total damage. More severe penalties were found necessary. Statute 36 Edward III (c. 13) enacted that King's escheators, guilty of waste, should " yield to the heir treble damages." If the boy was still a minor, his friends might bring a suit on his behalf; or after he was of full age he might bring it on his own account.[3]

(3) *Provision against recurrence of the waste.* It was only fair that reasonable precautions should be taken to prevent the heir who had already suffered hurt, from being similarly abused a second time. John promised to supersede the keeper guilty of waste, by two trustworthy freeholders on the heir's estate. These men, from their local and personal ties to the young heir, might be expected to deal tenderly with his property. The " unknown Charter " proposed a more drastic remedy : the lands were to be entrusted at once to four knights of the fief, without waiting until damage had been done. Even the milder provision of Magna Carta was an innovation, and there is no evidence that it was ever put in force.

CHAPTER FIVE.

Custos autem, quamdiu custodiam terre habuerit, sustentet domos, parcos, vivaria, stagna, molendina, et cetera ad ter-

[1] Edward I. c. 21. [2] Edward I. c. 5.

[3] Coke, *Second Institute*, p. 13, enunciates a doctrine at variance with this statute, holding that the heir who suffered damage could not, on coming of age, obtain triple damages, or indeed any damages at all, if the King had previously taken amends himself. Coke further maintains that even after waste, the person of the heir was left in the power of the unjust guardian, explaining that when the Charter took away the office "this is understood of the land, and not of the body."

ram illam pertinencia, de exitibus terre ejusdem; et reddat
heredi, cum ad plenam etatem pervenerit, terram suam
totam instauratam de carrucis et waynagiis, secundum quod
tempus waynagii exiget et exitus terre racionabiliter
poterunt sustinere.

> The guardian, moreover, so long as he has the wardship of
> the land, shall keep up the houses, parks,[1] fishponds, stanks,[2]
> mills, and other things pertaining to the land, out of the issues
> of the same land; and he shall restore to the heir, when he has
> come to full age, all his land, stocked with ploughs and "way-
> nage,"[3] according as the season of husbandry shall require, and
> the issues of the land can reasonably bear.

These stipulations form the complement, on the positive
side, of the negative provisions of chapter 4. It was not
sufficient to prohibit acts of waste; the guardian must
keep the estates in good repair.

I. *The Obligations of the Warden of a Lay-fief.* It was
the duty of every custodian to preserve the lands from
neglect, together with all the usual equipment of a medieval
manor. Outlay thus required formed, in modern language, a first charge on the revenues, before the balance was
appropriated by the " grantee," or paid to the exchequer by
the " committee."

This clause expands and improves the corresponding
Article of the Barons; but the obligation to restore the land
and its appointments " in as good order as the revenues
would bear " came to be regarded as too stringent, obliging
the guardian to use up surplus revenue in repairing waste
committed in the time of the deceased. Henry's charters
modified this: the guardian need only hand over the land
and appointments in as good condition as he had received
them.[4]

New methods of abusing wardship were invented after

---

[1] This term is explained, c. 47. *infra.*

[2] It is difficult to distinguish between *vivarium* and *stagnum.* By Coke, in the
Statutes at large, vivarium is translated " warren "; but that word has its Latin
form in *warrena.* Westminster II. (c. 4) speaks of *stagnum molendinæ* (a mill-
pond). Statute of Merton (c. 11) refers to poachers taken in *parcis et vivariis.*

[3] Discussed *infra,* under c. 20.　　　　[4] Cf. Blackstone, *Great Charter,* lxxviii.

Magna Carta. The Statute of Marlborough (c. 16) gave
to a ward, kept out of his heritage, an action of *mort
d'ancestor* against a mesne lord, but not against the Crown.[1]
The Statute of Westminster I. (c. 48) narrates that heirs
were often carried off bodily to prevent them raising actions
against guardians. The whole subject was regulated in
1549 by Statute 32 Henry VIII. c. 46, which instituted
the Court of Wards and Liveries, the expensive and dilatory
procedure of which caused increasing discontent, until an
order of both Houses of Parliament, dated 24th February,
1646, abolished it along with "all wardships, liveries,
primer seisins, and *ouster les mains."* [2] This ordinance
was confirmed at the Restoration by Statute 12 Charles II.
c. 24.[3]

II. *Wardships over Vacant Sees.* The church had its own
grievances. The Constitutions of Clarendon [4] had stipulated that each prelate should hold his Crown land *sicut
baroniam*; and this view ultimately prevailed. It followed
that all appropriate feudal burdens affected church fiefs
equally with lay fiefs. The lands of a see were, however,
the property of an undying corporation (to use the language
of a later age) : a minority was impossible, and therefore, so
it might be argued, wardships could never arise. Rufus
objected to this reasoning, and devised a substitute for
ordinary wardships by keeping sees long vacant, and
meanwhile appropriating the revenues. Henry I., while
renouncing all pretensions to exact reliefs, retained his
right of wardship, promising merely that vacant sees should
neither be sold nor farmed out. Stephen went further,
renouncing expressly all wardships over church lands; but
Henry II. ignored this concession, and reverted to the
practice of his grandfather. In his reign the wardship of
the rich properties of vacant sees formed a valuable asset of
the exchequer. During a vacancy the Crown drew not
only the rents and issues of the soil, but also the various
feudal payments which the under-tenants would otherwise

---

[1] Cf. *infra*, under c. 18. [2] See R. S. Gardiner, *Documents*, p. 207.

[3] See *infra*, under c. 37, for prerogative wardship.

[4] Article 11 : see *Select Charters*, 139.

have paid to the bishop.   The Pipe Roll of 14 Henry II.[1]
records " reliefs " of £30 and £20 paid by tenants of the
vacant see of Lincoln for six and four knights' fees
respectively.[2]

John reserved his wardships in his charter to the church;
and Stephen Langton thought, perhaps, it was unnecessary
to press for their renunciation, since the promise not to delay
elections would render such wardship unprofitable.[3]

The omission was supplied in 1216, when the provisions
applicable to lay fiefs were extended to vacant sees, with the
added proviso that church wardships should never be sold.

These provisions were supplemented by later acts.   An
Act of 14 Edward III. (stat. 4, cc. 4 and 5) gave to the dean
and chapter of a vacant see a right to pre-emption of the
wardship at a fair price.   If they failed to exercise this, the
King's right to appoint escheators or other keepers was
confirmed, but under strict rules as to waste.

CHAPTER SIX.

HEREDES maritentur absque disparagacione, ita tamen
quod, antequam contrahatur matrimonium, ostendatur
propinquis de consanguinitate ipsius heredis.

> Heirs shall be married without disparagement, yet so that
> before the marriage takes place the nearest in blood to that heir
> shall have notice.

The Crown's right to regulate the marriages of wards
had become an intolerable grievance.   The origin of this
feudal incident and its extension to male as well as female
minors have been elsewhere explained.[4]   John made a
regular traffic in the sale of wards—maids of fourteen and
widows alike.   The Pipe Roll of John's first year [5] records
how the chattels of Alice Bertram were sold because she
refused " to come to marry herself " at the King's summons.

---

[1] Cited by editors of the *Dialogus*, p. 223.   [2] Cf. under c. 43 *infra*.

[3] C. 46 of Magna Carta (see *infra*) confirmed *barons*, who had founded abbeys,
in their rights of wardship over them during vacancies.

[4] See *supra*, 26-3.   [5] Cited Madox, I. 565.

Only two expedients were open to those who objected to mate with the men to whom John sold them. They might take the veil, become dead in law, and forfeit their fiefs to escape the burdens inherent in them; or they might outbid objectionable suitors. Brief entries in John's Exchequer Rolls condense many a tragedy. In his first year, the widow of Ralph of Cornhill offered 200 marks, with three palfreys and two hawks, that she might not be espoused by Godfrey of Louvain, but remain free to marry whom she chose, and yet keep her lands. This was a case of desperate urgency, since Godfrey, for love of the lady or of her lands, had offered 400 marks, if she could show no reason to the contrary. It is satisfactory to learn that the lady escaped.[1]

Sometimes John varied his practice by selling, not the woman herself, but the *right* to sell her. In 1203 Bartholomew de Muleton bought for 400 marks the wardship of the lands and heir of a certain Lambert, along with the widow, to be married to whom he would, yet so that she should not be disparaged.[2]

Great stress was placed on " disparagement "—that is, forced marriage with one not an equal. William of Scotland, by the treaty of 7th February, 1212, conferred on John the right to marry prince Alexander to whom he would, " but always without disparagement." [3] Such proviso was understood where not expressed. It is not surprising, then, to find it confirmed in Magna Carta. The Articles of the Barons had, indeed, demanded that a royal ward should only be married *with consent* of the next of kin. In our text, this is softened down to the mere intimation of an intended marriage: the opportunity was still afforded of protesting against an unsuitable match. Insufficient as the provision was, it was omitted from the reissues of Henry's reign. The sale of heiresses went on unchecked.

Magna Carta made no attempt to define disparagement, but the Statute of Merton [4] gave two examples,—marriage

---

[1] See *Rotuli de Oblatis et Finibus*, p. 37, and *Pipe Roll*, 2 John, cited by Madox, I. 515.

[2] *Pipe Roll*, 4 John, cited by Madox, I. 324.   [3] See *infra*, c. 59.

[4] 20 Henry III. c. 6.

to a villein or a burgess.   This was not an exhaustive list.
Littleton [1] adds other illustrations :—" as if the heir that is
in ward be married to one who hath but one foot, or but one
hand, or who is deformed, decrepit, or having an horrible
disease, or else great and continual infirmity, and, if he be
an heir male, married to a woman past the age of child-
bearing."   Plenty of room was left for forcing on a ward
an objectionable spouse, who yet did not come within the
law's definition of " disparagement."   The barons argued
in 1258 that an English heiress was disparaged if married
to anyone not English born.[2]

Was it in the power of the far-seeing father of a prospec-
tive heiress, by bestowing her in marriage during his own
life-time, to render nugatory the Crown's right to nominate
a husband ?   Not entirely : the Charter of Henry I. reserved
the King's right to be consulted by the barons before they
bestowed the hand of female relations in marriage.   Magna
Carta is silent on the point.   Bracton [3] thus explains the
law :—No woman with an inheritance could marry without
the chief lord's consent, under pain of losing such inheritance ; yet the lord when asked was bound to grant consent,
if he failed to show good reason to the contrary.   He could
not, however, be compelled to accept homage from an
enemy or other unsuitable tenant.   The Crown's rights in
such matters were apparently the same as those of a mesne
lord.[4]

[1] *Tenures*, II. iv. s. 109.

[2] See Petition of the Barons (*Sel. Charters*, 383).   Gradually the conception of
disparagement expanded, partly from the natural development of legal principles
and partly from the increased power of the nobility.   Coke commenting on
Littleton (Section 107) mentions four kinds of disparagements : (1) *propter vitium
animi, e.g.* lunatics ; (2) *propter vitium sanguinis*, villeins, burgesses, sons of
attainted persons, bastards, aliens ; (3) *propter vitium corporis*, as those who had
lost a limb or were diseased or impotent ; and (4) *propter jacturam privilegii*, or
such a marriage as would involve loss of " benefit of clergy."   The last clause had
no connection with the law as it stood in 1215.   Marriage with a widow or
widower was deemed by the Church in later days an act of bigamy, and involved
loss of benefit of clergy, until this was remedied by the Statute 1 Edward VI.
c. 12 (sect. 16).

[3] II. folio 88.

[4] For further information on the age at which marriage could be tendered to a
ward, and the penalties for refusing, see Thomson *Magna Carta*, pp. 170-171.

CHAPTER SEVEN.

VIDUA post mortem mariti sui statim et sine difficultate habeat maritagium et hereditatem suam, nec aliquid det pro dote sua, vel pro maritagio suo, vel hereditate sua quam hereditatem maritus suus et ipsa tenuerint die obitus ipsius mariti, et maneat in domo mariti sui per quadraginta dies post mortem ipsius, infra quos assignetur ei dos sua.

> A widow, after the death of her husband, shall forthwith and without difficulty have her marriage portion and inheritance; nor shall she give anything for her dower, or for her marriage portion, or for the inheritance which her husband and she held on the day of the death of that husband; and she may remain in the house of her husband for forty days after his death, within which time her dower shall be assigned to her.

No forethought of a Crown tenant, setting his house in order, could rescue his widow from the unfortunate position into which his death would plunge her. He must leave her without adequate protection against the tyranny of the King, who might inflict terrible hardships by harsh use of rights vested in him for the safeguard of his feudal incidents. She might, if deprived of her "estovers," find herself in actual destitution, until she had made her bargain with the Crown. She had a right, indeed, to one-third of the lands of her husband (her *dos rationalis*) in addition to any lands she might have brought as a marriage portion; but she could only enter into possession by permission of the King, who had prior claims and could seize everything by his prerogative of primer seisin.[1] This chapter provides a remedy. Widows shall have their rights without delay, without difficulty, and without payment.

I. *The Widow's Share of Real Estate.* Three words are used:—*dos, maritagium,* and *hereditas.*

(1) *Dower.* A wife's dower is here the portion of her husband's lands set aside to support her in her widowhood. It was customary from an early date for a bridegroom to

[1] Cf. *supra,* 63-5.

make provision for his bride on the day he married her. The ceremony formed a picturesque feature of the marriage rejoicings, taking place literally at the church door, as man and wife returned from the altar. The share thus set apart for the young wife was known as her *dos* (or dowry), and would support her if her husband died. In theory, the transaction between the spouses partook of the nature of a contract. The wife's rôle, however, was a passive one : her concurrence was assumed. Yet, if no provision was made at all, the law stepped in, on the presumption that the omission had been unintentional, and fixed the dower at one-third of all his lands.[1]

John's Magna Carta contents itself with the brief enact- ment " that a widow shall have her dower." The Charter of 1217 goes farther, containing an exact statement of the law as it then stood : —" The widow shall have assigned to her for her dower the third part of all her husband's land which he had in his lifetime unless a smaller share had been given her at the door of the church." Lawyers of a later age have, by a strained construction of the words *in vita sua*, made them an absolute protection to a wife against all attempts to lessen her dower by alienations granted without her consent during the marriage.[2] Magna Carta contains no warrant for such a proposition, although a later clause (chapter 11) secures dower lands from attachment by the husband's creditors, Jews or others.

(2) *Maritagium*. It was customary for a land-owner to bestow marriage portions on his daughters. Land so granted was usually relieved from burdens of service and homage. It was hence known as " frank-marriage " (*liberum maritagium*), which almost came to be recognized as a separate form of feudal tenure. Such grants could be made without the consent of the tenant's expectant heirs. *Maritagium* was thus " a provision for a daughter—or per-

---

[1] See Pollock and Maitland, II. 422-3. The ceremony at the church door, when resorted to, was no longer an opportunity of giving material proof of affec- tion to a bride, but a means of cheating her out of what the law considered her legitimate provision, by substituting something of less value.

[2] Pollock and Maitland, II. 419.

haps some other near kinswoman—and her issue."[1] The husband was, during the marriage, treated as virtual owner; but, on his death, the widow had an indisputable title.

The obvious meaning, however, has not always been appreciated. Coke[2] reads the clause as allowing to widows of under-tenants a right denied (by chapter 8) to widows of Crown tenants—namely " freedom to marry where they will without any licence or assent of their lords." This interpretation is inherently improbable, since the barons at Runnymede desired to place restrictions on the King, not upon themselves; and it is opposed to the law as expounded by Bracton.[3]

Daines Barrington[4] invents an imaginary rule of law in order to explain a supposed exception. An ordinary widow, he declares, could not marry again within a year of her husband's death, but widows of landowners were privileged to cut short this period of mourning. " Maritagium " is thus interpreted as a landowning widow's right of speedily entering on second nuptials. This is a complete inversion of the truth; the possession of land really restricted freedom of marriage. Yet several later authorities follow Barrington's mistake.[5] This is the more inexcusable in view of the clear explanation given a century ago by John Reeves,[6] who distinguished between two kinds of marriage portion : *liberum maritagium*, whence no service whatever was exigible for three generations, and *maritagium servitio obnoxium*, liable to the usual services from the first,

---

[1] See Pollock and Maitland, II. 15, 16. *Liberum maritagium*, considered as a tenure, has various peculiarities. The lady's husband became the feudal tenant of her father. The issue of the marriage were heirs to the lands and would hold them as tenants of the heir of the donor. For three generations, however, neither service nor homage was due. After the third transmission, the land ceased to be "free"; the peculiar tenure came to an end; the new owner was subject to all the usual burdens.

[2] *Second Institute*, p. 16.   [3] See *supra*, p. 214.   [4] *Observations*, pp. 8-10.

[5] *E.g.* Thomson, *Magna Carta*, p. 172. Dr. Stubbs has his own reading of *maritagium*, namely, "the right of bestowing in marriage a feudal dependant." See Glossary to *Sel. Charters*, p. 545. The word may sometimes bear this meaning, but not in Magna Carta.

[6] See his *History of English Law*, I. 121 (3rd ed.).

although exempt from homage until after the death of the third heir.[1]

(3) *Hereditas.* Is the third item here mentioned simply another name for either *dos* or *maritagium*? Or, is it something different? It is possible that "the inheritance which her husband and she held on the day of the death of that husband" denotes lands that had come to the lady as heiress on the decease of relations, not as a gift at her marriage. Such lands might be described as held by both spouses; for a husband might even attend Parliament as a baron on the strength of his wife's barony.

II. *The Widow's Share of Personal Estate.* The present chapter says nothing of the widow's "peculiar" or share of her deceased husband's money and chattels; but chapter 26 secured to her the portion of one third allowed her by the existing law.

III. *Provision for the Widow's immediate Needs.* Intricate questions might arise before the land was divided into aliquot portions. Meanwhile, temporary provision must be made for her support. This was of two kinds: (1) *Quarantine.* Magna Carta confirmed her right to the family home for forty days, known to later lawyers as the widow's quarantine. The charter of 1216 notes an exception, on which John's Charter is silent: if the husband's place of residence had been a castle, the widow could not stay there; feudal strongholds were not for women. In such cases another residence must be substituted. In later days, widows were provided with a writ, "*de quarentina habenda,*" directing the sheriff to do her right.[2]

(2) *Estovers of Common.* The widow required more than the protection of a roof; until her dower lands had been assigned to her, no portion of the produce of her husband's manors could be strictly called her own. The estate was held "in common" between her and her husband's heir. It was only fair that, until her rights were ascertained, she

---

[1] Cf. *Ibid.*, I. 242, where Reeves rightly points out that Coke is mistaken, although he fails to notice the distinction drawn, in the passage criticized, between the Crown and mesne lords.

[2] See Coke, *Second Institute,* p. 16.

should be allowed a reasonable share of the produce. Neither John's Charter nor the first issue of Henry III. said anything on this head. The reissue of 1217 supplied the omission, expressly confirming her right to *rationabile estoverium suum interim de communi.* Many explanations of the word *estovers* might be cited : from Dr. Johnson, who defines it broadly as " necessaries allowed by law," to Dr. Stubbs, who narrows it to "firewood." [1] It was the right to supply one's personal or domestic wants : this varied in extent from full supply of all things necessary for the maintenance of life, down to a right to take one kind of produce for one specific purpose only. [2]

In this passage the word bears its wider signification. Such was Coke's view, [3] who held that it implied the widow's right to " sustenance " of every kind, including the right to kill such oxen on the manor as she required for food. Estovers " of common " should thus be read as extending the widow's right of consumption for her own and her household's use over every form of produce held " in common " by her and the heir's guardian prior to a final division. [4] She could not, however, cut down trees.

[1] See Glossary to *Select Charters*, p. 539 : " firewood ; originally provision or stuff generally."

[2] Several instances of the wider use may be given. Bracton (III. folio 137) explains that, pending the trial of a man accused of felony, his lands and chattels were set aside by the sheriff; meanwhile the imprisoned man and his family received "reasonable estovers." (Cf. *infra*, c. 32.) The Statute of Gloucester (6 Edward I. c. 4) mentions incidentally one method of stipulating for a return from property alienated, viz., estovers of meat or clothes. Blackstone, again (*Commentaries*, I. 441), applies the name *estovers* to the alimony made to a divorced woman "for her support out of the husband's estate." Sometimes the word was more restricted. Coke (*Second Institute*, p. 17) says, "when *estovers* are restrained to woods, it signifieth housebote, hedgebote, and ploughbote,"— that is, timber for repairing houses, hedges, and ploughs. Apparently it had an even more restricted scope when used to describe the right of those who dwelt in the King's forest, viz., to take dead timber as firewood. (Cf. *infra*, c. 44.)

[3] *Second Institute*, p. 17.

[4] There seems no reason to restrict her estovers to a right over "commons," in the sense of pastures and woods held "in common" by her late husband and the villeins of his manor. Some such meaning, indeed, attaches to the phrase "dower of estovers" met with in later reigns, *e.g.* in *Year Book* of 2 Edward II. (Selden Society), p. 58, where it was held that such a right (claimed as a permanent part of dower) did *not* belong to a widow.

CHAPTER EIGHT.

NULLA vidua distringatur ad se maritandum dum voluerit
vivere sine marito; ita tamen quod securitatem faciat quod
se non maritabit sine assensu nostro, si de nobis tenuerit,
vel sine assensu domini sui de quo tenuerit, si de alio
tenuerit.

> No widow shall be compelled to marry, so long as she prefers
> to live without a husband; provided always that she gives security
> not to marry without our consent, if she holds of us, or without
> the consent of the lord of whom she holds, if she holds of
> another.

Wealthy widows were glåd to escape from John's clutches
by agreeing to buy up the Crown's rights for a lump sum.
In the year of Magna Carta, Margaret, widow of Robert fitz
Roger, paid £1000;[1] and a few years earlier Petronilla,
countess of Leicester, had given 4000 marks.[2] The Pipe
Rolls mention numerous smaller sums; in 1200, Juliana,
widow of John of Kilpec, accounts for 50 marks and a
palfrey.[3] Horses, dogs, and falcons were frequently given
in addition to money fines, and testify eloquently to the
greed of the King, the anxiety of the victims, and the
extortionate nature of the system. In return, formal
charters were obtained, a good example of which is that
granted to Alice, countess of Warwick, dated 13th January,
1205,[4] containing concessions that she should not be forced
to marry; that she should be sole guardian of her sons;
that she should have one-third part of her late husband's
lands as her reasonable dower; and that she should be quit
from attendance at courts of shire and hundred, and from
payment of sheriff's aids during her widowhood. Another
charter, of 20th April, 1206, shows what a widow might
expect if she failed to make her bargain with the Crown:
John granted to Richard Fleming, an alien as his name

---

[1] See *Pipe Roll* of 16 John, cited Madox, I. 491.
[2] See *Pipe Roll* of 6 John, cited Madox, I. 488.
[3] See *Pipe Roll* of 6 John, cited Madox, I. 488.
[4] *New Rymer*, I. 91.

implies, the wardship of the lands of the deceased Richard Grenvill, with the rights of marriage of the widow and children.[1]

Magna Carta, in substituting a rule of law for the provisions of these private charters, repeated at greater length the promises made (and never kept) by Henry I. in his coronation charter: no widow was to be constrained to marry against her will. This liberty must not be used, however, to the prejudice of the Crown: the widow could not marry without the King's consent. Magna Carta provided that she must find security to this effect, an annoying, but not unfair stipulation. The Crown, in later days, compelled the widow, when having her dower assigned to her in Chancery, to swear not to marry without licence under penalty of a fine of one year's value of her dower.[2]

CHAPTER NINE.

Nec nos nec ballivi nostri seisiemus terram aliquam nec redditum pro debito aliquo, quamdiu catalla debitoris sufficiunt ad debitum reddendum; nec plegii ipsius debitoris distringantur quamdiu ipse capitalis debitor sufficit ad solucionem debiti; et si capitalis debitor defecerit in solucione debiti, non habens unde solvat, plegii respondeant de debito; et, si voluerint, habeant terras et redditus debitoris, donec sit eis satisfactum de debito quod ante pro eo solverint, nisi capitalis debitor monstraverit se esse quietum inde versus eosdem plegios.

Neither we nor our bailiffs shall seize any land or rent for any debt, so long as the chattels of the debtor are sufficient to repay the debt; nor shall the sureties of the debtor be distrained so long as the principal debtor is able to satisfy the debt; and if the principal debtor shall fail to pay the debt, having nothing wherewith to pay it, then the sureties shall answer for the debt; and let them have the lands and rents of the debtor, if they desire them, until they are indemnified for the debt which they have paid for him, unless the principal debtor can show proof that he is discharged thereof as against the said sureties.

[1] See New Rymer, I. 92. [2] See Coke, Second Institute, 18.

The Charter passes to another group of grievances. Chapters 9 to 11 treat of debts, usury, and the Jews, and should be read in connection with chapter 26, which regulates procedure for attaching personal estate of deceased Crown tenants who were also Crown debtors. The present chapter, although general in its terms, had special reference to cases where the Crown was creditor; while the two following chapters treat more particularly of debts contracted to money lenders.

The fact that John's subjects were indebted to his Exchequer did not imply that they had borrowed from the King. What with feudal incidents and scutages, and indiscriminate fines, a large proportion of Englishmen must have been permanently indebted to the Crown. At John's accession many northern barons still owed scutages imposed by Richard. John remitted none of the arrears, while imposing new burdens of his own: the attempts made to collect these debts intensified the friction between John and his barons.[1]

Three rules were laid down. (1) The personal estate of a debtor must be exhausted before his real estate or its revenues were attacked. To take away his land might deprive him of his means of livelihood; for chattels could not yield a permanent revenue.[2] This rule has not found a place in modern systems of law, which usually leave the option with the creditor. (2) The estate of the chief debtor had to be exhausted before proceedings could be instituted against his sureties. Magna Carta thus enunciated for English law a rule that has found favour in most systems of jurisprudence. The man who is only a surety for another's debt is entitled to immunity, until the creditor has taken all reasonable steps against the principal debtor. Such a right is known to the civil law as *beneficium ordinis*, and to Scots law as the "benefit of discussion." (3) If

---

[1] See *supra*, pp. 73-6.

[2] The *Dialogus de Scaccario*, II. xiv., half a century earlier, laid down rules even more favourable to the debtor in two respects: (1) the order in which moveables should be sold was prescribed ; and (2) certain chattels were absolutely reserved to the debtor, *e.g.* food prepared for use ; and, in the case of a knight, his horse with its equipment.

these sureties had, after all, to pay the debt in whole or part, they were allowed " a right of relief " against the principal debtor, being put in possession of his lands and rents. This rule has some analogy with the equitable principle of modern law, which gives to the surety who has paid his principal's debt, the right to whatever the creditor held in security.

Even when the Crown's bailiffs obeyed Magna Carta, they might still inflict terrible hardship upon debtors. Sometimes they seized goods valuable out of all proportion to the debt; and an Act of 1266[1] forbade this practice when the disproportion was " outrageous." Sometimes they attempted to extort prompt payment by selecting whatever chattel was most indispensable : oxen were taken from the plough and allowed to die of neglect. The practice of the Exchequer, in the days of Henry II., had been more considerate; oxen were to be spared as far as possible where other personal effects were available.[2] John's charter has no such humane provision,[3] and the abuse continued. The Act of 1266, already cited, forbade officers to drive away the owner who came to feed his impounded cattle at his own expense. The *Articuli super cartas*[4] went further, prohibiting seizure of beasts of the plough so long as other effects might satisfy the debt.[5]

CHAPTER TEN.

Si quis mutuo ceperit aliquid a Judeis, plus vel minus, et moriatur antequam illud solvatur, debitum non usuret

[1] 51 Henry III. stat. 4 (among "statutes of uncertain date" in *Statutes of Realm*, I. 197).

[2] See *Dialogus de Scaccario*, II. xiv.

[3] Cf., however, the rule as to amercements in c. 20.

[4] 28 Edward I. c. 12. Cf. Statute of Marlborough, 52 Henry III. c. 15.

[5] Henry's reissues make two small additions explaining certain points of detail : (1) the words "*et ipse debitor paratus sit inde satisfacere*" precede the clause giving sureties exemption ; and (2) the sureties are declared liable to distraint when the chief debtor can pay, but will not.

quamdiu heres fuerit infra etatem, de quocumque teneat;
et si debitum illud inciderit in manus nostras, nos non
capiemus nisi catallum contentum in carta.

> If one who has borrowed from the Jews any sum, great or
> small, die before that loan be repaid, the debt shall not bear
> interest while the heir is under age, of whomsoever he may
> hold;[1] and if the debt fall into our hands, we will not take
> anything except the principal sum [2] contained in the bond.

Usury, denied by law to Christians, was carried on by
Jews under disadvantages and risks. The rates of interest
were proportionately high, ranging in normal cases from
two to four pence per pound per week; that is, from $43\frac{1}{3}$
to $86\frac{2}{3}$ per cent. per annum.[3] During his nonage a ward
had nothing wherewith to discharge either principal or
interest, since he who had the wardship drew the revenue.
At the end of a long minority, an heir would have found
the richest estates swallowed up by a debt which had
increased automatically ten or twenty-fold.[4]

Magna Carta prevented this injustice to the ward; but,
in doing so, inflicted some injustice on the money-lenders.
During the minority no interest at all, it was provided,
should accrue to Jew or other usurer; while, if the debt
passed to the Crown, the King must not use his prerogative to extort more than a private debtor might; he must
confine himself to the principal sum specified in the document of debt. The provision that no interest should run

---

[1] The words "*de quocumque teneat*" include Crown-tenants and under-tenants,
and suggest that only freeholders were protected by this clause.

[2] *Catallum* and *lucrum* were the technical words for "principal" and "interest."
See Round, *Ancient Charters* (Pipe Roll Society, Vol. X.), No. 51, and John's
Charter to the Jews, *Rot. Chart.*, p. 93.

[3] See Pollock and Maitland, I. 452, and Round's *Ancient Charters*, notes to
Charter No. 51.

[4] The Crown was sometimes called in to enable a debtor, overwhelmed by the
accumulation of interest, to come to a settlement with his creditors. In 1199
Geoffrey de Neville gave a palfrey to the King to have his aid "in making a
moderate fine with those Jews to whom he was indebted." See *Rotuli de Finibus*,
p. 40. Ought we to view John's intervention as an attempt to arrange a reasonable composition with unreasonable usurers, or was it simply a conspiracy to cheat
Geoffrey's creditors?

during minorities was confirmed by the Statute of Merton,[1] which made it clear, however, that its provisions should not operate to discharge the principal sum or interest accrued before the ancestor's death. The Statute of Jewry, of uncertain date,[2] made interest irrecoverable by legal process. All previous acts against usury were repealed by the statute 37 Henry VIII. c. 9, which, however, forbade the exaction of interest at a higher rate than 10 per cent., and this remained the legal rate until reduced to 8 per cent. by 21 James I. c. 17.

I. *The History of the Jews in England.* In the policy of the Crown towards aliens of the Hebrew race, three periods may be distinguished. From the Norman Conquest to the coronation of Richard I., the Jews were fleeced and tolerated; during the reigns of Richard and John and the minority of Henry III., they were fleeced and protected; and finally they were fleeced and persecuted, this last stage ending with the ordinance of 1290, which banished Jews from England. The details of this long story of hardship and oppression, tempered fitfully by royal clemency, can be only glanced at here. There were Jews in England before the Norman Conquest; but the first great influx came in the reign of Rufus, whose financial genius recognized in them an instrument for his gain, and who would the more gladly protect them, as likely to prove a thorn in the side of his enemy the Church. A new immigration led to the disarming of Jews in 1181, a measure which left them at the mercy of the Christian rabble.

When a disturbance occurred at the coronation of Richard I., on 3rd September, 1189, a general massacre took place in London. York and other towns were not slow to follow this example. The King was moved to anger, not so much by the sufferings of the Jews, as by the destruction of their bonds; for the more the Jews had, the more could be extorted from them. Richard, returning from captivity a few years later, in urgent need of money, determined to prevent a repetition of such interference with a valuable source of revenue. His motive was selfish, but

---

[1] 20 Henry III. c. 5. [2] *Statutes of Realm*, I. 221.

P

that was no reason why the Israelites should not pay for
a measure designed for their own protection. Assembled
at Nottingham, they granted a liberal aid, in return for a
new expedient devised to secure their bonds. This scheme,[1]
for the details of which Richard was probably indebted to
the genius of his great justiciar, Archbishop Hubert
Walter, was of a comprehensive and practical character.
In London, York, and other important cities, offices or
bureaus were established under the Crown's protection,
containing treasure chests, called *archae*, fitted with triple
locks, to be opened in presence of custodians, known as
chirographers, who kept the keys. These were four in
number, two Christians and two Jews, chosen by juries
summoned for that purpose by the sheriff; and they were
obliged to find sureties. Only in their presence could loans
be validly contracted between Jews and Christians; and
it was their duty to see such bargains reduced to writing
in duplicate copies. No contract was binding unless a
written copy or chirograph had been preserved in one or
other of those repositories or arks, which thus served every
purpose of a modern register, and other purposes as well.
If the money-lender suffered violence and was robbed of
his copy of the bond, the debtor was still held to his obligations by the duplicate which remained. If the Jew and all
his relatives were slain, even then the debtor did not escape,
but was confronted by a new and more powerful creditor,
the King himself, armed with the chirograph. Lists of
transactions were preserved, and all acquittances and
assignments of debts, known from their Hebrew name as
" starrs," had to be carefully enrolled.[2] Stringent rules,
codified by Hubert Walter, were issued to the judges when
starting on their circuit in September, 1194.[3]

If this cunningly-devised system prevented the Christian
debtor from evading his obligations, it also placed the
Jewish creditor completely at the mercy of the Crown;
for the exact wealth of every Jew could be accurately

[1] Cf. *Cap. de Judaeis* (Sel. Ch. 262).

[2] Cf. J. M. Rigg, *Sel. Pleas of the Jewish Exchequer*, p. xix.

[3] *Sel. Charters*, 262.

gauged from a scrutiny of the contents of the *archae*. The King's officials knew, to a penny, how much it was possible to wring from the coffers of the Jews, whose bonds, moreover, could be conveniently attached until they paid the tallage demanded. The custom of fixing on royal castles as the places for keeping these arks, probably explains the origin of the special jurisdiction exercised over Jews by King's constables (" *qui turres nostras custodierunt* ").[1] In their dungeons, horrible engines were at hand for enforcing obedience. Such jurisdiction, however, extended legitimately over trivial debts only.[2] Important pleas were reserved for the officials of the exchequer of the Jews, a special government department, which controlled and regulated the whole procedure. Evidences of the existence of this separate exchequer have been traced back to 1198, although no record has been found of a date prior to 1218.[3] John, while despising the Jews, protected their wealth as a reservoir from which he might draw in time of need. Thus, by a charter dated 10th April, 1201, he took 4000 marks for confirming their privileges; and he obtained a similar amount after his rupture with Rome. The charter of 1201 was only a confirmation of rights already enjoyed by English Jews in virtue of the liberal interpretation put upon the terms of an earlier charter, granted by Henry I. to a particular father in Israel and his household, but subsequently extended, with the tacit concurrence of the Crown, to the whole Hebrew race. Under John's charter they enjoyed valuable and definite privileges, which exempted them from all jurisdictions except those of the King's justices and castellans.[4]

When a repetition of the massacres that had disgraced his brother's coronation was threatened in 1203, John promptly ordered the mayor of London to suppress all

---

[1] See John's Charter to the Jews of 10th April, 1201, in *Rotuli Chartarum*, p. 93.

[2] See Pollock and Maitland, I. 453 n.   [3] Rigg, *Op. cit.*, xx.

[4] See *Rot. Chart.*, I. 93. Complaints brought by Christians against Jews were to be judged " *per pares Judei*," a phrase which Harcourt, *Steward*, 228, interprets as equivalent to "the justices or custodes of the Jews," but see *infra* under c. 39.

such attempts: his promise of protection, " even though granted to a dog," must be held inviolate.[1] Protection was accorded, however, only that they might furnish a richer booty when the occasion came: suddenly John issued orders for a wholesale arrest of Jews throughout England. The most wealthy members of their community were brought together at Bristol, and, on 1st November, 1210, compelled to give reluctant consent to a tallage of the enormous sum of 66,000 marks. This amount had been fixed as the result of an exaggerated estimate of the contents of the *archae,* and was more than they could pay. The methods adopted by John's castellans to extort arrears are well known, especially the case of the unfortunate Jew of Bristol, from whom seven teeth were extracted, one each day, until he consented to pay the sum demanded.[2]

It was doubly hard that the race thus plundered and tortured by the King should be subjected to harsh treatment by the King's enemies on the ground that they were pampered protégés of the Crown. Yet such was the case: on Sunday, 17th May, 1215, when the insurgents on their way to Runnymede entered London, they robbed and murdered Jews, using the stones of their houses to fortify the city walls.[3] It is not to be wondered, then, that the same insurgents, in forcing on King John the demands that formed the basis of Magna Carta, included provisions against usury.

The advisers of the young Henry in 1216 omitted these clauses, but not from love of the Jews. They were unwilling to impair so useful a source of revenue, which has been compared to a sponge which slowly absorbed the wealth of the nation, to be quickly squeezed dry again by the King. The Jews were always willing to disgorge a portion of their gains in return for protection in the rest; but their lot became hard indeed when Henry III., urged by popular clamour and the wishes of the Pope, began a course of active persecution. In 1253, a severe ordinance inflicted vexatious regulations on the Hebrews, almost converting

---

[1] *Rot. Pat.*, I. p. 33, and *New Rymer*, I. 89. The date is 29th July, 1203.

[2] See Rigg, *ibid.*, xxiv.   [3] See Miss Norgate, *John Lackland*, p. 231.

their quarters in each great city into ghettos, like those of the Continent of Europe.

This was merely the commencement of oppressive measures, the outcome of the growing hatred with which Christians regarded Jews—a result partly of the heated imagination of the rabble, ready to believe unauthenticated stories of the crucifixion of Christian children, and partly of the fact that rich Jews, in spite of all persecution, had possessed themselves of the landed estates of freeholders and barons and claimed to act as lords of Christian tenants, enjoying wardships, escheats, and advowsons, as any Christian might have done. The scope of this enquiry excludes any detailed account of the stages through which repressive legislation passed. The Statute of Jewry, however,[1] was of exceptional importance; taking from usurers the right to recover interest by legal process, and limiting execution for the principal to one half of the debtor's lands and chattels. In return, some temporary concessions were granted. One by one, however, these privileges were again withdrawn, until the end came in 1290 with the issue of a decree of perpetual banishment by Edward I., who was compelled to sacrifice his royal preserve of Jews, in deference to national prejudice.

II. *Legal Position of the Jews.* All through these vicissitudes of fortune, the legal status of the Jews had remained unchanged in essentials. Their position was doubly hard; they were plundered by the Crown and persecuted by the populace. If John saved them from being robbed by his Christian subjects, it was that they might be better worth the robbing by a Christian king. Yet, for this protection, at once fitful and interested, the Jews had to pay a heavy price; not only were they liable to be tallaged arbitrarily at the King's will, without limit and without appeal, but they were hated by rich and poor as the King's allies. Such feelings would of themselves account for the unsympathetic treatment accorded to moneylenders by Magna Carta; two other reasons contributed. Usury was looked on in the Middle Ages as immoral

[1] *Statutes of Realm*, I. 221.

(although illegal only for Christians); while excessive interest was habitually exacted.

The feudal scheme of society had no place for Jews. They shared the disabilities common to aliens, in a form unmitigated by the protection extended to other foreigners by their Sovereigns and by the Church. As exiles in a foreign land, exposed to attacks of a hostile mob, they were forced to rely absolutely on the arm of the King. The Jews became the mere perquisites or chattels of the Crown, in much the same way as the villeins became the serfs or chattels of their lords. Rights they might have against others by royal sufferance, but they had no legal remedy against their master. In the words of Bracton,[1] "the Jew could have nothing of his own, for whatever he acquired, he acquired not for himself but for the king." His property was his merely by royal courtesy, not under protection of the law. When he died, his relations had no legal title to succeed to his mortgages, goods, or money; the exchequer, fortified by an intimate knowledge of the extent of his wealth (for that consisted chiefly in registered bonds), stepped into possession and could do what it pleased. The King usually, indeed, in practice contented himself with one-third of the whole; but if the relations of the deceased Jew received less than the balance of two-thirds, they would be well advised to offer no remonstrance. The Crown did not admit a legal obligation; and there was no one either powerful enough, or interested enough, to compel fulfilment of the tacit understanding that restricted the royal claims. Whatever the Jew had amassed belonged legally and potentially not to him but to the Crown. Magna Carta, in striking at money-lenders, was striking at the King.

CHAPTER ELEVEN.

Et si quis moriatur, et debitum debeat Judeis, uxor ejus habeat dotem suam, et nichil reddat de debito illo; et

[1] Folio 386b.

si liberi ipsius defuncti qui fuerint infra etatem remanserint, provideantur eis necessaria secundum tenementum quod fuerit defuncti, et de residuo solvatur debitum, salvo servicio dominorum; simili modo fiat de debitis que debentur aliis quam Judeis.

> And if anyone die indebted to the Jews, his wife shall have her dower and pay nothing of that debt; and if any children of the deceased are left under age, necessaries shall be provided for them in keeping with the holding of the deceased; and out of the residue the debt shall be paid, reserving, however, service due to feudal lords; in like manner let it be done touching debts due to others than Jews.

If the preceding chapter deprived Jews of part of their interest, the present one deprived them of part of the security on which they had lent the principal. The widow's dower lands were discharged from her husband's debts, only two-thirds of the original security thus remaining under the mortgage. Even this must submit to a prior claim, namely the right of the debtor's minor children to such " necessaries " as befitted their station in life. Magna Carta, at the same time, with characteristic care for feudal rights, provided that the full service due to lords of fiefs must not be prejudiced, whoever suffered loss. Finally, these rudiments of a law of bankruptcy were made applicable to Gentile creditors equally as to Jews. These provisions, with others injuriously affecting the royal revenue, were omitted in 1216, not to be restored in future charters: but they were re-enacted in their essential principle, though not in detail, by the Statute of Jewry, which limited a creditor's rights of execution to one moiety of his debtor's lands and chattels.

CHAPTER TWELVE.

NULLUM scutagium vel auxilium ponatur in regno nostro, nisi per commune consilium regni nostri, nisi ad corpus nostrum redimendum, et primogenitum filium nostrum militem faciendum, et ad filiam nostram primogenitam

semel maritandam, et ad hec non fiat nisi racionabile auxilium : simili modo fiat de auxiliis de civitate Londonie.

> No scutage nor aid shall be imposed on our kingdom, unless
> by common counsel of our kingdom, except for ransoming our
> person, for making our eldest son a knight, and for once
> marrying our eldest daughter ; and for these there shall not be
> levied more than a reasonable aid. In like manner it shall
> be done concerning aids from the city of London.

This is a famous clause, greatly valued at the time it was
framed because of its precise terms and narrow scope (which
made evasion difficult), and even more highly valued in
after days for different reasons.   It came indeed to be interpreted in a broad general sense by enthusiasts who, with
the fully-developed British Constitution before them, found
in it the modern doctrine that the Crown can impose no
financial burden on the people without consent of Parliament.   Before discussing how far such an estimate is
justified, it will be necessary to examine the historical
context, with special reference to two classes, feudal tenants
and the citizens of London respectively.

I. *Protection of Crown Tenants from arbitrary Exactions*.
Apart from payments such as reliefs and amercements, the
occasions of which were independent of the royal will,
feudal exactions were of two types : scutages and aids.
By these two expedients the King could arbitrarily increase
the burdens of his feudal tenants beyond the letter of the
original feudal contract. Recognized usage, however,
required the consent of the vassals before they were subjected to extraordinary exactions.   The barons were within
their rights in seeking to embody this general principle in
Magna Carta, although it would appear (from comparison
of the versions of 1215, 1216 and 1217) that they had
difficulty in devising a proper formula to give effect to it.
The present chapter attempts a rough compromise of the
question at issue, by requiring consent of the Crown tenants
to all scutages and also to aids other than the recognized
three.[1]

(1) *Feudal aids*. The three recognized aids are here

[1] See *supra*, p. 65.

specified, but no reform is attempted with regard tc them, and in particular (in marked contrast to the care taken in chapter two to define the exact rate of " relief "), nothing is said of the amount payable in name of " aid." It is only the extraordinary aids[1] that are regulated by this chapter : these are not to be taken without " common counsel " or the " Common Council "—for the Latin will bear either of these two meanings, which indeed in 1215 were probably not yet differentiated from each other. If the Crown tenants by " common counsel " could refuse a grant, they could *a fortiori* make one upon conditions; fixing, for example, the amount of an extraordinary aid as well as the occasions of its payment. So far as aids were concerned, there was here no innovation upon existing practice.

(2) *Scutage*. With regard to scutage, the requirement of consent was something very different. Scutage, in lieu of military service, was of the essence of the feudal relation : to make it impossible for the Crown ever to levy a scutage without consent of those who had to pay, was to go much beyond redress of the grievance suffered under John : it was to impose on him restrictions that his father had never acknowledged.[2]

The total omission of this chapter in 1216 may have been partly occasioned by the consciousness that it contained an innovation unwarranted by custom : the reissue of 1217 said nothing of aids, and contented itself, in regard to the vexed question of scutages, with the vague declaration that for the future these should be taken as had been the custom under Henry II.[3]

In spite, however, of the omission of chapter 12 from all reissues of the Great Charter, it was customary for Henry's advisers to consult " the Common Council " before exacting a scutage or aid. This was done, for example, in 1222,

---

[1] " Extraordinary aids " here mean all aids other than the three normal ones.

[2] Miss Norgate, *Minority*, 15, thinks the innovation so undoubted as to justify Innocent's Bull annulling the Great Charter. Cf. Adams, *Origin*, 276 n. : "a demand in regard to scutage which custom did not warrant." Cf. *ibid.*, 221-2, and *supra*, 71.

[3] See *supra*, p. 148.

when a Council granted an "aid for the Holy Land" of three marks for an earl, one mark for a baron, and twelve pence for a knight.[1] The consent of a Council, indeed, was usually taken even for one of the three recognized feudal aids.

II. *Protection of London from arbitrary Exactions.* Some attempt was made to protect the men of London from arbitrary demands : the insurgent leaders in this way discharged part of their debt to an ally with claims upon their gratitude.[2] The Articles of the Barons contained important provisions affecting London; and these were embodied in the Charter in slightly altered terms.[3] The present clause, for example, uses only one word, "aids," where the 32nd Article of the Barons referred to "tallages and aids." There is no evidence to show whether the omission had been deliberately planned, or was the result of inadvertence; and the ambiguity inherent in both words makes it dangerous to hazard a dogmatic opinion on the practical effect of the alteration. Yet a clearly-marked line can be traced between the respective meanings of the two terms when they are technically used.[4]

(1) "*Aid,*" a vague word, is applicable to any payment that can be regarded as, in any sense, a freewill offering. It embraced gifts to the Crown, whether from prelate or burgess or feudal baron. London was stimulated towards acts of generosity by Kings of England both before and after John. There were times when "voluntary" aids (like the "benevolences" of Tudor days) could not safely be withheld.[5]

---

[1] Miss Norgate, *Minority*, p. 194.   [2] See *supra*, p. 35.

[3] See Article 23 (which became c. 33), Article 31 (c. 41), and Article 32 (cc. 12 and 13), and cf. *supra*, p. 117. Whether Article 12 (c. 35) was more a benefit to, than a restraint upon, traders seems doubtful.

[4] See, however, Ballard (*British Borough Charters*, lxxx. ff.) who seems to make the two things shade into each other.

[5] Bracton, I. 288, holds that aids of this sort are personal not predial, for they look to persons not fiefs. *Auxilium burgorum* was sometimes a technical term, meaning sums paid by boroughs in lieu of 'Danegeld. See Round, *Eng. Hist. Rev.*, XVIII. 309. In our text, however, "aids" must be more broadly interpreted.

(2) *Tallage* would appear to mean a toll or exaction imposed on individuals who had no option of refusal. Villeins were talliable at their lord's caprice, without appeal. Liability to tallage, however, did not necessarily imply servile *status*; for the King could tallage all inhabitants of towns on royal demesne. London itself, for all its wealth, political importance, and chartered privileges, still shared this unwelcome liability.[1]

(3) *Comparison of Aid and Tallage.* The " aid," being a voluntary offering, differed fundamentally from tallage, which was a forced payment. In theory, the citizens were free to name the sum they proposed to pay. If the King was satisfied, the city collectively became responsible for assessing, collecting and paying over the money : the King's representatives had no need nor right to interfere with individual citizens. The amount of a tallage, on the contrary, was fixed by the King's Justices, assessed by them *per capita* on individual citizens, who were subject to direct distraint by the agents of the Crown. It was to the advantage of a borough to forestall, by a liberal aid, the Crown's anticipated demand for a tallage, for the hated tax-gatherer was thus kept outside the city gates. An aid was more to the King's advantage also than a tallage : not only was he saved the trouble, expense, and delay of collection, but he obviated risk of loss through the insolvency of some of the individuals fixed upon.

A story told by Madox[2] brings out the contrast. A dispute had arisen between the King and the Londoners in 1255. To Henry's demand for 3000 marks of " tallage," they at first replied by offering 2000 marks of " aid," which the King refused. The citizens then denied outright their liability to tallage, but were confronted with entries in Exchequer and Chancery Rolls which contradicted their contention. On the morrow, the mayor and citizens

---

[1] This statement, for which evidence is given *infra*, is not always admitted. Taswell-Langmead, *Eng. Const. Hist.*, p. 107, says : " The city of London can never have been regarded as a demesne of the Crown." For lists of prelates and barons paying tallage see Ludwig Riess, *Historische Zeitschrift*, Vol. 14, N.S. pp. 21 ff. (1904).

[2] I. 712, citing Mem. Roll 39 Henry III.

acknowledged that they were talliable, and paid the sum demanded.

(4) *London's attempts to escape tallage.* There is ample evidence that London in John's reign was galled by the liability to tallage, and was ready to seize any loophole of escape. John's letter to the city in 1206[1] refers to the serious damage done to his capital by the manner in which tallages had been assessed and collected. A document compiled about 1210, in the interests of London, partly from authentic sources, purporting to be a Charter by William I., declares that all freemen shall hold their lands and possessions " free from every unjust exaction and from every tallage." [2] Finally, Miss Bateson in 1902[3] called attention to a document of nine articles, which seem to be the heads of a petition prepared by the Londoners, probably in 1215, in which they ask *inter alia* the abolition of all tallages except *per communem assensum regni et civitatis.*

(5) *Effects of omission of " tallage " from Magna Carta.* Why, if not through pure inadvertence, was the word " tallage," occurring in *Articuli Baronum,* omitted from the Charter? Widely different answers have been given. Prof. G. B. Adams[4] ingeniously argues that the omission was deliberately made in the interests of London. That city, now a full-blown commune, enjoyed the *status* of a feudal vassal : though liable to aids, its burghers resented any allusion to the servile " tallage " in connection with themselves. If Prof. Adams here interprets their attitude aright, the Londoners were ill-advised to refuse, on any such punctilio, to secure in the Charter incorporation of a definite protection from arbitrary tallage by the Crown— a grievance from which they were destined to suffer for more than a century thereafter.

The true explanation, however, is more likely to lie in an opposite direction. The omission was, perhaps, made deliberately to the detriment of London, in deference to John's strong feeling on a point that did not affect the

[1] *Rot. Claus.,* I. 64.

[2] *Willelmi Articuli Londoniis Retractati,* in Liebermann, *Gesetze,* I. 490, c. 5.

[3] *Eng. Hist. Rev.,* XVII. 726.   [4] *Ibid.,* XIX. 702 ; *Origin,* 358 ff.

barons personally. John, for his part, would be readily persuaded to renounce the right to take "aids" from the wealthy traders of the capital, if he preserved the more drastic privilege of tallaging them at will. The word "tallage" was dropt from the Charter, not to gratify London's pride, but to enable the Crown to have access to the city's treasure chests.

(6) *Nature of the protection accorded to London.* The arrangement of this chapter is noteworthy : after securing redress of abuses pressing on the barons, a few comparatively careless words are added : "in like manner it shall be done concerning aids from the city of London." The words "in like manner" are difficult to interpret, for the two cases are far from parallel. Do they mean that no aid can be taken from London without the same "common counsel of the realm" previously stipulated for the taking of scutages from the tenants in chief? Probably not, for the method provided in chapter 14 for obtaining "the common counsel" would have been peculiarly ill-adapted to protect the Londoners, whose interests were not represented in the baronial assembly. The Petition of nine heads [1] had asked more than this, namely, that no tallage should be taken without common assent "of the kingdom" (that is, of the baronial assembly) and "of the city"—a double consent being thus required, as though "the common counsel" was not enough.

High authorities suggest a different explanation for the clause in chapter 12, which is read simply as an assertion that only "reasonable" aids should be taken from London.[2] If that be so, no criterion of reasonableness is suggested, and such might be difficult to find.[3] Subsequent history sheds no clear light on the intention of this clause. As the chapter was omitted from all reissues, no occasion ever arose of testing its meaning by actual practice.

In deciding between the two suggested explanations,

---

[1] See *supra*, p. 236.   [2] *Lords' Report on the Dignity of a Peer*, I. 65.

[3] In 1168, when Henry II. took an aid for the marriage of his daughter, London contributed £617 16s. 8d., which might afford a precedent for a "reasonable" aid. See *Pipe Roll*, 14 Henry II., cited Madox, I. 585.

however, it should be noted that, though " councils " framed
on the model of 1215 continued for half a century to meet,
they made no claim to interfere with the Crown's right to
tallage London.   Neither Henry nor Edward waited for the
" common counsel of the realm " before enforcing their
demands.

Whatever may have been the intention of the framers of
this clause with regard to London, it is notable that they
allowed that city to stand alone.   Magna Carta completely
ignored that provision of the Articles of the Barons which
extended the same protection " to citizens of other places
who thence have their liberties," meaning the boroughs
whose chartered privileges had been modelled upon those
of the metropolis.[1]   Here, again, the alteration was probably a concession to John made by the barons at their
allies' expense.[2]

(7) *Later history of the Crown's right to tallage the towns.*
The Crown continued at intervals to take tallages from
London until 1340.   It has sometimes been maintained,
indeed, that the *Confirmatio Cartarum* of 1297 was intended
to abolish this prerogative, and a document once considered an authoritative version of the *Confirmatio* bore the
suggestive title of *De tallagio non concedendo*.   It is now
well known that the latter document is unauthentic; while,
if the *Confirmatio* itself was intended to relieve the towns
from tallages, it signally failed.   Edward III. exacted
tallages from London and other towns.   Parliament,
however, succeeded, in 1340, in passing a statute which
abolished unparliamentary taxation of every kind.   This
act, sometimes styled by modern writers " the real *statutum
de tallagio non concedendo*," finally settled the law,[3] but
did not prevent the King from trying to break that law.

[1] Cf. however, Davis, *England under Normans*, 380.

[2] It might be argued that the last clause of chapter 13, extending to all towns a
confirmation of liberties and customs, was intended to embrace this provision as to
aids.   If so, the draftsman has expressed himself clumsily.

[3] See Stubbs, *Const. Hist.*, II. 548.   "Of the scope of this enactment there can
be no doubt ; it must have been intended to cover every species of tax not author-
ised by parliament, and . . . it seems to have had the effect of abolishing the royal
prerogative of tallaging demesne."

Edward frequently disregarded the restrictions placed upon his financial resources, and with varying success. He rarely did so, however, without meeting protests; and the rule of law laid down in the act of 1340 was never repealed.

III. *Magna Carta and the Theory of Parliamentary Taxation.* It is a commonplace of our text-books that chapters 12 and 14, taken together, amount to the Crown's absolute surrender of all powers of arbitrary taxation, and even that they enunciate a doctrine of the nation's right to tax itself.[1] Yet the very idea of "taxation" in its abstract form, as opposed to specific tallages and exactions, levied on definite things or individuals, is essentially modern. The doctrine of the day was that the King in normal times ought "to live of his own," like any other land-owning gentleman. A regular scheme of "taxation" to meet the ordinary expenses of government was undreamt of. It is too much to suppose, then, that our ancestors in 1215 sought to abolish something which, strictly speaking, did not exist. The famous clause treats, not of "taxation" in the abstract, but of the scutages and aids already discussed. It does not concern itself with the rights of Englishmen as such, but chiefly with the interests of barons who held freeholds of the Crown, and incidentally and inadequately with those of the citizens of London. Several considerations place this beyond reasonable doubt.

(1) The terms of the restriction are by no means wide or sweeping; but precise, accurate, and narrow. The "common counsel of the realm" was required for three exactions at the most: for scutages and for extraordinary aids from feudal tenants, and possibly also for aids from the city of London: that is all. Not a word is said of other forms of taxation or other groups of taxpayers. (2) If under-tenants received, by chapter 15, protection against mesne lords, they received none against the King. The Charter affected, not national "taxation," but feudal dues.

---

[1] *E.g.* Taswell-Langmead, *Engl. Const. Hist.*, 106. Dr. Stubbs, *Const. Hist.*, I. 573, considers that these words "admit the right of the nation to ordain taxation."

(3) The scant measure of protection did not extend even to all Crown tenants. The King's villeins were, of course, excluded; and so were even freeholders whose tenure was other than that of chivalry. Socage tenants were left liable to carucage, while the Crown's right to raise the " farms " of its own demesnes was reserved.[1]   (4) The Crown's initiative in " taxation " (here restricted in regard to " aids " and " scutages ") was, under many other names and forms, left intact.   The King required no consent before taking prises and custom dues from merchandise reaching or leaving England, or before taking tolls and fines at inland markets under the plea of regulating trade.   Tallages also were exigible at discretion from aliens and Jews, from tenants of demesne, from London and other chartered towns.   (5) The assembly to be convened for taking " common counsel " was a narrow body, representative neither of the ranks and classes of the community, nor of the separate national interests, nor yet of the various districts of England.   Its composition was homogeneous, an aristocratic council of the military tenants of the Crown, convened in such a way that only the greater among them were likely to attend.[2]

These facts serve as a warning not to read into Magna Carta modern conceptions which its own words will not warrant.   This famous clause was far from formulating any doctrine of self-taxation; it primarily affected impositions levied by John, not *qua* sovereign but *qua* feudal lord. Such as it was, it was omitted, along with its corollary (chapter 14), in 1216 and subsequent reissues.

CHAPTER THIRTEEN.

Et civitas Londonie habeat omnes antiquas libertates et liberas consuetudines suas, tam per terras, quam per aquas. Preterea volumus et concedimus quod omnes alie civitates,

---

[1] See *infra*, under c. 25.

[2] Even when an honour escheated, its tenants "were not suitors of the *Curia Regis*." See *Report on Dignity of a Peer*, I. 60.

et burgi, et ville, et portus, habeant omnes libertates et liberas consuetudines suas.

> And the city of London shall have all its ancient liberties and free customs, as well by land as by water; furthermore, we decree and grant that all other cities, boroughs, towns, and ports shall have all their liberties and free customs.

A full list of London's liberties and customs would be a long one; and to relate how each of these grew up and was confirmed by the Crown need not be here attempted. The most cherished of the privileges enjoyed in John's day by the citizens were the right to appoint a civic chief, who bore the name of mayor, and the right to choose the sheriffs who should collect the city's *firma* [1] (or annual rent payable to the exchequer), so as to obviate the intrusion of royal bailiffs. Only a brief account of the way in which the metropolis obtained these privileges is here required.

The chief feature of London before the Norman Conquest seems to have been lack of proper municipal organization. Dr. Stubbs describes the capital during the eleventh century as "a bundle of communities, townships, parishes, and lordships, of which each has its own constitution." [2] It was thus a collection of small administrative units, rather than one large unit. Some semblance of legal unity was, it is true, afforded by the folkmoot, in which the citizens regularly assembled; by its smaller council known as "husteng"; and perhaps also by its "cnihtengild" (if, indeed, this third body be not entirely mythical); while the existence of a "portreeve" shows that for some financial purposes the city was treated as one whole. London, however, prior to the reign of Henry I. was far from possessing the machinery of an efficient municipal government.

The first step towards a constitution is generally supposed to have been taken by the citizens when they obtained a charter from Henry I. in the last years of his reign (1130-35). This is not strictly accurate. London, indeed, by that

---

[1] *Firma* is explained *infra*, c. 25.

[2] Stubbs, *Const. Hist.*, I. 439. Round, *Commune*, 220, is in substantial agreement. Miss Bateson, however, thinks "there has been a tendency unduly to minimise the measure of administrative unity in the twelfth-century shire of London." See evidence produced by her, *Engl. Hist. Rev.*, XVII. 480-510.

grant gained valuable privileges; but it did not obtain a constitution. The chief rights actually conferred by Henry were as follows :—(1) The *firma* was fixed at the reduced rate of £300 per annum, the citizens obtaining a lease in perpetuity of their own city with the surrounding county of Middlesex—the grant being made to the citizens and their heirs; (2) they acquired the right to appoint the sheriffs of London and Middlesex, implying the exclusion of the King's tax-collectors by men of their own choosing; (3) a similar right of appointing their own nominee as justiciar was also conferred on them, to the exclusion apparently of the royal justices of eyre. Many minor privileges were confirmed which need not here be specified. Mr. J. H. Round[1] argues with convincing force that these concessions, important as they were, did not confer a civic constitution upon London. Henry's charter, in his opinion, confirmed the separate jurisdictions and franchises, perpetuating the old state of disunion, rather than creating a new principle of cohesion. Mr. Round proves, further, that the new concessions were cancelled by Stephen in 1141, when Geoffrey de Mandeville compelled Stephen to appoint him as sheriff and justiciar of London. Earlier in the same year, the citizens had risen against Matilda and tried to establish a sworn Commune, presumably of the continental type.[2] When London was placed in Earl Geoffrey's hands, all vestige of this would be swept away, along with any of the privileges granted by Henry I. that had endured till then.

Henry II., indeed, granted a charter in 1155, which is usually interpreted as a full confirmation of the concessions of the earlier Henry.[3] Mr. Round has proved the error of this opinion.[4] The charter of 1155 restricted, rather than enlarged, the privileges of London, being couched in cautious and somewhat grudging terms. The main concessions of the earlier charter were omitted : the citizens no longer elected their sheriffs or justiciar; the reduction of the

[1] *Geoffrey de Mandeville*, 356.   [2] William of Malmesbury, II. 576.
[3] See *e.g.* Miss Norgate, *Angevin Kings*, II. 471.
[4] *Geoffrey*, 367.

firma to £300 was not confirmed; and subsequent pipe rolls show that Henry doubled that amount.

The next crisis came early in Richard's reign. Then it was, perhaps, that London obtained its municipal constitution. Then also it may have regained the privileges precariously held under Henry I. and Stephen. The form in which the constitution came at last was, Mr. Round argues, borrowed from France, and was neither more nor less than the *Commune,* so well known on the Continent in the twelfth and thirteenth centuries. Mr. Round[1] has shown that these concessions were not, as has sometimes been supposed, voluntarily granted in 1189 by Richard I., but were extorted from his brother John, when that ambitious prince was bidding for powerful allies to support his claim to act as Regent. London, Mr. Round maintains, got its constitution on 8th October, 1191, under picturesque and memorable circumstances. While Richard tarried in the Holy Land, a scramble took place at home for the right to represent him. The Chancellor Longchamp had been appointed Regent; but John, wily and unscrupulous, ousted him, with the help of the men of London. At the critical moment, the metropolis had offered support on conditions, which included restoration of the short-lived privileges conferred by Henry I., and, in addition, a municipal constitution of the continental type.

Mr. Round, in a notable passage, describes the scene. " When, in the crisis of October, 1191, the administration found itself paralysed by the conflict between John, as the King's brother, and Longchamp, as the King's representative, London, finding that she held the scales, promptly named the ' Commune ' as the price of her support. The chronicles of the day enable us to picture to ourselves the scene, as the excited citizens, who had poured forth overnight, with lanterns and torches to welcome John to the capital, streamed together on the morning of the eventful 8th October at the well-known sound of the great bell, swinging out from its campanile in St. Paul's Churchyard. There they heard John take the oath to the ' Commune,'

---

[1] *Commune of London,* 222.

like a French king or lord; and then London, for the first time, had a municipality of her own." [1]

For any accurate definition of a Commune we look in vain to contemporary writers. Richard of Devizes [2] quotes with approval, "*Communia est tumor plebis, timor regni, tepor sacerdotii.*" Some insight has been gained in recent years, however, into its exact nature. A Commune was a town that had obtained recognition as a corporate entity, as a link in the feudal chain, becoming the free vassal of the King or other lord, and itself capable of having sub-vassals of its own. [3] Its chief institutions were a mayor and elective council, generally composed of twenty-four members, some or all of whom were known as *échevins* or *skivini*. Perhaps, the chief peculiarity of the Commune was the method of its formation, namely, by popular association or conspiracy, involving the taking of an oath of a more or less revolutionary nature by the citizens, and its subsequent ratification by those in authority. It is generally admitted that these communes, though revolutionary in origin, were not necessarily democratic in their sympathies.

From 1191 onwards, London was governed by its own mayor, an official chosen by the citizens, but holding office for life, until the citizens obtained a further concession in 1215. It has sometimes been argued that as a mayor was the natural head of a Commune, the continued existence of the one implied the existence of the other. It seems more likely, however, that if a Commune was actually set up in 1191, it did not long survive Richard's return from captivity. Mayors were to be found in the twelfth century ruling over boroughs that were not technically "Communes"; and Richard may have been willing to accept a mayor of London's choosing, while he repudiated the city's claim to independence as a Commune.

When John became King, he granted three charters to the capital for a *gersuma* (or slump payment) of 3000

---

[1] *Commune of London,* 224.   [2] *Select Charters,* p. 252.

[3] Luchaire, *Communes Françaises,* p. 97, defines it as "*seigneurie collective populaire.*"

marks.[1] All franchises specified in the charter of Henry I. were confirmed, with one exception : the liberty to appoint a justiciar of their own, now seen to be inconsistent with the Crown's centralizing policy, was abandoned. None of these charters made mention of mayor or commune, but they confirmed some minor privileges gained in Richard's reign.[2]

A fourth charter, dated 20th March, 1201, was of temporary interest. The fifth and last of the series came in the crisis of 1215, and some light is possibly shed on it by comparison with the petition of nine articles already mentioned,[3] which seems to represent the demands made by the Londoners at that date. Besides exemption from arbitrary tallage and several minor concessions, they demanded the control of Thames, the annual election of their mayor in the folkmoot, freedom of access for foreign traders, and the right to distrain for debt against the persons and property of debtors.

Some of these demands were granted by John's fifth charter, dated 9th May, 1215, some five weeks previous to Magna Charter, and representing the bait thrown by John to gain their support in this new crisis as he had gained it in the earlier crisis of 1191. The men of London obtained the right to appoint a mayor annually, and, if they chose, to depose him at the year's end and appoint another in his place, a right which Miss Norgate aptly calls " the crowning privilege of a fully constituted municipality." [4] The charter at the same time confirms all liberties already enjoyed, " as well within London as without, as well on water as on land, *salva nobis chamberlengia nostra*." The control of Thames and Medway, mentioned with more particularity in Magna Carta, seems to be here granted; while the freedom of access of foreign merchants is qualified

---

[1] Miss Bateson, *Engl. Hist. Rev.*, XVII. 508.

[2] *E.g.* removal of obstacles in Thames and Medway. Cf. *infra*, c. 33.

[3] *Supra*, p. 236.

[4] *John Lackland*, 228. From this date the list of mayors shows frequent, sometimes annual, changes. Serlo, the mercer, was mayor in May, 1215, when London opened its gates to the insurgents, while William Hardell had succeeded him before 2nd June, 1216.

by John's reservation of the right to take toll from them by appropriating such of their choicest wares as his chamberlain might select for the royal household.[1]

If the nine articles contain London's demands in 1215, the Charter of 9th May gives what John was willing to promise in return for the city's support; and the *Articuli Baronum* what the barons compelled him to grant to the city after it had preferred their alliance to his; while Magna Carta shows some slight modifications in the King's favour.

Such was the London whose privileges were confirmed by chapter 13 of Magna Carta in words that avoided details and confined themselves to a general confirmation of ancient "liberties and free customs." [2] Neither mayor nor Commune is mentioned; but the question has been raised whether by implication the Great Charter does not recognize the existence of one or both of these.

As the charter of 9th May had granted to London the right to elect a mayor, and as the mayor was appointed one of the 25 executors under chapter 61, it is clear that Magna Carta accepted that magistrate as head of the city's government; and the recognition of a mayor has sometimes been held to suggest also the recognition of a Commune. Professor Adams, on the other hand, has based an argument for the existence of a Commune after June, 1215, mainly upon the omission of the word tallage from chapter 12, which thus makes it possible to infer that an *auxilium* is the only imposition to be lawfully levied on London.[3] He seeks to show, further, that London lost this status of a Commune in 1216, when the charter was reissued without the chapter associating London with the payment of *auxilium* : " this clause was omitted, and with it London's legal right to a Commune fell to the ground." [4]

[1] See text of Charter in *Sel. Chart.*, 315.

[2] The meaning of both words is discussed *infra*, c. 39.

[3] See *supra*, p. 236. M. Petit-Dutaillis (*Studies Supplementary*, 102) doubts whether the citizens in 1215 had any wish to become a Commune, and holds that their desire was to escape burdensome exactions, no matter what these might be called. Prof. Adams (*Origin*, 367) maintains, in reply, that the only practicable method of effecting this exemption was to obtain recognition as a Commune.

[4] *Ibid.*, 361.

It is pertinent to note, however, that the Patent Rolls for 1221 [1] refer to " the mayor and Commune of London." If this implies the existence of a real Commune of the continental type, the date of its final abolition may possibly have been the year following, when London quarrelled with the young King's ministers and had difficulty in making peace.[2] On the whole, it must be left an open question whether or not the privileges granted to London in 1215 included the establishment of a Commune, and, if so, when that form of municipal government came to an end.

In this chapter of John's Magna Carta (in contrast with the last clause of chapter 12), London did not stand alone. "All other cities, boroughs, towns and ports " were confirmed in their liberties and free customs. A specification of these was, of course, impossible; each borough was left to prove its privileges as best it might. In the reissues of Henry, London shared the distinction of being mentioned by name with " the barons of the Cinque ports," who from their wealth, their situation, and their fleet, were allies worth conciliating. They played, indeed, a prominent part in the decisive naval victory gained by Hubert de Burgh on 24th August, 1217.[3]

Among the most cherished privileges claimed by the chartered boroughs were the rights to exact tolls and to place oppressive restrictions upon rival traders not members of their guilds, foreigners and denizens alike. The general confirmation of privileges in this chapter has been held to contradict chapter 41, which grants protection and immunities to foreign merchants.[4] The inconsistency, however, is perhaps greater in appearance than reality, since the later chapter aimed at abolition of " evil customs" inflicted by the King, not of those inflicted by the boroughs. At the same time, any favour shown to aliens would be bitterly resented by English traders. If the charter had been put in force in its integrity, the more specific privileges in favour of foreign merchants would have prevailed in

---

[1] *Rot. Pat.*, 303-4.

[2] See Norgate, *Minority*, 186, and authorities there cited.

[3] See *supra*, p. 145.   [4] Cf. Pollock and Maitland, I. 447-8.

opposition to the vague confirmation of borough " liberties," wherever the two conflicted.[1]

Other portions of John's Great Charter that specially affected Londoners were the last clause of chapter 12, and chapters 33 and 41; while many of the privileges granted or confirmed in other chapters were shared by them.

CHAPTER FOURTEEN.

ET ad habendum commune consilium regni, de auxilio assidendo aliter quam in tribus casibus predictis, vel de scutagio assidendo, summoneri faciemus archiepiscopos, episcopos, abbates, comites, et majores barones, sigillatim per litteras nostras; et preterea faciemus summoneri in generali, per vicecomites et ballivos nostros, omnes illos qui de nobis tenent in capite; ad certum diem, scilicet ad terminum quadraginta dierum ad minus, et ad certum locum; et in omnibus litteris illius summonicionis causam summonicionis exprimemus; et sic facta summonicione negocium ad diem assignatum procedat secundum consilium illorum qui presentes fuerint, quamvis non omnes summoniti venerint.

> And for obtaining the common counsel of the kingdom anent the assessing of an aid (except in the three cases aforesaid) or of a scutage, we will cause to be summoned the archbishops, bishops, abbots, earls, and greater barons, severally by our letters; and we will moreover cause to be summoned generally, through our sheriffs and bailiffs, all others who hold of us in chief, for a fixed date, namely, after the expiry of at least forty days, and at a fixed place; and in all letters of such summons we will specify the reason of the summons. And when the summons has thus been made, the business shall proceed on the day appointed, according to the counsel of such as are present, although not all who were summoned have come.

This chapter, which has no equivalent among the Articles of the Barons, appears here incidentally: it would never have found a place in Magna Carta but for the need of machinery to give effect to chapter 12.[2]

[1] Cf. *infra*, c. 41.

[2] On the whole subject of the *commune concilium*, cf. *supra*, 129-131 and 149.

As chapter 12 is frequently supposed to enunciate a general doctrine of *taxation,* so this one is cited as enunciating a doctrine of *parliamentary representation*; while the close connection between the chapters is taken as evidence that the framers of Magna Carta had grasped the essentially modern principle that taxation and representation ought always to go together.[1] In this view, the barons at Runnymede are given credit for anticipating the best features of modern parliamentary government. The text, however, will scarcely bear so liberal an interpretation.[2] Vital points of difference between the principles of Magna Carta and the modern doctrine of representation are revealed by analysis.

Under chapter 12, scutages and extraordinary aids could only be levied " with common counsel of our kingdom," and now chapter 14 fixes authoritatively the composition of an assembly charged with this function. The same Latin words which signify joint " consent " or counsel came to signify also the " Common Council," afterwards of vital constitutional importance, continuing under a new name the old *curia regis,* and passing in turn into the modern Parliament. The duties and constitutional importance of this *commune concilium* may be considered under six heads.

I. *Nature of the Summons.* Formal writs had to be issued, specifying the time, place, and reason of assembling, at least forty days in advance. Each of the really powerful men of the realm—archbishops, bishops, abbots, earls, and " other greater barons "—received a separate writ addressed to him individually, while the " smaller barons " were summoned collectively and indirectly through the sheriffs and bailiffs of each district.

II. *Composition of the Council.* It is clear that the meetings contemplated were purely baronial assemblies, since none but Crown tenants were invited to attend. " The common consent of my kingdom," in John's mouth, was

[1] *E.g.* Anson, *Law and Custom of the Constitution* (1st ed.), I. 14, declares that one of the two cardinal principles of the Charter is " that representation is a condition precedent to taxation." This has been altered in later editions.

[2] Prof. Adams (*Origin*, 276 n.) perhaps goes too far towards the opposite extreme in holding this chapter " an unnecessary addition to the Articles of the Barons and quite without importance." Contrast Round as cited *infra*, p. 251.

synonymous with "the consent of my barons."[1] The King's Council had by this time freed itself from any com-plicated theories as to its own composition, which may ever have hampered it. It was now entirely homogeneous, a feudal muster of Crown-vassals.[2]

It is unnecessary here to examine the rival theories pro-fessing to explain the composition of the Anglo-Saxon Witenagemot, or to discuss the exact connection between that institution and the *Curia Regis* of the Norman Kings. As matter of fact, the early constitution of the court of the Conqueror or of Rufus seems to have been monarchic rather than aristocratic or democratic; that is to say, it depended to a great extent on the personal will of the King. No evidence exists, of date anterior to the Great Charter, of any magnate thrusting himself unbidden into a royal council or forcing the King to issue a formal invitation. On one occasion, indeed, the action of Henry II. in omit-ting to issue a writ laid him open to criticism. This was in October, 1164, when a special council was summoned to Northampton to pass judgment upon questions at issue between the King and Thomas à Becket. The primate was ordered to appear for judgment; but the formal writ of summons, which every holder of a barony was wont to receive, was withheld. Apparently, contemporary opinion condemned this omission.[3] It is safer to infer, then, that as early as 1164, the method of issuing these writs had

---

[1] This is illustrated by comparison with the phrases in which Henry and his sons expressed "the common consent": *e.g.* (1) the Assize of Clarendon in 1166 (*Select Charters*, 143) bears to have been ordained by Henry II. "*de consilio omnium baronum suorum*"; (2) John's Charter to Innocent in 1213 declares that he acted "*communi consilio baronum nostrorum*" (*Select Charters*, 285); (3) Matthew Paris makes Earl Richard complain to Henry III. in 1255 that the Apulian business had been entered on "*sine consilio suo et assensu barnagii*" (*Chron. Maj.*, V. 520).

[2] Cf. Round (*Peerage and Pedigree*, 349 ff.), who speaks of this as creating "a harsh and artificial division of society." Its composition was stereotyped, and Mr. Round rejects alike the theory of Stubbs (*Const. Hist.*, I. 566) that the Council was being gradually extended, and that of Freeman (*Norman Conquest*, V. 419) that it was suffering contraction. Cf. also Adams, *Origin*, 226 n., and the authorities there collected.

[3] See Ramsay, *Angevin Empire*, p. 54, and authorities there cited.

become uniform, but this constitutional understanding was not reduced to writing until embodied in Magna Carta. It was in 1215 that the magnates of England formulated a distinct claim to be present at the King's councils; and even then the demand only referred to assemblies summoned for one specific purpose. Previously, attendance was reckoned not as a privilege, but rather as a burden incident to the possession of land.[1]

Mr. Round[2] maintains that under John "the writ of summons suddenly assumed a very real importance," and argues, with much plausibility, that the present chapter proves "that the Crown had been endeavouring to use the writ as a means of excluding its opponents from the assembly." The barons, on their part, unable to assert a right to attend uninvited, "insisted that they all must be summoned."

III. *Position of "Minor Barons."* Crown-tenants varied in power and position from the great earl, who owned the larger share of one or more counties, to the small freeholder with a few hides or acres of his own. A rough division was drawn somewhere in the midst; but the boundary was vague, and this vagueness was probably encouraged by the Crown, whose requirements might vary from time to time.[3] The Crown-tenants on one side of this fluctuating line were *barones majores*; those on the other, *barones minores*. The distinction had been recognized as early as the days of Henry II.;[4] but Magna Carta helped to stereotype it, and contributed to the growing tendency to confine the word "baron" to the greater men.[5] The smaller barons grudged the long journeys and the expense of attending Councils whose decisions they were powerless

---

[1] See L. O. Pike, *House of Lords*, 92, "There is no trace of any desire on the part of the barons to be summoned to the King's great Council as a privilege and an honour before the reign of John." Cf. also *Report on the Dignity of a Peer*, I. 389.

[2] *Peerage and Pedigree*, 355-6.   [3] See Prof. Medley, *Eng. Const. Hist.*, 123.

[4] *Dialogus de Scaccario*, II. x.D., "*baronias scilicet majores seu minores.*"

[5] Cf. *supra*, c. 2. Prof. Vinogradoff, *Law Quart. Rev.* XXI. 255, shows that "*baronia*" long remained a technical term for the body of freemen holding from the king, both great and small.

to influence; and they found a more fitting sphere for their energies in the meetings of the shire. For these reasons, they were prepared to ignore any summonses they might receive. In this respect, in Mr. Round's[1] opinion, the feudal theory "broke down in England."

Three distinct theories have been advanced as to the position occupied by the "minor barons" in the Common Council. (1) The duty of attendance was burdensome on the poorer Crown-tenants. It has been suggested that the device of inviting them by general summons was intended as an intimation that they need not come. This is the view taken by Prof. Medley.[2] (2) Dr. Hannis Taylor holds an opposite opinion, reading this chapter as an attempt "to rouse the lesser baronage to the exercise of rights which had practically passed into desuetude."[3] If such an attempt had really been made, and had succeeded, the result would have been to leave no room for the future introduction of the representative principle into the national council. (3) A third theory holds that the smaller Crown-tenants were called in a representative capacity. A few knights (probably elected for this purpose by their fellows) were expected to attend to represent the others. Dr. Stubbs seems predisposed towards this opinion, although he expresses himself with his usual caution.[4]

It may be suggested, even at the risk of seeming to invent a fourth theory in a series already too numerous, that to the great men who framed the clause it was a matter of supreme indifference whether their humbler fellow-tenants attended or stayed away. The general summons expressed neither an urgent desire for their presence, nor yet an intimation that they were not wanted; but merely conformed with established usage, and left with each "minor baron" the decision whether he should come or stay away.

---

[1] *Op. cit.*, 353. Cf. also his *King's Serjeanties*, 36; *Commune of London*; 252-3.

[2] *Eng. Const. Hist.*, 123. "The smaller tenants-in-chief would thankfully regard the general summons as an intimation to stay away."

[3] *Eng. Const.*, I. 466.

[4] See *Const. Hist.*, I. 666. "Whether or no the fourteenth Article of the Great Charter intended to provide for a representation of the minor tenants-in-chief by a body of knights elected in the county court," etc.

His presence would make little difference upon the deliberations of the magnates.

IV. *Representation*. It is well to hesitate before applying to ancient institutions a word so essentially modern as "representation." In a sense, the reeve and four best men of every village "represented" their fellows in the county court from an early age; and in a somewhat different sense the feudal lord "represented" his free tenants and villeins in the King's court; but in neither instance was there anything approaching the definite relation which exists at present between the member of Parliament and his constituents. Magna Carta shows no tendency whatever to adapt this expedient of representation, even in its crudest form, to the composition of the Common Council. The councillors whose summons was enjoined were all of one type, military tenants of the Crown, each of whom was to attend in his own interests not in those of his class, still less of his district or of the community as a whole. The barons, great and small, might be present, each man for himself; but the other contributors to the King's exchequer were ignored.[1]

V. *Powers of the Council*. It was not until long after the days of Magna Carta that Parliament secured the most important of those functions now deemed essential to its existence. No claim was made on behalf of the *commune concilium* to be consulted in the making of laws or in the performance of administrative duties by the Crown: no effort was made towards formulating any doctrine of ministerial responsibility. This assembly, narrow and aristocratic in composition, had only one right secured to it, a limited control over taxation. Even here, as we

[1] The writs of 7th November, 1213, are commonly regarded as introducing the representative principle into the national assembly, and in this view the barons' scheme embodied in Magna Carta has been considered as reactionary by comparison. Cf. Anson, *Law and Custom*, I. 44: "The provisions of 1215 described an assembly which was already passing away." There are difficulties, however, connected with the interpretation of those writs; and recent authorities are inclined to point to 1264, rather than to 1213, as the beginning of the systematic application of representation to Parliament. See Adams, *Origin*, 317, 340. Cf. also *supra*, 29-30.

have seen, no general claim was put forward. It had no right to control the national purse : the barons merely protected their own individual pockets against an increase of feudal burdens. A modern Magna Carta would have contained a careful list of the powers and privileges of " the common council of the realm." [1]

It would, indeed, have been an evil thing for England, if this narrow baronial assembly had established a claim to tax the important classes of the community, townsmen and vassals of mesne lords, who were totally unrepresented in it. Doubtless, it would have been ready enough to substitute, if it could, a scheme of taxation that relieved Crown-tenants of the burden of scutages and aids, at the expense of their humbler neighbours.

VI. *Rights of Majorities and Minorities.* The medieval conception of solidarity was defective; the King's council acted too much like a fortuitous gathering of unrelated individuals, and too little like a recognized organ of the body politic. " No new exactions without consent of the individual taxed " was nearer the ideals of 1215 than " no taxation without consent of Parliament." Each " baron " was summoned on his own behalf; and it is doubtful how far a dissenting minority could be bound by a decision of the rest. Accordingly, the framers of Magna Carta deemed it necessary to assert what would be too obvious to modern politicians to require assertion—namely, that when the *commune concilium* had been properly convened, its power to transact business should not be lost because a section of those summoned chose to stay away. " The business shall proceed on the day appointed, according to the advice of such as shall be present, although all that were summoned do not come." Not all business was competent, however, for the cause of summons had to be mentioned in the writs. If these writs were in order, the Council, so we may presume, had power to impose aids or scutages on those who were absent.[2]

---

[1] Cf. *Report on Dignity of a Peer*, I. 63.

[2] Cf. Stubbs, *Const. Hist.*, I. 607 : "Absence, like silence, on such occasions implies consent."

Nothing is said, however, as to the validity of a protest made by those who came and expressed disapproval. As the substance of this chapter was observed in practice (though omitted from subsequent confirmations), a precedent of the year 1221 may illustrate the interpretation put upon it by contemporary practice. A Council summoned by William Marshal had consented to a scutage, and the Bishop of Winchester was assessed at 159 marks for his knight's fees. He refused to pay, on the ground, quite untenable by modern standards, that he had dissented from the grant. The plea was accepted by the Regent, and the exchequer adjudged bishop Peter quit of the payment.[1] The incident shows how far the statesmen of the day were from realizing the principles of modern political theory. They had not yet grasped the conception of a Council endowed with constitutional authority to impose its will on a dissenting minority. Here it was apparently a minority of one.[2]

From this time forward the Common Council was almost invariably consulted before the Crown attempted to levy such contributions; and sometimes was bold enough to make conditions or to decline payment altogether, the first instance on record of an outright refusal taking place in a Parliament held at London in January, 1242.[3] The barons, in October, 1255, if Matthew Paris has not fallen into error, considered that the provisions of chapters 12 and 14 of John's Magna Carta were still in force, although they had been omitted in the reissues of Henry III. When the King asked a liberal aid in furtherance of his scheme for securing the Crown of Sicily for his son Edmund, those present at the Council deliberately refused, on the ground that some of their peers had not been summoned " according to the tenor of Magna Carta." [4]

[1] See *Pipe Roll* of 5 Henry III., cited Madox, I. 675.

[2] For the beginnings of the modern doctrine of the rights of majorities see *infra* under c. 61.

[3] See Prothero, *Simon de Montfort*, 67, and authorities there mentioned.

[4] See M. Paris, *Chron. Maj.*, V. 520. Note, however, that the version of the Charter given in his own history contains no such requirement. The barons in 1255 may have had access to the version of 1215.

CHAPTER FIFTEEN.

Nos non concedemus de cetero alicui quod capiat auxilium de liberis hominibus suis, nisi ad corpus suum redimendum, et ad faciendum primogenitum filium suum militem, et ad primogenitam filiam suam semel maritandam, et ad hec non fiat nisi racionabile auxilium.

> We will not for the future grant to any one licence to take an aid from his own free tenants, except to ransom his body, to make his eldest son a knight, and once to marry his eldest daughter; and on each of these occasions there shall be levied only a reasonable aid.

This chapter confers on the tenants of mesne lords protection similar to that already conferred on Crown-tenants: money is no longer to be extorted arbitrarily by their lords.[1] Different machinery, however, had here to be adopted, since the expedient of chapter 12 (" the common counsel of the realm ") was inapplicable.

I. *Points of difference between tenants-in-chief and under-tenants.* Tenants of mesne lords were in some respects better off than tenants of the King,[2] but in others their position was worse. Not only had they to satisfy demands of their own lord for " aids," but part of every burden laid by the King upon that lord's shoulders was transferred to theirs. In seeking to protect under-tenants, Magna Carta looked, not to the common council, but to the King. No mesne lord could compel his tenants to contribute to his necessities without written licence from the Crown; and the Crown was now forbidden to issue such licences except upon the usual three occasions.[3]

---

[1] The chapter is, therefore, on the one hand, a supplement of cc. 12 and 14; on the other, a particular application of the principle enunciated in c. 60, which extended to sub-tenants benefits secured to Crown-tenants by previous chapters.

[2] The exemptions enjoyed by them are explained under c. 43.

[3] By strict feudal theory the King had no right to interfere between the barons and their sub-tenants. (1) The need for royal writs was thus a usurpation. (2) Those writs were " only letters of request," not binding on sub-tenants. See Adams, *Origin*, 230-2.

Contrast this procedure with that which affected Crown-tenants :—

(1) While chapter 12 had spoken of " aids and scutages," this one speaks of " aids " alone. The omission can be readily explained : a mesne lord in England had no admitted right of private war, and was debarred from demanding scutage upon his own initiative. He might, indeed, allocate upon his freeholders part of any scutage which the Crown had taken from him ; but the barons who framed the Charter had no intention to renounce so just a right. The restriction of this clause to " aids " was thus intentional.

(2) It would have been absurd to require " the common counsel of the realm " for every aid paid by the freeholders of a manor. The embryo Parliament had no time for petty local affairs ; and the present chapter makes no such suggestion. Some substitute had, however, to be found. A natural expedient would have been to compel the mesne lord, who wished an aid, to take " the common consent " of the freeholders of his manor, assembled in court baron, as in a local Parliament. This course was sometimes followed. Henry Tracey, for example, in 1235 (although armed with a royal writ), convened his Devonshire knights and obtained their consent to an aid of 20s. per fee on his daughter's marriage.[1] No such obligation, however, had been placed on mesne lords by Magna Carta, which had sought a practical substitute for " the common counsel of the realm " in a different direction.

(3) A check upon such exactions was sought, not in the court baron, but in the need for a royal licence. The necessity for this may at first have been a practical, rather than a legal, one ; for executive power lay with the officers of the Crown alone, and the sheriff gave his services only at the King's command.[2] The Crown thus exercised what

---

[1] Bracton's *Note-book*, No. 1146, cited Pollock and Maitland, I. 331.

[2] In theory, in Henry II.'s reign at least, a royal writ was *not* required in the normal case. See *Dialogus*, II. viii., and the editors' comment (p. 191) : " Normally the levying of money under any pretext from a landowner gave him a right to make a similar levy on his under-tenants." As regards *scutage*, a distinc-

was virtually a power of veto over all aids taken by mesne
lords. Such a right, conscientiously used, would have
placed an effectual restraint on their rapacity. John,
however, sold writs to every needy lord who proposed to
enrich himself at his tenants' expense. Magna Carta forbade the two tyrants thus to combine against sub-tenants,
enunciating a hard-and-fast rule which, if duly observed,
would have struck at the root of the grievance : no writ
could be lawfully issued except on the three well-known
occasions.

II. *The Influence of Magna Carta upon later Practice.*
This chapter, along with chapters 12 and 14, was discarded
by Henry III.; and little difference, if any, can be traced
between the practices that prevailed before and after 1215.
Mesne lords invariably asked the Crown's help to collect
their aids. They could not legally distrain their freeholders, except through the sheriff, and this was, in part
at least, a result of Magna Carta.[1]

Henry III., however, disregarded the rule which forbade
the licensing of extraordinary aids. Like his ancestors,
he was prepared to grant writs on almost any plausible
pretext. From the *Patent* and *Close Rolls,* as well as from
other sources, illustrations of the Crown's earlier and later
practice can readily be collected : (1) *Scutages.* In 1217,
for example, Henry granted permission to all Crown
tenants who had served in person to collect scutage from
their knights.[2]

(2) *Ordinary Aids.* (a) John in 1204 authorized the
collection of " an effectual aid " from the knights and free-

---

tion was recognized. The lord who actually paid scutage might collect it from his
sub-tenants without a licence ; but, if he served in person, he could recover none
of his expenses except by royal writ. See *ibid.*, and cf. Madox, I. 675. It is
necessary, however, to avoid confusion between two types of writ, (a) that which
merely authorized contributions, *e.g.*, *de scutagio habendo* ; (b) that which commanded the sheriff to give his active help. In later practice, the sheriff often
collected scutage from the sub-tenants and paid it directly to the Crown. Pollock
and Maitland, I. 249-253.

[1] Cf. Pollock and Maitland, I. 331 : " The clause expunged from the Charter
seems practically to have fixed the law."

[2] *Close Rolls*, I. 306, cited Pollock and Maitland, I. 331.

holders of the Constable of Chester for the ransom of their lord.[1] (b) A royal writ in 1235 allowed Henry Tracey, as already mentioned, to take an aid for his daughter's marriage.

(3) *Special Aids.* (a) When a *fine* of sixty marks was incurred in 1206 by the Abbot of Peterborough, John allowed him to distrain his under-tenants.[2] (b) An heir, paying *relief*, might likewise take reasonable contributions from freeholders.[3] (c) The lord's *debts* were frequently paid by his tenants. The returns to the Inquest of 1170 contain particulars of "sums given individually by some forty burgesses of Castle Rising towards paying off the mortgages of their lord, the Earl of Arundel, who was clearly in the hands of the Jews "[4] while in 1234 the Earl of Oxford and the Prior of Lewes each obtained a letter patent distraining tenants to contribute to discharge their debts.[5] Evidence is thus preserved that Henry III. took full advantage of the omission from his own charters of this part of his father's promises. He did not question the justice of such writs, if good fees were paid. His letters authorized the taking of a " reasonable " aid, without hinting at any mode of determining what that was. This is illustrated by the procedure adopted by Henry Tracey in 1235, when he debated with his assembled knights of Devonshire the amount to be paid as "reasonable," and finally accepted 20s. per fee.[6] This same mesne lord, however, twelve years later, obtained a writ bidding the sheriff of Somerset assist him to collect " the scutage of Gascony " at 40s. per fee.[7]

The first Statute of Westminster virtually reverted to the rule laid down in 1215, for its terms imply that aids could only be taken on the three well-known occasions. Only

---

[1] *Patent Rolls*, 5 John, cited Madox, I. 615.

[2] *Close Rolls*, 7 John, cited Madox, I. 616.

[3] See Glanvill, IX. 8.   [4] See Round, *Commune of London*, 130.

[5] See Madox, I. 617, citing *Patent Rolls*, 18 Henry III. Various other examples are given by Pollock and Maitland, I. 331, *e.g.* "the earl of Salisbury, to enable him to stock his land."

[6] *Supra*, p. 257, and cf. Pollock and Maitland, I. 331.

[7] See Madox, I. 677.

20s. could be taken from a knight's fee and an equal sum from land held in socage of the annual value of £20. No aid for a knighthood could be taken before a son was 15 years of age, or for a marriage until a daughter was 7.

CHAPTER SIXTEEN.

NULLUS distringatur ad faciendum majus servicium de feodo militis, nec de alio libero tenemento, quam inde debetur.

> No one shall be distrained for performance of greater service for a knight's fee, or for any other free tenement, than is due therefrom.

For military tenants, the transition from scutage to service was a natural one. John declared that no freeholder should be constrained to do more service for his lands than he was legally bound to do. Disputes might arise, however, as to what extent of service actually was due in each particular case, and Magna Carta did nothing to remove such ambiguities. The difficulties of definition, indeed, were enormous, since the duration and conditions of service might vary widely, in consequence of special exemptions or special burdens which appeared in title deeds or rested upon immemorial usage. The barons could not enter on so intricate and laborious a task.

One grievance may have been specially in their minds. They had frequently objected to serve abroad, particularly during John's campaigns in Poitou.[1] To force them to serve in the south of France, or to fine them for staying at home, was, they may well have argued, to distrain them *ad faciendum majus servicium de feodo militis quam inde debetur.* When they inserted these words in the Charter, they doubtless regarded them as a prohibition of compulsory service in Poitou, at all events.[2] The clause was

---

[1] See the authorities cited *supra*, p. 68, n. 3, and 69, n. 1.

[2] In the so-called "unknown Charter of Liberties" (see Appendix) John concedes to his men " *ne eant in exercitu extra Angliam nisi in Normanniam et in Brittaniam,*" a not unfair compromise, which may possibly represent the sense in which the present chapter was interpreted by the barons. See, however, Adams, *Origin*, 232, who takes a different view.

wide enough, however, to include minor grievances. The barons did not confine its provisions to military service, but extended it to other forms of freehold tenure (" *nec de alio libero tenemento* "). No freeholder, whether in socage, serjeanty, or frankalmoin, could in future be compelled to render services not legally due.

If the barons thought they had thus settled the vexed questions connected with foreign service, they deceived themselves. Although this chapter (unlike those dealing with scutage) remained in all subsequent confirmations, it was far from preventing disputes. Yet the disputants in future reigns occupied somewhat different ground. From the days of William I. to those of Charles II., when the feudal system was abolished, quarrels frequently arose, the most famous of which, in 1297, led to Edward's unseemly wrangle with his hereditary Constable and Marshal, who refused to embark for Gascony except in attendance on the King's person.[1]

It has been shown in the Introduction[2] how the obligations of a military tenant fell naturally into three groups (services, incidents, and aids), while a fourth group (scutages) was added when the Crown commuted military service for its equivalent in money. Feudal grievances may be arranged in four corresponding groups, each redressed by special clauses of Magna Carta : abuse of *aids* by chapters 12, 14, and 15; of feudal *incidents*, by chapters 2 to 8; of *scutage*, by chapters 12 and 14; and of *service*, by the present chapter.

CHAPTER SEVENTEEN.

COMMUNIA placita non sequantur curiam nostram sed teneantur in aliquo loco certo.

Common pleas shall not follow our court, but shall be held in some fixed place.

[1] Walter of Hemingburgh, II. 121. Cf., on the whole subject of foreign service, *supra*, 67-76.

[2] *Supra*, 59-69.

An attempt was here made to render royal justice cheaper and more accessible. Law-suits in which the Crown had no special interest, common pleas, were to be held in some pre-appointed spot, and no longer to follow the King from place to place. The full extent of this boon will be better appreciated after a short consideration of the method of dispensing justice adopted by Henry II. and his sons.

I. *The Curia Regis as a Court of Law*. The evil complained of was a characteristically medieval one, and arose from the fact that all departments of government were centred in the King's household. This *Curia Regis*, indeed, united in itself the functions of the modern Cabinet, of the administrative departments (such as the Home Office, the Foreign Office, and the Admiralty), and of the various legal tribunals. It was the parent *inter alia* of the Court at St. James's and the courts at Westminster. Nothing could be done outside of the royal household, and that household never tarried long in any one spot. Everything was focussed to one point, but to a point constantly in motion. Wherever the King went, there the *Curia Regis*, with all its departments, went also. The entire machinery of royal justice followed Henry II., as he passed, sometimes on the impulse of the moment, from one of his favourite hunting seats to another. Crowds thronged after him in hot pursuit, since it was difficult to transact business of moment elsewhere.

This meant intolerable delay, annoyance, and expense. The case of Richard of Anesty is often cited in illustration. His own account is a graphic record of his journeyings in search of justice, throughout a period of five years, during which he visited in the King's wake most parts of England, Normandy, Aquitaine, and Anjou. The plaintiff, although ultimately successful, paid dearly for his legal triumph. Reduced to borrow from the Jews to meet enormous outlays, mostly travelling expenses, he had to discharge his debts with accumulations of interest at the ruinous rate of $86\frac{2}{3}$ per cent.[1]

II. *Common Pleas and Royal Pleas*. Long before 1215,

[1] Cf. J. F. Stephen, *Hist. of Crim. Law*, I. 88-9.

litigations conducted before the King's courts had come to be divided roughly into two classes, according as the royal interests were or were not specially affected by the issue. Those on one side of this fluctuating line were known as royal pleas, or " pleas of the Crown," provisions for holding which are contained in chapter 24, those on the other side as ordinary or " common pleas," to which alone the present chapter refers. As these ordinary suits did not require to be determined in the royal presence, it was possible to appoint a bench of judges to sit permanently in some fixed spot, selected to suit the convenience of litigants. No town was named in Magna Carta; but Westminster, even then the natural home of law, was probably intended from the first. It is Westminster that Sir Frederick Pollock has in mind when he writes : " We may also say that Magna Carta gave England a capital." [1] The barons in 1215, in asking this reform, were not insisting on any startling innovation, but demanding merely the observance of a rule long recognized. During most of John's reign, a court did sit at Westminster dispensing justice, with more or less regularity; and there most " common pleas " were tried, unless John ordered otherwise.[2] Magna Carta confirmed the understanding that " common pleas " should not dance attendance on the King, though it did not name any one fixed place where they should be tried.[3]

III. *Influences of Magna Carta on genesis of Courts of Common Law.* The ultimate consequences of this reform reached further than was foreseen. Intended to remove a practical grievance, it had important effects on the development of the English Constitution. By securing for common pleas a permanent home, it gave an impetus to

---

[1] *Jurisprudence and Ethics*, 209. Sometimes, however, another " fixed place " was substituted. The Court of Common Pleas sat once at York under Edward III. and once at Hertford under Elizabeth. See Maitland, *Select Pleas of the Crown*, xiii. The statute 2 Edward III. c. 11 enacted that it should not be removed to any new place without due notice.

[2] See Prof. Maitland, *Select Pleas of the Crown*, xiii.-xvi.

[3] See Pollock, *Expansion of Common Law*, 63 n. Cf. Holdsworth, I. 75.

the disintegrating tendencies already at work within the many-sided household of the King. It helped forward the cleavage destined to divide completely the future Courts of Westminster from the Court of St. James's and from Downing Street. Nor was this all : the special treatment accorded to " common pleas " emphasized the distinction between them and royal pleas, and so contributed to the splitting up of the same *Curia Regis,* on its judicial side, into two distinct tribunals. One little group of judges were set apart for hearing common pleas, and known as " the King's Judges of the Bench," or more briefly as " the Bench," and at a later date as the Court of Common Pleas. A second group, reserved for royal pleas, became the court *Coram Rege,* known subsequently as the Court of King's Bench. There were thus two benches : a common bench for common pleas and a royal bench for pleas of the Crown.[1]

The double process, by which these two small courts separated slowly from the parent court and from each other, began long prior to Magna Carta, and was not completed before the close of the thirteenth century. These benches were also closely linked with a third bench, known for centuries as the Court of Exchequer, which was in its origin merely one department of that government bureau, the King's financial Exchequer in which money was weighed and tested and the royal accounts drawn up. Many disputes or pleas affecting Crown debts had to be there decided, and a group of officials were set aside to try these. These men, called " barons of the exchequer," formed what was in fact, though not in name, a third bench or court of justice.

All three of the Courts of Common Law were thus off-shoots of the King's household. In theory, each of these ought to have confined itself to a special class of suits— royal pleas, common pleas, and exchequer pleas respectively ; but, by a process known to law-courts in all ages, each encroached on the jurisdictions and fees appropriate to the others, until they became, for most purposes, three sister courts of co-ordinate authority. They were bound

[1] Cf. *supra,* 90.

to decide all suits according to the technical and inflexible rules of common law; and their jurisdiction required a supplement, which was supplied by the genesis of the Court of Chancery, dispensing, not common law, but equity, which professed to give (and, for a short time, actually did give) redress on the merits of each case as it arose, unrestrained by precedents and legal subtleties.

IV. *The Evolution of the Court of Common Pleas.* The comment usually made upon the present chapter is that we have here the origin of the Court of Common Pleas. Now, legal institutions do not spring, full-fledged, into being: the Common Pleas, like its sister Courts of King's Bench and Exchequer, was the result of a long process of bifurcation from a common stem.

Three stages may be emphasized. (1) The earliest trace of a definite bench, set apart for common pleas, is to be found in 1178. Henry II., returning from Normandy, found that there had been irregularities. To prevent their recurrence, he effected changes, the exact nature of which is matter of dispute. A contemporary writer [1] relates how Henry chose two clerks and three laymen from the officials of his own household, and gave to these five men authority to hear all complaints and to do right " *and not to recede from his court.*" It was long thought that this marked the origin of the King's Bench,[2] but Mr. Pike [3] has conclusively proved that the bench thus established was the predecessor, not of the royal bench, but rather of the bench for common pleas.

In 1178, then, these five judges were set apart to hear ordinary suits; but they were specially directed not to leave Henry's court; so that common pleas still " followed the King," even ordinary litigants in non-royal pleas having to pursue the King in quest of justice as he passed from place to place in quest of sport or business.

It must not be supposed that the arrangement thus made

[1] Author of *Gesta Regis Henrici*, I. 207.

[2] Bigelow, *Procedure*, 89 ; Stubbs, *Gesta Regis Henrici*, I. lxxi.

[3] *House of Lords*, 32. See also Poole, *Exchequer*, 180, and Adams, *Origin*, 136 ff.

settled the practice for the whole period of thirty-seven years preceding the grant of Magna Carta. On the contrary, it was merely one of many experiments tried by that restless reformer, Henry of Anjou; and the separate bench then instituted may have been pulled down and set up again many times. It had probably, at best, a fitful and intermittent existence. There is evidence, however, that some such court did exist and did try common pleas in the reigns of Richard and John.[1] On the other hand, this tribunal had in John's reign ceased to follow the King's movements habitually, and established itself at Westminster.[2] It was in 1215 considered an abuse for John to try a common plea elsewhere.

(2) Magna Carta, in 1215, gave authoritative sanction to this understanding, and thus marks a stage in the evolution of the Court of Common Pleas.[3] Ordinary pleas were no longer to follow the King.[4] Young Henry renewed this promise, and his minority favoured its strict observance: a mere boy could not make progresses through the land dispensing justice as he went. Accordingly, all pleas continued for some twenty years to be heard at Westminster. The same circumstance may have temporarily arrested the process of cleavage between the two benches.

(3) About 1234, Henry began to follow the precedent, set by his ancestors, of moving through his realm with judges in his train. While one group went with him, another remained at Westminster: some method of allocating business had therefore to be found. Common pleas, in accordance with Magna Carta, remained stationary; while pleas of the Crown went on their travels. The split between the two benches now became absolute: from the

---

[1] See Prof. Maitland, *Sel. Pl. Crown*, xiii.-xvi. ; see also in *Pipe Roll*, 7 John (cited Madox, I. 791) how money was paid that a plea pending before the *Justiciarii de banco* might be heard *coram rege*. This entry proves the existence in 1205 of the *de banco* as distinct from the *coram rege*.

[2] See Maitland, *ibid.*

[3] Cf. Poole, *Exchequer*, 183, who insists, however, that "it said nothing about a distinct court."

[4] For attempts to evade this prohibition on the ground of the special character of particular pleas, see Bracton's *Note-book*, Nos. 1213 and 1220.

year 1234, two continuous series of distinct rolls can be traced, known respectively as *rotuli placitorum coram rege* and *rotuli placitorum de banco*. If any date in the history of one law court, which is in process of becoming two, can be reckoned as marking the point of separation, it should be that at which separate rolls appear. The court's *memory* lies in its records, which are thus closely associated with its identity. The common bench and the royal bench had become distinct.[1] While Henry and his justices sat in judgment at Worcester, in 1238, a litigant protested against his suit being tried before them. It was a "common plea" and therefore, he argued, ought not to follow the King, in violation of Magna Carta. At Westminster only, not at Worcester or elsewhere, could his case be heard.[2]

With royal pleas it was different: for long they continued to follow the King's person without any protest being raised; and the Court of King's Bench did not finally settle at Westminster for nearly a century after the Court of Common Pleas had been established there. It is doubtful whether, even in 1258, a separate royal bench had been constituted.[3] So late as 1300, Edward I. ordained, by the *Articuli super cartas*, that "the Justices of his Bench" (as well as his Chancellor) should follow him, so that he might have at all times near him "some sages of the law, which be able duly to order all such matters as shall come into the Court at all times when need shall require."[4] The matters here referred to were royal pleas: common pleas were tried at Westminster.

V. *Common Pleas and the Exchequer.* Records speak of the *curia regis* meeting for legal business *ad scaccarium* (that is, in the room where the business of the Exchequer of Accounts was normally transacted) long before the genesis of a separate Court of Exchequer.[5]

Formal sessions of the Exchequer for auditing the

---

[1] See Maitland, *Sel. Pl. Crown*, xviii.

[2] See *Placitorum Abbreviatio* (p. 105), 21 Henry III., cited Pike, *House of Lords*, p. 41 Cf. also Bracton's *Note-book*, pleas Nos. 1213 and 1220.

[3] Poole, *Exchequer*, 183. [4] 28 Edward I. c. 5.

[5] For stages in this genesis in 1234, 1236, and 1317, see Poole, *Exchequer*, 183.

Sheriffs' accounts could only be held at Westminster, where
the necessary apparatus was kept; but " the Exchequer,"
using that elastic word in a somewhat different sense, with
much of its impedimenta of writs and tallies, would
accompany the King on his progresses through the realm.
In 1210, for example, the Exchequer was at Northampton;
in 1266, at St. Paul's; in 1277, at Shrewsbury; and in
1299, at York.[1]

Now, the Exchequer, when it sat as a Court of law,
was ever willing—for a consideration—to place its potent
procedure, devised for the King's use, at the disposal of
private creditors, treating " common pleas " as " exchequer
pleas." Ordinary debtors, summoned to answer for their
debts before the *barones scaccarii* were subjected to more
rapid pressure than they would have experienced elsewhere.
Debtors were thus as anxious to escape the jurisdiction of
the Exchequer, as creditors were to invite it.

Both before and after Magna Carta, it would appear that
common pleas were sometimes tried at sessions of the
Exchequer, held not only at Westminster but also during
its wanderings in the King's train. It was natural enough
that defendants who found themselves hustled by the
stringent Exchequer process should seek shelter under the
present chapter of the Great Charter. That they did so
is proved by the words of the *Articuli super Cartas* of 1300,
which declared that no common pleas should henceforth be
held in the Exchequer " contrary to the form of the Great
Charter." [2]

The implication of this clause of the statute of 1300 has
sometimes been accepted literally.[3] Magna Carta, how-

---

[1] Stubbs, *Const. Hist.*, II. 281 n.

[2] See 28 Edward I. c. 4. Many previous attempts had been made to keep
common pleas out of the Exchequer, *e.g.* the writs of 56 Henry III. and 5
Edward I. (cited Madox, II. 73-4), and the so-called statute of Rhuddlan (12
Edward I.), see *Statutes of Realm*, I. 70.

[3] Thus Madox (II. 73-4) holds that c. 17 relates to the Exchequer ; so does Mr.
Bigelow (*History of Procedure*, 130-1), who explains the grievance as a difficulty
of getting speedy justice at the Exchequer, because the barons refused to sit after
their fiscal business had been finished. This seems to be an error : the Barons of
Exchequer made no difficulty about hearing pleas : quite the contrary. Plaintiffs

ever, in set terms at least, contains no such prohibition. If the present chapter excludes common pleas from the jurisdiction of a *travelling* Exchequer equally as from that of a travelling King's bench, its words cannot be so stretched as to apply to normal sessions of the Exchequer held at Westminster. The *Articuli super Cartas,* however, attempted what the Charter of 1215 did not. After 1300 it was clearly illegal to hold any pleas in the Exchequer, unless such as affected the Crown and its ministers. Subsequent statutes confirmed this; but their plain intention was always defeated by the ingenious use of legal fictions and the connivance of the barons of Exchequer, who welcomed the increase of fees that kept pace with the increase of business.[1]

CHAPTER EIGHTEEN.

RECOGNICIONES de nova dissaisina, de morte antecessoris, et de ultima presentacione, non capiantur nisi in suis comitatibus et hoc modo; nos, vel si extra regnum fuerimus, capitalis justiciarius noster, mittemus duos justiciarios per unumquemque comitatum per quatuor vices in anno, qui, cum quatuor militibus cujuslibet comitatus electis per comitatum, capiant in comitatu et in die et loco comitatus assisas predictas.

> Inquests of *novel disseisin,* of *mort d'ancestor,* and of *darrein presentment,* shall not be held elsewhere than in their own

were equally eager to purchase the writs which they were keen to sell: it was only defendants (debtors) who objected to the rapid and stringent procedure for enforcing payment adopted by this efficient court. The sheriffs and others waiting to render accounts before the Exchequer also protested against the congestion of business produced at the Exchequer by the eagerness of litigants who pressed there for justice. See Madox, II. 73. Plaintiffs had no reason to complain.

[1] The fiction of "Crown debtors" is well known : plaintiffs obtained a hearing in the exchequer for their common pleas by alleging that they wished to recover debts due to them "in order to enable them to answer the debts they owed to the king." See Madox, II. 192.

county-courts,[1] and that in manner following,—We, or, if we should be out of the realm, our chief justiciar, will send two justiciars through every county four times a year, who shall, along with four knights of the county chosen by the county, hold the said assizes in the county court, on the day and in the place of meeting of that court.

Provision is here made for holding before the King's travelling justices, frequently and in a convenient manner, three species of judicial inquests known as " petty assizes." These are of exceptional interest from their connection with the genesis of trial by jury and the Justices of Assize.

I. *The Curia Regis and the travelling Justices.* From an early date, certainly from the accession of Henry I., it was the Crown's practice to supplement the labours of its officials at the royal exchequer by the occasional despatch of chosen individuals to inspect the provinces, collecting information and revenue, and, incidentally, hearing law-suits. Justice was thus dispensed in the King's name by his delegates in every shire of England, and a distinction arose between two types of royal courts : (1) *the King's Council and its offshoots* (including the three courts of common law and the court of chancery), which at first followed the King's person, but gradually, as already shown,[2] found a settled home at Westminster; and (2) *the courts of the itinerant justices* which exercised such delegated authority as the Crown chose from time to time to entrust to them. The sphere of labour of these commissioners, as they passed from district to district, was the court of each shire, convened to meet them. They formed, in this way, a link between the old local popular courts and the system of royal justice. These travelling justices were of two types, Justices in Eyre and Justices of Assize respectively.

(*a*) *The Justices in Eyre* were the earliest form of travelling judges, though their original duties were rather financial and administrative, than strictly judicial. Their

[1] " *Comitatus* " indicates both the county where the lands lay and the court of that county. It was originally the sphere of influence of a *comes* or earl. Cf. *supra*, c. 2.

[2] See *supra*, c. 17.

history extends from Henry I. to the end of the fourteenth century.[1] Their outstanding characteristics were the sweeping nature of their commissions (*ad omnia placita*), the harsh and drastic way in which they used their authority, and their intense unpopularity. Their advent was dreaded like a pestilence : each district visited was left impoverished by fines and penalties. On one occasion, the men of Cornwall " from fear of their coming, fled to the woods." [2] An eyre was only resorted to at long intervals—seven years came to be the recognized term—and was a method of punishing delinquencies and miscarriages of justice and of collecting royal dues. It was not a visit from these hated Justices of Eyre that the barons in 1215 desired to have four times a year.

(b) *The Justices of Assize* also were travelling judges, but in their original form at least, possessed hardly another feature in common with the Justices in Eyre. Their history extends from a period not earlier than the reign of Henry II. down to the present day.[3] They seem to have been popular from the first, as they used a speedy and rational procedure; while the scope of their jurisdiction, although extended as their popularity increased, was limited by the terms of their commissions. They were regarded, not as royal tax-gatherers armed with harsh powers of coercion, but as welcome bearers of justice to the doors of those who needed it.

At first their duties were confined to enquiries of the kind mentioned in the text, known as " assizes "; and the new species of travelling judges were hence called " Justices of Assize," a name that has clung to them for centuries, although their jurisdiction has been gradually increased till it now includes both civil and criminal pleas of every description, and although meanwhile the invention of new forms of process has superseded the old " assizes," and at

[1] See W. S. Holdsworth (*History of English Law*, p. 115), who cites 1397 as the date of the final abolition of Eyres.

[2] This was in 1233 : see Pollock and Maitland, I. 181.

[3] Blackstone, *Commentaries*, III. 58, assigns 1176 (the assize of Northampton), as the date of their institution.

last necessitated their total abolition.[1] They are still "justices of assize" in an age which knows nothing of the old assizes.

II. *Nature and Origin of the Petty Assizes.* The institution of the "assizes"—particular forms of the sworn inquest—occupied a prominent place among the expedients by which Henry II. hoped to substitute a more rational procedure for the form of proof known as trial by combat.[2]

The *duellum,* introduced at the Norman Conquest, remained for a century the chief method in use among the upper classes for determining serious litigations. Gradually, however, it was confined to two groups of pleas, one civil and the other criminal : appeals of treason and felony on the one hand, and suits to determine title to land on the other.[3] The process of restriction was carried further by Henry II., who provided for the defendant or accused party, wherever possible, an option to trial by battle. Under chapter 36 will be explained the expedient adopted for evading combat in criminal cases. The present chapter relates to certain important groups of civil pleas,[4] namely, the three Petty Assizes, the frequent use of which was now insisted on, although the Grand Assize was still viewed askance, for reasons to be explained in connection with chapter 34.

[1] See statute 3 and 4 William IV. c. 27, §§ 36-7. The last actual case of a Grand Assize occurred in *Davies* v. *Loundes,* in 1835 and 1838 (1 Bing. N.C. 597, and 5 Bing. N.C. 161).

[2] The name "Assize" is sometimes a source of confusion, because of its various meanings. (1) Originally, it denoted a session or meeting of any sort. (2) It came to be reserved for sessions of the King's Council. (3) It was applied to any Ordinance enacted in such a session, *e.g.* Assize of Clarendon. (4) It was extended to every institution or procedure established by royal ordinance, but (5) more particularly applied to the procedures known as Grand Assize and Petty Assizes. (6) Finally, it denotes at the present day a "session" of these Justices of Assize, thus combining something of its earliest meaning with something of its latest. In certain contexts, it has other meanings still, *e.g.* (7) an assessment or financial burden imposed at a "session."

[3] See Neilson, *Trial by Combat,* 33-6, and authorities there cited.

[4] Cf. *supra,* p. 85, for the place of "combat" in legal procedure; and p. 89, for Henry's policy in discouraging it. For the later history of trial by battle, see *infra,* under c. 36.

(1) *The Grand Assize* is not mentioned in Magna Carta; but some acquaintance with it is necessary to an appreciation of the Petty Assizes. In the troubled reign of Stephen, lands changed hands frequently: there was hardly an important estate in England to which, at Henry's accession, two or more rival magnates did not lay claim. Constant litigations resulted, and the only legal method of deciding the issue was the *duellum*.

Henry II. introduced a startling innovation. The actual holder of a property *de facto,* when challenged to combat by a rival claimant, was allowed an option: he might force the claimant (if the latter persisted) to refer the matter to the oath of twelve knights of the neighbourhood. Henry's ordinance provided for the appointment of these recognitors. Four leading knights of the county were first to be chosen, on whom was placed the duty of selecting twelve knights of the particular district where the lands lay, and these, with all due solemnity and in presence of the King's justiciars, declared upon oath to which suitor the lands belonged. Their decision was final, and determined the question of ownership for all time.[1] The name Grand Assize was applied alike to the procedure and to the knights who gave the verdict.

The procedure was slow; many formalities and possibilities of delay intervened, involving expensive journeys to the central *Curia,* first by the four appointing knights and afterwards by the twelve appointed. Months and even years might elapse before the final verdict was obtained. To lighten these hardships in comparatively unimportant cases, the *Capitula* of 1194 authorized Justices of Eyre to hold Grand Assizes where the lands did not exceed £5 in annual value.[2]

Normally, however, this procedure was for the King's central *Curia,* neither for county court nor yet for baronial jurisdictions. For one thing, only magnates with wide

---

[1] See Glanvill, II. 7.

[2] *Sel. Chart.*, 259. The Assize of Northampton in 1176 (*ibid.* 152) had given them jurisdiction over estates of half a knight's fee or less, but nothing was there said of the mode of proof.

demesnes were likely to command the attendance of twelve knights (or even of twelve freeholders) from their own territories. In combination with the rule given by Glanvill,[1] that no plea concerning title to land could be commenced in any court without royal writ, and with the use made by the King of the writ *praecipe*,[2] the Grand Assize, while superseding trial by battle, became also an expedient for curtailing the jurisdiction of mesne lords. It is easy to understand why (unlike the petty assizes) it never became popular with the magnates.

Valuable boon as was the option to substitute the verdict of twelve knights for the *duellum* in questions of title to land, the reform had one obvious weak point : the option conferred might sometimes be usurped by the wrong man, if a turbulent claimant took the law into his own hands, evicted the holder by the rude method of self-help, and thereafter claimed the protection of Henry's ordinance. In such a case the man of violence—the holder *mala fide*—would enjoy the option intended for his innocent victim.

(2) *The petty assizes* may, perhaps, have been the outcome of Henry's determination to prevent misuse of his new engine of justice.[3] If a demandant alleged that the present possessor had usurped his place by violence, the King allowed the preliminary plea thus raised to be summarily decided by the oath of twelve local landowners, according to a procedure known as a petty assize. These petty assizes, of which three are here mentioned, related to questions of " possession," as opposed to " ownership."

(a) *Novel disseisin.* The word " seisin," originally synonymous with " possession " in general, was gradually restricted by medieval lawyers to the possession of real estate. " Disseisin " thus meant the interruption of seisin

---

[1] Glanvill, XII. 25.   [2] See *infra*, under c. 34.

[3] In the matter of actual date, the received opinion is that the " novel disseisin " procedure dates from 1166, and the Grand Assize came later. Round (*Athenaeum* for 28th Jany., 1899) suggests 1179. The evolution of the various writs was, however, a slow process, and steps in the chain are wanting. Under Geoffrey Plantagenet in Normandy various writs shade off into one another. See Haskins, *Amer. Hist. Rev.*, VIII. 613 ff. In any view, the *logical* sequence seems to be that given in the text.

(or possession) of land; and was the technical term applied to violent acts of eviction. " Novel " implies that such ejection was of recent date; for a summary remedy could be given only where there had not been undue delay in applying for it.[1]

The first of the petty assizes, then, was a rapid and peaceable method of ascertaining, by reference to sworn local testimony, whether an alleged recent eviction had really taken place or not. Without any of the law's delays, without any expensive journeys to the King's Court or to Westminster, but quickly and in the district where the lands lay, twelve local gentlemen determined upon oath all allegations of this nature. If the recognitors of the petty assize answered " Yes," then the evicted man would have " seisin " immediately restored to him, and along with " seisin " went the valued option of determining what proof should decide the " ownership,"—whether it should be battle or the Grand Assize. An ordinance instituting this most famous of the three petty assizes was issued probably in 1166, a year fertile in legal expedients.

(b) *Mort d'ancestor.* The protection afforded to the victim of " disseisin " did not remove all possibility of justice miscarrying; interested parties, other than the man ejected, were unprotected. An heir might be deprived of his tenement by his lord or by some rival claimant before he had an opportunity to take possession; never having been " in seisin," he could not plead that he had been disseised. For the benefit of such an heir, a second petty assize, known as " mort d'ancestor," was invented.[2] This is mentioned in article 4 of the Assize of Northampton, issued in 1176, where procedure, essentially similar to, though not quite so speedy as that already described, was put at the heir's disposal. If successful, he took the lands temporarily, subject to all defects in his ancestor's title, leaving as before the question

---

[1] In Normandy the corresponding period was "since the last harvest." See Maitland, *Equity*, 323.

[2] At so late a date as 1267 it was found necessary to recognize by statute the right of the heir, who had come of age, to oust his guardian from his lands by an assize of *mort d'ancestor.* See Statute of Marlborough, c. 16.

of absolute ownership to be determined (if challenged) by the more cumbrous machinery of the Grand Assize.

(c) *Darrein presentment.* Advowson (or the right of appointing to a vacant church) was then, as now, a species of real estate. Such patronage was highly prized, affording a living for a younger son or needy relative; or it might be converted into cash. Disputes often arose as to possession and ownership of advowsons. Any one who claimed the absolute property, as against the holder, must offer battle, as in the case of any other form of real estate; and the Charter says nothing on this head.[1]

The less vital question of possession was more rapidly determined: if a benefice fell vacant, and two proprietors claimed the patronage, the Church could not remain without a shepherd until the question was decided.[2] No; the man in possession was allowed to make the appointment. But who was the man in possession? Clearly he who had (or whose father had) presented a nominee to the living when the last vacancy occurred. Here, however, there might be a dispute as to facts. Twelve local men decided which claimant had made the last appointment (the " darrein presentment "); and the claimant thus preferred filled up vacancies, until ousted by battle or the Grand Assize.

All three forms of petty assize were merely new applications of the royal procedure known in England, since the Norman Conquest, as *inquisitio* or *recognitio*.[3]

III. *Aims of Magna Carta.* If the petty assizes were objects of suspicion when first invented by Henry II., public opinion, half a century later, had vindicated their wisdom. The insurgent barons in 1215 were far from demanding their abolition; their new grievance was rather that sessions

---

[1] Such was the law as late as 1285. Westminster II. c. 5 explains that, when any one had wrongfully presented to a vacant church, the real patron could not recover his advowson except by writ of right " *quod habet terminari per duellum vel per magnam assisam.*"

[2] A Lateran Council in 1179 authorized the diocesan bishop to appoint after three months' vacancy. Hence there was additional need of haste.

[3] The relations of the assizes to the ancient *inquisitio* and to the modern jury are discussed *supra*, pp. 134-8.

of assize were not held often enough. In prescribing the way in which these assizes must be held, several points were emphasized :—(1) No inquiry of the kind was to be held elsewhere than in the county where the property was situated. This was intended to meet the convenience of litigants, of those who served on assizes, and of all concerned.[1] Within two years it was seen that this provision went too far. It was more convenient to hold certain inquiries before the Bench at Westminster, and the reissue of 1217 made two modifications : (a) Assizes of darrein presentment were thereafter to be taken before " the Justices of the Bench "; (b) any novel disseisin or mort d'ancestor, revealing points of special difficulty, might also be reserved for the decision of the Bench. An element of uncertainty was thus introduced, of which the Crown took advantage. In a reported case of the year 1221, it was decided that an assize of mort d'ancestor should be held in its own county, not at Westminster.[2]

(2) John's Charter further insists on quarterly circuits of Justices of Assize; so that litigants in every county of England might have four opportunities each year of having their disputes thus settled. Such frequency involved expense and labour out of proportion to the good effected. The Charter of 1217, accordingly, provided that circuits should be made only once a year. In 1285, however, it was enacted that they might be held three times a year, but not oftener.[3]

(3) The Charter regulates the composition of the tribunal. Two justices appointed by the King (or by his chief justiciar) are directed to hold the assizes, along with four knights of the shire. The bench of six thus combines

---

[1] Thus two successive chapters of Magna Carta emphasize two divergent tendencies : c. 17 had demanded that "common pleas" should all be held at Westminster, while c. 18 demands that "assizes" should *not* be taken there. In both cases, the object was to consult the convenience of litigants.

[2] See Bracton's *Note-book*, No. 1478 ; cited Coke (*Second Institute, proem*). If this assize had presented points of special difficulty it might have been held at Westminster without violating Magna Carta, as amended in 1217.

[3] 13 Edward I. c. 30. Stephen, *History of Criminal Law*, 105-7, gives further details.

representatives of the *Curia* with local landowners. No
mention is made of the twelve recognitors : nor was this
necessary, as their functions and status were well known in
1215, and their verdict formed the essential feature of the
procedure.[1] Chapter 19 provides that the classes, from
whom recognitors had to be selected, should attend in
sufficient numbers " for the efficient making of judgments."

(4) The four knights were to be " elected " by the county
court (*quatuor militibus ... electis per comitatum*),[2] and
emphasis has been laid on this provision by historians
searching for ancient prototypes of modern institutions.
These knights have been incautiously welcomed as county
magistrates elected on a more or less extended suffrage.[3]

As the provisions of the reissue of 1217 are more carelessly expressed, and as in particular they contain no word
implying " election," it is sometimes assumed that a change
was intended; that a step tentatively taken towards representative local government in 1215 was deliberately retraced
two years later.[4] " *Electus,*" however, in medieval Latin
was a vague word, differing widely from the ideas usually
associated with a modern " election," and applied indiscriminately to all methods of appointment or selection, even
to the proceedings of officers engaged by Edward I. to compel the impressment of soldiers. The twelve knights were
to be " appointed," not " elected," in the county court; and
it remains doubtful whether the sheriff, the magnates, or
the body of the suitors, would have the chief share in the
appointment. No evidence is forthcoming that any
importance was attached in 1217 to the word " *electus,*" and
its omission may have been due to inadvertence.

[1] Cf. Assize of Northampton, c. 4.

[2] Cf. *infra*, c. 48, where twelve sworn knights are to be chosen *per probos homines ejusdem comitatus.* Cf. also *Forma Procedendi* of 1194 (*Sel. Charters*, 255).

[3] See, *e.g.* Stubbs, *preface* to R. Hoveden, IV. xcviii.; Blackstone, *Great Charter*, xxxvi.; Medley, *Eng. Const. Hist.*, 130.

[4] Blackstone, *ibid.*, points out these changes in the charter of 1217 : "the leaving indefinite the number of the knights and the justices of assize, the abolishing of the election of the former, and the reducing the times of taking assizes to once in every year."

IV. *Effects of Magna Carta.* The stipulations of the Great Charter were not strictly followed in practice. It was not the custom under Henry III. for the Crown to grant general commissions to hold petty assizes. On the contrary, each litigant was left to make separate application to the King, who would then assign a justice by letters patent to preside over that one particular plea. Hundreds of such commissions might be issued in one year, and recognitors were separately summoned for each one of these. In 1258 the Petition of the Barons (c. 19) complained of this, and an attempt was made at organization. The Statute of Westminster II. (c. 30) ordained that two sworn justices should be assigned, before whom and none others assizes of Novel Disseisin and Mort d'ancestor (along with attaints) should be taken. They were to go on circuit three times a year, and to associate with themselves one or more of the discreetest knights of each county—instructions which fall short of the stipulations of Magna Carta.[1]

V. *An Erroneous View.* Hallam, commenting on this chapter, seems to have misapprehended the issues at stake. " This clause stood opposed on the one hand to the encroachments of the King's court, which might otherwise, by drawing pleas of land to itself, have defeated the suitor's right to a jury from the vicinage : and, on the other, to those of the feudal aristocracy, who hated any interference of the Crown to chastise their violations of law, or control their own jurisdiction." [2] Hallam thus interprets the chapter as denoting a triumph of the old local popular courts over both the King's courts and the courts of the feudal magnates. It denoted no such thing, but marked in reality a triumph (so far as it went) of the King's courts over the tribunals of the feudal magnates—courts baron, as they were afterwards called. The assizes, it is true, were to be taken in the county court, but they were to be taken there by the King's justices. The county courts by this time had fallen completely under the King's domination, and were to all

---

[1] On the whole subject, see an admirable article by G. J. Turner, *Encycl. Laws of Engl.*, III. 76 ff.

[2] See *Middle Ages*, II. 464.

intents and purposes royal courts. The present chapter is thus conclusive evidence of the triumph of the King's justice, which was the best article in the market, and, in spite of all defects, deserved the popularity it had won.

VI. *Later History of the Justices of Assize.* Whatever may have been the exact date when there first went on tour throughout England travelling judges entitled to the description of "Justices of Assize," such circuits, once instituted, continued to be held at more or less regular intervals from the beginning of the thirteenth century to the present day. Their jurisdiction steadily widened under successive kings, from Henry II. to Edward III.; and they gradually superseded the older Justices of Eyre, taking over such functions as were not inconsistent with the change from the medieval to the modern system of justice.[1]

For centuries it was customary for the Crown to issue to the justices of each new circuit several commissions, each conferring jurisdiction over a different class of pleas. Founding on the authority of Sir Francis Bacon, historians have been wont to enumerate five distinct commissions.[2]

(1) The commission of assize, already discussed, allowed them to hold petty assizes, but not (in the normal case) the grand assize.[3]

(2) *Commission of Nisi Prius.* Under Statute Westminster II. c. 30, the sheriff was directed to summon jurors to Westminster "unless at an earlier date" (*nisi prius*) the justices of assize should happen to arrive in the county in question. This was interpreted as creating a jurisdiction in the justices of assize to try all non-criminal pleas of the county—a jurisdiction afterwards known as "*nisi prius.*" Thereafter, any such plea, whether begun in King's Bench or Common Pleas, might be determined locally in its appro-

---

[1] Cf. Coke, *First Institute,* 293b: "As the power of justices of assizes by many Acts of Parliament and other commissions increased, so these justices itinerant by little and little vanished away."

[2] On whole subject see Stubbs, *Sel. Chart.,* 141-3; Stephen, *Hist. Crim. Law,* I. 79-111; Holdsworth, I. 116-123. Contrast, however, Turner, *op. cit.,* III. 76 ff.

[3] For the exception where lands were under £5 in annual value, see *supra,* p. 273.

priate shire as well as at Westminster. According to the opinion generally received, a separate commission of "*nisi prius*" was issued to each group of justices of assize, but it has recently been urged that no separate commission was required, the one jurisdiction being merely incidental to the other.[1]

(3) *The commission of gaol delivery* was, subsequently to 1299, conferred on the justices of assize, in accordance with a statute of that year,[2] authorizing them to inspect all gaols and enquire into all charges against prisoners, and to set free those unjustly detained. Previously, similar powers had been spasmodically conferred on separate commissioners, who had too often abused their authority.

(4) *Commissions of Oyer and Terminer,* issued spasmodically from as early a date as 1285,[3] to more or less responsible individuals, were from 1329 onwards conferred exclusively on the justices of assize, who thus obtained authority[4] "to hear and determine" all criminal pleas pending in the counties they visited. This, combined with the commission of gaol delivery, amounted to a full jurisdiction over crimes and criminals of every kind and degree; just as the commission of assize (with or without an added commission of *nisi prius*) conferred full jurisdiction over civil pleas.[5]

(5) In the generally received opinion, a fifth commission was invariably issued to the justices, in the form of a special commission of the peace, from the reign of Edward III. onwards.[6]

[1] G. J. Turner, *ibid.*, p. 79.

[2] 27 Edward I. c. 3. For early history of gaol delivery, see Pollock and Maitland, II. 642.

[3] 13 Edward I. c. 39; see Stephen, *Hist. Criminal Law*, p. 106.

[4] Edward III. c. 2. *Ibid.*, 110.

[5] It is unnecessary to do more than notice the exceptional "commissions of trailbaston," supposed to date from the Statute of Rageman (1276), conferring special powers for the suppression of powerful wrongdoers. These were soon superseded by the commissions of oyer and terminer.

[6] Mr. Turner (*ibid.*, p. 79) suggests, however, that a separate commission was not needed, as "all justices of assize and gaol delivery were in the commission of the peace within the precincts of the court." In his view the justices received three distinct commissions, not five.

The justices of assize, from the small beginnings referred to in John's Great Charter, thus gathered to themselves the powers exercised originally by various sets of commissioners. They have continued for many centuries to perform the functions conferred by these various commissions, and form a characteristic part of the judicial system of England.

CHAPTER NINETEEN.

Et si in die comitatus assise predicte capi non possint, tot milites et libere tenentes remaneant de illis qui interfuerint comitatui die illo, per quos possint judicia sufficienter fieri, secundum quod negocium fuerit majus vel minus.

> And if any of the said assizes cannot be taken on the day of the county court, let there remain of the knights and freeholders, who were present at the county court on that day, as many as may be required for the efficient making of judgments, according as the business be more or less.

This supplement to the preceding chapter prescribed the course to be followed when press of business prevented some of the assizes on the agenda from being disposed of on the court day. The shiremoot lasted for one day only, and to hold an adjourned session of all the suitors would inflict hardship on those whose presence was required elsewhere. The framers of the charter here sought to provide for the presence of a sufficient supply of recognitors, without insisting on the continued attendance of the whole body of suitors. They were doing their best to give effect to two requirements of the *Articuli Baronum* not readily reconcilable, namely, that only those actually required as recognitors should be summoned (article 8); and that assizes should be " shortened " (article 13), implying the presence of sufficient recognitors for a rapid despatch of business.

The terms of Magna Carta made it clear that assizes in the normal case should be held in the county court—a point upon which the Articles had been silent. This was a salutary provision, since a healthy publicity accompanied the proceedings of the shiremoot.   If there was more business than could be got through in one day, a compromise must be made between the claims of litigants wishing their pleas hastened and the desire of other people to be discharged from further attendance.   The justices were directed to complete their labours on the morrow, but were forbidden to retain anyone in attendance except the actual parties to suits and a sufficient number of jurors.   Those whom Magna Carta thus compelled to wait a second day were exactly those whose presence the Articles had required upon the first day.   The discrepancy between the two documents might be explained on the supposition that the device of synchronizing the visit of the justices with the date of holding the monthly shiremoot was only thought of after the Articles of the Barons had been sealed.[1]

The Charter of 1217 made a different provision for the same contingency.   Unfinished assizes need no longer be taken in their own county on the day following the county court, nor, indeed, on any other day.   The judges received full authority to bring them to a conclusion elsewhere on their circuit according as it might suit their convenience. This concession to the justices, taken in connection with the further provisions of 1217, reserving all darrein presentments, together with other assizes of any difficulty, for the decision of the bench, shows a comparative disregard of the convenience of jurors, who might, in the option of the justices, find themselves compelled either to follow the assizes from shire to shire, or else to undertake the irksome journey to Westminster, from which the Charter of 1215 had relieved them.[2]

Subsequent practice did not conform to this rule.   One *novel disseisin*, or one *mort d'ancestor*, might be held by itself; and complaint was made in 1258 that the sheriffs proclaimed in the market places that all knights and freeholders must assemble for such an inquest, and when they came not, amerced them at will (*pro voluntate sua*).   See Petition of Barons, c. 19 (*Sel. Charters*, 385).

[2] Subsequent legislation vacillated between two policies, actuated at times by a desire to restrain the discretionary powers of the justices; and at others by experience of the hardships inflicted upon litigants by inflexible rules.   The Statute of Westminster II. (13 Edward I. c. 30) confirmed the power of the justices to reserve cases of mort d'ancestor for decision by the bench, and *per contra* allowed

CHAPTER TWENTY.

LIBER homo non amercietur pro parvo delicto, nisi secundum modum delicti; et pro magno delicto amercietur secundum magnitudinem delicti, salvo contenemento suo; et mercator eodem modo, salva mercandisa sua; et villanus eodem modo amercietur salvo waynagio suo, si inciderint in misericordiam nostram; et nulla predictarum misericordiarum ponatur, nisi per sacramentum proborum hominum de visneto.

> A freeman shall not be amerced for a slight offence, except in accordance with the degree of the offence; and for a grave offence he shall be amerced in accordance with the gravity of the offence, yet saving always his "contenement"; and a merchant in the same way, saving his "merchandise"; and a villein shall be amerced in the same way, saving his "wainage"—if they have fallen into our mercy: and none of the aforesaid amercements shall be imposed except by the oath of honest men of the neighbourhood.

This is the first of three chapters that seek to remedy abuses connected with royal amercements. To understand what these were requires some knowledge, not only of the system of legal procedure of which they formed part, but also of previous systems.

I. *Three stages of criminal law.* The efforts made in medieval England to devise machinery for suppressing crime took various forms. Three periods may be distinguished.

(1) *The bloodfeud.* The earliest method of redressing wrongs was retaliation, or the bloodfeud. The injured man, or his heir, took the law into his own hands and exacted satisfaction by the aid of battle-axe or spear.

assizes of darrein presentment to be taken "in their own counties." 6 Richard II. c. 5 curtailed the discretionary powers, directing that justices assigned to take assizes and deliver gaols should hold sessions in the county towns in which the shire courts were wont to be held. 11 Richard II. c. 11 once more relaxed this rule, alleging that it had resulted in the inconvenience of suitors. Authority was given to the chancellor, with the advice of the justices, to determine in what places assizes might be held.

(2) *Fixed money-payments*. At some early, but uncertain, date it became customary to accept money in lieu of vengeance. The new practice, at first exceptional, was gradually extended. It was made compulsory to offer solatium in money, and, finally, to accept it when offered. The right of private revenge was lawful only after the aggrieved individual had demanded, and been refused, compensation at the recognized rate. Various codes formulated rules for determining the amounts thus payable. Each man had his money value or *wer* (from the simple freeman, reckoned at 200 shillings, up to prelates and lay nobles, estimated at much higher figures). Slighter wrongs could be compensated by smaller sums, known as *bots* : so much for a foot, or an eye, or a tooth. The King or other lord exacted further payments from the wrong-doer, under the name of *wites*, which are sometimes explained as the price charged by the magistrate for enforcing payment of the *wer* or *bot*; sometimes as sums due to the community, on the ground that every evil deed inflicts a wrong on society in general, as well as upon its victim.

(3) *Amercements*. A third system succeeded. This is found in working order soon after the Norman Conquest, but was still regarded as an innovation at the accession of Henry I. It is known as the system of amercements. None of our authorities contains an entirely satisfactory account of how the change took place; but the following suggestions may be hazarded. The sums demanded from a wrong-doer, who wished to buy himself back under protection of the law, became increasingly burdensome. He had to satisfy claims of the victim's family, of the victim's lord, of the lord within whose territory the crime had been committed, of the church, mayhap, whose sanctuary had been invaded, of other lords who could show an interest of any sort, and finally of the King as lord paramount. It became practically impossible to buy back the peace once it had been broken. The Crown, however, stepped in, and offered protection on certain conditions : the culprit surrendered himself and all that he had to the King, placing himself " *in misericordiam regis*," and delivering a tangible

pledge (*vadium*) as evidence and security of the surrender.[1] Strictly speaking, the man's life and limbs and all that he had were at the King's mercy.[2] The Crown, however, found that it might defeat its own interests by excessive greed; and generally contented itself with moderate forfeits. Rules of procedure were formulated : the amounts taken were regulated partly by the wealth of the offender, and partly by the gravity of the offence. Further, it became a recognized rule that the amount should be assessed by what was practically a jury of the culprit's neighbours; and attempts were also made to fix a maximum.[3]

Thus a sort of tariff grew up, which the Crown usually respected in practice, without abandoning the right to demand more. Such payments were known as "amercements." For petty offences, men were constantly placed " in mercy " : for failure to attend meetings of hundred or county; for false or mistaken verdicts; for infringements of forest rights. The Charter of Henry I. (chapter 8) had promised a remedy, drastic indeed but of a reactionary and impossible nature. His promise, to abolish altogether the system of amercements (then of recent introduction) and to revert to the earlier Anglo-Saxon system of bots and wites, was made only to be broken.[4]

---

[1] See Charter of Henry I. c. 8, which, however, condemns the whole practice among the other innovations of the Conqueror and Rufus.

[2] See *Dialogus de Scaccario,* II. xvi.

[3] Cf. Pollock and Maitland, II. 511-4. There were, however, exceptions, *e.g.* Henry II. would not accept money payments for certain forest offences : mutilation was inflicted. See Assize of Woodstock, c. 1, and contrast Forest Charter of 1217, c. 10.

[4] Cf. Pollock and Maitland (II. 512), who describe Henry's promise as " a return to the old Anglo-Saxon system of pre-appointed wites." In order to avoid confusion, no mention has been made in the account given above of a classification of amercements into three degrees, which increases the obscurity surrounding their origin. The *Dialogus de Scaccario,* II. xvi., tells how (1) for grave crimes, the culprit's life and limbs were at the King's mercy, as well as his property ; (2) for less important offences, his lands were forfeited, but his person was safe ; while (3) for minor faults, his personal effects only were at the King's disposal. In the last case, the offender was "*in misericordia regis de pecunia sua.*" Thus to be "in mercy" did not always mean the same thing. Further, a villein or dependent freeman on a manor might fall into the " mercy " of his lord, as well as of the King. The records of manorial courts are full of amercements for petty transgressions of customs of the manor.

II. *Magna Carta and Amercements*. No one could expect to pass through life (perhaps hardly through a single year) without being subjected to amercements.[1] Three chapters of Magna Carta accordingly are occupied with remedies. Chapter 20 seeks to protect the ordinary layman; chapter 21, the barons; and chapter 22, the clergy—thus anticipating the conception of three estates of the realm;—commons, nobles, clergy. The "third estate" is analysed for purposes of this clause, into three subdivisions—the freeman, the villein, and the merchant.[2]

(1) *Amercement of freeholders*. The great object of the reforms here promised was to eliminate the arbitrary element; the Crown must conform to its own customary rules. With this object, safeguards were devised for freemen. (*a*) For a slight offence, only a petty sum could be taken. This was nothing new : the records of John's reign show that, both before and after 1215, very small amounts were often taken : threepence was a common sum. (*b*) For grave offences, a larger sum might be assessed, but not out of proportion to the offence. (*c*) In no case could the offender be pushed absolutely to the wall : his means of livelihood must be saved to him. Even if all other effects had to be sold off to pay the amount assessed, he was to retain his " contenement," a word to be afterwards discussed. (*d*) Another clause provided machinery for giving effect to these rules. The amount must be fixed, not arbitrarily by the Crown, but by impartial assessors, " by the oath of honest men of the neighbourhood." In the reissue of 1216 " honest men " became " honest and lawworthy (*legalium*) men," a purely verbal change.[3]

---

[1] " Very likely there was no clause in Magna Carta more grateful to the mass of the people than that about amercements." Maitland, *Gloucester Pleas*, xxxiv.

[2] Even Coke (*Second Institute*, p. 27) has to confess that for purposes of this chapter he must abandon the attempt made elsewhere (*ibid.*, p. 4 and p. 45) to bring villeins into the class of freemen.

[3] Adams, *Origin*, 257, thinks the addition made it clear that villeins could not amerce the *liber homo*; but were not the four *legaliores homines* of each village described in Assize of Clarendon, villeins? Harcourt, *Steward*, 221 n., insists that the clause does not secure "trial by peers" in the feudal sense, for the jury of neighbours need not be "peers of a tenure."

There were apparently two steps in the fixing of amercements. (*a*) In the case of a commoner, the penalty under normal circumstances would be assessed provisionally by the King's justices on circuit, with the assistance of the sheriff. It was their duty to see that the amount was proportionate to the gravity of the offence.[1] (*b*) Thereafter, the sheriff or his serjeants, in full county court, with the assistance of twelve neighbours, taxed the amercements, reducing them in accordance with their knowledge of the wrong-doer's ability to pay.[2]

The Pipe Rolls afford illustrations of the practice. In the fourteenth year of Henry II.[3] a certain priest (who, in this respect, stood on the same footing as a layman) had been placed "*in misericordiam*" of 100 marks by William fitz John, one of the King's justices, but that sum was afterwards reduced to 40 marks "*per sacramentum vicinorum suorum.*" It seems a safe inference that, on the priest pleading poverty, the question of his ability to pay was referred to local recognitors with the result stated. This priest was subsequently pardoned altogether "because of his poverty."[4]

Magna Carta in this chapter, treating of the amercements of freeholders, merchants and villeins, makes no reference to the part played by the King's justices, but only to the functions of the jury of neighbours.[5] All this is in marked contrast with the provisions of chapter 21, regulating the treatment to be accorded to earls and barons who made default.

(2) *Amercement of merchants.* The trader is in the same position as the *liber homo,* except that it is his "merchandise," not his "contenement," that is protected. The word

---

[1] Harcourt, *Engl. Hist. Rev.*, XXII. 733-4. See also *Dial. de Scac.*, p. 207 n.; Maitland, *Gloucester Pleas*, xxxiv. Amercements apparently might also be provisionally fixed by the justices of the bench or the barons of exchequer, who might (where arrears were still unpaid) reduce their figures of previous years.

[2] Harcourt, *ibid.*   [3] Madox, I. 527.

[4] See, however, on whole subject, Harcourt, *ibid.*

[5] Reeves, *History of English Law*, I. 248 (Third Edition) says: "Upon this chapter was afterwards framed the writ *de moderata misericordia*, for giving remedy to a party who was excessively amerced."

is capable of two somewhat different shades of meaning. Narrowly interpreted, it may refer to his wares, the stock-in-trade without which the pursuit of his calling would be impossible. More broadly viewed, it might mean his business itself, his position as a merchant. The difference is of little practical import : in either view the Charter saves to him his means of earning a living.[1]

Some boroughs, indeed, had anticipated Magna Carta by obtaining in their own charters a definition of the maximum amercement exigible, or in some cases of the amercing body. Thus, John's Charter to Dunwich of 29th June, 1200,[2] provides that the burgesses shall only be amerced by six men from within the borough, and six men from without. The capital had special privileges : in his Charter to London, Henry I. promised that no citizen *in misericordia pecuniae* should pay a higher sum than 100s. (the amount of his *wer*).[3] This was confirmed in the Charter of Henry II., who declared " that none shall be adjudged for amercements of money, but according to the law of the city, which they had in the time of King Henry, my grandfather." [4] John's Charter to London of 17th June, 1199, also referred to this ; [5] and the general confirmation of customs, contained in chapter 13 of Magna Carta, would further strengthen it. In all probability, the earlier grant covered trivial offences only (such as placed the offender in the King's hands *de misericordia pecuniae*). The present chapter is wider in its scope, applying to grave offences also, and embracing merchants everywhere, not merely the burgesses of chartered towns.

(3) *Amercements of villeins.* The early history of villeins as a class is enveloped in the mists that still surround the rise of the English manor. Notwithstanding the brilliant efforts of Mr. Frederic Seebohm [6] to find the origin of

---

[1] Cf. Professor James Tait, *Engl. Hist. Rev.* XXXVII., 720 ff., who thinks that any attempt to exempt merchant " wares " from amercement was inconsistent with the right to distrain goods for debt, as illustrated by many cases given by Gross, *Sel. Cases in Merchant Law* (Selden Society), *passim.*

[2] *Rotuli Chartarum*, 51.   [3] See *Select Charters*, 108.

[4] See Birch, *Historical Charters of London*, p. 5.

[5] *Ibid.*, p. 11.   [6] See *English Village Community*, *passim.*

T

villeinage in the status of the serfs who worked for Roman masters upon British farms long before the Teutonic immigrations began, an older theory still holds the field, namely, that the abject villeins of Norman days were descendants of free-born " ceorls " of Anglo-Saxon stock. On this theory, most of England was once cultivated by Anglo-Saxon peasant proprietors grouped in little societies, each of which formed an isolated village. These villagers were slowly sinking from their originally free estate during several centuries prior to 1066 : but the process of their degradation was completed rapidly and roughly by the Norman conquerors. The once free peasantry were crushed down into the dependent villeins of the eleventh and twelfth centuries.

Whichever theory may be the correct one, the position, economic, legal, and political, of villeins in the thirteenth century has been ascertained with certainty. Economically they were part of the equipment of the manor of their lord, whose fields they had to cultivate as a condition of being left in possession of acres, in a sense, their own. The services exacted, at first vague and undefined, were gradually specified and limited. They varied from century to century, from district to district, and even from manor to manor; but at best the life of the villein was, as a contemporary writer has described it, burdensome and wretched (*graviter et miserabiliter*). After his obligations were discharged, little time was left him for the ploughing and reaping of his own holding. The normal villein possessed his virgate or half virgate (thirty or fifteen scattered acres) under a tenure known as *villenagium,* sharply distinguished from the freeholder's tenures. He was a dependent dweller on a manor which he dared not quit without his master's leave.

It is true that he had rights of a proprietary nature in the acres he claimed as his own; yet these were determined, not by the common law of England, but by " the custom of the manor," or virtually at the will of the lord. These rights, such as they were, could not be pled elsewhere than before the court customary of that manor over which the lord's steward presided with powers wide and undefined. Politically his position was peculiar : allowed none of the privileges, he was yet expected to perform some of the duties, of the freeman. He attended the shire and hundred courts, and acted on juries, thus suffering still further encroachments on the scanty portion of time he might call his own, but preserving for a brighter day a vague tradition of his earlier liberty.

This chapter extends some measure of protection to villeins. Two questions, however, may be asked :—What measure? and from what motive? One point is clear : the villeins were protected from the abuse of only such amercements as John himself might inflict, not from the amercements of their manorial lords; for the words used are " *si inciderint in misericordiam nostram*." A villein in the King's mercy shall enjoy the same consideration as the freeholder or merchant in similar plight—his means of livelihood being saved to him. The word now used is neither " contenement " nor " merchandise," but " waynagium," the meaning of which has been the subject of discussion. Coke defined it as " the contenement of a villein; or the furniture of his cart or wain," and Coke has been widely followed. The word, however, has apparently no connexion with wains or wagons, but is merely a Latinized form of the French word " gagnage," of which Godefroy gives five meanings : (*a*) gain; (*b*) tillage; (*c*) crop; (*d*) land under the plough; (*e*) grain. Professor Tait is inclined to read the word, in its present context, as equivalent either to " crops " or to " lands under cultivation," and to translate the clause " saving his tillage." [1] What was the motive of these restrictions? It is usually

[1] See *Engl. Hist. Rev.*, XXXVII. 724, where Mr. Tait argues " for a broader and less concrete interpretation of the term . . . than has hitherto been put upon it." The villein was not to be ruined by impounding his seed-corn or growing crops any more than by depriving him of his plough or plough team. See also A. F. Pollard, *Engl. Hist. Rev.*, XXXVIII. 117, and cf. *waynagium* in c. 5, *supra*. The *Mirror of Justices*, p. 169, has a gloss on this passage, in which it is the villein's " gaigneur" that is saved to him, and this is apparently identified with the *villenagium* held by him. Mr. Tait's view has been adopted here ; but the word has sometimes a more restricted meaning, *e.g.* in Hoveden, iv. 48, where 100 acres of land are reckoned to the " waynage " of each plough.

supposed to have been clemency, the humane desire not to
reduce a poor wretch to absolute beggary. It is possible,
however, to imagine a different motive; the villein was the
property of his lord, and John must respect the vested
interests of others. That the King might do what he
pleased with his own property, his demesne villeins, seems
clear from a passage usually neglected by commentators,
namely, chapter 16 of the reissue of 1217. Four important
words were there introduced—*villanus alterius quam
noster*: the king was not to inflict crushing amercements on
villeins "*other than his own,*" thus leaving villeins on royal
manors unreservedly in his power.[1]

It must not be thought, however, that the position of
the King's villeins was worse than that of villeins of an
ordinary unroyal manor. On the contrary, it has been
clearly shown[2] that the King's peasants enjoyed privileges
denied to the peasants of other lords. Magna Carta protected a lord's villeins from the King, not from the lord
who owned them. That "great bulwark of the people's
rights" left the bulk of the rural population of England at
the mercy of their lords. The King must not take so much
from any lord's villeins as to destroy their usefulness as
manorial chattels; that was all.[3]

(4) *The difference between fines and amercements.* In the
thirteenth century, these terms were sharply contrasted.
"Amercement" was applied to sums imposed in punish-

---

[1] The view here taken of the motive for protecting villeins is strengthened by the
use of the peculiar phrase, "*vastum hominum*" in chapter 4 (*q.v.*). Thomson,
Magna Charta, p. 202, seems completely to have misunderstood this 16th chapter
of the reissue of 1217, construing the four interpolated words in a sense the Latin
will not bear, viz.: "A villein, *although he belonged to another.*"

[2] Notably by Professor Vinogradoff in his *Villeinage in England, passim.*

[3] The gulf which separated villein from freeman in this matter is shown by the
Pipe Roll of 16 Henry II. (cited Madox, I. 545); *Herbertus Faber debet j marcam
pro falso clamore quem fecit ut liber cum sit rusticus.* A villein might be amerced
for merely claiming to be free. It is difficult to reconcile any theory of the
villein's freedom with the doctrine of Glanvill, V. c. 5, who denies to everyone
who had been once a villein the right to "wage his law," even after emancipa-
tion, where any third party's interests might thereby be prejudiced. R. Hoveden,
iv. 46, speaking of the carucage of 1198, explains that for perjury a villein forfeited
his best ox to his lord (not to the King).

ment of misdeeds; the law-breaker had no option of refusing, and no voice in fixing the amount. " Fine," on the contrary, was used for voluntary offerings made to the King to obtain some favour or to escape punishment. Here the initiative rested with the individual, who suggested the amount to be paid, and was, indeed, under no legal obligation to make any offer at all. This distinction between fines and amercements, absolute in theory, could readily be obliterated in practice. The spirit of the restriction placed by this chapter and by the common law upon the King's prerogative of inflicting amercements could often be evaded. The Crown might imprison its victims for an indefinite period, and then graciously allow them to offer large payments to escape death by fever or starvation in a noisome gaol : enormous *fines* might thus be taken, while royal officials were forbidden to inflict arbitrary *amercements*.

With the gradual elimination of the voluntary element the word " fine " came to bear its modern meaning, while " amercement " dropped out of ordinary use."[1]

(5) *Contenement*. This word, which occurs in Glanvill [2] and in Bracton,[3] and also (in its French form) in the Statute of Westminster, I.,[4] as well as in Magna Carta, has formed a text for many commentators from Coke's days to our own. By comparing the entries from exchequer rolls brought together by Madox,[5] it appears that to save a man's " contenement " was to leave him sufficient for the sustenance of himself and those dependent on him. The word comes from the French " contenir," and has many shades of meaning, as capacity, maintenance, appearance, social condition or grade. A free man is not to be so crushed by an amercement that he cannot maintain himself in his former condition.[6] Several entries on Exchequer Rolls of Henry

---

[1] C. 55, which supplements this chapter, cancels amercements unjustly inflicted in the past.

[2] IX. 8.   [3] III. folio 116b.   [4] 3 Edward I. c. 6.   [5] See II. 208-9.

[6] Prof. Tait's conclusions (*op. cit.*) have here been accepted with some hesitation. " Contenement," he urges, " is not a compound from tenement." He admits, however, following Godefroy, that in one instance the word does mean " tenement." He does not notice the striking analogy between the use of " contenement " in this chapter and that of " tenement " in c. 11 *supra* ; nor does he discuss the evidence

III. and Edward I., collected by Madox,[1] throw light on the way in which a " contenement " might be saved to the man amerced. Thus in 40 Henry III. the officials of the exchequer, after discussing an offender's failure to pay an amercement of 40 marks, ordered inquiry to be made, " how much he was able to pay the King *per annum*, saving his own sustenance and that of his wife and children," an excerpt which illustrates the more humane side of exchequer procedure. In 14 Edward I. again, the officials of that day, when ferreting out arrears, found that certain poor men of the village of Doddington had not paid their amercements in full. An inquiry was set on foot, and the barons of exchequer were ordered to fix the dates at which the various debtors should discharge their debts (evidently an arrangement for payment by instalments) " *salvo contenemento suo.*" [2]

These illustrations of the procedure of later reigns, agreeing closely with the rules laid down by the Great Charter, show how a man's contenement might be saved to him without loss to the Crown. Magna Carta apparently desired that time should be granted in which to pay up debts by degrees. Meanwhile, the amerced freeman was not forced to part with what was necessary to maintain him, with his wife and family, in his proper station in life.

of the contemporary *Histoire de Guillaume le Maréchal*, where the word appears seven times with various meanings, *e.g.* capacity, manner of being, conduct, and equipment. M. Paul Meyer has collected these in his index. Mr. Tait goes too far when he asserts that to make freehold liable to amercement shows " a complete misconception of that form of punishment," p. 726. There were three degrees of amercement; and only for the mildest of the three was the forfeit limited to the culprit's personal estate (*de pecunia*). See *supra*, p. 286, n. Again, a man might be forced to sell his freehold to meet a heavy pecuniary mulct. Under Henry's Charter, in its final form, no ecclesiastic could be amerced except in accordance with his " tenement," which suggests an analogy with the saving of a freeman's " contenement " in the present passage.

[1] See II. 208-9.　　　　　　　　　[2] See Madox, *ibid.*

CHAPTER TWENTY-ONE.

COMITES et barones non amercientur nisi per pares suos, et non nisi secundum modum delicti.

> Earls and barons shall not be amerced except through their peers, and only in accordance with the degree of the offence.

Amercement of earls and barons. It is noteworthy that the *Articuli Baronum* contain no provisions corresponding to this chapter, which forms in one sense a supplement to chapter 20, and in another to chapter 39 of John's Charter. How is the omission from the earlier document to be explained? Was it an oversight? Was the present clause added at Runnymede as an afterthought for the sake of symmetry? Had the barons no personal grievances under this head to redress? Were they too disinterested to urge them? Or was the grievance of so notable a kind and so hard to remedy that they hesitated till the last moment before committing themselves to any form of expression? There is no contemporary evidence on which to base a conclusive answer to these questions; but much may be said for answering the last of them in the affirmative.

The equally natural question as to what the actual words of the Charter stood for in the minds of the barons is also hard to answer. When they mentioned amercement *per pares suos,* what exactly did they desire? Bracton[1] has a famous gloss on this chapter, in which these words seem at first sight to be replaced by the phrase " *et hoc per barones de scaccario vel coram ipso rege.*" Is this to be taken as an honest paraphrase? or does it represent a deliberate attempt by Crown lawyers to pervert the plain words of the Charter to authorize precisely what they had been originally intended to forbid?—to substitute the decision of a small knot of royal officials for that of the community of feudal barons? While the problem is

[1] III. folio 116b.

perhaps insoluble, some suggestions may be founded on a consideration of the actual practice before and after 1215.[1]

The plea rolls contain no distinct evidence of two stages in the amercement of barons, corresponding to those described in connexion with commoners. It is clear, however, that the justices on circuit had no power to fix the amercements imposed on them : in their case a blank was usually left to be afterwards filled in at the exchequer. " For this purpose, a separate roll or schedule was prepared containing the names of the amerced barons with the offences for which they were penalised, and this was sent to the exchequer with the other estreats." [2]

This was the course followed at an eyre held at Hertford in 1198-9 : when a list of the amerced was prepared and definite sums were entered after each ordinary offender's name, blanks were left after the names of Gerard de Furnivall and Reginald de Argenton, each of whom was reserved for special treatment " as a baron," and as such " to be amerced at the Exchequer for a disseisin." The Pipe Roll of John's first year shows that this procedure was carried out.[3]

Magna Carta, then, had good precedents for insisting that barons ought not to be amerced by the justices of eyre in the course of their circuits; but what exactly did it mean by demanding amercement " by their peers " ? In asking amercement *per pares suos*, were they merely acquiescing in John's current practice ? Did they desire to substitute the decision of a full *commune concilium*, as defined in chapter 14, for that of the King's professional justices ? Did they merely ask for the presence of a few barons at

---

[1] A valuable volume of evidence has been collected by Harcourt, *Eng. Hist. Rev.* XXII. 733 ff. ; though his conclusions are mainly negative. See also his *Steward*, ff. 289.

[2] Harcourt, *ibid.*, 736. Pike, *House of Lords*, 256-7, shows how barons were assessed sometimes—(a) before the barons of exchequer ; or (b) before the full King's Council ; or (c) at a later date, even before the justices of Common Pleas. They were never assessed, however, before the justices on circuit.

[3] See Pike, *House of Lords*, 255.

the exchequer, when one of their own class was being amerced? Or, did they refer to a second stage of procedure in which the amercements of barons should be taxed or reduced by other barons, just as (in the procedure referred to in chapter 20) amercements of commoners were taxed by a jury of neighbours?

If the last query could be answered in the affirmative, a clue would be afforded to the interpretation of Bracton's gloss :—"Comites vero vel barones non sunt amerciandi nisi per pares suos et secundum modum delicti et hoc per barones de scaccario vel coram ipso rege."[1] The words *" et hoc "* may here refer merely to the first stage in the process, the provisional fixing of the amount at the exchequer *secundum modum delicti,* while the function of the baron's " peers " was to " tax " this amount, with reference to the circumstances of the defaulting baron. If this interpretation of Bracton be admissible and if he has accurately paraphrased the substance of this chapter, then the barons were asking no more for themselves than they had already asked for their humble dependents. They were unlikely to ask less.

In the fourteenth century several cases are recorded in the course of which defaulters, in the hope of escaping with smaller payments, protested against being reckoned as barons. Thomas de Furnivall, for example, in the nineteenth year of Edward II. complained that he had been amerced as a baron " to his great damage, and against the law and custom of the realm," whereas he really held nothing by barony. The King directed the Treasurer and Barons of Exchequer " that if it appeared to them that Thomas was not a baron, nor did hold his land by barony, then they should discharge him of the said imposed amercement; provided that Thomas should be amerced according to the tenor of the great Charter of Liberties," [2] that is to say, as a simple freeholder according to the provisions of chapter 20. It is clear that Thomas de Furnivall was confident that a local jury would " tax " him at a lower figure than that fixed by the Exchequer barons. A few

---

[1] Bracton, f. 116b.   [2] Madox, I. 535-8.

years earlier the Abbot of Croyland had made a similar claim, but without success.[1]

At a later date, barons and earls were successful in securing by another expedient some measure of immunity from excessive exactions. They had established, prior to the first year of Henry VI., a recognized scale of amercements with which the Crown was expected, in ordinary circumstances, to content itself.[2] In the reign of Edward VI. a duke was normally amerced at £10, and an earl or a bishop at 100s.[3]

CHAPTER TWENTY-TWO.

Nullus clericus amercietur de laico tenemento suo, nisi secundum modum aliorum predictorum, et non secundum quantitatem beneficii sui ecclesiastici.

> A clerk shall not be amerced in respect of his lay holding except after the manner of the others aforesaid ; further, he shall not be amerced in accordance with the extent of his ecclesiastical benefice.

Amercement of the clergy. The churchman was to receive the same favourable treatment as the layman in all respects, and to enjoy one additional privilege. In proportioning the amercement to his means, no account was to be taken of the value of his " church benefice." There is room, however, for doubt as to the precise nature of this privilege, which seems to depend for its point on an antithesis between " lay tenement " and " ecclesiastical benefice."

In a well-known article of the Constitutions of Clarendon

---

[1] See Madox, *ibid.*, and also Pike, *House of Lords*, 257. Mr. Pike, p. 255, rightly says that what was originally a privilege had become a burden.

[2] See Pike, *ibid.*

[3] Madox, *Baronia Anglica*, 106, seems to view these sums as fixing a minimum, not a maximum. " If a baron was to be amerced for a small trespass, his amercement was wont to be 100s. at the least ; he might be amerced at more, not at less. This, I think, was the meaning of the term *amerciater ut baro.*" He adds that a commoner for a similar trespass would get off with 10s., 20s., or 40s.

(c. 9), a contrast is drawn between *laicum feudum* and *tenementum pertinens ad eleemosinam*. It is possible that Magna Carta means to observe the same distinction between "lay fee" and "frankalmoin," reckoning the former, but not the latter, in estimating a clerk's ability to pay amercements.

A more likely interpretation is that the contrast is drawn between lands owned by a clerk absolutely, and lands belonging to the church and held by the clerk in liferent. The plausibility of this conjecture is strengthened by alterations, apparently of a purely verbal nature, made in reissues of the Charter. The "*de laico tenemento*" of 1215 was omitted altogether in 1216; and in 1217, the provision took this final form : "Nulla ecclesiastica persona amerciatur secundum quantitatem beneficii sui ecclesiastici, sed secundum tenementum [1] suum et secundum quantitatem delicti." The substitution of ecclesiastical "person"—a word fast acquiring even then a connotation like that of the "parson" of present-day colloquial speech—for "clerk" has no significance, but the main antithesis drawn would seem to be between the "benefice" or mere liferent and the "tenement" or fief held in perpetuity. In taxing a clerk's amercement, no account was to be taken of possessions of which he was not really owner.

CHAPTER TWENTY-THREE.

NEC villa nec homo distringatur facere pontes ad riparias, nisi qui ab antiquo et de jure facere debent.

> No village or individual [2] shall be compelled to make bridges at river banks, except those who from of old were legally bound to do so.

[1] Stubbs, *Sel. Chart.*, 345, by a curious oversight reads "contenementum," in the issue of 1217, for which there seems to be no authority.

[2] The word "*villa*," used at first as synonymous with "manor," came to be freely applied not only to all villages, but also to chartered towns. Even London was described as a *villa* in formal writs. "*Homo*," though often loosely used, was the word naturally applied to a feudal tenant. The version given by Coke (*Second Institute*, p. 30) reads "*liber homo*," which is also the reading of one MS. of the *Inspeximus* of 1297 (25 Edward I.). See *Statutes of the Realm*, I. 114.

The object of this chapter is obvious; to compel the King to desist from his practice of illegally increasing the burden of the obligation to keep in repair all bridges over rivers. John might continue to exact what his ancestors had exacted; but nothing more. So much lies on the surface of the Charter, which explains, however, neither the origin of the obligation nor the reasons that made John keen to enforce it.

I. *Origin of Obligation to make Bridges.* The Norman kings seem to have based their claim to compel their subjects to maintain bridges upon the ancient tripartite obligation [1] (known as the *trinoda necessitas*). Three duties were required of all the men of England in the interests of the commonweal : attendance on the fyrd or local militia; the making of roads, so necessary for military purposes; and the repairing of bridges and fortifications. Gradually, as feudal tendencies prevailed, the obligation to construct bridges ceased to be a personal burden upon all freemen, and became a territorial burden.[2] The present chapter seems to be a particular application of the general principle enunciated in chapter 16. " Brigbot " required special treatment because of the prominence into which it had been forced by John.

II. *The King's interest in the Repair of Bridges.* Part at least of John's motives for making an oppressive use of this prerogative must be sought in his rights of falconry. Whenever John proposed to ride a-fowling, with his hawk upon his wrist, he issued letters compelling the whole country-side to bestir themselves in the repair of bridges. Several such writs of Henry III. are extant. The exact words vary somewhat, but comparison leaves no room for doubt either as to the nature of the commands conveyed or the reasons for issuing them. Addressed to sheriffs of such counties as the King was likely to visit, these letters

---

[1] See *Rot. Claus.*, 19 Henry III., cited by Moore, *History and Law of Fisheries*, p. 8.

[2] The Hundred Rolls illustrate the manner of its incidence; *e.g.* Omnes tenentes de Spaldinge debent ad reparacionem pontis illius, quilibet pro rata porcionis terrae suae contribuere, ita quod quaelibet acra erit par alterius. *Rot. Hund.*, I. 468.

gave instructions for repair of bridges, and a prohibition against the taking of birds before the King had enjoyed his sport. Both points are well brought out in a Letter Close of Henry III., dated 26th December, 1234, which directed "all bridges on the rivers Avon, Test, and Itchen to be repaired as was wont in the time of King John, so that when the lord King may come to these parts, free transit shall lie open to him for 'revaying' (ad riviandum) upon the said rivers." The sheriff is to issue a general prohibition against any one attempting to "revaye" along the river banks, previous to the coming of the King.[1] The Latin verb, for which the Old English word "revaye" or "ryvaye" is an exact equivalent, has been the subject of misconception; but conclusive evidence has recently been adduced to prove that it referred to the medieval sport of fowling, that is to the taking of wild birds in sport by means of hawks and falcons.[2]

These writs prove that the Crown claimed a preferential right to this form of sport along the banks of certain rivers; and these "preserved" rivers were said to be "in defence" (in defenso), a phrase which occurs also in a later chapter of Magna Carta.[3]

Two distinct hardships were thus imposed by the King's exercise of his rights of falconry, one negative and the other positive. Between the King's intimation and his arrival at the indicated rivers, the sport of other people was forbidden, while whole villages had to forsake their ploughs to reconstruct otherwise useless bridges. A wise king would be careful to use such rights so as to inflict a minimum of hardship. John knew no moderation, placing "in defence" not merely a few banks at a time, but many

[1] See Rot. Claus., 19 Henry III., cited in Moore, History and Law of Fisheries, p. 8.

[2] See Moore, ibid., 8-16. Two links in the chain of evidence are worthy of emphasis: (a) Writs of 13th November and 1st December, 1234, order repair of bridges for the transit of the King "along with his birds." (b) A writ of 28th October, 1283, contains a licence to 'the Earl of Hereford "during the present winter season to 'revaye' and take river-fowl throughout the rivers Lowe and Frome which are in defence."

[3] I.e. c. 47 (q.v.).

rivers indiscriminately, including those which had never been so treated in his father's day, and demanding that all bridges everywhere should be repaired, with the object, not so much of indulging a genuine love of sport, as of inflicting heavy amercements on those who neglected prompt obedience to his commands. Great consternation was aroused when John at Bristol in 1209 prohibited the taking of birds throughout the entire realm of England.[1]

Both grievances were redressed by Magna Carta. The present chapter promised not to impose the burden on those from whom it was not legally due.[2] Chapter 47, in which he agreed to withdraw his interdict from all rivers which had not been previously "in defence," and to disafforest all forests of his own creation, was entirely omitted in the Charter of 1216;[3] but in 1217 it reappeared in a new position and expressed in different words. The provision in the original chapter 47 that related to forests was relegated to the *Carta de Foresta*, and the other part of that chapter, relating to falconry, was joined to a clause which redressed another grievance growing from the same root. Chapter 19 of Henry III.'s Charter, in its final form, repeats word for word the terms of the present chapter of John, while in chapter 20 Henry proceeds to declare "that no river shall in future be placed in defence except such as were in defence in the time of King Henry, our grandfather, throughout the same places and during the same periods as they were wont in his day."

This express prohibition seems to have prevented the Crown from extending its prerogatives further in this direction. Yet Henry III. had ample opportunities of harassing his subjects by an inconsiderate use of the rights

---

[1] R. Wendover, II. 49 (R.S.), "*Ibi capturam avium per totam Angliam interdixit.*"

[2] Article 11 of the Barons had demanded that no *villa* should be *amerced* for failure to make illegal repairs, thus illustrating at once John's policy, and the point of connection between this provision and the immediately preceding chapters which dealt with amercements.

[3] It was, however, included among the subjects reserved for further consideration in "the respiting clause" (c. 42 of 1216) under the words "*de ripariis et earum custodibus.*" Cf. *supra*, 143.

still left to him. In many cases dubiety existed as to what banks had actually been "preserved" by Henry II., and a vague general command left in cruel uncertainty the district to be visited. Henry III. made important concessions: after the year 1241, he specified the particular river along whose banks he intended to sport, and sometimes announced the exact date at which he expected to arrive. As no writs appear subsequent to 1247, it is possible that he was induced to abstain from the exercise of a right which inflicted hardships out of all proportion to the benefits conferred on the King.[1]

The Crown, however, had not renounced its prerogatives, and several writs still exist to show that Edward I. occasionally allowed his great nobles to share in the royal sport. Licences were granted in 1283 to the Earl of Hereford and to Reginald fitz Peter, and in the following year to the Earl of Lincoln. On 6th October, 1373, Edward III. commanded the sheriff of Oxfordshire to declare that all bridges must be repaired and all fords marked out with stakes, for the crossing of the King "with his falcons" during the approaching winter.[2]

III. *Erroneous Interpretations.* It is not surprising that a pastime so passionately followed as falconry, should have left its traces on two chapters of Magna Carta, the full import of which has not been appreciated by commentators, partly from failure to read them together, but chiefly through the assumption that the words *ad riviandum* and *in defenso* referred to *fishing* rather than to fowling.[3]

It has been confidently inferred that the framers of Magna Carta, when forbidding additional banks to be put "in defence," equally as when demanding the removal of "weirs" from non-tidal waters,[4] intended to preserve public rights of fishing against encroachment. This is an error: in the Middle Ages, fishing was a means of procuring food, not a popular form of sport: to depict John and his action-

---

[1] Moore, *ibid.*, 9.   [2] Moore, *ibid.*, 12.

[3] The *Mirror of Justices* is cited as first suggesting this. See Moore, *ibid.*, 12-16. Coke, *Second Institute*, 30, misled by the *Mirror*, has misled others.

[4] Cf. *infra*, under c. 33.

loving courtiers as exponents of the gentle art of Isaac Walton is a ridiculous anachronism.

It is true that the value of fish as an article of diet led in time to legislation directed primarily to their protection; but apparently no statute with such a motive was passed previous to 1285.[1] It is further true that in the reign of Edward I. it became usual to describe rivers, over which exclusive rights of fishing had been established by riparian owners, as being *in defenso*;[2] but rivers might be " preserved " for more purposes than one.

From Edward's reign onwards, however, rights of fishing steadily became more valuable, while falconry was superseded by other pastimes. Accordingly a new meaning was sought for provisions of Magna Carta, whose original motive had been forgotten. So early as the year 1283 the words of a petition to the King in Parliament show that " fishing " had been substituted for " hawking," in interpreting the prohibition referred to in chapter 47 of John's Charter. The men of York complained that Earl Richard had interfered with their rights of fishing by placing *in defenso* the rivers Ouse and Yore "against the tenor of Magna Carta."[3] This error, which thus dates from 1283, has been accepted for upwards of five hundred years by all commentators on Magna Carta. The credit for dispelling it is due to Mr. Stuart A. Moore and Mr. H. S. Moore in their *History and Law of Fisheries,* published in 1903.[4]

CHAPTER TWENTY-FOUR.

NULLUS vicecomes, constabularius, coronatores, vel alii ballivi nostri, teneant placita corone nostre.

> No sheriff, constable, coroners, or others of our bailiffs, shall hold pleas of our Crown.

[1] This was 13 Edward I., stat. 1, c. 47, cited Moore, *ibid.*, 173.

[2] *Ibid.*, p. 6.   [3] *Ibid.*, p. 16.

[4] Lord Hale (Hargreaves, *Law Tracts,* p. 7) partly anticipated their conclusions, and he seems to have been followed by decisions of the New York Courts. See *Law Notes* (New York) for August, 1905.

The main object of this provision is not open to doubt :
men accused of crimes must be tried before the King's
judges and not by local magistrates of whatsoever kind.
Innocent men dreaded the jurisdiction of the local tyrants
whose harshness had earned widespread hatred. The
sheriffs and castellans deserved their bad repute : the
records of the age overflow with tales of their cruelties and
oppressions. It ought not to be forgotten, however, that
if this chapter contains a condemnation of the local administration of justice, it testifies to the comparative purity of
the justice dispensed by the King's own judges. So far
there is no difficulty; but differences of opinion exist as to
certain points of detail.

I. *Pleas of the Crown.* Pleas were royal or common
according as the interests of the Crown were or were not
involved. This classification has already been discussed
in connection with chapter 17. The present chapter concerns itself only with " pleas of the Crown," a phrase which
had, even in 1215, considerably altered its original meaning. In the eleventh century it had denoted royal business,
whether relating to judicial procedure or not, embracing
all matters connected with the King's household or his
estates, with the collection of his revenue, or the administration of his justice, civil as well as criminal. Gradually,
however, the usage of the word altered in two respects,
contracting in one direction, while expanding in another.
It ceased to be applied to financial business and even
to non-criminal, judicial business, and was reserved for
criminal trials held before the King's judges. This process of contraction had been nearly completed before the
accession of John.

A tendency in an opposite direction had been for some
time in progress; the distinction drawn in early reigns
between petty trespasses, which were left in the province
of the sheriff, and grave offences, which alone were worthy
of the King's attention, was being slowly obliterated.[1]
The central courts extended their activity over all misdeeds,
however trivial, until the whole realm of criminal law fell

[1] Traces may be found in Glanvill, I. c. 1.

U

under the description of " pleas of the Crown." In John's reign this process of expansion was far from complete : the words then, indeed, embraced grave criminal offences tried in the King's great courts, but not the petty offences disposed of in the sheriff's tourn or elsewhere.[1]

North of the Tweed the same phrase has had a different history : in modern Scots law its connotation is still a narrow one; and this is a result of the slow growth of the Scottish Crown in authority and jurisdiction, in notable contrast to the rapidity with which the English Crown attained its zenith. The Kings of Scotland failed to crush their powerful vassals, and pleas of the Scottish Crown, exclusively reserved for the High Court of Justiciary, formed a meagre list—the four heinous crimes of murder, robbery, rape, and arson. The feudal courts of the Scottish nobles long preserved their wide jurisdiction over all other offences. When the heritable jurisdictions were at last abolished, in 1748, the old distinction, so deeply rooted in Scots law, still remained. The sheriff court had no cognizance, until late in the nineteenth century, over the four crimes specially reserved for the King's judges.[2] Thus in Scotland the historic phrase " pleas of the Crown " is, even at the present day, confined to murder, robbery, rape, and fire-raising, while to an English lawyer it embraces the entire realm of criminal law.

II. *Keeping and Trying Criminal Pleas*. The machinery for bringing criminals to justice, as organized by Henry II., was somewhat elaborate. For our present purpose, it may be sufficient to emphasize two important stages in the procedure. An interval had always to elapse between the commission of grave crimes and the formal trial of the accused, for the coming of the itinerant justices took place only at intervals of about seven years. Meanwhile, pre-

---

[1] The triumph of royal justice over all rivals in the sphere of criminal law is thus symbolized by the extension of the phrase "pleas of the Crown," which can be traced through a series of documents—*e.g.* (*a*) the laws of Cnut ; (*b*) Glanvill, I. cc. 1, 2, and 3 ; (*c*) the Assizes of Clarendon and Northampton ; (*d*) the ordinances of 1194 ; and (*e*) Magna Carta.

[2] The *Criminal Procedure* (*Scotland*) Act, 1887 (50 and 51 Victoria, c. 35) gave him jurisdiction over three of them.

liminary steps were taken to collect and record evidence, which might otherwise be lost. The magistrate responsible for these preliminary steps was said to "keep" the pleas (*custodire placita*)—that is, to prevent them from passing out of mind[1] while waiting for the justices who would formally "hold" or "try" or "determine" them (*placitare* or *habere* or *tenere placita*).

Before the reign of John, the two functions had been entrusted to two distinct types of royal officials. The local magistrates of each district "kept" royal pleas, while only the King's justices could "hold" them. The process of differentiation was accelerated in consequence of the jealousy with which the Crown regarded the increasing independence of the sheriffs. The elaborate instructions issued in 1194 to the justices, whom Archbishop Hubert Walter was despatching through the counties, contain provisions intended to keep the pretensions of sheriffs within bounds:[2] they were expressly forbidden to act as justices within any counties in which they had acted as sheriffs since Richard's coronation.[3]

It is safe to infer that the "trying" of royal pleas was the province from which the sheriff was thus to be excluded. Even with regard to the "keeping" or preliminary stages of such pleas, the sheriff was by no means left in sole command. The justices received instructions[4] to cause three knights and one clerk to be chosen in each county as "*custodes placitorum coronae.*" It is possible that these new local officers, specially entrusted with the duty of "keeping" royal pleas, were intended rather to co-operate with, than to supersede, the sheriffs in this function; but, in any view, the sheriffs had no longer a monopoly of authority in their bailiwicks. Magistrates, to be afterwards known as coroners, were thenceforward associated with them in the administration of the county.[5]

---

[1] Cf. *infra*, 315-6, for details.

[2] See *Forma procedendi*, cc. 20 and 21 (*Sel. Chart.*, 260).

[3] *Ibid.*, c. 21.   [4] *Ibid.*, c. 20.

[5] The *Forma procedendi* is usually considered the earliest distinct reference to the office of coroner. Dr. Gross, however (*History of Office of Coroner*, 1892, and *Select Cases from Coroners' Rolls*, 1896) claims to have found traces of their

The ordinance of 1194 seems to have settled subsequent practice in both respects. Sheriffs, while still free to punish petty offenders in their half-yearly tourns or circuits, allowed the coroners to " keep " royal pleas, and the justices to " try " them. Public opinion of the day approved both rules. Yet John condoned and encouraged irregularities, allowing sheriffs to meddle with pleas of the Crown, even when no coroners were present to check their arbitrary methods; [1] and allowing them to give final judgments, involving loss of life or limb, without waiting for the Justices.[2] He employed the same men to visit as justices the very counties they had oppressed as sheriffs. The notorious Engelard of Cigogné, branded by name in chapter 50 of Magna Carta, acted as justice in his own county of Gloucester.[3]

The Articles of the Barons condemned such practices; and Magna Carta, in this first of a series of clauses directed against sheriffs' misdeeds, forbade them under any circumstances to try royal pleas.

III. *The Intention of Magna Carta.* The barons were merely demanding that the Crown should observe the rules it had laid down for its own guidance : caprice must give way to law. Sheriffs must not usurp the functions of coroners; nor must sheriffs and coroners together usurp those of King's justiciars. John's opponents associated these two irregularities, and may have assumed that expressly to abolish one implied an intention to abolish both. Some such supposition would explain a peculiar discrepancy between the Articles and the Charter. While Article 14 demanded redress of one grievance, Magna Carta granted redress of a different one. The earlier document required that coroners should always be associated with the sheriff when he meddled with pleas of the Crown : the Charter forbade sheriffs and coroners to " try " pleas

existence at a much earlier date. Maitland remained unconvinced (*Eng. Hist. Rev.*, VIII. 758, and Pollock and Maitland, I. 519).

[1] This inference is drawn from Article 14 of the Barons.

[2] This inference is drawn from c. 24 of Magna Carta.

[3] See Maitland, *Gloucester Pleas*, xx.

of this description. These two provisions are the complements of each other. Magna Carta would seem to be here incomplete.

The prohibition against sheriffs trying pleas of the Crown was repeated in all reissues of the Charter; and, although not strictly enforced in Henry's reign, soon became absolute. Thus sheriff Ralph Musard was one of seven justices of eyre who went on circuit in 1221, but he was prohibited from sharing the labours of his colleagues when they sat in Gloucestershire, where he was still sheriff.[1] Under Edward I. no one could determine such pleas unless armed with a royal commission to that effect;[2] and the commission would take the form either of gaol delivery, of trailbaston, or of oyer and terminer.[3]

IV. *An Erroneous View.* Hallam misunderstood the object of this provision. Commenting on Henry's Charter of 1225, he declares that the " criminal jurisdiction of the Sheriff is entirely taken away by Magna Carta, c. 17."[4] This is a mistake : both before and after the granting of the Charter, the sheriff exercised criminal jurisdiction, and that of two kinds. Along with the coroners, he conducted preliminary enquiries even into pleas of the Crown; while in his tourn (which was specially authorized to be held twice a year by chapter 42 of the very Charter quoted by Hallam) he was made responsible for every stage in the trial of trivial offences. He heard indictments and then condemned and punished petty offenders in a summary manner.[5] Several statutes of later reigns confirmed, even while regulating, the authority of the sheriff to take indictments at his tourns,[6] until this jurisdiction was transferred,

---

[1] *Ibid.*, p. x.

[2] See Coke, *Second Institute*, 30, and authorities there cited.

[3] For explanation of these terms, see *supra*, c. 18.

[4] See *Middle Ages*, II. 482 n.

[5] Cf. Stephen, *History of Criminal Law*, I. 83. The mistake made by Hallam and others may have been in part the result of their neglecting the important modification undergone by the phrase "pleas of the Crown" between 1215 and the present day.

[6] *E.g.* 13 Edward I. c. 13, and 1 Edward III., stat. 2, c. 17.

by an act of the fifteenth century, to the justices of peace assembled in Quarter Sessions.[1]

All that Magna Carta did was to insist that no sheriff or local magistrate should encroach on the province reserved for the royal justices, namely the final "trying" of such grave crimes as had now come to be recognized as "pleas of the Crown."[2] The Charter did not even attempt to define what these were, leaving the boundary between great and small offences to be settled by use and wont. In all this, it was simply declaratory of existing practice, making no attempt to draw the line in a new place.[3]

Professor Hearnshaw[4] propounds a theory that better fits the facts. He holds that this chapter defined and consolidated the sheriff's authority, giving him a recognized sphere of action of his own: in 1215 "leet jurisdiction came into existence. It was the jurisdiction left by the Great Charter to the sheriff in his tourn," while chapter 42 of the reissue of 1217, forbidding the tourn to be held oftener than twice a year, marked it off "from the ordinary civil jurisdiction of the three-weekly hundred court."

V. *Local Magistrates under John.* The urgent need of restricting the authority of the sheriffs can be abundantly illustrated from contemporary records. Ineffectual attempts had, indeed, been made more than once to restrain their evil practices, as in August, 1213, when directions were issued from the Council of St. Alban's commanding the sheriffs, foresters, and others, to abstain

---

[1] 1 Edward IV. c. 2.

[2] Contrast Coke, *Second Institute*, 32, who seems to suggest that one effect of Magna Carta was to take from the sheriff a jurisdiction over *thefts* previously enjoyed by him.

[3] Dr. Stubbs, *Const. Hist.*, I. 650, thinks that the Charter indicated a tendency towards judicial absolutism, only curbed by the growth of trial by jury. Yet the barons had no intention to enhance the royal power. The attitude of the insurgents in 1215 suggests rather that the sheriffs had now become instruments of royal absolutism to a greater extent than the King's justices themselves. Edward I., indeed, deftly turned this chapter to his own advantage, arguing that it cancelled all private jurisdiction over criminal pleas previously claimed by boroughs or individuals. See Coke, *Second Institute*, 31, and cases there cited.

[4] *Leet Jurisdiction*, 340.

from unjust dealing,[1] and, again, some two months later, when John, at the instance of Nicholas, the papal legate, promised to restrain their violence and illegal exactions.[2] Little or nothing, however, was effected; and Magna Carta, in addition to condemning specified evils, contained two general provisions: chapter 45, which indicated what type of men should be appointed as Crown officials, and the present chapter, which forbade local magistrates to encroach on the province of the King's justices. These local magistrates are comprehensively described under four different names.[3]

(1) *The Sheriff.* No royal officer was more justly hated than the sheriff. The chapter under discussion affords strong evidence alike of his importance and of the jealousy with which his power was viewed. A brief sketch of the growth of the office is all that is here possible. Long before the Conquest, in each shire of England, the interests, financial and otherwise, of the kings of the house of Wessex had been entrusted to an agent of their own appointing, known as a *scir-gerefa* (or shire-reeve). These officers were continued by the Norman monarchs with increased powers, under the new name of *vice comites*.[4]

In England, during the Anglo-Saxon period, the chief power over each group of shires had been shared among three officers—the bishop, the earl, and the sheriff. The bishop, by the natural differentiation of functions, soon confined his labours to spiritual affairs; while the policy of the Conqueror relegated the earl to a position of dignity severed from the possession of real power. Thus the sheriff was left without a rival within his shire. For a period of at least one hundred years after the Norman

[1] See *supra*, p. 28. [2] See W. Coventry, II. 214-5.

[3] Abuses by sheriffs and other bailiffs continued to be rife after 1215 as before it. Many later statutes afford graphic illustrations of the oppressive conduct they sought to control. In 1275 Edward found it necessary to provide "that the sheriffs from henceforth shall not lodge with any person, with more than five or six horses; and that they shall not grieve religious men nor others, by often coming and lodging, neither at their houses nor at their manors." See Statute of Westminster, c. 1, confirmed by 28 Edward I., stat. 3, c. 13.

[4] Cf. *supra*, pp. 15-16.

Conquest, he wielded an excessive local authority as the sole tyrant of the county. He was not indeed irresponsible, but it was difficult for his victims to obtain the ear of the distant King, who alone was strong enough to punish him.

To appreciate the full authority enjoyed by a sheriff who retained the King's confidence, we must remember the varied nature of his powers. He was not only local magistrate, local tax-gatherer and local judge, but he commanded the troops of his bailiwick. A royal favourite might have several counties and one or more royal strongholds in his custody. The military power of Fawkes de Breauté, for example, must have been enormous, for it embraced the forces of Northampton, Cambridge, Huntingdon, Bedford, Buckingham, and Oxford.[1] How powerful such men had become is shown by their pretensions after King John's death, when they claimed to hold their bailiwicks as matter of right throughout his son's minority. Preposterous as this demand seems, Henry's advisers gave effect to it, when they confirmed the appointment of all John's sheriffs (with the one exception of the notorious Stephen Harengod), thus weakening the central government at a time when it needed all its strength.[2]

The sheriff, however, had passed the zenith of his power before the reign of John. That King's father had been strong enough to show the disobedient sheriff his proper place, as he did notably in 1170. John, however, had his own reasons for giving a freer hand to the agents of his evil will, foreigners and desperadoes, whose services he rewarded in this way. This recrudescence of the sheriff's powers must be added to the causes contributing to the revolt of 1215.

It has already been explained how in 1194 the sheriff's powers were restricted. To the next year is usually traced the origin of the justices of the peace, who gradually took over the duties of the sheriff, until they practically superseded him as the ruling power in the county. In Tudor

[1] See G. J. Turner, *Trans. R. Hist. Soc.*, XVIII. 272.

[2] On this whole subject see the valuable remarks of Mr. Turner, *op. cit.*, p. 272.

days a new rival appeared in the Lord Lieutenant, then first appointed in each shire to represent the Crown in its military capacity. The fall of the sheriff was thus gradual, although finally complete. From presiding, as he did in his golden age, over all the business of the district—financial, administrative, military, and judicial—the sheriff has become, in England at the present day, a mere honorary figure-head of the county executive. A high sheriff is still chosen annually by King George for each county by pricking at random one name out of a list of three leading land-owners presented to him for that purpose. He is responsible, during his year of office, for the execution of all writs of the superior Courts within his county, including the execution of criminals, for returning the names of those elected to serve in the House of Commons, and for many other purposes; but his responsibility is chiefly theoretical. The real duties of his office are now performed by subordinates. What really remains to him is an empty and expensive honour, usually shunned rather than courted. In Scotland and America, the sheriff also exists at the present day, but his position and functions have in these countries developed in very different directions. In Scotland, in opposition to what has happened in England and America, the sheriff has remained emphatically a judicial officer, the judge of the local court of his shire, known as "the Sheriff Court." He has thus retained intact his judicial functions, to which such administrative duties as still remain to him are subordinate. In the United States of America, on the contrary, the sheriff is a purely executive official, possessing perhaps more real power, but notably less honour and social distinction, than fall to the lot of the English high sheriff. The duties of his office are sometimes performed by him in person; he may even set out at the head of the *posse comitatus* in pursuit of criminals. Three completely different offices have thus sprung from the same constitutional root, and all three are still known by one name.

(2) *The constable.* Portions of certain counties were exempted from the sheriff's bailiwick. Districts afforested

were administered by wardens, assisted by verderers, who excluded the sheriff and coroners; while royal fortresses, together with the land immediately surrounding them, were under command of officers known indifferently as castellans or constables.[1] The offices of warden of a particular forest and warden of an adjacent royal castle were frequently conferred on the same individual. Indeed, chapter 16 of the Forest Charter of Henry III. seems to use the term " castellans " as the recognized name of forest wardens, whom it forbids to hold " pleas of the forest."

The name constable has at different periods been applied to officers of extremely different types. The King's High Constable, a descendant of the horse-thegn of the Anglo-Saxon kings, was originally the member of the royal household responsible for the King's stables. At a later date, he shared with the Earl Marshal the duties of Commander-in-chief. The name of constable came to be applied also to commanders of small bodies of troops, whether in castles or elsewhere. At a later date the word was used in connection with duties of watch and ward : each hundred had its high constable and each village its petty constable in the fourteenth and fifteenth centuries.[2] The name is at the present day, confined to members of the police force.

The word, as used in Magna Carta, denoted the captain of a royal castle.[3] Such an office was one of trust; and wide powers were conferred upon its holder. He acted as gaoler of prisoners confided to the safe-keeping of his dungeons. He had authority, under certain ill-defined restrictions, to take whatever he thought necessary for provisioning the garrison—a privilege the exercise of which frequently led to abuses, guarded against by chapters 28

---

[1] These localities were independent of the ordinary executive authorities of the county ; partial exemption from the sheriff's control was enjoyed also by (a) chartered boroughs and (b) holders of franchises. The same man might, of course, be both sheriff and castellan.

[2] See H. B. Simpson, *Eng. Hist. Rev.*, X. 625, for authorities.

[3] Evidence collected by Coke, *Second Institute*, 31, proves the identity. See also Round, *Ancient Charters*, No. 55, where Richard I. in 1159 speaks of " *constabularia castelli Lincolniae.*"

and 29 of Magna Carta. He had also, to a limited extent, judicial authority. Not only did he try pleas for small debts to which Jews were parties, but he enjoyed a jurisdiction over all petty offences committed within the precincts of the castle, analogous to that of the sheriff within the rest of the county. The power of trying and punishing misdemeanours was not taken away by the Great Charter, and was confirmed by implication in 1300 by a statute which directed that the constable of Dover Castle should not hold, within the castle gate, "foreign" pleas of the county which did not affect "the guard of the castle."[1] The Articles of 1309 complained that constables of the King's castles took cognizance of common pleas.[2] In the reign of Henry IV. complaint was made that constables of castles were appointed justices of the peace, and imprisoned in one capacity the victims they had unjustly condemned in another. This practice was put down by statute in 1403.[3]

It would appear that at an earlier period the constable of the hundred sometimes acted as deputy-sheriff. Chapter 12 of the Assize of Northampton provided that when the sheriff was absent the nearest *castellanus* might take his place in dealing with a thief who had been arrested. His interference outside his own precincts must, however, have been regarded with great jealousy, and the coroners, after their appointment in 1194, would naturally act as substitutes during the sheriff's absence.

(3) *The coroners.* The coroners of each county, after their institution in 1194, seem to have shared with the sheriff most of the powers of which the latter had previously enjoyed a monopoly. They were appointed by the whole body of freeholders assembled in the county court,[4] and the nature of their duties is explained by the oath of office

---

[1] See *Articuli super cartas*, 28 Edward I. c. 7.

[2] Stubbs, *Const. Hist.*, II. 339.

[3] See 5 Henry IV. c. 10. Coke, *Second Institute*, 30, relates, as an indication of the authority and pretensions of these constables, that they had seals of their own "with their portraiture on horseback."

[4] See Stubbs, *Hoveden*, Pref. to Vol. IV. xcix.

sworn in the same words for many centuries, " *ad custodi-enda ea quae pertinent ad coronam.*" Their duty was to guard royal interests generally; and their " keeping " of royal pleas was merely one aspect of this wider function. Besides " attaching " those suspected of crimes—that is, receiving formal accusations and taking such sureties as might be necessary, it was their duty to make preliminary investigations; to examine the size and nature of the victim's wounds in a charge of mayhem;[1] and to keep a watchful eye on royal windfalls, including deodands, wrecks, and treasure-trove. They had also to appraise the value of chattels forfeited to the King. When felons took refuge in sanctuary, it was the coroner who arranged for their leaving the country on forfeiting all that they had. They kept a record of those who had been outlawed, and received " appeals " of criminal charges.[2]

Magna Carta forbade the coroner to determine pleas of the Crown; but, even after 1215, he sometimes did justice upon felons caught red-handed. An act of Edward I.[3] accurately defined his duties, empowering him to attach pleas of the Crown and to present criminals for trial, but forbidding him to proceed further alone.

The coroner's functions, originally so wide and varied, have been gradually narrowed down, until at the present day the duty usually associated with his office is the holding of inquests on dead bodies where there are suspicious circumstances.[4] He is still responsible for treasure-trove and he is also competent to act as the sheriff's substitute in case of illness or absence during the year of office.

(4) *The bailiffs.* The mention by name of three classes of local officers is supplemented by the addition of an indefinite word sufficiently wide to cover all grades of

[1] See Bracton, f. 122b.

[2] In 1197 Richard's Assize of Measures appointed six *custodientes* in each county and town. These were *coroners* over one class of offences, the use of false weights and measures. Cf. *infra*, under c. 35.

[3] Statute of Westminster, I. c. 10.

[4] Cf. Coke, *Second Institute*, 31, " In case when any man come to violent or untimely death, *super visum corporis.*"

Crown officials. The term "bailiff" may be applied to every individual to whom authority of any sort has been delegated by another. It would include the men who actually served writs, or distrained the goods of debtors; and also generally all local officials of every description, holding authority directly or indirectly from the Crown. The district over which his office extended was called his "bailiwick," a term often applied to the county considered as the sphere of the sheriff's labours.[1]

CHAPTER TWENTY-FIVE.

OMNES comitatus, hundrede, wapentakii, et trethingii, sint ad antiquas firmas absque ullo incremento, exceptis dominicis maneriis nostris.

> All counties, hundreds, wapentakes, and trithings (except our demesne manors) shall remain at the old rents, and without any additional payment.

This provision, directed against the sheriffs, shows a determination to get to the root of the disease, instead of merely attacking the symptoms. The rents at which the counties (or parts of them) were farmed out to the sheriffs must no longer be arbitrarily raised, but were to remain at the old figures which had become stereotyped from long usage. To understand how such increases would injuriously affect the inhabitants of the county, some explanation is necessary. Centuries before the Norman Conquest, England had been already mapped out into shires on lines substantially the same as those which still exist. Each county had been subdivided into smaller districts known as "hundreds" in the south, and as "wapentakes" in the Danish districts of the north; while intermediate divisions existed, exceptionally, in some of the large counties such as York and Lincoln, each of which had three "trithings" or ridings.

[1] Mr. G. J. Turner, speaking of the minority of Henry III., thinks "the term 'bailiff' as applied to a county at this period meant 'sheriff.'" *Transactions*, p. 274.

In commenting upon chapter 24, it has been explained how the Anglo-Saxon Kings entrusted their interests in each shire to an officer called a sheriff, and how a similar officer under the Norman Kings became the chief magistrate in the county. His financial duties, however, long remained the most important. Even before 1066, the sheriff had ceased to be a mere intermediary, who lifted the King's rents and paid over, pound by pound, the yearly varying sums he might receive. He had become a *firmarius*, buying for a yearly rent the right to appropriate to his own uses the revenues of the county. The Crown got the exact sum stipulated for, known as the *firma comitatus*; while the balance, if any, remained with the sheriff. In plain words, the sheriff speculated in the returns: it was his business, by fair means or foul, to make sure of a handsome surplus.

Authorities differ as to the exact list of items purchased by the *firma comitatus*; but the two chief sources of revenue were the profits of justice in the local courts, and the rents of royal manors.

William I. sharply raised the farms, and his successors endeavoured, whenever possible, to increase them further. Now, it might seem at first sight that these additional burdens concerned exclusively the Crown and the sheriff, but such was by no means the case. The sheriff took care to pass on the burden to the shoulders of those subject to his authority. His rule tended always to be oppressive, but his unjust exactions would be doubled when the amount of the *firma* had recently been raised.

Under the vigilant rule of Henry II., some measure of relief was obtained by the shires from the misdeeds of their local tyrants, since that far-seeing King knew that his own best interests called for curtailment of the sheriffs' pretensions. He punished their excesses and deprived them of office. John, on the contrary, appointed men of a less reputable type, and gave them rope. In return, he wrung more money from them. Not content with exacting the annual *firma* and the additional sum known as " increment," which had now become stereotyped as a fixed and recog-

nized payment,[1] John from 1207 onwards exacted a third
payment under name of *proficuum*, and allowed his sheriffs
to inflict new severities to recoup themselves for their additional outlay.

Magna Carta made no attempt to abolish the practice of
farming out the shires, but forbade alike the increase of the
farm and the exaction of *proficuum*. The barons here made
an innovation which was unfair to John. If it benefited the
men of the counties in dealing with their sheriffs, it gave
the sheriffs an undeserved advantage over the exchequer.
The total value of the various assets included in the *firma
comitatus* had greatly increased in the past, and would
probably continue to increase in the future. Therefore, it
was unfair to bind the Crown by a hard-and-fast rule which
would practically make a present of this future " unearned
increment " to the sheriff. To stereotype the *firma* was to
rob the Crown, which required increased revenues to meet
the increased cost of its expanding duties.[2]

Although this chapter was omitted from all reissues, the
Crown, during Henry III.'s minority, forbore to exact the
proficuum, reverting to the practice prior to the seventh
year of his father's reign. After he had been declared of
age, however, increased sums were again taken.[3] There
was, indeed, no valid reason why the unearned increment
should go to the sheriff rather than to the King : it was
sufficient to provide against the fixing of the amounts too
high. The *Articuli super cartas*, accordingly, while conceding to the counties the right of electing their own
sheriffs, declared that neither the bailiwicks and hundreds

---

[1] These extra payments appear under various names, *e.g. augmentum* or *incre-
mentum* in *Domesday Book* (cf. Ballard, *Domesday Inquest*, 75). The *Pipe Roll*
for 1166 (p. 11) records 200 marks paid as *gersuma* for Norfolk and Suffolk. See
evidence collected by Adams, *Origin*, 237 n. Huge sums were sometimes paid :
Archbishop Geoffrey in 1194 purchased the shrievalty of York for £2000. Ramsay,
Angevin England, 345.

[2] Cf. Sir James Ramsay, *Angevin Empire*, 476, who describes this provision as
"an impossible requirement." Dr. Stubbs' paraphrase is not entirely happy :
"the ferms of the counties and other jurisdictions are not to be increased." See
Const. Hist., I. 575.

[3] See Turner, *Trans. R.H.S.*, XVIII. 289.

of the King, nor those of great lords ought to be put to farm
at too high rates.   The evil, however, continued under a
new form; sheriffs, while only paying a moderate farm
themselves, sublet parts of their province at much higher
rates, thus appropriating the increment denied to the
exchequer, while the bailiffs who had paid the increase
could not " levy the said ferm without doing extortion and
duress to the people."[1] Three successive acts prohibited
this practice, declaring that hundreds and wapentakes must
either be kept in the sheriff's own hands, or sublet, if at all,
at the old fixed farms only.[2]

One exception to the scope of its own provisions was
deliberately made by Magna Carta—an exception of an
important and notable nature; the demesne manors of the
Crown were left exposed to arbitrary increases of their
annual rents.   Now, the chief items contained in the *firma*
were, as already explained, the rents of these manors and
the profits of the local courts.   It would thus appear, in the
light of this exception, that the aim of Magna Carta was to
prevent an increase under the second head—to prevent, that
is, the local courts being made the instruments of extortion;
and this apparently was the precise object of chapter 42 of
the reissue of 1217.

That chapter struck at one of the most fertile of the
sheriffs' expedients for swelling the profits of their office.
It was their practice to summon the various district courts
with unnecessary frequency and at inconvenient times and
places, fining every suitor who failed to attend.   The
Charter of 1217 reaffirmed the ancient usage [3] : no county
court should meet in future oftener than once a month; no
sheriff or bailiff should make his " tourn " through the
hundreds oftener than twice a year, to wit at Easter and
Michaelmas, and that only at the accustomed place; view
of frankpledge should only be held once a year at Michaelmas, and the sheriff must not seek " occasions," but content

---

[1] These are the words of the statute of 1330, cited below.

[2] 4 Edward III. c. 15; 14 Edward III. c. 9; 4 Henry IV. c. 5.

[3] For this usage see Cnut, II. 18 (Liebermann, *Gesetze*, I. 321); *Leges Henrici*,
7 and 8 (*ibid.*, 553); Writ of Henry I. (*ibid.*, 524).

himself with what he was wont to get for taking his " view " under Henry II.; all liberties must be respected; and any district in which the courts meet by custom less frequently than is normal, shall have the benefit of such exceptional local usage.[1]

In a curious case [2] that came before the justices in 1226, this clause was pleaded as a defence against a charge of impeding the sheriff of Lincoln in the performance of his duties of holding " counties," " thethings " (or courts of ridings), and wapentakes : the sheriff, against custom, was holding county courts oftener than once in five weeks and for more than one day at a time, and was holding a wapentake in Ancaster oftener than twice a year, and not according to the charter of liberty.

In another plea (1231) [3] juries testify that since the making of " carta de Runemede " (here evidently used for the Charter of 1217) the sheriff has come into the hundred twice instead of once a year (as the old custom was) to take view of frankpledge and to make attachments of pleas of the Crown.

After 1217, in absence of express royal grant or prescription to the contrary, the rule formulated in Henry's second reissue of Magna Carta fixed the times of holding the " tourn " of the sheriff, and this was extended also to the " leet " jurisdiction, which in the liberties took the place of the tourn.[4]

CHAPTER TWENTY-SIX.

Si aliquis tenens de nobis laicum feodum moriatur, et vicecomes vel ballivus noster ostendat litteras nostras patentes de summonicione nostra de debito quod defunctus nobis debuit, liceat vicecomiti vel ballivo nostro attachiare, et inbreviare catalla defuncti, inventa in laico feodo, ad

---

[1] See *supra*, p. 150.   [2] Bracton's *Note-book*, Plea 1730.

[3] *Ibid.*, No. 513.

[4] See Hearnshaw, *Leet Jurisdiction*, 79, 80, who reminds us, however (p. 147), that " even Magna Carta can be prescribed against."

valenciam illius debiti, per visum legalium hominum, ita
tamen quod nichil inde amoveatur, donec persolvatur nobis
debitum quod clarum fuerit; et residuum relinquatur executoribus ad faciendum testamentum defuncti; et, si nichil
nobis debeatur ab ipso, omnia catalla cedant defuncto, salvis
uxori ipsius et pueris racionabilibus partibus suis.

> If any one holding of us a lay fief shall die, and our sheriff or
> bailiff shall exhibit our letters patent of summons for a debt
> which the deceased owed to us, it shall be lawful for our sheriff
> or bailiff to attach and catalogue chattels of the deceased, found
> upon the lay fief, to the value of that debt, at the sight of law-
> worthy men, provided always that nothing whatever be thence
> removed until the debt which is evident[1] shall be fully paid to
> us; and the residue shall be left to the executors to fulfil the
> will of the deceased; and if there be nothing due from him to
> us, all the chattels shall go to the deceased, saving to his wife
> and children their reasonable shares.

The primary object of this chapter was to regulate the
procedure to be followed in attaching the personal estates of
Crown tenants who were also Crown debtors. Incidentally,
it throws light on the right of bequeathing property.

I. *Nature of the Grievance.* When a Crown tenant died
it was almost certain that arrears of scutages, incidents, or
other exactions remained unpaid. The sheriff and bailiffs
of the district, where deceased's estates lay, were in the habit
of seizing everything they could find on his manors, under
excuse of securing the interests of their royal master. They
attached and sold chattels out of all proportion to the sum
actually due. A surplus would often remain in the sheriff's
hands, which he refused to disgorge.

Magna Carta sought to make such irregularities impossible, by defining the procedure to be followed. The sheriff
and his bailiffs were forbidden to touch a single chattel of a
deceased Crown tenant, unless they came armed with legal
warrant in the form of royal letters patent vouching the
existence and the amount of the Crown debt. The officers
of the law were allowed to attach only as many chattels as
might reasonably be expected to satisfy the debt due to the
exchequer; and everything so taken must be carefully

---

[1] Cf. the use of the phrase "a liquid debt" in Scots law.

inventoried. All this was to be done " at the sight of lawful men," respectable, if humble, neighbours specially summoned for that purpose, whose function it was to form a check on the actions of the sheriff's officers, to prevent them from appropriating anything not included in the inventory, to assist in valuing each article and to see that no more chattels were distrained than necessary. A saving clause protected the interests of the Crown by forbidding the removal from the tenant's fief of any chattels, even those not so attached, until the full ascertained amount had been paid to the exchequer. Not till then could a division take place among the deceased man's relatives or legatees.

These provisions should be read in connection with chapter 9,[1] which provided that diligence for Crown debts must proceed against personal estate before the debtor's freehold was distrained, and laid down other equitable rules applicable alike to a deceased Crown debtor and to a living one.

II. *The Right to Bequeath.* The main interest of this chapter, for the historian of law and institutions, lies in a different direction; in the light thrown on the right of making Wills in 1215. The early law of England had difficulty in deciding how far it ought to acknowledge the claims made by owners of property, both real and personal, to direct its destination after death. Various influences were at work, prior to the Norman Conquest, to make the development of this branch of law illogical and capricious.[2] Of the law of bequests in the twelfth century it is possible to speak with greater certainty; definite principles had by that time received recognition. All testamentary rights over land or other real estate were then denied, not, as has sometimes been maintained, in the interests of the feudal lord, but rather of the expectant heir.[3] Many reasons contributed to this result. For one thing, it had become necessary to prevent churchmen from using their spiritual

---

[1] Cf. what is there said of the sheriff's oppressions.

[2] The subject is discussed by Pollock and Maitland, II. 312-353. See also Holdsworth, III. 418 ff. ; Makower, *Const. Hist. Church*, 427 ff.

[3] See Pollock and Maitland, II. 324.

influence to wring bequests from dying men to the impover-
ishment of the heir. Churchmen, in compensation as it
were for the obstacles thus opposed to their thirst for the
land of the dying, ultimately, but not before the reign of
Henry III., made good their claim to regulate all Wills
dealing with personal estate; that is money, goods, and
chattels.

Under Henry II. no such right had been admitted. The
Assize of Northampton (1176) directed that heirs should
divide the chattels according to the provisions made in the
Will, without any reference to the supervision of the bishop
or his clergy. Glanvill twice gives a writ directing the
sheriff to uphold the Will of a testator; but no trace of any
similar writ appears in the Registers of the early years of
Henry III.: "the state has had to retreat before the
church." [1]

This victory of the ecclesiastical courts was probably won
shortly after 1215. John's Charter makes no admission of
any right of the church in the " proving " of Wills; but it
does admit (in chapter 27) the church's right to "superintend" the division of the goods of intestates, an insidious
privilege, which was used as a lever during the minority
of Henry (a ward of Holy See), and thus helped to give
the courts Christian an excuse for deciding also as to
the validity of Wills. It was apparently in John's reign
that the practice of appointing executors to carry out the
Will of the deceased became general. Henry II. in his
own case had entrusted this duty to individuals whom he
named, but did not describe as " executors," a word, however, used in its technical sense in King John's Will.[2]

John claimed that his subjects could not make valid
Wills without his consent, which had, as usual, to be paid
for. Such, at least, is the inference to be drawn from the
existence of writs granting licences to make a Will, or
confirming one that had been made.[3] The King's interfer-

[1] Maitland, *Coll. Papers*, II. 139.   [2] Holdsworth, III. 418 ff.

[3] On 30th August, 1199 (*New Rymer*, I. 78) John confirmed the testament of
Archbishop Hubert Walter ; and on 22nd July, 1202 (*ibid.*, I. 86), he granted
permission to his mother, the dowager Queen Eleanor, to make a will.

ence in this province seems to have been regarded as an illegal encroachment.

Magna Carta declares that all the chattels (or the residue after paying Crown debts) " shall go to the deceased " for " the executors to fulfil the will of the deceased," but immediately adds the saving clause, that " all the chattels " means only what remains after deducting the " reasonable shares " of wife and children. This seems to exclude, by implication, the King's right to interfere on the plea that he had not licensed a Will, while it keeps alive an ancient rule that a testator could only dispose of part of his *pecunia* (or personal estate), his widow and children having absolute claims to the rest.

The Charter did not define these " reasonable shares " ; but custom had already fixed them at the same proportions of the whole as the law of Scotland observes at the present day. When a Scotsman dies, leaving wife and children, his movable or personal estate falls into three equal parts, known respectively as the widow's part (or *jus relictae*), the " bairns' " part (or *legitim*, the *legitima portio* of the Roman law), and " the dead's part." [1] If he attempts to dispose of his entire estate, wife and children may claim their legal rights, and " break the Will." Where a wife survives, but no children (or a child and no wife), the division is into two equal portions. Magna Carta recognizes a similar division ; and we know from Glanvill that, if the dead man's Will had attempted to defeat the just claims of wife or children, the writ *de rationabili parte bonorum* would give them relief.[2]

The conception of a " dead's part " or portion to be dispensed in charity and good works for the benefit of the deceased's soul was, of course, in great measure due to the influence of the church, which was not unwilling to stimulate the belief that one of the best methods of affecting this was to leave money to itself. Under Henry III. the bishop of the diocese made good his claim to " prove " Wills (that

[1] Cf. " *tota pars sua de pecunia sua* " in *Burton Abbey Surveys* (cited by Round, *Engl. Hist. Rev.*, XX. 279) ; Bateson, *Borough Customs*, II. xcvi.

[2] Glanvill, VII. 7.

is to determine whether they were valid), and to control the
" executors " in carrying out the dead man's instructions.
Where the testator's intentions were ambiguous, the
" ordinary " would see to it that deceased's soul did not
suffer through giving too little to the church.

The reissue of 1216 makes no alteration on this chapter
of John's Charter : that of 1217 omits " *et pueris,*" probably
through a clerical blunder, for the words were restored in
1225. As mere disuse does not abrogate an English statute,
this provision remained in force until repealed by implication by the Wills Act of 1837.[1]

Long subsequent to the thirteenth century, the laws of
England and Scotland as to the rights of succession of wife
and children seem to have remained identical : but, while
Scots law is unaltered to the present day, English law has,
by slow steps, the details of which are obscure, entirely
changed. The rule that acknowledged the children's right
to one third of the personal estate was gradually relaxed,
while the testator became sole judge what provision he
ought to make for his sons, until at last a purely nominal
sum of money was all that was required. The law of England, at the present day, does not compel a father to leave
son or daughter even the proverbial shilling. The phrase
" to cut off a son with a shilling," which still lives in popular
usage, may perpetuate the tradition of an intermediate stage
of English law, where some provision, however inadequate,
had to be made, if the Will was to be allowed to stand.

CHAPTER TWENTY-SEVEN.

SI aliquis liber homo intestatus decesserit, catalla sua per
manus propinquorum parentum et amicorum suorum, per
visum ecclesie distribuantur, salvis unicuique debitis que
defunctus ei debebat.

> If any freeman shall die intestate, his chattels shall be dis-
> tributed by the hands of his nearest kinsfolk and friends, under
> supervision of the church, saving to every one the debts which
> the deceased owed to him.

[1] See *Law Magazine*, Oct. 1905.

Here the Great Charter proceeds to remedy an evil connected with *intestate* succession, a natural sequel to the subject of *testate* succession.[1] In light of subsequent history, the words most worthy of notice are probably " *per visum ecclesiae,*" which appear also in the Articles of the Barons. There were good reasons for welcoming the intervention of the bishop's court as a substitute for the scramble that often took place for an intestate's chattels; but the jurisdiction thus gained by the church was quickly put to other uses.

The placing of this powerful weapon in the hands of the church was only incidental to the main purpose of this chapter. This was (while safeguarding the interests of creditors) to secure to the deceased's kinsmen and friends the right to make an equitable division of his chattels. By implication the Charter says " hands off " to John, and indeed to any lord superior, whether the King or another.

In the Middle Ages all classes of men, good and bad alike, exhibited an extreme horror of dying intestate.[2] Several causes contributed towards this frame of mind. Churchmen, from motives not unmixed, inculcated the belief that a dying man's duty was to leave part at least of his personal estate for religious and charitable objects. The bishop or priest, who had power to withhold extreme unction from dying men, was in a strong position to force advice upon penitents who believed the church to hold the keys of heaven. Motives of a more worldly nature lent their weight. If a man died intestate, his lord seized his chattels. Henry I. in his Coronation Charter renounced this right over Crown tenants under certain circumstances : if a baron or " man," cut off by war or infirmity (the words have a grudging, hesitating sound), had given no instructions for disposal of his *pecunia*, his wife and children and *legitimi homines* (or vassals) should divide it " for his soul " as seemed best to them.[3] Stephen, in his second or Oxford

---

[1] On whole subject, see Holdsworth, III. 418 ff. ; Makower, *Const. Hist. Church*, 427 ff.

[2] Pollock and Maitland, II. 354.

[3] See Appendix and *supra*, p. 98. Also Bateson, *Borough Customs*, II. cxlii-iii. Cf. Cnut, II. cc. 70 and 78 (Liebermann, *Gesetze*, 357-365).

Charter,[1] gave up all such claims, as regards the property of prelates and clerks, who were confirmed in their rights of making Wills.

These promises were not kept: in Glanvill's day, the King, like other feudal lords, appropriated the goods of intestates.[2] Henry II. continued to treat intestacy, especially in the case of clerks, as an excuse for forfeiture.[3] Magna Carta contained a clear pronouncement against this practice. The kinsmen and friends of the deceased, without royal interference, were to divide the chattels under supervision of the church : the King's courts were excluded. No scheme of intestate succession was set forth ; but where wife and children survived, the tripartite division was clearly implied. In the distribution of the dead's part, the prelates allowed themselves liberal discretion : something went to the poor, but more might be spent on masses, while a portion would be retained as remuneration for trouble expended.

In 1216 this provision of John's Charter was withdrawn. Why? Had a suspicion crossed the mind of William Marshal that it conferred a dangerously elastic privilege upon the church? Did the legate Gualo refuse to trust the English prelates with authority? Did the young King's

---

[1] See Appendix and *supra*, p. 102.   [2] Glanvill, VII. 16.

[3] See Pollock and Maitland, II. 354. Examples are readily found : "When Archbishop Roger of York died in 1182, Henry II. enjoyed a windfall of £11,000, to say nothing of the spoons and saltcellars" (Pollock and Maitland, I. 504). Royal prerogatives in the twelfth century were elastic. Henry II. used them freely, but on the whole fairly. His sons stretched every doubtful claim to its utmost limits. The Crown was the legal heir of all Jews (cf. c. 10) and apparently of all Christian usurers as well, at least of such as died unrepentant (see Pollock and Maitland, II. 486), and the making of a will was a necessary condition of a usurer's repentance. (See *Dialogus de Scaccario*, 224-5 nn.) The King, further, took the goods of all who died a felon's death (cf. c. 32) and of men who committed suicide (itself a felony). Madox (I. 346) cites an entry from the *Pipe Rolls* of 1172, recording 60 marks due to the exchequer as the value of the chattels of an intestate ; and, two years later, mention is made *de pecunia Gilleberti qui obiit intestatus*. There is nothing to show whether such men were, or were not, usurers. The Pope was another competitor for the personal estates of intestate clerks. In 1246 he issued an edict making this demand : even Henry III. (dependent and ally of Rome as he was) protested, and the edict was withdrawn. See Pollock and Maitland, II. 357.

advisers, conscious of their urgent need of money, determine to reserve what rights the indefinite earlier law allowed them of taking part in the scramble for the coin and chattels of intestates?

Irregularities continued during Henry's reign : Bracton [1] thought it necessary to urge that intestacy was not a crime. But his direct condemnation of the feudal lords' practice of seizing chattels is confined to cases of sudden death. Yet it was neither King nor barons, but the church that triumphed : the rule, enunciated in John's Charter, though omitted from all reissues, settled the practice of later years.[2] The personal estate of intestates was administered " under supervision of the church," and the same supervision was ultimately extended over the Wills and estates of men who had died testate.

CHAPTER TWENTY-EIGHT.

NULLUS constabularius, vel alius ballivus noster, capiat blada vel alia catalla alicujus, nisi statim inde reddat denarios, aut respectum inde habere possit de voluntate venditoris.

> No constable or other bailiff of ours shall take corn or other provisions from any one without immediately tendering money therefor, unless he can have postponement thereof by permission of the seller.

This chapter is the first of several that redressed abuses springing from the exercise of the royal right of purveyance.

I. *Purveyance in General.* The Norman and Angevin Kings of England were compelled by their administrative duties and induced by the pleasures of the chase to move constantly from district to district. The difficulties must have been great of finding sufficient food for the retinues surrounding the King in peace or war. It was to the

---

[1] F. 60.   [2] Pollock and Maitland, II. 355.   Cf. *supra*, p. 324.

interests of the community that the work of government should not be brought to a stand-still for want of supplies. No opposition was made when the King arrogated to himself the privilege of appropriating, under fair conditions, the necessaries his household might require. Such a right, not unlike that enjoyed in modern times by the commander of an army encamped in an enemy's country, was allowed to the Kings of England in their own land in time of peace. This was known as purveyance.[1] Unfortunately, the conditions under which supplies might be requisitioned were left vague : the privilege was subject to abuse. In theory it was a right of pre-emption; the provisions seized were to be paid for at the market rate : but practice tended to differ lamentably from theory. In the absence of a neutral arbitrator to fix the value of the goods, the unfortunate seller was thankful to accept any pittance offered by royal officials, who might subsequently, indeed, charge a higher rate against the Crown. Payment was often indefinitely delayed or made not in coin but in exchequer tallies, " a vexatious anticipation of taxation," since these could only be used in payment of Crown dues.

Magna Carta did not abolish purveyance, and placed no restrictions upon its use for the legitimate purpose of supplying the King's household. Some slight attempt to control its exercise was made sixty years later in the Statute of Westminster I.; but without producing much effect.[2] The Articles of 1309 [3] complained that the King's purveyors took great quantities of corn, malt, and meat without paying even by exchequer tallies. The grievances connected with purveyance continued, throughout four centuries, as a fertile source of vexation to the people and of friction between parliament and the King. An attempt, made by the House of Commons to induce James I. to surrender this prerogative for a money grant, ended in failure, with the abandonment of the abortive treaty known as " the Great Contract." In the general re-settlement of the revenue, however, at the Restoration, purveyance and pre-emption,

---

[1] See Blackstone, *Commentaries*, I. 287, for an often-quoted definition.

[2] 3 Edward I. c. 32.　　　　　　　[3] Stubbs, *Const. Hist.*, II. 339.

which had fallen into disuse during the Commonwealth, were abolished.[1] Yet in the following year a new statute [2] virtually revived one branch of the right under essential modifications : when royal progresses were necessary in the future, warrants might be issued from the Board of Green Cloth, authorizing the King to use such carts and carriages as he might require, at a fair rate of hire specified in the Act of Parliament.

II. *Branches of Purveyance restricted by Magna Carta.* A practice tolerated because of its absolute necessity, when confined to providing for the needs of the King's household, became intolerable when claimed by every castle-warden, sheriff, and local bailiff, for his own personal or official needs. Discretionary authority was vested by John in a class of officials least qualified to use it, unscrupulous foreign adventurers hired to intimidate the native population, responsible to no one save the King, and careful never to issue from their strongholds except at the head of their reckless soldiery. The Great Charter contained a few moderate provisions for checking the abuses of purveyance.

(1) *Provisioning of castles.* Commanders of fortresses were left free by Magna Carta to help themselves to such corn and other supplies as they deemed necessary for their garrisons. Immediate payment, however, must be made in current coin (not in exchequer tallies) for everything they requisitioned, unless the owner consented to postpone the date of payment. The Charter of 1216 made a slight modification in favour of castellans. Payment for goods taken from the town where the castle was situated might be legally delayed for three weeks, a term extended in 1217 to forty days. Such relaxation was perhaps necessary to meet the case of a warden with an empty purse called on to provide against an unexpected siege or other emergency; but the peaceful townsmen, over whose dwellings the dark walls of a feudal stronghold loomed, would not dare to press unduly for payment. Under Henry's Charters, as under that of John, immediate payment had to be tendered to owners

[1] 12 Charles II. c. 24, ss. 11-12. [2] 13 Charles II. c. 8.

who lived elsewhere than in this neighbouring town.[1]
(2) *Requisitioning horses and carts.* The provisions of
chapter 30, modified in subsequent reissues, sought to prohibit sheriffs from commandeering wagons that were the
property of freemen. (3) *Appropriation of timber.* The
succeeding chapter confined the King and his officers to
the use of such wood as they could obtain from the royal
demesnes.[2]

III. *Branches of Purveyance not mentioned in Magna
Carta.* A wide field was left alike for the use and the abuse
of this prerogative, after due effect had been given to these
moderate provisions. Two minor aspects of purveyance
came into prominence in later history.

(1) *Requisition of forced labour.* Hallam explains how
the King's rights of pre-emption were extended, by
analogy, to his subjects' labour. " Thus Edward III.
announces to all sheriffs that William of Walsingham had
a commission to collect as many painters as might suffice for
' our works in St. Stephen's chapel, Westminster, to be at
our wages as long as shall be necessary ' ; and to arrest and
keep in prison all who should refuse or be refractory ; and
enjoins them to lend assistance. Windsor Castle owes its
massive magnificence to labourers impressed from every
part of the kingdom. There is even a commission from
Edward IV. to take as many workmen in gold as were
wanted, and employ them at the King's cost upon the
trappings of himself and his household."[3] Perhaps, however, such demands did not form a legal branch of
purveyance, but were merely instances of illegal royal
encroachments.

(2) *Billeting of soldiers in private houses.* This practice,

---

[1] The Statute of Westminster I. (3 Edward I. c. 7) enacted " that no constable
or castellan from henceforth take any prise or like thing of any other than of such
as be of their own town or castle, and that it be paid or else agreement made
within forty days, if it be not ancient prise due to the king, or the castle, or the
lord of the castle," and further (c. 32) that purveyors taking goods for the King's
use, or for a garrison, and appropriating the price received therefor from the
exchequer, should be liable in double payment and to imprisonment during the
King's pleasure.

[2] For details, see under cc. 30 and 31.   [3] Hallam, *Middle Ages*, III. 221.

which may be considered a branch of purveyance, has always been peculiarly abhorrent to public opinion in England. It is as old as the reign of John; for, when that King visited York in 1201, he complained bitterly that the citizens neither came out to meet him nor provided for the wants of his crossbow-men. His threats and demands for hostages were with difficulty turned aside by a money payment of £100.[1] Charles I. made an oppressive use of this prerogative, punishing householders who refused to pay illegal taxes by quartering his dissolute soldiery upon them, a practice branded as illegal by the Petition of Right in 1628.[2]

CHAPTER TWENTY-NINE.

NULLUS constabularius distringat aliquem militem ad dandum denarios pro custodia castri, si facere voluerit custodiam illam in propria persona sua, vel per alium probum hominem, si ipse eam facere non possit propter racionabilem causam; et si nos duxerimus vel miserimus eum in exercitum, erit quietus de custodia, secundum quantitatem temporis quo per nos fuerit in exercitu.

> No constable shall compel any knight to give money in lieu of castle-guard, when he is willing to perform it in his own person, or (if he himself cannot do it from any reasonable cause) then by another responsible man. Further, if we have led or sent him upon military service, he shall be relieved from guard in proportion to the time during which he has been on service because of us.

Castle-guard, or the liability to serve in the garrison of a royal fortress, formed part of the feudal obligations of the owners of certain freeholds. This service was sometimes due in lieu of attendance in the army; more usually the tenant who owed garrison duty owed knight's service as well.[3] It was probably this duplication of duties that pre-

---

[1] See *Rotuli de oblatis et finibus*, 119.   [2] See 3 Charles I. c. 1.

[3] See the examples collected in Pollock and Maitland, I. 257. See also in *Rotuli de oblatis et finibus*, 107, how in 1200 Ralph de Bradel offered John 40 marks and a palfrey to be relieved of "the custody of the work of the castle of Grimsby."

vented castle-guard from hardening into a separate tenure.[1]
John preferred to commute personal service of castle-guard
for money payments (analogous to the scutage paid in lieu
of knight's service), and to man his feudal towers with
soldiers of fortune rather than with rebellious Englishmen.
Captains of royal castles were, therefore, in the habit of
demanding money even from those who offered personal
service. What was worse, when the freeholder followed
John on distant service, he was mulcted in a money payment because he had not stayed at home to perform garrison
duty during the same period. Both abuses were forbidden
in 1215.[2] In certain circumstances, however, this prohibition would have deprived the King of what was equitably
due to him. Suppose he had granted two fiefs to the same
tenant—one by simple knight's service, the other by castle-
ward. A double holding implied double service; the
tenant could not in fairness plead that the service of one
knight, rendered abroad, operated as the full discharge of
the services of two knights due from his two separate fiefs.
Castle-guard must in such a case be performed by an
efficient deputy, or else the usual compensation be paid.
The reissue of 1217 amended John's Charter to this effect.
Service with the army abroad operated as a discharge of
castle-guard at home, but not where the tenant owed two
services for two distinct fiefs.[3]

CHAPTER THIRTY.

NULLUS vicecomes, vel ballivus noster, vel aliquis alius,
capiat equos vel carectas alicujus liberi hominis pro cariagio
faciendo, nisi de voluntate ipsius liberi hominis.

> No sheriff or bailiff of ours, or other person, shall take the
> horses or carts of any freeman for transport duty, against the
> will of the said freeman.

[1] Cf. *supra*, p. 57 n.

[2] Adams, *Origin*, 238, contrasts the principle of this chapter with that of c. 12,
where no option is allowed the vassal of offering service in lieu of scutage—a
breach of strict feudal custom.

[3] *De feodo pro quo fecit servicium in exercitu.* This variation in the charter of
1217 seems to have escaped Dr. Stubbs' attention. See *Select Charters*, 346.

The Charter here returns to the subject of purveyance, one branch of which is practically abolished, except as affecting villeins. No carts or horses belonging to a free-man were to be requisitioned by any sheriff or bailiff for the King's use without the owner's consent; that is to say, they could not be requisitioned at all. Protection, however, was limited to freemen; the inference is that the horses and implements of villeins were left at the disposal of the Crown. The relative chapter of the reissue of 1216 partially restored this branch of purveyance; consent of the owner, even when a freeman, need not be obtained, provided hire was paid at rates that were fixed: 10d. *per diem* for a cart with two horses, 1s. 2d. for one with three.[1] The prerogative, though restored, was not to be abused.

In 1217 it was again slightly restricted in favour of the upper classes. No demesne cart of any " parson " (*ecclesiastica persona*), or knight, or lady, could be requisitioned by the bailiffs. The " demesne " carts were, of course, those that belonged to the owner of the manor as opposed to the carts of the villeins : the rights of villeins, if they had any, must not stand against the rights of the Crown. Yeomen and small freeholders were also left exposed to this annoying form of interference. Abuses continued. Purveyors would lay hands on all horses and carts in the countryside— far more than they required—choosing perhaps the season of harvest or some equally busy time. The owners, who urgently required them for their own purposes, had to pay ransom to regain possession. Edward I. enacted that perpetrators of such deeds should be "grievously punished by the marshals," if, as members of his household, they were amenable to the summary jurisdiction of his domestic tribunal, or, if not members, then they should pay treble damages and suffer imprisonment for forty days.[2]

[1] The rate fixed by 13 Charles II. c. 8, for the hire of carts or carriages requisitioned by the King, was 6d. per mile. This hire included six oxen, or alternatively two horses and four oxen, to each vehicle.

[2] See 3 Edward I. c. 32.

CHAPTER THIRTY-ONE.

Nec nos nec ballivi nostri capiemus alienum boscum ad castra, vel alia agenda nostra, nisi per voluntatem ipsius cujus boscus ille fuerit.

> Neither we nor our bailiffs shall take, for our castles or for any other work of ours, wood which is not ours, against the will of the owner of that wood.

Purveyance of timber growing elsewhere than on royal manors is here prohibited in absolute terms. In marked contrast with the limited restrictions placed upon other branches of purveyance, this branch is taken away, not merely from local officials, but from the King himself.[1] There was an obvious reason for greater stringency in this case : the King's own extensive demesne woods furnished timber in abundance, whether for building purposes or for firewood, leaving him no excuse for taking, especially if for nothing, the trees of other people.

The purveyors of James I., shortly after his accession, transgressed this provision of Magna Carta by requisitioning timber for repairing the fortifications of Calais. A decision against the Crown was given by the Barons of Exchequer in the second year of James's reign, and a proclamation was issued, bearing date 23rd April, 1607, disclaiming any right to such a prerogative. The guilty purveyors were brought before the Star Chamber.[2]

CHAPTER THIRTY-TWO.

Nos non tenebimus terras illorum qui convicti fuerint de felonia, nisi per unum annum et unum diem, et tunc reddantur terre dominis feodorum.

[1] Cf. Sir James Ramsay, *Angevin Empire*, p. 476, who considers that chapters 28 and 30, in the branches of prerogative with which they respectively deal, "leave the king's personal right open."

[2] See Coke, *Second Institute*, 36.

> We will not retain beyond one year and one day, the lands of those who have been convicted of felony, and the lands shall thereafter be handed over to the lords of the fiefs.

I. *The Crown's Claim to Property of Felons.* The Crown had established certain rights, not too well defined, in the property of criminals formally indicted and sentenced for felony. John, here as elsewhere, took advantage of the vagueness of the law to stretch prerogative to its limit. Magna Carta, therefore, attempted to define the exact boundaries of his rights. Custom gave the felon's land to his feudal lord, and his chattels to the lord who tried him. The Crown encroached on the rights of both, claiming the real estate of felons, as against mesne lords, and their personal estate, as against lords who had jurisdiction.

(1) *The felon's lands.* No difficulty arose when Crown tenants were convicted, for the King was lord of the fief as well as lord paramount, and claimed the whole lands as escheat. When the condemned man was the tenant of a mesne lord, however, a conflict of interests occurred, and here a distinction, which gradually became hard and fast, was drawn between treason and felony.[1] Treason was an offence against the person of the sovereign, and it was probably on this ground that the King made good his claim to seize as forfeit the entire estate, real and personal, of every one condemned to a traitor's death. With regard to ordinary felons, what looks like a compromise was arrived at. The King secured the right to lay waste the lands in question and to appropriate everything he could find there during the space of a year and a day; after which period he was bound to hand over the freehold thus devastated to the lord who claimed the escheat. Such was the custom during the reign of Henry II. as described by Glanvill,[2] who makes it perfectly clear that, before the lands were given up at the expiration of the year, houses were thrown down and

---

[1] Pollock and Maitland, II. 500, consider that the present chapter had a distinct influence in accentuating this twofold classification of crimes.

[2] Glanvill, VII. c. 17. Cf. Bracton, folio 129, for a graphic description of "waste," which included the destruction of gardens, the ploughing up of meadow land, and the uprooting of woods.

trees rooted up. The lord, when at last he entered into possession of the escheated lands found a desert, not a prosperous manor.[1]

Coke has attempted to give a more restricted explanation of the Crown's rights in this respect, maintaining that the " year and day " was not an addition to, but a substitute for, the earlier right of " waste," that the King renounced his barbarous claims in return for the undisputed enjoyment of the ordinary produce for one year only, and agreed, in return to hand over the land with all buildings and appurtenances intact.[2] The authorities he cites, however, are inconclusive, and the weight of evidence on the other side leaves little room for doubt. Not only does the phrase, " year, day, *and* waste " commonly used, create a strong presumption; but Glanvill's words in speaking of the earlier practice are quite free from ambiguity, while the document known as the *Praerogativa Regis* is equally explicit for a period long after Magna Carta.[3] Waste, indeed, was a question of degree, and the Crown was not likely to be scrupulous in regard to felons' lands, when it allowed wanton destruction even of Crown fiefs held in honourable wardship.[4]

Wide as were the legal rights of the Crown, John extended them illegally. When his officers had once obtained a footing in the felon's land, they refused to surrender it to the rightful lord after the year and day had expired. In 1205, Thomas de Aula paid 40 marks and a palfrey to get what he ought to have had for nothing, namely, the lands escheated to him through his tenant's

[1] Is it possible that the origin of "year and waste" can be traced to the difficulty of agreeing on a definition of "real" and "personal" estate respectively? The Crown would claim everything it could as "chattels"—a year's crops and everything above the ground.

[2] *Second Institute*, p. 36.

[3] See Pollock and Maitland, I. 316. "The apocryphal statute *praerogativa regis* which may represent the practice of the earlier years of Edward I." Bracto (folio 129) while stating that the Crown claimed both, seems to doubt the legality of the claim.

Cf. c. 4.

felony.[1] Magna Carta prohibited such abuses, and settled the law for centuries.[2] The Crown long exercised its rights, thus limited, and Henry III. sometimes sold his " year, day, and waste " for considerable sums. Thus, in 1229 Geoffrey of Pomeroy was debited with 20 marks for the Crown's rights in the lands of William de Streete and for his corn and chattels. This sum was afterwards discharged, however, on the ground that the King, induced to change his mind, doubtless by a higher bid, had bestowed these rights on another.[3]

(2) *The felon's chattels.* From an early date the King enjoyed, like other owners of courts, the right to the goods of the offenders he condemned. When Henry II. reorganized the system of criminal justice, and formulated, in the Assizes of Clarendon and Northampton, a scheme whereby all grave offenders should be formally indicted, and thereafter reserved for the coming of his own justices, he established a royal monopoly of jurisdiction over felons; and this logically implied a monopoly over their chattels—an inference confirmed by the express terms of article five of the earlier Assize. As the list of " pleas of the Crown " grew longer, so this branch of royal revenue increased proportionately, at the expense of the private owners of " courts leet." The goods of outlaws and fugitives from justice likewise fell to the exchequer—the sheriff who seized them being responsible for their appraised value.[4]

---

[1] Such at least is the most probable explanation of an entry on the *Pipe Roll* of 6 John (cited Madox, I. 488) ; although it is possible that Thomas only bought in "the year day and waste."

[2] Magna Carta is peculiar in speaking of year and day, without any reference to waste. If it meant to abolish " waste " it ought to have been more explicit. Later records speak of "*annum et vastum*," *e.g.* the *Memoranda Roll*, 42 Henry III. (cited Madox, I. 315), relates how 60 marks were due as the price of the "year and waste " of a mill, the owner of which had been hanged.

[3] *Pipe Roll*, 13 Henry III., cited Madox, I. 347. In Kent, lands held in gavelkind were exempt alike from the lord's escheat and the King's waste, according to the maxim, " The father to the bough, the son to the plough." See, *e.g. praerogativa regis*, c. 16. See also *Gloucester Pleas*, 114, where apparently the King's rights over half a hide were sold for 20s.

[4] Madox, I. 344-8, cites from the *Pipe Rolls* many examples.

The magnates in 1215 made no attempt to interfere with
this branch of administration, tacitly acquiescing in Henry
II.'s encroachments on their ancestors' criminal jurisdictions and perquisites. Under Henry III. and Edward I.,
the forfeited goods of felons continued to form a valuable
source of revenue. In 1290 the widow of a man who had
committed suicide, and therefore incurred forfeit as a *felo de
se,* bought in his goods and chattels for £300, a high price,
in addition to which the Crown specially reserved its "year,
day and waste." [1]

II. *Indictment, Conviction, and Attainder.* The Crown
could not appropriate the property of men merely suspected
of crime, however strong might be the presumption of guilt.
Mere accusation was not enough; a formal judgment was
required. The Charter refers to the lands of a "convicted"
offender, and conviction must be distinguished from indictment on the one hand, and from attainder on the other;
since these formed three stages in the procedure for determining guilt.

(1) *Indictment.* It has been already shown [2] how Henry
of Anjou tried to substitute, wherever possible, indictment
by a jury for private appeal in criminal suits. The Assize
of Clarendon authorized such indictments to be taken before
sheriffs, and we learn from Bracton that, immediately the
formal accusation had been made, the sheriff became responsible for the safety of the accused man's property, both real
and personal. With the help of the coroners and of law-
worthy men of the neighbourhood he must have the chattels
appraised and inventoried, and hold them in suspense until
the "trial," providing therefrom in the interval "estovers,"
that is, sufficient sustenance for the accused and his family.[3]

If the prisoner was acquitted or died before conviction,
the lands and chattels were restored to him or to his relatives, the Crown taking nothing. Reginald of Cornhill,
sheriff of Kent, was discharged in 1201 from liability for the
appraised value of the goods of a man who, after indictment
for burning a house, had died in gaol *non convictus.* As

---

[1] This case is cited by Madox, I. 347, from 18 Edward I.

[2] *Supra,* p. 88.   [3] See Bracton, II. folio 123, and folio 137.

the *Pipe Roll* states, his chattels did not pertain to the King.[1]

(2) *Conviction*. Only the justices could "try" the plea, that is, give sentence according to success or failure in the test appointed for the accused man to perform.[2] Prior to 1215 the usual test was ordeal of water in the ordinary case, or of the red-hot iron in the case of men of high rank and of women. If the suspected person failed, sentence was a mere formality; he had "convicted" himself of the felony. As a consequence of the condemnation of ordeal by the Lateran Council of 1215, the verdict of a petty jury became the normal "test" that branded an offender as *convictus*. This was long looked on as an innovation, and accordingly the law refused to compel the accused, against his will, to trust his fate to this new form of trial. He might refuse to "put himself upon his country," and by "standing mute" make his "conviction" impossible, saving himself from punishment and depriving the King of his chattels and "year and day." For centuries those responsible shrank from the obvious course of treating silence as equivalent to a plea of guilty; but while liberty to refuse a jury's verdict was theoretically recognized, barbarous measures were in reality adopted to compel consent. The Statute of Westminster in 1275[3] directed that all who refused should be imprisoned *en le prison forte et dure*. This statutory authority for strict confinement was liberally interpreted by the agents of the Crown, who treated it as a legal warrant for revolting cruelties. Food and drink were virtually denied, a little mouldy bread and a mouthful of impure water only being allowed upon alternate days; and at a later date the prisoner was slowly crushed to death under great weights "as heavy, yea heavier than he can bear." Brave men, guilty, or mayhap innocent, but suspicious of a corrupt jury, preferred thus to die in torments, that they might save to their wives and children the property which would upon conviction have fallen to the Crown. The fiction was carefully maintained that the victim of such barbarous treat-

---

[1] *Pipe Roll*, 2 John, cited Madox, I. 348. [2] Cf. *supra*, c. 24.
[3] 3 Edward I. c. 12.

ment was not subjected to "torture," always illegal at common law, but merely to *peine forte et dure*, a perfectly legal method of persuasion under the Statute of 1275. This procedure was not abolished until 1772; then only was an accused man for the first time deprived of his right to "have his law"—his claim to ordeal as the old method of proving his innocence. Until that date, then, a jury's verdict was treated as though it were still a new-fangled and unwarranted form of "test" usurping the place of the ordeal, although the latter had been virtually abolished early in the thirteenth century.[1]

(3) *Attainder.* Coke in commenting on this passage draws a further distinction between "conviction," which directly resulted from a confession or a verdict of guilty, and "attainder" which required a formal sentence by the judge. In his age, apparently, it was the attaint that implied forfeiture; looking as usual at Magna Carta through seventeenth-century glasses, he seems surprised to find "convicted" used where he would have written "attainted." Yet this distinction, if recognized in 1215, must have been immaterial then. It was under the Tudor sovereigns that the doctrine of the penal effects of attainder was elaborated. When sentence was passed on a felon, a blight fell on him : his blood was impure, and his kindred could inherit nothing that came through him. The Crown reaped the profit.[2]

Statutes of the nineteenth century modified the harshness with which this rule bore on the felon's innocent relations : [3] finally the Forfeiture Act of 1870[4] abolished "corruption of blood" and deprived the Crown of all interest in the estates of felons, alike in escheats and chattels. Thus the word "attainted" has become practically obsolete. A

---

[1] The Act 12 George III. c. 20, made standing mute equivalent to a plea of *guilty*. A later Act, 7 and 8 George IV. c. 28, made it equivalent to a plea of *not guilty*. See Stephen, *Hist. Crim. Law*, I. 298.

[2] This fiction of corrupt blood was apparently based in part on a false derivation of the word "attainder." See *Oxford English Dictionary*.

[3] *E.g.* 54 George III. c. 145, and 3 and 4 William IV. c. 106, s. 10.

[4] 33 and 34 Victoria, c. 23.

criminal who is fulfilling the term of his sentence is known, not as a man attainted, but simply as a " convict," the same word as was used in Magna Carta.

CHAPTER THIRTY-THREE.

OMNES kydelli de cetero deponantur penitus de Tamisia, et de Medewaye, et per totam Angliam, nisi per costeram maris.

> All kydells for the future shall be removed altogether from Thames and Medway, and throughout all England, except upon the sea shore.

The object of this provision is not open to doubt; it was intended to remove from rivers all obstacles likely to interfere with navigation. Its full importance can only be understood when the deplorable state of the roads is kept in view. The water-ways were the great avenues of commerce; when these were blocked, townsmen and traders suffered loss, while those who depended on them for necessaries, comforts, and luxuries, shared in the general inconvenience. Magna Carta mentions only one kind of impediments, namely, " kydells " (or fish-weirs), not because of the purpose to which these were put, but because they were the form of obstruction that called for repressive measures at the moment. This word seems to have been used by the framers of Magna Carta in a wide general sense, embracing all fixed contrivances or " engines " intended to catch fish, and likely by their bulk to interfere with the free passage of boats.[1]

It has been gratuitously assumed that the motive for prohibiting " kydells " must have been of a similar nature to the motive for constructing them; and that therefore the object of the present chapter was to prevent any monopoly in rights of fishing. Law courts and writers on jurisprudence for many centuries endorsed this mistaken

---

[1] The *Oxford English Dictionary* defines it as " a dam, weir, or barrier in a river, having an opening in it fitted with nets or other appliances for catching fish." For weirs in *Domesday Book*, see Ballard, *D. Inquest*, 175-6.

view, and treated Magna Carta as an absolute prohibition of the creation of " several " (or exclusive) fisheries in tidal waters.[1] Although this legal doctrine has been frequently and authoritatively enunciated, it rests on a misconception. The Great Charter sought to protect freedom of navigation, not freedom of fishing; and this is obvious from the last words of the chapter: kydells are to be removed from Thames and Medway and throughout all England "*except upon the sea-shore.*" It would have been a manifest absurdity to allow monopolies of taking fish in the open seas, while insisting on freedom to fish in rivers, the banks of which were private property. The sense is clear: no objection was taken to "kydells" so long as they did not interfere with navigation.

The erroneous view, however, had much to excuse it, and acquired plausibility from the circumstance that the destruction of obstacles to the free passage of boats incidentally secured also free passage for salmon and other migratory fish; and that *later* statutes, when legislative motives had become more complicated, were sometimes passed with both of these objects in view. The change is well illustrated by a comparison of the words of two statutes of 1350 and of 1472 respectively. The first of these repeats the substance of this chapter, and thus explains its object:—
" Whereas the common passage of boats and ships in the great rivers of England be oftentimes annoyed by the inhancing of gorces, mills, weirs, stanks, stakes, and kydells." [2] Here there is no allusion to fish or rights of fishing. The later Act, while confirming, under penalties, previous statutes for the suppression of weirs, not only states its own intention as twofold, namely, to protect

---

[1] Blackstone, *Commentaries*, IV. 424, declared that this chapter " prohibited for the future the grants of exclusive fisheries." Cf. *e.g.* Thomson, *Magna Charta*, 214, and Norgate, *John Lackland*, 217. See also Malcolmson *v.* O'Dea (1862), 10 *H. of L. Cas.*, 593, and Neill *v.* Duke of Devonshire (1882), 8 App. Ca. at p. 179,—cases cited in Moore, *History and Law of Fisheries*, p. 13, where the fallacy is exposed. For an unsuccessful attempt to extend the principle to Scotland, after the Act of Union, see an interesting review of the first edition of this work in *Jurid. Rev.* for March, 1905.

[2] 25 Edward III., stat. 3, c. 4.

navigation of rivers, and " also in safeguard of all the fry of fish spawned within the same," but retrospectively and unwarrantably attributes a like double motive to Magna Carta.[1]

So far as Thames and Medway were concerned, this provision contained nothing new. To the Londoners, indeed, the keeping open of their river for trade was a matter of vital importance. The right to destroy *kydelli* had been purchased from Richard I. for 1500 marks, and a further sum had been paid to John to have this confirmed. These charters (dated 14th July, 1197, and 17th June, 1199) " granted and steadfastly commanded that all kydells that are in the Thames be removed wheresoever they shall be within the Thames; also we have quit-claimed all that which the Warden of our Tower of London was wont yearly to receive from the said kydells. Wherefore we will and steadfastly command that no warden of the said Tower, at any time hereafter, shall exact anything of any one, neither molest nor burden nor make any demand of any person by reason of the said kydells." John's Charter went further than that of Richard, making it clear that the prohibition referred to Medway as well as to Thames, and granting the right to inflict a penalty of £10 upon anyone infringing its provisions.[2]

Magna Carta confirmed this provision and extended it to all rivers, and this was repeated in the reissues of Henry III. The citizens of London, not content with a clause in a general enactment, purchased for 5000 marks

[1] 12 Edward IV. c. 7. Apparently the earliest statute which refers to weirs as causing injury to fish was one passed in 1402, namely, 4 Henry IV. c. 11 ; see Moore, *Fisheries*, p. 175.

[2] It seems to have been generally assumed that these charters conferred positive as well as negative privileges on the citizens, including rights of administration and jurisdiction over the waters of Thames. See Noorthouck, *New History of London* (1773), 36. Luffman, *Charters of London* (1793), 13, says of Richard's grant in 1197 : " By this charter the citizens became conservators of the river Thames." This is an anachronism, but *Patent Rolls* of 33 Edward I., 5 Edward III., 8 Edward III., contain Commissions of Conservancy. See Moore, *op. cit.*, p. 176. In 1393 the statute of 17 Richard II. c. 9 granted authority to the Mayor of London to regulate weirs and generally to " conserve " the Thames from Staines downwards, and the Medway.

three new charters exclusively in their own favour. One of these, dealing with kydells in Thames and Medway, was issued by Henry on 18th February, 1227, in terms almost identical with those of Richard and John.[1]

CHAPTER THIRTY-FOUR.

BREVE quod vocatur *Precipe* de cetero non fiat alicui de aliquo tenemento unde liber homo amittere possit curiam suam.

> The writ which is called *praecipe* shall not for the future be issued to anyone, regarding any tenement whereby a freeman may lose his court.

The grievance here dealt with lay at the heart of the quarrel of 1215, and the remedy adopted proved a vital factor in the history of royal jurisdiction in England. In extorting from John a solemn promise to restrict the use of this particular writ, the barons gained something of infinitely greater value than a petty reform of court procedure; they committed their enemy to a reversal of a line of policy vigorously pursued for half a century. The process by which the jurisdiction of the King's courts was undermining that of the feudal courts was now to be arrested.[2] Magna Carta, by this apparently inoffensive clause, was grappling in reality with an urgent problem of the day, fraught with tremendous practical issues alike for King and barons. This can only be understood in connection with the technical details on which it hinges.

I. *Royal Writs and Feudal Jurisdictions*. In pleas of disputed titles to land, feudal theory gave sole jurisdiction to the lord of the fief. No principle was more absolutely established than this: no person, neither King nor Emperor, had any right to interfere, except on the one ground of failure of justice. Not even Henry II. dared to repudiate this universal rule; but he adopted expedients

---

[1] See *Rotuli Cartarum*, 11 Henry III.

[2] The *Histoire des ducs*, 149, paraphrases this chapter thus: "Toutes hautes justices vaurrent-ils avoir en lor tierres." Miss Norgate, *Minority*, 11, has not grasped the significance of this clause.

to render it inoperative. If Glanvill may be trusted, Henry was strong enough to obtain acquiescence in his prohibition of any plea, concerning ownership of a lay fee, being tried in a seignorial court without the licence of a royal precept.[1]

Henry also invented, or adopted from precedents of the Carolingian Emperors, two types of writ, the virtual effects of which were to evoke causes from the lords' courts to his own, without too open an infringement of feudal principle.[2] These were the Writ of Right and the Writ *Praecipe*. The Writ of Right proceeded on the principle that a lord superior was bound to see that his vassals dispensed justice to their rear vassals. When a freeholder, the tenant of a mesne lord, complained to the King that justice was refused him, the King formally commanded the remiss lord " to do full right " to the complainant, and added the threat that, unless he did so, the King himself would. The writ, known as a *breve de recto tenendo,* was thus issued to the owner of a feudal court; professed to afford him an opportunity of obedience by trying the plea in his court; and avoided conflict with feudal theory by justifying the proposed royal interference as "*pro defectu justitiae.*" It afforded, however, excellent opportunities for the insidious encroachments of the royal courts at the behest of powerful kings, who retained in their own hands the right to define what constituted a failure to do justice.[3]

The Writ *Praecipe* in its origin and antecedents differed fundamentally from the Writ of Right: it was addressed to the sheriff, not to the owner of a franchise; it was a more direct violation of feudal rights, for it made no allegation of failure of justice but simply ignored the lord's jurisdiction, bidding the sheriff command the tenant to restore the land in question to the demandant; or else to appear before the royal court to explain his reasons for disobedience. No opportunity was afforded the mesne lord of hearing the plea. The whole procedure, almost without disguise or excuse, was an open transference of the dispute from the

[1] Glanvill, XII. 25. See *supra,* p. 89. [2] Brunner, *Schwurgerichte,* 78 ff.
[3] The form of the writ is given in Glanvill, XII. 3.

manorial court to that of the King.[1] The writ, which on the surface reads merely as a summary and final command to hand over the estate to another, is really an " original writ " commencing a litigation in the King's court. One important effect of its issue was that all proceedings instituted in inferior tribunals must immediately stop.

The feudal lord, in whose court baron the plea would naturally have been decided, was thus robbed by the King of his jurisdiction. With it, he lost also authority over his tenants, and numerous fees and perquisites. The writ *praecipe* was thus an ingenious device for " evoking " a particular cause from the manorial court to the King's court.[2]

The two types of writ, *praecipes* and writs of right, at first contrasted as alternative methods of bringing a plea under royal jurisdiction, came in time to have entirely different relations. The person to whom the preliminary writ was issued, whether sheriff or lord of a franchise court, ceased to be of much importance, when the writ had become a mere formality. The essential feature of a Writ of Right came to be that it dealt with ownership as opposed to mere possession : all royal writs that originated pleas involving title to land were then reckoned Writs of Right, which now embraced an important species of the originally opposed genus of writs *praecipe*.[3] Thus, in one place, writs *praecipe* and writs of right overlapped each other.[4]

The motives of Henry II., in instituting his legal reforms, were probably mixed; and it is not easy to determine whether he favoured his new writs most because they really

---

[1] Cf. Stubbs, *Const. Hist.*, I. 576.

[2] Glanvill, I. 6, gives the form of a *praecipe*: *Rex vicecomiti salutem, Praecipe A. quod sine dilatione reddat B. unam hidam terrae in villa illa, unde idem B. queritur quod praedictus A. ei deforceat: et nisi fecerit, summone eum per bonos summonitores quod sit ibi coram me vel Justiciariis meis in crastino post octabas clausi Paschae apud locum illum, ostensurus quare non fecerit. Et habeas ibi summonitores et hoc breve. Teste Ranulpho de Glanvilla apud Clarendon.*

[3] Brunner, *Schwurgerichte*, 411 ; Maitland, *Col. Papers*, II. 129.

[4] Coke, *Sec. Inst.*, 40, gives three varieties of *praecipe*: (*a*) *praecipe quod reddat* ; (*b*) *quod permittat* ; (*c*) *quod faciat*. The first group includes one variety of Writs of Right and the various Writs of Entry. Writs of Right, on their part, are of three kinds : (1) writ of right patent, (2) writ *praecipe*, (3) little writ of right, applicable to villeins on ancient demesne.

stimulated the flow of justice in the feudal courts, or because they afforded facilities for sapping their strength. While reforming the entire administration of justice in England, the King hoped, by the same means, to destroy gradually the feudal privileges of his magnates. He intended to draw into his own courts all pleas relating to land. Questions of property were to be tried before his justices, by combat or, at the tenant's option, by the grand assize; questions of possession (without any option) by the appropriate petty assize. The barons showed no desire to dispute the Crown's assumption of a monopoly over the petty assizes; indeed they cordially acquiesced in this by the terms of chapter 18 of the Charter. The grand assize was another matter; they refused to be robbed of their right to determine, in their own courts baron, proprietary actions between their own tenants. Indeed, for such wholesale extension of the King's jurisdiction over pleas of land, Henry II. had absolutely no precedent. He had made the Crown strong and then used its power for his own aggrandizement. The King's courts had increased their authority, as a distinguished American historian has expressed it, " by direct usurpation, in derogation of the rights of the popular courts and manorial franchises, upon the sole authority of the King." [1]

While undermining the feudal courts, Henry was devising improved methods of dispensing justice in his own. Efforts were being successfully made, as has been shown,[2] to substitute the grand assize for trial by combat; and the desire for the more rational mode of proof favoured the King's policy of removing important litigations to his own court. The assize procedure must be taken along with the writ of right and the writ *praecipe* as parts of one scheme of reform.

II. *The Intention of Magna Carta.* The present chapter

---

[1] See Bigelow, *Hist. of Procedure*, 78. Glanvill, read between the lines, supports this view. Thus in I. c. 3, he speaks of the King's courts as normally dealing with "pleas of baronies"; in I. c. 5, he speaks of what he evidently considers an abnormal expansion of this jurisdiction to any plea anent a free tenement, if the Crown so desired.

[2] See *supra*, under c. 18.

says nothing of the Writ of Right, but guards against the abuse of the Writ *Praecipe*, without attempting to interfere with its employment within its legitimate sphere, that is to say, in settling disputes as to Crown fiefs. John might keep his own court, and issue *praecipes* to his own tenants; but let him respect the rights of other feudal lords and not use his writs as engines of encroachment upon manorial jurisdictions. For the future, such writs must not be issued "concerning any tenement whereby a freeman may lose his court." Writs *praecipe* might be freely used for any other purpose, but not for this. This one purpose, however, was exactly what had specially recommended them to King Henry.

The present chapter must, therefore, be regarded as one of the most reactionary in the Charter: the barons had forced John to promise a complete reversal of the deliberate policy of his father.

Here, then, under the guise of a small change in legal procedure, was concealed a notable triumph of feudalism over the centralizing policy of the monarchy—a backward step, which, if given full effect to, might have ushered in a second era of feudal turbulence such as had disgraced the reign of Stephen. We are told on high authority that John's acknowledgment of "the claims of the feudal lord to hold a court which shall enjoy an exclusive competence in proprietary actions" was one which "Henry II. would hardly have been forced into."[1] That may well be; but John had already more than once rejected this proposal with vehemence. In 1215, he could no longer strive against the inevitable, and agreed under compulsion to provisions which he had no intention to keep. The concession, although insincere, was nevertheless an important one. The substance of chapter 34 was repeated, with some trivial verbal alterations, in all future issues of Magna Carta.[2]

[1] Pollock and Maitland, I. 151.

[2] The version of 1216 speaks of a "free tenement," where that of 1215 spoke merely of a "tenement." The addition makes no change, since in no case could the King's courts try pleas affecting villeins of mesne lords. Perhaps the object is to make it clear that there was no interference with the King's rights over holdings of his own villeins.

Why did the barons, it may be asked, while attacking the writ *praecipe,* allow the writ of right patent to go unscathed? History is silent; but inferences may be drawn. The barons had no legal ground for condemning the legitimate use of the writ of right even when it deprived a baron or other freeman of his court. Feudal theory sanctioned this procedure, unless where it was abused; and it was difficult to define abuse of the procedure. If "*pro defectu justitiae*" was honestly alleged, the King had a right to interfere, well grounded in feudal law. The interference, too, even where unwarranted, was of a subtle nature, and difficult to guard against. Finally, encroachments initiated by this procedure had not been attempted before 1215 to any noticeable extent: the barons had no premonition of the new uses to which the writ of right would be put, after the channel of royal aggression by way of the *praecipe* had been closed. The writ of right patent was a cumbrous process, and its short day of usefulness came after the granting of Magna Carta.

III. *Expedients for evading Magna Carta.* One question remains: was this provision observed in practice? The answer is that its letter was stringently observed, but its spirit was evaded. Writs *praecipe* that deliberately evoked suits, other than those of Crown tenants, to the King's courts ceased to be issued, but the sphere denied to the writ was made as narrow as possible; and methods were devised for reducing seignorial courts practically to impotence, without direct violation of the terms of the Great Charter.

(1) *The letter of the law.* The Chancery, in obedience to Magna Carta, ceased to issue this particular form of writ in such a manner as to cause a freeman "to lose his court." It was still issued to Crown tenants; but strictly denied to under-tenants, who were thus left to find redress at the feudal court of the magnate from whom they held their land.[1]

[1] In translating the reissue of 1225, the *Statutes at Large* expand the word "*praecipe*" into "*praecipe in capite,*" for which there is no authority in any known text of Magna Carta, though it appears in Coke's version of Henry's charter (*Sec.*

The measure thus forced on the Crown in the selfish interests of the baronage, inflicted hardship on tenants of mesne lords : the court baron was now their only source of feudal justice, and in that court they could not get the benefit of the improved methods of royal procedure. In particular, the grand assize was a royal monopoly. The magnates, indeed, desired to adopt it, but they had difficulty in getting together twelve knights willing to act as jurors.[1] Whatever hopes the barons entertained of overcoming such difficulties were disappointed : in 1259 the Provisions of Westminster declared that freeholders should not be compelled to swear against their will " since no one can make them do this without the King's warrant."[2] It was the deliberate policy of Edward I. to exaggerate all such difficulties, putting every obstacle in the way of private courts, until he reduced their jurisdictions to sinecures.[3]

(2) *Evasion of its spirit.* While the letter of Magna Carta was strictly kept, its spirit was evaded. It was impossible to give loyal effect to an enactment that went

Inst., 38). Authorities differ as to what constitutes a *praecipe in capite.* Brunner, *Schwurgerichte,* sec. xx., declares it to be so called " because it begins with the word *Praecipe* " ; yet all *praecipes* so begin, even Writs of Entry, which are certainly not condemned by Magna Carta. Coke (*Sec. Inst.,* 38) seems (inconsistently with his own version of Magna Carta) to identify the *praecipe in capite* with a class of writs NOT prohibited in the Charter, namely, with those professing to deal with estates held directly under the Crown : no one ought to have it without taking oath " that the land is holden of the King *in capite.*" He cites illustrations from the reign of Edward I. Adams (*Origin,* 104), speaks of an " *in capite* " clause inserted in *praecipes* to evade the prohibition of Magna Carta. See also Holdsworth, III. 10.

[1] Such an attempt seems to have been made in 1207 by Walter de Lacy, Earl of Ulster, who set up in his Irish fief what is described as *nova assisa,* against which John protested. See *Rot. Pat.,* I. 72, for writ dated 23rd May, 1207. In one case John acquiesced in grand assizes being held in feudal courts : on 4th May, 1201, he granted licence to Hubert Walter to hold them for his tenants in gavelkind. See *New Rymer,* I. 83.

[2] See article 18 (*Select Charters,* 404). Cf. chapter 29 of the Petition of the Barons (*Select Charters,* 386), and Pollock and Maitland, I. 182 : " The voice of the nation, or what made itself heard as such, no longer, as in 1215, demanded protection for the seignorial courts."

[3] A partially successful attempt was made to revive feudal jurisdictions as late as the reign of Edward III. See Stubbs, *Const. Hist.,* II. 638-9.

directly counter to the whole stream of progress.   Manorial justice was falling into disrepute, while royal justice was becoming more efficient and more popular.   Under-tenants, deprived of access to the King's court by the direct road of the writ *praecipe*, sought more tortuous modes of entrance.   Legal fictions were devised.   The problem was how to evade Magna Carta without openly infringing it : the King's justices and would-be litigants in the King's courts formed a tacit alliance for this end, but had to proceed by wary steps, in the teeth of opposition from the powerful owners of seignorial courts.   Three methods were adopted by the Crown :—

(*a*) Magna Carta had not condemned the writ *praecipe*, but only its abuse; and abuse was sometimes difficult to define.   That writ remained the normal procedure in cases of Crown holdings,[1] and a liberal interpretation of this exception would sometimes pass unchallenged, though there seems no ground for supposing that any recognized legal fiction of this nature came into use.   Then, besides the later developments of the *praecipe* (to be afterwards described), the King claimed, in spite of Magna Carta, to grant *ex gratia speciali* the very writ complained of.[2]

(*b*) When the use of the writ *praecipe* was barred, the King could fall back on the more cumbrous procedure instituted by writ of right, the potentialities of which were developed after 1215.   Coke[3] cites an instance from the 34th year of Edward I., where a demandant admitted that the lands in dispute were not held of the King *in capite* but of his brother Edmund, and therefore he could not proceed by way of *praecipe*, but he might, if he so desired, proceed by writ of right patent in the King's *curia*.   This substitution of the writ of right for the *praecipe* is described by Professor Maitland[4] as " a victory of feudalism consecrated by the Great Charter."

When a tenant, whose title was challenged in his lord's court, applied to the King for a grand assize, the plea was practically certain, by one avenue or another, to reach the

---

[1] See, *e.g.* Madox, I. 793.   [2] Bracton, 404b.

[3] *Sec. Inst.*, 38.   [4] *Coll. Papers*, II. 129.

z

Curia Regis.[1] The rule that no one need defend his *liberum tenementum* unless summoned by a royal writ also worked towards the same end. But many difficulties lay in the path of the writ of right.[2] The Petition of the Barons of 1259 (chapter 29)[3] illustrates one attempt to make the most of these. Moreover, the whole procedure was dilatory, expensive, and inelastic, and it was gladly abandoned, after the invention of less direct but more convenient methods of effecting the same purpose.

(c) The procedure which rendered recourse to the writ of right unnecessary was instituted by one of various writs developed from the older *praecipe* and known as writs of entry. These writs instituted procedure in the King's court on the averment of some recent flaw in the tenant's title, which could be settled without opening up the whole matter of the ownership. This was a subterfuge, for the settling of the special point virtually decided the general question of ownership without appeal. Although probably not invented for the express purpose of defeating this chapter of the Great Charter, these writs were soon applied to that purpose. One of the most useful of their number was the writ of cosinage, devised by William of Raleigh, extending to others than the dispossessed heir the simple procedure of the petty assizes. As early as 1237, it was decided in the King's court that such a writ did not violate the Charter.[4] Writs of entry were thus, from the point of view of the magnate with his private court, wolves in sheep's clothing. They professed to determine a question of *possession*, but really decided a question of *ownership* At first, the pleas to which they could be applied were few and special. Steadily, new forms of action were devised to cover almost every conceivable case. The process of evolution was a long one, commencing soon after 1215, and virtually concluding with chapter 29 of the Statute of Marl-

---

[1] See Brunner, *Schwurgerichte*, 406 ; Maitland, *Coll. Papers*, II. 129.

[2] See Glanvill, XII. 7.   [3] *Sel. Chart.*, 386-7.

[4] See Bracton's *Note-book*, plea 1215, where the writ in question is cited at length : it contains the sentence, "*nec tollat alicui curiam suam ubi locum habere possit breve de recto.*"

borough, or rather with the liberal construction which Crown lawyers placed upon that statute in the following reign.

Edward I., at the height of his power, and eager to set his house in order, shrank from an open breach of the Great Charter, gladly adopting subtle expedients to oust mesne lords from rights secured to them by the present chapter. In Edward's reign the legal machinery was brought to perfection, so that thereafter no action relating to freehold was ever again tried in the courts baron of the magnates, but, in direct violation of the spirit of Magna Carta, decided in the courts of the King.[1]

The demandant had no need to infringe the prohibition against the older form of writ *praecipe* when he could obtain another writ, equally effective. A writ of entry was, indeed, to a peaceable demandant, preferable to a writ *praecipe*, which could only be issued to one prepared to *offer* battle, the option of accepting lying with his adversary. Crown tenants, even, who could obtain the original writ *praecipe*, came to prefer the modern substitute; and clause 34 of Magna Carta was virtually obsolete.

IV. *Influence on later legal development.* One of the indirect effects of the clause was of a most unfortunate nature. The necessity it created for effecting reforms by a tortuous path did great and lasting harm to the form of English law. Legal fictions have indeed their uses, by evading technical rules of law in the interests of substantial justice. The price paid for this relief, however, is usually a heavy one. Complicated procedures and underhand expedients have to be invented, and these lead in turn to new legal technicalities of a more irrational nature than the old ones. It would have been better in the interests of scientific jurisprudence, if so desirable a result could have been effected in a more straightforward manner. The authors of Magna Carta must bear the blame.[2]

[1] Technical details are given by Pollock and Maitland, II. 63-7. The whole family of writs were known as "writs of entry *sur disseisin*"; and these were applied to still wider uses after 1267 on the authority of the Statute of Marlborough, as "writs of entry *sur disseisin* on the *post.*" See also Maitland, Preface to *Sel. Pleas in Manorial Courts*, p. lv.

[2] Cf. Pollock and Maitland, I. 151, and *Sel. Pleas in Manorial Courts*, already cited.

CHAPTER THIRTY-FIVE.

UNA mensura vini sit per totum regnum nostrum, et una mensura cervisie, et una mensura bladi, scilicet quarterium Londonie, et una latitudo pannorum tinctorum et russetorum et halbergectorum, scilicet due ulne infra listas; de ponderibus autem sit ut de mensuris.

> Let there be one measure of wine throughout our whole realm; and one measure of ale; and one measure of corn, to wit, "the London quarter"; and one width of cloth (whether dyed, or russet, or "halberget"),[1] to wit, two ells within the selvedges; of weights also let it be as of measures.

This chapter confirmed the provisions of various ordinances that sought to regulate the sale of commodities. Assizes of bread and beer were issued from time to time, and also assizes of weights and measures, and of wines. Richard's Assize of Cloth, for example, of 20th November, 1197, was, according to modern conceptions of the proper sphere of government, partly commendable and partly ill-advised. It strove, on the one hand, to overcome the inconvenience experienced by traders, who met with varying standards as they moved their wares from place to place. What was of more importance, the Assize sought to obviate frauds perpetrated upon buyers under shelter of ambiguous weights and measures. The London quarter must, therefore, be used everywhere for corn; and one measure for wine or beer: so far, good. On the other hand, the ordinances of Richard went further than modern ideas of *laissez faire* would tolerate. In particular, freedom of trade was interfered with by the regulations reported by Roger of Hoveden.[2] No cloth, he tells us, was to be woven except of a uniform width, namely, "two ells within the lists."[3]

---

[1] This word, unknown to Ducange, seems to be connected with the "hauberk" or coat-of-mail. It may mean thick cloth worn under a coat-of-mail.

[2] R. Hoveden, IV. 33-4.

[3] At a later date cloth of an alternative standard width was also legalized, viz., of one yard between the "lists." Hence arose the distinction between "broadcloth" (that is, cloth of two yards) and "streits" (that is, narrow cloth of one

Dyed cloths, it was provided, should be of equal quality through and through, as well in the middle as at the outside. Merchants were prohibited from darkening their windows by hanging up, to quote the quaint language of the ordinance, " cloth whether red or black, or shields (*scuta*) so as to deceive the sight of buyers seeking to choose good cloth." Coloured cloth was only to be sold in cities or important boroughs. Here we have a sumptuary law meant to ensure that the lower classes went in modest grey attire. Six lawful men were to be assigned to keep the Assize in each county and important borough. These custodians of measures must see that no goods were bought or sold except according to the standards; imprison those found guilty of using other measures; and seize the chattels of defaulters, for the King's behoof. If the *custodes* performed their duties negligently they were to suffer amercement of their chattels.[1] Richard's Assize of Measures was supplemented in 1199 by John's Assize of Wine, which tried to regulate the price of wines of various qualities,[2] an attempt not repeated in Magna Carta.

The author who gives us the text of the ordinance of 1197, tells us that its terms were too stringent, and had to be relaxed in practice.[3] This was done in 1201 : the King's justices seized cloth that was less than the legal width. They compromised, however, by accepting money " to the use of the King and to the damage of many "; thus Hoveden denounces what he regards as an unlawful bargain between justices and traders for evading the strict letter of the ordinance.

The justices, indeed, were often more intent on collecting fines for its breach than on enforcing the Assize. In 1203, two merchants of Worksop were amerced each in half a

---

yard) (see Statute 1 Richard III. c. 8). The word "broadcloth" has, long since, changed its meaning, and now denotes material of superior quality, quite irrespective of width. See *Oxford English Dictionary*, under "Broadcloth."

[1] Cf. *supra*, c. 20, for "amercements," and *supra*, c. 24, for "custodes" of pleas (or coroners).

[2] See R. Hoveden, IV. 100.

[3] See Hoveden, IV. 172, and Stubbs, *Const. Hist.*, I. 616.

mark for selling wine contrary to the Assize, while the custodians of measures of the borough were mulcted in one mark for performing their duty negligently—an exact illustration of the words of the ordinance.[1] In the same year, a fine of one mark was imposed on certain merchants "for stretching cloth," in order, presumably, to bring it to the legal width.[2] Merchants frequently paid heavy fines to escape the ordinance altogether.[3]

When the barons in 1215 insisted upon John enforcing his brother's ordinance, they took a step in their own interests as buyers, and against the interests of the trade guilds as sellers. Although this provision was repeated in subsequent charters, evasion continued. One example may suffice : in the second year of Henry III.[4] the citizens of London paid 40 marks that they might not be questioned for selling cloth less than two yards in width. Here is an illustration of the practice of the judges to which Hoveden had objected, and which Magna Carta had apparently failed to put down. Sometimes, however, Richard's Assize of Measures[5] and John's Assize of Wine were enforced. In 1219, a Lincolnshire parson, with a liberal conception of his parochial duties, had to pay 40s. for wine sold *extra Assisam*.[6] Parsons, apparently, might engage in trade, but only if they conformed to the usual regulations.

[1] See *Pipe Roll*, 4 John, cited Madox, I. 566.

[2] See *ibid.*

[3] In 1203 the men of Worcester paid 100s. "*ut possint emere et vendere pannos tinctos sicut solebant tempore Regis Henrici*" ; and the men of Bedford, Beverley, Norwich and other towns made similar payments. See *Pipe Roll*, 4 John, cited Madox, I. 468-9.

[4] See *Pipe Roll*, cited Madox, I. 509.

[5] *Gloucester Pleas*, No. 501.

[6] *Pipe Roll*, 3 Henry III., cited Madox, I. 567.

CHAPTER THIRTY-SIX.

NICHIL detur vel capiatur de cetero pro brevi inquisicionis de vita vel membris, sed gratis concedatur et non negetur.

Nothing in future shall be given or taken for a writ of inquisition of life or limbs, but freely it shall be granted, and never denied.

This chapter has an important bearing upon trial by combat, and none at all upon *habeas corpus,* to which it is often supposed to be closely related. The writ upon which emphasis is here laid had been invented by Henry II. to obviate the judicial duel, by allowing the accused to refer the question of guilt or innocence to the verdict of his neighbours.

I. *Trial by Combat prior to the Reign of John.* The crucial moment in judicial proceedings during the Middle Ages arrived, as has already been explained,[1] when the "test" or "trial" (*lex*), appointed by the court, was attempted by one or both of the litigants. The particular form of proof to which the warlike Norman barons were attached was the *duellum,* and it was only natural that such of the old Anglo-Saxon aristocracy as associated with them on terms of equality should adopt their prejudices. "Combat" became the normal mode of deciding pleas among the upper classes. From the first, however, it seems not to have been competent for property of less than 10s. in value,[2] and it soon came to be specially reserved for two classes of disputes—civil pleas instituted by writ of right, and criminal pleas following on "appeal." The present chapter is concerned with the latter only.

An "appeal" in this connection was entirely different from the modern appeal from a lower to a higher court. It was a formal accusation of treason or felony made by a private individual on his own initiative, and was usually followed by judicial combat between the appellant and appellee, each of whom fought in person. Such a right was necessary in an age when the government had not

[1] See *supra*, pp. 84-6.   [2] See *Leges Henrici primi*, c. 69, §§ 15-16.

yet assumed a general responsibility for bringing ordinary
criminals to justice. The wronged person, not the magistrate, was the avenger of crime; and this explains several
peculiarities—why, for example, when the accused had
uttered " that hateful word craven," [1] thus confessing himself vanquished and deserving a perjurer's fate, the victori-
ous accuser was entitled to his vengeance, even in face of
a royal pardon. When Henry of Essex, constable and
standard-bearer of Henry II., in 1163, had been worsted
in the combat, the royal favour could not shield him, though
the King's connivance enabled him, by becoming a monk,
and therefore dead in law, to escape actual death by hanging.[2] At an early date the procedure resembled even more
closely a legalized private revenge: " the ancient usage
was, so late as Henry IV.'s time, that all the relations of
the slain should drag the appellee to the place of execution." [3]

The evils of trial by combat are obvious. From the first
it was dreaded by the traders of the boroughs, who paid
heavily for charters of exemption. Their aversion spread
to the higher classes, and was shared by Henry II. To
that statesman, endowed with the instincts of a reformer,
despising obsolete and irrational modes of procedure, and
devoid of reverence for tradition, trial by combat was
abhorrent. He would gladly have abolished it, but followed
the more subtle policy of undermining its vitality. For
this purpose, he used four expedients, which are of great
interest, in respect that they throw light on the process by
which trial by jury superseded trial by battle.[4] (1) Every
facility was afforded the parties to a civil suit to forego the
duellum voluntarily. Henry placed at their disposal, as a
substitute, a procedure which his ancestors had reserved for
the service of the Crown. Litigants might refer their rival
claims to the oath of a picked body of local neighbours:
the old recognitors thus developed into the *jurata*. This

---

[1] See Bracton, folio 531.   [2] See Jocelyn of Brakelond, 50-2.

[3] Blackstone, *Commentaries*, IV. 316. Cf. Bateson, *Borough Customs*, I. 73,
II. xxv., II. xxxiv.

[4] Cf. *supra*, p. 88, and also p. 272.

course was possible, however, only where both parties consented, and it had many features in common with a modern
arbitration. (2) In pleas relating to the title and possession
of land, Henry went further, granting to the tenant the
option of a peaceful settlement even when the demandant
preferred battle. The *assisa*, like the *jurata*, applied only
to civil pleas. (3) Attempts were made to discourage trial
by combat in criminal pleas also, by discouraging private
" appeal," its natural prelude. The corporate voice of the
accusing jury was made to supersede the individual complaint of the injured party. Only the near blood relation,
or the liege lord, of a murdered man was allowed to prove
the offender's guilt by combat; while a woman's right of
appeal was kept within narrow limits.[1] (4) A wide field
was still left for private appeal and battle; but Henry
endeavoured to narrow it by a subtle device. In appeals of
homicide, where the accusation was not made *bona fide*, but
maliciously or without probable cause, the appellee was
afforded a means of escaping the *duellum* : he might apply
for the writ that forms the subject of this chapter.

II. *The Writ of Life and Limb*. The writ here referred
to, better known to medieval England as the writ *de odio
et atia*,[2] was intended to protect from duel men unjustly
appealed of homicide. Many an appealed man was glad
to purchase escape by assuming the habit and tonsure of
a monk;[3] but Henry desired to save innocent men from
the risk of failure in the *duellum*, without this subterfuge.
If the accused asserted that his appellant acted " out of
spite and hate " (*de odio et atia*), he might purchase from
the chancery a writ to refer this preliminary plea to the

[1] See under c. 54.

[2] In identifying the writ spoken of by Magna Carta as that " of life and limbs "
with the well-known writ *de odio et atia*, most authorities rely on a passage in
Bracton (viz., folio 123). There is still better evidence. The Statute of Westminster, II. c. 29, ordains : " Lest the parties appealed or indicted be kept long
in prison, they shall have a writ *de odio et atia* like as it is declared in Magna Carta
and other statutes." Further, in 1231, twelve jurors who had given a verdict as to
whether an appeal was false, were asked *quo waranto fecerunt sacramentum illud
de vita et membris*, without the King's licence. See Bracton's *Note-book, case* 592.

[3] Madox, I. 505, has collected instances.

verdict of twelve recognitors. If his neighbours upheld the plea, further proceedings were quashed : the *duellum* was avoided.[1] A similar privilege was afterwards extended to those guilty of homicide in self-defence, or of homicide by misadventure.[2] Soon every man appealed of murder, whether guilty or not, alleged as matter of course that he had been accused maliciously, mere " words of common form." Virtually, the main issue of guilt or innocence, not merely the preliminary pleas, came to be determined by the neighbours' verdict,[3] which was treated as final. No further proceedings were necessary : none were allowed. The *duellum* had been elbowed aside, although it was not abolished until 1819.[4]

III. *Subsidiary Uses of the Writ.* This inquest of life and limb has been claimed as the direct antecedent of the procedure which became so valuable a bulwark of the subject's liberty, under the name *habeas corpus*. This is a mistake ; the modern writ of *habeas corpus* was developed out of an entirely different writ, which had for its original object the safe-keeping of the prisoner's body in gaol, not his liberation from unjust confinement.[5]

The opinion generally, though erroneously, held, is not without excuse ; for the writ mentioned by Magna Carta was put to a subsidiary use, which bears superficial resemblance to that of the *habeas corpus*. Considerable delay might occur between the appellee's petition for the writ of inquisition and the verdict upon it. In the interval, the man accused of murder had no right to be released on bail, a privilege allowed to those suspected of less grave crimes. This was hard where the accused was the victim of malice, or guilty only of justifiable homicide. Prisoners, in such

---

[1] Cf. Pollock and Maitland, II. 585-7, and Thayer, *Evidence*, 68.

[2] Feudal courts adopted a similar procedure in malicious appeals (although the King objected to their doing so without royal licence). Inquests were held shortly after the abolition of ordeal (1215) in the court of the Abbot of St. Edmund. See Bracton's *Note-book*, case 592.

[3] See Pollock and Maitland, II. 586.   [4] 59 George III. c. 46.

[5] The early history of *habeas corpus* is traced by Prof. Jenks, *Law Quarterly Review*, VIII. 164. The writ *de odio* was obsolete prior to the invention of the *habeas corpus*.

a plight, might purchase royal writs that would save them
from languishing for months or years in gaol.   The writ
best suited for this purpose was that *de odio et atia,* since
it was already applicable to presumably innocent appellees
for another purpose.[1]

As trial by combat became rapidly obsolete, the original
purpose of the writ was forgotten, and its once subsidiary
object became more prominent.   Before Bracton's day,
this change had taken place : the writ had come to be
viewed primarily as an expedient for releasing upon bail
homicides *per infortunium* or *se defendendo.*   Bracton, in
giving the form of the writ,[2] declares it to be iniquitous
that innocent men should be long detained in prison :
therefore, he tells us, an inquisition is wont to be made, at
the request of sorrowful friends, whether the accusation is
bona fide or has been brought *de odio et atia.*   This pleasing
picture of a king moved to pity by tearful friends of accused
men scarcely applies to John, who listened only to suitors
with long purses : the writs that liberated homicides had
become a valuable source of revenue.   Sheriffs were repri-
manded for releasing prisoners on bail without the King's
warrant, but, in spite of heavy amercements, they continued
their irregularities.   Thus, in 1207, Peter of Scudimore
paid to the exchequer 10 marks for setting homicides free
upon pledges, without warrant from the King.[3]   In that
year, John repeated his orders, strictly forbidding man-
slayers to be set free upon bail until they had received
judgment in presence of the King's justices.[4]

To John, then, the fees to be received for this writ, constituted its greatest merit; whereas the barons claimed, as
mere matter of justice, that it should be issued free of charge
to all who needed it.   John's acceptance of their demands
was repeated in all reissues, and apparently observed in
practice.   The procedure during the reign of Henry III. is
described by Bracton in a passage already cited.   After the
writ *de odio* had been received, an inquest, he tells us, must

[1] Cf. Brunner, *Schwurgerichte,* 471.   [2] See folio 123.
[3] See *Pipe Roll,* 8 John, cited Madox, I. 566.
[4] See *Rot. Pat.,* I. 76 ; Madox, I. 494.   The date is 8th Nov., 1207.

be held speedily, and if the jury decided that the accusation
had been made maliciously, or that the slaying had been in
self-defence or by accident, the Crown was to be informed
of this. Thereafter, from the chancery would be issued a
second writ (known in later days as the writ *tradias in bal-
lium*), directing the sheriff, on the accused finding twelve
good sureties of the county, to " deliver him in bail to those
twelve " till the arrival of the justices.

It should be noted that the provision granting gratuitous
writs was not construed as forbidding payments made by an
accused man for a special form of " trial." Prof. Maitland
has shown how " occasionally a person pays money to the
King that he may have an inquest, and it would seem that
he might still buy the right to be tried by a body constituted
in some particular way. He might pay to be tried by the
jurors of two hundreds, or of three hundreds, and because of
local enmities such a payment may sometimes have been
expedient."[1] A certain Reginald, Adam's son, in 1222,
offered one mark for a verdict of the three neighbouring
counties (it was a Lincolnshire plea), as to whether the
accusation was made because of " the ill-will and hate "
which William de Ros, appellant's lord, bore to Reginald's
father " *vel per verum appellum.*"[2]

A long series of later statutes enforced or modified this
procedure. These have been interpreted to imply frequent
changes of policy, sometimes abolishing and sometimes re-
introducing the writ and the procedure which followed it.[3]
This is a mistake; the various statutes wrought no radical
change, but merely modified points of detail; sometimes
seeking to prevent the release of the guilty on bail, and
sometimes removing difficulties from the path of the inno-

---

[1] *Gloucester Pleas*, xli., where cases are cited.

[2] See Bracton's *Note-book*, case 134, and cf. case 1548.

[3] Stephen, *Hist. Crim. Law*, I. 241 (following Foster, *Crim. Cases*, 284-5),
considers that it was abolished by 6 Edward I., stat. 1, c. 9. Coke, *Second
Institute*, 42, thought it was abolished by 28 Edward III. c. 9 (which, however,
seems not to refer to this at all), and restored by 42 Edward III. c. 1 (abolishing
all statutes contrary to Magna Carta). Coke, *ibid.*, and Hale, *Pleas of the Crown*,
II. 148, considered that the writ was not obsolete in their day. Cf. Pollock and
Maitland, II. 587 n.

cent. The Statute of Westminster, I., for example, after a preamble, which animadverted on sheriffs impanelling juries favourable to the accused, provided that inquests " shall be taken by lawful men chosen by oath (of whom two at least shall be knights) which by no affinity with the prisoners nor otherwise are to be suspected." [1] The Statute of Gloucester, on the other hand, ordered the strict confinement, pending trial, of offenders whose guilt was apparent.[2] The Statute of Westminster, II., once more favoured prisoners, providing by chapter 12 for the punishment of false appellants or accusers, and by chapter 29 that " lest the parties appealed or indicted be kept long in prison, they shall have a writ of *odio et atia*, like as it is declared in Magna Carta and other Statutes." [3] The writ in question was in use in 1314,[4] and seems never to have been expressly abolished, but to have sunk gradually into neglect, as appeals became obsolete and gaol deliveries were more frequently held.

IV. *Later History of Appeal and Battle.* The right of private accusation was restricted, not abolished, by Henry II. and his successors. It could not be denied to an injured man who was not suspected of abusing his right. Prosecutions by way of indictment and jury trial supplemented, without superseding, private prosecutions by way of appeal and battle. The danger of a second prosecution might hang over the head of an accused man after he had " stood his trial " and been honourably acquitted. It was unfair that he should be kept in such prolonged suspense; and, accordingly, the Statute of Gloucester provided that the right of appeal should lapse unless exercised within year and day of the commission of the offence.[5] To obviate all

---

[1] Edward I. c. 11. [2] 6 Edward I., stat. 1, c. 9.

[3] 13 Edward I. cc. 12 and 29. [4] See *Rot. Parl.*, I. 323.

[5] 6 Edward I. c. 9. Appeals were extremely frequent towards the close of the Plantagenet period, especially in the days of " the Lords Appellant." The proceedings on appeal sometimes took place before the Court of the Constable and Marshal and sometimes before Parliament. In neither case were they popular. One of the charges brought against Richard II. was that " in violation of Magna Carta " (that is, probably, of chapter 39) persons maliciously accused of treasonable words were tried before constable and marshal, and although " old and weak,

risk of a double prosecution, it was necessary that the Crown should delay to prosecute until the year and day had expired. This rule was followed in 1482. Such immunity from arraignment for twelve months would have produced a worse evil, by facilitating the escape of criminals from justice. After experience of its pernicious effects, the rule was condemned by the act of parliament which instituted the Star Chamber.[1]

This remedied the more recent evil, but revived the old injustice : the same statute enacted that acquittal should not bar appeal by the wife or nearest heir of a murdered man. Thus, once again, a man declared innocent by a jury might find himself exposed to a second prosecution. In 1817 the British public was startled to find that a long-forgotten procedure of the dark ages still formed part of the law of England. The body of a Warwickshire girl, Mary Ashford, was discovered in a pit of water under circumstances that suggested foul play. Suspicion fell on Abraham Thornton. After indictment and trial at Warwick Assizes on a charge of rape and murder, he was acquitted. The girl's brother, William Ashford, not satisfied by what was apparently an honest verdict, tried to secure a second trial, and claimed the appeal of felony, which the judges did not refuse. Ashford's attempt to revive this obsolete procedure was met by Thornton's revival of its equally obsolete counterpart. Summoned before the judges of King's Bench, he offered to defend himself by combat, throwing down as "wager of battle" a glove of approved antique pattern. Lord Ellenborough had to admit his legal right to defend himself against the appeal " by his body," and Thornton successfully foiled the attempt to force him to a second trial, as Ashford, a mere stripling, declined the

maimed or infirm," yet compelled to fight against appellants "young, strong, and hearty." See *Rot. Parl.*, III. 420, cited Neilson, *Trial by Combat*, 193. On the other hand, Statute 1 Henry IV. c. 14, provided that no appeals should be held before Parliament, but certain appeals might come before constable and marshal. Cf. Harcourt, *Steward*, 369.

[1] See 3 Henry VII. c. 1, s. 11 : the injured party, with the right of appeal, was "oftentimes slow and also agreed with, and by the end of the year all is forgotten which is another occasion of murder."

unequal contest with an antagonist of athletic build.[1] The unexpected revival of these legal curiosities led to their final suppression. In 1819 a Statute abolished proof by battle alike in criminal and in civil pleas : the right of appeal fell with it.[2]

CHAPTER THIRTY-SEVEN.

Si aliquis teneat de nobis per feodifirmam, vel per sokagium, vel per burgagium, et de alio terram teneat per servicium militare, nos non habebimus custodiam heredis nec terre sue que est de feodo alterius, occasione illius feodifirme, vel sokagii, vel burgagii ; nec habebimus custodiam illius feodifirme, vel sokagii, vel burgagii, nisi ipsa feodifirma debeat servicium militare. Nos non habebimus custodiam heredis vel terre alicujus, quam tenet de alio per servicium militare, occasione alicujus parve serjanterie quam tenet de nobis per servicium reddendi nobis cultellos, vel sagittas, vel hujusmodi.

If anyone holds of us by fee-farm, by socage, or by burgage, and holds also land of another lord by knight's service, we will not (by reason of that fee-farm, socage, or burgage,) have the wardship of the heir, or of such land of his as is of the fief of that other ; nor shall we have wardship of that fee-farm, socage, or burgage, unless such fee-farm owes knight's service. We will not by reason of any small[3] serjeanty which anyone may hold of us by the service of rendering to us knives, arrows, or the like, have wardship of his heir or of the land which he holds of another lord by knight's service.

In these provisions the Charter reverts to the subject of wardship, laying down three rules, which will be better understood when their sequence is altered, the second being taken first. (1) *Ordinary wardship*. The reason for claiming wardship from lands held in chivalry, namely, that a

---

[1] See Ashford *v*. Thornton, 1 *B. and Ald.*, 405-461.

[2] See 59 George III. c. 46.

[3] Pollock and Maitland, I. 304, read "*parva*" as an untechnical word. Round, *Serjeanties*, 35-6, finds in this chapter the origin of the distinction between "grand" and "petty" serjeanties, and compares the distinction made in c. 14 between greater and lesser barons.

boy could not perform military service, did not apply to fee-farm, socage, or burgage. There was much looseness of usage, however; and of this John took advantage. The Charter stated the law explicitly; wardship was not due from any such holdings, except in the anomalous case where lands in fee-farm expressly owed military service.[1] As petty serjeanties (although mentioned in the present chapter in a different connection) are not expressly said to share this exemption, it may be inferred that the barons admitted John's wardship over them, as over great serjeanties. By Littleton's time, the law had changed: petty serjeanties were then exempt.[2]

(2) *Prerogative wardship.* When the heir of a tenant-in-chivalry held military fiefs of different mesne lords, each of these lords enjoyed wardship over his own fief. This was fair to all parties: but, if the ward held one estate of the Crown, and another of a mesne lord, the King claimed wardship over both; and that, too, even when the Crown fief was of small value.[3] Such rights were known as " prerogative wardship," and, thus limited, were in 1215 perfectly legal, however inequitable they may now seem. (a) *Fee-farm, socage, and burgage.* John, however, pushed this right further, and exercised prerogative wardship over fiefs of mesne lords, not merely by occasion of Crown fiefs held in chivalry, but also by occasion of Crown fiefs held by any tenure. It was outrageous to claim prerogative wardship in respect of fee-farm, socage, or burgage lands, which were exempt even from ordinary wardship. John was made to promise amendment.[4] (b) *Small Serjeanties*[5] were in a different position. Magna Carta did not abolish the Crown's rights of ordinary wardship over these, but forbade

---

[1] Cf. *supra*, pp. 55-7 and 61-2.   [2] II. viii. s. 158.

[3] Cf. Glanvill, VII. c. 10. "When any one holds of the King *in capite* the wardship over him belongs exclusively to the King, whether the heir has any other lords or not; because the King can have no equal, much less a superior." Yet the King is not to have such wardship "because of burgage."

[4] Cf. *Petition of Barons* (1258), c. 2; *Prov. of West.* (1259), c. 12. Glanvill, VII. c. 10, had laid it down that burgage tenure could not give rise to prerogative wardship.

[5] See *supra*, p. 56.

that this should form an excuse for prerogative wardship over the wider fiefs of other lords.[1]

Prerogative wardship (even in the limited form admitted by Magna Carta) might involve a double hardship on the mesne lord. Suppose that the common tenant held lands from a mesne lord on condition of say, five knights' service, as well as his Crown fief. The King seized both fiefs on his death, nominally as a compensation for the loss of military service, which the minor heir could not render. Yet, when a scutage ran, the King demanded from the mesne lord payments in proportion to his full *quota* without allowing for the fees of five knights taken from him by prerogative wardship. This is no imaginary case: the barons in 1258 complained of the practice and demanded redress.[2]

CHAPTER THIRTY-EIGHT.

NULLUS ballivus ponat de cetero aliquem ad legem simplici loquela sua, sine testibus fidelibus ad hoc inductis.

[1] See Bracton, folio 87b. The *Note-book*, case 743, contains a good illustration. The motive for these restrictions was to prevent injustice to mesne lords. It was probably, however, an indirect consequence of Magna Carta that a similar rule came to be applied where no mesne lord was injuriously affected. In 1231 a certain Ralf of Bradeley died, who had held two separate freeholds of the Crown, (i) a small fee by petty serjeanty of twenty arrows a year, and (ii) land of considerable value held in socage. The Crown took possession of both estates, on the assumption that wardship over the petty serjeanty brought with it a right of wardship over the socage lands also (although these would have been exempt if they had stood alone). The King sold his rights for 300 marks. Ralf's widow claimed the wardship of the socage lands, on the ground that these were of much greater value than those held by serjeanty. Her argument was upheld, and the 300 marks refunded to the disappointed purchaser. See *Pipe Roll*, 5 Henry III., cited Madox, I. 325-6.

[2] See Petition of the Barons, Article 2 (*Select Charters*, 383). C. 53 of Magna Carta reverts to prerogative wardship, granting redress, although not summary redress, where John, or his father or brother, had illegally extended it by occasion of socage, etc. See also *supra*, p. 368. Round, *Eng. Hist. Rev.*, XXVIII. 156, cites from *Cal. Inq. post mortem*, III. 406-7, an interesting case of prerogative wardship decided against the Crown in 1301. Orpen, *Ireland*, II. 234, cites two Charters in which John renounces prerogative wardship. C. 43 *infra* (amended by c. 38 of 1217) guards against another abuse of prerogative wardship.

No bailiff for the future shall, upon his own unsupported complaint, put anyone to his "law," without credible witnesses brought for this purpose.

The exact nature of the abuse here condemned has been much discussed by commentators. Bailiffs (the word is probably used here in its widest sense [1]) were wont to abuse their authority: henceforth they shall put no man to his "*lex*" on their own initiative. The word *lex*, in its technical sense, applied to any form of judicial test, such as compurgation, ordeal, or combat, the precise meaning required in each particular case being determined by the context.[2] In the present chapter it seems to have this technical meaning of a judicial "proof" or "trial" of any sort:[3] henceforward no bailiff should have power "*simplici loquela sua*"[4] to put anyone to a "*lex*" of any kind. Authorities differ as to the exact nature of the irregularities which this clause was meant to suppress.

I. *Medieval Interpretations.* Ignorance of the exact

---

[1] Cf. *supra*, c. 24. It possibly includes sheriffs and their officers. The same men, apparently, were described as King's serjeants and sheriff's serjeants; one Roll records fines for a man buried "*sine visu servientum vicecomitis*," and for a robber hanged "*sine visu servientis regis*" (*Pipe Roll*, 31 Henry II). The word may also include the stewards who presided in manorial courts. If so, the unqualified "*ballivus*" of this passage should, perhaps, be contrasted with the "*noster ballivus*" of cc. 28 and 30. Coke, *Second Institute*, 44, following the doubtful *Mirror of Justices*, extends it to all King's justices and ministers.

[2] Dr. Stubbs (*Const. Hist.*, I. 576) translates "*lex*" in this passage by "compurgation or ordeal." Pollock and Maitland (II. 604 n.) explain that the word "does not necessarily point to unilateral ordeal; it may well stand for trial by battle." Thayer (*Evidence*, 199-200) extends it to embrace judicially appointed tests of every kind—battle, ordeal of fire or water, simple oath, oath with compurgators, charter, transaction witnesses, or sworn verdict. Bigelow (*Placita Anglo-Normanica*, 44) cites from *Domesday Book* cases where litigants offered proof *omni lege* or *omnibus legibus*, that is, in any way the court decided. Sometimes *lex* had a more restricted meaning; in the Customs of Newcastle-on-Tyne (*Select Charters*, 112) it seems to mean compurgation as opposed to combat. For its various meanings see also Harcourt, *Steward*, 232.

[3] In c. 55 "*lex*" would seem to bear a meaning more akin to the broader conception of "law" in modern jurisprudence; while in c. 39 its denotation is subject of controversy.

[4] Cf. the phrases "*per simplex verbum suum*" (Fordwick) and "*per vocem suam simplicem*" (Hereford) in Bateson, *Borough Customs*, I. 181. Cf. *ibid.*, II. xxxii.

nature of the abuse prohibited may well be excused at the present day, since it had become obscure within a century of the granting of the Charter. Some legal notes of the early fourteenth century, containing three alternative suggestions, have come down to us.[1]

(1) The first interpretation discussed, and apparently dismissed, in these notes, was that Magna Carta by this prohibition wished to ensure that no one should serve on a jury (*in juratam*) unless he had been warned by a timely summons. This far-fetched suggestion is clearly erroneous.

(2) The next hypothesis raised is that the clause prevented the defendant on a writ of debt (or any similar writ) from winning his case by his unsupported oath, where compurgators ought to have sworn along with him. Exception was, in this view, taken to the bailiff treating favoured *defendants* in civil pleas with unfair leniency.

(3) A third opinion is stated and eulogized as a better one, namely, that the Charter prohibited bailiffs from showing undue favour to *plaintiffs* in civil pleas. The defendant on a writ of debt (or the like) should not, in this interpretation of Magna Carta, be compelled to go to proof at all (that is, to make his " law ") unless the plaintiff had brought " suit " against him (that is, had raised a presumption that the claim was good, by production of preliminary witnesses or by some recognized equivalent).[2]

II. *Modern Interpretations.* If the chapter is read in a broad sense as prohibiting abuses of a generic kind, it is possible that more than one of its modern exponents may be substantially correct, in spite of apparent contradictions. (1) One theory would read the clause as forbidding magistrates to show undue favour to defendants of certain classes. Crown officials, under John, it is pointed out, favoured Jews against Christians with whom they went to law. The

---

[1] These appear as an Appendix to the Year Book of 32-3 Edward I. (p. 516); but the handwriting is supposed to be of the reign of Edward II.

[2] Cf. *supra*, p. 83. The necessity for such "suit" was not legally abolished until 1852 (by Statute 15 and 16 Victoria, c. 76, s. 55). In 1343 it had been decided that the "suit" must be in existence, but need not be produced in court; and that if they did appear they could not be examined. See Thayer, *Evidence*, 13-15.

Hebrew defendant in a civil suit "might purge himself by his bare oath on the Pentateuch, whereas in a similar case a Christian, as the law then stood, might be required to wage his law twelve-handed—*i.e.* with eleven compurgators."[1] Magna Carta, it has been suggested, struck at this preferential treatment of Jewish litigants, trebly hated as aliens, capitalists, and rejectors of Christ. If so, the attempt failed; for in 1275 a certain Hebrew, named Abraham, was allowed " to make his law single-handed on his Book of the Jewish Law " in face of the plaintiff's protest that this was contrary to the custom of the realm.[2]

- (2) On the other hand, the clause is sometimes made to prohibit undue favour shown to demandants in civil suits to the prejudice of defendants. A " suit " of witnesses (*secta-tores*) had to be produced in court by the plaintiff before any " trial " (*lex*) could take place at all. Bailiffs were forbidden to allow, through slackness, favour, or bribery, this rule to be relaxed. This interpretation, which was adopted by the author of the *Mirror of Justices*, and by the writer of the notes appended to the Year Book already cited, found favour with Chief Justice Holt in 1700.[3]

(3) A closely allied explanation treats the clause not as forbidding undue favour towards one party to an action, but rather as preventing bailiffs from favouring themselves. When it suited them, the King's officials were wont to dispense with the wholesome rule that demanded " suit " or its equivalent before a plea could be entertained. This practice was by no means confined to England, and has been discussed by Dr. Brunner.[4]

---

[1] See Rigg's *Sel. Pleas Jewish Exch.*, xii., and cf. *supra*, c. 10.

[2] Rigg, *ibid.*, 89, where the case is cited.

[3] See City of London *v.* Wood (12 *Modern Reports*, 669). Holt held the clause of Magna Carta to mean that the plaintiff, unless he had witnesses, could not put a defendant to his oath. Pollock and Maitland, II. 604, seem to concur, to the extent at least of counting this as one of the abuses condemned by c. 38 : " The rule which required a suit of witnesses had been regarded as a valuable rule ; in 1215 the barons demanded that no exception to it should be allowed in favour of royal officers."

[4] See his *Schwurgerichte*, 199-200. Cf. *ibid.*, 178 and 409-74. For a similar practice in Galloway, see G. Neilson on "Surdit de Sergaunt," *Scot. Antiq.*, XI.

(4) It is perhaps only another aspect of the same explanation to regard the clause as directed mainly against unfair treatment of accused men in criminal prosecutions. No one ought to be put to his " *lex,*" in the sense of " ordeal," on mere grounds of vague suspicion or on the unsupported statement of a royal bailiff. After 1166, at least, the voice of an accusing jury of neighbours was a necessary preliminary, under normal circumstances, before any one could be put to the ordeal in England. Magna Carta confirmed this salutary rule : no bailiff should put any one to the ordeal except after formal indictment, due evidence of which was presented at the diet of proof.[1]

III. *Nature of the grievance.* As already suggested, it seems not unlikely that two or more of these theories may require to be combined in order to furnish a complete explanation of the clause under discussion. Magna Carta may well have condemned alike the practice of compelling a man to defend a civil action unsupported by suit, and of sending him to the dreaded ordeal without indictment by his neighbours.

To the criminal aspect of the matter, the Assize of Clarendon (1166) seems to supply the key. Article 4 of that ordinance prescribes the procedure for trying robbers, thieves, and murderers : " the sheriff shall bring them before the justices; and with them they shall bring two law-worthy men of the hundred and of the village where they were apprehended, to bear the record of the county and of the hundred, as to why they had been apprehended; and, there, before the justices they shall make their law." This " law " is elsewhere in the ordinance clearly

155. The *Leges Quatuor Burgorum* would seem to guard against an evil of an opposite kind when (c. 76) they *forbid* the provost or bedells of a town (*prepositus vel precones*) to "bring witnesses to a claim against anyone," but direct that the defendant shall acquit himself *per legem.* This peculiar law would seem to be entirely unknown to previous commentators on this difficult passage of Magna Carta.

[1] This reading is supported by Pollock and Maitland, I. 130 n. There is no necessary inconsistency between the view here cited, and that already cited from *ibid.*, II. 604. The same clause of Magna Carta may have been aimed at irregularities of two kinds, in civil and criminal pleas respectively.

identified with ordeal;[1] and the purport of the whole was that accused men could not be put to ordeal except in presence of two lawful men who had been present at the indictment and had come before the justices specially to bear witness thereof. In other words, the sheriff's own report of the indictment "*sine testibus fidelibus ad hoc inductis*" was not sufficient. The "county" and the "hundred" which had heard the prisoner accused, must send representatives to bear record of the facts.[2]

The ordeal was a solemn affair, and every precaution must be taken against its abuse. Sheriffs or other royal bailiffs must be present, as well as members of the accusing jury. Lords of feudal courts, claiming this franchise, required apparently royal warrant for its exercise.[3] Practice, however, was loose : the King's justices would seem to have had a right to put suspects to the ordeal *ex officio* without the intervention of the accusing jury :[4] sheriffs and others, with the Crown's approval or connivance, exercised a similar privilege. In condemning these practices, Magna Carta would appear to have been, to some extent, modifying previous usage.[5] It was not enough thereafter that indictment should precede ordeal; members of the presenting jury, who had made the accusation at the first diet, must accompany the sheriff before the justices at the final diet, there to bear testimony both as to the nature of the crime and as to the fact of the indictment. Before anyone could

---

[1] See Article 12 where "*eat ad aquam*" is contrasted with "*non habeat legem*" of Article 13 (*Select Charters*, 144).

[2] The "*ad portandum recordationem comitatus et hundredi*" of the ordinance is exactly opposed to the "*simplex loquela sua*" of the Charter.

[3] Thus in 1166 (the year of the Assize of Clarendon) the "*Soca*" of Alverton was amerced because of a man placed "*ad aquam sine serviente*" (*Pipe Roll*, 12 Henry II., p. 49). In 1185 the "*villata*" of Preston paid 5 marks for putting a man "*ad aquam sine waranto*" (*Pipe Roll*, 31 Henry II., cited Madox, I. 547). In the same year a certain Roger owed half a mark for being present at an ordeal "*sine visu servientum regis*" : and heavy fines were exacted from those who had put a man "*injuste ad aquam*" (*ibid.*).

[4] See Miss Bateson, *Eng. Hist. Rev.*, XVII. 712.

[5] Miss Bateson (*Borough Customs*, II. xxxi.) speaks of the "right of accusation '*ex officio*' which belonged to the King's officers until Magna Carta, Art. 38, deprived them of it."

be put " to his law," the sheriff's formal report must be corroborated by the testimony of representative jurors.

The Charter of 1216 repeated this provision without alteration. In 1217 a change occurred, which was undoubtedly a consequence of the virtual abolition of the ordeal by the Lateran Council in 1215. The framers of Henry's second reissue found leisure to adjust points of administrative detail. The simple reference to ordeal was inappropriate now that new forms of trial were taking its place. The justices, indeed, scarcely knew what test to substitute for ordeal. They seem sometimes to have resorted to compurgation and sometimes to battle; but the sworn verdict of neighbours was fast occupying the ground left vacant. The Charter of 1217, then, made it clear that the provisions applied in 1215 to ordeal were to be extended to other tests. The " ad legem " of John's Charter became in the new version " ad legem manifestam nec ad juramentum." A " manifest law " might well mean either ordeal or any other actual physical test such as " battle," [1] while " juramentum " points to the sworn testimony of the jury, which was slowly taking the place of the discredited ordeal.[2]

CHAPTER THIRTY-NINE.

NULLUS liber homo capiatur vel imprisonetur, aut disseisiatur, aut utlagetur, aut exuletur, aut aliquo modo destruatur, nec super eum ibimus, nec super eum mittemus, nisi per legale judicium parium suorum vel per legem terre.

> No freeman shall be taken or [and] imprisoned or disseised or exiled or in any way destroyed, nor will we go upon him nor send upon him, except by the lawful judgment of his peers or [and] by the law of the land.[3]

[1] See Thayer, *Evidence*, 37 n., for a case of 1291, where "*ad legem manifestam*" can only mean trial by combat. Cf. *legem apparentem purgandus est* in Glanvill, XIV. ff. 112-114.

[2] Westminster I. (c. 12) described men refusing to put themselves on a jury's verdict, "*come ceaus qui refusent la commune ley de la terre.*"

[3] The usual English rendering has here been followed : Mr. Harcourt (*Steward*, 219) was possibly right in holding that " interpretation under the guise of translation

This chapter occupies a prominent place in law-books, and is of considerable importance, although its value has sometimes been exaggerated.[1]

I. *Its Main Object.* It has been usual to read it as a guarantee of trial by jury to all Englishmen; as absolutely prohibiting arbitrary commitment; and as solemnly undertaking to dispense to all and sundry an equal justice, full, free, and speedy.[2] The traditional interpretation has thus made it, in the widest terms, a promise of law and liberty and good government to every one.[3] A careful analysis of the clause, read in connection with its historical genesis, suggests the need for modification of this view. It was in accord with the practical genius of the Charter that it should here direct its energies, not to the enunciation of vague platitudes, but to the reform of a specific abuse. Its object was to prohibit John from resorting to what is sometimes whimsically known in Scotland as " Jeddart justice."[4] It

is in this case an inevitable snare." This does not, however, absolve the commentator from explaining the text. The Articles of the Barons (29) add "*vi*" ("*nec rex eat vel mittat super eum vi*" suggesting the fuller contemporary "*per vim et arma*"). This shows the inadequacy of the translation contained in the *Statutes at Large*, "nor will we pass upon him nor condemn him." The *Statutes of the Realm*, I. 117, suggest "deal with him" as an alternative. Coke, as explained *infra*, originated the error which thus connected "going" and "sending" with legal process.

[1] For a valuable discussion of alternative interpretations, see Adams, *Origin*, 256-274; also Pike, *House of Lords*, c. X. Mr. Harcourt's learned discussions (*Steward*, cc. VII. and VIII.) are worthy of careful study, though they are more useful in suggesting difficulties than in finding solutions.

[2] See, *e.g.* Coke, *Second Institute*, 55.

[3] Thus Blackstone, *Commentaries*, IV. 424 : " It protected every individual of the nation in the free enjoyment of his life, his liberty, and his property, unless declared to be forfeited by the judgment of his peers or the law of the land." Hallam, *Middle Ages*, II. 448, speaking of cc. 39 and 40 together, says they "protect the personal liberty and property of all freemen by giving security from arbitrary imprisonment and arbitrary spoliation." Creasy, *Eng. Const.*, p. 151 n. : "The ultimate effect of this chapter was to give and to guarantee full protection for person and property to every human being that breathes English air."

[4] The same grim tradition applied to Lidford as to Jedburgh :

> " I oft have heard of Lydford law,'
> How in the morn they hang and draw,
> And sit in judgment after."

See Neilson, *Trial by Combat*, 131, and authorities there cited.

forbade him for the future to place execution before judgment. Three aspects of this prohibition may be emphasized.

(1) *Judgment must precede execution.* In some cases John proceeded, or threatened to proceed, by force of arms against recalcitrants as though assured of their guilt, without waiting for legal procedure.[1] Complaint was made of arrests and imprisonments suffered " without judgment" (*absque judicio*); and these are the very words of the " unknown charter "—" *Concedit Rex Johannes quod non capiet homines absque judicio.*"[2] The Articles of the Barons and Magna Carta expand this phrase. *Absque judicio* becomes *nisi per legale judicium parium suorum vel per legem terrae*, thus guarding, not merely against execution without judgment, but also against John's subtler device for attacking his enemies by a travesty of judicial process. The Charter asks not only for a " judgment," but for a " judgment of peers " and " according to the law of the land." Two species of irregularities were condemned by these words; and these will be explained in the two following subsections.

(2) *Per judicium parium* : every judgment must be delivered by the accused man's " equals."[3] The need for " a judgment of peers" was recognized at an early date in England.[4] It was not originally a class privilege of the aristocracy, but a right shared by all grades of free-holders;

---

[1] Mr. Bigelow considers that such cases were numerous. See *Procedure*, 155: "The practice of granting writs of execution without trial in the courts appears to have been common."

[2] See Appendix.

[3] Mr. Harcourt (*Steward*, 218 ff.) has much to say on this phrase : for him a man's "peers" need not be his equals in rank (p. 220); while "judgment" is a vague word embracing widely opposed procedures : *e.g.* (p. 248), "In common parlance of the time a resolution of the King in Council to make war on a subject was a *judicium.*" He further instances, as examples of legal processes accepted in 1215 as equivalent to "judgment," the procedure for Crown debts under c. 9 ; outlawry under c. 42 ; the petty assizes under c. 19 ; and the special procedure in cc. 52, 56 and 59 (see *ibid.*, 220-3). Mr. Harcourt's conclusions are not clearly formulated, and some of them appear to be not well founded.

[4] The earliest known reference occurs in the *Leges Henrici* (c. 31) : *Unusquisque per pares suos judicandus est et ejusdem provinciae.*

whatever their rank, they could not be tried by their inferiors.[1] In this respect English custom did not differ from the procedure prescribed by feudal usage on the Continent of Europe.[2] Two applications of this general principle had, however, special interest for the framers of Magna Carta : the " peers " of a Crown tenant were his fellow Crown tenants, who would normally deliver judgment in the *Curia Regis*; while the " peers " of the tenant of a mesne lord were the other suitors of the Court Baron of the manor. In either case, judgments were given *per pares curiae*. John, resorting wholesale to practices used sparingly in earlier reigns, had set these rules at defiance. His political and personal enemies were exiled, or deprived of their estates, by the judgment of a tribunal composed entirely of Crown nominees. Magna Carta promised a return to the ancient practice.

The varied meanings conveyed by the word " peers " to a medieval mind, together with the nature of *judicium parium,* may be further illustrated by the special rules applicable to four exceptional classes of individuals :—(*a*) Jews of England and Normandy enjoyed under John's Charter of 10th April, 1201, the right to be judged by men of their own race; for them a *judicium parium* was a judgment of Jews.[3] (*b*) A foreign merchant, by later statutes, obtained the right to a jury of the " half tongue " (*de medietate linguae*), composed partly of aliens of his own country.[4] (*c*) The peers of a Welshman seem, in some disputes with the Crown, to have been men drawn from the marches : such at least is the plausible interpretation of the phrase " *in*

---

[1] Cf. Pollock and Maitland, I. 152. As there was no "peerage" in England (cf. *supra*, p. 186) until long after John's reign, it is obvious that the *judicium parium* of Magna Carta must be interpreted in a broader sense than any mere "privilege of a peer" at the present day. Freeholders holding of the same mesne lord were "peers of a tenure."

[2] See Stubbs, *Const. Hist.*, I. 578 n., for foreign examples of *judicium parium*.

[3] "If a Christian bring a complaint against a Jew, let it be adjudged by his peers of the Jews." See *Rot. Chartarum*, p. 93, and *supra*, p. 227 n. Harcourt, however (*ibid.*, 228), translates *pares Judei* as "justices or *custodes* of the Jews."

[4] See *Carta Mercatoria*, c. 8 ; 27 Edward III. stat. 2, c. 8 ; and 28 Edward III. c. 13; also Thayer, *Evidence*, p. 94.

marchia per judicium parium suorum," occurring in later chapters of Magna Carta, and granting to the Welsh redress of wrongful disseisins.[1] (*d*) A Lord Marcher occupied a peculiar position, enjoying rights denied to barons whose estates lay in more settled parts of England. In 1281 the Earl of Gloucester, accused by Edward I. of a breach of allegiance, claimed to be judged, not by the whole body of Crown tenants, but by such as were, like himself, lords marchers.[2] These illustrations show that a " trial by peers " had a wider and less stereotyped meaning in the Middle Ages than it has at the present day.[3]

(3) *Per legem terrae.* No freeman could be punished except " in accordance with the law of the land." The precise meaning of these often-quoted words ought, perhaps, still to be regarded as an open question. Two meanings are possible : one, narrow and technical; the other, of a loose and popular bearing. The more technical has already been explained.[4] Thus interpreted, the words of John's Charter promised a threefold security to all the freemen of England. Their persons and property were protected from the King's arbitrary will by the rule that execution should be preceded by a judgment—by a judgment of peers—by a judgment according to the appropriate time-honoured " test," battle, compurgation, or ordeal.[5]

[1] See *infra*, cc. 56, 57, and 58. Under c. 59 the barons of England were called peers of the King of Scots.

[2] See *Placitorum Abbrevatio*, p. 201, cited Pollock and Maitland, I. 393 n.

[3] See also a passage in the Scots Acts of Parliament (I. 318) attributed to David : "No man shall be judged by his inferior who is not his peer ; the earl shall be judged by the earl, the baron by the baron, the vavassor by the vavassor, the burgess by the burgess ; but an inferior may be judged by a superior."

[4] See *supra*, p. 84, and cc. 18, 36, and 38.

[5] See Thayer, *Evidence*, 200-1, for a discussion of the phrase " *lex terrae.*" See also Bigelow, *History of Procedure*, 155 n. : " The expression '*per legem terrae*' simply required judicial proceedings, according to the nature of the case ; the duel, ordeal, or compurgation, in criminal cases ; the duel, witnesses, charters, or recognition in property cases." The words occur at least twice in Glanvill, each time apparently with the technical meaning. In II. c. 19, the penalty for a false verdict includes forfeiture by jurors of their law (" *legem terrae amittentes*") ; while in V. c. 5, a man born a villein, though freed by his lord, cannot, to the prejudice of any stranger, wage his law (" *ad aliquam legem terrae faciendam*"). The stress placed on the accused's right to the time-honoured forms of *lex* is well

Much weight, however, must be allowed to the arguments of those who contend for interpreting " *lex terrae* " more in accordance with the vague and somewhat meaningless " law of the land " of popular speech at the present day. The phrase, they argue, was not confined to methods of procedure, but referred to the entire tone and substance of the law.[1] Advocates of both theories can point to other parts of Magna Carta where " *lex* " is used in the sense they claim for it in the present passage; for its purport was, in 1215, ambiguous. In chapters 18, 36, and 38, it refers primarily to procedure, whereas chapters 9, 45, 52, 56, and 59 suggest a broader interpretation.

Magna Carta is undoubtedly a loosely drawn document, and it is always possible that both meanings were in the minds of the framers. If so, the older, more technical signification was gradually forgotten, and " the law of the land " became the vague and somewhat meaningless phrase of the popular speech of to-day. It was only natural that this change of emphasis should be reflected in subsequent statutes reaffirming, expanding, or explaining Magna Carta. An important series of these, passed in the reigns of Edward III. and Richard II., shows how the *per legem terrae* of 1215 was read in the fourteenth century as equivalent to " by due process of law," and how the Great Charter was interpreted as prohibiting the trial of men for their lives and limbs before the King's Council on mere informal and irresponsible suggestions, sometimes made loosely or from malicious and interested motives.[2]

illustrated by the difficulty of substituting jury trial for ordeal. It has already been shown that the right of "standing mute," that is, virtually, of demanding ordeal, was only abolished in 1772. See *supra*, p. 342. Five and a half centuries were thus allowed to pass before the criminal law was bold enough, in defiance of a fundamental principle of Magna Carta, to deprive accused men of their "law."

[1] Mr. Harcourt (*Steward*, 220 ff.) has vehemently, and Prof. Adams (*Origin*, 266 ff.) judicially and moderately, maintained this view. Mr. Adams is influenced by his failure to discover any instance of "*per legem terrae*" in the technical sense, but "*per legem Angliae*" occurs in *Sel. Civil Pleas* (Selden Society), No. 104, where the reference is to ordeal of water.

[2] It would seem, however, from the words of these statutes that for this purpose the provisions of chapters 36 and 38 were used to supplement those of the present chapter, if they were not confused with them. See 5 Edward III. c. 9; 25

The Act of 1352, for example, after reciting this provision of Magna Carta, insisted on the " indictment or presentment of good and lawful people of the same neighbourhood where such deeds be done."   Coke,[1] founding apparently on these fourteenth-century statutes, makes *" per legem terrae "* equivalent to " by due process of law " and that again to " by indictment or presentment of good and lawful men," thus finding the grand jury enshrined in Magna Carta. The framers of the Petition of Right[2] read the same words as a prohibition, not only of imprisonment " without any cause showed " but also of proceedings under martial law, thus interpreting the aims of King John's opponents in the light of the misdeeds of King Charles.

Anachronisms such as these must be avoided.   Whatever may have been the exact grievances that bulked most largely in the barons' minds in 1215, their main contention was obvious.   John was no longer to take the law into his own hands : the deliberate judgment of a competent court of law must precede any punitive measures to be taken by the King against freemen of his realm.

(4) *The meaning of " vel."*   The peculiar use of the word *" vel "* introduced an unfortunate element of ambiguity. No proceedings were to take place " without lawful judgment of peers *or* by the law of the land "—" or " thus occurring where " and " might naturally be expected. Authorities on medieval Latin are agreed, however, that *" vel "* is sometimes equivalent to *et.*[3]   Comparison with the

---

Edward III. stat. 5, c. 4; 37 Edward III. c. 18; 38 Edward III. c. 3; 42 Edward III. c. 3; 17 Richard II. c. 6. See also Stubbs, *Const. Hist.*, II. 637-9, for the series of petitions beginning with 1351.

[1] *Second Institute*, p. 46.   [2] 3 Charles I. c. 1.

[3] Pollock and Maitland, I. 152 n., read the word as having *both* meanings in this passage. Cf. Gneist, *Engl. Const.*, chapter xviii. Mr. Pike, *House of Lords*, 170, takes a different view : " King John bound himself in such a manner as to show that judgment of peers was one thing, the law of the land another. The judgment of peers was . . . a very simple matter and well understood at the time. The law of the land included all legal proceedings, civil or criminal, other than the judgment of peers." The present writer rejects this antithesis, because the two things may be, and indeed must be, combined. The " trial " by a law and the " judgment " by equals were complementary of each other. The peers

terms of chapter 52 and with those of the corresponding Article of the Barons places the matter almost beyond doubt. The 25th of the Articles of the Barons had provided that all men disseised by Henry or Richard should " have right without delay by judgment of their peers in the king's court," giving no hint of any possible alternative to *judicium parium*. Chapter 52 of the Charter, in supplementing the present chapter, describes the evils complained of in both chapters as acts of disseisin or outlawry by the King " *sine legale judicio parium suorum*," leaving no room for ambiguity.

II. *The Scope of the Protection afforded*. The object of the barons was to protect themselves and their friends against the King, not to set forth a scientific system of jurisprudence : the *judicium parium* was interposed as a barrier against measures instituted by the King, not against appeals of private individuals. Pleas following upon accusations by the injured party were held in 1471 not to fall within the words of Magna Carta.[1] This was a serious limitation ; but as against the Crown the scope of the protection afforded by the Great Charter was very wide indeed. Care was taken that the three-fold safeguard should cover every form of abuse likely to be practised by John.[2]

(1) *Capiatur vel imprisonetur*. These words are followed in the text by a string of other verbs, each of which is introduced by " *aut* " (" *aut disseisiatur*," etc.). The contrast between " *vel* " and " *aut* " strengthens the suggestion that " *vel* " is used in this chapter conjunctively. The meaning would then be that no one could be arrested and imprisoned (that is, no one could be detained as a prisoner) without trial. If " *vel*," on the other hand, were to be read disjunctively while the two words it connects were literally

appointed the test and decided whether it had been properly fulfilled. See also, on opposite sides, Harcourt, *Steward*, 219 ff., and Adams, *Origin*, 262.

[1] See, *e.g.* Pike, *House of Lords*, 217, citing Littleton in *Year Book*, Easter, 10 Edward IV., No. 17, fo. 6.

[2] This chapter applied only to abuses of criminal process : cf. c. 21 for amercements and civil process.

interpreted and enforced, orderly government would be at an end.[1] Arrest normally precedes judgment, although judgment must precede permanent imprisonment following on arrest.

(2) *Aut disseisiatur.* Avarice was a frequent motive of John's oppressions : the machinery of justice was an engine for transferring land and money to his treasury. Crown-tenants frequently found their estates appropriated by the Crown as escheats. That this was a grievance to which the barons attached supreme importance is shown in many ways : by the care taken in the 25th Article of the Barons and in chapter 52 of the Charter to provide procedure for restoring " disseised "[2] estates, and by the terms of writs issued by John after the treaty at Runnymede, for the immediate restoration of " lands, castles, and franchises from which we have caused any one to be disseised *injuste et sine judicio.*"[3]

Later versions of Magna Carta (beginning with that of 1217) are careful to define the objects to be protected from disseisin : " free tenements, franchises, and free customs."[4] (a) *Liberum tenementum.* " Free " tenements were free-holds as opposed to the *villenagium* that passed into the modern copyhold. None of the possessions thus protected were more highly valued by the barons than their feudal strongholds.[5] Castles claimed by great lords as their own property are mentioned in many writs of the period, while chapter 52 of Magna Carta gives them a prominent place

---

[1] The wording of the 29th Article of the Barons, if not merely due to careless draftsmanship, seems, however, against this conjunctive interpretation. Cf. Adams, *Origin,* 262.

[2] For this word cf. *supra,* c. 18.

[3] See *Rot. Claus.,* I. 215. Mr. Pike (*House of Lords,* p. 170) maintains, indeed, that the prevention of disseisins "*sine judicio*" was the chief, if not the sole, object of the chapter under discussion : "The judgment of peers had reference chiefly to the right of landholders to their lands, or to some matters connected with feudal tenure and its incidents." This goes too far : the barons by no means confined the safeguard afforded by the *judicium parium* to questions of land. Pollock and Maitland, I. 393, countenance a broader interpretation.

[4] *De libero tenemento suo vel libertatibus vel liberis consuetudinibus suis.*

[5] Cf. *supra,* p. 151.

among the "disseisins" to be restored. (*b*) "*Libertates*"
covered feudal jurisdictions, immunities, and privileges of
various sorts, of too intangible a nature to be appropriately
described as "holdings." (*c*) *Consuetudines* had two
meanings, a broad general one and a narrower financial
one.[1] As the Charter of 1217 uses a proprietary pronoun
(no freeman shall be disseised of *his* free customs), it probably refers to such rights as those of levying tolls and
tallages. These vested interests were of the nature of
monopolies; and Coke, in treating this passage as a text
on which to preach the doctrine that monopolies have always
been illegal in England, aims wide of his mark. Commenting on the words "*de libertatibus,*" he declares that
generally all monopolies are against this Great Charter,
because they are against the liberty and freedom of the
subject and against the law of the land." [2]   In this error he
has been assiduously followed.[3]

(3) *Aut utlagetur, aut exuletur, aut aliquo modo
destruatur.* The declaration of outlawry, which could only
be made in the county court, was a necessary preliminary
to the forfeiture of the outlaw's lands and goods. The
expedient recommended itself peculiarly to John's genius;
it was his policy to terrify those with whom he had quarrelled, until they fled the country; to summon them three
times before the county court, knowing that they dared not
face his corrupt and servile officers; and finally to have
them formally outlawed and their property seized. Such
had been the fate of Robert Fitz Walter and Eustace de
Vesci, in the autumn of 1212.[4] The outlawed man was
outside the pale of society; anyone might slay him at
pleasure; in the grim phrase of the day, he bore "a wolf's
head" (*caput lupinum*), and might be hunted like a noxious
beast. A reward of two marks was offered for each outlaw's head brought to Westminster. This sum was paid

---

[1] Cf. *supra*, p. 246.   [2] *Second Institute*, p. 47.

[3] See, *e.g.* Creasy, *Hist. of Const.*, p. 151 n.: "Monopolies in general are
against the enactments of the Great Charter." See also Taswell-Langmead, *Eng.
Const. Hist.*, 108.

[4] See *supra*, p. 25.

in 1196 for the head of William of Elleford.[1] The word
" exiled " explains itself; and commentators have very properly noted the care taken to widen the scope of the clause by
the use of the words " or in any other way destroyed." [2]

(4) " *Nec super eum ibimus, nec super eum mittemus.*"
These words have been frequently misinterpreted. Read in
the light of historical incidents of the immediately preceding
years, they leave no room for ambiguity. Their object was
to prevent John from substituting violence for legal process : he must never again attack *per vim et arma* men
unjudged and uncondemned.

The meaning is plain. Yet Coke, following his vicious
method of assuming the existence, in Magna Carta, of a
warrant for every legal principle of his own day, misled
generations of commentators. He maintained that John
promised to refrain from raising, in his own courts, actions
in which he was personally interested. In elaborating this
error, he drew a distinction between the court of King's
Bench, otherwise known as *coram rege,* because the King
was in theory present, and other courts to which he had
" sent " a writ delegating authority. *Ibimus,* he seems to
think, applied in the former case; *mittemus* in the latter.
To quote his words, " No man shall be condemned at the
King's suit, either before the King in his bench, where the
pleas are *coram rege* (and so are the words, *nec super eum
ibimus,* to be understood) nor before any other commis-
sioner, or judge whatsoever (and so are the words, *nec super
eum mittemus,* to be understood), but by the judgment of
his peers, that is, equals, or according to the law of the
land." [3] Coke is in error; it was the use of brute force,

[1] See *Pipe Rolls,* 7 Richard I., cited by Madox, I. 201.

[2] *E.g.* Coke, *Sec. Inst.,* 48. For the early history of outlawry and exile, see
Liebermann, *Friedlosigkeit* (Brunner-Festschrift), and *Gesetze,* II. 413 ; A. Réville,
Abjuratio regni, Revue Hist., vol. 50 (1892). Harcourt (*Steward,* 221) charac-
terises "*destruatur*" as a "colloquial expression" covering even amercements,
if of excessive amounts.

[3] See *Second Institute,* p. 46. John Reeves, *History of English Law,* I. 249
(third ed.), while condemning Coke, gives an even more strained interpretation of
his own. Lingard, *History of England,* III. c. 1, deserves praise as the first
commentator who took the correct view.

not merely one particular form of legal process, which John
in these words renounced.

III. *What Classes enjoyed the Protection of Judicium
Parium?* No " freeman " was to be molested in any of the
ways specified; but how far in the social scale did this
description descend? Coke claims villeins as free for
purposes of this chapter and of chapter 1, while rejecting
them for the purposes of chapter 20.[1] Their right to the
status of freeman has already been disallowed, and any
possible ambiguity as to the present chapter is removed by
the words of the revised version of 1217. Chapter 35 of
that reissue, with the object of making its meaning clearer,
inserts after " *disseisiatur* " the words (already discussed)
" *de libero tenemento suo vel libertatibus vel liberis consuetudinibus suis.*" Mr. Prothero suggests that this addition implies an advance on the privileges secured in 1215 :
—" It is worth while to notice that the words in which
these liberties are stated in § 35 of the Charter of 1217 are
considerably fuller and clearer than the corresponding
declaration in the Charter of 1215." [2] It is safer to infer that
no change was here intended, but merely the removal of
ambiguity. If there is a change, it is rather a contraction
than an extension, making it clear that only " free " tenements are protected, and excluding the property of villeins
and even *villenagium* belonging to freemen.[3] It was made
plain beyond reasonable doubt that no villein should have
lot or part in rights hailed by generations of commentators
as the national heritage of all Englishmen.[4]

IV. *Reactionary Side of these Provisions.* To insist
that in all cases a judgment of feudal peers, either in King's
Court or in Court Baron, should take the place of a judgment by the King's professional judges, was to reverse one
of the outstanding features of the policy of Henry II. In

---

[1] *Second Institute*, pp. 4, 27, and 45.

[2] *Simon de Montfort*, 17 n. Cf. Blackstone, *Great Charter*, xxxvii., "the more
ample provision against unlawful disseisins."

[3] Cf. Pollock and Maitland, I. 340 n.

[4] Cf. *supra*, p. 118. Other verbal changes in the charter of 1217 show the same
care to exclude the villeins. *E.g.* c. 16 leaves the King's demesne villeins strictly
" in his mercy," that is, liable to amercement without any reservation.

this respect, the present chapter may be read in connection with chapter 34. The barons, indeed, were not strict logicians, and probably thought it prudent to claim more than they intended to enforce. Yet, a danger lurked in these provisions; the clause was a reactionary one, tending to restore feudal privileges and feudal usage, inimical alike to the Crown and to the growth of popular liberties.[1] John promised that feudal justice should be dispensed in his feudal court; and, if this promise had been kept, the result would have been to check the development of the small committees destined to become at no distant date the Courts of King's Bench and Common Pleas, and to revive the fast-waning jurisdictions of the manorial courts on the one hand and of the *commune concilium* on the other.[2]

V. *Genesis of this Chapter.* The interpretation here given is emphasized by comparison with certain earlier documents and events. The reigns of Richard and John furnish abundant examples of the abuses complained of. In 1191, Prince John, as leader of the opposition against his brother's Chancellor, William Longchamp, concluded a treaty that protected himself and his allies from the very evils which John subsequently committed against his own barons. Longchamp conceded in Richard's name that bishops and abbots, earls, barons, " vavassors " and free-tenants, should not be disseised of lands and chattels at the will of the King's justices or ministers, but only by judgment of the King's court according to the lawful customs and assizes, or by the King's command.[3]

---

[1] Mr. G. H. Blakesley, *Law Quarterly Review*, V. 125, perhaps goes too far : " It may reasonably be suspected that cap. 39 also was directed merely to maintain the lord's court against Crown encroachments."

[2] Mr. Pike, *House of Lords*, 170-4, shares this view of the reactionary nature of the clause, although he considers that the claim to *judicium parium* by a Crown tenant might be satisfied by the presence of one or more barons among the judges of the " Benches," and did not necessarily involve a full *commune concilium*. *Ibid.*, p. 204. If the " judgment " of the full court was requisite (and, in spite of the high authority of Mr. Pike, there is much to be said for that contention), then the reactionary feudal tendency is even more prominent.

[3] See R. Hoveden, III. 136.

Now, the main subject of the arbitration, ending in this treaty, was the custody of certain castles and estates. After the right to occupy each separate castle in dispute had been carefully determined, provision was then made, in the general words cited above, against this arrangement being disturbed without a judgment of the *curia regis*. Disseisin, and particularly disseisin of castles, was thus in 1191, as in 1215, a topic of special prominence.

Early in 1213, the King had attempted to take vengeance upon his opponents in a manner they are not likely to have forgotten, two years later at Runnymede. John, resenting the attitude of the northern barons who had refused alike to accompany him to Poitou and to pay scutage, determined to take the law into his own hands. Without summoning his opponents before a *commune concilium*, without even a trial and sentence by one of his Benches, he set out with an army to punish them. He had gone as far north as Northampton when, on 28th August, 1213, Stephen Langton persuaded him to defer forcible proceedings *until he had obtained a legal sentence* in a formal *Curia*.[1] That John again threatened recourse to violent methods may be inferred from the letter patent issued in May, 1215, when both sides were armed for war. He proposed arbitration, and promised a truce until the arbitrators had given their award. The words of this promise are notable; since, not only do they illustrate the procedure of August, 1213, but they agree closely with the clause of Magna Carta under discussion. The words are :—" Know that we have conceded to our *barons* who are against us, that we shall not take or disseise them or their men, nor shall we go against them *per vim vel per arma*, unless by the law of our kingdom, or by the judgment of their peers *in curia nostra*." [2] Magna Carta repeats this concession in more general terms, substituting "freemen" for the "barons" of the writ—an alteration which necessitated the omission from the Charter of the concluding words of the writ, " *in curia nostra* "; because the peers of ordinary

[1] Cf. *supra*, p. 29.

[2] The writ is dated 10th May, 1215, and appears in *New Rymer*, I. 128.

freemen would be found among the freeholders in the Court Baron.[1]

VI. *Later History of " Judgment of Peers."* The claim made by the barons at Runnymede was re-asserted on subsequent occasions. The phrase " judicium parium " which, probably in consequence of its use in Magna Carta, sprang into " sudden and extraordinary prominence "[2] was destined to have a long and distinguished career. Mr. Harcourt[3] thinks that " it was the obscurity of the chapter when reissued, the fact that it might mean so many things, which supplied the congenial soil wherein the principle of trial of peers was able to expand and grow to maturity," when " the Charter as a whole became the Bible of the constitution."

(1) *The baronial contention.* The earls and barons, throughout the reign of John's unhappy son, attempted to place a broad interpretation on the privilege secured to them by this chapter—claiming that all pleas, civil and criminal (such at least as were raised against them at the instance of the Crown) should be tried by their fellow earls and barons, and not by professional judges of lower rank. William de Braose in 1208 had declared himself ready to satisfy John " *secundum judicium curiae suae et baronum parium meorum.*"[4]

(2) *The royal contention.* The Crown, on the other hand, while not openly infringing the Charter, tried to narrow its scope. Judges appointed to determine pleas *coram rege,* no matter what their original status might be, became (so the Crown argued) by such appointment, the peers of any baron or earl. This doctrine was enunciated in 1233 when Peter des Roches denounced Richard, Earl Marshal, as a traitor, in a meeting (*colloquium*) of crown-tenants held at Gloucester on 14th August of that year. Thereafter, " *absque judicio curiae suae et parium suorum,*" as Matthew Paris carefully relates,[5] Henry treated Earl Richard and his friends as outlaws, and bestowed their

---

[1] Magna Carta also omits "*per vim et arma.*"

[2] Cf. Harcourt, *ibid.*, 235. [3] *Ibid.*, 236.

[4] M. Paris, II. 524. [5] *Ibid.*, III. 247-8.

lands on his own Poitevin favourites. An attempt was made, at a subsequent meeting held on 9th October, to have these proceedings reversed on the ground, already stated, that they had taken place *absque judicio parium suorum*.

The sequel makes clear a point left vague in Matthew's narrative : there had been a judgment previous to the seizure, but only a judgment of Crown officials *coram rege*, not of earls and barons in *commune concilium*. The justiciar defended the action of the government by a striking argument : " there were no peers in England, such as were in the kingdom of France," and, therefore, John might employ his justices to condemn all ranks of traitors.[1] Bishop Peter was here seeking to evade the provisions of Magna Carta without openly defying them, and his line of argument was that the King's professional judges, how-ever lowly born, were the peers of an English earl or baron.[2] Neither the royal view nor the baronial view entirely pre-vailed. A distinction, however, must be drawn between criminal and civil pleas.

(3) *Criminal pleas.* Offenders of the rank of barons partially made good their claim to a trial by equals; while ordinary freemen failed. A further distinction is thus necessary. (*a*) *Crown tenants.* The conflicting views held by King and baronage here resulted in a compromise. In criminal pleas, the Crown was obliged to recede from the high ground taken by Peter des Roches in 1233. Un-willingly, and with an attempt to disguise the fact of surrender by confusing the issue, Bracton in theory and Henry III. in practice admitted part of the barons' demand, namely, " that in cases of alleged treason and felony, when

---

[1] M. Paris, *Chron. Mag.*, III. 251-2.

[2] Pollock and Maitland, I. 393, hesitate to condemn this argument. " The very title of the ' barons ' of the Exchequer forbids us to treat this as mere insolence." Dr. Stubbs has no such scruples : " The Bishop replied contemptuously, and with a perverse misrepresentation of the English law " (*Const. Hist.*, II. 49). Else-where he makes him, not so much contemptuous, as ill-informed of the law— "ignorant blunder as it was" (II. 191). Yet Bishop Peter had presumably an intimate knowledge of the law he administered as justiciar in 1233. In the matter of amercements, at least, barons of exchequer acted as peers of earls and barons.

forfeiture or escheat was involved, they should be judged only by earls and barons.[1] Bracton does not admit that the King's justices were not " peers " of barons; but deduces their disability from the narrower consideration that the King, through his officials, ought not to be judge in his own behalf, since his interests in escheats might bias his judgment. This explains why " privilege of peers " has never extended to misdemeanours, since these involved no forfeiture to the Crown.

The *judicium parium* was secured to earls and barons in later reigns by bringing the case before the entire body of earls and barons in *commune concilium*. What the barons got at first was " judgment " by peers. The actual " trial " was the " battle," the fellow-peers acting as umpires and enforcing fair play.[2] Although new modes of procedure came to prevail, the Court of Peers continued its control, and the *judgment* of peers gradually passed into the modern *trial* by peers.[3] The subject has been further complicated by the growth of the modern conception of a " peerage," embracing various grades of " nobles." In essentials, however, the rights of a baron accused of crime have remained unchanged from the days of Henry III. to our own. The privilege of " trial by peers " still extends to treason and felony, and is still excluded from misdemeanours. When competent, it still takes place before a " Court of Peers "—namely, the House of Lords, if Parliament is in session, and the Court of the Lord High Steward, if not. Under these limitations the privilege of a peer has been for centuries a reality in England for earls and barons, and also for members of those other ranks of the modern " peerage " unknown in 1215—dukes, marquesses, and viscounts.[4]

---

[1] Pike, *House of Lords*, 173. See also Bracton, f. 119 ; Pollock and Maitland, I. 393.

[2] "The trial, therefore—the ascertaining of the fact—was, though under the direction and control of the Court of Peers, by battle ; but the judgment on the trial by battle was to be given by the peers." Pike, *House of Lords*, 174.

[3] Pike, *ibid.*, 174-9.

[4] The privilege was extended to peeresses by 20 Henry VI. c. 9.

(*b*) For *tenants of a mesne lord* no similar privilege has been established, even in a restricted form. In charges of felony, as in those of misdemeanour, all freemen outside the peerage are tried, and have been tried for many centuries past, in the ordinary courts of law. There is no privileged treatment for knight or landed gentleman : private feudal courts never recovered from the wounds inflicted by Henry II. The clauses of Magna Carta which sought to revive them were rendered nugatory by legal fictions or simply by neglect.

(4) *Civil pleas.* Various attempts were made by the barons to make good a claim to *judicium parium* in civil cases.[1] The chief anxiety, perhaps, of the men of 1215 was to save their estates and castles from disseisin consequent on such pleas. Yet the barons' efforts in this direction were unsuccessful. The House of Lords (except in cases involving the dignity or status of a peer) has never claimed to act as a court of first instance in civil cases to which a peer was a party. Noble and commoner here are on a level. No " peer of the realm " has, for many centuries, asked to plead before a special court of peers in any ordinary non-criminal litigation, whether affecting real or personal estate.

VII. *Erroneous Interpretations.* The tendency to vagueness and exaggeration has already been discussed. Two mistakes of unusual persistence require detailed notice.

(1) *The identification of* judicium parium *with trial by jury.* The words of the present chapter form the main, if not the sole, ground on which this traditional error has been based.[2] The mistake probably owes its origin to a tendency of later generations to explain what was unfamiliar in the Great Charter by what was familiar in their own experience. They found nothing in their own day to correspond with the *judicium parium* of 1215 ; and nothing in Magna Carta (unless it were this clause) to correspond

---

[1] The Earl of Chester claimed it in 1236-7, and the Earl of Gloucester (as a lord marcher) in 1281. See Pollock and Maitland, I. 393 n. See, however, Harcourt, *Steward*, 291.

[2] Cf. *supra*, pp. 134-5.

with trial by jury : therefore they identified the two.[1]   Mr.
Reeves, Dr. Gneist, and other writers long ago exposed
this error, but the most conclusive refutations are those
given by Prof. Maitland and Mr. Pike.   The arguments
of these writers are of a somewhat technical nature; [2] but
their importance is far-reaching.   They seem to be mainly
three :—

(a) The criminal petty jury cannot be intended in this
chapter, since it had not been invented in 1215 :[3] to introduce trial by jury into John's Great Charter is an unpardon-
able anachronism.   (b) The barons would have repudiated
trial by jury if they had known it.   They desired (here as
in chapter 21) that questions affecting them should be
" judged " before fellow barons, and in the normal case, by
the duellum.   They would have scorned to submit to the
verdict of " twelve good men " of their own locality.   Their
inferiors must have no voice in determining their guilt or
innocence.   This sentiment was shared by the tenants of
mesne lords.   (c) Judgment and verdict were essentially
different.   The function of a petty jury (after it had been
invented) was to answer a specific question.   The insurgent
barons demanded more than this :   they asked a decision
on the whole case.[4]   The " peers " who judged presided
over the proceedings from beginning to end, appointing
the proof they deemed appropriate, sitting as umpires while
its fulfilment was essayed, and giving a final decision as to
success or failure therein.

[1] The erroneous identification of judgment of peers with trial by jury can be
found far back in legal history.   Pollock and Maitland, II. 622-3 n., trace it to
within a century of Magna Carta.   "This mistake is being made already in
Edward I.'s day; Y. B. 30-1 Edward I., p. 531."   In spite of modern research
the error dies hard.   It appears, e.g., in Thomson, Magna Charta, 223 ; Taswell-
Langmead, Const. Hist., 110; Goldwin Smith, " The United Kingdom," I. 127.

[2] Pollock and Maitland, I. 152 n., and Pike, House of Lords, 169.

[3] Cf. supra, p. 134.

[4] Cf. Pike, ibid., 169.   "From the time when trial by jury first commenced,
either in civil or in criminal cases, to this present end of the nineteenth century,
no jury ever did or could give judgment on any matter whatsoever."   The difference between the ancient and modern conceptions of judgment, however, must
not be lost sight of.

(2) *Magna Carta and arbitrary commitment.* A second erroneous theory has still to be discussed. The Petition of Right, as already stated, treats Magna Carta as prohibiting the Crown from making arrests without a warrant showing the cause of detention; and the earlier commentators further interpreted it as making all acts of arbitrary imprisonment by the Crown absolutely illegal. Hallam, for example, declares that " It cannot be too frequently repeated that no power of arbitrary detention has ever been known to our constitution since the charter obtained at Runnymede." [1] Yet every King of England from John Lackland to Charles Stewart claimed and exercised the prerogative of summarily committing to gaol any man suspected of evil designs against Crown or Commonwealth. Even the famous protest of the judges of Queen Elizabeth, asserting the existence of legal limits to the royal prerogative of commitment, proves the lawfulness of the general practice to which it makes exceptions. Such rights inherent in the Crown were never seriously challenged until the struggle between Charles I. and his parliaments had fairly begun. Then only was it suggested that Magna Carta was intended to prohibit arbitrary commitments at the command of the Crown. Such was the argument deliberately put forth in 1627 during the proceedings known sometimes as Darnell's case and sometimes as the case of the Five Knights. Heath, the Attorney-General, easily repelled this contention : " the law hath ever allowed this latitude to the King, or his privy council, which are his representative body, in extraordinary cases to restrain the persons of such freemen as for reasons of state they find necessary for a time, without for this present expressing the causes thereof." [2] The parliamentary leaders, however, too grimly in earnest to be deterred by logic, were far from abandoning their error because Heath had exposed it. They embodied it, on the contrary, in the Petition of Right, which condemned the Crown's practice of imprisoning political offenders " without any cause showed " (other than *per speciale man-*

[1] *Const. Hist.*, I. 234.

[2] See *State Trials*, III. p. 1, and S. R. Gardiner, *History*, VI. 214.

datum regis), as contrary to the tenor of Magna Carta—
an effective contention as a political expedient, but unsound
in law.

CHAPTER FORTY.

NULLI vendemus, nulli negabimus, aut differemus, rectum
aut justiciam.

> To no one will we sell, to no one will we refuse or delay, right
> or justice.

This chapter, like the preceding, has had much read into
it that would have astonished its framers: application of
modern standards to ancient practice has resulted in complete misapprehension. The sums customarily received by
John, as by his predecessors, at every stage of legal procedure, were not always the wages of deliberate injustice.
Many such payments were not bribes to an unjust judge,
but merely expedients for hastening the law's delays, or to
ensure a fair hearing for a good plea, or to obtain some
unusual but not unfair expedient, such as a peculiarly potent
writ or the hearing of a case in the exchequer, which would
ordinarily have been tried elsewhere. If the royal courts
charged higher rates than the feudal courts, they supplied
a better article. When Henry of Anjou threw open the
doors of his court to all freemen who chose to pay for writs,
he found a ready market. These writs differed widely in
price. Some from an early date were issued whenever
applied for (writs *de cursu*) and at a fixed sum: others
were granted only as marks of favour or after a bargain
had been struck. Specially quick or cogent procedure had
to be specially paid for.

It would thus appear that the system of John was not
open to the unqualified and violent condemnatioi which it
usually receives. Hallam's language is too sweeping when
he says: " A law which enacts that justice shall neither
be sold, denied, nor delayed, stamps with infamy that
government under which it had become necessary." [1] In

[1] *Middle Ages*, II. 451.

the twentieth century, as in the thirteenth, justice cannot be had for nothing; and the would-be litigant with a good claim but a slender purse will be well advised to acquiesce in a small loss rather than incur certainty of losing as much again in extra-judicial outlays, and risk of losing many times more in the judicial expenses of a protracted litigation. The lack of " free justice " is a reproach which the men of to-day cannot with good grace fling at the administration of John.

As the evils complained of are often exaggerated, so also are the reforms promised by this chapter of Magna Carta. John is usually held to have agreed to the abolition of payments of every sort for judicial writs and other fees of court. Justice, unlike other valuable commodities, was, it would appear, to be obtained for nothing—an ideal never yet attained in any civilized community.

Those who framed this chapter desired to secure a more reasonable measure of reform : abuses of the system were to be redressed.[1] Unfortunately, it was not easy to define abuses—to determine where legitimate payments stopped and illegitimate ones began. Prohibitive prices ought not to be charged for writs *de cursu*; but was the Crown to have no right to issue writs of grace on its own terms ? Plaintiffs who had any special reason for haste frequently paid to have their suits heard quickly : was that an abuse ? [2]

Whatever the intention may have been, the practical effect of the clause was *not* to secure the abolition of the

---

[1] Cf. Madox, I. 455 : " By *nulli vendemus* were excluded the excessively high fines : by *nulli negabimus*, the stopping of suits or proceedings, and the denial of writs : by *nulli differemus*, such delays as were before wont to be occasioned by the counterfines of defendants (who sometimes would outbid the plaintiffs) or by the prince's will."

[2] Fines for this purpose were frequent under Henry II. and his sons. Madox, I. 447, cites many examples. Thus in 1166 Ralph Fitz Simon paid two marks "for speeding his right." The practice continued under Henry III. in spite of Magna Carta. Bracton's *Note-book* cites a hard case (No. 743) : Henry III. was claiming prerogative wardship where it was illegal under c. 37 of Magna Carta (*q.v.*). The court might have delayed hearing the mesne lord's plea until the wardship was ended ; but he paid five marks *pro festinando judicio suo*. The fine was said to be given " willingly " (*sponte*). Did the use of this word make possible an evasion of c. 40 of the Charter ?

sale of writs. The practice under Henry III. has been described by our highest authority :—"Apparently there were some writs which could be had for nothing; for others a mark or a half-mark would be charged, while, at least during Henry's early years, there were others which were only to be had at high prices. We may find creditors promising the King a quarter or a third of the debts that they hope to recover. Some distinction seems to have been taken between necessaries and luxuries. A royal writ was a necessary for one who was claiming freehold; it was a luxury for the creditor exacting a debt, for the local courts were open to him and he could proceed there without writ. Elaborate glosses overlaid the King's promise that he would sell justice to none, for a line between the price of justice and those mere court fees, which are demanded even in our own day, is not easily drawn. That the poor should have their writs for nothing, was an accepted maxim." [1]

Probably the practice before and after 1215 showed few material differences. Some of the more glaring abuses were checked: that was all.[2] Parliament in subsequent reigns had frequently to petition against the sale of justice in alleged breach of Magna Carta.[3] The King usually returned a politic answer, but never surrendered his right to exact large sums for writs of grace. Richard II., for example, replied : " Our lord the King does not intend to divest himself of so great an advantage, which has been continually in use in Chancery as well before as after the making of the said charter, in the time of all his noble progenitors who have been kings of England." [4]

It is evident that Magna Carta did not put down the practice of charging heavy fees for writs. Yet this chapter,

---

[1] Pollock and Maitland, I. 174. Cf. *ibid.*, II. 204, and authorities cited.

[2] Madox, I. 455, says : " And this clause in the great Charters seems to have had its effect. For . . . the fines which were paid for writs and process of law were more moderate after the making of those great Charters than they used to be before."

[3] Instances are collected by Sir T. D. Hardy in *Rot. de oblatis*, p. xxi. See also Stubbs, *Const. Hist.*, II. 636-7.

[4] *Rot. Parl.*, III. 116, cited Stubbs, *Const. Hist.*, II. 637.

although so frequently misunderstood and exaggerated, is still of considerable importance. It marks, for one thing, a stage in the process by which the King's courts outdistanced all rivals. In certain provinces, at least, royal justice was left in undisputed possession. In these the grievance was not that there was too much royal justice, but that it was sometimes delayed or denied. Here, then, even in the moment of John's bitter humiliation we find evidence of the triumph of the policy inaugurated by his father.

It is not to such considerations, however, that this chapter owes the prominence usually given to it in legal treatises; but rather to the fact that it has been interpreted as a universal guarantee of impartial justice to high and low; and because, when so interpreted, it has become in the hands of patriots in many ages a powerful weapon in the cause of constitutional freedom. Viewing it in this light, Coke throws aside his crabbed learning and concludes with what is rather a rhapsody than a lawyer's commentary : " as the gold-finer will not out of the dust, threads, or shreds of gold, let pass the least crumb, in respect of the excellency of the metal; so ought not the learned reader to pass any syllable of this law, in respect of the excellency of the matter." [1]

CHAPTER FORTY-ONE.

OMNES mercatores habeant salvum et securum exire de Anglia, et venire in Angliam, et morari et ire per Angliam, tam per terram quam per aquam, ad emendum et vendendum, sine omnibus malis toltis, per antiquas et rectas consuetudines, preterquam in tempore gwerre, et si sint de terra contra nos gwerrina; et si tales inveniantur in terra nostra in principio gwerre, attachientur sine dampno corporum et rerum, donec sciatur a nobis vel capitali justiciario nostro quomodo mercatores terre nostre tracten-

[1] Second Institute, 56.

tur, qui tunc invenientur in terra contra nos gwerrina; et
si nostri salvi sint ibi, alii salvi sint in terra nostra.

> All merchants shall have safe and secure exit from England,
> and entry to England, with the right to tarry there and to move
> about as well by land as by water, for buying and selling by the
> ancient and right customs, quit from all evil tolls, except (in
> time of war) such merchants as are of the land at war with us.
> And if such are found in our land at the beginning of the war,
> they shall be detained, without injury to their bodies or goods,
> until information be received by us, or by our chief justiciar,
> how the merchants of our land found in the land at war with us
> are treated; and if our men are safe there, the others shall be
> safe in our land.

Merchants and merchandise had suffered from John's
greed. The control of commerce was reserved for the
King's personal supervision : no binding rule of law or
traditional usage trammelled him in his dealings with
foreign merchants, who were dependent on royal favour,
not on the law of the land, for the privilege of trading and
even for personal safety. No alien could enter England
or leave it, nor take up his abode in any town, nor move
from place to place, nor buy and sell, without paying heavy
tolls to the King. This royal prerogative proved a profitable one.[1]

John increased the frequency and amount of such exactions, to the detriment alike of foreign traders and their
customers. Magna Carta, therefore, sought to restrain this
branch of prerogative, forbidding him to exact excessive
tolls for removing obstacles of his own creating. This
benefited merchants by securing to them certain privileges,
which may perhaps be analysed into three : safe-conduct,

[1] So far all authorities are agreed, though a difference of opinion exists as to the
source of these prerogatives. Thus (a) Stephen Dowell, *History of Taxation and
Taxes in England*, I. 75, considers that the duties on imports and exports were in
their origin of the nature of voluntary dues paid by foreign merchants in return for
freedom of trade and royal protection ; (b) Hubert Hall, *Customs Revenue of
England*, I. 58-62, justly reckons this prerogative as merely one aspect of purveyance, that is, of the King's right to take what he needed for himself and household.
Under an autocrat, however, facts count for more than theories. The prerogative
was measured by brute force : Kings took what they could with no jealous regard
for the exact letter of the law, and left future ages to invent theories to justify or
explain their conduct.

that is protection of their persons and goods from violence; liberty to buy and sell in time of peace; and a confirmation of the ancient stereotyped rates of " customs."

So far, the general purport of the enactment is undoubted; but discussions have arisen on several important points, such as the nationality of the traders in whose favour it was conceived; the exact nature of the " evil tolls" abolished; the motives for the rules enforced; and the relations between denizens and foreign traders.

I. *Magna Carta favours alien Merchants.* The better opinion would seem to be that this chapter applied to foreign traders from friendly states. Attempts have been made, indeed, to argue that denizens were to benefit equally with strangers : such was the purport of a learned discourse delivered in the House of Commons by William Hakewill, Barrister of Lincoln's Inn, in 1610, during the debate on John Bate's case.[1] His main argument was that certain statutes of Edward III.,[2] in seeking to confirm and expand the provisions of Magna Carta, did clearly embrace denizens as well as aliens. Yet the framers of an Act in the fourteenth century may well have misunderstood the tenor of John's Charter, or may have deliberately altered it.

Intrinsic and extrinsic evidences combine to create a strong presumption that here Magna Carta referred chiefly, perhaps exclusively, to merchants of foreign lands.[3] Denizens trading in England did not require those " safe conducts " which form the chief concession in this chapter. Their rights of buying and selling were already protected in another way; for independent traders were unknown, all merchants being banded into guilds in the various towns whose privileges (" *omnes libertates et liberas consuetudines* ") were guaranteed in a previous part of the Great Charter.[4] Alien merchants, however, required protection,

---

[1] See *State Trials*, II. 407-475, and especially 455-6.

[2] *E.g.* 2 Edward III. c. 9 and 14 Edward III., stat. 1, c. 21.

[3] Two-thirds of the chapter is occupied in explaining that merchant strangers of unfriendly States are not to benefit from it. Mr. Hakewill was aware of this, but sought to evade the natural inference by subtleties which are not convincing.

[4] See *supra*, under c. 13.

since they had, strictly speaking, no status in the eye of the law, and held their privileges from the King.[1] The policy of Henry II. and his sons was to favour merchant strangers, but to exact in return the highest dues possible, restrained only by an enlightened self-interest which stopped short at the point where trade would languish by becoming unprofitable. The exchequer and patent rolls afford illustrations of how individual traders or families made private bargains with the Crown for trading privileges. In 1181, Henry obtained two falcons for granting leave to export corn to Norway. In 1197, a certain Hugo Oisel owed 400 marks for licence to trade in England and Richard's other lands, in time of war as well as peace.[2]

At the commencement of John's reign, traders resident in England collectively obtained confirmation of their privileges. That King issued letters patent to the Mayor of London, to the magistrates of many smaller towns, and to the sheriffs of the southern counties of England, directing them, in terms closely resembling those of Magna Carta, to allow to all merchants, of whatsoever land, safe coming and going, with their wares.[3]

These arrangements were temporary. John did not intend that any general grant should prevent him from exacting further payments from individuals as occasion offered. For example, Nicolas the Dane promised a hawk each time he entered England, that he might come and go and trade " free of all customs which pertain to the King." [4] Such customary dues, at the usual rates, were not abolished by the Charter, but only the arbitrary additional payments for which there was no warrant.

On this point, then, Magna Carta contained no innovations, and the same is true of its provision for reprisals against traders from lands where English merchants were ill-treated. On the outbreak of war, the Charter directs

---

[1] For the legal position of aliens, see Pollock and Maitland, I. 441-450.

[2] See *Pipe Rolls*, 27 Henry II. and 8 Richard I., cited Madox, I. 467-8.

[3] See *Rot. Chart.*, 60 (5th April, 1200).

[4] See *Pipe Roll*, 6 John, cited Madox, I. 469, where other illustrations will be found. Cf. also *Rot. Pat.*, 170, 170b, 171, 172b.

that merchants of the enemy's nation should be detained until the King ascertained how his own subjects were treated in the enemy's territory. This is declaratory of previous practice, of which an illustration may be found in the terms of a writ of August, 1214, which directed the bailiffs of Southampton to detain all Flemings and their goods pending further instructions.[1] There were thus precedents for those rules for foreign traders, which have aroused the admiration of Montesquieu.[2]

II. *Customs and Tolls.* " *Consuetudines* " is in this passage used in its narrower, financial sense, relating to those duties on imports and exports still called " customs " at the present day, and to various local dues as well. " Tolls," when not stigmatized as " evil tolls " would seem to be practically synonymous with these customs. The Crown had at first taken whatever it thought fit. Practice soon established rules as to the normal rates considered fair in various circumstances. When a ship-load of foreign wine arrived, the normal toll was " one cask from a cargo of ten up to twenty casks, and two casks from a cargo of twenty or more." [3] From other merchandise a share was claimed of a fifteenth or sometimes a tenth of the whole. Such tolls, if originally a species of ransom, had in John's day come to be regarded as a legitimate branch of royal revenue. Any arbitrary increase, however, was condemned by public opinion, and ultimately by Magna Carta as a " *mala tolta.*"

The King was not the only one who exacted tolls. Every town in England, and many feudal magnates, by prescriptive usage or royal grant, levied payments on goods bought

---

[1] In the same writ John bade them allow to depart freely all vessels of the land of the Emperor or of the King of Scotland after taking security that they would sail straight to their own countries, with none but their own crews. See *Rot. Claus.*, I. 211, and cf. series of writs in I. 210.

[2] See *De l'Esprit des Lois*, II. 12 (ed. of 1750, Edinburgh), " *La grande chartre des Anglois défend de saisir et de confisquer en cas de guerre les marchandises des négociants étrangers, à moins que ce ne soit par représailles. Il est beau que la nation Angloise ait fait de cela un des articles de sa liberté !* "

[3] S. Dowell, *Hist. of Taxation*, I. 83, citing Madox, I. 525-9 (2nd ed. I. 765-770), and *Liber Albus*, I. 247-8.

or sold at fairs and markets, or that entered the city gates, or were unloaded at river wharves, or traversed certain roads. The ambition of every borough was to increase its own franchises at the expense of its neighbours. The free customs of Bristol, for example, meant not only that the men of that city should have freedom from tolls inflicted by others, but that they should have the right to inflict tolls upon those others. A whole network of such customs and restrictions impeded the free exchange of commodities in every part of England. Magna Carta had no intention of sweeping these away, so far as they were "just and ancient"; and it is probable that the prohibition against arbitrary increase of tolls was directed only against the Crown.

III. *The Motives prompting these Provisions.* It has been not unusual to credit the framers of Magna Carta with a policy of quite a modern flavour; they are made free-traders and credited with a knowledge of economic principles far in advance of their contemporaries. This is a misconception: Englishmen in the thirteenth century had formulated no far-reaching theories of the rights of the consumer, or the policy of the open door. The home traders were not consenting parties to this chapter, and would have bitterly resented any attempt to place foreigners on an equal footing with the protected guilds of the English boroughs. The barons acted on their own initiative and from purely selfish motives. Rich nobles, lay and ecclesiastic, desired that nothing should prevent the foreign merchants from importing wines and rich apparel that England could not produce. John, indeed, as a consumer of continental luxuries, partially shared their views, but his selfish policy threatened to strangle foreign trade by increasing the burdens attached to it, until it ceased to be remunerative. The barons, therefore, in their own interests, not in those of foreign merchants, still less in those of native traders, demanded that the customs duties should remain at their old fixed rates. In adopting this attitude, they showed their selfish indifference to the equally selfish claims of English traders, who desired a monopoly for themselves. Every favour shown to foreign merchants was an injury done to the guilds of the chartered boroughs. This chapter thus shows a lack of gratitude on the barons' part for the great service rendered by their allies, the citizens of London. John, on the other hand, would have little reluctance in punishing the men of his capital who, with the ink scarce dry on their new municipal charter, had not scrupled to desert his cause.[1] It must have been with grim pleasure that, on 21st July, 1215, in strict conformity with the tenor of Magna Carta, he addressed a writ to King Philip inviting reprisals upon London merchants in France in certain contingencies.[2]

In the reissue of 1216 the privileges conferred on merchant strangers were confined to such as had not been " publicly prohibited beforehand." This was a material alteration, the effect of which was to restore to the King full discretionary authority over foreign trade, since he had only to issue a general proclamation, and then to accept fines for granting exemption from its operation.

IV. *English Boroughs and Merchant Strangers*. The quarrel between home and alien traders underwent many vicissitudes during succeeding centuries, the Crown taking now one side, and now the other, as its pecuniary interests happened to dictate for the moment. No glimmerings of the doctrine of free trade can be traced : the merchants of each town, banded in their guilds, directed their endeavours towards securing rights of exclusive trading for themselves. It is true that the men of London were scarcely more jealous of the citizens of Rouen or Paris than of those of York or Lincoln ; their ambition was to inflict restrictions upon all rivals alike.

English traders were not yet merchant shippers and therefore did not prevent foreigners from undertaking the

---

[1] See *supra*, 34-35.

[2] See *New Rymer*, I. 135 : " Know that we have ordered the mayor and sheriffs of London to allow merchants of your land to remove their goods and chattels from London, without hindrance to doing thence their will; and that if they do not, you may, if it please you, grieve and molest the men of that town (*illius villae*) in your power, without our reckoning it a breach of truce on your part."

carrying trade between England and the Continent. Flanders bought English wool and sent back woven fabrics to rival which English looms could not aspire. Londoners, however, resold these goods at a profit and resented any attempt of aliens to encroach on their retail monopoly by coming into touch with English magnates or other consumers. Foreigners must be kept " at the wharf-head."

The *Liber Custumarum*, a compilation of the early thirteenth century, lays down minute rules for the regulation of foreign traders in London. The merchant stranger had to take up his abode in the house of a citizen. He was prohibited from purchasing articles in process of manufacture. He could buy only from those who had the freedom of the city, and could not re-sell within the borough walls. He was allowed to sell only to burgesses of London, except on three specified days of the week. Such were a few of the rules which the Londoners enforced on all traders within their gates. The King, however, intermittently encouraged foreigners. Under the fostering protection of Henry III., Lombards and Provençals settled in considerable numbers in the capital; and, with connivance of the King, infringed these rules. When the Londoners complained, Henry refused relief. Their loyalty thus shaken, they sided with the King's opponents in the Barons' War, and when the royalist cause triumphed at Evesham, the Capital shared in the punishment meted out to the Crown's opponents. Prince Edward in 1266 was nominated protector of foreign merchants. At the accession of that Prince, London bought itself back into favour, and an attempt was made to define what tolls might be taken by the Crown. In 1275, in Edward's first parliament, a tariff was fixed by "the prelates, magnates, and communities at the request of the merchants" on most of what then formed the staple exports of England : half a mark on every sack of wool, half a mark on every three hundred wool-fells (that is untanned skins with the fleeces on), and one mark on every load of leather.

These were subsequently called *magna et antiqua custuma*. The settlement of 1275 was by no means final.

New disputes arose; and in 1285 Edward I. confiscated the liberties of London, suppressed what he characterized as abuses, and favoured the aliens. In 1298 the franchises of the capital were restored, and very soon the abuses complained of began anew. Edward retorted in 1303 by a special ordinance known as the *Carta Mercatoria* in favour of their foreign rivals, by the terms of which the provisions of the present chapter of Magna Carta became at last a reality. This new charter, which was the result of a bargain struck between the Crown and the alien traders, conferred various privileges and exemptions in return for an increase of fifty per cent. of duty, known henceforth as *parva et nova custuma*. Edward I. made several attempts to exact the higher rates from denizens as well as strangers; but in this he failed. In 1309 a Petition of Parliament was presented against the exaction of the " new customs," declaring them to be in contravention of Magna Carta.

In 1311 a temporary community of economic and political interests resulted in an alliance between the English merchants and the English baronage, whose combined efforts forced the " Ordinances " upon Edward II., compelling him for a time to reverse his father's policy of favouring foreigners at the expense of native merchants. It is unnecessary to follow the checkered fortunes of these Ordinances, frequently enforced and as frequently abolished, according as the fortunes of the barons or of Edward II. were for the moment in the ascendant. During the reign of Edward III. the deep-rooted quarrel between home and alien merchants continued; and many changes of policy were adopted by the Crown. The statute of 1328, which abolished the " staples beyond the sea and on this side," provided " that all merchant strangers and privy may go and come with their merchandises into England, after the tenor of the Great Charter." [1] Seven years later, this was confirmed by an act which placed strangers and denizens on an exact equality in all branches of trade, both wholesale and retail, under the express declaration that no privileged rights of chartered boroughs should be allowed to interfere

[1] 2 Edward III. c. 9.

with its enforcement.[1] While this statute merely repeated and applied the general doctrine of the present chapter of Magna Carta, it directly infringed the provisions of chapter 13.[2] Such sweeping regulations were in advance of their age and could not be carried out without revolutionizing the medieval scheme of trade and commerce, which depended on merchant guilds, town charters and local monopolies. The influence of the English boroughs and their political allies was strong enough to make the strict enforcement of such legislation impossible; and later statutes, bowing to the inevitable, restored the privileges of the boroughs, while continuing to enunciate an empty general doctrine of free trade to foreigners.[3] The English boroughs, to which Parliament in the reign of Richard II. thus restored their franchises and monopolies, were able effectually to exclude foreign competition, in certain trades at least, from within their walls, for four centuries, until the Statute of 1835 ushered in the modern era of free trade.[4]

CHAPTER FORTY-TWO.

LICEAT unicuique de cetero exire de regno nostro, et redire, salvo et secure, per terram et per aquam, salva fide nostra, nisi tempore gwerre per aliquod breve tempus, propter communem utilitatem regni, exceptis imprisonatis et utlagatis secundum legem regni, et gente de terra contra nos gwerrina, et mercatoribus de quibus fiat sicut predictum est.

> It shall be lawful in future for any one (excepting always those imprisoned or outlawed in accordance with the law of the kingdom, and natives of any country at war with us, and

[1] See 9 Edward III. c. 1, and cf. 25 Edward III., stat. 4, c. 7.

[2] Cf. *supra*, pp. 247-8, where the inconsistency between the two parts of the Great Charter is pointed out. See also *supra*, p. 117.

[3] See 2 Richard II., stat. 1, c. 1, and 11 Richard II. c. 7.

[4] See 5 and 6 William IV. c. 76, s. 14.

merchants, who shall be treated as is above provided) to leave
our kingdom and to return, safe and secure by land and water,
except for a short period in time of war, on grounds of public
policy—reserving always the allegiance due to us.

The terms of this permission for free intercourse between
England and foreign lands are peculiarly wide, the exceptions being reasonable and necessary. Prisoners obviously
could not leave our shores, nor outlaws return to them :
the case of merchants from hostile states had already been
provided for in a liberal spirit; while the temporary restriction of intercourse with the enemy on the outbreak of
hostilities was eminently reasonable.

Although the provision is thus general in its scope, it
was peculiarly welcome to the clergy, as enabling them
without a royal permit to proceed to Rome, there to prosecute their appeals or press their claims for preferment.
Thus considered, it contains a virtual repeal of article 4
of the Constitutions of Clarendon of 1166, which forbade
archbishops, bishops, and parsons (*personæ*) of the kingdom to leave England without the King's licence.   The
grant of freedom of intercourse in 1215 opened a door
for the Church to encroach on the royal prerogative; and
for that reason it was omitted from the reissue of 1216,
never to be replaced. A boon was thus withdrawn from
all classes from fear that it might be abused by the ecclesiastics.   Henry III. took advantage of the omission in order
to restrain the movements of clergy and laity alike.   Those
who left the country without licence had frequently to pay
fines.[1]

The stringency with which the prerogative was at first
enforced tended afterwards to relax.   The King preserved
the right, but only exercised it by means of proclamations
over particular classes or on special occasions, the inference

---

[1] *E.g.* Coke (*Third Institute*, p. 179) cites from *Rot. finium* of 6 Henry III. and
Rot. Claus. of 7 Henry III. the following case : " *Willielmus Marmion clericus
projectus est ad regem Franciae sine licentia domini regis, et propterea finem fecit.*"
The practice had apparently been much the same prior to Magna Carta. *E.g.*
Madox (I. 3) cites from *Pipe Roll* of 29 Henry II. how " *Randulfus filius Walteri
reddit compotum de XX marcis, quia exivit de terra Domini Regis.*" See also
Makower, *Const. Hist. of Eng. Church,* 239-240 and notes.

being that all not actually prohibited were free to come and go as they pleased. Thus, in 1352 Edward III. had it proclaimed throughout every county of England that no earl, baron, knight, man of religion, archer, or labourer, should depart the realm under pain of arrest and imprisonment.[1] The fact that Edward found it necessary to issue such an ordinance, autocratic and abhorrent to modern ideals as its terms now appear, points to a decrease of royal power, as compared with that exercised by Henry II., John, or Henry III. A further curtailment of prerogative may be inferred from the terms of a Statute of Richard II.,[2] which, in confirming the King's power to prohibit free egress from England, does so, subject to wide exceptions. Under its provisions the Crown might prohibit the embarkation of all manner of people, as well clerks as others, under pain of forfeiture of all their goods, " except only the lords and other great men of the realm, and true and notable merchants, and the King's soldiers," who were apparently in 1381 free to leave without the King's licence, although earls and barons had been prohibited in 1352. Even if this statute confers on magnates, merchants, and soldiers, freedom to go abroad without royal licence (which is doubtful), the powers of veto reserved to the Crown were still, to modern ideas, excessive. The Act remained in force until 1606, when it was repealed under somewhat peculiar circumstances. After the union of the Crowns, King James, anxious to draw the bond closer, persuaded his first English parliament to abrogate a number of old laws inimical to Scottish interests. It was in this connection that the Act of Richard II. was declared (in words, however, not limited to Scotland) to be " from henceforth utterly repealed."[3] Coke stoutly maintains that this repeal left intact the Crown's ancient prerogative, not founded upon statute but on the common law, of which power the already-cited Proclamation of Edward III. had been merely an emanation. He seems almost, therefore, to argue that the King in the seventeenth century retained authority which

[1] See Coke, *ibid.*, citing the Close Roll of 25 Edward III.

[2] 5 Richard II., stat. I, c. 2.   [3] 4 James I. c. I, s. 22.

extended precisely over those classes mentioned in the
ordinance of 1352.

In any view, this prerogative has never been completely
abolished : yet the *onus* has been shifted. While, under
John or Henry III., the subject required, before embarking,
to obtain a licence from the Crown, under later Kings he
was free to leave until actually prohibited by a royal writ.
Coke [1] speaks of the form originally used for this purpose,
a form so ancient in his day as to be already obsolete, known
as *Breve de securitate invenienda quod se non divertet ad
partes externas sine licentia regis.* This was superseded by
the simpler writ *Ne exeat regno* which is still in use.[2] The
sphere of this writ was restricted and altered : it ceased to
be an engine of royal tyranny and was never issued except
as part of the process of a litigation pending in the Court of
Chancery. Regarded with suspicion by the courts of common law, it was for centuries the special instrument which
prevented parties to a suit in equity from withdrawing to
foreign lands. Some uncertainty exists as to the proper
province of these writs since the Judicature Acts have
merged the Court of Chancery in the High Court of
Justice.[3] The perfect freedom to leave the shores of England and return at pleasure, accorded by John's Magna
Carta, but immediately withdrawn as impracticable for that
age, has thus in the course of centuries been fully realized.[4]

Two phrases, occurring in this chapter, call for comment :
(1) *Salva fide nostra.* This short-lived clause of Magna
Carta very properly provided that mere absence from England should absolve no one from allegiance to his King.
The old doctrine of nationality was stringent : *nemo potest
exuere patriam.* Everyone born in the land owed allegiance to its King—and this tie continued unbroken until
severed by death. A breach of allegiance, which was

---

[1] *Third Institute*, p. 178.

[2] Its origin is obscure. See Beames, *Brief view of the writ of Ne Exeat*,
passim.

[3] See *Encyclopaedia of Laws of England*, IX. 79.

[4] On the whole subject of these writs, see Stephen, *Commentaries*, II. 439-40
(ed. of 1899), and authorities there cited.

consequent thus on the mere accident of birth, might expose the offender to the inhuman horrors inflicted upon traitors.

A series of statutes, culminating in the Naturalization Act of 1870, have entirely abrogated this ancient doctrine. A native of Great Britain is now free to become the subject of any foreign state; and the mere fact of his doing so, deliberately and with all necessary formalities, denudes him of his British nationality, severs the tie of allegiance, and frees him from the operation of the law of treason. The words " *salva fide nostra* " no longer apply.

(2) *Propter communem utilitatem regni.* The Charter, in placing restriction on the right of free egress in time of war, declared that such restriction was to be imposed for the common good of the kingdom, thereby enunciating what is regarded as a modern doctrine : John was to take action, not for his own selfish ends, but only *pro bono publico.*

CHAPTER FORTY-THREE.

Si quis tenuerit de aliqua eskaeta, sicut de honore Walling-fordie, Notingeham, Bolonie, Lancastrie vel de aliis eskaetis, que sunt in manu nostra, et sunt baronie, et obierit, heres ejus non det aliud relevium, nec faciat nobis aliud servicium quam faceret baroni si baronia illa esset in manu baronis; et nos eodem modo eam tenebimus quo baro eam tenuit.

> If anyone holding of some escheat (such as the honour of Wallingford, Nottingham, Boulogne, Lancaster, or of other escheats which are in our hands and are baronies) shall die, his heir shall give no other relief, and perform no other service to us than he would have done to the baron, if that barony had been in the baron's hand ; and we shall hold it in the same manner in which the baron held it.

This chapter reaffirms a distinction recognized by Henry II. but ignored by John. Crown-tenants were divided into two classes, according as their holdings had been originally granted by the Crown, or by some mesne lord whose barony had subsequently escheated. The latter class received preferential treatment from Henry II. for reasons to be immediately explained. A mesne lord had no right to appropriate the holdings of sub-tenants of a tenant who had incurred escheat; but the Crown did not submit to this just restriction. The King treated all sub-tenancies as wiped out by the mere fact that their lord's fief had escheated to the Crown.

Henry II. mitigated in practice the full severity of this theory, confirming as of grace, or from motives of policy, or in return for money, claims which he refused to admit as matter of right. The tenants of escheated baronies were accepted as tenants *in capite* of the Crown.[1] Not only so; but Henry did not allow them to be prejudicially affected by the change. The King would only take from them those services and feudal dues which they had been wont to render to the lord of the barony previous to its escheat. This just and lenient policy explains the origin of the division of royal tenants into two classes; tenants who held of Henry *ut de corona*, and tenants who held of him *ut de escaeta, ut de honore*, or *ut de baronia* (phrases used synonymously).[2] In respect of such obligations as were heavier for ordinary Crown tenants than for tenants of mesne lords, holders of Crown fiefs *ut de escaeta* were placed on the more favoured footing. Two illustrations may be given. While tenants *ut de corona* under Henry had to pay large and arbitrary reliefs, those *ut de escaeta* paid no more than 100s. per knight's fee.[3] Nor was their

---

[1] Royal clemency in this respect could not be relied on by the sub-tenants of *small* escheated fiefs (not reckoned as honours or baronies). This seems to be the opinion of Madox, *Baronia Anglica*, 199: "If a fee holden of the Crown *in capite* escheated to the King and was not an Honour or Barony, then such fee did not (that is to say, I think it did not) vest in the Crown in the same plight in which it was vested in the said tenant *in capite*." Cf. also *ibid.*, 203.

[2] See Madox, *Baronia Anglica*, 169-171; also Pollock and Maitland, I. 261, and authorities there cited.

[3] See *Dialogus*, II. x. F, and *ibid.*, II. xxiv. The same rule applied to sub-tenants of baronies in wardship (which was analogous to temporary escheat): when the see of Lincoln was vacant in 1168, the heirs of sub-tenants paid to Henry only what they would have paid to the bishop; one giving £30 for six fees, and another 30 marks for four. See *Pipe Roll*, 14 Henry II., and cf. *supra*, c. 2. In the

obligation of " suit " to be increased : " the tenants of any honour or manor which had come by escheat to the Crown, were not suitors of the Curia Regis, but of the court of the honour or manor which had so escheated." [1]

John ignored this distinction, extending to tenants *ut de escaeta* the more stringent rules applicable to tenants *ut de corona*. Magna Carta reaffirmed the distinction ; and, not content with enunciating a general principle, made two particular applications of it : neither reliefs nor services of former tenants of baronies were to be augmented by reason of the fact that such baronies had escheated to the Crown.[2] Henry III.'s Charter of 1217 emphasized a third application of the general rule, declaring that he would not, by reason of an escheated barony, claim escheat or custody over the sub-tenants of that barony.[3] To understand this concession, it must be remembered that under Henry III. sub-tenants of baronies were still liable to have their titles reduced through the escheat of their lord ; while sub-tenants of those who were themselves sub-tenants were not exposed to a similar mischance. Here also, the position of

---

matter of scutage, also, a distinction was recognized : while tenants *ut de corona* might be compelled to serve in person without an option, Crown-tenants *ut de honore* (and, *a fortiori*, sub-tenants also) might claim exemption on tendering scutage. See case of Thomas of Inglethorpe in 12 Edward II., cited by Madox, *Baronia Anglica*, 169-171.

[1] *Report on the Dignity of a Peer*, I. 60.

[2] The need for this reference to relief is not, at first sight, obvious, since c. 2 of Magna Carta, by forbidding John to exact from Crown-tenants of either class the arbitrary sums taken by his father, would seem to have already secured them from abuse. Probably, however, c. 43 sought to prevent John from treating each tenant of the escheated barony as holder of a new barony of his own, and therefore liable to a baron's relief of £100 instead of the £25 he ought to pay for his five fees, or £50 for his ten fees, or as the case might be. The case of William Pantol (see *Pipe Roll*, 9 Henry III., cited Madox, I. 318) seems to illustrate this. He was debited with £100 of relief, but protested that he held nothing of the Crown save five knights' fees of the land which was of Robert of Belesme. This plea was upheld, and £75 of the amount debited was written off.

[3] See c. 38 of 1217, and cf. the gloss given by Bracton (II. folio 87b) which makes the meaning somewhat less obscure. The Charter of 1217 contained a saving clause : "unless the holder of the escheated barony held directly of us elsewhere." Bracton added a second proviso, namely, unless the said sub-tenants (now Crown-tenants *ut de escaeta*) had been enfeoffed by the King himself.

Crown fiefs *ut de escaeta* was to be assimilated to that of fiefs of mesne lords, and differentiated from that of Crown fiefs *ut de corona*. Sub-tenancies of escheated baronies were not to be wiped out, but to subsist, and the Crown (or its grantee) would take the escheat, subject to all liabilities to, and rights of, sub-tenants.

The Crown seems not to have strictly observed this rule in practice. Article 12 of the Petition of the Barons in 1258[1] complained that Henry had granted charters conferring rights not his to give (*aliena jura*), but which he claimed as escheats. An act of the first year of Edward III. narrated how the Crown had confiscated, from purchasers, tenements held of the Crown " as of honours," thus treating them " as though they had been holden in chief of the King, as of the Crown." Redress was promised by the statute :[2] but irregularities continued throughout the earlier Tudor reigns; and the first Parliament of Edward VI. passed an act to protect purchasers of lands appertaining to honours escheated to the Crown.[3]

CHAPTER FORTY-FOUR.

HOMINES qui manent extra forestam non veniant de cetero coram justiciariis nostris de foresta per communes summoniciones, nisi sint in placito, vel plegii alicujus vel aliquorum, qui attachiati sint pro foresta.

> Men who dwell without the forest need not henceforth come before our justiciars of the forest upon a general summons, except those who are impleaded, or who have become sureties for any person or persons attached for forest offences.

These provisions were intended to redress one of many abuses connected with the oppressive forest laws.

I. *The Royal Forests.* The word " forest " had acquired an exact technical meaning, and was applied to certain

---

[1] See *Sel. Charters*, 384 ; but see Adams, *Origin*, 344 n.

[2] See 1 Edward III., stat. 2, c. 13, *Statutes of Realm*, I. 256.

[3] See 1 Edward VI., c. 4, *Statutes of Realm*, III. 9.

wide districts, scattered irregularly throughout England, reserved to the Crown for purposes of sport. Here the wild boar and deer of various species found shelter, in which they were protected by the severe regulations of the " Forest Law." It was the prevalence of this code which marked off the districts known as royal forests from all that lay *extra forestam*; and this made an accurate definition possible. A " forest " was a district where this law prevailed to the exclusion of the common law which ruled outside. The forests with their inhabitants had been omitted from the process by which the rest of England had been assimilated under a uniform *lex terrae* : this was the root from which many evils grew.

From this definition of a forest as a *legal,* not a *physical,* entity, it follows that the word is far from synonymous with terms such as " wood " or " covert," implying merely natural characteristics. A forest was not necessarily covered with trees throughout the whole or even the greater part of its extent. Miles of moorland and heath and undulating downs might be included, and even fertile valleys, with ploughed fields and villages nestling among them. The same forest, indeed, might contain many woods, some of them on royal demesne and some the property of private owners. Within the imaginary line the King's power was supreme, and he used it frankly for the preservation of beasts of the chase. The men who happened to dwell there were subject to a law, in the expressive words of Dr. Stubbs, " cruel to man and beast." If accused of forest offences, they had no protection from the common law of England any more than from the law of a foreign land. It was something, however, that even in these high places of prerogative, customary rules grew up, obtained authoritative recognition, and hardened into laws which set some limits to royal caprice. Before John's time the forest code, as set forth in the Assize of Woodstock, had taken its place as a definite system of law, distinct from common law and canon law alike.[1]

[1] A convenient, short account of the forests, with their special laws, special officials, and special courts, will be found in W. S. Holdsworth's *History of English Law*, I. 340-352. For fuller information see *Dialogus de Scaccario*, I. xii. ; John

II. *Origin of the Forests*. Before the Norman Conquest the Kings of England do not seem to have laid claim to any exclusive prerogative in this respect. The only ordinance of Canute on the subject, admitted to be authentic, enacted merely that every man should have his own hunting, while the King should have his.[1] The rights of the Crown, however, were strengthened by the events of 1066, and by the hardening of feudal theory which followed. All unoccupied waste lands became royal property; and these were the natural resorts of the larger sorts of game. The King established a claim to an exclusive right to hunt the more important species of animals *ferae naturae*, known as " beasts of the forest "—embracing the red deer (harts and hinds), the fallow deer (bucks and does), the roe deer of both sexes, and the wild boar, with, exceptionally in one forest, the ordinary hare.[2] Henry I. formulated the forest law, and it was probably due to him that " forest " acquired its technical meaning. With the special meaning came the express claim to a monopoly of hunting, together with supreme and exclusive jurisdiction. The disorders of Stephen's reign lowered the Crown's authority, and Henry II. found the forests much curtailed. He had no intention to acquiesce in this, but it was not till 1184 that he attempted, by the Assize of Woodstock, to formulate the rules of the forest law. In this sphere, as in so many others, Henry II. built on foundations laid by his grandfather. John's attitude to the forest laws was not consistent. The monk of Barnwall relates how, in 1212, John allowed some relaxation in the severity of the forest code.[3] More characteristic of his normal attitude was the order issued on 28th June, 1209, that hedges should be burned and ditches levelled, so that, while men starved, the beasts might fatten upon the crops and fruits.[4]

Manwood, *Book of the Forests* (1598) ; Coke, *Fourth Institute*, 289-317 ; Liebermann, *Constitutiones de Foresta* (1894) ; G. J. Turner, Preface to *Select Pleas of the Forest* (1901) ; and an article in the *Edinburgh Review* for April, 1902.

[1] *Select Charters*, 156.   [2] *Select Pleas of the Forest*, xiii.

[3] See W. Coventry, II. 207, and Stubbs' Preface, lxxxvii.

[4] R. Wendover, III. 227. This, however, is clearly a hostile account of the King's resumption of forest tracts illegally put under cultivation by way of purpresture.

III. *Forest officials.* The local magistrates who administered the rest of England were excluded from the forests by a separate set of officials. At the head of this special organization was placed, in early times, the Forest Justiciar (called the chief forester in chapter 16 of the *Carta de Foresta*), whose duties were divided in the year 1238, after which there were two provinces separated by the river Trent.[1] His appointment was permanent, and his duties, which continued between the eyres, were administrative rather than judicial. He had discretionary authority to release trespassers imprisoned for offences against the forest law.[2] Under his general supervision each forest, or group of forests, was governed by a separate *warden*, aided by a number of petty officials known as *foresters*, whose duties were analogous to those of a modern gamekeeper, but with magisterial powers in addition. Wardens were of two classes—" the one appointed by letters patent under the great seal, holding office during the King's pleasure; the other hereditary wardens." [3] There was situated in or near each forest of any extent a royal residence which, in the Middle Ages, naturally took the form of a stronghold. It was convenient that the office of warden should be combined with that of constable of this neighbouring castle.[4] " The wardens were the executive officers of the King in his forests. Writs relating to the administration of forest business, as well as to the delivery of presents of venison and wood, were in general addressed to them." [5]

The office was one of authority and profit, usually paid in kind rather than by a salary. The warden often held

---

[1] See *Select Pleas of the Forest*, xiv. The permanent routine work performed by this functionary must not be confused with the intermittent duties of the Justices of Forest Eyres, although he was usually a member of the commission who went on circuit: *e.g.* chapter 16 of the Forest Charter speaks of the Chief Forester holding pleas of the forest.

[2] *Select Pleas*, xv.   [3] Turner, in *Select Pleas*, xvii.

[4] Engelard de Cigogné, for example, whose name appears in chapter 50, occupied this double position. Chapter 16 of *Carta de Foresta* forbids *castellans* to determine pleas of the forests, thus strengthening the presumption that wardens were usually constables.

[5] *Select Pleas*, xix.

a fief by a tenure connected with the service, and enjoyed rights and perquisites always of a valuable nature, though varying with each forest. These were sufficient to provide him with an income adequate to his position, and to allow him to find the wages of his under-keepers, who ought thus to have been paid officials. Such was the theory; as matter of fact, the foresters, instead of receiving wages, paid large sums to the warden, and recouped themselves by extortions from the dwellers in their bailiwicks.[1] These unpaid foresters were expressively said to " live upon the country." They may be classified in various ways, as, into riding and walking foresters, or into foresters nominated by the wardens, and foresters in fee. These last had vested interests which the Forest Charter was careful to respect; as, where chapter 14 reserved to them the right to take " chiminage," or way-leave, denied to other types of foresters. They might still enjoy, but not abuse, the " vested rights " reserved to them.[2]

With these professional gamekeepers there co-operated, in later times at least, several groups of unpaid magistrates appointed from the knights and freeholders of the district. Of these honorary officials, whose original function was to supply supplementary machinery for protecting the rights of the Crown, but whose position as county gentleman, with a stake in the district, led them also to act to some extent as arbitrators between the King and outside parties, there were three recognized kinds. (a) Towards the close of the twelfth century officers known as *verderers* (usually four for each forest) become prominent. They appear in the *Carta de Foresta* of 1217, but had not been mentioned in the Assize of Woodstock of 1184. It is probable that the office was devised in the interval as a check on the warden's power; just as the office of coroner had been instituted in the reign of Richard as a drag on the sheriff. In other important respects the duties of the verderers within the forests resembled those of coroners within the rest of the county. They were not royal employees, but local land-owners whose unpaid magisterial services were required

[1] *Select Pleas*, xxi.   [2] The same chapter, however, fixed the rates of " chiminage."

only on special occasions. They were responsible directly to the King, not to the warden; and were appointed in the county court, their " election " taking place in accordance with the terms of the writ " *de viredario eligendo*." They attended the forest courts and swanimotes, and it appears from chapter 16 of Henry's forest charter that it was their duty to bring before the Justices in Eyre lists of all offenders indicted in the lower courts. These " rolls of attachment" were certified by their seals.[1] (*b*) The *Regarders* were twelve knights appointed in each forest county to make tours of inspection every third year, finding answers to a series of questions known as the " Chapters of the Regard." In this way they reviewed the Crown's interests alike in " the venison and the vert " (the technical names for game and growing timber respectively), and reported upon all encroachments : upon hawks and falcons, bows and arrows, greyhounds and mastiffs (with special reference to " expeditation " or cutting of their claws),[2] and generally upon everything owned by private individuals likely to harm the beasts of the forest.[3] (*c*) The *Agistors* are mentioned in the same clause of the Assize of Woodstock which mentions the Regarders. Four knights were appointed to protect the King's interests in all matters connected with the pasturing of swine or cattle within the royal woods. For thirty days at Michaelmas, pigs were turned loose to feed on acorns and beech mast, on payment by their owners of a small fixed sum per head. The four knights were required to take note of sums thus due, known as " pannage," and to collect them at Martinmas.[4]

[1] For the earliest notice of verderers see *Select Pleas of the Forest*, xix. n. Their appointment in county court may indicate that they acted in some measure as a check on the professional foresters in the interests of the people generally, as well as a check on the warden in the interests of the King. Within the forest the warden, with the verderers and foresters, offered an exact parallel to the sheriff with the coroners and bailiffs (or serjeants) in other parts of a county.

[2] See *Carta de Foresta*, c. 6.

[3] After 1217, if not before, it was their duty to fix the number of foresters required, so that the inhabitants need not groan under a heavier burden than necessary.

[4] In one document they were styled *agistatores precii* (*Select Pleas*, p. l.), which suggests that fixing the rate was their chief duty. " Agist" was a general term ; it was apparently correct to speak of "agisting a wood," of "agisting cattle," and of "agisting the money due."

Mention ought, perhaps, to be made of the private foresters also, whom owners of woods within the forests were obliged to appoint. These "wood wards," as they were sometimes called, while paid for by the owner of the wood, were expected to protect the King's interests. In particular, they must prevent trees from being destroyed or wasted : these formed shelter for the game.

IV. *Forest Courts.* The judicial side of the forest system was developed in a manner equally elaborate. Three sets of tribunals must be distinguished : (1) *The Court of Attachments* (or "view of attachments") was a petty tribunal, the chief duty of which was the taking of evidence to be laid in due course before a higher court. Exceptionally, however, it had power to inflict fines for small trespasses against the "vert"—namely, for acts of waste not exceeding the value of fourpence. It met once in every forty days,[1] which seems in practice to have been interpreted as once every six weeks, the meetings being always held on the same day of the week.[2] (2) *Courts of Inquisitions.* When a serious trespass was discovered, a special court was, in early days, immediately summoned. The foresters and verderers conducted the inquiry, but it was their right and duty to assemble the men of the neighbouring townships to help them. In strictness, all inhabitants might be compelled to attend. In practice, it was sufficient if four men and the reeve represented each of the four adjoining villages. Whenever a "beast" was found dead in the forest, twenty men had thus to assemble, to the neglect of their own affairs. In one district at least (Somerton) the definition of beasts of the chase extended to the ordinary hare; and we read[3] how four townships sat in solemn judgment, and found "that the said hare died of murrain, and that they know of nothing else except misadventure," and how, this verdict not giving satisfaction, the townships were fined on the pretext that they were not fully represented. The real offence was their failure to disclose the culprit. Some alleviation of the

---

[1] *Carta de Foresta,* c. 8. [2] *Select Pleas of the Forest,* xxx.

[3] *Select Pleas of the Forest,* p. 42.

burden was effected when, at some date posterior to 1215, *special inquisitions* were superseded by one *general inquisition*, held at regular intervals (usually every six weeks), to cover all trespasses committed during the interval. These courts of inquiry (whether special or general) only " kept " pleas without " trying " them—that is to say, they received and recorded accusations, while judgment was reserved for the justices. (3) *Courts of the forest justices in eyre.* As the smaller courts, in the normal case, received verdicts and reports, without punishing the offences reported, it is evident that the whole system ultimately depended on the justices. Their eyres, however, were held at wide intervals—apparently once every seven years during the reign of Henry III. A full attendance of forest officials and of the public was summoned to meet them. The evidence, stored up as a result of the work of the smaller courts, supplemented by the Rolls of the Regard, was laid before the justices, who summarily judged " pleas of the vert," and " of the venison." These eyres came to be known as " Courts of Justice Seat," but not until long after the reign of John. No juries were present; the justices punished offenders already convicted by juries at a lower court.

In addition, there should be mentioned two other kinds of assemblies which performed duties administrative rather than judicial, as these terms are now understood. (4) The *regard,* held once every three years—not by Crown officials, but by what was practically a jury of local knights—has already been referred to. These tours of inspection, sometime known as *visitationes nemorum,*[1] and sometimes even as " views of expedition," were of great practical importance. The resulting report was placed before the justices of eyre as evidence of forest trespasses. (5) Three times every year, meetings, known from an early date as " *Swanimotes,*" were held to regulate the pasturing of swine and cattle within the royal woods. A fortnight before Michaelmas, the agistors met the foresters and verderers to provide for the agisting of the King's woods, a process that lasted

---

[1] *Dialogus,* I. xi. E.

for thirty days—fifteen before and fifteen after Michaelmas. At Martinmas the agistors collected the pannage in presence of the same officials. A third meeting was held in June to make arrangements for excluding cattle from the King's woods when the deer were fawning, but at this the presence of the agistors were not required.[1]

The *Carta de Foresta* applies to these assemblies, and to none other, the name "Swanimotes"—a word whose correct use has been the subject of much discussion. Its authoritative appearance in 1217 affords strong evidence of the original sense which it bore. In later days, however, it was more loosely used, being applied to inquisitions and also to courts of attachment. This has led to much confusion, while its derivation has also been the subject of discussion. Bishop Stubbs derived it from "swain," on the supposition that courts so called were resorted to by swains or country people. As matter of fact (whatever doctrine may be correct philologically), these assemblies were connected, not with "swains," but with "swine." The peasantry were specially exempted; whereas all three meetings sought to regulate the entry or exclusion of pigs from the woods.

V. *Chases, Parks, and Warrens*. Forests were necessarily royal monopolies and must on this and other grounds be distinguished from three things with which they are apt to be confused. (1) A "chase" was a district, once a royal forest, which had, without any formal act of disafforestation, been granted by the King to a private individual. The result was to transfer the monopoly of hunting to the grantee, while modifying the nature of the rights transferred. The full force of the forest laws was abated, although the extent and direction of this diminution was nowhere strictly defined, but varied from chase to chase. Such provisions of the forest law as continued to be binding were no longer enforced by royal officials and royal courts, but by those of the magnate, who obtained a franchise over

[1] It is stated in *Carta de Foresta* (1217) that only verderers and foresters need be present at the June moot, and the same officers, with the agistors, at the two others. The public were exempted.

the chase and the royal beasts it contained.[1] (2) A " park " was any piece of ground enclosed with a paling, or hedge, whether with the object of protecting wild beasts or otherwise, and the right to effect this was quite independent of royal grant. If the owner of a manor in the near neighbourhood of a royal forest wished to keep deer of his own, which he might kill at pleasure, whether for sport or for food, without infringing the forest laws, he had to stock an enclosure with beasts legally his own, and to keep them under conditions which made confusion with the King's deer impossible.[2] In 1234 the barons asserted their right to keep private gaols for poachers taken in their parks (*in parcis et vivariis suis*), but the King refused to allow this.[3] (3) A " warren," which might belong either to the King or to any private owner, carried with it exclusive rights of hunting within its bounds all wild animals, except those technically defined as " beasts of the forest." [4] In practice it chiefly embraced hares and foxes.[5] Neither parks nor warrens were protected by the forest law, but by that part of the common law which related to theft and trespass. This was, however, vigorously administered, passing gradually into the modern Game Laws.[6] Dr. Stubbs held, apparently, too narrow a conception of warren, when he read it in its modern sense of " a rabbit warren." [7] It was a tract of land wherein exclusive rights of hunting lesser game (together with rabbits and other vermin) were preserved to its owner. The King might, and did, have his warrens and warreners, just as any subject might; and these royal warreners might inflict cruel injustice on the common people; [8] but their power was less than that of foresters, as they were dependent on the common law. The forest code did not apply even to royal warrens.[9]

---

[1] *Select Pleas of the Forest*, cix. *et seq.*   [2] *Ibid.*, cxvii.

[3] Statute of Merton, c. 11.   [4] *Select Pleas of the Forest*, cxxiii.

[5] *Ibid.*, cxxviii.-cxxix.   Wild cats should perhaps be added.

[6] See W. S. Holdsworth, *History of English Law*, I. 346.

[7] See *Select Charters*, 552.

[8] Some of these Magna Carta sought to guard against.   See c. 48.

[9] Rights of hunting were conferred on subjects over territory not their own. Richard I. granted permission to Alan Basset to hunt foxes, hares, and wild cats throughout the realm.   Round, *Ancient Charters*, No. 18.

VI. *Forest Rights and Forest Grievances*. It is not difficult to understand the store which the Kings of England set upon their forests. They prized them not merely as a pleasure ground, but also as a source of revenue. Fines and amercements, individually small, but amounting to a large sum in the aggregate, flowed into the Exchequer. Great as were the pleasure and the profit to the King, the burden and loss inflicted upon the people were greater out of all proportion. Not only were the interests of forest-dwellers sacrificed to the royal hunting, not only were legal fines rendered trebly burdensome by the galling and wasteful manner of their collection; but the men who paid them were victims of illegal exactions in addition. These grievances may be considered under seven heads:—(1) *The extent of the forests*. The Crown constantly strove to extend the boundaries; the people to contract them. The Conqueror and Rufus each "afforested" wide tracts of land, of which the New Forest is only one example. In the Charter of 1100, Henry bluntly declared:—"I retain in my hand, by the common consent of my barons, my forests as my father had them." This consent of the magnates would suggest that the barons were allowed some share in royal rights of hunting, which led them here to make common cause with the Crown. Henry, as matter of fact, retained not only the forests of his father but those of Rufus, and created new ones of his own.[1] Stephen, while retaining the forests of the two Williams, renounced those added by Henry I. Under Henry II., afforestation began anew.[2] The words of the Great Charter leave no doubt that Henry of Anjou had extended the boundaries of Stephen's forests; and that both Richard and John

---

[1] This is implied in the terms of Stephen's Oxford Charter. An example of an act of afforestation by Henry is given in *Select Pleas*, 45, which shows how "a district could be afforested in a moment by the mere word of the monarch; it took centuries to free it from the royal dominion." See *Edinburgh Review*, vol. cxcv. (1902), p. 459. Even the Forest Charter (cc. 1 and 3) admitted the Crown's right to afforest woods on its own demesne—reserving, indeed, common of pasture to those with legal rights thereto.

[2] The policy of Henry I., Stephen, and Henry II. respectively is well illustrated by the case of Waltham forest in Essex. See Round, *Geoffrey de Mandeville*, 377-8.

carried the process further, bringing within the circle of the cruel law, not only waste and moor, but also " woods " belonging to private owners. These royal encroachments were the more oppressive, occurring in an age when population was increasing and seeking outlet in the reclamation of waste places on the debateable land that surrounded the forests. The vagueness of the frontier aggravated this grievance, as it was often difficult for the honest reclaimer of barren land to know when he was committing a trepass for which he might be punished by a crushing fine.[1]

(2) *The monopoly of hunting.* The Crown also made the law more stringent. The Crown's insistence on a strict monopoly may not seem an important grievance, but it was one likely to exasperate the sport-loving nobles. John, in 1207, admitted that his barons still retained some share in the hunting of royal beasts.[2] These rights were formally recognized and defined in 1217. Chapter 11 of the *Carta de foresta* allowed each magnate when passing through a forest to take one or two beasts at sight of the foresters, or, if these officials could not be found, then after blowing a horn to show that nothing underhand was being done.

(3) *Interference with rights of property.* Freeholders whose lands lay in districts which the King was successful in afforesting, retained their freeholds, but their proprietary rights lost half their value. They could not root out trees, to clear their own lands for cultivation; for that was to commit an *assart.* They could not plough up waste land or pasture (even outside the covert) and turn it into arable, nor build a mill, nor take marl or lime from pits, nor make fishponds, nor enclose any space with hedge or paling; for these acts of ownership were *purprestures* or encroachments on the King's rights. They could not destroy a tree or

---

[1] This group of grievances was partly remedied by chapters 47 and 53 of Magna Carta. The former provided for the summary disafforestation of all districts made forests by Richard and John, while the latter showed a more judicial spirit in the undoing of the similar work effected by their father. The *Carta de Foresta* of 1217 contained clauses which took the place of these somewhat crude provisions.

[2] See *Rot. Claus.*, I. 85 (dated 11th June, 1207).

lop off branches (except under stringent conditions), without being guilty of *waste*.[1] They could not agist their woods until a fortnight after Michaelmas, when the agisting of the King's demesnes was over (thus reserving for him the best market and " pannage dues ").[2] Heavy tolls were, under the name of " chiminage," taken from carts and sumpter-horses passing through the woods. The Great Charter endeavoured to strike at the abuse of these Crown rights by providing machinery for the abolition of " evil customs." The *Carta de foresta* entered more into detail. Not only were past trespasses of all three kinds—wastes, purprestures, and assarts—to be condoned, but the law was altered for the future. The long list of purprestures was curtailed : it was made lawful for a man to make (on his own freehold in the forest) mills, ponds, lime pits, ditches, and arable lands, provided these were not placed within the covert and did not infringe on any neighbour's rights.[3] He might also keep eyries for breeding falcons and other birds of prey, and take honey found on his own ground—rights previously denied.[4]

(4) *Interference with the pursuits of the poor*. If the rich suffered injury in their property, the poor suffered in a more pungent way : stern laws prevented them from supplying three of their primary needs; food, firewood, and building materials. On no account could they kill deer; while difficulties surrounded the taking of timber from the woods.[5] It is true that even the Assize of Woodstock allowed them the privilege of " estovers " (that is of cutting firewood), but only under stringent rules. All waste was prohibited; and " waste " was a wide word covering, not merely wanton destruction, but all sales or gifts of logs; while nothing could be taken except at sight of the forester,

---

[1] For detailed information as to wastes, purprestures, and assarts with their ascending scale of penalties, see *Select Pleas*, lxxxii.

[2] See Assize of Woodstock, article 7.   [3] See *Carta de Foresta*, c. 12.

[4] *Ibid.*, c. 13; another clause (c. 14) forbade ordinary foresters to exact chiminage, and fixed the rates payable to those with vested rights at two pennies for each cart per half-year, and one half-penny for each sumpter horse.

[5] See Assize of Woodstock, article 3.

whose consent would not be procured for nothing. This may be illustrated from a period sixty years later than John's reign : Hugh of Stratford, who paid two and a half marks of yearly rent to the Warden for his post, recouped himself by taking " from the township of Denshanger for every virgate of land one quarter of wheat in return for their having paling for their corn and for collecting dead wood for their fuel in the demesne wood of the lord king; and from the same town he took from every house a goose and a hen in every year." [1] A sum might be taken for every load of sticks; the men of Somerset complained that " from the poor they take, from every man who carries wood upon his back, sixpence." [2] Dwellers within or near the forests were prohibited from keeping dogs, unless their value for other pursuits, as well as for hunting, was destroyed by the removal of three claws of the forefoot.[3] Nor could they keep bows or arrows, so necessary for their protection amid the dangers that beset the inhabitants of lonely districts throughout the Middle Ages.[4] No tanner or bleacher of hides could reside in forest districts, unless within a borough.[5]

(5) *Attendance at forest courts.* At every inquisition, representatives from neighbouring townships must be present, while the entire population were compelled to meet the justices on their forest eyres. Henry II. enforced this duty upon those outside the boundaries as well as on those within. The Assize of Woodstock admits no exemption for earl or baron, for knight or freeholder, nor even (according to one version) for archbishop or bishop. The double duty of doing suit at county courts and forest courts meant double loss of time, and double risk of amercement. This 11th Article of the Assize was repealed by chapter 44 of Magna Carta, which restricted the obligation to denizens of the forests, a concession confirmed in 1217.[6]

---

[1] See *Select Pleas*, 123 (6 Edward I.).

[2] *Select Pleas*, (127 (1278-9). This was a heavy rate, the more remarkable in face of the provisions against " chiminage " in *Carta de Foresta*, c. 14.

[3] Assize of Woodstock, article 14. Cf. *Carta de Foresta*, c. 6.

[4] *Ibid.*, article 2.   [5] *Ibid.*, article 15.   [6] See *Carta de Foresta*, c. 2.

(6) *Fines and punishments.* Frequent exactions ground down the dwellers in royal forests to abject poverty. If they failed to attend one of the numerous inquisitions or to disclose the guilty poacher, they paid a fine. If they gave false information; sold or gave away timber; kept grey hounds or mastiffs, which had not been " lawed," they paid a fine.[1] If a bow or arrow were found in their keeping; if they committed any one of the numerous forms of waste or trespass, they paid a fine.

The Northampton Eyre Roll of 1209 illustrates how a township might suffer severely for no fault of their own. " The head of a hart recently dead was found in the wood of Henry Dawney at Maidford by the King's foresters. And the forester of the aforesaid Henry is dead. And because nothing can be ascertained of that hart, it is ordered that the whole of the aforesaid town of Maidford be seized into the King's hand, on the ground that the said Henry can certify nothing of that hart." [2] There was a strong inducement to find someone guilty.

In certain cases Henry II. would not accept a fine, but inflicted mutilation upon violators of the King's monopoly. It was often better to kill a fellow-man than a boar or stag. Article 1 of the Assize of Woodstock announced that the full rigour of the laws would be enforced, as under Henry I., while article 12 laid down more definitely that sureties would only be accepted twice. For the third offence nothing would suffice save the body of the offender. John's Magna Carta made no regulation on this head; but chapter 10 of the *Carta de foresta* in 1217 conceded that no one should henceforth lose life or limb for such offences. The culprit should lie in prison for year and day, and thereafter find sureties for his good behaviour, or be banished the realm.

(7) *Arbitrary government and illegal exactions.* If the laws of Henry's code were stringent and the legal pay-

---

[1] It had been the practice to exact an ox in reparation of such transgression, thus leaving the peasant without means of tilling his land. The Forest Charter (c. 6) limited the fine to 3s.

[2] See *Select Forest Pleas*, p. 4.

ments onerous, it was a worse evil that the law could be defied by Crown officials, and that payments of a perfectly illegal nature might be freely exacted. Within the forest bounds, the peasantry lived in daily fear of the discretionary authority of officials, whose most unreasonable wishes they dared not oppose. Sometimes a local tyrant established a veritable reign of terror. This happened in the forest of Riddlington under Peter de Neville, as the records of•the Rutland Eyre, held in 1269, disclose. One item, taken almost at random from the long list of his evil deeds, will suffice : "The same Peter imprisoned Peter, the son of Constantine of Liddington, for two days and two nights at Allexton, and bound him with iron chains on suspicion of having taken a certain rabbit in Eastwood; and the same Peter the son of Constantine, gave two pence to the men of the aforesaid Peter of Neville, who had charge of him, to permit him to sit upon a certain bench in the gaol of the same Peter, which is full of water at the bottom." [1]   Other examples are only too abundant. In 1225, Norman Samson, a petty official of the forest of Huntingdon, put men to the torture without cause, and only released them from their torments in return for heavy bribes. If such things could happen after the Charters of 1215 and 1217, it is not likely that foresters were more merciful before. John was always too indifferent or too busy to redress such wrongs. The only guarantee against their recurrence was that honest officials should be selected. Chapter 45 of Magna Carta, which tried to effect this, was withdrawn in 1216.

Some good must have resulted from chapter 16 of the Forest Charter, which forbade wardens to hold pleas of the forest. This prevented wardens from being judges in their own cause; but their arbitrary acts continued to be plentiful under Henry III., as has been already shown. Sixty years after Magna Carta, the men of Somerset complained that "foresters come with horses at harvest time and collect every kind of corn in sheaves within the bounds of the forest and outside near the forest, and then they make their ale from that collection, and those who do not

[1] *Select Pleas*, 50.

come there to drink and do not give money at their will, are sorely punished at their pleas for dead wood, although the King has no demesne; nor does anyone dare to brew when the foresters brew, nor to sell ale so long as the foresters have any kind of ale to sell; and this every forester does year by year to the great grievance of the country." [1] Each one of these abuses had been forbidden by chapter 7 of the *Carta de foresta*, which had prohibited the making of "scotale" and the collection of corn, lambs, and pigs. Such rules were easier to enunciate than enforce.

VII. *Later History of Forests and Forest Laws*. The Forest Charter signally failed to secure a pure administration of the law; but two ameliorating processes were at work. The long struggle to define the boundaries ended, in the reign of Edward II., in the defeat of the King, who consented to the frontier being drawn to suit the barons.[2] Within these restricted limits, time and the progress of civilization softened the severity of the forest code, many customs becoming obsolete.[3] Charles I. made an ill-judged attempt to revive some of the Crown's long-forgotten rights. Justice-seats were held by the Earl of Holland, accompanied by amercements and attempts to extend the forest bounds.[4] The result was a drastic act of the Long Parliament, limiting them to their old extents.[5] This statute, however, abolished neither the forests, the forest laws, nor the forest courts. After the Restoration a Justice-seat actually took place *pro forma* before the Earl of Oxford. Blackstone declares this to be the last ever held,[6] although the offices of justice and warden of the forests were not abolished till 1817.[7] The forests, much curtailed in extent, are still Crown property, now administered in the interests of the public by

---

[1] *Select Pleas*, 126. [2] See *infra*, under c. 47.

[3] "*Assisa et consuetudines forestae*," issued by Edward I. in 1278, although declaratory, may have done something towards curtailing discretionary authority. *Statutes of Realm*, I. 243; Bémont, *Chartes*, lxv.

[4] See S. R. Gardiner, *Hist. Engl.*, VII. 363, and VIII. 282.

[5] 16 Charles I. c. 16. [6] *Commentaries*, III. 72.

[7] By 57 George III. c. 61.

Commissioners of Woods and Forests.[1] The operation of the common law is, of course, no longer excluded from their confines, the old antithesis between forest law and the law of England being a thing of the past.[2]

CHAPTER FORTY-FIVE.

Nos non faciemus justiciarios, constabularios, vicecomites vel ballivos, nisi de talibus qui sciant legem regni et eam bene velint observare.

> We will appoint as justices, constables, sheriffs, or bailiffs only such as know the law of the realm and mean to observe it well.

The object of this plainly worded clause was to prevent the appointment of unsuitable men to responsible posts under the Crown. The list of officers is a comprehensive one—justices, sheriffs, constables and bailiffs—embracing all royal ministers and agents, both of the central and of the local government, from the chief justiciar down to the humblest serjeant.[3] This clause was directed in particular against John's foreign favourites such as the Poitevin Bishop of Winchester, Peter des Roches, who had wielded the authority of chief justiciar in 1214 when the King was abroad,[4] or such as Engelard de Cigogné, stigmatized by name in a later part of Magna Carta.[5] Such men had no interests at stake in England, and little love for its customs and free traditions. In future John must choose a different type of servants, avoiding all such unscrupulous men, whether Englishmen or foreigners, as were ready to break the law in their master's interests or their own. But what class were to fill their places?

Bishop Stubbs credits the framers of the Charter

---

[1] In virtue of a series of Acts of which 14-15 Victoria c. 42 is the latest.

[2] See Stephen, *Commentaries*, II. 465-6.

[3] Constable and bailiff are discussed *supra*, c. 24, and shown to include forest magistrates, *supra*, c. 44.

[4] See *supra*, p. 30, and cf. Blackstone, *Great Charter*, viii.

[5] See c. 50.

with, an intention to secure the appointment of men well versed in legal science: " on this principle the steward of a court-leet must be a learned steward." [1] The clause of Magna Carta, however, refers to royal nominees, not to the officers appointed by mesne lords to preside over their feudal courts. The barons appointed their own stewards and bailiffs, and had no wish to hamper their own freedom of choice; but only that of the King. Further, the barons did not desire that John should employ men steeped in legal lore, but plain Englishmen with a rough-and-ready knowledge of insular usage, who would avoid arbitrary acts condemned by the law. The barons at Runnymede desired precisely what the council of St. Albans had desired on 4th August, 1213, when it issued formal writs to sheriffs and foresters to observe the laws of Henry I. and abstain from unjust exactions; [2] and these laws of Henry were but the laws of Edward Confessor (or, in reality, of Canute) slightly amended.

The attitude of John's barons was the same as that of Henry's barons, when the latter declared, in 1234, in emphatic terms, that they did not wish the laws of England to be changed. [3] They were far from desiring to be governed by ministers deeply versed in the science and literature of jurisprudence, since these would necessarily have been churchmen and civilians.

This well-meaning provision of Magna Carta disappeared in 1216 (without any comment in the so-called " respiting clause "). Even if it had remained intact, it would not have effected much, in the absence of adequate machinery to ensure its enforcement. In promising the appointment of such ministers as knew the law and meant to keep it, John remained sole judge of the men appointed and their intentions. The clause indicated no standard of fitness, no neutral arbitrator to decide between fit and unfit, [4] and no

[1] *Const. Hist.*, I. 578 n.   [2] Cf. *supra*, p. 28.

[3] " *Nolunt leges Anglie mutare que usitate sunt et approbate.*" See Statute of Merton, c. 9.

[4] It would have been a notable anticipation of modern constitutional theory if the barons in 1215 had referred such questions to the decision of the *Commune Concilium* summoned as in c. 14 (*q.v.*).

sanction to enforce compliance on an unwilling King. Half a century later, the Provisions of Oxford gave proof of some advance in political theory. They contained an expedient, crude enough it is true, for constraining royal officials to keep the law : forms of an oath of office to be taken by castellans and ministers of all grades were carefully provided.[1] Even this was only a first step towards settling a problem not completely solved until the modern doctrine of ministerial responsibility was firmly established.[2]

CHAPTER FORTY-SIX.

OMNES barones qui fundaverunt abbatias, unde habent cartas regum Anglie, vel antiquam tenuram, habeant earum custodiam cum vacaverint, sicut habere debent.

> All barons who have founded abbeys, concerning which they hold charters from the kings of England, or of which they have long-continued possession, shall have the wardship of them, when vacant, as they ought to have.

Religious houses of various orders (abbeys, priories, and convents), which had increased rapidly in number since the reign of Henry I., fell naturally into two classes, according as they had been founded by the King or by private individuals. The King or the great baron, in bestowing lands on a religious foundation, reserved, either expressly or by implication, valuable rights of property : of these the control over the election of the abbot or prior, together with the wardship of the fief during vacancies, were the most important. King John, while by his charter to the clergy he renounced control over election of bishops, reserved his rights of wardship; and the barons insisted that the proprietary rights of mesne lords who had founded religious houses, should also be respected. John, however,

---

[1] See *Select Charters*, 388-391, and Madox, II. 149, with authorities there cited.

[2] Prof. Adams seems to make too much of this chapter (*Origin*, 259-260). It is only a vague promise to employ honest officials : it confers no constitutional veto upon anyone. Had the function of defining fit ministers been conferred on the Common Council, it would have been a notable innovation.

wherever he had any plausible pretext, usurped the wardship over private foundations. It would appear, from the
terms of a later chapter,[1] that in 1215 the Crown actually
held in ward certain abbeys founded by mesne lords. The
present chapter looks to the future, forbidding new usurpa-
tions of this nature.

In reissues of the Charter verbal changes occur, but it is
not clear that they imply changes of substance. In 1216
the words " and as it has been above declared " were added,
implying that the rights of mesne lords were to be restricted
by the rules previously laid down in chapter 5, as to wardship—rules particularly applied to the lands of bishoprics
and religious houses in 1216 by a clause which had no
parallel in John's Charter.[2] In 1217 three other small
changes tend to define and perhaps to widen the scope of
the clause. The " barons who have founded abbeys "
become " the patrons of abbeys "; royal " charters "
become more explicitly " charters of advowson "; " ancient
tenure " is expanded into " ancient tenure or possession." [3]
These alterations seem to indicate an effort towards greater
verbal accuracy, and do not involve any change of principle.
It should, perhaps, be noted, however, that the words
" *patroni* " and " *de advocatione*," occurring in 1217, contain
a tacit assertion of lay patronage of which there was no hint
in 1215; but it would not be safe to conclude from this alone
that there had been any change of attitude on the question
of canonical election.

The object of this chapter was to define the relations
between the King and the barons as to wardship, not those
between the lay and ecclesiastical authorities as to rights of
appointment. It seems to have made little difference, if
any, in practice: Henry III. never observed in its fullness
the doctrine here enunciated, but claimed wardship over
abbeys and priories founded by earls and barons on their
own fiefs.[4] On the closely allied question of lay patronage,

[1] See *infra*, c. 53.   [2] Cf. *supra*, p. 212.
[3] See Appendix for final form in charter of 1225.
[4] See Petition of Barons, c. 11 (*Sel. Chart.*, 384); Maitland, *Sel. Pleas Man.
Courts*, lxxvii. For the practice in Normandy, see authorities cited by Adams,
Origin, 246 n.

not directly raised in any version of Magna Carta, Henry's practice seems not to have differed from his father's. John interfered freely between abbeys and their founders. On 16th August, 1200, he granted to William Marshal the privilege of bestowing the pastoral staff of Nuthlegh Abbey, which lay within that earl's fief; this shows that he forbade appointments without royal licence.[1] The barons in 1258 protested against similar conduct on the part of Henry III.[2]

CHAPTER FORTY-SEVEN.

OMNES foreste que afforestate sunt tempore nostro, statim deafforestentur; et ita fiat de ripariis que per nos tempore nostro posite sunt in defenso.

> All forests that have been made such in our time shall forth-with be disafforested; and a similar course shall be followed with regard to river-banks that have been placed "in defence" by us in our time.

An analogy may be traced between the prerogatives of hunting and of falconry here brought together. William the Conqueror claimed wide and ill-defined rights to "afforest" whole districts at his discretion; and for pro-tecting his preferential rights of fowling, whole rivers might be placed "in defence." The parallel must not be pushed too far. River-banks were preserved only for such limited period as was covered by the King's express command; and, although wardens were appointed to guard them,[3] the Crown never established such absolute control over the banks of rivers as it did within districts declared "afforested."

The provision of the present chapter, defining what river-banks might be "defended," disappeared, together with the

---

[1] See *New Rymer*, I. 81. John had also interfered "in the time of the interdict" with what Robert fitz Walter considered his rights of patronage over Binham Priory (a cell of St. Albans). See J. H. Round, *Eng. Hist. Rev.*, XIX. 710-11.

[2] Petition of Barons, c. 11 (*Sel. Chart.*, 384).

[3] Mention of these officers is made in c. 48. The phrase "in defence" is explained *supra*, pp. 301-3.

relative clause of chapter 48 ("*ripariis et earum custodibus*"), from the reissue of 1216; but, in the "respiting" clause there was promised further deliberation, which resulted in its replacement in chapter 20 of the final version of Magna Carta.[1]

More attention is usually paid to the bearing of the present chapter upon the limits of the forests. John, if he had created no new forests, had extended the boundaries of the old ones. All such encroachments are to be immediately given up. This summary redress should be contrasted with the more judicial procedure appointed by chapter 53 for determining encroachments made by Henry II. and Richard. A somewhat similar distinction is also to be found in the corresponding provisions of the Forest Charter of 1217 (chapters 1 and 3); but the line is there differently drawn. Chapter 1 of the *Carta de foresta* extends the summary methods of redress to the disafforesting of all forests created by Richard as well as those created by John. The terms of the later document are also more detailed. Both seem to be directed against encroachments on the rights of landowners, affording no protection to the poor. While they deny the Crown's right to afforest private woods "to the damage of any one" (that is, of barons or freeholders owning them), they admit the legality of past acts, whether of Henry, of Richard, or of John, in afforesting Crown lands, subject always to a saving clause in favour of freeholders in right of common of pasturage.[2]

Even if Henry III. had cordially co-operated with his barons to disafforest all tracts of ground afforested by Henry II. and his sons, difficulties of definition would still have made the task tedious. As it was, struggles to settle boundaries embittered the relations between Crown and Parliament, until the very close of Edward Plantagenet's reign. Only the leading steps in the slow process by which the opposition triumphed need here be mentioned.

[1] Cf. *supra*, p. 147.

[2] G. J. Turner, *Select Pleas of Forest*, xciii., points out that although forests included open country as well as woods, yet *Carta de foresta* spoke only of "woods" in this connection.

After the issue of *Carta de foresta* on 6th November, 1217,[1] machinery was set in motion, in obedience to its terms, to ascertain the old boundaries and disafforest recent additions. The work of redress continued for some years, suffering no interruption from the issue of the new royal seal at Michaelmas, 1218.[2] In face of many difficulties, only slow progress was possible. More strenuous efforts followed the reissue of the Charters on 11th February, 1225;[3] for, five days later, justices were appointed to make new perambulations, which resulted in the disafforestation of wide tracts. Henry considered himself, and with some reason, unjustly treated by these justices, or by the local juries on whose verdicts they had relied. After he had proclaimed himself of age in January, 1227, he challenged their findings; and this has been misinterpreted as an attempt to annul the Forest Charter.[4]

Some of the knights who had perambulated the forests were persuaded or coerced into acknowledging that they had made mistakes; and, after further inquiry, Henry restored the wider bounds. His reactionary measures went on for two years; but thereafter the frontiers were fixed, in spite of many complaints, until strong pressure compelled Edward I. to reopen the whole question. Perambulations in 1277 and 1279 produced apparently no results. Renewed complaints were followed by new perambulations in 1299-1300, the reports of which were laid before a Parliament at Lincoln on 25th January, 1301. The King on 14th February confirmed the Forest Charter, and agreed to the reduced boundaries as defined by the most recent inquests. Edward had acted under constraint: on this plea he subsequently obtained from Pope Clement V. a bull, dated 29th December, 1305, revoking all concessions made at Lincoln.[5] The Crown seemed thus to triumph once more; but the barons refused to accept defeat, forcing upon Edward II. the acceptance of the narrower bounds as defined at his father's

---

[1] Cf. *supra*, p. 146.   [2] Cf. *supra*, p. 153, and see *Select Pleas*, xcv.

[3] Cf. *supra*, p. 154.   [4] Cf. *Select Pleas*, xcix. ; and see also *supra*, p. 156.

[5] See *Select Pleas*, cv. Mr. Turner's account of Edward's conduct may be compared with the estimate of M. Bémont, *Chartes*, xlviii.

Parliament in 1301. This settlement was confirmed by
statute in the first year of Edward III.[1] and that King
failed in all attempts to escape from its provisions. Thus
the authoritative pronouncement made in 1301 by the
Parliament of Lincoln furnished the basis on which the
protracted controversy was finally determined.[2]

The further history of the forest boundaries may be told
in a few sentences. No changes were made until the sixteenth century. When Henry VIII. afforested the districts
surrounding Hampton Court in 1540, he did so by consent
of Parliament, and on condition of compensating all who
suffered damage. The same course was followed by
Charles I. in creating the Forest of Richmond in 1634.
Finally, as a result of attempts of the Stewarts to revive
obsolete rights, a statute of the Long Parliament, reciting
the Act of 1327, " ordained that the old perambulation of
the forest in the time of King Edward the First should be
thenceforth holden in like form as it was then ridden and
bounded."[3]

CHAPTER FORTY-EIGHT.

OMNES male consuetudines de forestis et warennis, et de
forestariis et warennariis, vicecomitibus et eorum ministris,
ripariis et earum custodibus, statim inquirantur in quolibet
comitatu per duodecim milites juratos de eodem comitatu,
qui debent eligi per probos homines ejusdem comitatus, et
infra quadraginta dies post inquisicionem factam, penitus,
ita quod numquam revocentur, deleantur per eosdem, ita
quod nos hoc sciamus prius, vel justiciarius noster, si in
Anglia non fuerimus.[4]

　　All evil customs connected with forests and warrens, foresters
　　and warreners, sheriffs and their officers, river-banks and their

---

[1] 1 Edward III., stat. 2, c. 1.

[2] See *Select Pleas*, cvi. There was one exception. On 26th December, 1327,
Edward III. had to submit to further disafforestations in Surrey.

[3] 16 Charles I. c. 16.

[4] The last sixteen words, inclusive of "*per eosdem*," appear at the foot of both of
the Cottonian versions of Magna Carta. Cf. *supra*, p. 166.

wardens, shall immediately be inquired into in each county by twelve sworn knights of the same county chosen by the honest men of the same county, and shall, within forty days of the said inquest, be utterly abolished, so as never to be restored, provided always that we previously have intimation thereof, or our justiciar, if we should not be in England.

This chapter is mainly, though not exclusively, a forest one. It provides in a sweeping and drastic manner for the abolition of "evil customs," three groups of which are specially emphasized : (a) those connected with forests and warrens (presumably royal warrens only), or with their officials; (b) those connected with sheriffs and their subordinates; and (c) those connected with river-banks and their guardians. The word "customs" is obviously here used in its wider sense, embracing all usages and procedure, whether specially connected with pecuniary exactions or not.[1] The word "evil" is not defined, but machinery is provided for arriving at a definition. In each county a local jury of twelve knights was to be immediately chosen by "the good people" of that county, and these twelve received a mandate to hold a comprehensive inquest into "evil customs" : practices condemned by them were to be abolished within forty days of the inquiry, "so that they shall never be restored."

At the end of the chapter appears a proviso that, before actual abolition, notice must be sent to the King, or, in his absence, to his justiciar. Although such intimation was necessary, both on grounds of policy and of ordinary courtesy, this clause is written (apparently as an afterthought) at the foot of two of the copies of the Great Charter.

John lost no time in instituting machinery for effecting this part of the reforms. On the very day on which terms of peace were concluded at Runnymede, namely, on 19th June, 1215, he began the issue of writs to sheriffs, warreners, and river bailiffs. Within a few days every one of these had been certified of the settlement arrived at, and had received commands to have twelve knights chosen in the first county court to make sworn inquest into evil customs.[2]

---

[1] Contrast the more restricted meaning of the same word in c. 41.

[2] See *Rot. Pat.*, I. 180, cited also *Select Charters*, 306-7. Cf. *supra*, p. 42.

The knights appointed seem to have taken a liberal view
of their functions, claiming to share with the sheriffs the
exercise of the whole executive authority of the county.
Some warrant for these pretensions may be found in the
terms of a second series of writs issued in the King's name
on 27th June and following days. These were addressed
to the sheriff and the twelve knights jointly, commanding
them to make instant seizure of all who refused to take, as
required in the previous writs, the oath of obedience to the
twenty-five executors of the Charter.[1] The revolutionary
committee of the central government had thus, in each
county, local agents in the twelve knights whose original
duties had been to see evil customs abolished.

The hatred to the forest laws is well illustrated by the
iconoclastic spirit in which these knights set about the
remedy of abuses. Moderate-minded men began to fear
that sweeping changes would abolish the royal forests.
Accordingly, the leading prelates issued a written protest
that this chapter must be understood by both parties "as
limited," and "that all those customs shall remain, without
which the forests cannot be preserved."[2] What effect, if
any, this protest had, is not known. The country was soon
plunged in civil war, during the continuance of which
neither side had leisure for the reform of abuses. In 1216
the subject was "respited" for future consideration, and in
1217 an attempt was made to specify in detail the evil customs to be abolished. The dangerous experiment of leaving
the definition to local juries in each district was not
repeated.

[1] Cf. *infra*, c. 61.

[2] Cf. *supra*, p. 43. The text is given *Rot. Claus.*, 17 John, m. 27 d. and *New
Rymer*, I. 134. It runs in name of the archbishops of Canterbury and Dublin,
and the bishops of London, Winchester, Bath, Lincoln, Worcester and Coventry,
comprising (with one exception) those mentioned in the preamble to Magna
Carta. For text, see Appendix.

CHAPTER FORTY-NINE.

OMNES obsides et cartas statim reddemus que liberate fuerunt nobis ab Anglicis in securitatem pacis vel fidelis servicii.

We will immediately restore all hostages and charters delivered to us by Englishmen, as sureties of the peace or of faithful service.

A feature of John's system of government was the constant demand for hostages as guarantees of his subjects' loyalty. Such an expedient was, indeed, naturally resorted to in the Middle Ages upon special occasions, as, for example, to secure the observance of a recent treaty, or where the leaders of a rebellion, newly suppressed, had been spared on condition of future good behaviour. Thus the Conqueror, in 1067, during a forced absence from England, took with him Edgar Atheling and the Earls Morkere and Edwin. Such cases were, however, exceptional, until John resorted to such a policy, not merely in face of danger, but as a constant and normal practice in times of peace.

John lived in his native England like a conqueror in the midst of a hostile race, keeping sons and daughters in his clutches to answer for their parents' attempts at revolt. This ingenious but unfair practice accords well with what we know of John's character and general policy. It was a measure of almost devilish cunning for obtaining his immediate ends, but likely to recoil on himself whenever a critical state of his fortunes arrived. Its efficacy lay in this, that it forced the hand of discontented magnates, compelling them to decide, upon the instant, between the desperate expedient of open rebellion and delivery of their children to an unscrupulous enemy, thus renouncing, perhaps for ever, the possibility of resistance or revenge, thereafter to be purchased at too dear a price—the life of the hostage. By thus paralyzing his enemies one by one, John hoped to render disaffection innocuous.[1]

[1] The only magnates not exposed to this dilemma were the prelates, whose celibacy cut them adrift from acknowledged family ties. They had no hostages

The history of the reign shows of what excessive practical importance this question of hostages had become. Thus, in 1201, John seized the castles of certain of his barons; and one of them, William of Albini, only saved his stronghold of Belvoir by handing over his son as a hostage.[1] In the same year, the men of York offended the King by omitting to meet him in procession when he visited their city, and by their failure to provide for the billeting of his archers. John, as usual, demanded hostages, but ultimately allowed the citizens to escape on payment of £100, to buy good-will.[2]

Hardly a year passed without similar instances; but, apparently, it was not until 1208 that the practice was enforced wholesale. In that year, the King's abject fear of the effects of the Pope's absolution of his barons from their allegiance, led to his demand that every leading man in England should hand over his sons, nephews, or other blood relations to the King's messengers.[3]

The danger of failure to comply with such demands is illustrated by the fate of Maud of Saint-Valery, wife of William de Braose, who refused point-blank to hand over her grandchildren to a King who, she was unwise enough to say, "had murdered his captive nephew."[4] Two years later John, after failing to extort enormous sums in name of fines, caused her, with her eldest son, to be starved to death, a fate to which her own imprudence had doubtless contributed.[5] John's drastic methods of treating his hostages may also be illustrated from the chronicles of his reign, for example, from the fate of the youths he brought from Wales in June, 1211. When he heard of the Welsh rebellion of the following year, he ordered his levies to meet him at Nottingham. At the muster, early in September, John found awaiting him a great concourse, who were treated to

---

to give, and were, further, in the normal case, exempt from fear of personal violence.

[1] See R. Hoveden, IV. 161.   [2] See *Rotuli de Finibus*, p. 119.

[3] See R. Wendover, III. 224-5, and M. Paris, II. 523.

[4] R. Wendover and Matthew Paris, *ibid.*

[5] See authorities cited by Miss Norgate, *John Lackland*, p. 288.

an object lesson which long might haunt their dreams. His passion at white heat, John incontinently hanged eight-and-twenty defenceless boys of the noblest blood of Wales.[1] This ghastly spectacle could not have been forgotten, when later in the same month the King, in the throes of sudden panic, fled to London; and, secure in the fast-nesses of the Tower, demanded hostages wholesale from all the nobles whose fidelity he doubted. Eustace de Vesci and Robert fitz Walter preferred to seek safety in flight.[2] The others, with the Nottingham horror fresh in their memories, were constrained to hand over sons and daughters to the tender mercies of John, cunning and cruel by nature, and rendered doubly treacherous by suspicion intensified by fear.

The defects of this policy, in the long run, may be read in the events which preceded Magna Carta. When John's hold on the hostages was relaxed, because of the campaign of 1214, ending as it did in discomfiture, the disaffected were afforded their long-desired opportunity, and were stimulated to rapid action by the thought that such a chance might never occur again. John, on his return, held com-paratively few hostages, and the northern barons saw that they must act, if at all, before their children were once more in the tyrant's clutches.

Even in June, 1215, however, John had still a few hostages, and this chapter demands the immediate restora-tion of those of English birth (the Welsh receiving separate treatment), together with the charters which John held as additional security. This provision of Magna Carta was immediately carried out. Letters were dispatched to the custodians of royal hostages, ordering an immediate release.[3] The practice of taking hostages, however, by no means ended with the granting of the Great Charter. Before a year had run, some of the insurgent nobles, repenting of their boldness, succeeded in making terms with John by the payment of large sums of money and the delivery of their sons and daughters in security for their

[1] Cf. *supra*, p. 25.   [2] Cf. *supra*, p. 25.

[3] See letter of 23rd June to Stephen Harengod in Appendix.

future loyalty. Simon fitz Walter, for example, thus gave up his daughter Matilda.[1]

CHAPTER FIFTY.

Nos amovebimus penitus de balliis parentes Gerardi de Athyes, quod de cetero nullam habeant balliam in Anglia; Engelardum de Cygony, Petrum et Gionem et Andream, de Cancellis, Gionem de Cygony, Galfridum de Martinny et fratres ejus, Philippum Marci et fratres ejus, et Galfridum nepotem ejus, et totam sequelam eorundem.

> We will entirely remove from their bailiwicks, the relations of Gerard of Athée (so that in future they shall have no bailiwick in England); namely, Engelard of Cigogné, Peter, Guy, and Andrew of Chanceaux, Guy of Cigogné, Geoffrey of Martigny with his brothers, Philip Mark with his brothers and his nephew Geoffrey, and the whole brood of the same.

Chapter 45 sought to secure the appointment of suitable men to posts of trust under the Crown; the present chapter definitely excludes from bailiwicks (a comprehensive term embracing all grades of local magistracies) one particular group of royal favourites. This clause was omitted from future reissues, along with chapter 45.

The Charter does not explain the reasons that had rendered these men obnoxious; but the testimony of contemporary Plea Rolls and Pipe Rolls amply supplies the omission. Each one of them can be shown to have held places of profit under the Crown as sheriffs of counties, forest wardens, and commanders of royal garrisons. They formed a group of kinsmen who, after John had lost his French dominions, preferred to follow their royal master to England. The three villages of Athée, Cigogné, and Chanceaux lie close together in Touraine, in the modern department of Indre-et-Loire, not far from the cities of Tours and Loches. The group of men here named all came

[1] See *Rotuli de Finibus*, 571. The custody of hostages might be a desirable office; in 1199 Alan, the earl's son, offered three greyhounds for the custody of a hostage of Brittany, *Rotuli de Finibus*, p. 29.

from this district. " They were neither courtiers nor politicians, but soldiers of experience, whom the barons feared
with good cause." [1]

The career of Engelard de Cigogné may be taken as
typical of the rest. He was a nephew of Gerard of Athée,
whom he succeeded, in 1209, as sheriff of Gloucester and
Hereford, an office he held until about the time of Magna
Carta. The Plea Roll of the Gloucestershire Eyre of 1221
covers the period of his shrievalty, and contains a striking
and detailed picture of his misdeeds and extortions.[2] He
accounted for the *firma burgi* of Bristol,[3] which seems to
imply interference with its chartered liberties. He also
held pleas of the Crown for Gloucestershire,[4] in violation of
the ordinance of 1194 forbidding any sheriff to act as
justiciar in his own county.[5] Several entries tell of barrels
of wine which he took as " prise " from ships entering the
port of Bristol, and thereafter sold to the King. For
example, the exchequer officials allowed him to deduct from
the *firma*, the sum of 60s., in respect of four tuns of red
wine, as certified by the King's writ.[6] Engelard guarded a
rich treasure for the King at Bristol, probably as constable
of the castle there, sums being paid to him *ad ponendum in
thesauro regis*.[7] On one occasion he was entrusted with
more than 10,000 marks of the King's money.[8] Hostages,
as well as bullion, were placed under his care; a writ dated
18th December, 1214, directed him to liberate three noble
Welshmen whom it mentioned by name.[9]

In the civil war to which the treaty of peace sealed at
Runnymede was a prelude, Engelard, then constable of
Windsor Castle and warden of the adjacent forest of
Odiham, proved active in John's service. He successfully
defended Windsor from the French faction, making vigor-

[1] G. J. Turner, *Trans. R.H.S.*, XVIII. p. 254.

[2] See *Gloucester Pleas*, edited by Maitland, *passim*.

[3] *Pipe Roll*, 12 John, cited Madox, I. 333.

[4] *Pipe Roll*, 12 John, cited Madox, II. 146.   [5] *Gloucester Pleas*, xiii. ff.

[6] *Pipe Roll*, 12 John, cited Madox, I. 766.

[7] *Ibid.*, I. 606.   [8] *Ibid.*, I. 384.

[9] *Rot. Pat.*, 16 John, m. 9 (I. 125), and *New Rymer*, I. 126.

ous sorties until relieved by the King.[1] He requisitioned supplies to meet the royal needs; and a plea was brought against him so long afterwards as 1232, in connection with twelve hogsheads of wine thus taken.[2] He acted as sheriff of Surrey under William Marshal, but was suspended from this office in 1218, in consequence of a dispute with Earl Warenne.[3] He remained warden of the castle and forests for twenty years after the accession of Henry III.,[4] and his long services were rewarded with grants of land: in the county of Oxford he held the manor of Benzinton, with four hundreds and a half, during the King's good pleasure;[5] while his son Oliver received the lucrative post of guardian over the lands and heirs of Henry de Berkley.[6]

In 1221, however, acting in consort with Falkes de Bréauté, Philip Mark, and other castellans, Engelard supported earl William of Aumâle in his resistance to the demands of Henry's ministers, that all royal castles should be restored to the King. Notwithstanding the secrecy with which he sent men to the earl at Biham castle,[7] he fell under suspicion of treason, and found hostages that he would hold the castle of Windsor for the King.[8] In 1236, he was relieved of some of his offices, but not of all, for in 1254 he was two years in arrears with the *firma* of the manor of Odiham.[9] In that year, apparently, he died; for the patent roll contains a writ granting him permission to make his will, and an entry in 1255 relates how " for good service done to the King by Engelard of Cigogné in his lifetime, the King granted to his executors that they should be quit of all accounts to be rendered by them at the exchequer, and of all averages of accounts, and of all debts and imposts." [10] Engelard thus died, as he had lived, the

---

[1] See M. Paris, II. 665, who calls him " *Ingelardus de Athie* " and describes him as *vir in opere martis probatissimus.* Cf. *Rot. Pat.*, 9 Henry III. m. 9.

[2] See Bracton's *Note-book*, No. 684.   [3] See *Rot. Pat.*, 2 Henry III. m. 7.

[4] *Ibid.*, 19 Henry III.   [5] See *Testa de Neville*, p. 18, and *ibid.*, p. 120.

[6] *Rot. Pat.*, 9 Henry III. m. 6.   [7] R. Wendover, IV. 66.

[8] *Annals of Dunstable*, III. 68.

[9] *Mem. Roll*, 28 Henry III., cited Madox, II. 201.

[10] *Mich. Communia*, 29 Henry III., cited Madox, II. 229.

trusted servant and favourite of kings. His career illustrates how the very same men who had incurred odium as partisans of John became, when the civil war was over, instruments of his son's misgovernment.[1]

CHAPTER FIFTY-ONE.

ET statim post pacis reformacionem amovebimus de regno omnes alienigenas milites, balistarios, servientes, stipendiarios, qui venerint cum equis et armis ad nocumentum regni.

> As soon as peace is restored, we will banish from the kingdom all foreign-born knights, cross-bowmen, serjeants, and mercenary soldiers, who have come with horses and arms to the kingdom's hurt.

John here binds himself to disband his foreign troops, the agents of his tyrannies. These men, who had garrisoned royal castles, are to be banished "as soon as peace is restored," an indication that a state of virtual war was recognized. This promise was partially fulfilled : on 23rd June writs were issued for disbandment of the mercenaries.[2] The renewal of the civil war, however, was followed by enrolment of new bands of foreigners, whose presence was one of the main causes of the rebellion of 1224, after the suppression of which most of them were again banished with their ringleader, Falkes de Bréauté.

The words used to describe these soldiers are comprehensive. *Stipendiarii* embraced mercenaries of every kind : *balistarii* were cross-bowmen. This weapon, imported into England as a result of the crusades, quickly superseded the

---

[1] Some particulars respecting the other individuals named will be found in Thomson, *Magna Charta*, 244-5. Philip Mark was Constable of Nottingham (R. Wendover, III. 237), and Sheriff both before and after 1215 (see, *e.g.*, *Rot. Claus.*, I. 412), while Guy de Chanceaux in 1214 accounted for scutage of the honour of Gloucester (Madox, I. 639), and for the rent of the barony of William of Beauchamp (*ibid.*, I. 717). See also Petit-Dutaillis, *Louis VIII.*, p. 116; *Gloucester Pleas, passim* ; Turner, *op. cit. passim*.

[2] See *Rot. Pat.*, 17 John, m. 23 (*New Rymer*, I. 134).

earlier short bow, but had, in turn, to succumb to the long bow, which was apparently derived from Wales by Edward I., who gained by means of it many battles against the Scotch and Welsh, and made possible the later triumphs of the Black Prince and Henry V.

CHAPTER FIFTY-TWO.

Si quis fuerit disseisitus vel elongatus per nos sine legali judicio parium suorum, de terris, castellis, libertatibus, vel jure suo, statim ea ei restituemus; et si contentio super hoc orta fuerit, tunc inde fiat per judicium viginti quinque baronum, de quibus fit mencio inferius in securitate pacis : de omnibus autem illis de quibus aliquis disseisitus fuerit vel elongatus sine legali judicio parium suorum, per Henricum regem patrem nostrum vel per Ricardum regem fratrem nostrum, que in manu nostra habemus, vel que alii tenent que nos oporteat warantizare, respectum habebimus usque ad communem terminum crucesignatorum; exceptis illis de quibus placitum motum fuit vel inquisicio facta per preceptum nostrum, ante suscepcionem crucis nostre : cum autem redierimus de peregrinacione nostra, vel si forte remanserimus a peregrinacione nostra, statim inde plenam justiciam exhibebimus.

If any one has been dispossessed or removed [1] by us, without the legal judgment of his peers, from his lands, castles, franchises, or from his right, we will immediately restore them to him ; and if a dispute arise over this, then let it be decided by the five-and-twenty barons of whom mention is made below in the clause for securing the peace.[2] Moreover, for all those possessions, from which any one has, without the lawful judgment of his peers, been disseised or removed, by our father, King Henry, or by our brother, King Richard, and which we retain in our hand (or which are possessed by others, to whom we are bound to warrant them) we shall have respite until the usual term of crusaders ; excepting those things about which a plea has been

[1] The *elongatus* of the Charter replaces the *prolongatus* of the Articles.

[2] The so-called "executive clause," the "*forma securitatis ad observandum pacem*" of the Articles, which became chapter 61.

raised, or an inquest made by our order, before our taking of the cross; but as soon as we return from our expedition (or if perchance we desist from the expedition) we will immediately grant full justice therein.

Chapter 39, in so far as it relates to illegal disseisins, is here supplemented: remedy is provided for everyone dispossessed by the Crown " *sine legali judicio parium suorum.*" Yet, a distinction is drawn between wrongs inflicted by John himself (where summary methods are to rule) and by his predecessors (where less precipitate procedure must take its course).

The Articles of the Barons had recognized the same distinction, while providing somewhat different treatment. Those disseised by Henry or Richard were to get redress " according to the judgment of their peers in the King's court "; those disseised by John, " according to the judgment of the twenty-five barons." Both cases were, in the Articles, qualified by a stipulation which calls for comment. John had taken the crusader's vow a few months before, and now claimed the usual three years' " respite " from all legal proceedings. The barons, viewing John's vow as a notorious perjury, rejected his claim. The Articles referred the question to arbitration. The prelates, whose *judicium* on this point was declared to be final (" *appellatione remota* "), and who were bound to give an early decision (" *ad certum diem* "), might not unreasonably have been suspected of partiality, since " taking the cross " was not a step to be belittled by churchmen. Yet they seem to have acted in a spirit of not unfair compromise, if the clause as it finally appeared in John's Magna Carta may be taken as giving the substance of their award.

In cases where John himself had been the disseisor, the twenty-five executors might decide forthwith. Respite was allowed, however, in respect of disseisins of Henry and Richard (except where legal proceedings were already pending).[1] The Charter says nothing of the procedure at the close of the three years; but there was probably no

---

[1] This " benefit of a crusader " was extended to John in three other sets of complaints, specified in c. 53 (*q.v.*).

2 F

intention to depart from the terms of the Articles in this respect, namely, " judgment of peers in the King's court."

John had good reason to consider as unfair the mode here appointed for deciding disputes as to the other class of disseisins, namely, those effected by him : many delicate points would be referred to the summary decision of a baronial committee, sure to be composed of his most bitter enemies—the very men, perhaps, who claimed to have been dispossessed. If the " judgment of the twenty-five" meant for the barons " the judgment of peers," it meant for the King the judgment of inferiors and enemies.[1]

CHAPTER FIFTY-THREE.

EUNDEM autem respectum habebimus, et eodem modo de justicia exhibenda de forestis deafforestandis vel remansuris forestis, quas Henricus pater noster vel Ricardus frater noster afforestaverunt, et de custodiis terrarum que sunt de alieno feodo, cujusmodi custodias hucusque habuimus occasione feodi quod aliquis de nobis tenuit per servicium militare, et de abbaciis que fundate fuerint in feodo alterius quam nostro, in quibus dominus feodi dixerit se jus habere; et cum redierimus, vel si remanserimus a peregrinacione nostra, super hiis conquerentibus plenam justiciam statim exhibebimus.[2]

> We shall have, moreover, the same respite and in the same manner in rendering justice concerning the disafforestation or retention of those forests which Henry our father and Richard our brother afforested, and concerning the wardship of lands which are of the fief of another (namely, such wardships as we have hitherto had by reason of a fief which anyone held of us by knight's service), and concerning abbeys founded on other fiefs than our own, in which the lord of the fee claims to have

---

[1] This chapter embraced not merely estates retained in John's possession, but also those granted out anew. If the former owner recovered these, the Crown was bound to make good the loss caused by the eviction. The case of Welshmen is specially treated in c. 56 (*q.v.*).

[2] The words, "*et eodem modo, de justicia exhibenda,*" and "*vel remansuris forestis*" are written at the foot of both the Cottonian versions. Cf. *supra*, 195 n. They make clear, rather than add to, the meaning of the rest.

right; and when we have returned, or if we desist from our expedition, we will immediately grant full justice to all who complain of such things.

This chapter makes an addition to the Articles of the Barons, extending to three additional kinds of abuses, the respite provided in chapter 52 for redressing acts of illegal disseisin. The " close time " secured to John in virtue of his crusader's vow is to cover (a) inquiries into boundaries of forests alleged to have been extended by his father or his brother; (b) wardships over lands usurped by illegal extensions of prerogative wardship; and (c) abbeys founded by mesne lords but seized by John during vacancies.[1]

CHAPTER FIFTY-FOUR.

Nullus capiatur nec imprisonetur propter appellum femine de morte alterius quam viri sui.

> No one shall be arrested or imprisoned upon the appeal of a woman, for the death of any other than her husband.

The object of this chapter was to find a remedy for what the barons evidently considered an unfair advantage enjoyed by women appellants, who were allowed to appoint some champion to act for them in the *duellum*, while the accused man had to fight for himself. The connectioɩ. between appeal and battle, and the distinction between battle following on appeal and battle on a writ of right, have already been explained.[2] In civil pleas, neither party could fight in person : champions were essential, although *hired* champions were condemned.[3] In criminal pleas, the parties must fight in their own persons. This distinction is not so illogical as it seems at first sight, for the appellant himself, in the one case, and the champion who fought for

---

[1] It thus supplements three previous chapters (a) c. 47 ; (b) c. 37 ; and (c) c. 46 respectively.

[2] Cf. *supra*, c. 36.

[3] Bracton, folio 151b, cites the case of a champion sentenced to mutilation of a foot because he confessed that he was paid to appear. Statute of Westminster, I. (c. 41), enacted that champions need not swear to personal knowledge. Neilson, *Trial by Combat*, 48-51.

him, in the other, were both supposed to be eye-witnesses of the facts.[1]

In a case of homicide, no private accuser would be heard unless he alleged that he had seen the accused actually do the deed. The stringency of this rule was, however, modified by legal fictions. The near relation, or the feudal lord, of the slain man, was treated as constructively present at his slaying. This, at least, is the most plausible interpretation of Glanvill's words : " No one is admissible to prove the accusation unless he be allied in blood to the deceased or be connected with him by the tie of homage or lordship, *so that* he can speak of the death upon testimony of his own sight." [2]

The rule which required an appellant to offer proof by his own body was also relaxed in certain cases; women, men over sixty, and those with broken bones or who had lost a limb, an ear, a nose, or an eye, might fight by proxy.[3] The privilege accorded to women was looked on with disfavour : accordingly, the man accused by a woman might, in Glanvill's words, elect either " to abide by the woman's proof or to purge himself by the ordeal." [4] This option was freely used; an appellee in 1201 was allowed to go to the ordeal of water,[5] while two years later when the widow of a murdered man offered to prove her accusation " as the court shall consider," the accused " elected to bear the iron."[6] After the virtual abolition of ordeal in 1215, appeals by women were usually determined *per patriam* : such is the doctrine of Bracton,[7] whose authority is borne out by recorded cases. Thus in 1221, a man accused by a woman of her husband's murder offered fifteen marks for a verdict of the jurors.[8]

---

[1] The appellant "in all cases except murder, that is, secret homicide, made oath as a witness that he had seen and heard the deed." Neilson, *Trial by Combat*, 48.

[2] Glanvill, XIV. c. 3.

[3] See Bracton, II. ff., 142b, 145b; also Neilson, *Trial by Combat* 47, and authorities there cited.

[4] Glanvill, XIV. c. 3.   [5] *Sel. Pleas of the Crown*, No. 1.

[6] *Ibid.*, No. 68. Cf. No. 119.   [7] Bracton, folio 142b.

[8] *Select Pleas of the Crown*, No. 130.

A woman's right of accusation (even when thus safe-guarded from abuse) was restricted to two occasions, the murder of her husband and the rape of her own person. Magna Carta mentions only one of these two grounds of appeal; but silence on the subject of assault need not be interpreted as indicating any intention to deprive women of their rights in such cases.[1]

The present chapter of the Great Charter confines itself to appeals of murder, declaring that no woman has the right to institute proceedings in this way for the death of father, son, or friend, but only for that of her husband. Hard as this rule may seem, the barons here made no change on existing law. Glanvill does not recognize a woman's appeal save for the death of her husband:[2]— "A woman is heard in this suit accusing anyone of her husband's death, if she speak as being an eye-witness to the fact, because husband and wife are one flesh"—another example of constructive presence.[3]

There seems to be no authority for Coke's hasty infer-ence, that previous to 1215 a woman had an appeal for the death of any of her " ancestors " :[4] this chapter was purely declaratory. Yet its provisions were by no means gallant. The barons were more careful to guard themselves against risk than to champion the cause of women.[5]

---

[1] The Act 6 Richard II. c. 6, to prevent the woman's connivance, extended the right of appeal in such cases to a woman's husband, father, or other near relative ; but denied the appellee's right to the option of defending himself by battle—thus proving no exception to the policy of discouraging the *duellum* wherever possible.

[2] Glanvill, XIV. c. 3.

[3] Fleta I. c. 33 seems to indicate the same doctrine when he speaks " *de morte viri sui inter brachia sua interfecti*," although laboured explanations are some-times attempted, *e.g.* Coke, *Second Institute*, 93. Pollock and Maitland (I. 468 n.) dismiss the phrase *inter brachia sua* as " only a picturesque common form."

[4] See Coke, *Second Institute*, p. 68, and contrast Pollock and Maitland, I. 468. John's justices rejected in 1202 a woman's claim to appeal for her father's death, and some ten years later two claims for the death of sons. See *Select Pleas of the Crown*, Nos. 32, 117, and 118 ; yet *Gloucester Pleas* (No. 482) records n 1221 a woman's appeal for a sister's death.

[5] A peculiarity of wording should, perhaps, be noticed. It restricts explicitly not appeals, but " arrest and imprisonment " following on appeal.

CHAPTER FIFTY-FIVE.

OMNES fines qui injuste et contra legem terre facti sunt nobiscum, et omnia amerciamenta facta injuste et contra legem terre, omnino condonentur, vel fiat inde per judicium viginti quinque baronum de quibus fit mencio inferius in securitate pacis, vel per judicium majoris partis eorundem, una cum predicto Stephano Cantuariensi archiepiscopo, si interesse poterit, et aliis quos secum ad hoc vocare voluerit : et si interesse non poterit, nichilominus procedat negocium sine eo, ita quod, si aliquis vel aliqui de predictis viginti quinque baronibus fuerint in simili querela, amoveantur quantum ad hoc judicium, et alii loco eorum per residuos de eisdem viginti quinque, tantum ad hoc faciendum electi et jurati substituantur.

> All fines made with us unjustly and against the law of the land, and all amercements imposed unjustly and against the law of the land, shall be entirely remitted, or else it shall be done concerning them according to the decision of the five-and-twenty barons of whom mention is made below in the clause for securing the peace, or according to the judgment of the majority of the same, along with the aforesaid Stephen, archbishop of Canterbury, if he can be present, and such others as he may wish to bring with him for this purpose, and if he cannot be present the business shall nevertheless proceed without him, provided always that if any one or more of the aforesaid five-and-twenty barons are in a similar suit, they shall be removed as far as concerns this particular judgment, others being substituted in their places after having been selected by the rest of the same five-and-twenty for this purpose only, and after having been sworn.

The thirty-seventh of the Articles, forming the draft of this chapter, refers specially to fines exacted by John from widows for the peaceful enjoyment of their own and their husband's estates ("*pro dotibus, maritagiis, et hereditatibus*") : it forms thus a natural supplement to chapter 7. The earlier chapter had confirmed widows in their rights for the future; this one remits fines unjustly taken in the past. It is probable that the Articles of the Barons did not intend to limit their own operation to this one group of unjust fines; and they mention amercements without qualification. In any view, the terms of Magna Carta were broadened out to embrace illegal fines and amercements of every sort.[1]

The distinction between fines and amercements has been explained in a former chapter.[2] The system of arbitrary fines culminated in the reign of John, whose talents were well suited to the development of its ingenious and mean details. Dr. Stubbs describes the product of John's labours as "the system of fines which was elaborated into that minute and grotesque instrument of torture which all the historians of the reign have dwelt on in great detail,"[3] and Hallam has a passage which has become classical :—" The Bishop of Winchester paid a tun of good wine for not reminding the King (John) to give a girdle to the countess of Albemarle; and Robert de Vaux five best palfreys, that the same King might hold his peace about Henry Pinel's wife. Another paid four marks for leave to eat (*pro licentia comedendi*)."[4]

Unique procedure was provided by the present chapter for deciding disputes as to the legality of fines and amercements. Authority to decide was vested in a board of arbitrators to consist of thirteen or more of the twenty-five executors, together with Stephen Langton and such others as he chose to summon. No mention is made of the maximum number whom the primate might nominate, and there is no attempt to define their powers relative to the other members, a somewhat unbusinesslike omission, but one which testifies to the confidence placed in Langton by those who approved its terms. Care is taken to prevent members of the twenty-five from sitting in judgment on suits arising from circumstances resembling their own.

[1] In its expanded form the clause becomes a supplement also to cc. 20, 21, and 22 (which defined procedure at amercements), and to cc. 36 and 40 (which condemned John's practice of refusing writs and justice until heavy fines were offered).

[2] See *supra*, c. 20.   [3] See Preface to W. Coventry, II. lxix.

[4] *Middle Ages*, II. 438. Hallam's examples are all drawn from Madox, I. 507-9. Other illustrations of fines and amercements may be found under several of the foregoing chapters. Every man who began a plea and lost it, or abandoned it, was amerced.

This chapter, like others addressed to special needs of John's reign, found no echo in future charters.

CHAPTER FIFTY-SIX.

Si nos disseisivimus vel elongavimus Walenses de terris vel libertatibus vel rebus aliis, sine legali judicio parium suorum, in Anglia vel in Wallia,[1] eis statim reddantur; et si contencio super hoc orta fuerit, tunc inde fiat in marchia per judicium parium suorum, de tenementis Anglie secundum legem Anglie, de tenementis Wallie secundum legem Wallie, de tenementis marchie secundum legem marchie. Idem facient Walenses nobis et nostris.

> If we have disseised or removed Welshmen from lands or liberties, or other things, without the legal judgment of their peers in England or in Wales, they shall be immediately restored to them; and if a dispute arise over this, then let it be decided in the marches by the judgment of their peers; for tenements in England according to the law of England, for tenements in Wales according to the law of Wales, and for tenements in the marches according to the law of the marches. Welshmen shall do the same to us and ours.

Three chapters, redressing wrongs suffered by Welshmen, testify to the importance attached by the barons to the Welsh alliance. Restoration is to be made (a) of illegal disseisins effected by John (chapter 56); (b) of those effected by Henry II. and Richard I. (chapter 57); and (c) of hostages and charters delivered to John as pledges of peace (chapter 58).

This chapter does for Welshmen dispossessed by John what chapter 52 did for Englishmen, but substitutes "in marchia per judicium parium suorum" for the "per judicium viginti quinque baronum" of the earlier chapter. The "venue" was thus fixed in the marchland for all Welshmen's cases, although different kinds of law were to be applied according to the situation of the property in

---

[1] The words "in Anglia vel in Wallia" are written at the foot of one of the Cottonian versions (cf. supra, 166 n.); but they appear in situ in the Articles of the Barons.

dispute. This indication of the existence of three distinct bodies of law, one for England, another for Wales, and a third for the marches, shows that the unifying task of the common law had not yet been completed. Interesting questions of a nature analogous to those treated by the branch of modern jurisprudence known as International Private Law must constantly have arisen.

All three classes of alleged disseisins (whatever the law involved) were to be decided by a *judicium parium*; but the "peers" of a Welshman were not defined—a vital omission.[1]

CHAPTER FIFTY-SEVEN.

DE omnibus autem illis de quibus aliquis Walensium disseisitus fuerit vel elongatus sine legali judicio parium suorum per Henricum regem patrem nostrum vel Ricardum regem fratrem nostrum, que nos in manu nostra habemus, vel que alii tenent que nos oporteat warantizare, respectum habebimus usque ad communem terminum crucesignatorum, illis exceptis de quibus placitum motum fuit vel inquisicio facta per preceptum nostrum ante suscepcionem crucis nostre : cum autem redierimus, vel si forte remanserimus a peregrinacione nostra, statim eis inde plenam justiciam exhibebimus, secundum leges Walensium et partes predictas.

> Further, for all those possessions from which any Welshman has, without the lawful judgment of his peers, been disseised or removed by King Henry our father, or King Richard our brother, and which we retain in our hand (or which are possessed by others, to whom we are bound to warrant them) we shall have respite until the usual term of crusaders ; excepting those things about which a plea has been raised or an inquest made by our order before we took the cross ; but as soon as we return, (or if perchance we desist from our expedition), we will immediately grant full justice in accordance with the laws of the Welsh and in relation to the foresaid regions.

The provisions for Welshmen unjustly dispossessed by Henry or Richard are identical with those made in the

[1] Cf. Harcourt's comment, "A bad piece of work this" (*Steward*, 220).

latter part of chapter 52 for Englishmen, except for the last words, " in accordance with the laws of the Welsh in relation to the foresaid districts " : no machinery is here specified for declaring or applying these laws.

The Articles of the Barons had, however, mentioned the procedure to be adopted; and a comparison of articles 25 and 44 with this chapter suggests the antithesis between " *per judicium parium suorum in curia regis* " for Englishmen, and " *in marchia per judicium parium suorum* " for Welshmen.

CHAPTER FIFTY-EIGHT.

Nos reddemus filium Lewelini statim, et omnes obsides de Wallia, et cartas que nobis liberate fuerunt in securitatem pacis.

> We will immediately give up the son of Llywelyn and all the hostages of Wales, and the charters delivered to us as security for the peace.

The treatment of hostages in general and Welsh hostages in particular has already been illustrated.[1] The patent and close rolls show a constant coming and going of these living pledges of the peace. A writ of 18th December, 1214, for example, bade Engelard of Cigogné restore three Welsh nobles to Llywelyn.[2] Since then, new hostages, including Llywelyn's son, had been handed over; and charters also had been pledged.

The Articles of the Barons had treated this question as an open one, referring it to the arbitration of Stephen Langton and others he might nominate. The point had apparently been decided in favour of the Welsh before the Charter was engrossed in its final form.[3] John is now

---

[1] See *supra*, p. 441.　　　　　　[2] See *supra*, p. 445.

[3] No. 45 of the Articles is connected by a rude bracket with No. 46 (relating to Scotland) ; and a saving clause, thus made applicable to both, is added with some appearance of haste : " *nisi aliter esse debeat per cartas quas rex habet, per judicium archiepiscopi et aliorum quos secum vocare voluerit.*" Cf. *supra*, p. 38. So far as related to Scotch affairs, the King's *caveat* found its way, in an altered form, into Magna Carta. See c. 59.

made to promise an immediate surrender of hostages and charters.

The Welsh prince must have breathed more freely when this was fulfilled. Soon, with a light heart, his son by his side, he renewed hostilities. Gualo, on 11th November, 1216, laid interdict on the whole of Wales for holding with the barons.[1] By the treaty of Lambeth, Louis was to send a copy of the peace to Llywelyn and the other Welsh princes.[2]

CHAPTER FIFTY-NINE.

Nos faciemus Alexandro regi Scottorum de sororibus suis, et obsidibus reddendis, et libertatibus suis, et jure suo, secundum formam in qua faciemus aliis baronibus nostris Anglie, nisi aliter esse debeat per cartas quas habemus de Willelmo patre ipsius, quondam rege Scottorum; et hoc erit per judicium parium suorum in curia nostra.

> We will do towards Alexander, King of Scots, concerning the return of his sisters and his hostages, and concerning his franchises, and his right, in the same manner as we shall do towards our other barons of England, unless it ought to be otherwise according to the charters which we hold from William his father, formerly King of Scots; and this shall be according to the judgment of his peers in our court.

The barons welcomed allies whether from Wales or Scotland; and this chapter was dictated by a desire to conciliate Alexander. John was forced to promise to restore to the King of Scots his sisters and other hostages, together with his franchises and his " right."

Opinions have been, and still are, sharply divided as to whether, or in what degree, Scotland was subject to feudal overlordship. David I. and his successors, Kings of Scotland, had been wont to do fealty and homage to the Kings of England; but this fact has received different interpretations. Such homage, it is argued, was performed in respect of certain English baronies which happened to belong by hereditary right to the Kings of Scotland,

[1] Annals of Waverley, *sub anno* 1216.   [2] *New Rymer*, I. 148.

namely, the earldom of Huntingdon, and the counties of Northumberland, Cumberland, and Westmoreland. The terms of homage did not indicate for what fiefs it was sworn—whether for the English earldoms alone, or for the country north of Tweed as well.

The position of the Kings of Scots remained ambiguous, until William the Lion was placed at a terrible disadvantage by his capture at Alnwick in 1174. To gain release, he ratified the Treaty of Falaise on 8th December, of that year, by which he agreed to hold his territories as fiefs of the English Crown. All his tenants in Scotland were to take oath to Henry; while hostages were surrendered, along with the castles of Berwick, Roxburgh, Jedburgh, Edinburgh, and Stirling.[1]

Henry's diplomacy was undone by his successor. Richard, preparing for his crusade of 1190, sold recklessly every right that would fetch a price : William bought back the independence of his kingdom; but this restoration of the relations that prevailed previous to 1174, involved a restoration of the old ambiguities. When Richard died, William despatched ambassadors to England, pressing claims upon the northern counties, promising to support John's title in return for their admission, and adding threats.[2] John avoided committing himself until his position in England was assured; thereafter he commanded William to do homage unconditionally. The Scots King disregarded the first summons, but yielded to a second, yet " reserving always his own right." [3] The saving clause left everything vague as before.

In April, 1209, the King of Scots incurred John's displeasure. William's only son, Alexander, was demanded as a hostage, or alternatively three border castles must be delivered up. After a refusal, the old King gave in on

---

[1] See Ramsay, *Angevin Empire*, 183-4. In the spring of 1185 Henry confirmed William's claim to Huntingdon, and the Scots King transferred it to his brother David ; *ibid.*, 226 n.

[2] See Miss Norgate, *John Lackland*, 66.

[3] See Stubbs, *Const. Hist.*, I. 596 n., and Norgate, *John Lackland*, 73, 78. Cf. the words " *salvo jure suo* " with the " *et jure suo* " of Magna Carta.

7th August, 1209.[1] Alexander did homage on behalf of his father " for the aforesaid castles and other lands which he held," and found sureties for the payment of 15,000 marks. William's daughters, Margaret and Isabel, became wards of John, who had the right to bestow them in marriage.[2] There seems to have been an understanding that one of them should wed John's eldest son.[3] Margaret and Isabel, though virtually prisoners in Corfe Castle, were honourably treated there. The Close Rolls contain orders for supplying them with articles of comfort and luxury. Thus on 6th July, 1213, John instructed the Mayor of Winchester to despatch in haste, for the use of his niece Eleanor and of the two Scots princesses, robes of dark green (tunics and super-tunics) with capes of cambric and fur of miniver, together with twenty-three yards of good linen cloth, with light shoes for summer wear, " and the Mayor is to come himself with all the above articles to Corfe, there to receive the money for the cost of the same." [4]

Meanwhile, events in Scotland had favoured English pretensions. In 1212, Cuthred, a claimant for the Scottish throne, endeavoured to dethrone King William. English succour was asked and paid for by a treaty sealed at Norham on 7th February, 1212, by which William granted to John the right to marry the young Alexander, then fourteen years of age, " *sicut hominem suum ligium*," to whomsoever he would, at any time within the next six years, but always " without disparagement." [5] William pledged himself and his son to keep faith and allegiance to John's son, Henry, " as their liege lord " against all mortals.[6] William had saved his Crown, but Scotland was sinking into the position

---

[1] *New Rymer*, I. 103, where "Northampton" is apparently a mistake for "Norham." See Ramsay, *Angevin Empire*, 421 n.

[2] Ramsay, *ibid.*, and authorities there cited.

[3] Ramsay, *Angevin Empire*, 421, and authorities.

[4] *Rot. Claus.*, I. 144, and I. 157. This Eleanor was the sister of Prince Arthur. The fortunes of war had in 1202 placed both of them in John's hands. Arthur disappeared—murdered it was supposed ; Eleanor remained a prisoner for life ; the Scots princesses were virtually her fellow-prisoners for a time in Corfe Castle.

[5] See *supra*, c. 6.

[6] *New Rymer*, I. 104. See also W. Coventry, II. 206.

of a vassal state. On 28th October, 1213, Innocent III. ordered the King of Scotland and his son to show fealty and devotion to King John.[1]

William the Lion died at Stirling on 4th December, 1214, and Alexander's peaceful succession was facilitated by the knowledge that he had the support of John. Such was the position of affairs when John was brought to bay at Runnymede. The barons were willing to bid for the alliance of Alexander; yet it was unnecessary to bid high. John was made to promise to restore Alexander's sisters and other hostages unconditionally, but words were used which committed him on none of the disputed points.[2] Franchises and "right" were to be restored only in so far as accorded with William's "charters," as interpreted by the judgment of the English barons in the court of the English King.

The allusion in the text to the Scottish King as one among " our other barons of England" need not be pressed against Alexander, any more than similar expressions should be pressed against John, whose position as Duke of Normandy and Aquitaine in no way made England a fief of the French Crown or prevented him becoming a vassal of Rome. In questions affecting his feudal position in France, John's peers were the dukes and counts of that country; and similarly those who had a right to sit in judgment as Alexander's peers over his claims to English fiefs were the English earls and barons. Such a tribunal was not likely to give decisions favourable to Scots pretensions, at the expense of England.[3]

Alexander, though no party to the treaty at Runnymede,

---

[1] See *New Rymer*, I. 116.

[2] Both ladies, however, remained prisoners after Henry III.'s accession. Peter de Maulay, constable of Corfe Castle, was, in that King's fifth year, credited with sums expended on their behalf. *Rot. Claus.*, I. 466; see also I. 483. Both found permanent homes in England—Margaret as wife of Hubert de Burgh, Isabel as wife of Roger Bigod. See Ramsay, *Angevin Empire*, 421, and authorities there cited.

[3] No. 46 of the Articles referred the question of Alexander's "right" to the judgment of Langton and his nominees, for which Magna Carta substituted "judgment of his peers in our court."

was willing to profit by it : on 7th July, 1215, he despatched the Bishop of St. Andrews and five laymen to John "concerning our business which we have against you to be transacted in your court."[1] Nothing came of this; and Alexander invaded England in order to push his claims. John swore his usual oath, "by God's teeth," that he would "chase the little red-haired fox-cub from his hiding-holes."[2]

By the treaty of Lambeth (12th September, 1217), Louis and Henry were each to send a copy of the peace to Alexander that he might be included in its terms on his restoring castles, lands, and prisoners, taken by him in the war.[3] On 23rd September, they joined in urging him to restore Carlisle, and Alexander, anxious to preserve his English honour of Huntingdon, was constrained to yield.[4] The deeper question at issue between England and Scotland was still unsolved when the relations between the two countries entered on a new phase, as a consequence of the attempts at annexation made by Edward I., "the hammer of the Scots."

CHAPTER SIXTY.

OMNES autem istas consuetudines predictas et libertates quas nos concessimus in regno nostro tenendas quantum ad nos pertinet erga nostros, omnes de regno nostro, tam clerici quam laici, observent quantum ad se pertinet erga suos.

> Moreover, all these aforesaid customs and liberties, the observance of which we have granted in our kingdom as far as pertains to us towards our men, shall be observed by all of our kingdom, as well clergy as laymen, as far as pertains to them towards their men.

It would have been as impolitic as it was obviously unfair for the barons, in their capacity of mesne lords, to inflict upon their own tenants those very exactions which they compelled the King to abjure as against themselves. Accordingly, the benefit of the "customs and liberties"

---

[1] *New Rymer*, I. 135. [2] M. Paris, II. 642.
[3] *New Rymer*, I. 148. [4] *Rot. Pat.*, I. 93.

conceded by John to his feudal tenants was—in a somewhat perfunctory manner, it is true—extended to the feudal tenants of all other magnates, whether cleric or lay. Although the reference to " customs and liberties " was quite general in its terms, it seems natural to infer that feudal grievances were chiefly meant, since the view of society indicated is feudal rather than national.[1]

These considerations suggest that too liberal a view has sometimes been taken of the scope of this chapter. Coke treated it as affecting not merely freeholders, but the whole mass of the people :—" This is the chief felicity of a kingdom, when good laws are reciprocally of prince and people (as is here undertaken) duly observed." [2] In this view, he has had many followers; and the present chapter has received undue emphasis as supporting a democratic interpretation of Magna Carta.[3] It has been referred to as " the only clause which affects the whole body of the people." [4] The better view is that its provisions were confined to feudal sub-tenants.

Even authors who interpret the chapter in this restricted application are still prone to exaggerate its importance. (1) The clause is sometimes regarded as springing directly from the barons' own initiative : Dr. Stubbs, contrasting it with Henry I.'s Charter of Liberties, holds that it was " adopted by the lords themselves." [5] Such praise is unmerited; the barons inserted it because they had need of allies. (2) On the other hand, credit for the clause, equally unwarranted, has been sometimes bestowed on John. Dr. Robert Henry says that " this article, which was highly reasonable, was probably inserted at the desire of the King." [6]

The substance of this chapter appears in the reissues of

[1] Harcourt, *Steward*, 221, treats this chapter as extending to manorial courts the principles regulating the *judicium parium* and amercements.

[2] *Second Institute*, 77.   [3] Cf. *supra*, p. 113.

[4] Thomson, *Magna Carta*, 269, and authorities there cited.

[5] *Const. Hist.*, I. 570. Cf. *supra*, p. 117.

[6] *History of Great Britain*, VI. 74 (1823). See also Henshall, *History of South Britain*, cited Thomson, *Magna Carta*, 268-9.

1217 and 1225; but its force there is possibly somewhat impaired by the addition of a new clause reserving to archbishops, bishops, abbots, priors, templars, hospitallers, earls, barons, and all other persons as well ecclesiastical as secular, all the franchises and free customs they previously had [1]—a "saving clause" that might be turned to various uses.

CHAPTER SIXTY-ONE.

Cum autem pro Deo, et ad emendacionem regni nostri, et ad melius sopiendam discordiam inter nos et barones nostros ortam, hec omnia predicta concesserimus, volentes ea integra et firma stabilitate in perpetuum [2] gaudere, facimus et concedimus eis securitatem subscriptam; videlicet quod barones eligant viginti quinque barones de regno quos voluerint, qui debeant pro totis viribus suis observare, tenere, et facere observari, pacem et libertates quas eis concessimus, et hac presenti carta nostra confirmavimus, ita scilicet quod, si nos, vel justiciarius noster, vel ballivi nostri, vel aliquis de ministris nostris, in aliquo erga aliquem deliquerimus, vel aliquem articulorum pacis aut securitatis transgressi fuerimus, et delictum ostensum fuerit quatuor baronibus de predictis viginti quinque baronibus, illi quatuor barones accedant ad nos vel ad justiciarum nostrum, si fuerimus extra regnum, proponentes nobis excessum, petent ut excessum illum sine dilacione faciamus emendari. Et si nos excessum non emendaverimus, vel, si fuerimus extra regnum justiciarius noster non emendaverit, infra tempus quadraginta dierum computandum a tempore quo monstratum fuerit nobis vel justiciario nostro si extra regnum fuerimus, predicti quatuor barones referant causam illam ad residuos de illis viginti quinque baronibus, et illi viginti quinque barones cum communa tocius terre distringent et gravabunt nos modis omnibus quibus pote-

---

[1] See c. 46 of 1217.

[2] The words "*in perpetuum*" are written at the foot of one of the Cottonian versions. See *supra*, 166 n.

runt, scilicet per capcionem castrorum, terrarum, possessionum, et aliis modis quibus poterunt, donec fuerit
emendatum secundum arbitrium eorum, salva persona
nostra et regine nostre et liberorum nostrorum; et cum
fuerit emendatum intendent nobis sicut prius fecerunt.
Et quicumque voluerit de terra juret quod ad predicta
omnia exequenda parebit mandatis predictorum viginti
quinque baronum, et quod gravabit nos pro posse suo cum
ipsis, et nos publice et libere damus licenciam jurandi
cuilibet qui jurare voluerit, et nulli umquam jurare pro-
hibebimus. Omnes autem illos de terra qui per se et
sponte sua noluerint jurare viginti quinque baronibus, de
distringendo et gravando nos cum eis, faciemus jurare
eosdem de mandato nostro, sicut predictum est. Et si
aliquis de viginti quinque baronibus decesserit, vel a terra
recesserit, vel aliquo alio modo impeditus fuerit, quominus
ista predicta possent exequi, qui residui fuerint de predictis viginti quinque baronibus eligant alium loco ipsius,
pro arbitrio suo, qui simili modo erit juratus quo et ceteri.
In omnibus autem que istis viginti quinque baronibus
committuntur exequenda, si forte ipsi viginti quinque
presentes fuerint, et inter se super re aliqua discordaverint,
vel aliqui ex eis summoniti nolint vel nequeant interesse,
ratum habeatur et firmum quod major pars eorum qui
presentes fuerint providerit, vel preceperit, ac si omnes
viginti quinque in hoc consensissent; et predicti viginti
quinque jurent quod omnia antedicta fideliter observabunt,
et pro toto posse suo facient observari. Et nos nichil
impetrabimus ab aliquo, per nos nec per alium, per quod
aliqua istarum concessionum et libertatum revocetur vel
minuatur; et, si aliquid tale impetratum fuerit, irritum sit
et inane et numquam eo utemur per nos nec per alium.

Since, moreover, for God and the amendment of our kingdom
and for the better allaying of the quarrel that has arisen between
us and our barons, we have granted all these concessions, de-
sirous that they should enjoy them in complete and firm endurance for ever, we give and grant to them the under-written security,
namely, that the barons choose five-and-twenty barons of the
kingdom, whomsoever they will, who shall be bound with all their
might, to observe and hold, and cause to be observed, the peace

and liberties we have granted and confirmed to them by this ou present Charter, so that if we, or our justiciar, or our bailiffs or any one of our officers, shall in anything be at fault toward anyone, or shall have broken any one of the articles of the peace or of this security, and the offence be notified to four barons of the foresaid five-and-twenty, the said four barons shall repair to us (or our justiciar, if we are out of the realm) and, laying the transgression before us, petition to have that transgression redressed without delay. And if we shall not have corrected the transgression (or, in the event of our being out of the realm, if our justiciar shall not have corrected it) within forty days, reckoning from the time it has been intimated to us (or to our justiciar, if we should be out of the realm), the four barons aforesaid shall refer that matter to the rest of the five-and-twenty barons, and those five-and-twenty barons shall, together with the community of the whole land, distrain and distress us in all possible ways, namely, by seizing our castles, lands, possessions, and in any other way they can, until redress has been obtained as they deem fit, saving harmless our own person, and the persons of our queen and children ; and when redress has been obtained, they shall resume their old relations towards us. And let whoever in the country desires it, swear to obey the orders of the said five-and-twenty barons for the execution of all the aforesaid matters, and along with them, to molest us to the utmost of his power ; and we publicly and freely grant leave to every one who wishes to swear. and we shall never forbid anyone to swear. All those, moreover, in the land who of themselves and of their own accord are unwilling to swear to the twenty-five to help them in constraining and molesting us, we shall by our command compel the same to swear to the effect foresaid. And if any one of the five-and-twenty barons shall have died or departed from the land, or be incapacitated in any other manner which would prevent the foresaid provisions being carried out, those of the said twenty-five barons who are left shall choose another in his place according to their own judgment, and he shall be sworn in the same way as the others. Further, in all matters, the execution of which is intrusted to these twenty-five barons, if perchance these twenty-five are present and disagree about anything, or if some of them, after being summoned, are unwilling or unable to be present, that which the majority of those present ordain or command shall be held as fixed and established, exactly as if the whole twenty-five had concurred in this ; and the said twenty-five shall swear that they will faithfully observe all that is aforesaid, and cause it to be observed with all their might. And we shall procure nothing from anyone, directly or indirectly, whereby any part of these concessions and liberties might be revoked or diminished ; and if any such thing has been procured, let it be void and null, and we shall never use it personally or by another.

This important chapter stands by itself, providing machinery for enforcing all that precedes it. It thus forms what modern jurisprudence would describe as the " sanction " of the whole, but what was known in the current phrase of its own day as " the form of security " (*forma securitatis ad observandum pacem et libertates*).[1] It contains the only executive clause of the Charter, the sole constitutional machinery.[2]

I. *The " Security " or legal Sanction.* The procedure devised for enforcing the Charter was crude : John conferred upon twenty-five of his enemies a legal right to organize rebellion, whenever in their opinion he had broken any one of the provisions of Magna Carta. Violence might be legally used against him, until he redressed their alleged grievances " to their own satisfaction " (*secundum arbitrium eorum*). If it had been possible to put so violent an expedient into practice, the " sovereignty," or supreme power in England, would have been split into two. John would have held the sceptre only until his opponents declared that he had broken the Charter, when, by his own previously-granted mandate, it would pass to the twenty-five barons forming what has been variously styled a " Committee of Remonstrance and Constraint " or a " Committee of Rebellion." [3]

The procedure for redressing grievances is described in some detail ; the wronged party must make known his case to four barons of the twenty-five, who would then make it known to the King, and ask redress. If John refused or

---

[1] This phrase occurs in the 49th (and last) of the Articles, as the title of a clause separated from the others by a blank of the width of several lines of writing : " *Haec est forma securitatis*," etc. The words are not used as a heading in the present chapter itself, but c. 52 refers to c. 61 as the clause " *in securitate pacis*," and c. 62 refers to it as " *super securitate ista*."

[2] *Histoire des ducs*, 150, has a commentary on this chapter : " Over and above all this they desired that 25 barons should be chosen, and by the judgment of these 25 the King should govern them in all things, and through them redress all the wrongs that he should do to them, and they also, on the other hand, would through them redress all the wrongs that they should do to him. Also they further desired, along with all this, that the King should never have power to appoint a bailiff in his land except through the 25." Cf. *supra*, p. 123 and p. 177.

[3] Cf. S. R. Gardiner, *Short History of England*, 183 : " a permanent organization for making war against the King."

unduly delayed, compulsion might be used. On the matter of undue delay, the Articles of the Barons said " within a reasonable time to be determined in the Charter." The Charter did determine this, naming forty days. Compulsion might take any form, except violence against the person of the King, or of his wife or children.

II. *Minor details*. Although the whole expedient seems chimerical to the modern mind, the opposition leaders in 1215 evidently thought they had devised a practicable scheme of government. This is shown by the care with which they elaborated the procedure.

(1) *Appointment of the twenty-five executors*. The members of the committee were to be, in the first instance, " elected " by the " barons." Vacancies were to be filled by the method now known as " co-optation ": the committee, once appointed, would form a close corporation; no one uncongenial to the majority could gain admission —an arrangement with a thoroughly oligarchic flavour. The provision for supplying vacancies caused by death proves that the scheme was not to be temporary.

Writs, issued to the sheriffs on 19th June, command the enforcement of the oath to the twenty-five barons, but do not mention them by name. Matthew Paris supplies the omission, and though he does not disclose the source of his information, it is unlikely that so comprehensive a list could be entirely a work of the imagination.[1] They occur in the following order, the earls of Hertford, Aumâle, Gloucester, Winchester, Hereford, Norfolk, and Oxford, William Marshall the younger, Robert fitz Walter the elder, Gilbert de Clare, Eustace de Vesci, Hugh Bigod, William of Mowbray, William Hardell (Mayor of London), William de Lanvalei, Robert de Ros, John de Lacy (Constable of Chester), Richard de Perci, John fitz Robert, William Mallet, Geoffrey de Say, Roger de Mumbezon, William of Huntingfield, Richard de Muntfitchet, and William of Albini.[2] There are here no churchmen and

---

[1] R. Wendover, from whom Paris borrows so freely, gives no list.

[2] The list is from Matthew Paris, II. 604-5, as corrected by Blackstone, *Great Charter*, p. xx, after collation with a marginal note on the Harleian MS. of the

no members of the moderate party whose names appear in the preamble. All except two, or at most three, were declared enemies of John.[1] It was an oligarchy of disaffected Crown tenants, whose baronial homogeneity was only broken by the presence of the Mayor of London. Such a committee was not likely to use its powers to further other interests than its own.

(2) *A majority to form a quorum.* Driven by necessity the barons devised, or stumbled upon, a peculiarly modern expedient. Unanimity would be difficult to obtain. It was provided, accordingly, that the will of the majority of those present should prevail. It would be inaccurate to say, in modern phraseology, that thirteen formed a quorum, since the quorum varied with the number of those present. No provision was made for summoning or constituting this committee, and room was thus left for packed meetings: one faction, hurriedly convened, might usurp the rights of the whole body. The precedent tentatively introduced, for allowing a majority to act for the whole, was followed only timidly and at intervals. Still, its appearance in John's Charter marks a stage in the advance of the principle of modern politics which substitutes the " counting of heads for the breaking of them." [2]

(3) *The sub-committee of four.* Four of the twenty-five executors were to act as intermediaries between aggrieved individuals and the King. Such a position involved discretionary powers; for, if the four refused to endorse the justice of any complaint, John also would be in safety to refuse.[3]

charter (cf. *supra*, p. 168 n.). For biographical information, see Thomson, *Magna Carta*, 270-312.

[1] These three were Earl Aumâle (a title sometimes exchanged for Earl of York, see Round, *Geoffrey de Mandeville*, 157 n.), William of Albini, and Geoffrey de Say (see Stubbs, *Const. Hist.*, I. 583).

[2] This is not the earliest reference in English law to the binding power of a majority; Liebermann, *Gesetze*, II. 575, points to *Leges Henrici*, c. 5, s. 6 (*ibid.*, I. 549) as formulating the principle.

[3] An alternative explanation is possible, namely, that the function of intermediary might be exercised by *any* four of the twenty-five. In that view, an aggrieved individual might place pressure on the King if he persuaded any four to support his claim.

(4) *Local agents of the twenty-five executors.* In each county the twelve knights, whose original function was to preside at inquiries into "evil customs," came to act as local representatives of the revolutionary committee, being armed with power to constrain the sheriff to carry out the provisions of Magna Carta, very much as the twenty-five were authorized to constrain the King. In particular, these knights were charged with enforcement of the oath of obedience to the revolutionary committee, and with confiscating the property of all who refused.[1]

(5) *The part to be played by the public.* John authorized his subjects to side against him, if he should violate the Charter : his general mandate was granted to the twenty-five " *cum communa totius terræ,*" while licence was "freely and publicly" bestowed on everyone so disposed, to swear obedience to the executors. Two aspects of this provision require attention : (*a*) *Its relation to allegiance and treason.* John solemnly authorized his subjects, in certain circumstances, to transfer their allegiance from himself to the committee of his foes. If they refused, he agreed to their compulsion ; and on 27th June, 1215, writs were actually issued instructing the seizure of the lands and goods of all who would not swear to obey the twenty-five.[2] (*b*) *Communa totius terræ.* The "community of the whole land" was thus to afford active help in subjecting the King to the reign of law ; and the phrase has been pressed into the service of democracy by enthusiasts, who seek to magnify modern conceptions by finding their roots in the past. Few words of medieval Latin offer a more tempting field to enquirers than this *communa*, which, with its English and French equivalents, holds the key to many problems of constitutional origins. The appearance in Magna Carta of a body described as a "commune," in conjunction with an oath of obedience to a revolutionary committee, suggests comparison with the form of civic constitution known in that age as "the sworn commune."[3] The "communa" referred to in chapter 61

[1] Cf. *supra*, c. 48.　　　　　[2] See Appendix.

[3] It was fourteen years since London had extorted its "commune," in this sense, from Prince John ; cf. *supra*, c. 13.

was something widely different : to the barons at Runnymede it may have meant either the entire body of feudal
tenants or only the magnates ; but medieval analogies make
it impossible that the word could embrace the free peasantry,
still less the villeins of England. The occurrence of such
a word is far from proving that the Charter rests on any
broad or popular basis.

III. *Relations to Contemporary Theory*. Clumsy and
impracticable as the whole scheme appears to modern eyes,
it was quite in accord with medieval theory. The conception of a relation founded upon contract between lord and
vassal lies at the root of feudalism. If either party glaringly
broke the terms of the compact, the other was justified in
repudiating the relationship, but he must observe due
formalities. *Diffidatio*, intimated to his lord, must precede
any attempt of the vassal to redress his wrongs by force.
The barons at Runnymede, having complied with this preliminary, had for the moment ceased to owe fealty to John.
In reserving power to appoint an Executive Committee
(even if this be regarded as implying a right of legalized
rebellion), as a condition precedent to a renewal of allegiance, they moved in the direction of legal restraint as
opposed to revolutionary violence. The right here recognized by John, likely as it might be to lead to hostilities,
was in theory and intention an honest effort to obviate war
by recourse to the nearest approximation to constitutional
action then available. It was, further, an attempt to substitute united action of the body of feudal tenants (*communa totius terræ*) for the individual vassal's right of
private judgment, claimed and sometimes exercised in that
age, on the European continent, and actually confirmed in
1222 by Andreas II. of Hungary by his *Bulla Aurea*.[1]

The expedient contained in this chapter is a logical deduc-
tion from the vassal's right of defiance as a prelude to
private war against a lord who has wronged him. It was
no innovation, but something found by the barons in feudal
law.[2] Foreign parallels have been found for it, not only in

---

[1] Hantos, *Magna Carta*, 149, 198. Cf. Gneist, *Eng. Const.*, 251.

[2] Adams, *Origin*, 181 ff.

the more anarchic procedure of the Hungarian *Bulla Aurea*, but also in the institutions of Aragon and elsewhere.[1] When the baronial leaders in 1263 performed *diffidatio*, they echoed the words of this chapter, " *salva persona regis, reginae et liberorum suorum.*" [2]

This chapter has been acclaimed as embodying for the first time the idea that formed " the true corner stone of the English Constitution," [3] namely, the right to compel an erring King to bow to a body of law that lies outside his will.   There is much to be said for this view.   It is quite consistent, however, to combine an appreciation of the value of this conception, with an admission of the defective and clumsy nature of the machinery by which a first attempt was made to realize it.[4]

IV. *Modern Criticism.*   Until the last twenty-five years or so, commentators were wont to credit the framers of Magna Carta with anticipating most of the cardinal principles of the modern Constitution.   In combating such exaggerations, it would not be unnatural to lay emphasis on the extent to which the machinery of this chapter is condemned by the standards of the nineteenth century. Yet it is well to steer a middle course, neither praising the men of 1215, nor blaming them for failing to achieve the impossible.

The faults of the scheme, whether viewed from the side of modern theory or of modern practice, are obvious.   It was a violent measure, full of immediate dangers, and calculated to exercise a baneful influence on constitutional development in the future.   The fact that Magna Carta provided no better sanction for its own enforcement than the right of legalized rebellion, has already been discussed as its cardinal defect.[5]   It is instructive to note a few of its other defects in detail.

(1) The scheme challenged hostility by its want of

---

[1] Hantos, *op. cit.*, 150.   Adams, *Origin*, 181 n., suggests a parallel from the kingdom of Jerusalem.   Dr. Riess, *Historische Zeitschrift*, 1906, p. 170, compares also the Ephors of Sparta.

[2] *Liber de Antiquis Legibus*, 53.   [3] Adams, *Pol. Hist. Eng.*, II. 439.

[4] Cf. Adams, *Origin*, 276 n.   [5] See *supra*, p. 129.

moderation. On every vexed political question of the day, John's authority would have been superseded by that of twenty-five of the most hostile faction of the baronage. If the King thought himself aggrieved in anything, he would require to plead his cause before a tribunal in which his opponents sat as judges.[1] The scheme was thus repugnant to loyal Englishmen, who cherished a respect for the monarchy. No King would submit tamely to remain a sovereign, whose "sovereignty" existed on sufferance of his enemies. The powers thus conferred in 1215 were more sweeping than those conferred on a similar committee in 1258, and yet the Parliament which appointed the latter has been branded as "the Mad Parliament," because of the violence of its measures.

(2) Rebellion, even where morally justified, is necessarily illegal; to attempt to map out for it a legitimate sphere of action is to attempt the logically impossible. The barons had failed to rise to the true conception of a limited monarchy; their scheme recognized a King still absolute in some matters, but in others powerless and abject. The powers of the twenty-five, a body which received no proper organization, were those of aggression rather than of administration. Viewed in this modern light, the claims of the barons to constructive statesmanship rank low.

(3) The powers of the revolutionary committee, excessive though ill-defined, backed by the sworn obedience of all classes of the nation, would tend completely to paralyze the King. The nominal sovereign, nervous under this sword of Damocles, would lose all power of initiative, while the committee, powerful to reduce him to impotence, would be powerless to goad him into action or to act in his stead. The revolutionary committee had been planned as a drag on a bad executive, not as a good executive to take its place.

(4) Even as a drag, the efficiency of the committee would have been neutralized in either of two contingencies: if the barons composing it disagreed among themselves, or, if the

---

[1] Dr. Riess, *Historische Zeitschrift*, 1906, p. 170, thinks this goes too far. Cf., however, Adams, *Origin*, 179 : John "was reduced to the function of executing the judgments of a court not his own."

King refused to surrender. Not a step to restrain the King could legally be taken, until he had received formal intimation followed by an interval of forty days, during which he might complete his preparation for war without fear of interruption.

(5) If the scheme of the barons seems ill-suited to the needs of the hour of its conception, it was fraught with even greater dangers to the future development of the English constitution. The problem it sought to solve was one of no transient or unimportant nature : the barons sought the best method of turning royal promises into laws which succeeding Kings must obey. In attempting this, Magna Carta moved along lines that were radically wrong ;[1] which, if not departed from in time, would have rendered any enduring progress impossible. The statesmanship which, while leaving one King on the throne, subjected him to the dictation of " five-and-twenty over-kings " was crude and ill-advised. It is true that the party of reform, throughout the long reign of Henry III., clung to the same erroneous solution ; but they met with no success. After half a century of unrest, a settlement seemed as far distant as before. The dangers of schemes like those of 1215, 1244, and 1258 are clearly seen in contrast with the more tactful efforts of Edward I. towards a true solution, along lines leading in due time to complete success.

The true policy for the barons was to use the King's own administrative machinery and the King's own servants to control the King. The principle was slowly established that the sovereign could perform no single act of prerogative except through the agency of a particular officer or organ of the royal household; while very gradually the doctrine of ministerial responsibility grew up, compelling each officer of the Crown to obey not only the law of the land, but also the *Commune Concilium*, fast changing into the modern Parliament. The credit of starting the constitution on its right line of development is in great measure due to Edward I.[2]

[1] Cf. Adams, *Origin*, 179 : " It was not finally to be the way of the constitution."

[2] Cf. *supra*, pp. 159-164, for a sketch of Edward's policy.

V. *Failure of the Scheme.* Almost before John's Charter had been engrossed and sealed, the futility of its " sanction " was recognized. Each side grew suspicious and demanded new " sanctions " not contained in the Charter.

(1) *Quis custodiet ipsos custodes?* Magna Carta, assuming apparently that perfect trust could be placed in the revolutionary committee, provided no machinery for controlling them, no guarantee that they would observe the Charter. The futility of this complacency was soon manifest. One tyrant had brought distress on the whole nation; and now he was to be superseded by five-and-twenty. Who was to restrain the new tyrants? A second committee was nominated, partly to assist and partly to control the twenty-five. Matthew Paris [1] describes it as composed of thirty-eight " *Obsecutores et Observatores,*" including the Earl Marshal, Hubert de Burgh, the earls of Arundel and Warenne, and other prominent members of the moderate party, not unfriendly to the King. Dr. Stubbs dismisses their relations to the executors with the remark that they " swore to obey the orders of the twenty-five." [2] Miss Norgate takes what seems to be a better view, in emphasizing, as the chief reason for their appointment, the duty of compelling " both the King and the twenty-five to deal justly with one another." [3] The thirty-eight were required to constrain the twenty-five, as the twenty-five constrained the King. [4]

(2) *Suspicions of the barons' good faith.* There is evidence that the King was distrustful of the barons' good faith, and desired on his part some " sanction " that they would not again renounce allegiance. The barons' promise to grant John security, and the written protest against their breach of faith, made by Langton and other prelates at John's request, have already been described. [5]

---

[1] *Chron. Maj.*, II. 605-6. [2] *Const. Hist.*, I. 583 n. [3] *John Lackland*, 236.

[4] One version of the narrative of Matthew Paris is fuller than the other. " *Isti omnes juraverunt quod obsequerentur mandato viginti quinque baronum*" of the first becomes " *Omnes isti juraverunt cogere si opus esset ipsos* xxv. *barones ut rectificarent regem. Et etiam cogere ipsum si mutato animo forte recalcitraret*" in the second, II. 606 n.

[5] See *supra*, p. 43, and Protest in Appendix.

(3) *Suspicions of John's good faith.* The barons, on their part, soon came to the conclusion that the Committee, in spite of all its powers, formed an inadequate sanction against John. They demanded further " security." The city of London was placed in their hands, and the Tower of London in the neutral custody of the primate, as pledges of John's good faith, until 15th August or longer if need were. Those terms were reduced to writing in a document entitled " *Conventio facta inter Regem Angliae et barones ejusdem regni,*" which thus supplied a new " form of security," supplementing, if not superseding, that contained in chapter 61.[1]

(4) *Precautions against papal intervention.* The Articles of the Barons afford evidence of the framers' suspicions that John would apply to Rome for release from his bargain. They demanded that the English prelates and the papal legate should become the King's sureties, that he would not invite the Pope to invalidate the Charter. If Pandulf, as the Pope's accredited agent, had put seal to such a document, he would have seriously embarrassed his august master.

Two important alterations in the completed Charter were effected, however, whether at John's instance, or at that of Pandulf, or of the English prelates, is matter of conjecture. All mention of Innocent by name was omitted, the clause being made quite general in its terms : John promised to procure a dispensation " from no one "; while the question of sureties was ignored. Innocent was left free to support John's policy of repudiation.[2]

[1] See *supra*, p. 43. The text is given in Appendix. Thirteen of the twenty-five executors are mentioned by name as agreeing to this new treaty ; cf. Wendover, III. 319. A third sanction appears in the garbled versions of the Charter given by Wendover (III. 317) and M. Paris (II. 603) : the constables of the four royal castles of Northampton, Kenilworth, Nottingham, and Scarborough were to swear to hold these strongholds under orders of the twenty-five. This clause has not been found in any known copy of any issue of Magna Carta : cf. Luard's Preface to M. Paris, II. xxxiii to xxxvi.

[2] Cf. *supra*, p. 45.

CHAPTER SIXTY-TWO.

Et omnes malas voluntates, indignaciones, et rancores ortos inter nos et homines nostros, clericos et laicos, a tempore discordie, plene omnibus remisimus et condonavimus. Preterea omnes transgressiones factas occasione ejusdem discordie, a Pascha anno regni nostri sextodecimo usque ad pacem reformatam, plene remisimus omnibus, clericis et laicis, et quantum ad nos pertinet plene condonavimus. Et insuper fecimus eis fieri litteras testimoniales patentes domini Stephani Cantuariensis archiepiscopi, domini Henrici Dublinensis archiepiscopi, et episcoporum predictorum, et magistri Pandulfi, super securitate ista et concessionibus prefatis.

> And all the ill-will, hatreds, and bitterness that have arisen between us and our men, clergy and lay, from the date of the quarrel, we have completely remitted and pardoned to everyone. Moreover, all trespasses occasioned by the said quarrel, from Easter in the sixteenth year of our reign till the restoration of peace, we have fully remitted to all, both clergy and laymen, and completely forgiven, as far as pertains to us. And, on this head, we have caused to be made for them letters testimonial patent of the lord Stephen, archbishop of Canterbury, of the lord Henry, archbishop of Dublin, of the bishops aforesaid, and of Master Pandulf as touching this security and the concessions aforesaid.

The clauses that follow the *forma securitatis* are of a formal nature. The present chapter, after making a well-meant declaration that bygones should be bygones, so that peace and goodwill should everywhere prevail—a pious aspiration doomed to speedy disillusion—proceeds to authorize the prelates to issue, under their seals, certified copies of the Great Charter. Such letters were actually issued, and their terms are preserved in the Red Book of the Exchequer.[1]

---

[1] See folio 234. Compare *supra*, p. 41: also R. L. Poole in *Engl. Hist. Rev.*, XXVIII. 448 ff. The text, as reproduced by Bémont, *Chartes*, 35, runs as follows: "Omnibus Christi fidelibus ad quos presens scriptum pervenerit, Stephanus Dei gratia Cantuariensis archiepiscopus, tocius Anglie primas et sancte romane ecclesie cardinalis, Henricus, eadem gratia Dublinensis archiepiscopus,

CHAPTER SIXTY-THREE.

QUARE volumus et firmiter precipimus quod Anglicana ecclesia libera sit et quod homines in regno nostro habeant et teneant omnes prefatas libertates, jura, et concessiones, bene et in pace, libere et quiete, plene et integre sibi et heredibus suis, de nobis et heredibus nostris, in omnibus rebus et locis, in perpetuum, sicut predictum est. Juratum est autem tam ex parte nostra quam ex parte baronum, quod hec omnia supradicta bona fide et sine malo ingenio observabuntur. Testibus supradictis et multis aliis. Data per manum nostram in prato quod vocatur Ronimede, inter Windlesoram et Stanes, quinto decimo die Junii, anno regni nostri decimo septimo.

> Wherefore it is our will, and we firmly enjoin, that the English Church be free, and that the men in our kingdom have and hold all the aforesaid liberties, rights, and concessions, well and peaceably, freely and quietly, fully and wholly, for themselves and their heirs, of us and our heirs, in all respects and in all places for ever, as is aforesaid. An oath, moreover, has been taken, as well on our part as on the part of the barons, that all these conditions aforesaid shall be kept in good faith and without evil intent. Given under our hand—the above-named and many others being witnesses—in the meadow which is called Runnymede, between Windsor and Staines, on the fifteenth day of June, in the seventeenth year of our reign.

This last of the sixty-three chapters into which Magna Carta has been divided by modern commentators, contains little that calls for remark. Beginning with a repetition of the declarations made in chapter one that the English

Willelmus Londoniensis, Petrus Wintoniensis, Joscelinus Bathoniensis et Glastoniensis, Hugo Lincolniensis, Walterus Wigorniensis, Willelmus Coventriensis et Benedictus Roffensis, divina miseracione episcopi, et magister Pandulfus domini pape subdiaconus et familiaris, salutem in Domino. Sciatis nos inspexisse cartam quam dominus noster Johannes illustris rex Anglie fecit comitibus, baronibus et liberis hominibus suis Anglie de libertate sancte ecclesie et libertatibus et liberis consuetudinibus suis eisdem ab eo concessis sub hac forma . . . . [Here follows the text of John's Magna Carta] . . . . . . Et ne huic forme predicte aliquid possit addi vel ab eadem aliquid possit subtrahi vel minui, huic scripto sigilla nostra apposuimus."

church should be free (omitting, however, any second reference to canonical election) and that *homines in regno nostro*
should have and hold all of the aforesaid liberties, rights
and concessions, it records that both parties had taken oath
to observe its contents in good faith.[1]   The magnates named
in the preamble were thereafter, along with many others
unnamed, referred to collectively as witnesses.   The
Charter concludes with a declaration that it has been " given
by our hand," and the place and date are specified.   The
actual " giving " by John's hand was effected by impress of
his great seal.[2]

[1] Cf. *supra*, p. 40.

[2] There are no signatures to the document.   The frequent references to " the
signing of the Great Charter " are thus inaccurate, if " signing " is taken in its
modern sense of "subscribing," but may perhaps be justified by a reference to
signum in its original meaning of "a seal."   To imprint a seal was, in a sense,
" to sign."   Reasons have already been given for holding that Magna Carta, in
spite of its mention of its own date as 15th June, was actually sealed on the 19th.
See *supra*, pp. 48-9.

APPENDIX.

DOCUMENTS RELATIVE TO, OR ILLUSTRATIVE OF, MAGNA CARTA.

I. THE CHARTER OF LIBERTIES OF HENRY I.[1]
(1100.)

HENRICUS Dei gratia rex Anglorum omnibus baronibus et fidelibus suis tam Francigenis quam Anglis salutem.

1. Sciatis me Dei misericordia et communi consilio baronum regni Anglie ejusdem regni regem coronatum esse. Et quia regnum oppressum erat injustis exactionibus, ego, respectu Dei et amore quem erga vos omnes habeo, sanctam Dei ecclesiam imprimis liberam facio : ita quod nec vendam nec ad firmam ponam nec, mortuo archiepiscopo sive episcopo sive abbate, aliquid accipiam de dominio ecclesie vel de hominibus ejus, donec successor in eam ingrediatur. Et omnes malas con- suetudines, quibus regnum Anglie injuste opprimebatur, inde aufero ; quas malas consuetudines ex parte hic pono :

2. Si quis baronum meorum, comitum, sive aliorum qui de me tenent, mortuus fuerit, heres suus non redimet terram suam sicut faciebat tempore fratris mei, sed legitima et justa releva- tione relevabit eam. Similiter et homines baronum meorum legitima et justa relevatione relevabunt terras suas de dominis suis.

3. Et si quis baronum vel aliorum hominum meorum filiam suam nuptum tradere voluerit, sive sororem, sive neptem, sive cognatam, mecum inde loquatur. Sed neque ego aliquid de suo pro hac licentia accipiam, neque defendam ei quin eam

---

[1] The text is taken from Liebermann, *Gesetze*, I. 521. Cf. *Trans. R.H.S.* viii. 21 ff., for an exhaustive discussion of the various copies of the lost charter. For commentary, cf. *supra*, pp. 96-101. Liebermann shows the striking variations of the opening and ending clauses : the preamble varied with the persons to whom each copy was addressed. Cf. R. L. Poole, *Eng. Hist. Rev.*, XXVIII. 444 ff.

2 H

det, excepto si eam vellet jungere inimico meo. Et si, mortuo barone vel alio homine meo, filia heres remanserit, illam dabo consilio baronum meorum cum terra sua. Et si, mortuo marito, uxor ejus remanserit et sine liberis fuerit, dotem suam et maritationem habebit; et eam non dabo marito, nisi secundum velle suum.

4. Si vero uxor cum liberis remanserit, dotem quidem et maritationem suam habebit, dum corpus suum legitime servaverit; et eam non dabo, nisi secundum velle suum. Et terre et liberorum custos erit sive uxor sive alius propinquorum, qui justius esse debebit. Et precipio ut barones mei similiter se contineant erga filios et filias vel uxores hominum suorum.

5. Monetagium commune quod capiebatur per civitates et comitatus, quod non fuit tempore regis Eadwardi, hoc ne amodo sit, omnino defendo. Si quis captus fuerit, sive monetarius, sive alius, cum falsa moneta, justicia recta inde fiat.

6. Omnia placita et omnia debita que fratri meo debebantur condono exceptis rectis firmis meis et exceptis illis que pacta erant pro aliorum hereditatibus, vel pro eis rebus que justius aliis contingebant. Et si quis pro hereditate sua aliquid pepigerat, illud condono, et omnes relevationes que pro rectis hereditatibus pacte erant.

7. Et si quis baronum vel hominum meorum infirmabitur, sicut ipse dabit vel dare disponet pecuniam suam, ita datam esse concedo. Quodsi ipse, preventus vel armis vel infirmitate, pecuniam suam non dederit nec dare disposuerit uxor sua sive liberi aut parentes aut legitimi homines ejus eam pro anima ejus dividant, sicut eis melius visum fuerit.

8. Si quis baronum vel hominum meorum forisfecerit, non dabit vadium in misericordia pecunie sue, sicut faciebat tempore patris mei vel fratris mei, sed secundum modum forisfacti, ita emendabit, sicut emendasset retro a tempore patris mei, in tempore aliorum antecessorum meorum. Quodsi perfidie vel sceleris convictus fuerit, sicut justum fuerit, sic emendet.

9. Murdra etiam retro ab illa die qua in regem coronatus fui omnia condono; et ea que amodo facta fuerint juste emendentur secundum lagam regis Eadwardi.

10. Forestas communi consensu baronum meorum in manu mea retinui, sicut pater meus eas habuit.

11. Militibus qui per loricas terras suas deserviunt terras dominicarum suarum quietas ab omnibus geldis et ab omni opere, proprio dono meo, concedo, ut, sicut tam magno grava-

mine alleviati sunt, ita equis et armis se bene instruant, ut apti et parati sint ad servitium meum et ad defensionem regni mei.

12. Pacem firmam in toto regno meo pono et teneri amodo precipio.

13. Lagam regis Eadwardi vobis reddo cum illis emendationibus quibus pater meus eam emendavit consilio baronum suorum.

14. Si quis aliquid de meo vel de rebus alicujus post obitum regis Willelmi, fratis mei, cepit, totum cito reddatur absque emendatione.   Et si quis inde aliquid retinuerit, ille super quem inventum fuerit graviter michi emendabit.

Testibus Mauricio Lundonie episcopo, et Gundulfo episcopo, et Willelmo electo episcopo, et Henrico comite, et Simone comite, et Waltero Giffardo, et Rodberto de Monfort, et Rogero Bigoto, et Henrico de Portu, apud Westmonasterium, quando coronatus fui.   Valete !

II. THE SECOND OR OXFORD CHARTER OF STEPHEN.[1]
(1136.)

EGO Stephanus Dei gratia, assensu cleri et populi in regem Anglie electus, et a Willelmo Cantuariensi archiepiscopo et sancte Romane ecclesie legato consecratus, et ab Innocentio sancte romane sedis pontifice postmodum confirmatus, respectu et amore Dei sanctam ecclesiam liberam esse concedo, et debitam reverentiam illi confirmo. Nichil me in ecclesia vel rebus ecclesiasticis simoniace acturum vel permissurum esse promitto. Ecclesiasticarum personarum et omnium clericorum et rerum eorum justiciam et potestatem et distributionem bonorum ecclesiasticorum in manu episcoporum esse perhibeo et confirmo.   Dignitates ecclesiarum privilegiis earum confirmatas et consuetudines earum antiquo tenore habitas inviolate manere statuo et concedo.   Omnes ecclesiarum possessiones et tenuras, quas die illa habuerunt qua Willelmus rex avus meus fuit vivus et mortuus, sine omni calumpniantium reclamatione, eis liberas et absolutas esse concedo.   Si quid vero de habitis vel possessis

[1]The text is founded on that of the *Statutes of the Realm*, I. 3, which follows the Exeter version.   Cf. Bémont, *Chartes*, 8-10, who discusses the various editions. Dr. R. L. Poole has noted the variants of an original of the Charter preserved in the muniment room of Salisbury Cathedral ; see *Report on Manuscripts in Various Collections*, I. 384-5 (Historical Manuscripts Commission, 1901).   Two of these variants have been here adopted : (*a*) "*regem Anglie*" for "*regem Anglorum*" and (*b*) "*postmodum*" added after "*pontifice.*"

ante mortem ejusdem regis quibus modo careat, ecclesia deinceps repetierit, indulgentie et dispensationi mee vel restituendum vel discutiendum reservo. Quecunque vero post mortem ipsius regis liberalitate regum vel largitione principum, oblatione vel comparatione, vel qualibet transmutatione fidelium eis collata sunt, confirmo. Pacem et justiciam me in omnibus facturum et pro posse meo conservaturum eis promitto.

Forestas quas Willelmus avus meus et Willelmus avunculus meus instituerunt et habuerunt mihi reservo. Ceteras omnes quas rex Henricus superaddidit, ecclesiis et regno quietas reddo et concedo.

Si quis episcopus vel abbas vel alia ecclesiastica persona ante mortem suam rationabiliter sua distribuerit vel distribuenda statuerit, firmum manere concedo. Si vero morte preoccupatus fuerit, pro salute anime ejus, ecclesie consilio, eadem fiat distributio. Dum vero sedes propriis pastoribus vacue fuerint, ipsas et earum possessiones omnes in manu et custodia clericorum vel proborum hominum ejusdem ecclesie committam, donec pastor canonice substituatur.

Omnes exactiones et injusticias et meschenings sive per vicecomites vel per alios quoslibet male inductas funditus exstirpo. Bonas leges et antiquas et justas consuetudines in murdris et placitis et aliis causis observabo et observari precipio et constituo. Hec omnia concedo et confirmo, salva regia et justa dignitate mea.

Testibus Willelmo Cantuariensi archiepiscopo, et Hugone Rothomagensi archiepiscopo, et Henrico Wintoniensi episcopo, et Rogero Saresberiensi episcopo, et Alexandro Lincolniensi episcopo, et Nigello Eliensi episcopo, et Evrardo Norwicensi episcopo, et Simone Wigorniensi episcopo, et Bernardo episcopo de S. Davide, et Audoeno Ebroicensi episcopo, et Ricardo Abrincensi episcopo, et Roberto Herefordiensi episcopo, et Johanne Rovecestriensi episcopo, et Athelulfo Carlolensi episcopo, et Rogero cancellario, et Henrico nepote Regis, et Roberto comite Gloecestrie, et Willelmo comite de Warenna, et Rannulfo comite Cestrie, et Rogero comite de Warewic., et Roberto de Ver., et Milone de Gloecestria, et Brientio filio Comitis, et Roberto de Oilly conestabulis, et Willelmo Martello, et Hugone Bigot, et Hunfredo de Buhun, et Simone de Belcamp dapiferis, et Willelmo de Albiniaco, et Eudone Martello pincernis, et Roberto de Ferreriis, et Willelmo Pevrello de Notingeham, et Simone de Saintliz, et Willelmo de Albamarla, et Pagano filio Johannis, et Hamone de Sancto Claro, et Ilberto de Laceio. Apud Oxeneford. Anno ab incarnatione Domini M.C. XXXVI., set regni mei primo.

III. CHARTER OF HENRY II.[1]
(CIRCA 1154.)

HENRICUS Dei gracia rex anglie, dux Normannie et Aquitanie, et comes Andegavie, omnibus comitibus, baronibus et fidelibus suis Francis et Anglicis, salutem. Sciatis me, ad honorem Dei et sancte Ecclesie, et pro communi emendacione tocius regni mei, concessisse et reddidisse et presenti carta mea confirmasse Deo et sancte ecclesie et omnibus comitibus et baronibus et omnibus hominibus meis omnes concessiones et donaciones et libertates et liberas consuetudines, quas rex Henricus avus meus eis dedit et concessit. Similiter eciam omnes malas consuetudines, quas ipse delevit et remisit, ego remitto et deleri concedo pro me et heredibus meis. Quare volo et firmiter precipio quod sancta ecclesia et omnes comites et barones et omnes mei homines omnes illas consuetudines et donaciones et libertates et liberas consuetudines habeant et teneant libere et quiete, bene et in pace et integre, de me et heredibus meis, sibi et heredibus suis, adeo libere et quiete et plenarie in omnibus, sicut rex Henricus avus meus eis dedit et concessit, et carta sua confirmavit. Teste Ricardo de Luci apud Westmonasterium.

IV. THE SO-CALLED "UNKNOWN CHARTER OF LIBERTIES" OF JOHN.[2]
(CIRCA 1214-1215.)

1. Concedit Rex Johannes quod non capiet hominem absque judicio, nec aliquid accipiet pro justitia, nec injustitiam faciet.

[1] The text is taken from that given in *Statutes of the Realm*, I. 4, which is founded on a copy of the original preserved in the British Museum (Cotton, Claudius D. II., folio 107). Cf. Bémont, *Chartes*, 12-14.

[2] For a discussion of the nature, date, and historical context of this document see *supra*, pp. 171-5 and Index. The text is founded upon that published by Mr. J. H. Round in the *English Historical Review*, VIII. 288, but effect has been given to most of the emendations suggested by Mr. Hubert Hall and Mr. G. W. Prothero. Cf. *ibid.*, IX. 117 and 326. The twelve clauses are here numbered for convenience of reference, although no numbers appear in the MS.

2. Et si contingat quod meus baro vel homo meus moriatur et haeres suus sit in aetate, terram suam debeo ei reddere per rectum releveium absque magis capiendi.

3. Et si ita sit quod haeres sit infra aetatem, debeo iiij^or militibus de legalioribus feodi terram bajulare in custodia, et illi cum meo famulo debent mihi reddere exitus terrae sine venditione nemorum et sine redemptione hominum et sine destructione parci et vivarii; et tunc quando ille haeres erit in aetate terram ei reddam quietam.

4. Si foemina sit haeres terrae, debeo eam maritare, consilio generis sui, ita non sit disparagiata. Et si una vice eam dedero, amplius eam dare non possum, sed se maritabit ad libitum suum, sed non inimicis meis.

5. Si contingat quod baro aut homo meus moriatur, concedo ut pecunia sua dividatur sicut ipse diviserit; et si praeoccupatus fuerit aut armis aut infirmitate improvisa, uxor ejus, aut liberi, aut parentes et amici propinquiores pro ejus anima dividant.

6. Et uxor ejus non abibit de hospitio infra xl. dies et donec dotem suam decenter habuerit, et maritagium habebit.

7. Adhuc hominibus meis concedo ne eant in exercitu extra Angliam nisi in Normanniam et in Britanniam et hoc decenter; quod si aliquis debet inde servitium decem militum, consilio baronum meorum alleviabitur.

8. Et si scutagium evenerit in terra, una marca argenti capietur de feodi militis; et si gravamen exercitus contigerit, amplius caperetur consilio baronum regni.

9. Adhuc concedo ut omnes forestas quas pater meus et frater meus et ego afforestaverimus, deafforesto.

10. Adhuc concedo ut milites qui in antiquis forestis meis suum nemus habent, habeant nemus amodo ad herbergagia sua et ad ardendum; et habeant foresterium suum; et ego tantum modo unum qui servet pecudes meas.

11. Et si aliquis hominum meorum moriatur qui Judaeis debeat, debitum non usurabit quamdiu haeres ejus sit infra aetatem.

12. Et concedo ne homo perdat pro pecude vitam neque membra.

V. THE ARTICLES OF THE BARONS.[1]
(1215.)

Ista sunt Capitula que Barones petunt et dominus Rex concedit.

1. Post decessum antecessorum heredes plene etatis habebunt hereditatem suam per antiquum relevium exprimendum in carta.

2. Heredes qui infra etatem sunt et fuerint in custodia, cum ad etatem pervenerint, habebunt hereditatem suam sine relevio et fine.

3. Custos terre heredis capiet rationabiles exitus, consuetudines, et servitia, sine destructione et vasto hominum et rerum suarum, et si custos terre fecerit destructionem et vastum, amittat custodiam; et custos sustentabit domos, parcos, vivaria, stagna, molendina et cetera ad terram illam pertinentia, de exitibus terre ejusdem; et ut heredes ita maritentur ne disparagentur et per consilium propinquorum de consanguinitate sua.

4. Ne vidua det aliquid pro dote sua, vel maritagio, post decessum mariti sui, sed maneat in domo sua per .xl. dies post mortem ipsius, et infra terminum illum assignetur ei dos; et maritagium statim habeat et hereditatem suam.

5. Rex vel ballivus non saisiet terram aliquam pro debito dum catalla debitoris sufficiunt; nec plegii debitoris distringantur, dum capitalis debitor sufficit ad solutionem; si vero capitalis debitor defecerit in solutione, si plegii voluerint, habeant terras debitoris, donec debitum illud persolvatur plene, nisi capitalis debitor monstrare poterit se esse inde quietum erga plegios.

6. Rex non concedet alicui baroni quod capiat auxilium de liberis hominibus suis, nisi ad corpus suum redimendum, et ad faciendum primogenitum filium suum militem, et ad primogenitam filiam suam semel maritandam, et hoc faciet per rationabile auxilium.

7. Ne aliquis majus servitium faciat de feodo militis quam inde debetur.

8. Ut communia placita non sequantur curiam domini regis, sed assignentur in aliquo certo loco; et ut recognitiones capiantur in eisdem comitatibus, in hunc modum: ut rex mittat duos justiciaros per .iiii^or. vices in anno, qui cum .iiii^or. militibus ejusdem comitatus electis per comitatum, capiant assisas de nova

---

[1] The text is taken from that of the *Statutes of the Realm*, I. 7-8, which is founded on the original in the British Museum. See *supra*, pp. 170-1. Cf. Bémont, *Chartes*, 15-23.

dissaisina, morte antecessoris, et ultima presentatione, nec aliquis ob hoc sit summonitus nisi juratores et due partes.

9. Ut liber homo amercietur pro parvo delicto secundum modum delicti, et, pro magno delicto, secundum magnitudinem delicti, salvo continemento suo; villanus etiam eodem modo amercietur, salvo waynagio suo; et mercator eodem modo, salva marcandisa, per sacramentum proborum hominum de visneto.

10. Ut clericus amercietur de laico feodo suo secundum modum aliorum predictorum, et non secundum beneficium ecclesiasticum.

11. Ne aliqua villa amercietur pro pontibus faciendis ad riparias, nisi ubi de jure antiquitus esse solebant.

12. Ut mensura vini, bladi, et latitudines pannorum et rerum aliarum, emendetur; et ita de ponderibus.

13. Ut assise de nova dissaisina et de morte antecessoris abbrevientur; et similiter de aliis assisis.

14. Ut nullus vicecomes intromittat se de placitis ad coronam pertinentibus sine coronatoribus; et ut comitatus et hundredi sint ad antiquas firmas absque nullo incremento, exceptis dominicis maneriis regis.

15. Si aliquis tenens de rege moriatur, licebit vicecomiti vel alii ballivo regis seisire et imbreviare catallum ipsius per visum legalium hominum, ita tamen quod nichil inde amoveatur, donec plenius sciatur si debeat aliquod liquidum debitum domino regi, et tunc debitum regis persolvatur; residuum vero relinquatur executoribus ad faciendum testamentum defuncti; et si nichil regi debetur, omnia catalla cedant defuncto.

16. Si aliquis liber homo intestatus decesserit, bona sua per manum proximorum parentum suorum et amicorum et per visum ecclesie distribuantur.

17. Ne vidue distringantur ad se maritandum, dum voluerint sine marito vivere, ita tamen quod securitatem facient quod non maritabunt se sine assensu regis, si de rege teneant, vel dominorum suorum de quibus tenent.

18. Ne constabularius vel alius ballivus capiat blada vel alia catalla, nisi statim denarios inde reddat, nisi respectum habere possit de voluntate venditoris.

19. Ne constabularius possit distringere aliquem militem ad dandum denarios pro custodia castri, si voluerit facere custodiam illam in propria persona vel per alium probum hominem, si ipse eam facere non possit per rationabilem causam; et si rex eum

duxerit in exercitum, sit quietus de custodia secundum quantitatem temporis.

20. Ne vicecomes, vel ballivus regis, vel aliquis alius, capiat equos vel carettas alicujus liberi hominis pro cariagio faciendo, nisi ex voluntate ipsius.

21. Ne rex vel ballivus suus capiat alienum boscum ad castra vel ad alia agenda sua, nisi per voluntatem ipsius cujus boscus ille fuerit.

22. Ne rex teneat terram eorum qui fuerint convicti de felonia, nisi per unum annum et unum diem, sed tunc reddatur domino feodi.

23. Ut omnes kidelli de cetero penitus deponantur de Tamisia et Medeweye et per totam Angliam.

24. Ne breve quod vocatur " Precipe " de cetero fiat alicui de aliquo tenemento unde liber homo amittat curiam suam.

25. Si quis fuerit disseisitus vel prolongatus per regem sine juditio de terris, libertatibus, et jure suo, statim ei restituatur; et si contentio super hoc orta fuerit, tunc inde disponatur per juditium .xxv. baronum, et ut illi qui fuerint dissaisiti per patrem vel fratrem regis, rectum habeant sine dilatione per juditium parium suorum in curia regis; et si rex debeat habere terminum aliorum cruce signatorum, tunc archiepiscopus et episcopi faciant inde juditium ad certum diem, appellatione remota.

26. Ne aliquid detur pro brevi inquisitionis de vita vel membris, sed libere concedatur sine pretio et non negetur.

27. Si aliquis tenet de rege per feodi firmam, per sokagium, vel per burgagium, et de alio per servitium militis, dominus rex non habebit custodiam militum de feodo alterius, occasione burgagii vel sokagii, nec debet habere custodiam burgagii, sokagii, vel feodi firme; et quod liber homo non amittat militiam suam occasione parvarum sergantisarum, sicuti de illis qui tenent aliquod tenementum reddendo inde cuttellos vel sagittas vel hujusmodi.

28. Ne aliquis ballivus possit ponere aliquem ad legem simplici loquela sua sine testibus fidelibus.

29. Ne corpus liberi hominis capiatur, nec imprisonetur, nec dissaisietur, nec utlagetur, nec exuletur, nec aliquo modo destruatur, nec rex eat vel mittat super eum vi, nisi per juditium parium suorum vel per legem terre.

30. Ne jus vendatur vel differratur vel vetitum sit.

31. Quod mercatores habeant salvum ire et venire ad emen-

dum vel vendendum, sine omnibus malis toltis, per antiquas et rectas consuetudines.

32. Ne scutagium vel auxilium ponatur in regno, nisi per commune consilium regni, nisi ad corpus regis redimendum, et primogenitum filium suum militem faciendum, et filiam suam primogenitam semel maritandam; et ad hoc fiat rationabile auxilium. Simili modo fiat de taillagiis et auxiliis de civitate Londonie, et de aliis civitatibus que inde habent libertates, et ut civitas Londonie plene habeat antiquas libertates et liberas consuetudines suas, tam per aquas, quam per terras.

33. Ut liceat unicuique exire de regno et redire, salva fide dominis regis, nisi tempore werre per aliquod breve tempus propter communem utilitatem regni.

34. Si quis mutuo aliquid acceperit a Judeis plus vel minus, et moriatur antequam debitum illud solvatur, debitum non usurabit quamdiu heres fuerit infra etatem, de quocumque teneat; et si debitum illud inciderit in manum regis, rex non capiet nisi catallum quod continetur in carta.

35. Si quis moriatur et debitum debeat Judeis, uxor ejus habeat dotem suam; et si liberi remanserint, provideantur eis necessaria secundum tenementum; et de residuo solvatur debitum salvo servitio dominorum; simili modo fiat de aliis debitis; et ut custos terre reddat heredi, cum ad plenam etatem pervenerit, terram suam instauratam secundum quod rationabiliter poterit sustinere de exitibus terre ejusdem de carucis et wainnagiis.

36. Si quis tenuerit de aliqua eskaeta, sicut de honore Walinge-ford, Notingeham, Bononie, et Lankastrie, et de aliis eskaetis que sunt in manu regis et sunt baronie, et obierit, heres ejus non dabit aliud relevium, vel faciet regi aliud servitium quam faceret baroni; et ut rex eodem modo eam teneat quo baro eam tenuit.

37. Ut fines qui facti sunt pro dotibus, maritagiis, heredi-tatibus, et amerciamentis, injuste et contra legem terre, omnino condonentur; vel fiat inde per juditium, .xxv. baronum, vel per juditium majoris partis eorumdem, una cum archiepiscopo et aliis quos secum vocare voluerit ita quod, si aliquis vel aliqui de .xxv. fuerint in simili querela, amoveantur et alii loco illorum per residuos de .xxv. substituantur.

38. Quod obsides et carte reddantur, quae liberate fuerunt regi in securitatem.

39. Ut illi qui fuerint extra forestam non veniant coram justiciariis de foresta per communes summonitiones, nisi sint in

placito vel plegii fuerint; et ut prave consuetudines de forestis et de forestariis, et warenniis, et vicecomitibus, et rivariis, emendentur per .xii. milites de quolibet comitatu, qui debent eligi per probos homines ejusdem comitatus.

40. Ut rex amoveat penitus de balliva parentes et totam sequelam Gerardi de Atyes, quod de cetero balliam non habeant, scilicet Engelardum, Andream, Petrum, et Gyonem de Cancellis, Gyonem de Cygony, Matheum de Martiny, et fratres ejus; et Galfridum nepotem ejus et Philippum Mark.

41. Et ut rex amoveat alienigenas, milites, stipendiarios, balistarios, et ruttarios, et servientes qui veniunt cum equis et armis ad nocumentum regni.

42. Ut rex faciat justiciarios, constabularios, vicecomites, et ballivos, de talibus qui sciant legem terre et eam bene velint observare.

43. Ut barones qui fundaverunt abbatias, unde habent cartas regum vel antiquam tenuram, habeant custodiam earum cum vacaverint.

44. Si rex Walenses dissaisierit vel elongaverit de terris vel libertatibus, vel de rebus aliis in Anglia vel in Wallia, eis statim sine placito reddantur; et si fuerint dissaisiti vel elongati de tenementis suis Anglie per patrem vel fratrem regis sine juditio parium suorum, rex eis sine dilatione justiciam exhibebit, eo modo quo exhibet Anglicis justiciam de tenementis suis Anglie secundum legem Anglie, et de tenementis Wallie secundum legem Wallie, et de tenementis Marchie secundum legem Marchie; idem facient Walenses regi et suis.

45. Ut rex reddat filium Lewelini et preterea omnes obsides de Wallia, et cartas que ei liberate fuerunt in securitatem pacis . nisi aliter esse debeat per cartas quas rex habet per

46. Ut rex faciat regi Scottorum de obsidibus reddendis, et de libertatibus suis, et jure suo, secundum formam quam facit baronibus Anglie . . . . . juditium archiepiscopi et aliorum quos secum vocare voluerit.

47. Et omnes foreste que sunt aforestate per regem tempore suo deafforestentur, et ita fiat de ripariis que per ipsum regem sunt in defenso.

48. Omnes autem istas consuetudines et libertates quas rex concessit regno tenendas quantum ad se pertinet erga suos, omnes de regno tam clerici quam laici observabunt quantum ad se pertinet erga suos.

[Here, there occurs a blank space in the original.]

49. Hec est forma securitatis ad observandum pacem et libertates inter regem et regnum. Barones eligent .xxv. barones de regno quos voluerint, qui debent pro totis viribus suis observare, tenere et facere observari, pacem et libertates quas dominus rex eis concessit et carta sua confirmavit; ita videlicet quod si rex, vel justiciarius, vel ballivi regis, vel aliquis de ministris suis, in aliquo erga aliquem deliquerit, vel aliquem articulorum pacis aut securitatis transgressus fuerit, et delictum ostensum fuerit .iiii^or. baronibus de praedictis .xxv. baronibus, illi .iiii^or. barones accedent ad dominum regem, vel ad justiciarium suum, si rex fuerit extra regnum; proponentes ei excessum, petent ut excessum illum sine dilatione faciat emendari; et si rex vel justiciarius ejus illud non emendaverit, si rex fuerit extra regnum, infra rationabile tempus determinandum in carta, predicti .iiii^or. referent causam illam ad residuos de illis .xxv. baronibus, et illi .xxv. cum communa totius terre distringent et gravabunt regem modis omnibus quibus poterunt, scilicet per captionem castrorum, terrarum, possessionum, et aliis modis quibus poterunt, donec fuerit emendatum secundum arbitrium eorum, salva persona domini regis et regine et liberorum suorum; et cum fuerit emendatum, intendant domino regi sicut prius. Et quicumque voluerit de terra jurabit se ad predicta exequenda pariturum mandatis predictorum .xxv. baronum, et gravaturum regem pro posse suo cum ipsis; et rex pubblice et libere dabit licentiam jurandi cuilibet qui jurare voluerit, et nulli umquam jurare prohibebit. Omnes autem illos de terra qui sponte sua et per se noluerint jurare .xxv. baronibus de distringendo et gravando regem cum eis, rex faciet jurare eosdem de mandato suo sicut predictum est. Item si aliquis de predictis .xxv. baronibus decesserit, vel a terra recesserit, vel aliquo modo alio impeditus fuerit quominus ista predicta possint exequi, qui residui fuerint de .xxv. eligent alium loco ipsius pro arbitrio suo, qui simili modo erit juratus quo et ceteri. In omnibus autem que istis .xxv. baronibus committuntur exequenda, si forte ipsi .xxv. presentes fuerint et inter se super re aliqua discordaverint, vel aliqui ex eis vocati nolint vel nequeant interesse, ratum habebitur et firmum quod major pars ex eis providerit vel preceperit, ac si omnes .xxv. in hoc consensissent; et predicti .xxv. jurabunt quod omnia antedicta fideliter observabunt et pro toto posse suo facient observari. Preterea rex faciet eos securos per cartas archiepiscopi et episcoporum et magistri Pandulfi, quod nichil impetrabit a domino papa per quod aliqua istarum conventionum revocetur vel

minuatur, et, si aliquid tale impetraverit, reputetur irritum **et** inane et numquam eo utatur.

VI. WRITS SUPPLEMENTARY OF JOHN'S GREAT CHARTER.

(1) *Writ to Stephen Harengod, dated 23rd June, 1215, announcing that terms had been arranged.*[1]

REX Stephano Harengod etc., Sciatis quod firma pax facta est per Dei gratiam inter nos et barones nostros die Veneris proximo post festum Sancte Trinitatis apud Runemed., prope Stanes; ita quod eorum homagia eodem die ibidem cepimus. Unde vobis mandamus firmiter precipientes quod sicut nos et honorem nostrum diligitis et pacem regni nostri, ne ulterius turbetur, quod nullum malum de cetero faciatis baronibus nostris vel aliis, vel fieri permittatis, occasione discordie prius orte inter nos et eos. Mandamus etiam vobis quod de finibus et tenseriis nobis factis occasione illius discordie, si quid superest reddendum, nichil capiatis. Et si quid post illum diem Veneris cepistis, illud statim reddatis. Et corpora prisonum et obsidum captorum et detentorum occasione hujus guerre, vel finium vel tenseriarum predictarum, sine dilatione deliberetis. Hec omnia predicta, sicut corpus vestrum diligitis, faciatis. Et in hujus etc., nobis mittimus. Teste meipso apud Runemed., xxiij. die Junii anno regni nostri xvij.

(2) *Writ to Hugh de Bova, dated 23rd June, 1215, ordering disbandment of mercenaries.*[2]

Rex Hugoni de Bova, salutem. Mandamus vobis quod in fide qua nobis tenemini non retineatis aliquem de militibus vel servientibus qui fuerunt apud Dover., sed in patriam suam in pace sine dilatione ire faciatis. Et in hujus, etc. Teste meipso apud Runimed. xxiij. die Junii anno regni nostri xvij^mo.

---

[1] The text follows that of *New Rymer*, I. 133, but has been collated with *Rot. Pat.*, I. 143 (17 John, m. 23) and two corrections made. This writ is referred to *supra*, p. 41 n., where its date is discussed.

[2] See *supra*, p. 42. The text is given in *New Rymer*, I. 134, and in *Rot. Pat.*, I. 144 (17 John, m. 23).

(3) Writs issued to the sheriffs of counties on 19th June, 1215.[1]

Rex vicecomiti, forestariis, warennariis, custodibus ripariarum et omnibus baillivis suis in eodem comitatu, salutem. Sciatis pacem firmam esse reformatam per Dei gratiam inter nos et barones et liberos homines regni nostri, sicut audire poteritis et videre per cartam nostram quam inde fieri fecimus, quam etiam legi publice precepimus per totam bailliam vestram et firmiter teneri; volentes et districte precipientes quod tu vicecomes omnes de baillia tua secundum formam carte predicte jurare facias xxv. baronibus de quibus mentio fit in carta predicta, ad mandatum eorundem vel majoris partis eorum, coram ipsis vel illis quos ad hoc atornaverint per litteras suas patentes, et ad diem et locum quos ad hoc faciendum prefixerint predicti barones vel atornati ab eis ad hoc. Volumus etiam et precipimus quod xii milites de comitatu tuo, qui eligentur de ipso comitatu in primo comitatu qui tenebitur post susceptionem litterarum istarum in partibus tuis, jurent de inquirendis pravis consuetudinibus tam de vicecomitibus quam eorum ministris, forestis, forestariis, warennis et warennariis, ripariis et earum custodibus, et eis delendis, sicut in ipsa carta continetur. Vos igitur omnes sicut nos et honorem nostrum diligitis, et pacem regni nostri, omnia in carta contenta inviolabiliter observetis et ab omnibus observari faciatis, ne pro defectu vestri, aut per excessum vestrum, pacem regni nostri, quod Deus avertat, iterum turbari contingat. Et tu, vicecomes, pacem nostram per totam bailliam tuam clamari facias et firmiter teneri precipias. Et in hujus, etc. vobis mittimus. Teste me ipso apud Runimede, xix. die Junii, anno regni nostri xvij^mo.

(4) Writs issued to the sheriffs of counties on 27th June, 1215.[2]

Rex vicecomiti Warewic. et duodecim militibus electis in eodem comitatu ad inquirendum et delendum pravas consuetudines de vicecomitibus et eorum ministris forestis et forestariis warennis et warennariis ripariis et earum custodibus salutem. Mandamus vobis quod statim et sine dilatione sais-

---

[1] See *supra*, p. 42. The text is given by *New Rymer*, I. 134, and in *Rot. Pat.*, I. 134 (17 John, m. 21). A French version appears in D'Achery, *Spicilegium*, XII. 573, and in Bémont, *Chartes*, XXIV. n.

[2] See *supra*, pp. 42-3, and 440. The text is taken from *Rot. Pat.*, I. 180 (17 John, m. 23 d.). It will be found also in *New Rymer*, I. 134, and in Stubbs' *Sel. Chart.*, 306-7.

iatis in manum nostram terras et tenementa et catalla omnium
illorum de comitatu Warewic. qui jurare contradixerint viginti
quinque baronibus secundum formam contentam in carta nostra
de libertatibus vel eis quos ad hoc atornaverint. Et si jurare
noluerint statim post quindecim dies completos preterquam
terre et tenementa et catalla eorum in manu nostra saisita
fuerint, omnia catalla sua vendi faciatis et denarios inde pre-
ceptos salvo custodiatis, deputandos subsidio terre sancte.
Terras autem et tenementa eorum in manu nostra teneatis,
quousque juraverint. Et hoc provisum est per judicium
domini Cantuar. archiepiscopi et baronum regni nostri. Et in
hujus etc. Teste meipso, apud Winton. xxvij die Junii anno
regni nostri xvij^{mo.}

Idem mandatum est omnibus vicecomitibus Anglie.

(5) *Conventio facta inter Regem Anglie et barones ejusdem*
   regni.[1]

Hec est conventio facta inter dominum Johannem regem
Anglie, ex una parte, et Robertum filium Walteri, marescallum
exercitus Dei et sancte ecclesie in Anglia, et Ricardum comitem
de Clare, Gaufridum comitem Essex. et Glouc., Rogerum
Bigot comitem Northfolc. et Suthfolc., Saherum comitem
Wint., Robertum comitem Oxon., Henricum comitem Hereford., et barones subscriptos, scilicet Willielmum Mariscallum
juniorem, Eustachium de Vescy, Willielmum de Mobray, Johannem filium Roberti, Rogerum de Monte Begonis, Willielmum
de Lanvalay, et alios comites et barones et liberos homines totius
regni, ex altera parte, videlicet quod ipsi comites et barones et
alii prescripti tenebunt civitatem London. de baillio domini regis,
salvis interim domino regi firmis redditibus et claris debitis suis,
usque ad assumptionem beate Marie anno regni ipsius regis
xvij^{mo.} et dominus Cant. tenebit similiter de baillio domini regis
turrim London. usque ad predictum terminum, salvis civitati
London. libertatibus suis et liberis consuetudinibus suis, et salvo
cuilibet jure suo in custodia turris London., et ita quod interim
non ponat dominus rex munitionem vel vires alias in civitate
predicta vel in turri London. Fiant etiam infra predictum terminum sacramenta per totam Angliam viginti quinque baronibus
sicut continentur in carta de libertatibus et securitate regno con-

---

[1] See *supra*, pp. 43, and 477. The text is taken from *New Rymer*, I. 133, on
the authority of *Rot. Claus.*, 17 John, m. 27 d. It is printed by Blackstone,
Great Charter, 25-6.

cessis vel attornatis viginti quinque baronum sicut continentur in literis de duodecim militibus eligendis ad delendum malas consuetudines de forestis et aliis. Et preterea infra eundem terminum omnia que comites et barones et alii liberi homines petunt a domino rege que ipse dixerit esse reddenda vel que per xxv barones aut per majorem partem eorum judicata fuerint esse reddenda reddantur secundum formam predicte carte. Et si hec facta fuerint vel per dominum regem non steterit quo minus ista facta fuerint infra predictum terminum tunc civitas et turris London. ad eundem terminum statim reddantur domino regi salvis predicte civitati libertatibus suis et liberis consuetudinibus suis sicut prescriptum est. Et si hec facta non fuerint et per dominum regem steterit quod ista non fiant infra predictum terminum barones tenebunt civitatem predictam et dominus archiepiscopus turrim London. donec predicta compleantur. Et interim omnes ex utraque parte recuperabunt castra terras et villas quas habuerunt in initio guerre orte inter dominum regem et barones.

(6) *Protest by archbishops of Canterbury and Dublin, and other prelates, that chapter 48 of the Great Charter was to be interpreted by both sides as limited.*[1]

Omnibus Christi fidelibus ad quos presentes littere pervenerint, Stephanus, Dei gracia Cantuar. archiepiscopus, tocius Anglie primas et sancte Romane ecclesie cardinalis et H. eadem gracia, archiepiscopus Dublin., W. quoque London., P. Winton., J. Bathon et Glaston., H. Lincoln., W. Wygorn., et W. Coventr., ejusdem gracie dono episcopi, salutem in Domino. Cum dominus Rex concesserit et per cartam suam confirmaverit, quod omnes male consuetudines de forestis, et forestariis et eorum ministris, statim inquirantur in quolibet comitatu, per duodecim milites juratos de eodem comitatu; qui debent eligi per probos homines ejusdem comitatus; et infra xl. dies post inquisitionem factam penitus, ita quod nunquam revocentur, deleantur per eosdem; dum tamen dominus Rex hoc prius sciat; universitati vestre notum fieri volumus, quod articulus iste ita intellectus fuit ex utraque parte, quum de eo tractabatur, et expressus, quod omnes consuetudines ille remanere debent, sine quibus foreste servari non possint: et hoc presentibus litteris protestamur.

[1] See *supra*, pp. 43, and 440. The protest is recorded in *Rot. Claus.*, 17 John m. 27 d., and is printed in *New Rymer*, I. 134.

(7) Protest by the archbishops and other prelates that the barons repudiated their promise to ratify their oaths by formal charters.[1]

Omnibus Christi fidelibus etc. Stephanus, Dei gracia Cantuar. archiepiscopus, totius Anglie primas et sancte Romane ecclesie cardinalis, Henricus Dublin. archiepiscopus, Willielmus London., Petrus Winton., Joscelinus Bathon. et Glaston., Hugo Lincoln., Walterus Wigorn., Willielmus Coventr., Ricardus Cicestr., episcopi et magister Pandulfus domini Pape subdiaconus et familiaris, salutem. Noverit universitas vestra, quod quando facta fuit pax inter dominum regem Johannem et barones Anglie, de discordia inter eos orta, idem barones, nobis presentibus et audientibus, promiserunt domino Regi, quod quamcumque securitatem habere vellet ab eis de pace illa observanda, ipsi ei habere facerent, preter castella et obsides. Postea vero quando dominus Rex petiit ab eis, ut talem cartam ei facerent :—

"Omnibus etc. Sciatis nos astrictos esse per sacramenta et homagia domino nostro Johanni Regi Anglie, de fide ei servanda de vita et membris et terreno honore suo, contra omnes homines qui vivere possint et mori; et ad jura sua et heredum suorum, et ad regnum suum custodiendum et defendendum."

Ipsi id facere noluerunt. Et in hujus rei testimonium id ipsum per hoc scriptum protestamur.

VII. THE GREAT CHARTER OF HENRY III.[2]
(THIRD REISSUE, 11TH FEBRUARY, 1225.)

Henricus Dei gratia rex Anglie, dominus Hibernie, dux Normannie, Aquitanie, et comes Andegavie, archiepiscopis, epis-

---

[1] See *supra*, p. 43. The protest is printed in *Rot. Pat.*, I. 144 (17 m. 21 d.), and also in *New Rymer*, I. 134.

[2] This is the definitive form of the Great Charter, as confirmed by Edward I. in 1297 and many times thereafter. See *supra*, p. 154. The text is taken from *Statutes of the Realm*, I. 22-25. Words not found in the Charter of 1215 are here printed in italics. The footnotes (in preparing which frequent reference has been made to Bémont's *Chartes*) give the principal variants occurring in the Charters of 1215, 1216, and 1217, as compared with that of 1225. The numbers commonly used (and here adopted) for the chapters of the issue of 1225 do not agree with those used for similar chapters of the issue of 1217. The numbers in brackets are those of corresponding chapters of 1215.

copis, abbatibus, *prioribus,* comitibus, baronibus,[1] vicecomitibus, prepositis, ministris et omnibus ballivis et fidelibus suis *presentem cartam inspecturis,* salutem. Sciatis [2] quod nos, intuitu Dei et pro salute anime nostre et *animarum* antecessorum et successorum nostrorum, ad exaltationem sancte ecclesie et emendationem regni nostri, *spontanea et bona voluntate nostra, dedimus et concessimus archiepiscopis, episcopis, abbatibus, prioribus, comitibus, baronibus et omnibus de regno nostro has libertates subscriptas tenendas in regno nostro Anglie in perpetuum.*

1 (1). In primis *concessimus* [3] Deo et hac presenti carta nostra *confirmavimus* [4] pro nobis et heredibus nostris in perpetuum quod anglicana ecclesia libera sit, et habeat *omnia* [5] jura sua integra

[1] *Justiciariis, forestariis* follow *baronibus* in the issues of 1215 and 1216, both of which omit *prioribus.*

[2] The sentence following "*sciatis*" differs in each preamble. For that of 1215, see *supra,* pp. 185-6.

The Charter of 1216 reads: Sciatis nos, intuitu Dei et pro salute anime nostre et omnium antecessorum et successorum nostrorum, ad honorem Dei et exaltationem sancte ecclesie et emendationem regni nostri, per consilium venerabilium patrum nostrorum domini Gualonis titulo sancti Martini presbiteri cardinalis, apostolici sedis legati, Petri Wintoniensis, Reineri de Sancto Asapho, Jocelini Batthoniensis et Glastoniensis, Simonis Exoniensis, Ricardi Cicestriensis, Willelmi Coventriensis, Benedicti Roffensis, Henrici Landavensis, Menevensis, Bangorensis et Sylvestri Wygorniensis episcoporum, et nobilium virorum Willelmi Mariscalli, comitis Penbrocie, Ranulfi comitis Cestrie, Willelmi de Ferrariis comitis Derebie, Willelmi comitis Albemarle, Huberti de Burgo justiciarii nostri, Savarici de Maloleone, Willelmi Brigwerre patris, Willelmi Brigwerre filii, Roberti de Crutenay, Falkesii de Breaute, Reginaldi de Vautort, Walteri de Lascy, Hugonis de Mortuomari, Johannis de Monemute, Walteri de Bellocampo, Walteri de Clifford, Roberti de Mortuomari, Willelmi de Cantilupo, Mathei filii Hereberti, Johannis Mariscalli, Alani Bassett, Philippi de Albiniaco, Johannis Extranei et aliorum fidelium nostrorum: (i) Imprimis concessisse Deo et hac presenti carta confirmasse . . . .

The Charter of 1217 reads: Sciatis quod, intuitu Dei et pro salute anime nostre et animarum antecessorum et successorum nostrorum, ad exaltationem sancte ecclesie et emendationem regni nostri, concessimus et hac presenti carta confirmavimus pro nobis et heredibus nostris in perpetuum, de consilio venerabilis patris nostri domini Gualonis titulo Sancti Martini presbiteri cardinalis et apostolice sedis legati, domini Walteri Eboracensis archiepiscopi, Willelmi Londoniensis episcopi et aliorum episcoporum Anglie, et Willelmi Mariscalli comitis Pembrocie, rectoris nostri et regni nostri, et aliorum fidelium, comitum et baronum nostrorum Anglie, has libertates subscriptas tenendas in regno nostro Anglie in perpetuum.

[3] *Concessisse,* in 1215 and 1216.   [4] *Confirmasse,* in 1215 and 1216.

[5] *Omnia,* omitted also in 1216 and 1217.

et libertates suas illesas.[1] Concessimus etiam omnibus liberis hominibus regni nostri pro nobis et heredibus nostris in perpetuum omnes libertates subscriptas, habendas et tenendas eis et heredibus suis de nobis et heredibus nostris *in perpetuum*.[2]

2 (2). Si quis comitum vel baronum nostrorum sive aliorum tenencium de nobis in capite per servicium militare mortuus fuerit, et, cum decesserit, heres *ejus* [3] plene etatis fuerit et relevium debeat, habeat hereditatem suam per antiquum relevium, scilicet heres vel heredes comitis de baronia comitis integra per centum libras, heres vel heredes baronis de baronia integra per centum libras,[4] heres vel heredes militis de feodo militis integro per centum solidos ad plus; et qui minus debuerit minus det secundum antiquam consuetudinem feodorum.

3 (3). Si autem heres alicujus talium fuerit infra etatem,[5] *dominus ejus non habeat custodiam ejus nec terre sue antequam homagium ejus ceperit; et, postquam talis heres* fuerit in custodia, cum ad etatem pervenerit, *scilicet viginti et unius anni,* habeat hereditatem suam sine relevio et sine fine, *ita tamen quod, si ipse, dum infra etatem fuerit, fiat miles, nichilominus terra remaneat in custodia dominorum suorum usque ad terminum predictum.*

4 (4). Custos terre hujusmodi heredis qui infra etatem fuerit non capiat de terra heredis nisi rationabiles exitus et rationabiles consuetudines et rationabilia servicia, et hoc sine destructione et vasto hominum vel rerum; et si nos commiserimus custodiam alicujus talis terre vicecomiti vel alicui alii qui de exitibus *terre* illius nobis debeat respondere, et ille destructionem de custodia fecerit vel vastum, nos ab illo capiemus emendam, et terra committetur [6] duobus legalibus et discretis hominibus de feodo illo qui de exitibus nobis respondeant vel ei cui eos assignaverimus; et si dederimus vel vendiderimus alicui custodiam alicujus talis terre, et ille destructionem inde fecerit vel vastum, amittat ipsam

---

[1] For the important clause occurring in 1215 between *illesas* and *Concessimus*, see *supra*, p. 190.

[2] *In perpetuum*, omitted also in 1216 and 1217.   [3] *Suus*, in 1215.

[4] The *Inspeximus* of 1297 reads "*marcas*" in place of "libras." See *supra*, p. 201.   Cf. Bracton, II. c. 36, and other authorities cited by Bémont, *Chartes*, 47 n.

[5] *Et* connects *etatem* and *fuerit in custodia* in 1215, the intervening words being omitted.

[6] *Committatur*, in 1215, 1216 and 1217.

custodiam et tradatur duobus legalibus et discretis hominibus de feodo illo qui similiter nobis respondeant, sicut predictum est.

5 (5). Custos autem, quamdiu custodiam terre habuerit, sustentet domos, parcos, vivaria, stagna, molendina et cetera ad terram illam pertinencia de exitibus terre ejusdem, et reddat heredi, cum ad plenam etatem pervenerit, terram suam totam instauratam de carucis [1] *et omnibus aliis rebus, ad minus secundum quod illam recepit. Hec omnia observentur de custodiis archiepiscopatuum, episcopatuum, abbatiarum, prioratuum, ecclesiarum et dignitatum vacancium que ad nos pertinent, excepto quod hujusmodi custodie vendi non debent.*

6 (6). Heredes maritentur absque disparagatione.[2]

7 (7). Vidua post mortem mariti sui statim et sine difficultate *aliqua* habeat maritagium suum et hereditatem suam, nec aliquid det pro dote sua vel pro maritagio suo vel pro hereditate sua, quam hereditatum maritus suus et ipsa tenuerunt [3] die obitus ipsius mariti, et maneat in capitali mesagio mariti sui [4] per quadraginta dies post obitum ipsius mariti sui, infra quos assignetur ei dos sua, *nisi prius ei fuerit assignata, vel nisi domus illa sit castrum; et si de castro recesserit, statim provideatur ei domus competens in qua possit honeste morari, quousque dos sua ei assignetur secundum quod predictum est,[5] et habeat rationabile estoverium suum interim de communi. Assignetur autem ei pro dote sua tercia pars tocius terre mariti sui que sua fuit in vita sua, nisi de minori dotata fuerit ad hostium ecclesie.*

(8). Nulla vidua distringatur ad se maritandam,[6] dum vivere voluerit sine marito, ita tamen quod securitatem faciet quod se non maritabit sine assensu nostro, si de nobis tenuerit, vel sine assensu domini sui,[7] si de alio tenuerit.

8 (9). Nos vero vel ballivi [8] nostri non seisiemus terram aliquam nec redditum pro debito aliquo quamdiu catalla debitoris *presencia* sufficiant [9] ad debitum reddendum *et ipse debitor para-*

---

[1] Different ending in 1215; see *supra*, p. 210.

[2] An additional clause occurs in 1215; see *supra*, p. 212.

[3] *Tenuerint*, in 1216 and 1217.

[4] *In domo mariti sui*, in 1215 and 1216; *in capitali mesuagio mariti sui*, in 1217.

[5] The words *et habeat* to *ad hostium ecclesie* are omitted also in 1216.

[6] *Maritandum*, in 1216; a contraction occurs in 1217, which may stand for either termination.

[7] *De quo tenuerit*, in 1215.   [8] *Nec nos nec ballivi*, in 1215.

[9] *Sufficiunt*, in 1215, 1216 and 1217.

tus sit inde satisfacere; nec plegii ipsius debitoris distringantur quamdiu ipse capitalis debitor sufficiat[1] ad solutionem debiti; et, si capitalis debitor defecerit in solutione debiti, non habens unde reddat *aut reddere nolit cum possit,* plegii respondeant pro[2] debito; et, si voluerint, habeant terras et redditus debitoris quousque[3] sit eis satisfactum de debito quod ante pro eo solverunt,[4] nisi capitalis debitor monstraverit se inde esse quietum versus eosdem plegios.

9[5] (13). Civitas[6] Londonie habeat omnes antiquas libertates et liberas consuetudines suas.[7] Preterea volumus et concedimus quod omnes alie civitates, et burgi, et ville, *et barones de quinque portubus,* et *omnes* portus, habeant omnes libertates et liberas consuetudines suas.

10[8] (16). Nullus distringatur ad faciendum majus servicium de feodo militis nec de alio libero tenemento quam inde debetur.

11 (17). Communia placita non sequantur curiam nostram, set teneantur in aliquo loco certo.

12 (18). Recognitiones de nova disseisina *et* de morte antecessoris[9] non capiantur nisi in suis comitatibus, et hoc modo : nos, vel si extra regnum fuerimus, capitalis justiciarius noster, mittemus[10] justiciarios per unumquemque comitatum *semel in anno,*[11] qui cum militibus comitatuum capiant in comitatibus assisas predictas. *Et ea que in illo adventu suo in comitatu per justiciarios predictos ad dictas assisas capiendas missos terminari non possunt, per eosdem terminentur alibi in itinere suo; et ea que per eosdem propter difficultatem aliquorum articulorum terminari non possunt, referantur ad justiciarios nostros de banco, et ibi terminentur.*

13. *Assise de ultima presentatione semper capiantur coram justiciariis nostris de banco et ibi terminentur.*

14[12] (20). Liber homo non amercietur pro parvo delicto nisi secundum modum *ipsius* delicti, et pro magno delicto, secundum

---

[1] *Sufficit,* in 1215.   [2] *De,* in 1215.   [3] *Donec,* in 1215.

[4] *Solverint,* in 1215, 1216 and 1217.

[5] Three additional chapters (10, 11 and 12) occur in 1215.

[6] *Et civitas,* in 1215.   [7] *Tam per terras, quam per aquas,* in 1215.

[8] Two additional chapters (14 and 15) occur in 1215.

[9] *Et de ultima presentacione,* added in 1215.   [10] *Duos justiciarios,* in 1215.

[11] *Per quatuor vices in anno,* in 1215, which concludes somewhat differently, see *supra,* p. 296.   The charter of 1216 is practically the same, here, as that of 1215; while that of 1225 reproduces that of 1217.

[12] An additional chapter (19) occurs in 1215.

magnitudinem delicti, salvo contenemento suo; et mercator eodem modo salva mercandisa sua; et villanus *alterius quam noster*[1] eodem modo amercietur salvo wainagio suo, si inciderit[2] in misericordiam nostram : et nulla predictarum misericordiarum ponatur nisi per sacramentum [3] proborum *et legalium* hominum de visneto.

(21). Comites et barones non amercientur nisi per pares suos, et non nisi secundum modum delicti.

(22).[4] *Nulla ecclesiastica persona* amercietur *secundum quantitatem beneficii sui ecclesiastici, set secundum laicum tenementum suum, et secundum quantitatem delicti.*

15 (23). Nec villa, nec homo, distringatur facere pontes ad riparias nisi qui ex antiquo et de jure facere debet.[5]

16.[6] *Nulla riparia decetero defendatur, nisi ille que fuerunt in defenso tempore regis Henrici avi nostri, per eadem loca et eosdem terminos sicut esse consueverunt tempore suo.*

17 (24). Nullus vicecomes, constabularius, coronatores vel alii ballivi nostri teneant placita corone nostre.

18[7] (26). Si aliquis tenens de nobis laicum feodum moriatur, et vicecomes vel ballivus noster ostendat litteras nostras patentes de summonitione nostra de debito quod defunctus nobis debuit, liceat vicecomiti vel ballivo nostro attachiare et inbreviare catalla defuncti inventa in laico feodo ad valenciam illius debiti per visum legalium hominum, ita tamen quod nichil inde amoveatur donec persolvatur nobis debitum quod clarum fuerit, et residuum relinquatur executoribus ad faciendum testamentum defuncti ; et si nichil nobis debeatur ab ipso, omnia catalla cedant defuncto, salvis uxori ipsius et pueris suis [8] rationabilibus partibus suis.

---

[1] *Alterius quam noster*, omitted also in 1216 ; first inserted in 1217.

[2] *Inciderint*, in 1215. [3] *Sacramenta*, in 1217.

[4] This reads in 1215 : *Nullus clericus amercietur de laico tenemento suo, nisi secundum modum aliorum predictorum, et non secundum beneficii sui ecclesiastici.*

In 1216 : *Nullus clericus amercietur, nisi secundum formam predictorum, et non secundum quantitatem beneficii sui ecclesiastici.*

The Charter of 1217 is here identical with that of 1225, except that *sed* takes the place of *set*.

[5] *Debent*, in 1215.

[6] Compare with last clause of c. 47 of 1215, which was omitted in 1216. The Charter of 1217 here resembles that of 1225.

[7] An additional chapter (25) occurs in 1215 ; see *supra*, p. 317, which should be compared with c. 35 of 1225.

[8] Omitted in 1216.

19 [1] (28). Nullus constabularius vel ejus ballivus [2] capiat blada vel alia catalla alicujus *qui non sit de villa ubi castrum situm est,* nisi statim inde reddat denarios aut respectum inde habere possit de voluntate venditoris ; *si autem de villa ipsa fuerit, infra quadraginta dies precium reddat.* [3]

20 (29). Nullus constabularius distringat aliquem militem ad dandum denarios pro custodia castri, si *ipse eam* facere voluerit [4] in propria persona sua, vel per alium probum hominem, si ipse eam facere non possit propter rationabilem caus. ͫ, et, si nos duxerimus eum [5] vel miserimus in exercitum, erit quietus de custodia secundum quantitatem temporis quo per nos fuerit in exercitu *de feodo pro quo fecit servicium in exercitu.* [6]

21 (30). Nullus vicecomes, vel ballivus noster, vel alius [7] capiat equos vel carettas alicujus [8] pro cariagio faciendo, nisi [9] *reddat liberationem antiquitus statutam, scilicet pro caretta ad duos equos decem denarios per diem, et pro caretta ad tres equos quatuordecim denarios per diem.* [10] *Nulla caretta dominica alicujus ecclesiastice persone vel militis vel alicujus domine capiatur per ballivos predictos.*

(31). Nec nos nec ballivi nostri *nec alii* [11] capiemus alienum boscum ad castra vel alia agenda nostra, nisi per voluntatem illius [12] cujus boscus ille fuerit.

22 (32). Nos non tenebimus terras eorum [13] qui convicti fuerint de felonia, nisi per unum annum et unum diem ; et tunc reddantur terre dominis feodorum.

23 (33). Omnes kidelli decetero deponantur penitus per Tamisiam et Medeweiam [14] et per totam Angliam, nisi per costeram maris.

---

[1] An additional chapter (27) occurs in 1215 ; see *supra*, p. 326.

[2] *Alius ballivus noster,* in 1215, which omits *ejus.*

[3] In 1216 the last phrase reads : *si autem de villa fuerit, teneatur infra tres septimanas precium reddere.*

[4] *Si facere voluerit custodiam illam,* in 1215.

[5] *Eum* comes after *miserimus* in 1215.

[6] The words in italics here are omitted also in 1216.

[7] *Aliquis alius,* in 1215.   [8] *Alicujus liberi hominis,* in 1215.

[9] *Nisi de voluntate ipsius liberi hominis,* in 1215.

[10] This chapter is not in 1216, but first occurs in 1217.

[11] *Nec alii,* omitted also in 1216.   [12] *Ipsius,* in place of *illius,* in 1215.

[13] *Illorum,* in place of *eorum,* in 1215.   [14] *De Tamisia, et de Medewaye,* in 1215.

24 (34). Breve quod vocatur Precipe decetero non fiat alicui de aliquo[1] tenemento, unde liber homo *perdat*[2] curiam suam.

25 (35). Una mensura vini sit per totum regnum nostrum, et una mensura cervisie, et una mensura bladi, scilicet quarterium London., et una latitudo pannorum tinctorum et russettorum et haubergettorum, scilicet due ulne infra listas; de ponderibus *vero*[3] sit ut de mensuris.

26 (36). Nichil detur[4] de cetero pro brevi inquisitionis *ab eo qui inquisitionem petit*[5] de vita vel membris, set gratis concedatur et non negetur.

27 (37). Si aliquis teneat de nobis per feodifirmam vel soccagium, vel per burgagium, et de alio terram teneat per servicium militare, nos non habebimus custodiam heredis nec terre sue que est de feodo alterius, occasione illius feodifirme, vel soccagii, vel burgagii, nec habebimus custodiam illius feodifirme vel soccagii vel burgagii, nisi ipsa feodifirma debeat servicium militare. Nos non habebimus custodiam heredis *nec*[6] terre alicujus quam tenet de alio per servicium militare, occasione alicujus parve serjanterie quam tenet de nobis per servicium reddendi nobis cultellos, vel sagittas, vel hujusmodi.

28 (38). Nullus ballivus ponat decetero aliquem ad legem *manifestam vel ad juramentum* simplici loquela sua, sine testibus fidelibus ad hoc inductis.

29 (39). Nullus liber homo *decetero* capiatur vel inprisonetur aut disseisiatur *de aliquo libero tenemento suo vel libertatibus vel liberis consuetudinibus suis*,[7] aut utlagetur, aut exuletur aut aliquo *alio* modo destruatur, nec super eum ibimus, nec super eum mittemus, nisi per legale judicium parium suorum, vel per legem terre.

(40). Nulli vendemus, nulli negabimus aut differemus rectum vel[8] justiciam.

30 (41). Omnes mercatores, *nisi publice antea prohibiti fuerint,* habeant salvum et securum exire de Anglia, et venire in Angliam, et morari, et ire per Angliam tam per terram quam per aquam[9] ad emendum *vel*[10] vendendum sine omnibus toltis

---

[1] *Libero* follows *aliquo,* in 1297.

[2] *Amittere possit,* in 1215; *omittere possit,* in 1216.   [3] *Autem,* in 1215.

[4] *Vel capiatur,* after *detur,* in 1215.

[5] The words in italics are omitted also in 1216.

[6] *Et* for *nec,* in 1216; *vel* in 1217.

[7] The words in italics are omitted also in 1216.   [8] *Aut,* in 1215.

[9] *Aquas,* in 1216.   [10] *Et,* in 1215 and 1217.

malis[1] per antiquas et rectas consuetudines, preterquam in tempore gwerre, et si sint de terra contra nos gwerrina; et si tales inveniantur in terra nostra in principio gwerre, attachientur sine dampno corporum vel rerum, donec sciatur a nobis vel *a* capitali justiciario nostro quomodo mercatores terre nostre tractentur, qui tunc invenientur in terra contra nos gwerrina; et, si nostri salvi sint ibi, alii salvi sint in terra nostra.

31[2] (43). Si quis tenuerit de aliqua escaeta, sicut de honore Wallingefordie, Bolonie, Notingeham, Lancastrie, vel de aliis[3] que sunt in manu nostra, et sint baronie, et obierit, heres ejus non det aliud relevium nec fiat[4] nobis aliud servicium quam faceret baroni, si *ipsa*[5] esset in manu baronis; et nos eodem modo eam tenebimus quo baro eam tenuit; *nec nos, occasione talis baronie vel escaete, habebimus aliquam escaetam vel custodiam aliquorum hominum nostrorum, nisi alibi tenuerit de nobis in capite ille qui tenuit baroniam vel escaetam.*[6]

32.[7] *Nullus liber homo decetero det amplius alicui vel vendat de terra sua quam ut de residuo terre sue possit sufficienter fieri domino feodi servicium ei debitum quod pertinet ad feodum illud.*

33[8] (46). Omnes *patroni abbatiarum* qui habent cartas regum Anglie *de advocatione,* vel antiquam tenuram *vel possessionem,* habeant earum custodiam cum vacaverint, sicut habere debent, *et sicut supra declaratum est.*

34[9] (54). Nullus capiatur vel imprisonetur propter appellum femine de morte alterius quam viri sui.

---

[1] *Malis toltis,* in 1215.

[2] An additional chapter (42) occurs in 1215.

[3] *Eskaetis,* after *aliis,* in 1215.

[4] *Faciat,* for *fiat,* in 1215.

[5] *Si baronia illa esset,* in 1215; *si terra illa esset,* in 1216; *si illa esset,* in 1217.

[6] The words in italics are omitted also in 1216.

[7] Two additional chapters (44 and 45) occur in 1215.

[8] The charter of 1215 reads: *omnes barones qui fundaverunt abbatias, unde habent cartas regum Anglie, vel antiquam tenuram, habeant earum custodiam cum vacaverint, sicut habere debent.*

[9] Seven additional chapters (47 to 53) occur in 1215. The charter of 1216 omits cc. 32 and 33 of 1225, but has instead of them three chapters of which c. 36 is the same as c. 44 of 1215, except that *sunt* appears for *sint*; c. 37 is the same as c. 46 of 1215, as quoted in last note, except that the words *et sicut supra declaratum est* are added at the end; c. 38 is of the same tenor as c. 47 of 1215, except that John's *tempore nostro* is changed to meet the altered circumstances.

35.[1] *Nullus comitatus decetero teneatur, nisi de mense in mensem; et, ubi major terminus esse solebat, major sit. Nec aliquis vicecomes vel ballivus faciat turnum suum per hundredum nisi bis in anno et non nisi in loco debito et consueto, videlicet semel post Pascha et iterum post festum sancti Michaelis. Et visus de franco plegio tunc fiat ad illum terminum sancti Michaelis sine occasione, ita scilicet quod quilibet habeat libertates suas quas habuit et habere consuevit tempore regis Henrici avi nostri, vel quas postea perquisivit. Fiat autem visus de franco plegio sic, videlicet quod pax nostra teneatur, et quod tethinga integra sit sicut esse consuevit, et quod vicecomes non querat occasiones, et quod contentus sit eo quod vicecomes habere consuevit de visu suo faciendo tempore regis Henrici avi nostri.*

36. *Non liceat alicui decetero dare terram suam alicui domui religiose, ita quod eam resumat tenendam de eadem domo, nec liceat alicui domui religiose terram alicujus sic accipere quod tradat illam ei[2] a quo ipsam recepit[3] tenendam. Si quis autem de cetero terram suam alicui domui religiose sic dederit, et super hoc convincatur, donum suum penitus cassetur, et terra illa domino suo illius feodi incurratur.*

37. *Scutagium decetero capiatur sicut capi solebat[4] tempore regis Henrici avi nostri. Et salve[5] sint archiepiscopis, episcopis, abbatibus, prioribus, templariis, hospitalariis, comitibus, baronibus et omnibus aliis tam ecclesiasticis quam secularibus personis libertates et libere consuetudines quas prius habuerunt.*

(60). Omnes autem istas consuetudines predictas et libertates quas concessimus in regno nostro tenendas quantum ad nos pertinet erga nostros, omnes de regno nostro tam clerici quam laici observent quantum ad se pertinet erga suos.[6] *Pro hac*

[1] The charter of 1216 (like that of 1215) omits cc. 35, 36, and 37 of 1225 (all of which occur in 1217). C. 35 of 1225, however, should be compared with c. 25 of 1215, and c. 37 of 1225 with c. 12 of 1215.

The charter of 1215 has five additional chapters here (55 to 59), of which c. 56 appears in 1216 as c. 40, with the alteration made necessary by the new reign.

[2] *Eam illi* (in place of *illam ei*), in 1217.

[3] *Receperit* (in place of *recepit*), in 1217.

[4] *Consuevit* (in place of *solebat*), in 1217.

[5] The last sentence, from *Et salve* onwards, is omitted in 1217.

[6] After *erga suos*, each charter proceeds differently. The charter of 1215 has three additional chapters (61, 62, and 63, *q.v.*).

The charter of 1216 has one additional chapter : Quia vero quedam capitula in priori (*sic*) carta continebantur que gravia et dubitabilia videbantur, scilicet de *autem concessione et donatione libertatum istarum et aliarum libertatum contentarum in carta nostra de libertatibus foreste, archiepiscopi, episcopi, abbates, priores, comites, barones, milites, libere tenentes, et omnes de regno nostro dederunt nobis quintam decimam partem omnium mobilium suorum. Concessimus etiam eisdem pro nobis et heredibus nostris quod nec nos nec heredes nostri aliquid perquiremus per quod libertates in hac carta contente infringantur vel infirmentur; et, si de aliquo aliquid contra hoc perquisitum fuerit, nichil valeat et pro nullo habeatur.*

Hiis testibus domino Stephano Cantuariensi archiepiscopo, Eustachio Lundoniensi, Jocelino Bathoniensi, Petro Wintoniensi, Hugoni Lincolniensi, Ricardo Sarrisberiensi, Benedicto Roffensi, Willelmo Wigorniensi, Johanne Eliensi, Hugone Herefordiensi, Radulpho Cicestriensi, Willelmo Exoniensi episcopis, abbate sancti Albani, abbate sancti Edmundi, abbate de Bello, abbate sancti Augustini Cantuariensis, abbate de Eveshamia, abbate de Westmonasterio, abbate de Burgo sancti Petri, abbate Radingensi, abbate Abbendoniensi, abbate de Maumeburia, abbate de Winchecomba, abbate de Hida, abbate de Certeseia, abbate de Sireburnia, abbate de Cerne, abbate de

scutagiis et auxiliis assidendis, de debitis Judeorum et aliorum et de libertate exeundi de regno nostro, vel redeundi in regnum, et de forestis et forestariis, warrenis et warrenariis, et de consuetudinis comitatum, et de ripariis et earum custodibus, placuit supradictis prelatis et magnatibus ea esse in respectu quousque plenius consilium habuerimus; et tunc faciemus plenissime tam de hiis quam de aliis que occurrerint emendenda, que ad communem omnium utilitatem pertinuerint et pacem et statum nostrum et regni nostri. Quia vero sigillum nondum habuimus, presentem cartam sigillis venerabilis patris nostri domini Gualonis tituli sancti Martini presbiteri cardinalis, apostolice sedis legati, et Willelmi Mariscalli comitis Penbrocie, rectoris nostri et regni nostri, fecimus sigillari, Testibus omnibus prenominatis et aliis multis, Datum per manus predictorum domini legati et Willelmi Mariscalli, comitis Penbrocie apud Bristollum duodecimo die novembris anno regni nostri primo.

The charter of 1217 has two additional chapters (46 and 47):

C. 46: Salvis archiepiscopis, episcopis, abbatibus, prioribus, templariis, hospitalariis, comitibus, baronibus, et omnibus aliis, tam ecclesiasticis personis, quam secularibus, libertatibus et liberis consuetudinibus quas prius habuerunt—(which may be compared with the last clause of c. 37 of 1225, *supra*).

C. 47: Statuimus etiam, de communi consilio tocius regni nostri, quod omnia castra adulterina, videlicet ea que a principio guerre mote inter dominum Johannem patrem nostrum et barones suos Anglie constructa fuerint vel reedificata, statim deruantur. Quia vero nondum habuimus sigillum, hanc sigillis domini legati predicti et comitis Willelmi Mariscalli rectoris et regni nostri fecimus sigillari.

Abbotebiria, abbate de Middletonia, abbate de Seleby, abbate de Wyteby, abbate de Cirencestria, Huberto de Burgo justiciario, Ranulfo comite Cestrie et Lincolnie, Willelmo comite Sarrisberie, Willelmo comite Warennie, Gilberto de Clara comite Gloucestrie et Hertfordie, Willelmo de Ferrariis comite Derbeie, Willelmo de Mandevilla comite Essexie, Hugone Le Bigod comite Norfolcie, Willelmo comite Aubemarle, Hunfrido comite Herefordie, Johanne constabulario Cestrie, Roberto de Ros, Roberto filio Walteri, Roberto de Veteri ponte, Willielmo Brigwerre, Ricardo de Munfichet, Petro filio Herberti, Matheo filio Herberti, Willielmo de Albiniaco, Roberto Gresley, Reginaldo de Brahus, Johanne de Munemutha, Johanne filio Alani, Hugone de Mortuomari, Waltero de Bellocampo, Willielmo de sancto Johanne, Petro de Malalacu, Briano de Insula, Thoma de Muletonia, Ricardo de Argentein., Gaufrido de Nevilla, Willielmo Mauduit, Johanne de Baalun.

Datum apud Westmonasterium undecimo die februarii anno regni nostri nono.

VIII. CARTA DE FORESTA.[1]
(6 NOVEMBER, 1217.)

HENRICUS Dei gratia rex Anglie, dominus Hibernie, dux Normannie, Aquitanie et comes Andegavie, archiepiscopis, episcopis, abbatibus, prioribus, comitibus, baronibus, justiciariis, forestariis, vicecomitibus, prepositis, ministris, et omnibus ballivis et fidelibus suis, salutem. Sciatis quod, intuitu Dei et pro salute anime nostre et animarum antecessorum et successorum nostrorum, ad exaltacionem Sancte Ecclesie et emendacionem regni nostri, concessimus et hac presenti carta confirmavimus pro nobis et heredibus nostris in perpetuum, de consilio venerabilis patris nostri domini Gualonis tituli sancti Martini presbiteri cardinalis et apostolice sedis legati, domini Walteri Eboracensis archiepiscopi, Willelmi Londoniensis episcopi, et aliorum episcoporum Anglie, et Willelmi Marescalli comitis Penbrocie, rectoris nostri et regni nostri, et aliorum fidelium comitum et baronum nostrorum Anglie, has libertates subscriptas tenendas in regno nostro Anglie, in perpetuum :

1. In primis omnes foreste quas Henricus rex avus noster

[1] See *supra*, pp. 146-7. The text is taken from the *Statutes of the Realm*, I. 20-21. Bémont, *Chartes*, 64 ff., gives in footnotes the variants in the reissue of 1225.

afforestavit videantur per bonos et legales homines; et, si boscum aliquem alium quam suum dominicum afforestaverit ad dampnum illius cujus boscus fuerit, deafforestentur. Et si boscum suum proprium afforestaverit, remaneat foresta, salva communa de herbagio et aliis in eadem foresta, illis qui eam prius habere consueverunt.

2. Homines qui manent extra forestam non veniant decetero coram justiciariis nostris de foresta per communes summoniciones, nisi sint in placito, vel plegii alicujus vel aliquorum qui attachiati sunt propter forestam.

3. Omnes autem bosci qui fuerunt afforestati per regem Ricardum avunculum nostrum, vel per regem Johannem patrem nostrum usque ad primam coronacionem nostram, statim deafforestentur, nisi fuerit dominicus boscus noster.

4. Archiepiscopi, episcopi, abbates, priores, comites et barones et milites et libere tenentes, qui boscos suos habent in forestis, habeant boscos suos sicut eos habuerunt tempore prime coronacionis predicti regis Henrici avi nostri, ita quod quieti sint in perpetuum de omnibus purpresturis, vastis et assartis factis in illis boscis, post illud tempus usque ad principium secundi anni coronacionis nostre. Et qui de c .tero vastum, purpresturam, vel assartum sine licencia nostra in illis fecerint, de vastis et assartis respondeant.

5. Reguardores nostri eant per forestas ad faciendum reguardum sicut fieri consuevit tempore prime coronacionis predicti regis Henrici avi nostri, et non aliter.

6. Inquisicio, vel visus de expeditacione canum existencium in foresta, decetero fiat quando debet fieri reguardum, scilicet de tercio anno in tercium annum; et tunc fiat per visum et testimonium legalium hominum et non aliter. Et ille, cujus canis inventus fuerit tunc non expeditatus, det pro misericordia tres solidos; et de cetero nullus bos capiatur pro expeditacione. Talis autem sit expeditacio per assisam communiter quod tres ortilli abscidantur sine pelota de pede anteriori; nec expeditentur canes de cetero, nisi in locis ubi consueverunt expeditari tempore prime coronacionis regis Henrici avi nostri.

7. Nullus forestarius vel bedellus decetero faciat scotale, vel colligat garbas, vel avenam, vel bladum aliud, vel agnos, vel porcellos, nec aliquam collectam faciant; et per visum et sacramentum duodecim reguardorum quando facient reguardum, tot forestarii ponantur ad forestas custodiendas, quot ad illas custodiendas rationabiliter viderint sufficere.

8. Nullum suanimotum de cetero teneatur in regno nostro nisi ter in anno; videlicet in principio quindecim dierum ante festum Sancti Michaelis, quando agistatores conveniunt ad agistandum dominicos boscos nostros; et circa festum Sancti Martini quando agistatores nostri debent recipere pannagium nostrum; et ad ista duo suanimota conveniant forestarii, viridarii, et agistatores, et nullus alius per districtionem; et tercium suanimotum teneatur in inicio quindecim dierum ante festum Sancti Johannis Baptiste, pro feonacione bestiarum nostrarum; et ad istud suanimotum tenendum convenient forestarii et viridarii et nulli alii per districtionem. Et preterea singulis quadraginta diebus per totum annum conveniant viridarii et forestarii ad videndum attachiamenta de foresta, tam de viridi, quam de venacione, per presentacionem ipsorum forestariorum, et coram ipsis attachiatis. Predicta autem suanimota non teneantur nisi in comitatibus in quibus teneri consueverunt.

9. Unusquisque liber homo agistet boscum suum in foresta pro voluntate sua et habeat pannagium suum. Concedimus eciam quod unusquisque liber homo possit ducere porcos suos per dominicum boscum nostrum, libere et sine inpedimento, ad agistandum eos in boscis suis propriis, vel alibi ubi voluerit. Et si porci alicujus liberi hominis una nocte pernoctaverint in foresta nostra, non inde occasionetur ita quod aliquid de suo perdat.

10. Nullus de cetero amittat vitam vel menbra pro venacione nostra; set, si aliquis captus fuerit et convictus de capcione venacionis, graviter redimatur, si habeat unde redimi possit; et si non habeat unde redimi possit, jaceat in prisona nostra per unum annum et unum diem; et, si post unum annum et unum diem plegios invenire possit, exeat a prisona; sin autem, abjuret regnum Anglie.

11. Quicunque archiepiscopus, episcopus, comes vel baro transierit per forestam nostram, liceat ei capere unam vel duas bestias per visum forestarii, si presens fuerit; sin autem, faciat cornari, ne videatur furtive hoc facere.

12. Unusquisque liber homo decetero sine occasione faciat in bosco suo, vel in terra sua quam habeat in foresta, molendinum, vivarium, stagnum, marleram, fossatum, vel terram arabilem extra cooperatum in terra arabili, ita quod non sit ad nocumentum alicujus vicini.

13. Unusquisque liber homo habeat in boscis suis aereas, ancipitrum et spervariorum et falconum, aquilarum, et de hey-

rinis et habeat similiter mel quod inventum fuerit in boscis suis.

14. Nullus forestarius de cetero, qui non sit forestarius de feudo reddens nobis firmam pro balliva sua, capiat chiminagium aliquod in balliva sua; forestarius autem de feudo firmam nobis reddens pro balliva sua capiat chiminagium, videlicet pro careta per dimidium annum duos denarios, et pro equo qui portat sumagium per dimidium annum unum obolum, et per alium dimidium annum obolum, et non nisi de illis qui de extra ballivam suam, tanquam mercatores, veniunt per licenciam suam in ballivam suam ad buscam, meremium, corticem vel carbonem emendum, et alias ducendum ad vendendum ubi voluerint : et de nulla alia careta vel sumagio aliquod chimunagium capiatur : et non capiatur chiminagium nisi in locis illis ubi antiquitus capi solebat et debuit. Illi autem qui portant super dorsum suum buscam, corticem, vel carbonem, ad vendendum, quamvis inde vivant, nullum de cetero dent chiminagium. De boscis autem aliorum nullum detur chiminagium foristariis nostris, preterquam de dominicis bocis nostris.

15. Omnes utlagati pro foresta tantum a tempore regis Henrici avi nostri usque ad primam coronacionem nostram, veniant ad pacem nostram sine inpedimento, et salvos plegios inveniant quod de cetero non forisfaciant nobis de foresta nostra.

16. Nullus castellanus vel alius teneat placita de foresta sive viridi sive de venacione, sed quilibet forestarius de feudo attachiet placita de foresta tam de viridi quam de venacione, et ea presentet viridariis provinciarum et cum irrotulata fuerint et sub sigillis viridariorum inclusa, presententur capitali forestario cum in partes illas venerit ad tenendum placita foreste, et coram eo terminentur.

17. Has autem libertates de forestis concessimus omnibus, salvis archiepiscopis, episcopis, abbatibus, prioribus, comitibus, baronibus, militibus et aliis tam personis ecclesiasticis quam secularibus, Templariis et Hospitalariis, libertatibus et liberis consuetudinibus in forestis et extra, in warennis et aliis, quas prius habuerunt. Omnes autem istas consuetudines predictas et libertates, quas concessimus in regno nostro tenendas quantum ad nos pertinet erga nostros, omnes de regno nostro tam clerici quam laici observent quantum ad se pertinet erga suos. Quia vero sigillum nondum habuimus, presentem cartam sigillis venerabilis patris nostri domini Gualonis tituli Sancti Martini

presbiteri cardinalis, apostolice sedis legati, et Willelmi Marescalli comitis Penbrok, rectoris nostri et regni nostri, fecimus
sigillari. Testibus prenominatis et aliis multis. Datum per
manus predictorum domini legati et Willelmi Marescalli apud
Sanctum Paulum London., sexto die Novembris, anno regni
nostri secundo.

SELECT BIBLIOGRAPHY AND LIST OF AUTHORITIES REFERRED TO.

I. COMMENTARIES AND OTHER WORKS ON MAGNA CARTA (CHRONOLOGICALLY ARRANGED).

The Mirror of Justices, edited by Whittaker, W. J. (Selden Society); 1895.

Coke, Sir Edward, *Second Institute*, 1641; 17th edition, 1817.

Cooke, Edward, *Magna Charta made in the ninth year of King Henry III. and confirmed by King Edward I. in the twentieth year of his reign*; 1684.

Blackstone, Sir William, *The Great Charter and Charter of the Forest, to which is prefixed the History of the Charters*; 1759.

Barrington, Daines, *Observations upon the Statutes from Magna Charta to 21 James I.*; 1766.

Sullivan, F. S., *An Historical Treatise on the Feudal Law, with a Commentary on Magna Charta*; 1772.

Thomson, Richard, *An Historical Essay on the Magna Charta of King John*; 1829.

Lau, Thaddaeus, *Die Entstehungsgeschichte der Magna Charta*; 1856.

Bémont, Charles, *Chartes des Libertés Anglaises*; 1892.

Hantos, Elemér, *The Magna Carta of the English and of the Hungarian Constitution*; 1904.

II. CHRONICLES AND ANNALS.

Annals of Dunstable, edited by H. R. Luard (Rolls Series); 1866.

Annals of Waverley, edited by H. R. Luard (Rolls Series); 1865.

Benedict Abbot, *Gesta Regis Henrici Secundi*, edited by William Stubbs (Rolls Series); 1867.

Histoire de Guillaume le Maréchal, edited by Paul Meyer; 1891.

Histoire des ducs de Normandie et des rois d'Angleterre, edited by F. Michel; 1840.

Jocelyn of Brakelond, *Chronica de rebus gestis Samsonis Abbatis Monasterii Sancti Edmundi*, edited by J. G. Rokewode (Camden Society); 1840.

Matthew Paris, *Chronica Majora*, edited by H. R. Luard (Rolls Series); 1872.

Memorials of St. Dunstan, edited by William Stubbs (Rolls Series); 1874.

Ralph of Coggeshall, *Chronicon Anglicanum*, edited by Joseph Stevenson (Rolls Series); 1875.

Roger of Hoveden, *Chronica*, edited by William Stubbs (Rolls Series) ; 1868-1871.

Roger of Wendover, *Chronica sive Flores Historiarum*, edited by H. O. Coxe (Eng. Hist. Society) ; 1841.

Walter of Coventry, *Memoriale*, edited by William Stubbs (Rolls Series) ; 1872.

Walter of Hemingburgh, *Chronicon de Gestis Regum Angliae*, edited by H. C. Hamilton (Eng. Hist. Society) ; 1848-9.

William of Malmesbury, *Gesta Regum Anglorum*, edited by William Stubbs (Rolls Series) ; 1887-9.

III. COLLECTIONS OF STATUTES, CHARTERS, AND TREATIES.

Statutes of the Realm (Record Commission) ; 1810-28.

Statutes at Large.

Die Gesetze der Angelsachsen, edited by F. Liebermann ; 1898-1912.

Acts of the Parliament of Scotland from 1124 to 1707, edited by Thomas Thomson and Cosmo Innes ; 1814-75.

Rotuli Litterarum Clausarum in Turri Londinensi Asservata, edited by Thomas Duffus Hardy (Record Commission) ; 1833.

Rotuli Litterarum Patentum in Turri Londinensi Asservata, edited by T. D. Hardy (Record Commission) ; 1835.

Rotuli Chartarum in Turri Londinensi Asservata, edited by T. D. Hardy (Record Commission) ; 1837.

Rotuli de Oblatis et Finibus, edited by T. D. Hardy (Record Commission) ; 1835-6.

Rotuli Parliamentorum ; 1832.

Rotuli Hundredorum (Record Commission) ; 1812-18.

Testa de Neville sive Liber Feodorum (Record Commission) ; 1807.

The Red Book of the Exchequer, edited by Hubert Hall (Rolls Series) ; 1896.

Munimenta Gildhallae Londoniensis : Liber Albus, Liber Custumarum et Liber Horn, edited by H. T. Riley (Rolls Series) ; 1859-62.

Rymer, Thomas, *Foedera, Conventiones, Litterae, et cujuscunque generis acta publica* ; 4th edition (Record Commission) ; 1816-69 (referred to throughout as " New Rymer ").

Ancient Charters, Royal and Private, edited by J. H. Round (Pipe Roll Society, vol. 10) ; 1888.

D'Achery, J. L., *Vetorum Scriptorum Spicilegium* ; 1655-77.

Hemingi Chartularum Ecclesiae Wigornensis, edited by Thomas Hearne ; 1723.

Potthast, A., *Regesta Pontificum Romanorum* ; 1874-5.

Teulet, Alexandre, *Layettes du Trésor des Chartes* ; 1863-1902.

Stubbs, William, *Select Charters and other Illustrations of English Constitutional History* ; 7th edition, 1890.

Prothero, G. W., *Select Statutes and other Constitutional Documents illustrative of the reigns of Elizabeth and James I.* ; 1894.

Gardiner, S. R., *The Constitutional Documents of the Puritan Revolution* ; 1889.

Birch, W. de G., *Historical Charters and Constitutional Documents of the City of London* ; 1887.

IV. COLLECTIONS OF PLEAS, TRIALS, AND OTHER RECORD EVIDENCE.

Placitorum Abbreviatio, Richard I. to Edward II. (Record Commission) ; 1811.

Bigelow, M. M., *Placita Anglo-Normannica* ; 1879.

Bracton's Note Book : a Collection of Cases, edited by F. W. Maitland ; 1887.

Howell, T. B and T. J., *Complete Collection of State Trials* ; 1809-28 (referred to as " State Trials ").

Pleas of the Crown for the County of Gloucester, edited by F. W. Maitland ; 1884.

Select Pleas of the Crown, edited by F. W. Maitland (Selden Society) ; 1888.

Select Pleas in Manorial and other Seignorial Courts, edited by F. W. Maitland (Selden Society) ; 1889.

Select Pleas of the Forest, edited by G. J. Turner (Selden Society) ; 1901.

Select Pleas, Starrs, and other Records from the Rolls of the Exchequer of the Jews, edited by J. M. Rigg (Selden Society) ; 1902.

Year Books of the Reign of Edward I., edited by A. J. Horwood and L. O. Pike (Rolls Series) ; 1863-1901.

Year Books of Edward II., 1307-1309, edited by F. W. Maitland (Selden Society) ; 1903.

Great Roll of the Pipe for the Twelfth Year of Henry II. (Pipe Roll Society, vol. 9) ; 1888.

Madox, Thomas, *History and Antiquities of the Exchequer of the Kings of England* ; 2nd edition, 1769 (referred to throughout as " Madox ").

Madox, Thomas, *Firma Burgi* ; 1726.

Madox, Thomas, *Baronia Anglica* ; 1741.

V. LEGAL TREATISES—MEDIEVAL.

Glanvill, Ranulf, *Tractatus de Legibus et Consuetudinibus Regni Angliae.*

Richard, son of Nigel, *De necessariis Observantibus Scaccarii Dialogus* (commonly called *Dialogus de Scaccario*), edited by A. Hughes, C. G. Crump, and C. Johnson ; 1902.

Bracton, Henry de, *De legibus et consuetudinibus Angliae*, edited by Sir Travers Twiss (Rolls Series) ; 1878-83.

Fleta, *Commentarius Juris Anglicani* ; edition of 1647.

Littleton, Thomas, *Treatise of Tenures* ; edition of 1841.

VI. LEGAL TREATISES—MODERN.

Anson, Sir W. R., *The Law and Custom of the Constitution* ; 2nd edition, 1892.

Blackstone, Sir William, *Commentaries on the Laws of England* ; edition of 1826.

Coke, Sir Edward, *Institutes of the Laws of England* ; 17th edition, 1817. (The *First Institute* is generally referred to as " Coke on Littleton.")

Encyclopaedia of the Laws of England, edited by A. W. Renton ; 1897-8.

Hale, Sir Matthew, *Historia Placitorum Coronae* ; 1736.

Jenks, Edward, *Modern Land Law* ; 1899.

2 K 2

Manwood, John, *A Treatise and Discourse of the Laws of the Forest* ; 1598.

Stephen, H. J., *Commentaries on the Laws of England* ; 13th edition, 1899.

Thayer, J. B., *A Preliminary Treatise on Evidence at the Common Law* ; 1898.

VII. LEGAL AND CONSTITUTIONAL HISTORIES.

Bigelow, M. M., *History of Procedure in England* ; 1880.

Brunner, Heinrich, *Die Entstehung der Schwurgerichte* ; 1871.

Creasy, Edward, *Progress of the English Constitution* ; 1874.

Gneist, Rudolf, *The History of the English Constitution*, translated by P. A. Ashworth ; edition of 1891.

Gneist, Rudolf, *The English Parliament in its Transformations through a Thousand Years*, translated by A. H. Keane ; 1887.

Holdsworth, W. S., *A History of English Law*, vol. 1 ; 1903.

Medley, D. J., *A Student's Manual of English Constitutional History* ; 2nd edition, 1898.

Moore, S. A. and H. S., *The History and Law of Fisheries* ; 1903.

Pollock, Sir F., and Maitland, F. W., *The History of English Law before the time of Edward I.* ; 1st edition, 1895 (referred to throughout as " Pollock and Maitland ").

Pike, L. O., *A Constitutional History of the House of Lords, from original sources* ; 1894.

Reeves, John, *History of English Law* ; 3rd edition, 1783-4.

Stephen, Sir J. F., *A History of the Criminal Law in England* ; 1893.

Stubbs, William, *The Constitutional History of England in its Origin and Development* : (*a*) vol. 1, 6th edition, 1897 ; (*b*) vol. 2, 4th edition, 1894 ; (*c*) vol. 3, 5th edition, 1896.

Taswell-Langmead, T. P., *English Constitutional History from the Teutonic Conquest to the Present Time* ; 5th edition, 1896.

Taylor, Hannis, *The Origin and Growth of the English Constitution* ; 1898.

VIII. GENERAL HISTORIES.

Brady, Robert, *Complete History of England* ; 1685.

Care, Henry, *English Liberties in the Freeborn Subjects' Inheritance* ; 1719.

Green, J. R., *A Short History of the English People* ; edition of 1875.

Henry, Robert, *History of Great Britain* ; 6th edition, 1806.

Lingard, John, *A History of England to 1688* ; 1819-30.

Mackintosh, James, *History of England* ; edition of 1853.

Smith, Goldwin, *The United Kingdom : a Political History* ; 1899.

Tyrrell, James, *History of England*, 1697-1704.

IX. HISTORIES OF SPECIAL PERIODS.

Bateson, Mary, *Mediaeval England* (Story of the Nations Series) ; 1903.

Freeman, E. A., *The Norman Conquest of England* ; 1870-9.

Freeman, E. A., *The Reign of William Rufus* ; 1882.

Gardiner, S. R., *History of England from the Accession of James I. to the Outbreak of the Civil War* ; 1883-4.

Hallam, Henry, *View of the State of Europe during the Middle Ages* ; 7th edition, 1837.

Kemble, J. M., *Saxons in England* ; 1849.

Norgate, Kate, *England under Angevin Kings* ; 1887.

Norgate, Kate, *John Lackland* ; 1902.

Norgate, Kate, *The Minority of Henry III.* ; 1912.

Pearson, Charles, *A History of England during the Early and Middle Ages* ; 1867.

Petit-Dutaillis, Charles, *Étude sur la vie et la règne de Louis VIII.* ; 1894.

Powicke, F. M., *The Loss of Normandy* ; 1913.

Prothero, G. W., *The Life of Simon de Montfort, Earl of Leicester* ; 1877.

Ramsay, Sir J. H., *The Foundations of England* ; 1898.

Ramsay, Sir J. H., *The Angevin Empire* ; 1903.

X. MISCELLANEOUS.

Adams, G. B., *The Origin of the English Constitution* ; 1912.

Brady, Robert, *A Full and Clear Answer* ; 1683.

Boutmy, Émile, *Études de Droit Constitutionnel* ; 1885.

Burke, Edmund, *Works* ; edition of 1837.

Chadwick, H. Munro, *Studies on Anglo-Saxon Institutions* ; 1905.

Dowell, Stephen, *History of Taxation and Taxes in England* ; 1884.

Gross, Charles, Preface to *Select Cases from the Coroners' Rolls* (Selden Society) ; 1896.

Hall, Hubert, *History of the Customs Revenue in England* ; 1885.

Harcourt, L. W. V., *His Grace the Steward and Trial of Peers* ; 1907.

Hearnshaw, F. J. C., *Leet Jurisdiction in England* ; 1908.

Lapsley, G. T., *The County Palatine of Durham* ; 1900.

Luard, H. R., Preface to vol. 2 of Matthew Paris, *Chronica Majora* (Rolls Series) ; 1872.

Luchaire, Achille, *Communes Françaises* ; 1890.

Luffman, John, *Charters of London* ; 1793.

Neilson, George, *Trial by Combat* ; 1890.

Noorthouck, John, *A New History of London* ; 1773.

Macy, J., *The English Constitution ; a Commentary on its nature and growth* ; 1897.

Maitland, F. W., *Township and Borough* ; 1898.

Maitland, F. W., in *Social England*, edited by Henry Duff Trail, vol. 1 ; 1st edition, 1893.

Maitland, F. W., Preface to *Select Pleas of the Crown* (Selden Society) ; 1888.

Maitland, F. W., Preface to *Select Pleas in Manorial and other Seignorial Courts* (Selden Society) ; 1889.

Maitland, F. W., Preface to *The Mirror of Justices* (Selden Society) ; 1895.

Maitland, F. W., *Collected Papers*, 3 vols. ; 1911.

Maitland, F. W., *Equity* ; 1909.

Orpen, G. H., *Ireland under the Normans* ; 1911.

Petit-Dutaillis, Charles, *Studies and Notes Supplementary to Stubbs' Constitutional History*, translated by W. E. Rhodes ; 1908.

Pollock, Sir F., *Essays in Jurisprudence and Ethics* ; 1894.

Poole, R. L., *The Exchequer in the Twelfth Century* ; 1912.

Rigg, J. M., Preface to *Select Pleas, Starrs, and other Records from the Rolls of the Exchequer of the Jews* (Selden Society) ; 1902.

Rössler, Oskar, *Kaiserin Mathilde und das Zeitalter der Anarchie in England* ; 1897.

Round, J. H., editorial notes to *Ancient Charters, Royal and Private* (Pipe Roll Society, vol. 10) ; 1888.

Round, J. H., *Geoffrey de Mandeville : a Study of the Anarchy* ; 1892.

Round, J. H., *Feudal England : Historical Studies of the Eleventh and Twelfth Centuries* ; 1895.

Round, J. H., *The Commune of London and other Studies* ; 1899.

Round, J. H., *Peerage and Pedigree* ; 1910.

Round, J. H., *The ̄ .ngs' Serjeants and Officers of State* ; 1911.

Seebohm, Frederic, *The English Village Community : an Essay on Economic History* ; 1883.

Stubbs, William, Preface to Walter of Coventry, *Memoriale* (Rolls Series) ; 1972.

Turner, G. J., Preface to *Select Pleas of the Forest* (Selden Society) ; 1901.

Vinogradoff, Paul, *Villainage in England : Essays in English Mediaeval History* ; 1892.

Vinogradoff, Paul, *The Growth of the Manor* ; 1905.

Vinogradoff, Paul, *English Society in the Eleventh Century* ; 1908.

XI. REPORTS, BIBLIOGRAPHIES, AND DICTIONARIES.

Reports from the Lords' Committee appointed to search the Journals of the House, Rolls of Parliament, and other Records for all matters touching the Dignity of a Peer ; 1st Report, 1820.

Reports from the Select Committee appointed to inquire into the state of the Public Records of the Kingdom (Record Commission) ; 1900.

Report on Manuscripts in Various Collections (Historical Manuscripts Commission) ; 1901.

Gross, Charles, *The Sources and Literature of English History* ; 1900.

Watt, Robert, *Bibliotheca Britannica* ; 1824.

Lowndes, W. T., *The Bibliographer's Manual of English Literature* ; 1857-64.

Dictionary of National Biography, edited by Leslie Stephen and Sidney Lee ; 1885-1900.

INDEX OF STATUTES.

			PAGE
20 Henry III.	c. 6,	-	63, 213.
	c. 7,	-	- 64 n.
	c. 8,	-	- 64 n.
	c. 9,	-	- 432 n.
	c. 11,	210 n.,	423 n.
52 Henry III.	c. 15,	-	- 223 n.
	c. 16,	64 n.,	211, 275 n.
	c. 29,	-	- 355 n.
3 Edward I.	c. 1,	-	- 311 n.
	c. 6,	-	293.
	c. 7,	-	- 332 n.
	c. 10,	-	316.
	c. 11,	-	365.
	c. 12,	-	341, 375 n.
	c. 21,	-	- 209.
	c. 32,	330, 332 n.,	335 n.
	c. 36,	-	- 66.
	c. 48,	-	211.
4 Edward I.	(Rageman),	-	281 n.
6 Edward I.	c. 4,	-	55, 219 n.
	c. 5,	-	- 209.
	c. 9,	364 n.,	365 n.
7 Edward I.	-	-	150 n.
13 Edward I.	c. 5,	-	- 276 n.
	c. 12,	-	365 n.
	c. 13,	-	- 309 n.
	c. 29,	361 n.,	365 n.
	c. 30,	- 277 n.,	283.
	c. 39,	-	- 281.
	c. 47,	210 n.,	304 n.
18 Edward I.	-	-	150 n.
27 Edward I.	-	-	c. 3, 281.
28 Edward I.	c. 4,	-	- 268 n.
	c. 5,	-	- 267 n.
	c. 7,	-	- 315 n.
	c. 12,	-	223.
	c. 14,	-	319.
	stat. 3,	c. 13,	311 n.

Statutes of uncertain date:
Statute of Jewry, - 229, 231.
Praerogativa Regis, 339 n.
Consuetudines et Assisae de foresta, - - - 430.

			PAGE
1 Edward III.	stat. 2, c. 1,	438 n.
	c. 13,	413 n.
	c. 17,	309 n.
2 Edward III.	c. 2,	- 281 n.
	c. 9,	400 n., 406 n.
	c. 11,	- 263 n.
4 Edward III.	c. 15,	- 320.
5 Edward III.	c. 9,	- 380 n.
9 Edward III.	c. 1,	- 407 n.
14 Edward III.	stat. 1, c. 9,	320.
	c. 21,	400 n.
	stat. 2,	238.
	stat. 4, c. 4,	212.
	c. 5,	212.
25 Edward III.	stat. 3, c. 4,	344.
	stat. 4, c. 7,	407 n.
	stat. 5, c. 4,	380-1 n.
	c. 11,	66.
27 Edward III.	stat. 2, c. 8,	378 n.
28 Edward III.	c. 13,	- 378 n.
37 Edward III.	c. 9,	- 364 n.
	c. 18,	- 381 n.
38 Edward III.	c. 3,	- 381 n.
42 Edward III.	c. 1,	- 159, 364 n.
	c. 3,	- 381 n.
2 Richard II.	stat. 1, c. 1,	407 n.
6 Richard II.	c. 5,	- 284 n.
	c. 6,	- 453 n.
11 Richard II.	c. 7,	- 407 n.
	c. 11,	- 284 n.
17 Richard II.	c. 6,	- 381 n.
	c. 9,	- 345 n.
1 Henry IV.	c. 14,	- 366 n.
4 Henry IV.	c. 5,	- 320 n.
	c. 11,	- 345 n.
5 Henry IV.	c. 10,	- 315 n.
1 Edward IV.	c. 2,	- 310 n.
12 Edward IV.	c. 7,	- 345 n.
1 Richard III.	c. 8,	- 356-7 n.
3 Henry VII.	c. 1 (s. 11),	- 366 n.
32 Henry VIII.	c. 46,	- 211.
1 Edward VI.	c. 4,	- 413.
3 Charles I.	c. 1,	333, 381 n., 394.
16 Charles I.	c. 16,	430 n., 438.
12 Charles II.	c. 24,	55, 211, 331 n.

PAGE

13 Charles II.   c. 8, 331 n., 335 n.

12 George III.   c. 20, -   - 342 n.

54 George III.   c. 145,   - 342 n.

57 George III.   c. 61, -   - 430 n.

59 George III.   c. 46, - 362 n., 367.

7 and 8 George IV., c. 28, - 342 n.

3 and 4 William IV. c. 27, - 272 n.

           c. 106 (s. 10), 342 n.

PAGE

5 and 6 William IV. c. 76 (s. 14),
    407 n.

14 and 15 Victoria, c. 42, - 431 n.

15 and 16 Victoria, c. 76, - 371 n.

33 and 34 Victoria, c. 14, - 411.

            c. 23, - 342 n.

50 and 51 Victoria, c. 35, - 306 n.

INDEX.

Abbeys (rights of founders of), 433-5, 451.
Advowson, 276, 434. (See also Presentment.)
Aesop, 4.
Agistors, 419.
Aids (feudal), 59, 65-7, 232-4, 248, 256-60, 261.
Aids (general), 234-9.
Alexander II. (King of Scots), 213, 459, 461-3.
Aliens. (See Foreigners.)
Allegiance, 409, 410-11.
Amercements, 71, 118, 284-99, 453-6.
Anglo-Saxon period, 4-5, 6, 8.
Anselm, 17.
Anson, Sir William R., 107 n., 249 n., 253 n.
Appeal (to a higher court), 8, 12.
Appeal (or accusation), 89, 135-6, 316, 360, 365-7, 451-3.
Arbitrary imprisonment. (See Imprisonment.)
Archbishops. (See Dunstan, Lanfranc, Anselm, Becket, Hubert Walter, Stephen Langton.)
Aristotle, 5.
Arthur (John's nephew), 188, 207, 442, 461 n.
Arthur (King), 24.
Articles of the Barons; impressed with John's seal, 37-8.
    relation to schedule of 27 April, 1215, 37.
    relation to "unknown charter," 175.
    relation to Magna Carta, 37, 39, 41, 42 n., 196, 198, 236, 248, 282-3, 308, 382, 449, 451, 454, 469, 477.
    leave some points undecided, 38-9.
    selfish in motive, 119.
    omits provisions of Charter, 129-130, 191, 248, 451.

history of MS. of, 170-1.
    as affecting the Church, 191.
    on relief, 198.
    on wardship, 213.
    on rights of London, 234, 236.
    on tallage, 236.
    on petty assizes, 282-3.
    on coroners, 308.
    on judgment of peers, 377, 382, 449, 458.
    on estates unjustly disseised, 383, 449.
    on unjust fines, 454-5.
    on rights of Welshmen, 458.
    on rights of King of Scots, 462 n.
    on "the form of security," 468 n.
    text of, 487-493.
Articuli super Cartas, 223, 319.
Ashford v. Thornton, 366-7.
Assize (various meanings of), 272 n.
Assize of Arms, 12.
Assize of Clarendon, 250 n., 340.
    on ordeal, 60, 373.
    on Crown pleas, 88, 339.
    on jury of accusation, 135.
    on chattels of felons, 339, 340.
    article 4 of, 373.
    article 5 of, 339.
Assize of Measures, 316 n., 356-8.
Assize of Northampton, 271 n., 278 n.
    on Crown pleas, 88.
    on jury of accusation, 135, 339.
    on wardship, 206.
    on mort d'ancestor, 275.
    on powers of castellans, 315.
    article 4 of, 206, 275, 278 n.
    article 12 of, 315.
Assize of Wine, 356-8.
Assize of Woodstock, 286 n., 415-6, 418, 426, 427 n., 428.
Assize (Grand), 90, 137, 272-6, 353.
Assizes (Petty), 90-2, 137-8, 269-83, 347. (See also Justice of Assize.)
Attainder, 60, 342.

Bailiffs, 304, 316-7, 319, 369-75.
  definition of, 316-7.
  duties of, 369-75.
  abuses by, 329, 369, 431.
  type of men to be appointed, 431.
Baronia, meanings of, 200, 251 n.
Barons (legal position of), 85, 130-1,
    196, 200, 251.
  amercement of, 295-8.
Barons (minor), 251-3.
Barons (under John and his son).
  their motives, 49, 51, 116-7, 119.
  their grievances, 48-92, 389.
  their policy, 51, 67-8, 88, 120, 389.
  their factions, 189.
Barons' War (against Henry III.),
    142-3, 405.
Barony, 200. (See also *Honour*.)
Barrington (Daines), 179, 208 n.,
    217.
Bateson, Miss Mary, 56, 241 n.,
    360 n.
Battle. (See *Trial by combat*.)
Bec, Abbey of, 17.
Becket (Thomas à), 13, 192-3, 250.
Bémont, Charles, 177, 180.
Bench. (See *King's Bench* and
    Common Pleas.)
Benefit of clergy. (See *Clergy*.)
Bigelow, M. M., 268 n., 349 n.,
    370 n., 377 n., 379 n.
Bishops.
  as holders of baronies, 17, 62, 68,
    202, 211.
  election of, 17-19, 141, 194, 213-4.
  wardship over their lands, 62,
    97-8, 103, 192-3, 211-2, 434.
  liable for scutage, 70.
  not for relief, 202-3, 211-2.
Blackstone, Sir William.
  on the sensation caused by Char-
    ter of Henry I., 28 n.
  on the barons' *diffidatio*, 34.
  compares John's Charter with
    Articuli, 39.
  on forest clauses in John's char-
    ter, 44.
  on antecedents of Charter, 47.
  on tenure, 53.
  on feudal incidents, 59 n., 64.
  on nature of Magna Carta, 111,
    113.
  on loss of John's seal, 144 n.
  on different versions of Charter,
    155 n., 168, 171 n., 210 n., 278,
    386 n.
  his book, 176, 179.
  on estovers, 219 n.
  on justices of assize, 271 n., 278.
  on c. 33, 344 n.

  on c. 39, 376 n., 386 n.
  on feudal appeal, 360 n.
  on forest courts, 430.
  on executors of charter, 469 n.
Blench tenure (in Scotland), 56 n.
Bloodfeud, 284-5.
Boroughs, 234-48.
  monopoly of, 357.
  privileges of, 240-1, 357, 404-7.
    (See also under *Firma*.)
Bot, 285.
Boutmy, Émile, 106.
Bouvine (battle of), 30.
Bracton, 208, 214, 219 n., 230, 293,
    297, 329, 340, 360 n., 364 n.,
    413 n., 452 n.
Bréauté, Falkes de, 446.
Bridges, obligation to repair, 299-
    304.
Brewer, William, 153.
Burgage tenure, 57, 62, 367-9.
Burgess, 115, 213-4. (See also
    Merchant.)
Burgh, Hubert de.
  at Runnymede, 36.
  becomes Justiciar, 42.

Canonical election, 18, 25, 32. (See
    also *Bishops*.)
Canute (King), 6, 14.
Capitulary of Kiersey, 59.
Carta de foresta. (See *Forest*.)
Cartae (of 1166), 12.
Castellans. (See *Constables*.)
Castle-guard (tenure of), 333-4.
Castles (private), 218, 442.
Castles (royal), 226-7, 333-4.
Central government, problem of,
    13-16.
Champions (in *duellum*), 451.
  King's, 56.
Chancery, 11, 89, 342.
  Court of, 264-5, 410.
Charter, John's Great.
  date when sealed, 37-41.
  historical antecedents of, 3-5, 48-
    92.
  its prototypes, 93-104.
  historical sequel to, 139-64.
  form of, 104-9.
  contents of, 109-20.
  characteristics of, 109-20.
  how far a baronial manifests,
    113-6.
  its value, 120-9.
  its defects, 129-31.
  its traditional interpretations,
    132-3.
  how far declaratory, 111-2
    310-2, 345-6.

Charter, John's Great.—*contd.*
  relations to Henry II.'s reforms, 111-2, 270-8.
  how far reactionary, 112-3.
  its practical nature, 120, 131 n., 376.
  attitude towards Church and clergy, 116, 190-4, 408-11, 434.
  towards boroughs and traders, 42, 117, 234-9, 240-8, 398-407.
  towards tenants of mesne lords, 116-7, 255-60, 411-4, 463-5.
  towards villeins, 113, 118-9.
  towards lower classes generally, 113-4, 118.
  its sanction, 115-6, 129-31, 465-70.
  variations from articles of Barons, 39, 116-7, 130, 191, 234, 236, 248, 282-3, 299, 308, 451, 458-9.
  exaggerated estimates of, 120-3.
  four copies of, 41.
  manuscripts of, 165-75.
  restored by Prince Louis, 146.
  (See also *Table of Contents.*)
Charter, the so-called " unknown charter of John." (See *Unknown*.)
Charter of Henry I. ; granting of, 97.
  exhibited by Langton, 28, 32.
  Blackstone on, 28 n., 48.
  a model for Magna Carta, 32, 95.
  its general tenor, 97.
  its chief provisions, 97-101.
  on rights of church, 203.
  on marriage, 98.
  on wardships, 98, 203, 206.
  on reliefs, 197, 203.
  on amercements, 286.
  on forests, 424.
  on rights of sub-tenants, 464.
  text of, 481.
Charter of Henry II., 101.
  text of, 485.
Charter, Henry III.'s first reissue (1216), 139-44.
  its additions, 204, 218, 223 n., 434.
  its omissions, 141-4, 228, 231, 233, 236, 255, 258.
  its respiting clause, 143.
  on homage, 204.
  on wardship, 204, 212, 434.
  on Church and clergy, 212, 434.
  on marriage, 213.
  on widows' quarantine, 218.
  on debtors, 223 n.
  on Jews, 228, 231.
  on aids and scutages, 233, 236, 255, 258.
  on merchants, 404.
Charter, Henry III.'s second reissue, (1217), 145-52.
  its omissions, 130, 151, 326.
  its additions, 147-51, 216, 219, 331, 440, 465.
  reactionary clauses of, 148-9.
  on widows' rights, 216, 219.
  on scutages, 148-9, 233.
  on petty assizes, 277-8.
  on villeins, 119, 292, 386.
  on clergy, 299.
  on *Commune Concilium*, 130.
  on purveyance, 331, 335.
  on forests, 302.
  on amercements, 299.
Charter, Henry III.'s third reissue (1225), 152-7.
  the final form of Magna Carta, 155.
  price paid for, 154-5.
  text of, 497-508.
Charter of Stephen, 101-3, 188.
  text of, 483-5.
Chase, distinguished from " forest," 422.
Chatham, Lord, 113.
Chattels, forfeit of felon's, 339.
  in intestacy, 326-9.
Church, English.
  growth of conception of National Church, 191-2.
  gains power under Stephen, 18.
  Henry II.'s struggle with, 13.
  relations to State, 16, 17, 194, 324.
  relations to Rome, 16, 17, 194, 408-9.
  freedom of, 18, 32, 97, 102, 116, 141, 191-4.
  national character of, 192.
  question of investitures, 17.
  influence upon the Great Charter, 191, 326-9, 408.
  relations to Crown, 96, 194, 408.
  relations to John, 32, 116.
  John's charter to, 32.
  relations to barons, 50.
  its control of wills and property of intestates, 326-9.
  canonical election. (See *Bishops.*)
  (See also *Clergy.*)
Cigogné, Engelard de, 417 n., 444-7.
Clarendon. (See *Constitutions of* and *Assize of.*)
Clergy, amercement of, 298-9.
  their right to go to Rome, 407-11.
  " benefit of clergy," 18, 214 n.
Cnut. (See *Canute.*)

Coinage, private, 8.
Coke (Chief Justice).
  on tenures, 54, 57 n.
  on primer seisin, 65 n.
  on Magna Carta, 113, 133, 178, 181, 190, 464.
  on c. 39, 381, 385, 386.
  on c. 40, 398.
  on c. 54, 453.
  on villeins, 118, 287 n., 386.
  on Knights' fees, 201.
  on waste, 209 n., 338.
  on disparagement, 214.
  on rights of widows, 217, 219.
  on justices of assize, 280 n.
  on attainder, 342.
  his unhistorical method, 178, 385.
Combat. (See *Trial by combat.*)
Comitatus. (See *Shire, Shire Court,* and also *Earldom.*)
Commissions of Justices, 280-2.
Committee of Executors. (See *Executors.*)
Common law, growth of, 12.
  courts of, 263-9.
Common pleas, 90, 261-9.
  Court of, 11, 90, 265-7.
Commune, 116, 243-5, 471.
Commune Concilium, 231-40, 248-55.
  functions of, 130-1, 163, 254-5.
  composition of, 250-5.
Commune of London. (See *London.*)
Compurgation, 85, 370.
Confirmatio Cartarum, 69, 238.
Constables, different uses of word, 313-5.
  their functions and powers, 314, 329, 333.
  and purveyance, 329-31.
  and castle-guard, 333.
Constitutions of Clarendon, 18-19, 202 n., 211, 298-9, 408.
Contenement, 284.
  meaning of, 293-4.
Copyhold, 53.
Coronation oath, 95-6.
Coroner, 16, 304, 315.
  his functions, 315-6.
Council of St. Albans (1213), 28, 432.
Council of Oxford (1213), 30.
Councils, Lateran. (See *Lateran.*)
County. (See *County Court,* also *Firma Comitatus.*)
County Court, 77, 81, 282-3.
  to appoint knights to reform abuses, 42, 439-40.
  to appoint knights for assizes, 277-8.
Courts, three rival systems of, 77-92.

Courts, Christian, 323-4.
Courts, local. (See *County* and *Hundred.*)
Courts, royal. (See *Curia Regis, Chancery, Common pleas, Exchequer, King's Bench.*)
Criminal law. (See *Pleas of the Crown.*)
Crusaders, 449-50.
  effects of vow, 33, 449.
Curia Regis.
  appeals to, 8.
  altered by Henry I., 9.
  under Henry II., 11, 50.
  powers of, 188-9, 262, 264, 388.
  relation to Witenagemot, 188, 250.

Danish influence, 6.
Darrein presentment. (See *Presentment.*)
David I. (King of Scots), 460.
Debtors, 223-5, 321-3.
  and Court of Exchequer, 268.
Diffidatio.
  nature and effects of, 34.
  by barons on 5th May, 1215, 34.
Disparagement, 212-3, 461.
Disseisin, 119, 274-5, 383, 386, 450.
Disseisin (Assize of Novel), 269, 274-5, 277.
Domesday Book, 10.
Dominus, meaning of, 187-9.
Dower, 215-7, 230-1, 454.
Duellum. (See *Trial by combat.*)
Dunstan, 14, 95.
Dymoke (Family of), 55.

Earldormen, 8, 14.
Earls, amercement of, 130, 295-8.
  definition of, 201.
  relief due from, 196-202.
  members of *Commune Concilium,* 248-51.
  relation to county, 270 n.
Earls Palatine, 7, 15, 64 n.
Edgar (King), 14.
Edward Confessor, 6, 7, 14.
  his laws confirmed, 27, 32, 111-2.
Edward I.
  his reforms, 159-64.
  his attitude to the Charter, 161-4.
  his Parliaments, 162-3.
  his *Inspeximus* of the Charter, 168-9, 198 n., 299 n.
  quarrels with Constable and Marshal, 69, 261.
  relations with London, 405.
  his influence on the Constitution, 162-4, 475.

Edward II., 406, 430, 437.
Edward III., 238, 303, 332, 406, 409, 438.
Election, meaning of word, 278.
 in relation to kingship, 118-9.
 of jurors, 277-8.
 of knights to reform abuses, 42, 438-40.
 of knights to hold assizes, 278.
England, growth of a united, 4-6.
English Church. (See *Church*.)
English law. (See *Law*.)
English Monarchy. (See *Monarchy*.)
Escheat, 59-61, 336-9, 411-3.
Estovers, definition of, 218-9.
 widows' rights of, 218.
 of firewood, 426.
Exchequer, under Henry I., 9-10.
 Court of, 263-5, 267-9.
Executors of the Charter, 465-77.
 references to, 40, 42, 44.
 their excesses, 44.
 their local agents, 440.
 their powers, 449, 455, 465-77.
Eyres. (See *Justices of Eyre*.)

Falconry. (See *Fowling*.)
Fee-farm, 55, 57, 368-9.
Felony, 336-43.
Feudal aids. (See *Aids*.)
Feudal grievances, 58-92, 121.
Feudal incidents, 59-65. (See also *Reliefs, Escheats, Wardships, Marriages, Primer Seisins*, and *Fines for Alienations*.)
Feudal jurisdictions. (See under *Jurisdictions* and under *Courts*.)
Feudal obligations, 52-76, 116-7. (See also *Services, Incidents*, and *Aids*.)
Feudal services, 12, 52-3, 67-9, 199, 260-1.
Feudal tenures. (See *Tenures*.)
Feudalism in England, 7-9, 52-3, 54, 57.
Fictions (legal), 269 n.
Fines, 454-6.
 differ from amercements, 292-3.
Fines for alienations, 65.
Firma burgi, 241-2, 320, 445.
Firma comitatus, 317-21.
Fishing, 303-4, 343-6.
Fitz-Aylwin, Mayor of London, 34.
Fitz-Peter, Geoffrey, 29.
Fitz-Walter, Robert.
 escapes from John, 25.
 reinstated, 26.
 commands barons' army, 34.
 outlawed, 384.

one of the executors of Charter, 469.
Flambard, Ralph.
 his feudal innovations, 9, 58, 203, 206.
Foreign merchants.
 their position in London, 247.
 favoured by Magna Carta, 400-7.
Foreign service, 69, 260-1.
Forest Charters, issued in 1217, 146.
 its repudiation feared, 155-6.
 provisions of, 425, 426, 428, 430, 436.
 text of, 508-12.
Forest Courts, 420-2, 427.
Foresters, 417-20, 428-30.
Forests, 414-31, 435-40.
 protests by prelates regarding, 43.
 text of protests, 496-7.
 boundaries of, 156, 437.
Fowling, King's rights of, 299-304, 435-8.
Frankalmoin, 55, 298-9.
Free socage. (See *Socage*.)
Freehold, 53-8.
Freeman, definition of, 114-5, 195, 287 n., 299 n., 386.
 rights of, 284, 287-9, 334-5, 346-7, 375 ff.
 obligations of, 300.
Fyrd, 12, 300.

Godwin, 14.
Government, ideal form of, 5.
 " mixed," 5.
 (See also *Local government*.)
Grand Assize. (See *Assize*.)
Grand Jury. (See *Jury*.)
Grand Serjeanty. (See *Serjeanty*.)
Great Charter. (See *Charter*.)
Green, John Richard, on Richard I.'s reign, 21.
Grey, John de, 23.
Gualo (papal legate), 46, 47, 139, 144, 145.
Guardian, 219. (See also *Wardship*.)
Guilds, 400, 404, 407.

Habeas corpus. (See *Writ of*.)
Hardell (William), Mayor of London, 245 n., 469.
Harold, King, 7.
Hawking. (See *Fowling*.)
Henry I.
 his character, 9.
 his title, 96, 196.
 reforms, 9-10, 15.
 relations with church, 17, 192, 203.

Henry I.
   and canonical election, 18.
   his attitude towards the forests,
      424.
   scutage under, 70.
   charter to Jews, 227.
   charter to London, 241-2.
   organizes Exchequer, 9.
   his Charter of Liberties. (See
      Charter.)
Henry II.
   his character, 11.
   and Becket, 19, 250.
   policy in regard to church, 18-19,
      211.
   military reforms, 12.
   legal reforms, 11-12, 88-92, 273,
      306, 347.
   administrative reforms, 11-12,
      19-20.
   his new legal procedure, 11-12,
      88-92.
   opposes hereditary principle,
      15.
   discourages trial by combat, 273,
      360-1.
   undermines private jurisdictions,
      12, 273, 347.
   takes aids, 66.
   levies scutages, 69-70.
   founder of trial by jury, 134-8,
      273.
   charter to London, 242-3.
   opens royal courts to freeholders,
      12, 77, 80-1, 87, 395.
Henry III.
   his coronation, 139.
   his minority, 143, 266.
   his advisers accept the Charter,
      47, 139.
   takes aids, 66.
   levies scutage, 143, 258.
   takes fees for writs, 259, 397.
   his attitude to Magna Carta,
      153-9, 160.
   his attitude to the Jews, 228.
   protects foreign merchants, 405.
   his alliance with Rome, 328 n.
   his rights of fowling, 303.
   his attitude towards the forests,
      437-8.
   declared of age, 153.
   (See also under *Charter.*)
Honorius III., 153.
Hostages, 25, 441-4, 458, 459.
Hubert de Burgh. (See *Burgh.*)
Hubert, Walter (Archbishop).
   his reforms, 21, 307.
   his testament, 324 n.
   his death, 23.

Hundred, 317-8.
   Court of, 78-9.

Imprisonment (arbitrary), 133,
   401-2.
Incidents. (See *Feudal incidents.*)
Indictment, 340-1.
Innocent III. nominates Stephen
   Langton, 23-4.
   releases John's subjects from
      allegiance, 24, 25.
   excommunicates John, 26.
   his reconciliation with John, 26.
   appealed to by malcontents, 33.
   supports John, 33, 46, 462, 477.
   suggested as umpire by John,
      34.
   annuls the Great Charter, 45.
   excommunicates barons, 46.
   interferes with Scots King, 462.
Inquest of Service (1212), 24, 75-6.
Inquest of Sheriffs. (See *Sheriff.*)
Inquisitio. (See *Recognitio.*)
Interest, 223-5. (See also *Jews* and
   Usury.)
Interregnum (theory of), 96.
Investitures (question of), 17.
Isabel, Princess. (See *Scotland.*)
Ivo, Bishop of Chartres, 17.

James I., 58 n., 336.
Jarls (Danish), 15.
Jews, 223-31, 378.
Joan (John's natural daughter), 25.
John, his character, 48.
   his bad faith, 42-3.
   his power, 24.
   his policy, 21, 48, 50.
   his incapacity, 22.
   his title to the Crown, 186-9.
   his exactions, 22, 31, 49.
   his straits for money, 32.
   his levies of scutage, 31, 69-76.
   charters to English Church, 32,
      33, 194, 211-2.
   charters to London, 34, 244-5,
      345.
   relations with his barons, 24, 29,
      31, 34, 49.
   refuses their demands, 33.
   meets barons at Runnymede,
      36-41.
   takes Crusader's vow, 33, 46.
   relations with English Church, 23,
      24, 50, 212.
   relations with Rome, 23.
   the quarrel, 24.
   the reconciliation, 26, 50.
   his surrender to Innocent, 26, 29,
      50.

John asks Innocent to annul charter, 44.
hangs Welsh hostages, 25, 442-3.
loses Normandy, 22.
confiscates church property, 24.
restores it, 28.
issues writs for a Council in Nov. 1213, 29.
and county representation, 29.
his death, 47.
Judgment (in medieval law), 84-6.
Judgment of peers. (See *Peers.*)
Jurisdiction, royal, 80-1. (See also *Courts.*)
Jurisdictions, private, 78-80. (See also *Courts.*)
Jury, trial by.
relation to *recognitio*, 87, 135.
relation to writ *de odio*, 89, 136, 361-2.
relation to Magna Carta, 134-8.
Jury (of accusation or presenting jury), 135-7.
Jury (Civil), 137-8.
Jury (Grand), 136.
Jury (Petty), 136-8, 360-1.
Justice, three systems of, 77-81. (See also *Courts* and *Jurisdictions.*)
Justices of the Peace, 16, 281.
Justices, itinerant (or of Eyre), 270-1.
Justices of Assize, 270-83.
commissions of, 280-1.

Kiersey, capitulary of, 59.
King's Bench, 11, 263-7.
Knight's fee, 199-200, 260.
Knight's service, 54, 199.
Kydells. (See *Weirs.*)

Lanfranc, 17, 96.
Langton. (See *Stephen.*)
Lateran Council (1099), 17.
Lateran Council (1215), 46, 341.
Law (*lex*), technical meaning of, 84, 369-70, 379-81. (See also *Trial.*)
Leasehold, 53-6.
Legal fictions. (See *Fictions.*)
Legal procedure. (See *Procedure.*)
Leofric, 14.
Letters testimonial, 41.
text of, 478 n.
Llywelyn, 25, 458.
Local government, problem of, 13-16.
London.
receives rebel army, 35.
accepts Louis as King, 47.

liable to tallage, 117, 234-9.
granted by John as security, 42, 477.
John's charters to, 34, 244-7, 345.
taxation of, 231-2, 234-9.
privileges of, 240-8, 345.
Longchamp, 51.
Lords (House of), 392.
Louis, son of French king, 46, 140, 145.
confirms Magna Carta, 47.

Magna Carta. (See *Charter.*)
Manorial courts, 77-80, 87. (See also *Courts* and *Jurisdictions.*)
Maritagium, 216-8, 454.
Marriage, feudal incident of, 62 3, 212-4.
Marshal (William, Earl Marshal), 32, 33, 35.
mediator between King and barons, 33, 35, 36, 476.
acts as Regent, 139-41, 145, 255.
Matilda (daughter of Henry I.), supplanted by Stephen, 10-11.
her prodigal grants, 137.
Merchants. (See *Foreign merchants, London,* and *Boroughs.*)
Ministerial responsibility, doctrine of, 129, 161-3, 433.
Minorities, rights of, 254-5.
Monarchy, two types of, 4-5.
Monarchy (English).
growth of, 5-13.
strong under Normans, 5.
and Angevins, 13.
weak under Anglo-Saxon kings, 4-5, 13.
Monopolies.
attitude of Magna Carta towards, 384.
claimed by native merchants, 117, 398-407.
Montfort, Simon de, 161-2.
Mort d'ancestor, 269-70, 275-6, 283 n.
Municipalities. (See *Boroughs.*)

National Church. (See *Church.*)
National unity in England, 5-6.
Nicholas (Papal legate), 311.
Norgate, Miss Kate.
on writs of November 1213, 29.
on date of Magna Carta, 41 n.
on John's misconduct, 48 n.
on John's levies of scutage, 74 n., 75 n.
on privileges of London, 245.
on the twenty-five executors, 476.
on the price paid for the charter of 1225, 154 n.

Norman Conquest, effects of, 5.
Novel disseisin. (See *Disseisin*.)

Oligarchic elements in England, 4.
Ordeal, 84-5, 136, 369-75.
Original writs. (See *Writs*.)
Outlaws, 384-5.

Pandulf (Papal legate), 26, 45.
Papal Bull, annulling Charter, 45-6.
Papal legates. (See *Gualo, Nicholas, Pandulf*.)
Parks, distinguished from forests, 422.
Parliament.
  its development, 162.
  functions of, 162, 253-4.
  composition of, 162.
Parliamentary taxation. (See *Taxation*.)
Parliamentary representation. (See *Representation*.)
Peasantry. (See *Villeins*.)
Peers, amercement by, 130, 295-8.
  as a separate class, 186 n.
Peers, judgment of, 375, 377-9, 386-95.
  confused with jury trial, 134 n.
Peter des Roches (Bishop of Winchester), 30, 41, 45, 48, 255, 389, 431.
Peter of Wakefield, 26.
Peter's pence, 17.
Petition of Barons (1258), 198 n., 214, 283 n., 414, 435.
Petty Assizes. (See *Assize*.)
Petty Jury. (See *Jury*.)
Petty Serjeanty. (See *Serjeanty*.)
Philip (King of France), 26, 27, 30, 46.
Pipe Rolls, of 1130, 9.
  revived by Henry II., 11.
Pleas. (See *Common pleas*.)
Pleas of the Crown, 88-92, 266-7, 304-21.
  in Scots law, 306.
Pleas of the forest, 313-4.
Popes. (See *Honorius* and *Innocent*.)
Presentment (darrein), 193, 269, 276-7, 283.
  nature of, explained, 276.
Primer seisin, 63-5.
Procedure (legal), 81-6.
  Henry II.'s reforms, 86-92.
Proof (in medieval law), 84-6. (See also *Trial*.)
Protests by the prelates in John's favour, 43, 476.
  text of, 496-7.

Provisions of Oxford (1258), 160, 433.
Purprestures, 425.
Purveyance, 329-32, 334-6.

Quarantine, widow's, 218.
Queen's gold, 198.

Recognitio (principle of), 28, 86, 135-8.
Regarders, 417-22.
Relief (feudal incident of), 59-61, 203-5, 211-2.
  not due from bishop-elect, 97-8, 202-3.
  not due after wardship, 203.
  definition of sums due, 196-203.
Representation, parliamentary, 248-55.
Responsibility. (See *Ministerial*.)
Richard I., 51, 66, 73, 197, 243, 460.
  lessons of his reign, 20-1.
Richard II., 407.
Roches (Peter des). (See *Peter*.)
Roger, bishop of Salisbury, 9.
Rolls. (See *Pipe Rolls*.)
Royal justice. (See *Courts* and *Jurisdiction*.)
Royal writs. (See *Writs*.)
Runnymede, 36-8, 44, 52, 479.

Saladin tithe, 20.
Salisbury, Roger, bishop of. (See *Roger*.)
Schedule of grievances (27 April, 1215), 33, 37, 38, 173.
Scotland, relations to England, 459-63.
  kings of. (See *Alexander, David,* and *William*.)
  Princesses Margaret and Isabel, 459.
Scutage, 69-76, 231-4.
  grand sergeanties not liable for, 55-6.
  in charter of 1215, 231-4, 248.
  in charter of 1217, 148-9.
  by sub-tenants, 256.
Scutum. (See *Knight's fee*.)
Seal (king's great), 143-4, 153.
Seisin. (See *Primer Seisin* and *Disseisin*.)
Serjeanty (grand), 55-7, 64 n., 199, 261.
Serjeanty (petty), 56-7, 64 n., 199, 261, 367-8.
Service. (See under *Feudal service, Foreign service,* and *Knight's service*.)

Sheriff, 311-3, 431.
  history of the office of, 311-3.
  chief magistrate of county, 311.
  his powers, 16, 304-10.
  curtailed by the charter, 304, 317, 334.
  his " tourn," 320-1.
  his tyrannies, 15-16, 311, 320, 334.
  his qualifications, 431-3.
  his gradual decline, 16, 312-3.
  forbidden to hold pleas of the Crown, 304.
  in America, 313.
  in Scotland, 313.
  accountable to Exchequer, 9.
  under William I., 15.
  under Henry II., 15-16.
  Inquest of, 16.
Shire. (See *County*.)
Socage, 54-5, 57, 66, 199, 261, 367-9.
Statutes. (See separate Index of Statutes.)
Stephen (King).
  supplants Matilda, 10, 101.
  his title, 102, 188.
  relations with Church, 18, 102.
  (See also *Charters of*.)
Stephen Langton.
  nominated by Innocent, 23.
  received by John, 27.
  his alliance with the barons, 28.
  exhibits charter of Henry I., 28, 32.
  consolidates the opposition, 51.
  mediates between King and barons, 29, 32, 33, 36, 38, 45.
  at Runnymede, 36, 38.
  trusted by both sides, 38-9, 43, 51, 462 n.
  influence on Great Charter, 39, 191, 212.
  Tower of London placed in his custody, 43.
  suspended from office, 45.
  goes to Rome (1215), 45.
  asks Henry III. to confirm the Charters, 153.
  cares for interests of English Church, 191, 212.
Stubbs (Bishop William).
  on Henry I.'s compromise with Anselm, 18.
  on the coalition of John's opponents, 44.
  on John's submission to Innocent, 51.
  on scutage, 69-71.
  on charter of Henry I., 97, 464.
  on " national " character of Charter, 113, 117 n., 125.
  on the barons' unselfishness, 117 n., 464.
  on villeins under the Charter, 119 n.
  on reissue of 1216, 140 n., 143 n.
  on treaty of Lambeth, 145.
  on witnesses to the Charter, 189.
  on *maritagium*, 217 n.
  on estovers, 219.
  on constitution of London, 241.
  on the Common Council, 252, 254.
  on c. 24, 310.
  on c. 45, 431.
  on meaning of " *lex*," 370 n.
  on judgment of peers, 390 n.
  on meaning of " warren," 423.
  on the twenty-five executors, 476.
Succession, intestate, 141-2, 326-9.
  testate, 321-6.
Suit and service, 67-9.
Suit (or forewitnesses), 84, 369-75.
Swanimotes, 421.
Synod of Whitby, 6.

Tallage, 235-9.
Taxation.
  common Council's rights over, 231-40.
  parliamentary, 238-9.
Tenserie, definition of, 40 n.
Tenure by barony, 54.
Tenure by castle-ward, 57 n.
Tenure in chivalry. (See *Knight's service*.)
Tenures, 53-9. (See also *Burgage, Fee-farm, Frankalmoin, Knight's service, Serjeanty, Socage, Villeinage*, also under *Freehold*.)
Tourn. (See *Sheriff's tourn*.)
Treason, 60, 337-9.
Trial (in medieval procedure), 83-6, 136, 359, 369.
Trial by combat, 89, 136-7, 272, 360-7, 451-3.
Trial by jury. (See *Jury*.)

" Unknown charter of Liberties " (so-called), referred to, 29.
  theories as to its nature and origin, 171-5.
  text of, 485-6.
Usury, 223-5. (See also *Jews*.)

Verderers, 314, 418.
Vesci, Richard de, 25, 26, 33, 384, 443, 469.
Vicecomes. (See *Sheriff*.)
Villeinage, 54, 290, 386.

Villeins, 289-92
  not freemen, 118-9.
  methods of " wasting," 208 n.
  amercement, of, 289-92.
  attitude of charter to, 119, 335, 386, 386 n.

Wales, 25, 456-9.
Wapentake, 78, 135, 317.
Warden, 417. (See also *Constable* and *Guardian*.)
Wardship, 61-2, 63.
  tenures subject to, 55, 57, 367-8.
  conditions of, 204.
  attitude of charter to, 205-12, 367-9, 450.
  over vacant sees, 97-8, 211-2.
  over abbeys, 433-5.
  prerogative wardship, 368-9, 450-1.
Warrens, meaning of, 210 n., 423.
  distinguished from forest, 423.
  charter on, 438-440.
Waste, of ward's lands, 207-9.
  of felon's lands, 336-9.
  of forests, 426-7.
Watling Street, 6.
Waynage, 291-2.
Weirs, 343-6.
Welshmen. (See *Wales*.)
Wergeld, 285-6.
Whitby, Synod of, 6.

Widows' rights, 215-21, 230-1, 325.
William I., 6.
  outline of reign, 6-9.
  his policy of balancing, 7-8.
  relations to feudalism, 7.
  to Domesday Book, 10.
  local government under, 13-14, 15.
  relations with Rome, 17.
  his innovations, 86.
  title to English Crown, 7, 95-6.
  relations with Witenagemot, 7-8, 14.
William II., relations with the Church, 17, 203.
  features of reign, 8-9.
William the Lion, King of Scots, 460-3.
Wills, 321-6.
Witenagemot, 14.
  attitude of William I. to, 7-8.
  powers of, 188-9.
Wites, 285-6.
Witnesses, 84.
Writ *de odio et atia*, 89, 136, 361-5.
Writ *ne exeat regno*, 409-10.
Writ of *habeas corpus*, 362-3.
Writ of entry, 354-5.
Writ of right, 347-9, 353-4.
Writ *praecipe*, 346-55.
Writs of November 1213, 29-30.

PRESS NOTICES OF FIRST EDITION

MAGNA CARTA: A Commentary on the Great Charter
of King John, with an Historical Introduction. By William Sharp McKechnie, M.A., LL.B., D.Phil., Lecturer on Constitutional Law and History in the University of Glasgow.

" A book remarkable alike for its solid learning, its fertility in suggestion, and its characteristic note of moderation and sweet reasonableness. . . . No one will close the book without feeling that his knowledge of Magna Carta has been greatly amplified and enriched. . . . One of the most important contributions to medieval history in recent years."—*The Times*.

" Of the great merit and value of the present essay there can, we think, be little doubt. The historical and juridical methods adopted by the author are sound and intelligent, and naturally in striking contrast with those of earlier commentators. His style is attractive and sufficiently concise, whilst his equipment for such a formidable task is very considerable. As the result of these elaborate studies, we have an entirely new view of the Great Charter in its legal and constitutional aspects and political environment."—*Athenaeum*.

" Mr. McKechnie's work is of such great value that no historian can afford to neglect its clear and reasoned statements on all the questions which centre round the scene at Runnymede, and on the economic facts which led up to, and away from, that momentous conference."—*Spectator*.

" Bears with it the collective wisdom of all the commentaries, ancient and modern, dispassionately scrutinised and sifted with close and varied learning on medieval institutions. . . . It is a great theme, and to say that it is at last adequately treated, from the constitutional side, is well merited praise."—*Juridical Review*.

" Dr. McKechnie has placed students of constitutional law and history under deep obligations. . . . There can be no doubt that his work comes to fill a long-felt want in legal and historical literature."—*Outlook* (New York).

" Few more readable books—except to those who can read nothing but fiction—have ever been written."—*Liberty Review*.

" Students of the historical development of the law of the British Constitution owe a welcome to the appearance of this learned treatise, a work which brings the interpretation of a prime document of political liberty abreast of recent advances in knowledge which, in legal history no less than in other departments of inquiry, have brought in new views of old facts."—*Scotsman*.

" Dr. McKechnie has given very satisfactory explanations of most of the knotty points of the Charter, and we may specially commend the sanity of his exposition of the constitutional clauses. Altogether his book is a useful and solid help in the study of the numerous difficulties involved in the text of the Great Charter."—*Manchester Guardian*.

PRESS NOTICES OF FIRST EDITION

" One of the most important contributions to English diplomatics that has appeared within the last five years."—*Westminster Review*.

" It has already won its place as the standard treatise on the Great Charter."—*Scottish Law Review*.

" Dr. McKechnie has performed a real and needed service to historical and legal scholarship. The manner in which he has performed his task is as admirable as the matter. He writes in a clear and direct style, well adapted to his subject. The book is printed in attractive form."—*Law Notes* (New York).

" It may be said at once that our author has succeeded in giving us a very sound and useful commentary instead of the antiquated ones of Blackstone and of Thomson. . . . His book is sure to be used and to last."—Professor Vinogradoff in the *Law Quarterly Review*.

" The labor of anyone who comments in the future on the clauses of the Great Charter has been greatly lightened by the careful and learned work of Dr. W. S. McKechnie."—Professor G. B. Adams of Yale, in *The Origin of the English Constitution*.

" Of permanent value to students of English constitutional history."—*Annual Register*.

" An admirable commentary on Magna Carta."—H. A. L. Fisher, Fellow of New College, Oxford, in an editorial note to Maitland's *Constitutional History of England*.

" A work on Magna Carta of unparalleled excellence in both its historical and expository matter."—Hon. Fred. A. Baker in *The Gateway* (Michigan).

" We question whether another commentary will venture to attempt to displace this one until some generations of historical students have been at work on new material. . . . Anyone who turns to these pages for help in particular difficulties will find enough to persuade him that he had better read every section."—The late Miss Mary Bateson, Fellow of Newnham College, Cambridge, in *Scot. Hist. Rev.* iii. p. 229.

" Mr. McKechnie may justly claim to have provided us with a most adequate commentary on Magna Carta."—H. W. C. Davis, Fellow and Tutor of Balliol College, Oxford, in *English Historical Review*, xxi. p. 150.

" Im ganzen eine Arbeit, die jeder Erforscher der mittelalterlichen Rechts- und Verfassungsgeschichte Englands dankbar brauchen wird."—Professor Felix Liebermann, of Berlin, in *Historische Vierteljahrschrift*.

" C'est un livre qu'il faudra consulter pour l'histoire des institutions politiques et administratives de l'Angleterre au xiie et au xiiie siècle ; il a sa place marquée à côté de Stubbs dans la bibliothèque des érudits."—Professor Charles Bémont, of the Sorbonne, in *La Revue Historique.*